A Critique of Postcolonial Reason

A Critique of Postcolonial Reason

Toward a History of the Vanishing Present

Gayatri Chakravorty Spivak

HARVARD UNIVERSITY PRESS
Cambridge, Massachusetts
London, England

LIBRARY OF CONGRESS CATALOGING-IN-PUBLICATION DATA
Spivak, Gayatri Chakravorty.
A critique of postcolonial reason : toward a history of the
vanishing present / Gayatri Chakravorty Spivak.
p.   cm.
Includes bibliographical references and index.
ISBN 0-674-17763-0 (alk. paper).
ISBN 0-674-17764-9 (pbk. : alk. paper)
1. Postcolonialism.   2. Feminist criticism.
3. Women and literature.   4. Feminism and literature.
5. Philosophy, Modern—19th century.
6. Philosophy, Modern—20th century.
7. Politics and culture.
JV51.S58   1999
325'.3—dc21   98-31566

Tarak Nath Sen

Paul de Man

CONTENTS

Preface / ix

1 Philosophy / 1

2 Literature / 112

3 History / 198

4 Culture / 312

Appendix:
The Setting to Work of Deconstruction / 423

Index / 433

PREFACE

My aim, to begin with, was to track the figure of the Native Informant through various practices: philosophy, literature, history, culture. Soon I found that the tracking showed up a colonial subject detaching itself from the Native Informant. After 1989, I began to sense that a certain postcolonial subject had, in turn, been recoding the colonial subject and appropriating the Native Informant's position. Today, with globalization in full swing, telecommunicative informatics taps the Native Informant directly in the name of indigenous knowledge and advances biopiracy. Therefore the foreclosure that I see operative in Chapter 1 continues, rather more aggressively. The *Encyclopedia of Life Support Systems* projected by UNESCO "defines" the Aboriginal period of human history as the "timescale of the *far past* . . . associated with *inactive* approaches in which there is no concern for environmental degradation and sustainability." It was of course as impossible for the Aboriginal to think sustainability as it was for Aristotle to "decipher . . . the secret of the expression of value," because of "the historical limitation inherent in the society in which [they] lived."[1] Yet the practical philosophy of living in the rhythm of the ecobiome must now be dismissed as "no concern."

Assaulted by this dynamic, my book charts a practitioner's progress

---

1. *Encyclopedia of Life Support Systems: Conceptual Framework* (Whitstable: Oyster Press, 1997), p. 13; Karl Marx, *Capital: A Critique of Political Economy*, tr. Ben Fowkes, vol. 1 (New York: Vintage, 1976), p. 152.

from colonial discourse studies to transnational cultural studies. The latter position, a "moving base" that I stand on as the text seeks to catch the vanishing present, has asserted itself in narrative footnotes. Some will find this irritating and confusing; some, I hope, will share the challenge. The implied reader whose face I discover in Chapter 4 is too diversified to be assigned a definite interest, a definitive preparation. Based on my own uncertain scholarship, I sometimes conjure up a lexicon-consulting reader for the new cultural studies. The book tries also to address the "sanctioned ignorance" of the theoretical elite and of the self-styled academic "practitioner." The sanctions too are of heterogeneous provenance. Thus the reader's place is as unsecured as the writer's. But is that not the status of all texts, resisted in the writing and the reading?

The first chapter looks at philosophy: how Kant foreclosed the Aboriginal; how Hegel put the other of Europe in a pattern of normative deviations and how the colonial subject sanitized Hegel; how Marx negotiated difference.

The second chapter reads a cluster of literary texts to show how colonialism and postcoloniality are figured: Brontë, Mary Shelley, Baudelaire, Kipling, Rhys, Mahasweta, Coetzee. In my reading, Mary Shelley joins the last three on that list in not presenting the ethics of alterity as a politics of identity: a lesson for our struggle. Today, I would have added at least Jamaica Kincaid's *Lucy*, a powerful paratactic text that loses nothing of its cutting edge against the exploiters, because it dares, in closing, to dissolve the central character's proper name by an alterity beyond its choice, so that it can claim, in the subjunctive, the right/responsibility of loving, denied to the subject that wishes to choose agency from victimage.

The third chapter follows a nineteenth century hill queen through the archives and ponders the management of widow burning. I should perhaps mention that it contains a revision of "Can the Subaltern Speak?" which was originally published in *Marxism and the Interpretation of Culture*, edited by Cary Nelson and Lawrence Grossberg (Urbana: University of Illinois Press, 1988).

The fourth chapter looks at postmodern fashion and the place of woman in the history of textile.

In addition to "Can the Subaltern Speak?" earlier versions of portions of this text have been published as follows: "The Rani of Sirmur:

An Essay in Reading the Archives," *History and Theory* 24, no. 3 (1985): 247–272; "Three Women's Texts and a Critique of Imperialism," *Critical Inquiry* 12, no. 1 (Autumn 1985): 243–261; "Imperialism and Sexual Difference," *Oxford Literary Review* 7 (1986): 225–240; "Versions of the Margin: J. M. Coetzee's *Foe* reading Defoe's *Crusoe/Roxana*," in *Consequences of Theory*, edited by Johnathan Arac and Barbara Johnson (Baltimore: Johns Hopkins University Press, 1991), pp. 154–180; and "Time and Timing: Law and History," originally published in *Chronotypes*, edited by John Bender and David E. Wellbery, used with the permission of the publishers, Stanford University Press, © 1991 by the Board of Trustees of the Leland Stanford Junior University.

These chapters do not stand alone. They are loosely strung on a chain that may be described this way: the philosophical presuppositions, historical excavations, and literary representations of the dominant—insofar as they are shared by the emergent postcolonial—also trace a subliminal and discontinuous emergence of the "native informant": autochthone and/or subaltern. This is not a trope expressed through the speech, writing, and images of "third world literature." How it displaces itself from impossible perspective to resistant networks as well as super-exploited objects is part of the story. The problematic of text-ile seems to contain a coda. In the telling, the chain cuts often—but the cut threads reappear, I hope.

This is a feminist book. Feminist issues are "pre-emergent" (Raymond Williams's word) in the first chapter. They are the substance of the rest. In the fourth, a critique of contemporary culturalist universalist feminism is offered.

This book belongs on the same shelf as the work of bell hooks, Deniz Kandiyoti, Ketu Katrak, Wahneema Lubiano, Trin-ti Minh-ha, Chandra Talpade Mohanty, Aiwah Ong, Sara Suleri. During the years of writing this book, these women and others that I have not named here have advanced postcolonial feminist studies greatly. Suleri and I concentrate more on mainstream texts. Unacknowledged similarities between these scholars' work and mine are proof that we are in a common struggle.

But I concentrate more on mainstream texts even as I try to probe what subaltern is strategically excluded from organized resistance. The feminism we inhabit has something like a relationship with the tradition of the cultural dominant, even when adversarial. Chandra Mohanty has an eloquent passage about SEWA (Self-Employed Women's Association) in her new book.[2] It was precisely because, in spite of the leaders' repeated admonition to the then young lawyer Ella Bhatt— "But how will you organize them? These women have no employers!"—that Ms. Bhatt brought into being the category "self-employed" and, as the first move in her unique revolutionary project, exhorted these women to put together a bare minimum in order to found a bank. Otherwise, they would have remained strategically excluded from the organized labor movement. And today, I have heard Nicola Armatrod of Women's World Banking repeatedly cite SEWA when asked what social work WWB undertakes and cite "Chandra Behn" of SEWA as holding her hand and saying that the WWB is their benefactor! It is my belief that a training in a literary habit of reading the world can attempt to put a curb on such superpower triumphalism only if it does not perceive acknowledgment of complicity as an inconvenience. My book is therefore a "critique" in that it examines the structures of the production of postcolonial reason.

Without this power to proceed minus the cleanest bill of health, we are caught between two problems: on the one hand, theories, however subtly argued, that support the idea that upward class mobility—mimicry and masquerade—is unmediated resistance; on the other, a failure to "recognize . . . the passing of an era when the West, and particularly the Americans, were willing to tolerate the rhetoric of the third world."[3] The task of the teacher of literary reading is placed in the aporia of an uncoercive rearrangement of the will as student and teacher shuttle between freedom-from and freedom-to; not in congratulating the will to U.S. class-power as unmediated resistance.

Thus, although both Aijaz Ahmad and I criticize metropolitan postcolonialism, I hope my position is less locationist, more nuanced with a productive acknowledgment of complicity. I always attempt to look

---

2. Chandra Mohanty, "Women Workers and Capitalist Scripts: Ideologies of Domination, Common Interests, and the Politics of Solidarity," in M. Jacqui Alexander and Chandra Talpade Mohanty, eds., *Feminist Genealogies, Colonial Legacies, Democratic Futures* (New York: Routledge, 1997), pp. 26–27.

3. James Traub, "Kofi Annan's Next Test," *The New York Times Magazine*, March 29, 1998, p. 46.

around the corner, to see ourselves as others would see us. Not, however, in the interest of work stoppage, but so that work is less clannish.
What I continue to learn from deconstruction is perhaps idiosyncratic,
but it remains my rein.

I am not erudite enough to be interdisciplinary, but I can break rules.
Can anything be learned from this? I ask my two former students who
suffered through most of the earlier parts of the book in the form of
classroom teaching: Jenny Sharpe and Tres Pyle. And for the last part,
my thanks to the three who have made possible my other learning:
Mahaswetadi, Farida, Farhad.

CHAPTER ONE

Philosophy

I

Postcolonial studies, unwittingly commemorating a lost object, can become an alibi unless it is placed within a general frame. Colonial Discourse studies, when they concentrate only on the representation of the colonized or the matter of the colonies, can sometimes serve the production of current neocolonial knowledge by placing colonialism/imperialism securely in the past, and/or by suggesting a continuous line from that past to our present. This situation complicates the fact that postcolonial/colonial discourse studies is becoming a substantial subdisciplinary ghetto. In spite of the potential for cooptation, however, there can be no doubt that the apparently crystalline disciplinary mainstream runs muddy if these studies do not provide a persistent dredging operation. Because this dredging is counterproductive when it becomes a constant and self-righteous shaming of fully intending subjects, deconstruction can help here. (It is not accidental that, in spite of Derrida's repeated invocations of disciplinary matters and the crisis of European consciousness, the few attempts at harnessing deconstruction to these ends are not considered germane to deconstructive literary or philosophical critique.)[1]

---

1. For disciplinary matters see *Qui a peur de la philosophie?* (Paris: Flammarion, 1977); "The Principle of Reason: The University in the Eyes of Its Pupils," *Diacrit-*

The mainstream has never run clean, perhaps never can. Part of mainstream education involves learning to ignore this absolutely, with a sanctioned ignorance. Therefore in this opening chapter I read three central texts of the Western philosophical tradition, texts that sanction. In conclusion to "The Three Worlds," Carl Pletsch writes

> Our challenge is not merely to cast aside this conceptual ordering of social scientific labor [into three worlds], but to criticize it. And we must understand the task of criticism in the Kantian, Hegelian, and Marxist sense here. We must, in other words, overcome the limitations that the three worlds notion has imposed upon the social sciences as a matter of course.[2]

It is beyond the scope of this book to demonstrate how the new North-South divide in the post-Soviet world imposes new limitations, although my argument will constantly seek to escape that caution.[3] We

---

ics 13.3, (1983); and "Mochlos; or, The Conflict of the Faculties," in Richard Rand, ed., *Logomachia* (Lincoln: Univ. of Nebraska Press, 1992). Apart from the texts discussed in Chapter 2, imperialist matters are most strongly invoked in "Racism's Last Word," *Critical Inquiry* 12 (Autumn 1985): 290–299, and "The Laws of Reflection: Nelson Mandela, in Admiration," in Derrida and Mustapha Tlili, eds., *For Nelson Mandela* (New York: Seaver Books, 1987). In fact, my argument in this paragraph and this book, that third-worldist/colonial-discursivist criticism unwittingly "(con)states," in the form of an alibi, what neo-colonialism is performing and has already performed, is also to be found in the last piece: "The properly *performative* act [of the institution of a modern nation-state] must produce (proclaim) what in the form of a *constative* act it merely claims, declares, gives the assurance of describing. . . . It cannot make itself be forgotten [*se faire oublier*], as in the case of states founded on a genocide or a quasi-extermination" (p. 18; translation modified). So much at first writing. Derrida's later work has taken this line further. I have noted that trajectory in text and footnote throughout the book.

2. Carl Pletsch, "The Three Worlds, or the Division of Social Scientific Labor, circa 1950–1975," *Comparative Studies in Society and History* 23.4 (October 1981): 588.

3. This sentence was written at the start of final revision, itself dislocated by the author's current active shuttling between North and South. This book is a "practitioner's progress from colonial discourse studies to transnational cultural studies." I report, therefore, that, in the last chapter, in the globalized, electronified, virtualized name of woman, my reach exceeded my grasp and the caution gave way. The footnotes got longer, more narrative, pushing into the text. To those interested in deconstruction, given that I regularly maul the necessary but impossible model so

may, however, suggest that our grasp on that process is made more secure if we in the humanities (Pletsch writes of the social sciences) see the "third world" as a displacement of the old colonies, as colonialism proper displaces itself into neocolonialism. (By neocolonialism I always mean the largely economic rather than the largely territorial enterprise of imperialism. The difference between colonialism and imperialism, crucial to historians, is not of the last importance here.) The post-Soviet situation has moved this narrative into the dynamics of the financialization of the globe.[4] These "great narratives" are becoming increasingly more powerful operating principles, and we in the U.S. academy are participants in it. This is also why it may be interesting to read Kant, Hegel, Marx as remote discursive precursors, rather than as transparent or motivated repositories of "ideas."[5] I keep hoping that some readers may then discover a constructive rather than disabling

---

grievously, I ask: is this a vulgar version of what was with intent undertaken in "Border Lines" and "Circumfessions" (Derrida, "Living On/Border Lines," in Harold Bloom et al., *Deconstruction and Criticism* [New York: Seabury Press, 1979], pp. 75–176; and "Circumfessions," in Derrida and Geoffrey Bennington, *Jacques Derrida* [Chicago: Univ. of Chicago Press, 1993])?

4. Thus industrial (and specifically postindustrial) capitalism is now in an interruptive *différance* with commercial capital; World Trade with finance capital markets. To notice this *différance* is to learn from Derrida; yet Derrida's own resolute ignoring of the difference between the two is caught within it. This inside/outside relationship with something called "deconstruction," to be mentioned in an anticipatory footnote, is also one of the driving motors of this book. (For "interruption" in this sense, see Marx's description of the relationship between the three circuits of capital in Karl Marx, *Capital: A Critique of Political Economy*, tr. David Fernbach, New York: Viking, 1979, vol. 2, p. 109 and *passim*. For this sense of *différance*, see Derrida, "Differance," in *Margins of Philosophy*, tr. Alan Bass, Chicago: Univ. of Chicago Press, 1982, p. 17. We must grapple practically with the curious "fact" that *différance* cannot have a "sense," not just cover incomprehension with mockery. For Derrida's apparent ignorance (or ignoring) of the difference between industry and finance, see Spivak, "Limits and Openings of Marx in Derrida," in *Outside, in the Teaching Machine* (New York: Routledge, 1993), pp. 97–119, and "Ghostwriting," *Diacritics* 25.2 (Summer 1995): 65–84.

5. As always and in general, I find most useful the (later discredited) notion of discursive formations in part 3 of Michel Foucault, *The Archaeology of Knowledge*, tr. A. M. Sheridan Smith (New York: Pantheon, 1972). By "discursive production" I mean something that is among the conditions as well as the effect of "a general system of the formation and transformation of statements [*énoncés*]" (Foucault, *Archaeology*, p. 130).

complicity between our own position and theirs, for there often seems no choice between excuses and accusations, the muddy stream and mudslinging.

As the century spanning the production of Kant and Marx progresses, the relationship between European discursive production and the axiomatics of imperialism also changes, although the latter continues to play the rôle of making the discursive mainstream appear clean, and of making itself appear as the only negotiable way. In the course of this unceasing operation, and in one way or another, an unacknowledgeable moment that I will call "the native informant" is crucially needed by the great texts; and it is foreclosed.

I borrow the term "foreclosure" *(forclusion)* from Lacanian psychoanalysis. I read psychoanalysis as a technique for reading the pre-emergence (Raymond Williams's term) of narrative as ethical instantiation.[6] Let me sketch this technique briefly by way of the entry for "Foreclosure" in a still useful general lexicon of the passage between Freud and Lacan, *The Language of Psycho-Analysis.*[7] My implied reader, who figures herself forth in Chapter 4, will be obliged to consult lexicons.

As *Language* points out,

> [t]he sense brought to the fore by Lacan, . . . [is to be found] for instance, in [what] Freud writes . . . [about] "a much more energetic and successful kind of defence. Here, the ego rejects [*verwirft*] the incompatible idea *together with the affect* and behaves as if the idea had never occurred to the ego at all." . . . The work from which Lacan has most readily derived support for his . . . idea of foreclosure is the case-history of the "Wolf-Man." (Emphasis mine.)

The idea of the rejection of an affect can direct us into the dis-locating of psychoanalytic speculation from practical science (for which specialized training is recommended) to ethical responsibility (a burden of

---

6. I have discussed this approach in "Echo," in Donna Landry and Gerald MacLean, eds., *The Spivak Reader* (New York: Routledge, 1995), p. 178 and *passim.* I repeat some of that general argument later in this chapter.

7. Jean Laplanche and J.-B. Pontalis, *The Language of Psycho-Analysis,* tr. Donald Nicholson-Smith (New York: Norton, 1974), pp. 166–169. All the quotations about foreclosure are from these pages.

being human). It is also useful to remember that it was the history of the Wolf-Man analysis that led Nicolas Abraham and Maria Torok into the thinking of cryptonymy, the encrypting of a name.[8] Derrida, who works this dis-location by disclaiming "responsibility" within the circuit of the production and consumption of psychoanalytic practice, mimes the encrypting of the patronymic and the search for the impossible matronymic in a text of mourning for his father.[9] In this chapter, I shall docket the encrypting of the name of the "native informant" *as the name of Man*—a name that carries the inaugurating affect of being human. *We* cannot diagnose a psychosis here, but we can supplement the ethical Freud who wrote *The Un-ease [Unbehagen] of Civilization* with this thought: that this rejecion of affect served and serves as the energetic and successful defense of the civilizing mission.

As the lexicon traces the development of the idea in Freud, it mentions that the idea comprises an inner-outer switch: an internal withdrawal of cathexis [*Besetzung*] that becomes a "'disavowal [*Verleugnung*] of the real external world.'"[10] "How, in the last reckoning, are we to understand this sort of 'repression' into the external world. . . . [T]he withdrawal of cathexis [*Besetzung*] is also a withdrawal of significance [*Bedeutung*]."

Taking this inside-outside two-step as his guide, "Lacan defines foreclosure . . . a translation [of Freud] into his own language. . . . [as] 'what has been foreclosed from the Symbolic reappears in the Real.'" Thus foreclosure relates to a Freudian "'primary process' embodying two complementary operations: 'the *Einbeziehung ins Ich*, introduction into the subject, and the *Ausstoßung aus dem Ich*, expulsion from the subject.'" The Real is or carries the mark of that expulsion.

---

8. Nicolas Abraham and Maria Torok, *The Wolf Man's Magic Word: A Cryptonymy*, tr. Nicholas Rand (Minneapolis: Univ. of Minnesota Press, 1986).

9. I discussed this in Spivak, "*Glas*-piece; A *Compte-rendu*," *Diacritics* 7.3 (Fall 1977): 22–43. As Derrida elaborates in *The Gift of Death*, tr. David Wills (Chicago: Univ. of Chicago Press, 1995), p. 85f., the situation between father and son is a basic site of the conflict between ethics and sacrifice in the Jewish tradition.

10. One might think this withdrawal within the circuit of *Besetzung* (occupation) :: *Gesetz* (law) :: *Setzung* (positing) → *Satz* (proposition). The native informant ("lesser breeds beyond the law?") slips out of the *énoncé*/*Satz*/statement of being human.

I think of the "native informant" as a name for that mark of expulsion from the name of Man—a mark crossing out the impossibility of the ethical relation.

I borrow the term from ethnography, of course. In that discipline, the native informant, although denied autobiography as it is understood in the Northwestern European tradition (codename "West"), is taken with utmost seriousness. He (and occasionally she) *is* a blank, though generative of a text of cultural identity that only the West (or a Western-model discipline) could inscribe. The practice of some benevolent cultural nativists today can be compared to this, although the cover story there is of a fully self-present voice-consciousness. Increasingly, there is the self-marginalizing or self-consolidating migrant or postcolonial masquerading as a "native informant." I am discovering the native informant clear out of this cluster. The texts I read are not ethnographic and therefore do not celebrate this figure. They take for granted that the "European" is the human norm and offer us descriptions and/or prescriptions. And yet, even here, the native informant is needed and foreclosed. In Kant he is needed as the example for the heteronomy of the determinant, to set off the autonomy of the reflexive judgment, which allows freedom for the rational will; in Hegel as evidence for the spirit's movement from the unconscious to consciousness; in Marx as that which bestows normativity upon the narrative of the modes of production. These moves, in various guises, still inhabit and inhibit our attempts to overcome the limitations imposed on us by the newest division of the world, to the extent that, as the North continues ostensibly to "aid" the South—as formerly imperialism "civilized" the New World—the South's crucial assistance to the North in keeping up its resource-hungry lifestyle is forever foreclosed. In the pores of this book will be the suggestion that, the typecase of the foreclosed native informant today is the poorest *woman* of the South. But the period and texts under our consideration in this chapter will produce—to cite Gramsci's uncanny insight—the native informant(s) as a site of unlisted traces. To steer ourselves through the Scylla of cultural relativism and the Charybdis of nativist culturalism regarding this period, we need a commitment not only to narrative and counternarrative, but also to the rendering (im)possible of (another) narrative.

As my opening quotation from Pletsch betrays, our sense of critique is too thoroughly determined by Kant, Hegel, and Marx for us to be able to reject them as "motivated imperialists," although this is too often the vain gesture performed by critics of imperialism. A deconstructive politics of reading would acknowledge the determination as well as the imperialism and see if the magisterial texts can now be our servants, as the new magisterium constructs itself in the name of the Other.[11]

Foucault's historical fable locates the breakdown of the discourse of sovereignty and the emergence of the micrology of power at the end of the French and British eighteenth century. In the same fabulating spirit, one might suggest that the end of the "German" eighteenth century (if one can speak of "Germany" as a unified proper name in that era) provides material for a narrative of crisis management: the "scientific" fabrication of new representations of self and world that would provide alibis for the domination, exploitation, and epistemic violation entailed by the establishment of colony and empire.

As we move within the great narratives of cultural self-representation, it is appropriate to note that Germany's imperialist adventures did not consolidate themselves until the latter part of the nineteenth century.[12] The narrative of "German" cultural self-representation, within the Western European context, is therefore one of difference. Its very singularity provides a sort of link with that earlier scenario of self-representation that would not allow the name "German," a lack of unified nationhood that could only find a fuller founding through the rediscovery of a German antiquity; a lack of participation in the European Renaissance that would nonetheless allow a modern and active reenactment of the Renaissance.[13]

---

11. See, once again, Derrida, *Of Grammatology*, tr. Spivak (Baltimore: Johns Hopkins Univ. Press, 1976), p. 24; "Otobiographies: The Ear of the Other," in *The Ear of the Other: Otobiography: Transference: Translation*, tr. Peggy Kamuf (New York: Schocken Books, 1985); and Derrida, "The Principle of Reason."

12. See John Noyes, *Colonial Space: Spatiality in the Discourse of German Southwest Africa* (1884–1915) (Philadelphia: Harwood Publishers, 1992) as a starting point. Although theoretically derivative, its documentation is helpful. As its title indicates, it does not cover all of Germany's colonial adventure.

13. In "Onto-Theology of National-Humanism: Prolegomena to a Hypothesis," *Oxford Literary Review* 14.1–2 (1992), Derrida quotes Karl Grün, against whom "Marx ironises with some verve," as typical of a specifically German trend,

It is hard to plot the lines by which a people (metonymically that group within it that is self-consciously the custodian of culture) construct the explanations that establish its so-called cultural identity. Yet it cannot be denied that such lines are drawn and redrawn. If we think of the ways in which our own cultural identities and rôles are negotiated and renegotiated, implicitly and explicitly, by way of great narratives ranging from the popular to the scholarly, it is not implausible to make the following suggestion. Cultural and intellectual "Germany," the place of self-styled difference from the rest of what is still understood as "continental" Europe and Britain, was the main source of the meticulous scholarship that established the vocabulary of proto-archetypal ("comparative" in the disciplinary sense) identity, or kinship, without direct involvement in the utilization of that other difference, between the colonizer and the colonized; in the nascent discourses of comparative philology, comparative religion, even comparative literature. The difference in tone between a William Jones (1746–1794) and a Herder (1744–1803)—taxonomizing Sanskrit and thinking alterity by way of language/culture, respectively—will bring home my point. "Africa" remained a place apart on this network of possible identity, a place that provoked bafflement or hysteria.[14]

The field of philosophy as such, whose model was the merging of science and truth, remained untouched by the comparative impulse. In this area, Germany produced authoritative "universal" narratives where the subject remained unmistakably European. These narratives—Kant's cosmopolitheia, Hegel's itinerary of the Idea, Marx's socialist

---

which he locates earlier in Fichte, and by way of which, "in the name of an apolitical people which is not a people . . . the national-philosophical assertion as cosmopolitanism states its paradoxes which are also . . . paradigms for the future. . . . We shall find the recurrent effects of this on the most opposite sides, in Heidegger as well as Adorno" (pp. 17, 22). Jürgen Habermas, whose work presents itself as a paradigm for the future from within postwar West Germany, may perhaps also be read with this trend in mind.

14. See V. Y. Mudimbe, *The Invention of Africa: Gnosis, Philosophy, and the Order of Knowledge* (Bloomington: Indiana Univ. Press, 1988) for a philosophical account of the resistance to this phenomenon. For a careful analysis of the contemporary fallout of this separation in the academic subdivision of labor, see *The Yearbook of Comparative and General Literature* 43 (1995).

homeopathy—neither inaugurated nor consolidated a specifically scholarly control of the matter of imperialism.

Carl Pletsch's admonition to us to be Kantian, Hegelian, and Marxist in our dismantling of third-worldist talk is yet another example of their influence in the formation of the European ethico-political subject. In my estimation, these source texts of European ethico-political selfrepresentation are also complicitous with what is today a self-styled postcolonial discourse. On the margins of my reading is the imagined and (im)possible perspective I have called the native informant. Ostentatiously to turn one's back on, say, this trio, when so much of one's critique is clearly if sometimes unwittingly copied from them, is to disavow agency, declare kingdom come by a denial of history.

On the other hand, to imagine that the positioning of the other remains the same in all their work is to assume that the only real engagement with the other is in the "objective" social science disciplines, after all. My point is that we in the humanities, dealing with the position of the other as an implied "subject"(ive) position, must also vary our assumptions depending upon the text with which we are dealing. Paradoxically, every questioner who enters the book trade does so as a species of "native informant" or has been trained from infancy, for hours every day, even if reactively, in some version of an academic culture that has accommodated these three fellows, often in their radical margins but sometimes also in their conservative centers. I write in the conviction that sometimes it is best to sabotage what is inexorably to hand, than to invent a tool that no one will test, while mouthing varieties of liberal pluralism.

I will call my reading of Kant "mistaken." I believe there are just disciplinary grounds for irritation at my introduction of "the empirical and the anthropological" into a philosophical text that slowly leads us toward the rational study of morals as such. I rehearse it in the hope that such a reading might take into account that philosophy has been and continues to be travestied in the service of the narrativization of history. My exercise may be called a scrupulous travesty in the interest of producing a counternarrative that will make visible the foreclosure of the subject whose lack of access to the position of narrator is the condition of possibility of the consolidation of Kant's position. If "the combination of these talents [among them "mixing up the empirical with the rational"] in one person produces only bunglers," let us remember that "bungling" may be a synonym for intervention.[15]

Kant's *Critique of Pure Reason* charts the operation of the reason that cognizes nature theoretically. *The Critique of Practical Reason* charts the operation of the rational will. The operations of the aesthetic judgment allow the play of concepts of nature with concepts of freedom.

The Critique of Judgment is divided into the Aesthetic and the Teleological; the section on aesthetic judgment is further divided into considerations of the Beautiful and the Sublime.[16] In the experience of the beautiful the subject, without cognizing itself, constructs a seeming object of cognition without objective reference; pleasure in the beautiful is pleasure at the subject's capacity to represent an object of cognition without the reference necessary for true cognition. Here we see the connection between the aesthetic judgment and the realm of theoretical reason: the subject *represents* an object for cognition—art allows the *ungrounded* play of the concept of nature—by which things can be cognized.

In the moment of the Sublime the subject accedes to the rational will. It has often been noted that the rational will intervenes to cover over a moment of deprivation. There is, strictly speaking, no full experience of the Sublime. "The feeling of the sublime is . . . a feeling of pain arising from the want of accordance between the aesthetical estimation . . . formed by the imagination and the same formed by reason." But since this "judgment of the inadequacy of our greatest faculty of sense" is reasonable and correct, "a pleasure [is] excited." The superiority of the rational over the sensible "arouses in us the feeling of our supersensible determination [*Bestimmung*]" (*CJ* 96–97).[17] It is not too excessive to say that we are programmed or, better, tuned, to feel the inadequacy

---

15. Kant, *Foundations of the Metaphysics of Morals with Critical Essays*, tr. Lewis White Beck (New York: Bobbs-Merrill, 1969), p. 5.

16. Kant, *The Critique of Judgment*, tr. J. H. Bernard (New York: Hafner Press, 1951). All references to this text are incorporated into my own. Translations have been modified where necessary.

17. *Bestimmung*—"determination"—is translated many different ways in English. Because of the consistency of the metaphor in the concept in German, resounding in *Stimme* (voice), and *Stimmung*—among other things a suggestion of "tuning"—I indicate the word whenever it occurs in Kant's text.

of the imagination (thus tripping the circuit to the superiority of reason) through the pain incited by the Sublime. The language is persistently one of inescapable obligation, although the concept in question is that of freedom. "The tendency for this determination [*Bestimmung*] lies in our nature, while its development and exercise remains incumbent and obligatory" (*CJ* 102). *Anlage*, the word often used by Kant and generally translated as "tendency," carries the sense of a blueprint or program as well.

Such a model, of the *programmed* access to the concept of freedom as the pleasure of "reason . . . exercis[ing] dominion over sensibility" (*CJ 109*) implicitly presupposes that "freedom"—generated by a determination or programming—is a trope of freedom. Indeed, "the feeling of the sublime in nature" is a clandestine metalepsis (substitution of effect for cause). It is "a respect for our own determination [*Bestimmung*] which, by a certain subreption, we attribute to an object of nature." It is a dissimulated "exchange [*Verwechselung*] of respect for the *object* [natural sublime] for respect for the idea of humanity in our *subject*" (*CJ* 96; emphasis mine).

All this relates to the sublime in magnitude, not to the superior category of the "dynamic" sublime. I should like, however, to emphasize a few aspects of Kant's descriptive morphology that remain common to all that he wrote about the human access to the rational will. This access is structured like the programmed supplementation of a structurally necessary lack. To denominate this supplementation a feeling for nature is at best a metalepsis, by a certain "subreption." "Subreption" is rather a strong word that, in Ecclesiastical Law, means the "suppression of truth to obtain indulgence" *(OED).*[18]

Indeed, in his discussion of the dynamic sublime—"as might that has

----

18. In the *Inaugural Dissertation*, "by analogy with the accepted meaning of the term subreption," Kant is hard on "the metaphysical fallacy of subreption. . . . Such hybrid axioms (hybrid, in that they proffer what is sensitive as being necessarily bound up with the intellectual concept) I call a surreptitious axiom. Those principles of intellectual error that have most harmfully infested metaphysics have, indeed, proceeded from these spurious axioms" (Kant, *Inaugural Dissertation and Early Writings on Space*, tr. John Handyside [Chicago: Open Court, 1929], p. 74). On the next page Kant goes on to propose "[t]he principle . . . of the reduction of any surreptitious axiom." I consider its elaboration in the text.

no dominion over us"—Kant similarly marks the moment of improper displacement of the epithet upon nature, as he implies a certain inevitability of usage in it: "Everything that excites this feeling [of superiority to nature within and without us] in us . . . is called then (although *improperly*) sublime" (*CJ* 104; emphasis mine).

The structure of the sublime is a troping. The sublime in nature is operated by a subreptitious impropriety. Our access to morality is operated by rhetoric and clandestinity. The *Critique of Judgment* repeatedly cautions us therefore against any attempt at *cognitive control* of the rational will.[19]

"The tuning of the mind [*die Stimmung des Gemüts*; the metaphor is the same as in *Bestimmung*, or determination] to the feeling of the sublime"—the necessary structure of supplementation and compensation that I have described above—"requires its receptivity [*erfordert eine Empfänglichkeit desselben*] to ideas" (*CJ* 104). This receptivity, a "natural" possibility as part of the programming of determinate humanity, is actualized only by culture [*Kultur* rather than *Bildung* (education or formation)]:

> Reason exerts a power over sensibility [*Sinnlichkeit*] in order to intend it adequately [*angemessen*] to its proper realm (the practical), and to let it [*lassen*] look out upon [*auf*] the infinite, which is for it an abyss. . . . But although the judgment upon the sublime in nature *needs* culture . . . it is not therefore primarily *produced* by culture. . . . It has its foundation [*Grundlage*] in human *nature* . . . in the tendency [*Anlage*] to the feeling for (practical) ideas, i.e., to the moral [*zu dem Moralischen*]. (*CJ* 105)

Let us note this rather special inscription of a judgment programmed in nature, needing culture, but not produced by culture. It is not possible to *become* cultured in this culture, if you are *naturally* alien to it. We should read Kant's description of the desirability of the proper humanizing of the human through culture within this frame of paradox: "Without *development* of moral ideas, that which we, prepared by cul-

---

19. In this connection, see Patrick Riley's critique of Hannah Arendt's *Lectures on Kant's Political Philosophy* in "On De Leue's Review of Arendt's *Lectures on Kant's Political Philosophy,*" *Political Theory* 12 (August 1984).

ture, call sublime presents itself to man in the raw [*dem rohen Menschen*] merely as terrible" (*CJ* 105; emphasis mine). The adjective *roh* is suggestive. It is generally translated "uneducated." In fact in Kant, the "uneducated" are specifically the child and the poor, the "naturally uneducable" is woman.[20] By contrast, *der rohe Mensch*, man in the raw, can, in its signifying reach, accommodate the savage and the primitive.

To claim that the moral impulse in us is cognitively grounded is,

---

20. In *Le Respect des femmes (Kant et Rousseau)* (Paris: Galilée, 1982), Sarah Kofman discusses the sublime as something the access to which is made possible by keeping woman at a distance. In this text, as well as in Genevieve Lloyd's *The Man of Reason: "Male" and "Female" in Western Philosophy* (Minneapolis: Univ. of Minnesota Press, 1984), and Beverley Brown's "Kant for the Eighties: Comments on Hillis Miller's 'The Search for Grounds in Literary Studies,'" *Oxford Literary Review* 9 (1987): 137–145, the treatment of (the theme and figure of) woman is shown to be demonstrated abundantly by Kant's text, even if often in the ruse of disavowal. As I hope to show, the figure of the "native informant" is, by contrast, foreclosed. Rhetorically crucial at the most important moment in the argument, it is not part of the argument in any way. Was it in this rift that the seeds of the civilizing mission of today's universalist feminism were sown? At best, it is a recoding and reterritorializing of the native-informant-as-woman-of-the-South, so that she can be part of the argument. I consider the rôle of the UN-style initiative in the New World Order in the pores of this book. The wholesale Americanizing of Southern babies through adoption is another issue. Although the personal goodwill, indeed obsession, is, in most of these cases, unquestionable, one is also reminded of Cecil Rhodes's remark, mutatis mutandis, of course: "I contend that we are the first race in the world, and that the more of the world we inhabit the better it is for the human race. . . . If there be a God, I think that what he would like me to do is to paint as much of the map of Africa British red as possible" (quoted in L. S. Stavrianos, *Global Rift: The Third World Comes of Age* [New York: Morrow, 1981], p. 263). In the domestic context, the problem was approached by what has now become a classic: Gloria T. Hull et al., eds., *All the Women Are White, All the Blacks Are Men, But Some of Us Are Brave: Black Women's Studies* (Old Westbury N.Y.: Feminist Press, 1982). I am not suggesting that Kant's expressed view on the matter of colonialism and race, to be found, for example, in relatively peripheral texts such as the "Third Definitive Article for a Perpetual Peace" (in *Perpetual Peace and Other Essays on Politics, History, and Morals*, tr. Ted Humphrey [Indianapolis: Hackett Publishing, 1983]) or "On the Distinctiveness of Races in General" (in Earl W. Count, ed., *This Is Race: An Anthology Selected from the International Literature on the Races of Man* [New York: Henry Schuman, 1950]) should be ignored, although their assumptions are historically interpretable as well. I am suggesting that a revised politics of reading can give sufficient value to the deployment of rhetorical energy in the margins of the texts acknowledged to be central.

then, to fail to recognize that its origin is a supplement. And uncritically to name nature sublime is to fail to recognize the philosophical impropriety of the denomination. Yet these cognitive failures are a part of developed culture and can even have a functional rôle in them. As Kant will argue later, they may be "wholesome illusions" (*CJ* 313). Only the cultured are susceptible to these particular errors and to their correction. The metalepsis that substitutes respect for the object for respect for humanity (in the subject) is a *normative* catachresis, a "wholesome" abuse of a figurative move. (The dictionary defines a "catachresis" as, among other things, "abuse or perversion of a trope or metaphor.") The distinction between a correct and an incorrect denomination might itself be indeterminate here. On the other hand, the mistake made by the *raw* man, for whom the abyss of the infinite is fearful rather than sublime, must be corrected through culture itself, although on the threshold of such a project stands the peculiar relationship between productive and natural culture cited earlier. (One of the ideological consequences of this relationship might be the conviction that the cultural mission of imperialism can never really succeed, but it must nonetheless be undertaken. Further consequences of this position for the postcolonial and current predicaments will be examined later in the book.)

Those who are cooked by culture can "denominate" nature sublime [*erhaben nennen*], although necessarily through a metalepsis. To the raw man the abyss comes forth [*erhaben vorkommen*] as merely terrible.[21] The raw man has not yet achieved or does not possess a subject whose *Anlage* or programming includes the structure of feeling for the moral. He is not yet the subject divided and perspectivized among the three critiques. In other words, he is not yet or simply not the subject as such, the hero of the *Critiques*, the only example of the concept of a natural yet rational being. This gap between the subject as such and the not-yet-subject can be bridged under propitious circumstances by culture.

---

21. Did this metaphor leap to my eyes because of the Vedic tradition of cooking the world in/as sacrificial fire as the specific task of the *brāhmana*, who might loosely translate as "the philosopher?" Charles Malamoud has masterfully laid out this tradition for the Western reader in *Cuir le monde: Rite et pensée en Inde ancienne* (Paris: Découverte, 1989), although he does not comment on its rôle in sustaining social hierarchy.

As Freud noted, the transformation of the abyss (of nature's infinity) from fearful to sublime through the supplementing mediation of reason—a violent shuttling from *Abgrund* to *Grund*—bears more than a resemblance to the Oedipal scene.[22]

Schiller has been criticized for anthropomorphizing the narrative implicit in Kant's discussion of the sublime.[23] And indeed, Kant's version of the access to the sublime can only too easily be read as a narrative whose adequate representation in programs of education will produce the correct empirico-psychological reflexes. Here Kant's own warnings against such practices should perhaps be heeded.[24] In spite of Schiller's careful specification of his own project as *aesthetic* education,

---

22. "Kant's Categorical Imperative Is Thus the Direct Heir to the Oedipus Complex," in Sigmund Freud, *The Standard Edition of the Complete Psychological Works*, tr. James Strachey et al. (New York: Norton, 1961–1976), vol. 19, p. 167; this edition hereafter cited as *SE*. Freud does not notice the specific play of sexual difference with Nature as the abyss of the fearful mother. See also Kofman, *Le respect*, pp. 42–44. It has often been noticed that section 27 of the "Analytic of the Sublime" is full of images of violence.

23. Paul de Man, "Kant and Schiller," in *Aesthetic Ideology* (Minneapolis: Univ. of Minnesota Press, 1996), pp. 129–162.

24. These warnings deal with violent revolution. It is well known that, according to Kant, "one should view neither the united will of the people nor the contract as empirical quantities. Such an understanding would not only be incorrect from a philosophical point of view but also politically dangerous. . . . Kant welcomes the principles of the French Revolution but condemns the Jacobin terror" (Ottfried Höffe, *Immanuel Kant*, tr. Marshall Farrier [Albany: SUNY Press, 1994], pp. 183–184). It can perhaps be argued that there "is" a radical discontinuity—if discontinuity can be spoken of in the mode of being—between all ethical programs and decisions to implement them in practice. Indeed, this is Derrida's argument about decisions in "The Force of Law" (see Appendix). In Kant, this rift is avoided by assigning justice itself (rather than accountability in law) to the constitutionally collective calculus alone; or rather, to keep to the Kantian vocabulary, "the acknowledged duty of the human soul . . . [to] the evolution of a constitution in accordance with natural law" (Kant, *The Conflict of the Faculties*, tr. Mary J. Gregor [New York: Abaris Books, 1979], p. 157). For a discussion of the relationship between natural and positive law, we loop back to Derrida, "Force of Law," p. 927f. One of the chief problems with preference-based ethical theories is their inability to work this into their calculations in order to destabilize them *productively*. See, for example, Amartya Sen and Bernard Williams, eds., *Utilitarianism and Beyond* (Cambridge: Cambridge Univ. Press, 1982), an otherwise brilliant collection from a variety of points of view.

which would, presumably, raise it out of empirical psychology, his reading practice, according to Paul de Man, betrays him in the end.

De Man implies that Schiller's aberrant reading might be a necessary supplement to—a substitution that is possible for—something already there in Kant's text:

> Kant was dealing with a strictly philosophical concern, with a strictly philosophical, epistemological problem, which he chose to state for reasons of his own in interpersonal, dramatic terms, thus telling dramatically and interpersonally something which was purely epistemological and which had nothing to do with the pragma of the relationship between human beings. Here, in Schiller's case, the explanation is entirely empirical, psychological, without any concern for the epistemological implications. And for that reason, Schiller can then claim that in this negotiation, in this arrangement, where the analogy of danger is substituted for the real danger, where the imagination of danger is substituted for the experience of danger, that by this substitution, this tropological substitution, that the sublime succeeds, that the sublime works out, that the sublime achieves itself, and brings together a new kind of synthesis. . . . Schiller appears as the ideology of Kant's critical philosophy.[25]

To correct such an aberration by deciding to avoid anthropomorphism altogether, which seems consonant with de Man's practice, one might come to a reversal of Schiller's problem and therefore its legitimation. I am proposing to "situate" rather than expurgate (or excuse: "Kant chose to state for reasons of his own . . .") the anthropomorphic moment in Kant. Such a moment is irreducible in his text, as it is in any discursive practice, including, of course, de Man's or mine. The best we can do is to *attempt* to account for it. Not to do so is to stop at Kant's tropology or figurative practice and ignore the dissimulated history and geography of the subject in Kant's text. If we call this "the politics of the subject," then such an attempt would be simply to follow Althusser's old directive about how to read philosophy: "Everything which touches on politics may be fatal to philosophy, for philosophy lives on poli-

---

25. De Man, "Kant and Schiller," pp. 143, 147.

tics."[26] From within the discipline of philosophy, such a reading can never justify itself.

Since part of the task of this book is to show how deconstruction can serve reading, we might notice here that in an early essay where Derrida takes a whole generation to task for naively anthropologizing philosophy, he also outlines the possibility of doing so strategically. The reasons he gives seem to offer a provisional justification for my attempt: "the anxious and busy multiplication of colloquia in the West is doubtless an effect of [a] difference . . . *of an entirely other order than that of the internal or intra-philosophical differences of opinion* . . . that is bearing down, with a mute, growing and menacing pressure, on the enclosure of Western collocution. The latter doubtless makes an effort to interiorize this difference, to master it, . . . by affecting itself with it."[27]

In the end, speaking presumably for "the West" (everything defined by the "we" of humanism) in 1968, Derrida writes: "Perhaps we are between [the guard mounted around the house—critical vigilance?— the awakening to the day that is coming—radical practice?]. . . . But who, we?"[28] Twenty years later, Derrida seems to construct an answer by playing a *fort-da* game with the figure of the hybrid, the migrant.[29]

---

26. Louis Althusser, *Lenin and Philosophy and Other Essays,* tr. Ben Brewster (New York: Monthly Review Press, 1971), pp. 29–30.

27. Derrida, "The Ends of Man," *Margins of Philosophy,* p. 113. Emphasis mine.

28. Ibid., p. 136.

29. *The Other Heading: Reflections on Today's Europe,* tr. Pascale-Anne Brault and Michael B. Naas (Bloomington: Indiana Univ. Press, 1992) is the book that starts this thematic of the split self as migrant hybrid: "I feel European *among other things,* would this be, in this very declaration, to be more or less European? . . . It is up to others, in any case, and up to me *among them,* to decide" (p. 83). *Aporias,* tr. Thomas Dutoit (Stanford, Calif.: Stanford Univ. Press, 1993), pulls it back into an earlier text of hybridity—Catholic Spain—and introduces the Marrano: "If one, figuring, calls Marrano [*si l'on appelle marrane, par figure*] anyone who remains faithful to a secret he has not chosen, in the very place where he lives" (p. 81; translation modified). By the graphic of this figure (if not the logic of the metaphor) it is possible to think that the utterly persuasive dominant discourse of Derrida's critique of Western metaphysics contains signs (or at least signals) of a prior identity hidden by collective covenant in response to shared menace. Given the importance of the Father-Son situation as the site of contestation of ethics by sacrifice, and Derrida's insistent iteration of the texts of Hegel, Freud, Nietzsche, Genet, as well

Let me point beyond the argument here to suggest that an unquestioning privileging of the migrant may also turn out to be a figure of the effacement of the native informant.

My attempt to read the anthropological moment in Kant is consonant with Paul de Man's version of deconstruction as well. Especially in his analysis of Rousseau, de Man has shown how the discovery that something that claims to be true is a mere trope is the first (tropological) step in what de Man called deconstruction.[30] The second (performative) step is to disclose how the corrrective impulse within the

---

as his own bio-graphy in his concatenations, it may not be without meaning that he has made it public that his son showed him a text of the Marrano. Does this then name, make specific—and necessarily efface—in an affect-rich "narrow" sense, the general graphematic that all disclosure is also effacement (without derivation from an original)—by way of a differance that "is" not, or a gift, if there is any? The slippery negotiation between general and narrow seems there between the first and second phrases of location in the following sentence, but am I reading what I want to read? Does one not, often?: "in the underived night [*nuit sans contraire*] where the radical absence of any historical witness keeps him [*le tient* does not warrant 'him or her']"—general sense—"in the dominant culture that by definition holds the calendar [*dispose du calendrier*]"—narrow sense—"this secret keeps the Marrano even before he keeps it"—whatever I seem to intend there is that other text at work (p. 81; see also p. 77). In the mean time, as it were, the graphic of the hybrid migrant is also generalized, earlier in the same text, as the absolute *arrivant* who "does not cross a threshold scparating two identifiable places" (p. 34). The passage about the Marrano makes it clear that the sense of the *arrivant* there is not "absolute" by specifying the Marrano's home as "the home of the first or of the second *arrivant*" (p. 81), and therefore presumably from and/or to "an identifiable place(s)." From this it is a step to inscribe Marx as migrant and Marrano—whose Abrahamic messianism re-vectors "The Jewish Question." "We" are, then, the Marrano as old European. Since I argue in this book that the "postcolonial" as a figure masquerades as and overwrites the foreclosed position I am calling the "native informant," it seems appropriate to mention that none of this possible Derridian itinerary is "postcolonial" in the narrow sense. Algeria is not inscribed on it as a recently liberated nation-state. In that inscription, Derrida's rôle is that of an honorable and well-placed Eurocentric economico-cultural migrant: making his immense reputation count for migrant activism, and organizing public and academic fora; susceptible only to the general critique of the place of migrant activism with reference to counter-globalization resistance, which Chapter 4 will open.

30. De Man, "Allegory of Reading: *(Profession de Foi),*" in *Allegories of Reading: Figural Language in Rousseau, Nietzsche, Rilke, and Proust* (New Haven: Yale Univ. Press, 1979), p. 236 and *passim.*

tropological analysis is obliged to act out a lie in attempting to establish it as the corrected version of truth. De Man tracked the laying out of this double structure in a handful of writers: Rousseau, Nietzsche, Hölderlin, Proust, Yeats. In Kant, it is the presupposition of the nascent axiomatics of imperialism that gives the tropological deconstruction the lie. This is most clearly seen in the last part of *The Critique of Judgment*—"Critique of the Teleological Judgment."

"The Critique of the Teleological Judgment" occupies a curious place in the architectonics of Kant's critical system, laid out in the conclusion to the Introduction to *The Critique of Judgment* (*CJ* 34, translation modified), all the more interesting because written *after* the book:

The following table may facilitate the review of all the higher faculties according to their systematic unity.

ALL THE FACULTIES OF THE MIND

Cognitive faculties	Desiring faculty [*Begehrungsvermögen*]

Feeling of pleasure and unpleasure [*Unlust*]

COGNITIVE FACULTIES

Understanding	Judgment	Reason

A PRIORI PRINCIPLES

Conformity to law	Purposiveness	Final purpose

APPLICATION TO

Nature	Art	Freedom

The place of *The Critique of Judgment* is in the middle column above. According to the table, the only application of the faculty of judgment seems to be to Art. Yet Art is the subject matter only of a *part* of *The Critique of Judgment*, namely the First Book, the second part of the Second Book of the First Division and the entire Second Division—all three belonging to Part 1 ("Critique of the Aesthetical Judgment"). Strictly speaking, the "Analytic of the Sublime"—where the being's accession to the moral law is first outlined in its structure—is outside the scope of application of judgment by the table above, for "the deduction of aesthetical judgments on the objects of nature must not be directed to what we call sublime in nature, but only to the beautiful" (*CJ* 120). There are no examples of sublime art in Kant.

But it is teleological judgment that most significantly falls outside of the scope of the application of judgment as specified in the table. It has nothing to do with Art at all. Its subject is the possibility of purposiveness in nature and of an intelligent author of the world. Both are cases of supplementation, paralleling the structure outlined in the analytic of the Sublime.

"The Critique of the Teleological Judgment" is thus developed in a space that is both inside and outside of the perceived closure of Kant's system as outlined in the third *Critique*. It is curious that Kant puts the most crucial issues of judgment—politics and religion, natural/social and divine justice—in such a structurally indeterminate place. It is almost as if the subreption or suppression that otherwise unaccountably wins art the legitimate place of application of judgment is thus made *structurally* manifest, although the *declaration* of the text securely places not only Art, but *beautiful* art—purposiveness *without* purpose—as the only legitimate field of play of the *a priori* principle of purposiveness. I say this, of course, because the sublime is confined, although improperly, to a judgment about *Nature*. By this lacuna in the table, the exceptional is perhaps made the rule and the legitimate exceptionalized. Indeterminacy informs the question of the moral in Kant in more than one way. The larger part of *The Critique of Judgment* would be docketed "by Kant" as outside of the proper scope of judgment, if the summarizing outline were strictly followed. It may, however, be supplemented as philosophy.[31]

In "The Critique of the Teleological Judgment," our thoughts of a purpose in nature, a purpose in human life, and the sense of an intelligent author of the world are shown to occupy the site of a desire, our very capacity to desire—*Begehrungsvermögen*—the faculty of desire it-

---

31. If this seems too fanciful, one might note Kant's repeated and peculiar admissions of non-seriousness in regard to his political writings, as recorded by Hans Saner, *Kant's Political Thought: Its Origins and Development*, tr. E. B. Ashton (Chicago: Univ. of Chicago Press, 1973), p. 1.

self—practical reason becoming effective through the judgment fashioning teleologies:

> [to] suppose [man] to be the final purpose of creation, in order to have a rational ground for holding that nature must harmonize with his happiness if it is . . . an absolute whole according to principles of purposes . . . is only the capacity of desire [*Begehrungsvermögen*—generally translated "faculty of desire"]. . . . It is that worth which he alone can give to himself and which consists in . . . how and according to what principles he acts, and that not as a link in nature's chain but in the *freedom* of his faculty of desire. That is, a good will is that whereby alone his being [*Dasein*] can have an absolute worth and in reference to which the being of the world can have a *final purpose*. (*CJ* 293)

There is a quiet slippage between the capacity to desire and a good will. The former is an inbuilt characteristic of the mind, the latter a deliberative or characterological property. How the one *must* present itself as the other is part of the argument of this section. In passages such as the above, Kant's own text seems to be rehearsing the scenario that it lays bare. If we read this as the text signalling to us its own vulnerability to the system it describes, it becomes part of the grandeur of Kantian ethics.

Kant calls the source of our sense of *duty* "a commanded *effect*" (*CJ* 321; emphasis mine)—*eine gebotene Wirkung*—rather than a mere command or a commanding cause. I have been at pains to trace the supplementary production of the concepts of practical reason as *effects* of a structuring, of an *Anlage*. If we keep that necessarily-groundless-yet-necessarily-supplemental structure in mind, Kant's own description of exposing the supplementary production of the concept of freedom becomes interpretable as itself a supplementing of the abyss: "It is the *duty* of the philosopher . . . to expose the above illusion, however wholesome" (*CJ* 314). A few lines above, the illusion, too, is described as a "supplementation [*Ergänzung*]," albeit an "arbitrary" one (*CJ* 313).

The freedom of desire is the condition of possibility of the concept of freedom. Yet there are many passages where the functioning of this freedom is described as a compulsion: ". . . in order to account for . . . the existence of things commensurate with [*gemäss*] *a final purpose*, we *must* assume, not only first an intelligent Being (for the possibility of things of nature for which we are *compelled* to judge of *as purposes*), but also a *moral* Being, as author of the world" (*CJ* 306; I have italicized "must" and "compelled").

The compulsion to be free operates through an obligation to supplement. Kant's inscription of indeterminacy in his description of faith, re-writing an older thematics of absurdity, is well known:

> It is therefore the persistent [*beharrlich*] principle of the mind to assume as true, because *obligated* to do so [*wegen der Verbindlichkeit zu demselben*], that which [it] is necessary to presuppose as condition of the possibility of the highest moral final purpose, although its *possibility as well as* [*so wohl auch*] *its impossibility*, cannot be looked into by us [*von uns nicht angesehen werden kann*] (*CJ* 324; emphasis added)

This double bind of practical reason, which must beg all final questions, can therefore work only by analogy, not through cognition (*CJ* 307*)* or the ascription of "proper signification" (*CJ* 315–316). Yet the capacity to desire (the faculty of desire) is compelled to supplement every absence and is compelled to solve every antinomy generated by that move.

The crucial antinomy is that we *must* think a final purpose and yet we *can* not know it. That part of judgment which must think nature purposive by mechanical laws "for the purposive employment of our cognitive faculties" (*CJ* 232) is autonomous *because* it "has mere subjective validity" (*CJ* 236), *because* it is "objectively quite in want of a law or of a concept" (*CJ* 232). This want is supplemented by the part of judgment that is heteronomous—"which must adjust [*richten*] itself according to laws" heterogeneous to itself, "given . . . by understanding" (*CJ* 236). This latter kind of judgment is called "determinant," although its persistence would be better grasped by the reader of today's English if it were called "determining," for the German *bestimmend*. (We have noticed that it is itself determined or "tuned" thus to determine.) The philosopher "must expose and undo [*auflösen*]" any confusion between the two kinds of judgment.

Kant is careful to fix the limits of reason, to see it as free yet bound, determined to supplement what must always remain a lack. The human being is moral only insofar as he cannot cognize himself. Kant does not give cognitive power to the subject of reason, and indeed he makes his own text susceptible to the system of determined yet sometimes wholesome illusions he seeks to expose. This may be called a tropological deconstruction of the concept of freedom.

In physicotheology and ethicotheology rather than philosophy the supplementation of lacks is arbitrary and inadequate, unable to bestow "proper signification." According to Kant, there *is*, as it were, a "proper supplement," and its name is God. This is what fills the abyss of fearful infinity with sublime denomination. The echo of the Analytic of the Sublime is unmistakable in passages like the following:

> We may then suppose a righteous man [*einen rechtschaffenden Mann annehmen*] . . . who holds himself firmly persuaded that there is no God . . . He wishes, rather, disinterestedly to establish the good to which [the moral] law directs all his powers. But his effort is bounded. . . . Deceit, violence, and envy will be his style [*ihn im Schwange gehen*], although he himself will be honest, peaceable, and benevolent [*wohlwollend*]; and the righteous men with whom he meets will, notwithstanding all their worthiness of happiness be yet subjected by nature . . . just like the other [*den übrigen*] beasts of the earth. So it will be until one wide grave devours [*verschlingt*] them together . . . into the abyss [*Schlund*] of the purposeless chaos of matter from which they were drawn. . . . If he wishes to remain devoted [*anhanglich*] to the call of his moral inner determination . . . he must . . . assume the being [*Dasein*] of a *moral* author of the world, that is, a God. (*CJ* 303–304)

The abyss here *is* the place we were drawn from—nature's womb—and the grave—the devouring mouth [*Schlund*]—rather than merely the groundlessness of the *Abgrund*, the German word for abyss used in the passage on the Sublime. The God that must be presupposed to assert the law of our moral being seems, in a paragraph such as the above, to be beyond a wholesome illusion that the philosopher must expose; although by the systematicity of the argument he must be that as well. The philosopher's position is less assured here; he seems obliged to participate in the *need* to assume a moral author of the world, since he too is righteous within the limits of the womb and the grave. He cannot fully describe God's denomination as subreptive metalepsis, although the structure signals at this possibility. His position is similarly compromised when the discourse of desire turns to faith. Toward the end of the book, in a sober footnote, speculative reason itself is put in second place. The moral law cannot be a wholesome illusion. It is real because it can be thought without contradiction.

"We have therefore in us a principle," runs the concluding paragraph of the section immediately preceding the General Remarks that conclude *The Critique of Judgment,*

> capable of determining the idea of the supersensible within us, and through it [*dadurch*] also that of the supersensible without us, for knowledge, although only in a practical point of view—a principle this of which mere speculative philosophy (which could give a merely negative concept of freedom) must despair. Consequently the concept of freedom . . . can extend reason beyond those bounds within which every natural (theoretical) concept must remain hopelessly limited. (*CJ* 327)

This can certainly be read as an example of the abyss of the infinity of Nature being re-inscribed as the boundlessness of the concept of freedom. Can it not be said that it is only in the "Critique of the Teleological Judgment," in the indeterminate (no)-place seemingly outside of the system, across the bridge of the discussion of the aesthetic though not on it, that nature and freedom can be brought together, and (the practice of the production of) Philosophy itself can thus become the example of the sublime? Yet the philosopher of the sublime is also obliged to indicate that to call it by that epithet is to supplement an impropriety by subreption. Thus, the qualifying tag remains: Philosophy performing the rôle of the subject in the sublime can do so "only in a practical point of view." The entire *Critique of Judgment* has been a commentary on the precariousness of that point of view.

Even these apparently recuperative gestures, if read against the grain of the text, can be seen as signals given to the reader for the text's own deconstruction, or even as the bold suggestion that, even in the practical field, theory (analyzing the sublime) is always already normed by practice (having to assume a moral being). Toward the end of the book, speculative reason is situated more overtly in terms of the language of compulsion and determination that we have come to expect:

[the speculative reason] would regard the moral law itself as the mere deception of our reason in its practical aspect [*in praktischer Rücksicht ansehen*]. But since the speculative reason fully convinces that [this] can never take place, but that on the other hand those ideas whose object lies beyond nature [*über die Natur hinaus liegt*] can be though without contradiction, it *must for its own practical law and the task imposed through it* [*die dadurch auferlegte Aufgabe*], recognize those ideas as real *in order not to* come into contradiction with itself (*CJ* 323–324; emphasis added*)*

It is only if we acknowledge these indefinitely repeated moves of a tropological deconstruction that problematizes the text's performance and performs the text as (self) problematized, that we can see in what an overt way an unacknowledged differentiation within the subject as such moves Kant's text.

Let us return to what I have called the double bind of practical reason. It can work only by analogy, not through cognition or the ascription of "proper signification." Yet the faculty of desire is compelled to supplement every absence. This generates antinomies between "physical and teleological . . . methods of explanation." Kant removes any possibility of an antinomy by indicating the autonomy of the *reflective* judgment (*CJ* 236). By contrast, the heteronomy of the determinant judgment "must adjust itself according to the laws . . . given to it by understanding" (*CJ* 236). To define and control Kant's double bind and its solution through abyssal tropological deconstruction as a "bourgeois symptom" is to ignore our own situation within it, in the New post-Soviet World Order. This must persist as one of the driving theses of this book.

If we remain within *determinant* judgment, the antinomy poses itself as follows: "To judge of a thing as a natural purpose on account of its internal form is something very different from taking the existence of that thing to be a purpose of nature. For the latter assertion we require, not merely the concept of a possible purpose, but the cognition [*Erkenntnis*] of the final purpose (*scopus*) of nature. This requires a reference to something supersensible that far surpasses [*übersteigt*] all our teleological cognition [*Erkenntnis*] of nature" (*CJ* 225).

Through the remaining thirty-odd sections of the *Critique*, Kant develops that cognition-surpassing supersensible referent—the proper supplement—God. There is, however, one and only one example of what a legally adjusted and grounded determinant judgment would produce:

> Grass is needful for the ox, which again is needful for man as a means of existence; but then we do not see why it is necessary that men should exist (a question which is not so easy to answer if we cast our thoughts by chance [*wenn man etwa . . . in Gedanken hat*] on the New Hollanders or the inhabitants of Tierra del Fuego). Such a thing is then [*alsdem ist ein solches Ding*] not even a natural purpose; for it (or its entire species [*Gattung*—the connotation of "race" as in "human race" cannot be disregarded here]) is not to be regarded as a natural product. (*CJ* 225)

Here the raw man of the Analytic of the Sublime—stuck in the *Abgrund*-affect without subreptitiously shuttling over to *Grund*—is named. He is only a *casual* object of thought, not a paradigmatic example. He is not only not the subject as such; he also does not quite make it as an example of the thing or its species as natural product. If you happen to think of him, your determinant judgment cannot prove to itself that he, or a species of him, need exist. Of course, the "proper" reading of philosophy will dismiss this as an unimportant rhetorical detail. But if in Kant's world the New Hollander (the Australian Aborigine) or the man from Tierra del Fuego could have been endowed with speech (turned into the subject of speech), he might well have maintained that, this innocent but unavoidable and, indeed, crucial example—of the antinomy that reason will supplement—uses a peculiar thinking of what man is to put him out of it. We find here the axiomatics of imperialism as a natural argument to indicate the limits of the cognition of (cultural) man. The point is, however, that the New Hollander or the man from Tierra del Fuego *cannot* be the subject of speech or judgment in the world of the *Critique*.[32] The subject as such in Kant

---

32. It is possible that Kant chose the inhabitants of these two specific areas for reasons of euphony, although as his mention of "the Greenlander, the Lapp, the Samoyede, the inhabitant of Yakutsk, etc." (*CJ* 215) in the section on the "Relative as Distinguished from the Inner Purposiveness of Nature" shows, his construction of the noumenal subject is generally dependant upon the rejection [*Verwerfung*] of

is geopolitically differentiated. (Let us remind ourselves of that peculiar paragraph immediately following the Analytic of the Sublime on na-ture-culture-convention and *Anlage* [see page 11].) Kant's text cannot quite say this and indeed cannot develop this argument. But its crucial presence in *The Critique of Judgment* cannot be denied. It provides the

---

the Aboriginal. In German the two words are *Neuholländer* and *Feuerländer*. One might think here of Jakobson's famous pronouncement: *"the poetic function projects the principle of equivalence from the axis of selection into the axis of combination"* ("Clos-ing Statement: Linguistics and Poetics," in Thomas A. Sebeok, ed., *Style in Lan-guage* [Cambridge: MIT Press, 1960], p. 370), and consider the irony of its possible use in the choice of the heteronomous examples that cannot serve as autonomous examples of the human as rational being. For a brilliant speculation on Kant's difficult usefulness for "the Western subject," we must consult the work of Jean-Luc Nancy, especially *L'impératif catégorique* (Paris: Flammarion, 1983). See also Eduardo Cadava et al., eds., *Who Comes after the Subject?* (New York: Routledge, 1991), which "present[s] the current research of nineteen contemporary French philosophers on one of the great motifs of modern philosophy: the critique or the deconstruction of subjectivity" (p. vii). All the essays acknowledge the importance of "the remote condition of possibility of Kant himself at the beginning of the 'Western' as such" (p. 1). Many of the essays are aware that some strategic exclusion was at work. Vincent Descombes goes so far as to say "as long as political actions are not performed, the question *Who?* cannot be posed" (p. 132). But, like most analytical philosophers, he cannot consider the discontinuity between ethical pro-grams and decisions (see note 23), and, like many Euro-U.S. thinkers of the global, he is caught in the national. Sylviane Agacinski can name the excluded as woman (p. 16). Sarah Kofman risks "stupidity" (pp. 178–197) with Descartes as I risk "mis-take" with Kant. Nancy asks: "'Before/after the subject': *who* . . . : not a question of essence, but one of identity. . . . The place is *place*" (p. 7). I learn a great deal from the delicacy of these readings, from Nancy's acknowledgment of the risks of the imperative, but I have indeed thought of who will have come after the subject, if we set to work, in the name of who came before, so to speak. Here is the simple answer that Nancy calls for in such complicated syntax: the Aboriginal. And therefore have those two proper names of peoples, possibly fortuitous, invaginated my text. Worse than Schiller, I took these for real names and started reading about them. One thing became clear at the outset. The question as to whether these peoples were human was part of a general European debate. Kant was simply answering it in the nega-tive, in a philosophical rather than empirical way, "which he chose to state for his own reasons, in [anthropological] terms," as de Man would say ("Kant and Schiller," p. 143). The languages and textualities of the Aboriginal inhabitants— how is one to deal with this word? Paradoxically, Kant bestowed upon them an absurd national identity (*Neuholländer*, no more absurd than the modern hyphena-

only example of "that natural dialectic . . . , an unavoidable illusion which we must expose and resolve in our *Critique,* to the end that it may not deceive us" (*CJ* 233). Indeed, it provides the representative example of a conclusion of the determinant judgment that the autonomy of the philosopher's reflective judgment will correct. (And thus foreclose: *Ein-*

------

tion of the migrant, except that there is no exodus here)—are so heterogeneous that the manuscript got stalled for years. In the process I found, of course, that, like any people on earth, the Koorie today is also class heterogeneous, and divided in its ambitions. I realized that, as for all peoples who are not the felicitous subject of the European Enlightenment, their perennially blocked path to "modernity" has been hybrid, not "European." (Indeed, if one understands hybridity as an absolute, the so-called European path of modernity is hybrid as well.) When the Warlpiri describe "the coming of the Europeans [as] 'the end of the Jukurrpa,'" they are both theorizing their hybrid modernity and describing it as a loss of their dominant. "When Rosie Napurrurla said this at Lajamanu, she explained that this did not mean there was now nothing to be learned from the Jukurrpa but that, from that time, Warlpiri people have no longer been living in it" (*Yimikirli: Warlpiri Dreamings and Histories,* tr. Peggy Rockman Napaljarri and Lee Cataldi [San Francisco: HarperCollins, 1994], p. xx). I cannot write upon this, because I cannot learn their languages with the same commitment and skill with which I have learned English, and, to a rather lesser extent, German. I have therefore felt enabled by the notion of "losing language" as it is used by the early inhabitants of the East Kimberley region, as I discuss in my last chapter. As for the Fuegans, the story of how they were wiped out, as outlined in José Emperaire in *Les nomades de la mer* (Paris: Gallimard, 1955), is not to be believed. When *The New York Times* describes a naturalists' tour of this area, the ecstatic account of the flora and the fauna cover over completely the bloody history of the erasing of a people so casually abused by one of our greatest ethical philosophers (Mary Ellen Sullivan, "Magellan's Route in Tierra del Fuego," 9 October 1994, sec. 5, pp. 10, 38). Michael Taussig's theoretically sophisticated *Mimesis and Alterity: A Particular History of the Senses* (New York: Routledge, 1993) makes visible the specularity of the colonial encounter but stalls us there. In Chapters 2 and 3, I have commented on the limitations of this. There are photographs of the last Fuegans in *Les nomades.* I do not share the characterological conventions that can read the smile of Kostora, crouching naked with her child between pp. 160 and 161. The hybrid path to modernity allows a viewer to put an expressive interpretation upon—"the sullen and cunning?"—look of Kyeakyewa between pp. 96 and 97. I cannot write that other book that bubbles up in the cauldron of Kant's contempt. Just looking at the documentation of two very different books such as Ronald M. and Catherine H. Berndt, eds., *Aborigines of the West: Their Past and Present* (Nedlands: Univ. of Western Australia Press, 1979) and Günter Schilder, *Australia Unveiled: The Share of the Dutch Navigators in the Discovery of Australia,* tr.

beziehung ins Ich, introduction into reflective judgment; and *Ausstoßung aus dem Ich*, expulsion from the subject, into the noumenon.) In the late eighteenth century this is not a fortuitous example.[33]

(By contrast, Kant has a firm and examined answer, rooted in patriarchy, to the question of sexual difference, to which he ascribes a unique place, which is in no way crucial to the functioning of his system:[34]

> There is only one external purposiveness which is connected with the internal purposiveness of organization, and yet serves in the external relation of a means to a purpose, without the question necessarily arising as to what end this being so organized must have existed for. This is the organization of both sexes in their mutual relation for the propagation of their kind. . . . Why must such a pair exist? The answer is: This pair first constitutes an *organizing* whole, though not an organized whole in a single body. [*CJ* 275]

Olaf Richter (Amsterdam: Theatrum Orbis Terrarum, 1976) with a novice's lack of judgment gives one a sense of the enormity of the task if one wants to escape politically correct anthropology, philosophy, colonial discourse: the academic subdivision of labor; and the prisonhouse of academic identity politics. And in the general scholarship, observations are in the order of "the Critique of Aesthetic Judgment provides a much richer context for reflective judgment, and a more satisfactory conception of human nature. . . . Kant's concept of man *was* enriched in the *Critique of Judgment*" and so on (Frederick P. Van de Pitte, *Kant as Philosophical Anthropologist* [The Hague: Nijhoff, 1971], pp. 75, 77). One tiny detail may give Kant's dismissal the lie: "[U]ntil José Emperaire no one [except themselves, of course] knew what name they gave themselves: *Kaweskar*, the People" (Jean Raspail, *Who Will Remember*, tr. Jeremy Leggatt [San Francisco: Mercury House, 1988], p. ix).

33. For a vigorous description of Kant's felicitous subject, see Jean-François Lyotard, *Lessons on the Analytic of the Sublime*, tr. Elizabeth Rottenberg (Stanford: Stanford Univ. Press, 1994), p. 24f.

34. Lyotard's reading of the Third Critique is exemplary, indeed "helpful in avoiding certain errors in the reading of Kant's text" (*Ibid.*, p. ix). Yet, in view of the place of Woman in European philosophy, it seems peculiarly unfair to give to the imaginative counterpart of the philosopher's reflective judgment a female rôle: "She 'reflects' and he 'determines.' The (paternal) moral law determines itself and determines thought to act. . . . But the mother, the free, reflective imagination, knows only how to deploy forms without prior rules and without a known or knowable end" (p. 179).

After this, the question, "wherefore is there [*ist da*] a thing" is once again broached, leading finally to the answer: "so man, although in a certain reference he might be esteemed a purpose, yet in another has the rank of a means" [*CJ* 277]. The New Hollander and the inhabitant of Tierra del Fuego make their appearance in answer to the first articulation of this question. The discontinuity between sex- and race-differentiation is one of the arguments in this book. When the Woman is put outside of Philosophy by the Master Subject, she is argued into that dismissal, not foreclosed as a casual rhetorical gesture. The ruses against the racial other are different.)

If we let the de Manian version of deconstruction master what is "outside" the text "by affecting itself with it," then, in this structurally indeterminate part of the text, Kant's system performs what it deconstructs and, if we read against the grain, can be made to deconstruct what it performs. If, however, we take note of and question the historical and geographical differentiation of the subject as such, there is no possibility of that second step. The possibility of the production of the native informant by way of the colonial/postcolonial route and thus, ultimately, books such as this one, is lodged in the fact that, for the real needs of imperialism, the in-choate in-fans ab-original para-subject cannot be theorized as functionally *completely* frozen in a world where teleology is schematized into geo-graphy (writing the world). This limited access to being-human is the itinerary of the native informant into the post-colonial, which remains unrecognized through the various transformations of the discussions of both ethics and ethnicity. Thanks to this sanctioned inattention, the philosopher's duty, articulated in its place, seems to apply to all men, in the interest of being able to presuppose equality: it is the philosopher's duty to help men turn the fearful abyss of Nature the mother into the sublime, through reason, with the use of the assumption of God the Father (though with no cognizable ground of his presence)—thus to resolve practically the contradiction between what *can* be known and what *must* be thought. If on the individual level this is the passage into manhood, of this Kant speaks little in the *Critique*. The project of initiation into humanity is rather the project of culture (with that unacknowledged proviso for limited access for the non-European), civil legislation, and faith. Schiller will call this aesthetic education, "aesthetic" because, according to the morphology of the naming of the sublime, teleologies can only be approached through the mediation of the aesthetic.

If, as de Man suggests, Schiller flattens out the Kantian project by anthropomorphizing it in an unproblematic way, the critique of Kant as the philosopher of bourgeois society must also overlook the specifically geo-politically differentiated subject. For example, if, as per Manfred Riedel's astute suggestion, "Kant tacitly re-introduces empirical concepts into the normative approach" in order to cover over the aporia of norm and fact in his concept of civil society, what is important to our reading is that it is through the figure of the "citizen" or *Bürger* as "independent" that this re-introduction is performed.[35]

For Kant the project of culture as the training of speculative reason to see its own "limits" and the moral reason's "boundlessness" presupposes an "uncultivated [or unconstructed—*unangebautet*] reason" (*CJ* 310) belonging to earlier (or other) societies.

> But they could never think any other principle [*Prinzip*, not *Grundsatz*] of the possibility of the unification of nature with its inner ethical laws [*innere Sittengesetz*] than a supreme cause governing the world according to moral laws, because a final purpose in them assigned [*aufgegeben*] as duty, and a Nature without any final purpose external to them [*ausser ihnen*], in which nevertheless [*gleichwohl*] that purpose is to be [*soll*] actualized, stand in contradiction [*im Widerspruche stehen*]. (*CJ* 310)

In the two sentences following, Kant gives us his invariable scenario. The other civilizations produced senseless supplements. Graduation into philosophy would fill up the gap of that contradiction with the proper supplement, the moral law emerging only when speculative reason has been trained not to be fearful of its own limits. Polytheism is here defined as demonology and Christian monotheism as "wondrous" [*wundersam*] because, in a certain sense, it is almost philosophy, philosophy's supplement, not really needed as specifically a religion by those who are ready for it (*CJ* 325, n. 33; *CJ* 310).

---

35. Manfred Riedel, "Transcendental Politics? Political Legitimacy and the Concept of Civil Society in Kant," *Social Research* 48 (1981): 602.

The civil organization of society in *bürgerliche Gesellschaft* is recommended for societies that have already acceded to a general level of culture.[36] Kant's philosophical project, whether sublime or bourgeois, operates in terms of an implicit cultural difference.

The systematic description of practical reason and its project (*CJ* 34) must assume man as noumenon as its subject as such. Although there is no discussion of cultural differences here, it is clear that the raw man is reduced out of this definitive arena. Conversely, the uncultivated reason of this raw man cannot conceptualize man as noumenon either. In fact, if *we* introduced him into the discussion of man as noumenon, we would be engaging in precisely the determinant-reflective confusion that a critical philosophy is supposed to expose and resolve. The bind is more than double. Of "man considered as noumenon . . . it *can* no longer be asked why . . . he exists" (*CJ* 285, emphasis mine). Yet this man does enter a certain "anthropological" sphere, for this is undoubtedly the subject whose "good will" and "common sense" the philosopher relies upon (*CJ* 293). "This common sense is constantly presupposed by the *Critique*, which nevertheless holds back the analysis of it. It could be shown that this suspension ensures the complicity of a moral discourse and an empirical culturalism. This is a permanent necessity."[37]

Once arrived at the noumenal man, the system can work: "Since now it is only as moral being that we recognize man as the purpose of creation, we have in the first place a ground (at least the chief condition) for regarding the world as a whole connected according to purposes and as a *system* of final causes" (*CJ* 294). If the New Hollander and the inhabitant of Tierra del Fuego could have had an opinion on the matter (of course that would be anthropomorphism, and these two do not even qualify as the proper anthropos in whose form a mistaken anthropo-

---

36. To repeat a point I have made earlier and will make later, this "general level" expresses an articulation of sexism and classism. Quite apart from Kant's expressed opinion on race or colonization, I am noting here the mysterious working of the savage and the named savage in the *central* text on *the* subject's access to the rational will and its consolidation as the transcendental subject.

37. Derrida, "Parergon," in *The Truth in Painting* tr. Geoff Bennington and Ian McLeod (Chicago: Univ. of Chicago Press, 1987), p. 35.

morphism would work), what concept-metaphor would seem implicit in the following passage of "pure" philosophy, where metaphor has no place? "Only in man, and only in him as subject of morality [*Moralität*], do we meet with *unconditioned legislation* in respect of purposes, which therefore makes him alone [*allein*] capable of being an end purpose to which the whole of nature is teleologically subordinated" (*CJ* 286). If we took the subject to be the undifferentiated subject of [European] culture in the determinant judgment, and then shifted to the undifferentiated [European] subject in reflective judgment, a passage such as the above would seem a canny warning against a desire *adequately* to represent philosophy in political action, against the empirico-transcendental confusion that, for Michel Foucault, is among the marks of the discursive formation of modernity.[38] If, on the other hand, it is seen with the globally differentiated subject in mind, a subject that is to say, who is (almost) human *only by nature*, it might seem a justification for Europe to be the global legislator. This latter is the conclusion from the impossible (because historically and discursively discontinuous) perspective of the native informant turned reader rather than evidence. (You cannot "prove" it in a court of philosophic law, for the verdict, offered with appropriate embarrassment or amusement, depending on the philosopher-judge's unacknowledged politics, would be, "a category mistake!" It would also, of course, be seen as a mistake if we concentrated too much on rhetoric and metaphor in the text of a philosophy that would only convince, not persuade.)

Within the European cultural context, it is "the *archaeologist* of nature," not the philosopher, who

> can suppose the womb [*Mutterschoss*] of the earth, as she passed out of her chaotic state (like a great animal), to have given birth in the beginning to creatures of less purposive form, that these again gave birth to others which cultivated [*ausbildeten*] themselves more appro-

---

38. Michel Foucault, *The Order of Things: An Archaeology of the Human Sciences*, tr. anon. (New York: Vintage, 1973), p. 318f. (See also note 22.) We will see later that the colonial and postcolonial subjects are produced by the slow dislocation of this discursive historical discontinuity. The transnational agent negotiates its representation.

priately [*angemessener*] to their state of generation [*Zeugungsplatz*] and their relationship to each other. Until this uterus [*Gebärmutter*] itself, becoming torpid and ossified reduced [*eingeschränkt*] its births to determined [*bestimmt*] species degenerating no further [*fernehin nicht ausartend*]. (*CJ* 268)

The philosopher's task, on the contrary, is no more and no less than to bestow the *name* of man to man by thinking him as noumenon and the subject of philosophy.

The aporia between the discontinuous texts of the raw man and the subject as such should make Kant's critique of judgment unreadable in the strictest sense. Its readability is bought by ignoring the aporia, passing through it by way of the axiomatics of imperialism. Kant's own account of this unreadability must still exclude any consideration of his framing or differentiation of the subject as such. In his own account we have something like the two-part scheme in Rousseau analyzed by de Man in *The Allegory of Reading*. First, the production of *gods* through the troping logic of fear. Next, this tropology corrected by the production of God through the tropological deconstruction of *reason*. At this stage, "the inner *moral* [*moralische*] purposive determination [*Bestimmung*] of man's being [*Dasein*] supplemented [*ergänzte*] that in which the cognition of nature [*Naturerkenntnis*] was deficient" (*CJ* 298). I have tried to notice, in recognition of the grandeur of Kant's text, that it performs this dependency upon supplementation even when the seemingly developmental stage of humanity is long past. Structurally and crucially, however, the nature/culture-differentiated para-subject remains outside the work, *par[a-]ergonal*, to use Derrida's word.

In terms of the organic human body, Derrida argues for "vomit . . . as a parergon of the third *Critique* considered as a general thesis of transcendental idealism." If the third *Critique* is read as the indirect orchestration of a universalist teleology, the *parergon* that it yields is the raw man. In the Derridian reading, this "possibility of a vicariousness" is "unnameable."[39] I am suggesting that when the "pure" "hetero-affection" toward the wholly other is "from above," rather than "from below" as a "*sollen* [thou shalt] projected to infinity," the violent moment

---

39. Derrida, "Economimesis," *Diacritics* 11 (June 1981): 21, 25.

of naming is not avoided. New Holland and Tierra del Fuego are throwaway names that are simply introducing a note that will be sounded often in this book. Yet the "relationship without relationship" [*rapport sans rapport*] remains just as crucial to the system. In my argument, the vicariousness that Derrida writes of becomes the (im)possibility of a vicarious (un)reading, the perspective of the "native informant." No account of Kant's universalism can account for this moment. Deconstruction allows me to appropriate it to this end by proposing that

> no "theory," no "practice," no "theoretical practice" can effectively intervene in [the] field [of historical, economic, political inscription] if it does not weigh up and bear on the frame [*parergon*], which is the decisive structure of what is at stake, at the invisible limit to (between) the interiority of meaning (put under shelter by the whole hermeneuticist, semioticist, phenomenologicalist, and formalist tradition) *and* (to) all the empiricisms of the extrinsic which, incapable of either seeing or reading, miss the question completely.[40]

But does deconstruction necessarily lead to appropriations? We will consider this at the end of this chapter, when we come to Marx.

When the famous justification of civil society is broached, it is *within* the developed cultural context *inside* the frame. The passage is too well known for extended quoting here. Let us remind ourselves of the "splendid misery" of "inequality among men," which is "bound up with the development of the natural tendencies [*Naturanlagen*] of the human race," and the speculation that war might be "designed" by "supreme wisdom" to furnish "a drive [*Trieb*] for developing all talents serviceable for culture" (*CJ* 282–283). This design, in this circumscribed setting, is also the philosophical task of "the freeing of the will from the despotism of desires" (*CJ* 282), so that the capacity to desire can be turned to the service of reason. It is also within this circumscribed context that Kant lists despotic desire—*Suchten* (sick addictions), *Ehrsucht* (ambition), *Herrschsucht* (lust of dominion), *Habsucht* (avarice). These are the desires gone wrong of those "who have power [*Gewalt*]" (*CJ* 280). It is also in this context of the developed world that he proposes the "voluntar[y]

---

40. Derrida, "Parergon," p. 35; extract from p. 61.

submi[ssion] to . . . a cosmopolitan [*weltbürgerlich*] whole, i.e. a system of all states that are in danger of acting injuriously upon each other" (*CJ* 282).

When "civil legislation" becomes an analogy for a "moral teleology," "reason takes for final purpose the furthering of happiness in harmony [*Einstimmung*] with morality" (*CJ* 299, 302). As we begin to move into the discourse of faith, Kant begins a global project for the subject—as such—of reason, man as noumenon, that would, if that shadowy New Hollander and the Fuegan could read and think (we know why it is a mistake to introduce them here), seem to them like an entitlement for the project of transforming them from the raw to the philosophical. For imperialism as social mission, God's image is that of the governor: "an author and governor of the world, who is at the same time a moral lawgiver" (*CJ* 307).[41] Now "the *highest good*, in the world, to be actualized by freedom [*durch Freiheit zu bewirkende*]" is a "*thing of faith*" (*CJ* 321). Although "the mind"—undifferentiated—must accept the indeterminacy of the final purpose, "faith (to put it in a word [*schlechthin so genannt*]), is a trust in the attainment of a design, the furthering [*Beförderung*] of which is a duty, but the possibility of the execution [*Ausführung*] of which . . . is not to be *understood* [*einzusehen*] by us" (*CJ* 324). This is because, "although the necessity of duty is very plain for the practical reason, yet the attainment of its final purpose, so far as it is not altogether in our own power, is only assumed with a view to the [*zum Behuf des*] practical use of reason, and therefore is not so practically necessary as duty itself" (*CJ* 323).

The last sentence of this section tells us that to "a *doubtful faith* . . . the absence of conviction by grounds of speculative reason is only a hindrance, and for this a critical insight into the limits of this faculty can remove its influence upon conduct, and can put in its place as a substitute [*zum Ersatz hinstellen*] a truth-assumption [*Fürwahrhalten*]"

---

41. I have discussed an interesting use of God as governor by Freud in "Psychoanalysis in Left Field; and Fieldworking: Examples to Fit the Title," in Michael Münchow and Sonu Shamdasani, eds., *Speculations after Freud* (New York: Routledge, 1994), pp. 59–60.

(*CJ 325*). I wish to conclude my remarks on Kant with a tribute to the delicacy of his distinction between faith, assuming the truth of an indeterminacy, and doubtful faith, working by provisional truth-assumptions. Attention to the consistency of detail forbids him the use of the pervasive discourse of supplementation [Ergänzung] here. This is only a fake, an ersatz, not only not faith, but not even belief. Yet I must not give up my insistence that a travesty is implicit in the delicacy, a travesty that appears in the mere translation: the definitive English version of *überwiegendes praktisches Fürwahrhalten* turns out to be "paramount practical belief"!

I have not tried to diagnose Kant's hidden "beliefs" here. I have constructed a version of a script within which his text may be seen as held. To read a few pages of master discourse allowing for the parabasis operated by the native informant's impossible eye makes appear a shadowy counterscene. Yet the binary opposition between master and native cannot bear the weight of a mere reversal. Kant "was no crook; indubitably, as he embarked on his great voyages of discovery, he was the great civilizer, a Prospero of the Enlightenment."[42] And, although Shakespeare was great, we cannot merely continue to act out the part of Caliban. One task of deconstruction might be a persistent attempt to displace the reversal, to show the complicity between native hegemony and the axiomatics of imperialism. To consider this I will turn to Hegel's remarks on the *Srimadbhagavadgitā*. India had its own Fuegans, its own New Hollanders. The Indian Aboriginal did not flourish in pre-British India. As I will argue by way of Samir Amin in the next section, there is something Eurocentric about assuming that imperialism began with Europe.

II

"Time" is a word to which we give flesh in various ways. The Kant that philosophized the relationship between theoretical and practical reason

---

42. Gananath Obeysekere, *The Apotheosis of Captain Cook: European Mythmaking in the Pacific* (Princeton: Princeton Univ. Press, 1992), p. 24. He is writing about Captain Cook.

taught the European that he could not be or think or act without this first gesture.[43] Freud unhooked this lesson from its easy reading—the primacy of real lived time as giving us life itself—by suggesting that "real lived time" is produced by the machinery of the mental theater.[44] One common way of grasping life and ground-level history as events happening to and around many lives is by fleshing out "time" as sequential process. Let us call this "timing." This feeling for life and history is often disqualified, in a dominant interest, in the name of the real laws of motion of "time," or rather, "Time." It is my contention that Time often emerges as an implicit Graph only miscaught by those immersed in the process of timing. I have sketched this tyranny of the "visible," of the "good writing," in a text of Hegel on the *Srimadbhagavadgitā* as well as in the *Srimadbhagavadgitā* itself.[45]

Radical critiques of the tyranny of the visible or of writing over the merely lived covers the kind of gesture I will uncover in Hegel and the *Gitā*. The open-ended deconstructive notion of writing as the structure that assures the possibility of meaning in the absence of the sender is also a critique of that gesture, but not in the name of the "lived." It would poke below, beside, around, perhaps even beyond the impression

---

43. "Time is not an empirical concept that has been derived from any experience, for neither coexistence nor succession would ever come within our perception, if the representation of time were not the a priori grounding [*zum Grunde lage*]. . . . Time is a necessary representation which grounds [*zum Grunde liegt*] all intuition." From Kant, "Time," *Critique of Pure Reason*, tr. Norman Kemp Smith (New York: St. Martin's Press, 1965), p. 74. I always use the shocking "he" when that is true to the spirit of the author. Kant's system cannot be made socio-sexually just by pronominal piety, without violating the argument. (See, for example, Lloyd, *Man of Reason*, esp. chap. 4.) This also reminds some of us, as we speculate about the ethics of sexual difference, that traditional European ethical philosophy simply disavows or benevolently naturalizes its sexual differentiation.

44. The best explanation of this argument is still Derrida, "Freud and the Scene of Writing," in *Writing and Difference*, tr. Alan Bass (Chicago: Univ. of Chicago Press, 1978), pp. 196–231.

45. For the "good and bad writing" argument, see Derrida, *Of Grammatology*, tr. Spivak (Baltimore: Johns Hopkins Univ. Press, 1976), pp. 15–18, hereafter *OG*, with page numbers following.

of the "lived," so that the authority of the "lived" is also undermined, although its importance is never denied.[46]

Insofar as deconstructions can be undertaken, they are always asymmetrical by way of the doer's (in this case the reader's) "interest." On the track of the native informant, my interest drives me to deconstruct the opposition between Hegel and the *Gitā* rather than undo the human agent Arjuna's sense of "lived timing" in the text. This openly declared interest makes my reading the kind of "mistake" without which no practice can enable itself. It is my hope that to notice such a structural complicity of dominant texts from two different cultural inscriptions can be a gesture against some of the too-easy West-and-the-rest polarizations sometimes rampant in colonial and postcolonial discourse studies. To my mind, such a polarization is too much a legitimation-by-reversal of the colonial attitude itself.

The usual political critique of the Hegelian dialectic is to say that it finally excuses everything.[47]

Another way of putting it is that because Hegel places all of history and reality upon a diagram, everything fits in. Thus, in the Hegelian pictures of the journey of the *Geist* given in *The Philosophy of History*, *The Philosophy of Right*, and *Aesthetics*, the laws of motion of history are made visible as, concurrently, the Hegelian morphology is fleshed out.[48] The Time of the Law has the spaces of a rebus, the active reading of

---

46. As I point out in the Appendix, (the word) experience (without scare-quotes) has silently come to mark the productive discontinuity between other and subject—alterity and the agent—in Derrida's later work.

47. Max Horkheimer said this powerfully over fifty years ago: "The attempt to afford justification to every idea and every historical person and to assign the heroes of past revolutions their place in the pantheon of history next to the victorious generals of the counterrevolution, this ostensibly free-floating objectivity conditioned by the bourgeoisies's stand on two fronts against absolutist restoration and against the proletariat, has acquired validity in the Hegelian system along with the idealistic pathos of absolute knowledge" ("On the Problem of Truth," in *The Essential Frankfurt School Reader*, eds. Andrew Arato and Eike Gebhart [New York: Urizen Books, 1978], p. 418).

48. Hegel, *The Philosophy of History*, tr. J. Sibree (New York: Dover, 1956); *The Philosophy of Right*, tr. T. M. Knox (Oxford: Clarendon Press, 1962); *Aesthetics:*

which will produce the timing of history. In Hegel's own words, "the intelligible [*das Verständige*] remains [*stehenbleiben*] in concepts in their fixed determinateness and difference from others [*von anderen*]; the dialectical [*das Dialektische*] exhibits them in their transition and dissolution."[49] As a literary critic by training, I will concentrate on a couple of paragraphs from the *Lectures on the Aesthetic*. Because I am Indian and was born a Hindu, I will also attempt to satisfy the increasing, and on occasion somewhat dubious, demand that ethnics speak for themselves, by focusing on a bit in Hegel on Indian poetry. The native-informant / postcolonial here is affected as a centrally interpellated voice from the margin.

According to Hegel, there are three moments in a work of art. The form or *Gestalt*, the content (*Gehalt* or *Inhalt*), and the meaning or *Bedeutung*. The true meaning, not only of a work of art, but also of any phenomenal appearance, is the situation of the spirit on the graph of its course toward "self-knowledge." (This, too is basically a graphic intuition: It is not that the spirit, in a subjective model, "knows itself" progressively. It is rather a graph leading toward the exact coincidence of the spirit and its knowing, when superimposed.)

Starting from a situation where content and form are intertwined in an unacknowledged unity as meaning, the elements must separate with some violence so that the conciliation may finally be effected with knowledge. At that stage of adequate superimposition or "identity," there is no separation between sign (content/form) and the transcendental meaning (spirit-in-self-knowledge), and therefore there is no art. "Art" is the name or the sign of the lack of fit between the two axes of the graph—spirit and its knowing.

It is well known that the spirit or *Geist* that acts out the scenario of self-knowledge is not something like a grand individual subject. It is rather like the principle of subjectivity, in other contexts given a world historical nuance.

Lectures on Fine Arts, tr. T. M. Knox, 2 vols. (Oxford: Clarendon Press, 1975). All references to the last of the three are included in my text as *LA*, followed by page number.

49. Hegel, *The Philosophical Propadeutic*, tr. A. V. Miller (Oxford: Blackwell, 1986), p. 126. All translations, including this one, have been modified when considered necessary.

What we have in Hegel's narrative of the development of art forms, then, is not an epistemology, an account of how an individual subject or subjects know(s) or knew and produce(d) commensurate art, but an epistemography, a graduated diagram of how knowledge (an adequate fit between sign and varieties of meaning) comes into being. Art marks the inadequacies on the way. It is a dynamic epistemograph: the emergence of the finally adequate relationship between sign (spirit) and meaning (knowledge) is the result of much straining on the part of both to achieve a fit. Each new configuration steps forth in the sublation of the earlier stages of the struggle. The "deviations"—lack of fit—are therefore "normative" in view of the telos of the system.[50]

Upon this epistemograph, a graduated diagram of the coming-into-being of knowledge, the art of Persia, India, and Egypt are not granted the status of being produced *by* the spirit, however un-fitting such art might be to the graph of true knowledge. They are all normative deviations in the area of the *un*conscious symbolic. In Derrida's latest language, one may say that they cryptically carry a secret—the Spirit's itinerary—that they have not chosen and cannot know. The task of the Hegelian philosopher of art is to analyse the cryptonym, decipher the epistemograph, spell the spirit's paraphe, on its way to Europe's signature. The relationship between form and content in this art can only be evidence of a struggle toward signification rather than an intended collective sign of a stage in the journey toward adequation.

By the time we get to India, the shape *(Gestalt)* is perceived (by the *Geist* as subject, not Indian individuals) to be separate from the meaning. Indian art seeks to give an *externally* adequate representation, ac-

50. I have signaled a relationship between a political unconscious and the Hegelian epistemograph in Spivak, *In Other Worlds: Essays in Cultural Politics* (New York: Methuen, 1987), pp. 258–259. Surprisingly, there is an acceptance of "normative deviations" in Fredric Jameson, *Marxism and Form: Twentieth-Century Dialectical Theories of Literature* (Princeton: Princeton Univ. Press, 1971), pp. 329–330. It is, I think, this conviction or presupposition that surfaces in the by-now notorious essay "Third World Literature in the Era of Multinational Capital," *Social Text* 15 (Fall 1986), contested by Aijaz Ahmad, "Jameson's Rhetoric of Otherness and the 'National Allegory,'" in *In Theory: Classes, Nations, Literatures* (New York: Verso, 1992), pp. 95–122. The terms of the contestation are, in this reading, a questioning of the "scientific" claims of the Hegelian epistemograph, however disguised.

cording to Hegel, to the grandeur of a meaning that is perceived as beyond phenomenality. Thus, unlike the scenario as run by the proper inner process, Indian art cannot supersede or sublate the contradiction between shape and meaning. The contradiction "is supposed to produce a genuine unification . . . yet," in Indian art, "from one side it is driven into the opposite one, and out of this is pushed back again into the first; without rest it is just thrown hither and thither, and in the oscillation and fermentation of this striving for a solution thinks it has already found appeasement" (*LA* 1:333–334). Therefore, "the Indian knows no reconciliation and identity with Brahma [the so-called Hindu conception of the Absolute] in the sense of the human spirit's reaching *knowledge* of this unity" (*LA* 1:335). (Who this "Indian" might be is of course an irrelevant question here.)[51]

The *verstandlose Gestaltungsgabe*, translated by Knox as "unintelligent talent for configuration," that Hegel sees as the *Geist*'s normative aesthetic/epistemic representation in this *static* "Indian" moment on the chronograph spans some millennia—from at least the second millennium B.C. to fifth century A.D.—embracing scattered examples from the *Vedas*, the fantastic cosmogonies of the *Purānas*, the *Srimadbhagavadgitā* and Kalidasa's play *Sakuntalā* (the last translated by Goethe). In Kant, Captain Cook's voyages produce a rhymed couplet, a passively constitutive moment not worthy of research. This expanded and apparently

---

51. What Hegel is producing and presupposing here is an "orientalist," semitized, nearly monotheist, homogeneous religion called "Hinduism." See *Seminar* (September 1985). A somewhat psychologistic account of the construction of this religion is also to be found in Ashis Nandy, *The Intimate Enemy: Loss and Recovery of Self under Colonialism* (Delhi: Oxford Univ. Press, 1983). "Taking brahmin documents as representative of all Indian society" is of course still common practice (Damodar Dharmanand Kosambi, *Myth and Reality: Studies in the Formation of Indian Culture* [Bombay: Popular Prakashani, 1983], p. 38, n. 3). This approach is to be strictly distinguished from analyzing such documents as ingredients of a regulative psychobiography—as in Chapter 3—where a coercive element in cultural production as performance rather than formation is presupposed. "All production is at once desiring and social" (Gilles Deleuze and Félix Guattari, *Anti-Oedipus: Capitalism and Schizophrenia*, tr. Robert Hurley et al. [Minneapolis: Univ. of Minnesota Press, 1986], p. 296). To confuse the two approaches is to be tendentious.

thoroughly researched "moment" marks the difference between critical and historical philosophy. Yet, the difference might share a generic similarity. For, by predictable contrast to the millennial span of the Indian moment, there is, in Hegel's text, a detailed account of the various stages of Christianity and a careful distinction between Greece and Rome.

Of Hegel's "Indian" readings, I have chosen his comments on two passages on the *Gitā*, because they dramatize most successfully my thesis that Time graphed as Law manipulates history seen as timing in the interest of cultural political explanations, both in the Hegelian and the high Hindu contexts.

Hegel quotes two rather beautiful passages from the *Gitā*. By contrast with the deeply offensive passages about Africa and history in *The Philosophy of History*, for example, the tone of Hegel's comments is ostensibly benevolent.[52]

So it is said, e.g., of [sic] Krishna . . . : "Earth, water and wind, air and fire, spirit, understanding, and self-hood are the eight syllables of my essential power; yet recognise thou in me another and a higher being who vivifies the earth and carries the world: in him all beings have their origin; so know thou, I am the origin of this entire world and also its destruction; beyond me there is nothing higher, to me this All is linked as a chaplet of pearls on a thread; I am the taste in flowing water, the splendour in the sun and the moon, the mystical word in the holy scriptures, in man his manliness, the pure fragrance in the earth, the splendour in flames, in all beings the life, contemplation in the penitent, in living things the force of life, in the wise their wisdom, in the splendid their splendour; whatever natures are genuine, are shining or dark, they are from me, I am not in them, they are in me. Through the illusion of these three properties the whole world is bewitched and mistakes me the unalterable but even the divine illu-

---

52. Hegel, *Philosophy of History*, p. 99. I have touched upon the differentiation between Asia and Africa in the modern context in "Marginality in the Teaching Machine," in *Outside*, pp. 53–54. For a general discussion of *The Philosophy of History* on the matter of India, see Perry Anderson, *Lineages of the Absolutist State* (London: Verso, 1974), pp. 469–479.

sion, Maya, is my illusion, hard to transcend [*duratyaya*—difficult to cross]; but those who follow me [shelter in me] go forth beyond illusion [*mayametam taranti*—cross over this illusion]."[53] Here [the] substantial unity [of the formless and the multiplicity of terrestrial phenomena] is expressed in the most striking way, in respect both of immanence in what is present and also the stepping over [*hinwegschreiten*] everything individual. In the same way, Krishna says of himself that amongst all different existents he is always the most excellent: "Among the stars I am the shining sun, amongst the lunary signs the moon, amongst the sacred books the book of hymns, amongst the senses the inward, Meru amongst the tops of the hills, amongst animals the lion, amongst letters I am the vowel A, amongst seasons of the year the blossoming spring," etc. (*LA* 1:367)

However benevolent or admiring Hegel's remarks might be, they still finally point at the mindless gift for making shapes [*verstandlose Gestaltungsgabe*] and an absence of the push into history.

Obviously, Hegel has to quote lists because he needs to say that the Spirit-in-India makes monotonous lists in a violently shuttling way. Hegel's conclusions from these rather difficult passages can be summarized as follows: the recitation of the height of excellence, like the mere change of shapes in which what is to be brought before our eyes is always one and the same thing over again, remains, precisely on account of this similarity of content, extremely monotonous, and on the whole, empty and wearisome.

The alternative to Hegel's reading is not necessarily to propose a reading that would pronounce the *Gītā* politically, philosophically, or yet aesthetically correct, profound, and fine. One constructive alternative is, I think, to gain enough sense of the *Gītā* and its place within a historical narrative to realize that the *Gītā* itself can also be read as another dynamic account of the quenching of the question of historical verification. In fact, such a sense of the place of the *Gītā* within a historical narrative is provided by its setting within the epic *Mahāb-*

---

53. As Knox notes, Zaehner has translated this last bit as follows: "By these three states of being inhering in the constituents the whole universe is led astray and does not understand that I am far beyond them and that I neither change nor pass away." This translation can also be questioned.

hārata. The *Gitā* is a tightly structured dialogue in the middle of the gigantic, multiform, diversely layered account of the great battle between two ancient and related lineages. Here the battle is stalled so that the merely human Prince Arjuna can be motivated to fight by his divine charioteer Krishna. All around the *Gitā* is myth, history, story, process, "timing." In the halted action of the text is the unfurling of the Laws of Motion of the transcendence of timing, the Time of the Universe. The *Gitā* too substitutes immanent philosophical significance in the interest of a political intervention where killing becomes a metonym for action as such.[54]

(I should like to distinguish my approach from two that I have chosen as representative of innovative or re-constellative readings of the *Gitā*. One is used in D. D. Kosambi's "Social and Economic Aspects of the Bhagavad-Gitā," an essay from which I have already quoted. The other is developed in Bimal Krishna Matilal's last work on the study of contemporary Indian cultural formation through the Indian epics.[55] Because I have given them this representative status, I will occasionally refer to them.

For the general reader, Kosambi's essay remains the best guide to the non-exemplary character, indeed the elusiveness, of the *Gitā* in its "appropriate historical and geographical context." He establishes the peculiar contradictory interpretability of the *Gitā* and concludes: "The Gita furnished the one scriptural source which could be used without violence to accepted Brahmin methodology, [as also] to draw inspiration

---

54. An argument concentrating on the logic of the metonym would point out that the figurative energy of the text pushes the "earlier" semiotic field of lineage into the "later" one of the nascent state (Romila Thapar, *From Lineage to State: Social Formations in the Mid-First Millennium B.C. in the Ganga Valley* [Bombay: Oxford Univ. Press, 1984]). In question here is the killing of blood kin, forbidden in the earlier formation. Krishna himself might be a mark of "the transition from mother-right to patriarchal life, [which] allowed the original cults to be practised on a subordinate level" (Kosambi, *Myth*, p. 28). Part of the figurative logic might be based on the possible regulative norm of sanctioned suicide (it is allowed to kill and be killed when you know that the soul is immortal), which I discuss in Chapter 3. Whatever else it might be, it is not a *monotonous* argument.

55. Forthcoming in Bimal Krishna Matilal and Spivak, *Epic and Ethic: Indian Examples* (New York: Routledge, n.d.).

and justification for social actions in some way disagreeable to a branch of the ruling class. . . . It remains to show how the document achieved this unique position." His answer is that "the utility of the Gitā derives from its peculiar fundamental defect, namely dexterity in seeming to reconcile the irreconcilable."[56] The way to this answer, apart from laying out the expedient ambivalence of all overt idealisms, is, for him, through realistic and characterological narrative analysis.

My goal, by contrast, is specific to my pedagogic-institutional situation. I repeatedly attempt to undo the often unexamined opposition between colonizer and colonized implicit in much colonial discourse study. Therefore I must show that there are strategic complicities between Hegel's argument and the structural conduct of the Gitā. I also make an attempt to fill the empty place of the discourse of the colonized, in however imperfect a way, and suggest a method appropriate to departments of English or culture studies, obviously not to the expert historian of India. By contrast to Kosambi's realism, and emphasis on character study, therefore, my way is to point out the moves in the *structure* and *texture* of the text—performative in the sense that the Gitā is an island of *diagesis* in a sea of *poiesis*, the tremendous episodic narrative mass of the *Mahābhārata*, that will persuade the assenting reader or receiver of the epic to transform myth into scripture.

Matilal's work attempts, among other things, to deconstruct the opposition between colonialists and nationalists, as well as between developmental realists and mystical culturalists, by pointing at what he perceives to be a "dissident voice" within the text. I must contrast this to my own position as well. Matilal's new politics of reading may be useful in the Indian context. Upon the disciplinary scene of British philosophy—Matilal was a specialist in Indian philosophy who taught at Oxford—Matilal's last work related to the ethical arguments within analytic philosophy as spelled out by writers like Bernard Williams or Thomas Nagel, whose positions are unremittingly Euramerican. My disciplinary placing, as far as I can understand it myself, I have already sketched.)

The *Srimadbhagavadgitā*, the full name of the text, is a considerably

56. Kosambi, *Myth*, pp. 15, 17.

later dramatic narrative addition to the epic *Mahābhārata*.[57] The rest of the immense poem is ostensibly sung by the poet Vyāsa. This bit is sung by God, the graceful lord—that is the meaning of the full title. The short title simply means "sung," but implies, of course, the full designation, where the subject is so powerful that it cannot be actively forgotten even when absent. The "intent" of this addition to the epic is clearly to anagogize the political. It is a text composed for interpretation (and therefore designated as one of the "Vedāntas"—teaching the ultimate scope of the *veda*, that which is discovered and constituted as knowledge—wrenched out of its "appropriate context").[58]

In accordance with my general project, I will construct below a crudely "dialectical" reading of the actual narration of the *Gītā* in terms of the play of law and history. Had Hegel the wherewithal to read it this way? I think so. The reading that I am going to propose is considerably less complicated than, say, the celebrated reading of *Antigone* in the *Phenomenology* and requires no more knowledge of the "Indian background" than Hegel himself professed to possess. It requires merely an impossible anachronistic absence of the ideological motivation to prove a fantasmatic India as the inhabitant of what we would today call the "pre-conscious" of the Hegelian Symbolic.[59]

Because "Hegel" (the name is a world-historical metonym here) wants and needs to prove that "India" is the name for this stop on the spirit's

---

57. J. A. B. van Buitenen, tr., *The Bhagavadgītā in the Mahābhārata* (Chicago: Univ. of Chicago Press, 1981) is the definitive bilingual edition accessible to the nonspecialist. I have offered my own translations of the Sanskrit because often this is the only way to cut through the solemnity that informs the best translations of the great texts of classical antiquity. I have tried to follow the contemporary phonetic transcriptions of Sanskrit words, except with such words as "Sanskrit" or "Krishna," that are well known to the nonspecialist reader in these non-specialized spellings. I apologize for the inconsistency but, since this is recognizably not an expert Indianist book, I felt that consistency would have been an affectation.

58. See, for example, Sarvepalli Radhakrishnan, *The Hindu View of Life* (London: Allen & Unwin, 1961), p. 18, from which I will quote at greater length later.

59. Hegel's traffic with India is ably criticized by Michel Hulin, *Hegel et l'orient: Suivi de la traduction annotée d'un essai de Hegel sur le Bhagavad-Gita* (Paris: Vrin, 1979). Hulin includes Hegel's two reviews on the subject of the *Gita* and on its relationship to the philosophy of India. Any serious consideration of the specific

graphic journey, he makes his "India" prove it for him. (For example, just as Hegel telescopes 2,500 years to prove that Indians cannot move history, so also does he base his evidence for the Indian "recurring description of national *generation* instead of the idea of a spiritual *creation*" on absent passages that he could not have read: "(This passage the English translator had no mind to translate word for word because it is all too wanting in decency and shame.) . . . Schlegel has not translated this part of the episode" (*LA* 1:344).

---

topic of Hegel's orientalism would have to examine these essays in detail. My interest is in noticing how the well-known texts are woven with the axiomatics of imperialism, and therefore I keep to the *LA*. It is clear from Hegel's letters that he was well acquainted with contemporary German scholars of Sanskrit. I use "pre-conscious" to distinguish Indian from Persian art in the Hegelian morphology. The "luminous essence" that provides the pre-originary space for that scene of fire has been delicately discussed by Werner Hamacher (unpublished lecture, Stanford University, 10 May 1988). I might mention in passing here that, although I am deeply interested in the usual deconstructive focus (not always shared by Derrida) on the "moments" (I use this word where no word will suffice) of "stalling" (Hamacher's word) at beginning and end ("différance" and "aporia" are only two names for these moments), I am more interested in the generating of a shaky middle by way of an irreducible "mistake" (not to be derived from some prior "correct" step). I have touched on this issue in "Feminism and Deconstruction, Again," in *Outside*, p. 131f. Eight years after first writing, it is worth mentioning that Derrida's own questions have moved to the shaky middle. In "Finis," in *Aporias*, p. 14, the piece he delivered at the second ten-day Derrida colloquium in 1992 (the first one was in 1982), he offers a summary of his earlier tendency, and signals this move by way of the cryptic question, "[w]hat if there was no other concept of time than the one that Heidegger calls 'vulgar'?," whereas in 1968 he had written "perhaps there is no 'vulgar concept of time'" (could he have meant "the same thing"?), and gone on to evoke "presence [as] . . . the trace of the trace, the trace of the erasure of the trace" ("*Ousia* and *Grammè:* Note on a Note from *Being and Time*," in *Margins*, pp. 63, 66). It is beyond the scope of this book to discuss this latest Derridian move, whose most poignant staging may be in "Circumfessions," in Derrida and Geoffrey Bennington, *Jacques Derrida*, tr. Geoffrey Bennington (Chicago: Univ. of Chicago Press, 1993). Let this remain a parenthesis, in a note, on the note on a note in "*Ousia* and *Gammè*." The reading of *Antigone* is in *The Phenomenology of Mind*, tr. A. V. Miller (Oxford: Oxford Univ. Press, 1977), pp. 261–262, 284–289.

Such moves are not unusual among the ideologues of imperialism, then and now. Yet the question must be asked: given the immense importance of the Hegelian morphology, is it mean-spirited, unduly polemical, and ultimately mistaken to fix on these time-bound details? I think so, if it involves rejecting the morphology altogether. To critique it from within, to turn it away from itself, one must notice that these so-called time-bound bits are crucial to the system.

Such a reading is of course also "mistaken" because it attempts to engage the (im)possible perspective of the "native informant," a figure who, in ethnography, can only provide data, to be interpreted by the knowing subject for reading.[60] Indeed, there *can* be no correct scholarly model for this type of reading. It is, strictly speaking, "mistaken," for it attempts to transform into a reading-position the site of the "native informant" in anthropology, a site that can only *be* read, by definition, for the production of definitive descriptions. It is an (im)possible perspective. In Kant, we made no claim to restore the "miraculated" perspective of a native Australian or Fuegan.[61] Here, too, we are not proposing the restoration of the plausible perspective of a Hindu contemporary of Hegel's bemused by the reading. (In fact, a few decades later, the slow epistemic seduction of the culture of imperialism will produce modifications of the *Gitā* that argue for its world historical role in a spirit at least generically though not substantively "Hegelian." And these will come from Indian "nationalists." If the student of culture wishes to pursue this further, the scrupulous difference between the figuration of the native informant in the text of Kant and Hegel should lead her to investigating the differences in the oppression of the Australian Aborigine and groups like the Fuegans and the production of the dominant Hindu colonial subject, rather than positing a unified "third world," lost, or, more dubiously, found lodged *exclusively* in the ethnic minorities in the First.)

The native informant may be figured here as an implied reader "contemporary" with the *Gitā*. It gives him—gender advised—a span of

---

60. For the value of the "(im)", see Spivak, *In Other Worlds*, p. 263.

61. For "miraculation," see Deleuze and Guattari, *Anti-Oedipus*, p. 10 and *passim*.

some two centuries to float about in, still less than the Hegelian arrested space of India on the graph. Such a reader or listener acts out the structure of the hortatory ancient narrative as the recipient of its exhortation. The method is structural rather than historical or psychological, for we cannot know if any contemporary reader or listener behaved quite this way. But, (a) if he did, we can surmise that he would be bemused that a text that was the site of the most obvious negation and sublation of history (if he can think English he can be imagined to think Hegel) should be adduced as proof of eons of a-historicity and, (b) Hegel himself and many present-day readers of the exotic literatures of the past did and do assume such an implausible, if often unacknowledged, contemporary reader: contemporary with the text, and far removed from "our" time; and further, (c), refusing the centralized interpellation to be a native informant, as a teacher I am calling for a critic or teacher who has taken the trouble to do enough homework in language and history (not necessarily the same as specialist training) to be able to produce such a "contemporary reader" in the interest of active interception and reconstellation; rather than teach the producers of neo-colonialist knowledge to chant in unison, "one cannot truly know the cultures of other places, other times," and then proceed to diagnose the hegemonic readings into place.

It is interesting that both Kosambi and Matilal presuppose the figure of such a reader. Here is Kosambi: "The lower classes were necessary as an audience, and the heroic lays of ancient war drew them to the recitation. This made the epic a most convenient vehicle for any doctrine which the brahmins wanted to insert."[62] And Matilal: "Perhaps the historian has to eavesdrop on the dialogue between the past and the then present of earlier times."

The implied receiver of the exhortation in the text is Arjuna, the prince unwilling to kill his relatives in battle. The sender of the exhortation is Krishna, not only god-turned-charioteer, but also prince of a House not included among the two main contenders in the battle. There is a crucial moment in the nearly unbroken exhortation where the narrative makes Arjuna ask the question of history in the simplest

---

62. Kosambi, *Myth*, p. 18.

way. In search of evidential verification from history as sequence or timing for Krishna's transgression of the historical, Arjuna asks Krishna, "Your birth was later and the birth of the sun was earlier. How should I know that you said all this first?" (This version of the question of history, asked within the story as performed, must be strictly distinguished from the question of historicity, seeking to establish the locatable truth-value of the story as illocution.)

The "all this" in question is the third canto of the poem, Krishna's long lesson on how to act knowingly but without desire. Arjuna's question is placed at the beginning of the fourth canto, to provide an opening for Krishna, to give him a chance to clinch the lesson of Canto 3, by speaking of renunciation through knowing action. The question is ostensibly provoked by Krishna's claim that he had told this unchanging way of knowing (lawful) action to the sun.[63]

It is quite appropriate to bring up the question of history here. Krishna is not offering his account in a more primordial mode of being where time has not yet been caught in the thought of sequentiality. In fact, Krishna's claim traps heliocentric time into genealogical time through the mediation of the law. The Law in this case is Krishna's secret passed on by the immutably law-abiding sun to the mythic human law-encoder Manu. That is the substance of Krishna's speech, and the ostensible reason for Arjuna's question, as represented by the text. Manu passes the relay to Iksvāku, the eponymous progenitor of the Sun dynasty, where "Sun" has become an honorific proper name for the best genealogy of kings. Thus it is proper here to presuppose a certain connection between truth and history-as-timing and ask, "how shall I know (the truth of) what you say? How should I verify what you say, since you came after?"

To this Krishna gives three kinds of answer, which subordinate history as timing to law as the graph of time:

1. We come and go many times. I know them; you do not. One cannot obtain sequential verification by means of just *this* history.

---

63. "Unchanging way of knowing" is *avyaya yoga* in the original, meaning something more like "undiminishing technique." The problem of translating *yoga* is well known. It might interest the reader to know that, in grammatical terminology, the qualifier for the noun is the participial nominative for the indeclinable particle.

Krishna invokes his own superiority or perfection as proper agent or subject of knowledge.

2. I become by inhabiting my own nature through my own phenomenal possibility, although I am not born but am of immutable (the epithet is explained in note 63) spirit and am the head of all (already-been) beings.

I hope it is obvious from my carefully awkward translation that heavy philosophical issues are entailed in answer number two. An informed discussion of such issues is irrelevant here (as it is not in the case of Kant), to the figuration of the perspective named "native informant."[64] It seems enough to notice that human historicity is shown here to be of limited usefulness as explanatory or verificatory model. For here the privileged or exceptional subject of knowledge is also claiming to be the subject of exceptional genesis by a self-separated auto-affection. The divine male separates itself from itself to affect a part of itself and thus create. What in the human male would be nothing more than the dead inscription of spilled seed becomes, in God, self-origin and self-difference.[65] Nature (prakrti) in this is already available as the female principle (as well as roughly the two most common senses of "nature" in English) over against (specifically male or phallic) "man" (purusa). The word I translate "inhabit" (adhisthāna), does carry the sense of "properly placed," as a genius loci is properly placed in its locus. And if the self-generating subject properly inhabits the female in itself in order to

---

64. Rather than foreclosing the "native informant," Hegel is transvaluing cultural texts by appropriating them into a scale. To trace the foreclosure of the "Aboriginal," you step into Hegel's Africa, or the Gitā's description of the sūdra. We are on the track of the colonial subject, who certainly mimics the Master's racism (and classism) by reterritorializing his own. (Sexism is used to recode the divide.)

65. My "native informant" should be able to think Derrida if Derrida's notions of good divine writing as set up against bad human writing, of which male auto-affection is a case, has any logical plausibility. I hope the reader is able to distinguish this suggestion from the appropriation of "deconstruction" to legitimize exotic texts. As far as I can tell, there is no recriminatory pathos against masturbation in "Hindu" regulative psychobiography. For the authoritative injunction against masturbation, see The Laws of Manu, tr. G. Buhler (Oxford: Clarendon Press, 1886), canto 2, ll. 180–181, p. 63. I am grateful to Bimal Krishna Matilal for this reference.

become, the instrument is his own *māyā*. I have translated this word as "phenomenality," but in the *Gitā*'s Sanskrit it already carries the charge of "illusion," as indeed does *Schein* in *Erscheinung*, the German word most commonly translated "phenomenal appearance." Working with the metaphors that hold the metaphysics here, rather than merely conceptualizing the allegory, one could say that historical verification by temporal presence is being dismissed not only by Krishna's statement that the human being is present many times around, but also by further adducing that when *I* am present it is by a mechanism different from any other. *I* give the *logos* outside of historical temporality because *I* carry the phallus outside of physiological obligations.[66] Our native-informant-cum-contemporary reader would not have this specific vocabulary, but Hegel would.

3. I make myself whenever the Law is in decline.

This three-part phallogocentric negation and sublation of history can be grasped easily. Yet even such a sublation, of history as timing through the mediation of law—the vanishing moment of sequential human temporality into a catachresis named Time, is not the final hortatory instrument of the text. Krishna *shows* the exception at an important point by giving in to human error. Offering a structural summary of a highly repetitive exchange, let us say that Krishna, the privileged and exceptional subject of Time, withdraws into mere human timing and the arena of history by way of a staging of the indulgence of acknowledged error. We move toward this in Canto 10, where Krishna inserts himself into *one* model of sequentiality, if not the temporal, by describing himself as the best of a bewildering number of

---

66. My own bilingual copy of the *Gitā*, purchased in my teens when I was profoundly taken by nineteenth-century semitized Hinduism, offers the standard conceptual anagogical reading within that framework: "Though I am unborn, of changeless nature and Lord of beings, yet subjugating My Prakriti, I come into being by My own Maya" (*Shrimad-Bhagavad-Gitā*, tr. Swami Swarupananda [Calcutta: Advaita Ashrama, 1956], p. 99). The point might be made that this translation is perhaps more marked by the West than a reading using Greek words carrying *for the moment* a "Derridean" flavor. Van Buitenen's authoritative translation is: "Although indeed I am unborn and imperishable, although I am the lord of the creatures, I do resort to nature, which is mine, and take on birth by my own wizardry" (p. 87).

discontinuous series. (This is one of the passages Hegel quotes as simply a monotonous repetition of what goes on in millennia of Indian aesthetic representation.) In Canto 11, Arjuna's reaction to the entire "transcendental" or "exceptionalist" supra-historical first part of the narrative is one of acknowledged error and a prayer for indulgence:

> evam etad yathattha tvam ātmanam paramesvara
> drastum icchami te rupam aisvaram purushottama

The strongest burden of this couplet is the most emphatically implied "yet" between the two lines. The first line says, "Yes, Lord, you *are* as you say": by the mechanics of transcendental non-representability you *are* the holder of, and the singular example of, a special law. The second line says, "I want to see this divine form." The relation between the two lines is, "Sorry, I know it's wrong (a category mistake? lack of faith? human frailty?) but . . ." It is in response to this important self-excusing request that the text stages Krishna showing himself as cosmograph and indeed, in a peculiar way as an ontograph that can contain a historiograph. (This is the other passage that Hegel quotes as proof of the monotonous repetition of the same monstrous representation in millennia of static "Indian" aesthetic representation.) In apparent indulgence to the history-bound human insistence on timed verification, here in a somewhat unreally prolonged present, Time as exceptionalist graph must be negated into this more vulgar graphic gesture (showing himself)—the famous *viswarupadarsana* (the vision of the universal form) in the *Gitā*.[67]

---

67. Much can be made of the fact that *darsana*—vision—is usually translated "philosophy," although that usage would be clearly inappropriate here. The alternative usage, the felicity of constituting the transcendental object as object of the gaze, at once points at the difficulty of violating a cultural text by translation (*darsana* = philosophy = idolatrous reverence; ergo India [= Sanskritic Hinduism] has no philosophy but only religion/superstition); and offers the possibility of a deconstructive lever on the model of *pharmakon* (drug/poison), supplement (addition/hole-filler), *différance* (effacement/ disclosure), and the like. (Can the "same thing" be done with *theorein*—to see? I do not know.) Since I am not offering a deconstructive reading of the *Gitā* here, but rather using deconstruction as an excuse for the figuration of my perspective, I have no interest in pursuing this line of speculation. I should also mention that the reward for human frailty topos is used, abundantly in the *Gitā* and elsewhere, as the legitimization of *bhaktiyoga*,

Let me offer a detailed explanation of the abominable neologisms in "an ontograph that can contain a historiograph."

When, in response to an unendorsable request, Krishna shows himself to Arjuna as containing the universe, he must also expand the dimensions of his own body (I am aware that this is an epic topos): having a thousand arms and a thousand eyes, and so on, dismissed by Hegel as "monstrosity without aim and measure" (*LA* 1:338)—in fact a cultural idiomatic ruse in the dialectic between law and history. Of much greater interest to me is the move that makes Krishna *contain* all origins, all developments, *and* also the present moment.

Here is Arjuna in the battlefield. He is watching the two sides. *There* are his own people—*there* are his cousins on the other side.

All these sons of Dhrtarāstra [Arjuna's uncle, the father of his enemies], with hosts of kings, Bhisma, Drona, [Karna] the *Suta*-son, as well as our own chief warriors, are hastening into your terrifying and tusky mouth. Some can be seen sticking in the gaps between your teeth with their heads crushed to powder.

This vivid and memorable passage is a description of the actual phenomenal present in which Arjuna is standing. He is *seeing* an alternative version of *this* Krishna as chewing up all *these* people in his mouth. Krishna as a graphic representation of (a) transcendental Being [ontograph] contains the fluid present-in-time [historiograph]. No explanation is needed here: the graph is evidence, as required. Being is being-eaten. The graph of Time is a devouring of time as timing.

The human agent in his present-in-time (his here and now) can no longer trust the here and now as the concrete ground of verifiability. It is structurally most appropriate, *and* a support to the hortatory power of the text for the "contemporary receiver," that Arjuna speaks as follows, now, to Krishna, a person who had hitherto been his friend. These most

---

commonly translated as "the path of devotion." Kosambi points out that, "to hold [feudal—this term is now contested by Indian historians] society and its state together, the best religion is one which emphasizes the role of *bhakti*, personal faith, even though the object of devotion may have clearly visible flaws" (Kosambi, *Myth*, p. 32). As the following pages will I hope make clear, this is different from my analysis of the foregrounding of human error as the rhetorical motor of a shift from the transcendental to the social.

moving lines are an apology for action justified by the phenomenality of mere affect: "If, thinking you friend [*sakheti*], I have too boldly cried, hey Krishna, hey Yādava [almost a patronymic], friend [*sakheti*]; and if, through ignorance of this greatness of yours, or through sheer love or absence of mind, I did wrong [*asatkrta*] for the sake of fun,—on walks, in bed, sitting or eating, alone and in company,—since you are boundless, forgive me, I beg you."[68]

Through the grotesquely phenomenal representation (*by Arjuna*) of Krishna masticating the details of the immediately perceptible phenomenal reality in time and space, the authority of the here and now is undermined and, in the reaction (*by Arjuna*), the phenomenality of affect is denied and produced as excuse. (It is to be noticed that, in the first line of the quoted passage, Arjuna uses *sakheti* [as (if) a friend] not merely as an adverbial phrase modifying *yaduktam* [whatever I said] but also as a mode of address, a noun in the vocative case—"you who are *as if* a friend." It is all the more noticeable because the second occurrence is, strictly speaking, grammatically "incorrect" and "unnecessary," or merely semi-grammatical. Here the Jakobsonian poetic function"—"as if friend" repeated twice apparently for the sake of symmetry—underscores the illusoriness of judgments based on the phenomenality of affect.)

In what interest is this graphic or visible sublation (negation and preservation on another register) of the apparent phenomenality of lived time and affect performed in the poem? Again, doing injustice to a complex and repetitive text, it can be advanced that it is in the interest of the felicitous presentation of a *concrete* social order, within a frame that has now been disclosed as an indulgent allowance to human error. This section of the *Gītā* is not much celebrated in the current conjuncture, as indeed "The Critique of Teleological Judgement" is not the

---

68. Arjuna is speaking here of the difference between human and divine. With all due respect, it seems to me to be merely pedantic to explain this with reference to mere "matters of [social] precedence" as does van Buitenen, p. 167, n. 9. Kosambi's down-to-earth approach necessarily flattens the text, for it does not read closely: "the moral is pointed by the demoniac God himself: that all the warriors on the field had really been destroyed by him; Arjuna's killing them would be a purely formal affair whereby he could win the opulent kingdom" (*Myth*, p. 17).

most perused part of *The Critique of Judgment*. I suggest that in this section the actual *social* exhortation comes, framed, not as a betrayal or contradiction of the abundantly celebrated transcendental sections, but as an appropriate concession, an acknowledgement of human error, an indulgence. The tone of the narrative becomes much more "temporal" (to use that charged adjective) after this. (The "bad" social writing, as opposed to the "good" transcendental writing, is indulgently and clandestinely inserted in response to human error. The "human" produces an *alibi* for what is *in illo tempore*.)

It is through these cantos, then, that the four castes—*Brāhman, Ksatriya, Vaisya, Sudra*—can at last be named as such:

> Control of mind and senses, austerity, purity, patience, uprightness, knowledge, insight, and belief in a hereafter are born of the proper being [*svabhāva*] of the brahman. Prowess, energy, perseverance, capability, steadfastness in battle, gift-giving, and feelings of lordship are born of the proper being of the *ksatriya*. Agriculture, cattle-herding, and trade are born of the proper being of the *vaisya*. The proper being of the *sudra* generates work whose essence is to serve others.[69]

The happiness that is proper to the being named *sudra* is elaborated thus: "the happiness which, first and last, arises from the confusion of sleep, sloth, and delusion."

---

69. Hitherto only the proper name *ksatriya* (warrior) is used a number of times, not as one caste marker among four, but as a general interpellation in ideology for Arjuna. The enunciative strategy of the verse (4.13) that is invariably chosen, by Radhakrishnan and many others, as proof of the liberating and flexible vocational definition of caste offered by Krishna in the *Gitā* (*Hindu View*, p. 79), should be carefully analyzed before any claim is made. Matilal locates a critical tradition within Brahmanical orthodoxy itself, however defined. His treatment of the field of battle as the field of *dharma* (*dharmakshetra*), as, in its turn, a field of rule following; his critique of Max Weber by way of a commentary on the relationship between caste and Karma; his astute tracking of the slippage between *svadharma* and *svabhāva*, relate his study, as I have already suggested, to the study of the formation of culture on the Indian subcontinent, and its diasporic and global variants today. Hegel's general position on caste is to be found in *The Philosophy of History*, p. 168.

These vignettes are far indeed from transcendental graphing. They are customarily taken to be proof of the functional heteropraxy of Hindu social behavior. My point is that, in this authoritative text, taken as static and monotonous by Hegel, such summaries are allowed by way of a textual ruse of the self-excusing unendorsable erring request endorsed as an indulgence of a human error that must nonetheless deny the phenomenality of affect and deny the ground of verification by the so-called concrete lived present. The proper name of the caste stands as a mark to cover over the transition from a tribal society of lineage, where one cannot kill one's own kin, to something more like a state where one's loyalties are to abstracter categories for self-reference.[70]

Through this crudely dialectical reading of a moment in the *Gitā*, I have attempted to deconstruct Hegel's graphic self-differentiation from the subject in India (*one* stage of the unconscious symbolic). I have attempted to show that "Hegel" and the "*Gitā*" can be read as two rather different versions of the manipulation of the question of history in a political interest, for the apparent disclosure of the Law.

One of the differences is the *Gitā*'s exceptionalism in the place of Hegel's Euro-teleological normativity. In Chapter 3, I discuss the possibility that, in the context of gendering, exceptionalism might be one part of the Indic regulative psychobiography.[71]

In an early passage of his critique of Hegel, Marx writes in a way that is coherent with a graphic image of the Hegelian system. If the orchestration of the marxian passage in its context is attended to, I believe it can

---

70. It would be interesting to work this into the alliance-affinal dialectic of territorialization and coding in Deleuze and Guattari, *Anti-Oedipus*, p. 145f. Let us remember, however, that although they are critical of the connections between ethnography and psychoanalysis, they themselves share some of the historical prejudices (such as a faith in "oriental despotism") sustained by the culture of imperialism. See, for example, Deleuze and Guattari, *A Thousand Plateaus: Capitalism and Schizophrenia*, tr. Brian Massumi (Minneapolis: Univ. of Minnesota Press, 1987), p. 351f.

71. Matilal's notion of Krishna as emulable moral agent and this idea of Krishna as exceptionalist regulator nicely point up the difference between analytic and deconstructive studies of culture (see Spivak and Matilal, *Epic and Ethic*, chap. 2.)

then be seen as suggesting that that system makes appear the Being estranged from itself [*sich entfremdetes Wesen*—Being not adequate to its own proper outlines, as it were] even as it seems to present Being coming home to itself through a process of necessary othering and sublating [*Entäusserung/Aufhebung*]: "It is the confirmation [*Bestätigung*] of apparent being or *self-estranged* being in its negation [*Verneinung*] . . . and its transformation into the subject."[72]

An interesting reading is produced if Marx's use of *Verneinung* is related to Freud's later use of the term (with which it is not inconsonant), now often translated as "denegation": "A negative judgement [*die Verurteilung*] is the intellectual substitute for repression; its 'no' is the hall-mark [*Merkzeichen*] of repression, a certificate of origin—like, let us say, 'Made in Germany.'"[73] By this line of reasoning, the judgment becomes a visible graphic mark of the negation.

If Marx is read retrospectively with this Freudian passage in mind, the Hegelian graph may be said to make visible the repressed certificate of origin: "Made in (or for—effect or condition) Capitalism." Marx shows this by shifting the system to "the sphere of political economy" to show up the estrangement of the system, its derailment, so that the results computed by it are reversed to the extent of irrelevance: "In the sphere of political economy [the] realization [*Verwirklichung*] of labour appears as a *loss of reality* [*Entwirklichung*] for the worker, objectification [*Vergegenständlichung*] as *loss of and bondage to the object* [*Verlust und Knechtschaft des Gegenstandes*], and appropriation [*Aneignung*] as *estrangement* [*Entfremdung*], as *alienation* [*Entäusserung*]."[74]

Freud had indicated the usefulness of denegation as follows: "By means of [*vermittels*] the symbol of negation, thinking frees itself from the restrictions of repression and enriches itself with material that is indispensible for its proper functioning." It is perhaps in acknowl-

---

72. Marx, *Early Writings*, tr. Rodney Livingstone and Gregor Benton (Harmondsworth: Penguin, 1975), p. 393.

73. Freud, *SE* 19:236.

74. Marx, *Early Writings*, p. 324; emphasis Marx's. This is not the place to pursue my conviction that *Entfremdung* (estrangement) and *Entäusserung* (alienation) generally carry separate charges in Marx—the first an ontological error perpetrated by philosophy in collaboration with political economy, the second an ontological necessity for the very predication of (the human) being and doing.

edgement of an enriched and proper functioning that owes something to denegation (in a proto-Freudian rather than a strictly "philosophical" sense) that, in the sentence that follows my quotation, Marx dockets the Hegelian system in the narrative timing of *das Aufheben*—the effort of sublating—rather than the graphic Time of *Aufhebung*, the accomplished sublation.

One of the most scandalous examples of such a slippage between the effort of sublating and accomplished sublation (if there may be such an accomplishment) is the access of the colonized, along lines of class-alliance and class-formation, to the heritage and culture of imperialism. In other words, it is not only in the sphere of political economy as such that *"Aneignung* [appropriation] becomes *Entfremdung* [estrangement]." If one assumes an "own-ness" (or *Eigenschaft*) of cultural ground—an assumption no more than strategically necessary for this calculation—everything gained through this classed access to the culture of imperialism was an estrangement. Every attempt at consolidating a cultural ground by these means defined out the peoples without access as constituents *of*, and indeed *to*, that presumed ground, in a parody of the foreclosure in Kant. This estrangement and foreclosure are now being re-played as varieties of "fundamentalism," a return of the repressed. The current mood, in the radical fringe of humanistic Northern pedagogy, of uncritical enthusiasm for the Third World, makes a demand upon the inhabitant of that Third World to speak up as an authentic ethnic fully representative of his or her tradition. This demand in principle ignores an open secret: that an ethnicity untroubled by the vicissitudes of history and neatly accessible as an object of investigation is a confection to which the disciplinary pieties of the anthropologist, the intellectual curiosity of the early colonials and the European scholars partly inspired by them, *as well as* the indigenous elite nationalists, by way of the culture of imperialism, contributed their labors, and the (proper) object (of investigation) is therefore "lost."

There is a great deal to be said about this unexamined negotiation between U.S. Third Worldism—carried as an alternative to, as well as an expression of, "the Left"—and the construction of the object of colonialism/nationalism, each legitimizing the other. I will draw attention to only one point here: that the current negotiation may be no more and, of course, no less, than a displacement of the negotiation between colonialism and nationalism, even as the latter was ostensibly and, in its context, powerfully, taking a stand against the former:

> The contradictory pulls on nationalistic ideology in its struggle against the dominance of colonialism [led to] . . . a resolution which was built around a separation of the domain of culture into two spheres—the material and the spiritual. It was in the material sphere that the claims of Western civilization were the most powerful. Science, technology, rational forms of economic organization, modern methods of statecraft—these have given the European countries the strength to subjugate non-European peoples and to impose their dominance over the whole world. To overcome this domination, the colonized people must learn those superior techniques of organizing material life and incorporate them within their own cultures. This was one aspect of the nationalist project of rationalizing and reforming the traditional culture of their people. But this could not mean the imitation of the West in every aspect of life, for then the very distinction between the West and East would vanish—the self-identity of national culture would itself be threatened. In fact, as Indian nationalists in the late 19th century argued, not only was it not desirable to imitate the West in anything other than the material aspects of life, it was not even necessary to do so, because in the spiritual domain the East was superior to the West. What was necessary was to cultivate the material techniques of modern Western civilization while retaining and strengthening the distinctive spiritual essence of the national culture. This completed the formulation of the nationalist project, and as an ideological justification for the selective appropriation of Western modernity it continues to hold sway to this day.[75]

Within this scenario, the *Gītā* once again comes to occupy an important place in the representation of the spiritual and cultural sphere.[76] It is now declared by prominent nationalists to have a timeless core that is

---

75. Partha Chatterjee, *The Nationalist Resolution of the Women's Question*, occasional paper 94 (Calcutta: Centre for Studies in Social Sciences, 1987), p. 6. See also Kumari Jayawardena, *Feminism and Nationalism in the Third World* (London: Zed, 1986), pp. 254–261 and *passim*.

76. Nandy, *Intimate Enemy*, p. 47.

supra-historical rather than not-yet-historical, as in Hegel. My concept-metaphor of the graphing of time operates here, however vestigially, by way of the notion of the perennial structures of the universal human mind. I would argue that just as nationalism in many ways is a displaced or reversed legitimation of colonialism, this approach is a displacement of what we have, metonymically, named "Hegel."

To repeat, neither the colonial, nor the postcolonial subject inhabits the (im)possible perspective of the native informant or the implied contemporary receiver. "Hegel" is refracted into the colonial subject. Here are quotations from three sources: first, *Essays on the Gitā* (1916), a meditative text by the celebrated nationalist-activist turned sage, Aurobindo Ghose; second, *The Hindu View of Life* (1927), an authoritative text by nationalist-philosopher turned statesman Sarvepalli Radhakrishnan; and, finally, *Marxism and the Bhagvat Geeta*, a mechanical marxist text, published in 1982, that would be held in tolerant contempt by the indigenous sophisticate.[77]

In the first passage, like the colonized body politic, the text of the *Gitā* itself has been divided into the material and the spiritual. Its structure has been flattened out. What is now diagnosed as the time-bound material aspect of the text has nothing to do of course with the rusing structural liveliness that I have been at pains to point out. Here is Sri Aurobindo:

> No doubt, [in our attempt at reading the Gitā] we may mix a good deal of error born of our own individuality and of the ideas in which we live, as did greater men before us, but if we steep ourselves in the spirit of this great Scripture and, above all, if we have tried to live in that spirit, we may be sure of finding in it as much real truth as we are capable of receiving as well as the spiritual influence and actual help that, personally, we were intended to derive from it. And that is after all what Scriptures were written to give; the rest is academical disputation or theological dogma. Only those Scriptures, religions, philoso-

---

77. Aurobindo Ghose, *Essays on the Gitā* (Pondicherry: Sri Aurobindo Ashram, 1972); Sarvepalli Radhakrishnan, *The Hindu View;* and S. G. Sardesai and Dilip Bose, *Marxism and the Bhagvat Geeta* (New Delhi: People's Publishing House, 1982). For a successful entry into continuous academic discourse, see, for example, Hiralal Haldar, *Neo-Hegelianism* (London: Heath Cranton, 1927). This is the person mocked by Kipling in *Kim*.

phies which can be thus constantly renewed, relived, their stuff of permanent truth constantly reshaped and developed in the inner thought and spiritual experience of a developing humanity, continue to be of living importance to mankind. The rest remain as monuments of the past, but have no actual force or vital impulse for the future. In the Gītā there is very little that is merely local or temporal and its spirit is so large, profound and universal that even this little can easily be universalised . . .'[78]

It is almost as if the entire Hegelian graph of the spirit's journey has been sea-changed into a de-racialized universalism where the cultured colonial nationalist can denegate colonialism. "The spiritual experience of a developing humanity" is neither Hindu nor Hegel but a bit of both.

By 1927, the voice of "academical disputation" itself is carrying the torch of legitimation. Here is Radhakrishnan, writing from Oxford University:

> The Hindu method of religious reform helps to bring about a change not in the name but in the content. While we are allowed to retain the same name, we are encouraged to deepen its significance. To take a familiar illustration, the Yahveh of the Pentateuch is a fearsome spirit. . . . The conception of the Holy One who loves mercy rather than sacrifice, who abominates burnt offerings, who reveals himself to those who yearn to know him asserts itself in the writings of Isaiah and Hosea. In the revelation of Jesus we have the conception of God as perfect love. The name "Yahveh" is the common link which connects these different developments. When a new cult is accepted by Hinduism, the name is retained though a refinement of the content is effected. To take an example from early Sanskrit literature, it is clear that Kali in her various shapes is a non-Aryan goddess. But she was gradually identified with the supreme Godhead. . . . Similarly Krsna becomes the highest Godhead in the *BhagavadGitā* whatever his past origin may have been.[79]

It is possible for Radhakrishnan to draw a clear and adequate parallel between the development from pre-Aryan to Aryan and that from Judaism to Christianity. The model of a developing spirit of humanity is

---

78. Ghose, *Essays*, p. 3.
79. Radhakrishnan, *Hindu View*, pp. 32–33.

aligned, in narrative inspiration, to that very "Hegel" who claimed to Humboldt that modern scholarly findings had removed the grounds for claiming transcendental grandeur for the philosophy of the Hindus, a myth perpetrated by Pythagoras and followers (see note 59). The agent of Hinduism is the high colonial/nationalist subject who "refines" the religion into its universalist lineaments. (One might note that "Sanskritization" is, literally, "refinement.") The *Gītā* is now the fountainhead of the philosophy of the Aryans, where caste is re-inscribed as the secret of freedom quite in keeping with Marx's famous line: "Man makes his own history but not of his own free will."[80]

There is often a certain loss of style in the descent or shift from the high culture of nationalism within territorial imperialism to that search for "national identity" that confuses religion, culture, and ideology in the newly independent nation. Although the ingredients of the earlier universalization of the *Gītā* can still be encountered, more typical is a muscular fundamentalism or nativism. Pitted against it is an equally muscular "marxist" idiom that is routinely and perhaps understandably impatient with the folds and pleats of ancient texts. Commenting on the relatively exceptionalist model of the *sthitaprajna* or the stable-in-knowledge offered by the absolutely exceptional Krishna, such an approach has this to say:

> We have the famous verse which says, "What is night for all creatures is wakefulness for him. What is wakefulness for the creatures is night for him." So, what is light for you and me is darkness for the *sthitaprajna*, what is darkness for us is light for him. The implication is clear. The masses are sunk in ignorance, greed, voluptuousness, temptation, violence, and what not. The one who has seen Light is untouched by all human weaknesses.[81]

None of the philosophical presuppositions of the Hegelian or nationalist fabulations is called into question here. The extraordinary ways in which the text wins assent are necessarily ignored. Indeed, the nationalist admiration for the *Gītā*, in the interest of preserving a sense of

---

80. Marx, *Surveys from Exile*, tr. David Fernbach (New York: Vintage, 1974), p. 146.
81. Sardesai and Bose, *Marxism*, p. 24.

"national continuity," however spurious, is seen as an ennobling alibi in its time and place.

The impulses toward a new U.S. pedagogy of the "Third World" cannot not articulate itself in the chain of displacements that I put together here in such broad linkings. Its critical role—precisely not to undertake to restore a lost "historical Indian" obliterated by the Hegelian chronotypograph and lurking in the generalized indigenous soul today—has perhaps produced too uncritical a celebration of the "hybrid," which inadvertently legitimizes the "pure" by reversal. The nativist can then forget that there is no *historically* available authentic (*eigentlich*) Indian point of view that can now step forth (*hervortreten*) and reclaim its rightful place in the narrative of world history. If as literary critics and teachers, we could have taught ourselves and our students the way to informed *figurations* of that "lost" perspective, then the geopolitical postcolonial situation could have served as something like a paradigm for the thought of history itself as figuration, figuring something out with "chunks of the real."

Writing in the metropolis or in the former colony, many of us are trying to carve out positive negotiations with the epistemic graphing of imperialism. For some of the shadow areas in the micrology of the manipulation of law and history, cutting across the body of the great narrative of imperialism, no good word can be said. And our disciplinary goodwill can become complicitous with those areas without the vigilance I attempt to dramatize here. I cannot illuminate those shadow areas in any detail in this broad focus. Let me rather make an impertinent move. Since the strategy of this book is, at least in part, to attempt to persuade through the discontinuity of odd connections or reconstellation, I will invite the student or scholar of cultural studies to figure out the relationship between my account of the narrative of the chronotypography of imperialism and the story told in the following report of the International Commission of Jurists and the Christian Conference of Asia:

In some countries [of the south and southeast Asian region] the denial [of basic civil and democratic rights to the variously disenfranchised] is built into the constitution and the laws, while in some areas it masquerades under the guise of religious fundamentalism [I have been arguing, with the support of writers such as Chatterjee and Jayawardena that the two are displacements of each other in the post-colonial discursive formation]. . . . In some cases, the legislations carry the same names—like the Official Secrets Act in Malaysia and India—or similar names (e.g., National Security Act of India; Public Security Act of Nepal; National Security Law of South Korea; Internal Security Act of Malaysia and Singapore; Internal Security Act of Pakistan). . . . Religion, or tyrannical doctrines in the name of religion, are being woven into the constitutions of some countries to suppress [these] rights [to ethnic minorities, women, and so on].[82]

Look now at the language being used by the indigenous "Third World" elite to describe the foundations of such practices: "the mono-doctrine of 'Panchshila,' a compulsory state ideology which comprises: 'Belief in the one supreme God, just and civilized humanity, and the unity of [the nation] . . .'"

If we remain *caught* in the shuffle between claims and counter-claims upon a legiferant and adjudicating chronotypography—no disciplinary formation can *fully* avoid it—the only alternative to the hyperbolic admiration for the authentic ethnic might be to proclaim: "This challenged giant [the United States] . . . may, in fact, be on the point of becoming a David before the growing Goliath of the Third World. I dream that our children will prefer to join this David, with his errors and impasses, armed with our erring and circling about the Idea, the Logos, the Form: in short, the old Judeo-Christian Europe. If it is only an illusion, I like to think it may have a future."[83]

It is in order to take a distance from this reasonable binary opposition that we might be able to make use of the (im)possible perspective of the native informant. The *possibility* of the native informant is, as I have already indicated, inscribed as evidence in the production of the scien-

---

82. "Internationalism of Oppressors," *Economic and Political Weekly* 23. 4 (23 Jan. 1988): 108. The details of contemporary Indonesian politics, and the place of "religion" there, is so intricate that it is quite beyond my scope. Let this slight intrusion stand here marking the range of the speculations I have ignorantly launched.

83. Julia Kristeva, "My Memory's Hyperbole," in Domna C. Stanton, ed., *The Female Autograph: Theory and Practice of Autobiography from the Tenth to the Twentieth Century* (Chicago: Univ. of Chicago Press, 1987), p. 235. These words take on added violence at the time of revision, in full deployment of "Operation Desert Storm." Kristeva's exhortation on behalf of "foreigners"—included in the catalogue for the second Johannesburg Biennale—remains as bewilderingly Eurocentric.

tific or disciplinary European knowledge of the culture of others: from field-work through ethnography into anthropology. That apparently benign subordination of "timing" (the lived) into "Time" (the graph of the Law) cannot of course be re-traced to a restorable origin, if origin there is to be found.[84] But the resistant reader and teacher can at least (and persistently) attempt to undo that continuing subordination by the figuration of the name—"the native informant"—into a reader's perspective. Are we still condemned to circle around "Idea, Logos, and Form," or can the (ex)orbitant at least be invoked?

III

Marx keeps moving for a Marxist as the world moves. I keep wanting to write this section differently. One way would be to begin with a citation from *The Communist Manifesto*: "The less the skill and exertion of strength implied in manual labour, in other words, the more modern industry becomes developed, the more is the labour of men superseded by that of women."[85] Although this passage immediately follows a description of the *pre*-Fordist factory, Marx's prescience is fulfilled in postfordism and the explosion of global homeworking. The subaltern woman is now to a rather large extent the support of production.

Next a reading of Marx's reading of the commodity-form as the locus of the homeopathy that would monitor the *différance* of capitalism and socialism. That imperialism introduces mobility toward socialization

---

84. This type of assertion provokes resentment in metropolitan anti-colonialists as well as a growing body of indigenous urban intellectuals who are themselves critical of hegemonic nationalism in India and yet are paradoxically susceptible to identifying "India" with the view from the urban centers where they live and teach. This can, on occasion, turn into a rather insidious brand of nationalism disqualifying all diasporic analysis. Without prejudice to the further development of an argument analyzing this position, I should like to offer as appeasement the assurance that such assertions are also about the nature of "real" origins in general, and work against the authority of abundantly established dominant origins such as "Hegel." Our vigilance is so that counter-claims to alternative origins, mouthed by the indigenous dominant as self-chosen representative of the subordinate, do not legitimize the vanguardism of established "origins" by a mere reversal.

85. Marx, *The Communist Manifesto*, ed. Frederic L. Bender (New York: Norton, 1988), p. 62.

has proved itself, I would suggest, in the cases of both international communism and international capitalism. And, in the new new international economic order after the dissolution of the Soviet Union, it is the labor of the patriarchally defined subaltern woman that has been most effectively socialized.

I would expand this, by way of a Marxist theorization of reproductive engineering and population control as the socialization of reproductive laborpower. (The nonexhaustive taxonomy that such a theorization has allowed me, tentatively, to formalize in the classroom, I offer here in shorthand, in the hope that Marxist-feminists active in global economic resistance will be able to reproduce the analysis. But will they be interested in Kant and Hegel? At any rate, here is the shorthand taxonomy of the coded discursive management of the new socialization of the reproductive body: (a) reproductive rights (*metonymic* substitution of abstract average subject of rights for woman's identity); (b) surrogacy (*metaphoric* substitution of abstract average reproductive labor power as fulfilled female subject of motherhood); (c) transplant (displacement of eroticism and generalized presupposed subject of immediate affect); (d) population control (objectification of female subject of exploitation to produce alibi for hypersize through demographic rationalization); and (e) postfordist homeworking (classical coding of the spectrality of reason as empiricist individualism, complicated by gender ideology). It is only after a discussion of a possible taxonomy of the recoding of this socialization that I would describe the theater of global resistance where these issues are now paramount.[86]

This current reinscription of the perspective called the "native informant," I would suggest, has been foreclosed in the tradition of Marxism

---

86. The commodity-form is the locus of the sustained homeopathic monitoring of the chronic differance between socialism and capitalism—because, with things, it generates "more" (*Mehrwert* = surplus-value), and with people, it permits abstraction and thus separation from individual intention. Etienne Balibar's magisterial "In Search of the Proletariat" can take this on board if it pushes off the residual commodity pietism that stands in its way (in Balibar, *Masses, Classes, Ideas: Studies on Politics and Philosophy before and after Marx*, tr. James Swenson [New York: Routledge, 1994]). Let us unfix the binary opposition between "labor-power [as] *only* a commodity" and the heterogeneous hierarchies of race-gender-migrancy (p. 147; emphasis author's), and see a shuttle where the rational calculus of commodification

and continues to be excluded. For Marx was the organic intellectual of European capitalism. (This too would need discussion.) I would cite, in demonstration of this foreclosure, the electoral left in the developing world, as well as the UN conference on Population and Development in Cairo (1994) and on Women in Beijing (1995); Jacques Derrida's

---

protects from the dangers of a merely fragmented identity politics—and not in the economic sphere alone. Balibar describes "the term 'proletariat' [as] only connot[ing] the 'transitional' nature of the working class, . . . accentuat[ing] the difficulty in holding together, without aporia or contradiction, historical materialism and the critical theory of *Capital*" (pp. 126–127). Why are Marxist intellectuals interested in holding things together, when "history," "culture,' "real life" (big, difficult words) are forever on the move, is a question I ask Fredric Jameson in Chapter 4. Balibar sees this transitionality as an inability "to formulate the concept of *proletarian ideology* as the ideology *of proletarians*" (p. 148; emphasis author's). We must read it as the moment where the Marxian text transgresses its own protocols— so far Balibar is our guide—so that it can be turned around and let the subaltern (who is not coterminous with the proletarian) enter in the colonial phase, and today make room for the globe-girdling nationalist-under-erasure Southern (rather than only the Eurocentric migrant) subject who would dislocate Economic Citizenship by constant interruption, "permanent parabasis" (de Man, *Allegories*, p. 301). Then the shift from World Trade to finance market—the signature of the post-Soviet conjuncture—does not have to be described in the residual language of the buck passing from the economic to the political sphere. Of course the "subject of 'capital'" (p. 143) is "formal," and all that follows from it. Marx's project is to dislocate a restricted definition of the subject (which would ignore "superadequation," that it is worth more ([*Mehrwert* = surplus-value] than itself) from the intent of the agent, so that it can occupy (*besetzen*—"cathect?") this subject-position for others, not just selves. We would say that this cannot last through change of mode of production (economic) or government (political) alone; although these calculuses provide the support. Therefore differance, not sublation once and for all. This is how we counter Balibar's astute critique of the "myth of the 'integrated' working class" (p. 149), not by positing "'population movements' [as] the main basis of explanation for 'mass movements'" (p. 146). Raymond Williams appropriated Marxism for Britain a generation ago by inscribing it as *The Country and the City* (New York: Oxford Univ. Press, 1973). Postcolonial Eurocentric migration is historical, just as much "an organic aspect of [the post-]modern form [of the capitalist relations of production]" as was the "integrated" working class of the "modern" (p. 149). Unless we go one better than Samir Amin, who zooms this explanation out to the history of the world before Europe (see page 89) and look at the sketched idea of movements before the (ab)-original. As Mahasweta, Toni Morrison, and Coetzee (among many others) know, "history" moves into "geology" here (see Chapter 2 and Spivak, "Acting Bits / Identity Talk," in Henry Louis Gates, Jr. and Anthony Appiah, eds., *Identities* (Chicago: Univ. of Chicago Press, 1995), p. 171. In fact, a

Specters of Marx as well as Stanley Aronowitz's "The Situation of the Left in the United States;" as examples of "the perspective which views the dominant system not as a globalized local tradition, but as a universal tradition."[87]

The socialized woman as "native informant" would then invaginate this book.[88] She would take it beyond its outlines, for in the current version, the last chapter looks toward her as it ends. But I can do no more than leave this mark of that possible invagination, for it is too late to undertake so radical a rewriting. In insufficient recompense, I have quietly changed "sublation" to *"différance"* as the name of the relationship between capitalism and socialism. That change is all the more urgent in the context of the global project as such: planetary financialization.

Here, then, is the earlier text.

Carl Pletsch urged us to do a Kantian, Hegelian, Marxian deconstruction of the division of the world into three. I put aside the problem that one cannot "do" a "deconstruction" of anything. I set myself to show rather, that even as we use a Kantian or a Hegelian vision to understand this division, we must also know how to read the great European philosophers' complicity in the sustenance of that division. I argued that the figure of the native informant was crucial yet foreclosed—a necessarily "lost" object—in Kant's third Critique and

---

useful critique of the homeopathy of commodification emerges from "the country" in the current conjuncture. Marx thought of the capitalization of land as part of the pre-history of capital. In today's exploitation, appropriation, and contamination of biodiversity, the linearity of this narrative is challenged by way of the postmodernization of technology. And, since soil is irreplaceable and unmotivated, the circuit of more-worth only depletes it. A limit, (as) ground. This is the book that I cannot write.

87. Derrida, *The Specters of Marx: The State of the Debt and the New International,* tr. Peggy Kamuf (New York: Routledge, 1994); Stanley Aronowitz, "The Situation of the Left in the United States," *Socialist Review* 23.3 (1994): 5–79; Vandana Shiva, *Monocultures of the Mind: Perspectives on Biodiversity and Biotechnology* (London: Zed, 1993), p. 10.

88. As always, my definition of "invaginate" follows Derrida's in "The Law of Genre," in Derek Attridge, ed., *Acts of Literature* (New York: Routledge, 1992), pp. 227–228. What is a part also contains the whole, in a chiastic (as in the rhetorical figure of chiasmus) relationship.

Hegel's discussion of the Unconscious Symbolic. One cannot comment on the texts of Marx in quite the same way. Marx has been global in a way that Kant and Hegel have not been. And one of the major stakes in that globality has been an understanding of the nature and content of the narrative of history and the construction of a non-Atlantic country as the subject (agent) of history. Where and how will a non-European country insert itself into the predictive blueprint of what is understood as the Marxist promise to a certain kind of historical agency? The question of the native informant as revolutionary subject is institutionalized in Marxism in the name of a vanguard—a more sophisticated method of foreclosure, perhaps—although Marx himself seemed more interested in the question of agency (institutionally validated action).

In Marx's case, I am therefore not going to analyze a bit of text. I am going to look at the implications of a notorious phrase that Marx probably used only once: "the Asiatic Mode of Production."[89] Since the term ranged in scope of application over most of the non-European globe at one time or another, it would be rather difficult to imagine a native informant's perspective here. I will next consider the notion of the "value-form" in Marx, which can be useful for expanding the field of investigation available to such a perspective.

Marxist literary criticism never had much interest in either of the terms. For Marxist literary criticism, the question of the "Asiatic Mode" was usually considered settled by tendentious but easily available books such as Karl Wittfogel's *Oriental Despotism.*[90] In 1986, at a time when interest in global cultural studies was being felt widely in more privileged institutions of higher learning in the United States, Fredric Jameson had this to say in a rather influential essay:

In the gradual expansion of capitalism across the globe, then, an economic system confronts two very distinct modes of production that pose two very different types of social and cultural resistance to its influence. These are so-called primitive, or tribal societies on the one

---

89. Marx, *A Contribution to the Critique of Political Economy*, tr. S. W. Ryazanskaya (New York: International Publishers, 1970), p. 21.

90. Karl August Wittfogel, *Oriental Despotism: A Comparative Study of Total Power* (New Haven: Yale Univ. Press, 1951).

hand, and the Asiatic mode of production, or the great bureaucratic imperial systems on the other. African societies and cultures, as they became the object of systematic colonization in the 1880s, provide the most striking example of the symbiosis of capital and tribal societies; while China and India offer the principal examples of another and quite different sort of engagement of capitalism with the great empires of the so-called Asiatic mode. . . . Latin America offers yet a third kind of development.[91]

This is an effort at inserting non-Europe (no more graceful word will suffice) into an Eurocentric normative narrative—"our economic system . . . and social and cultural resistances to its influence." The "Asiatic Mode" is simply accepted as a taxonomic term here. China and India are conflated. Yet it cannot be denied that Jameson is himself resolutely against Atlantic-European dominance. In order to understand globality, then, should we resurrect that tired old Asiatic mode? Perry Anderson wrote about this mode, in 1974: "These elementary contrasts [outlined in his book], of course, in no way constitute even the beginnings of a comparison of the real *modes of production* whose complex combination and succession defined the actual social formations of these huge regions outside Europe. They merely . . . preclude any attempt to assimilate them as simple examples of a common 'Asiatic' mode of production. Let this last notion be given the decent burial that it deserves."[92]

The Asiatic mode of production marks a venerable moment in theorizing the other. The usual way of accounting for it is to say that Marx and Engels came up with this phrase precisely in answer to the question: why did the normative logic of Capital not determine itself in the same way everywhere? Or, more "theoretically," is the history of the world uni- or multi-linear? Like Rousseau's question about the origin of languages, the question that led to the largely unsatisfactory formulation of the Asiatic Mode of Production is: why is there difference? why is "Europe" not the only self-identical "same?" Why is there

---

91. Jameson, "Third-World Literature" *Social Text* (1986): 68–69.
92. Anderson, *Absolutist State*, p. 548.

"Asia?" It is well known that "Asia" in this formulation soon lost any resemblance to any empirically recognizable space.[93]

How did Marx get to the question of difference? And was the Asiatic Mode the only form in which this question was asked by him? In order to construct an answer to these questions, I will pass through a schematic view of Marx's early life.

[Marx] has perhaps been alone in putting his name . . . on the line, . . . particularly for the political future of what he left to be signed. How can one avoid taking . . . this into account when reading [Marx's] texts? One reads [them] only by taking it into account . . . [T]o make an immense bio-graphical paraph out of all that [he] has written on [social justice or injustice]—this is . . . what we have to put on active record. . . . We would . . . be mistaken if we understood it as a simple presentation of identity, assuming that we already knew what is involved in self-presentation and a statement of identity ("Me, such a person," male or female, an individual or collective subject, "Me, psychoanalysis," "Me, metaphysics[,]" [Me, communism]).[94]

Let us approach Marx's entry into his proper name through the question of bio-graphy understood in this way. Then the Economic and Philosophical Manuscripts of 1844 can be read as "an outwork, an *hors d'oeuvre*, an exergue or a flysheet whose topos, like (its) temporality,

---

93. Questions about difference, one or multiple origins and histories, are of course the by-product of imperialism. In the London of the 1860s, the conflict between the Ethnological Society of London and the Anthropological Society of London provides an example of this. Their concern was whether difference could be articulated in terms of language, rather than in terms of race. "The creation of the Anthropological Institute [of Great Britain and Ireland in 1871] healed the wound made by the Anthropological Society and returned organized anthropology to the traditional British pattern of scientific societies that deal only with scientific issues" (Ronald Raingere, "Race, Politics, and Science: The Anthropological Society of London in the 1860s," *Victorian Studies* [Autumn 1978]: 70). The native informant questions even "the traditional British pattern."

94. Derrida, "Otobiographies," pp. 6–7, 10. Derrida is writing of Nietzsche here, who staged this paraph in his work. Pressing this into the service of reading, I have made the appropriate changes in strict accordance with his general argument.

strangely dislocates what we, with our tranquil assurance, would like to understand as the time of life and the time of life's *récit*, of the writing of life by the living."[95]

Even for those who hold that the "correct" Marx begins with *Capital*, "Marx as such" begins with the Economic and Philosphical Manuscripts. From the protocol of his texts, how might Marx have made sense of his life's course, his *curriculum vitae*, up to this point? What might have been his self-presumed subject-position? Much later, in the famous Second Postface to *Capital* 1, when he was fifty-five, he described himself, by implication, as "representing . . . the proletariat."[96] I think it can be claimed that, for the twenty-six-year-old Marx of 1844, everything "made sense" only as dynamic instantiations of the dialectical rhythm: position-negation-sublation (negation of the negation—destroying and preserving on another level, continuing the rhythm). How might he have plotted his own life on this rhythm? Position as philosopher, negation as activist (the energy of the negation supplied by the discovery of injustice in the Faculty of Philosophy), and sublation as philosopher of activism who destroys philosophy even as he preserves it on quite another level—to speculate on a philosophy of practice that will be pertinent to human beings in general, not just people who resemble him in the empirical here and now. The energy of this sublation is provided by the discovery of cautious compromises in merely topical activism.

(If the concern of these pages were only Marx's paraphs, the reader would have to consider an itinerary of errancy. The re-reading lesson of the Economic and Philosophical manuscripts yields us documents out of which two have claimed global attention. *The Communist Manifesto*—emphasizing the dialectical embrace of the bourgeoisie and the proletarian on the one hand, and the impracticality of winning back the patriarchal or artisanal workshop on the other, takes it away from the romantic anticapitalists of various kinds. *The German Ideology* mocks the uselessness and inflated rhetoric of egologico-philosophical solutions to

---

95. Ibid., p. 11.
96. Marx, *Capital: A Critique of Political Economy*, tr. Ben Fowkes, 3 vols. (New York: Viking Penguin, 1977), 1:98.

social evils.[97] As "The Eighteenth Brumaire of Louis Bonaparte," and indeed all the writings on the Civil War in France show, the failure of 1848 moved him away from a confidence in the inevitable outcome of the bourgeois-proletarian embrace.[98] The intervening years saw another effort at re-reading, as we see in the notebooks called the *Grundrisse*;[99] to train the proletarian into transforming circumstantial overdeterminations into a dialectical embrace between bourgeoisie and proletarian, we see the establishment of the International Workingmen's Association (if I were writing this section today, I would smell out here a foreclosure of the woman who will be the agent of Marxism today in the inevitable docketing of European as "international" and organized internationality as "men's") in 1866 and the tremendous effort at writing a textbook for the International and its program in the publication of *Capital* in 1867, the year of the founding of "the German Empire." In this last we see the emergence of an understanding of the commodity-form, and thus an understanding of labor-power as a lever for maneuvering the différance of capital and socialism. Then came the disappointment of 1871, the failure of the Paris Commune, itself a *nationalist* re-play of the Jacobin Commune of 1793, squashed by the very same "modern" royalist (Orleanist) section of the bourgeoisie against whom Marx had warned in 1852. It was time for Marx to be errant again. The headquarters of the International are moved to New

---

97. In his mature theoretical texts, he is not centrally concerned with ideology, but rather with the positive task of acquiring the rational x-ray vision that would cut through the fetish-character of the commodity. The worker would understand and set to work the circuit of commodity capital. Consider the rôle of rendering transparent assigned to rationality in the following passage: "The commodity capital, as the direct product of the capitalist production process, recalls its origin and is therefore more rational in its form, less lacking in conceptual differentiation, than the money capital, in which every trace of this process has been effaced. . . . The expression $M \ldots M'(M = m)$ is irrational, in that, within it, part of a sum of money appears as the mother of another part of the same sum of money. But here this irrationality disappears" (Marx, *Capital* 2:131).

98. Marx, "The Eighteenth Brumaire of Louis Bonaparte," in *Surveys from Exile*, pp. 143–249.

99. Marx, *Grundrisse: Foundations of the Critique of Political Economy*, tr. Martin Nicolaus (New York: Viking, 1973).

York, outside of Europe altogether. In the brilliant and ruminant analyses of the three circuits of capital published by Engels as part of - *Capital 2*, and in the historical situating of "class struggle" in *Capital 3*, this Marx focuses almost entirely on the commodity-form as *pharmakon*, and on the differantial relationship between capitalist and socialist modes of production of capital. By the time nationalist Europe breaks the International in 1914, Marx is dead, the errancy is given over to Marxist intellectuals or communist state-builders, the emphasis shifts to ideology, until we get such absurd arguments as Marx the inventor of the symptom, or such pathetic figures as Marx the illegal alien, and the foreclosure of the "native informant" is sealed.[100] With *Capitals* 2 and 3 unread, Marx is turned into a personalist naif by followers, detractors, self-styled heirs, and post-Marxists alike. There is no one left to write the Eighteenth Brumaire of the Bolshevik Revolution in the aftermath of 1989.

But I cannot rewrite the Marx section of this chapter today. Let us return to the earlier text and Marx in 1844.

Thus Marx in the subject-position of sublator/sublation opens textbooks of political economy in order to perceive, paradoxically, the work of the negative in the constitution of the human essence. The proper bearer of his argument has two aspects: natural and human, Species-Life and Species-Being. Both are marked by ipseity rather than alterity. The first, inaccessible to the social, is where nature is the human being's "great body without organs."[101] In this aspect of the human, nature is the paradoxical Subject, without voice-consciousness, only inscribed

---

100. Georg Lukács's influential *History and Class Consciousness: Studies in Marxist Dialectics*, tr. Rodney Livingstone (Cambridge: MIT Press, 1985) would in fact allow for a strong reading of the commodity form. But given the philosophical presuppositions of a Western Marxist readership, his theory of reification has not been read as accommodating the dynamic rôle of labor power as commodity. It is also true that his occasional references to vol. 2 of *Capital*—there is only one in the chapter on "Reification" (pp. 106–107)—betray a privileging of use-value as the concrete.

101. Marx, *Early Writings*, p. 328. Since Nature is exactly not "inorganic," there can be no doubt that *unorganisch* means "without organs." The next passage is from the same page, and the translation has been modified.

to relate to itself through the human being's physical and mental life (as it does through the physical and mental life of all living things?).

> Man *lives* from nature, i.e. nature is his *body*, and he must remain in a continuous process [*in beständigem Prozeß bleiben*] with it if he is not to die. To say that man's physical and mental life is linked to nature simply means that nature is linked to itself, for man is a part of nature.

This idea, that the human is the living element that can be instrumental in animating (or operating) inscriptions, whether positive or negative and however vectored, remains crucial to Marx (although in later work the emphasis moves from individual subject to collective agent), as the often-quoted later passage about the capitalist logically operating as the mind of capital demonstrates:

> [T]he circulation of money as capital is an end in itself, for the valorization of value takes place only within this constantly renewed movement. The movement of capital is therefore limitless. . . . [I]t is only in so far as the appropriation of abstract wealth [*des abstraktes Reichtums*] is the sole driving force behind his operations that he functions as a capitalist, i.e. as capital personified and endowed with consciousness and a will.[102]

This is the fundamental critique of the intending subject that sustains all Marx's thought. It can readily be seen that the notion of ideology *and* class-consciousness are other individuations of this model. The model is the way "the human" works—in Nature, in Society, in History, in Ideology—animating, but not with full intent, rather by inscription. To understand this (know) and to take control of this (do) can only be a *critical* enterprise, in the strongest sense, for it is against the way things are, the way the human element works. To argue that the rational is therefore the spectral, the ghostly grasping of the technological in the "human essence" is beyond the scope of this version.

At twenty-six, graphing himself into the seat of *Aufhebung*, Marx sees

---

102. *Capital*, 1:253–254.

the necessity for this critical enterprise in the specifically "human" character of the human—Species-Being. His debt to classical German philosophy in his conception of Species-Being is immediately recognizable. "Man is a species-being . . . because he looks upon himself as a *universal* and therefore free being."[103] It is thus the definitive predication of being-human to take the singular self as general or universal. As we have seen above, a philosophy that concerns itself with the noumenal subject can simply operate this as the formal possibility of ethics. The young activist philosopher, wishing to insert the historical narrative within philosophy, violating its form, as it were, to verify it in the strictest sense, perceives that, given social inequity, it is not possible for each human being to take himself (we would add "or herself") as the *correct* general case of being-human as such. (Later it will be the human capacity for the difference between needing and making, the secret of the capitalization of the commodity-form, that will be seen as the general case.) The narrative of history introduces difference within the self-sameness or self-identity of the normative (ethical?) subject. It is not difficult to perceive here a guiding principle of Marx's thought. Marx's own ostensible project, in this early phase, seems to be to establish self-identity through access to a self-determination that will annul the difference established by history. (Like the contradiction between subject and structure pointed out by Perry Anderson, this contradiction—between a critique of the intending subject in every presupposition, and a telos based on the intending subject, also drives Marxism apart from the inside, perhaps also because action as creative performance of a given script is learned in a responsibility-based rather than a right-based system, and Marx's intuition is toward the former from within convictions spawned by the latter.)[104] At this early stage, before the formulation of the notion of value, Marx's goal for socialism is to undertake this annulment, although he does not see his way clear.

Because Hegel keeps the possibility of irresolvable difference at bay by confining philosophy to an exclusive sphere, his system is on the way

---

103. Marx, *Early Writings*, p. 327.

104. Perry Anderson, *In the Tracks of Historical Materialism* (Chicago: Univ. Of Chicago Press, 1984), pp. 32–55.

to *Aufhebung—das Aufheben*—not accomplished sublation. By contrast, Marx will be in search of a system that will remove difference *after* taking it into account. Thus the exigency of accounting for difference lies at the heart of Marx's system.

This is why a mere burial of the notion of the AMP, showing it as empirically or theoretically insufficient, or as unimportant to Marx, will not take care of the problem as I have outlined it above. It is not merely a question of supplying Fredric Jameson with a reading list. The Asiatic Mode of Production, however brief its appearance, is the name and imaginary fleshing out of a difference in terms that are consonant with the development of capitalism and the resistance *appropriate* to it as "the same." To see it at work one must look at Stalin's speeches on nationalism and multiculturalism, and the justification for the hierarchical division of the USSR. It operates both Eurocentric economic migration as well as the financialization of the globe through "Development" and economic restructuring. The fact that this crucial item could not just be foreclosed as unimportant but took on a special kind of importance when "the different" wanted to become agents within "the same" richly testifies to this. The name, emerging more than a decade after the early manuscripts, marks the desire to theorize the other so that the object, remaining lost in its own space, can become an "Asia" that can break into the circuit of the same by way of the crises of Revolution or Conquest. That "Africa" is excluded emerges in the generalization "tribal mode of production" in Jameson's passage.

The Marx of Volumes 1 and 2 of *Capital* may seem much more taken up with developing the notion of value than with accounting for difference. Once the notion of value is thought through, a seemingly alternative predication of being-human is established. When human self-conscious activity (Species-Being) appears in the value-form, value being a simple contentless "thing" which is open to measure and exchange, it shows itself capable of producing value in excess of what is needed to sustain being-natural in Species-Life (subsistence). Yet it is a difference between need and making that means not only the possibility of exchange, but also the possibility of a surplus accessible to further exchange (or use). Marx presupposes this predication and focuses on the economic coding of value. The logic of economic coding leads to the development of capital, which, Marx argues, can be sublated beyond capital*ism*. Thus both socialism and communism—within which each human being can be the example of the human as such—presuppose capital. Capital*ism* creates class-difference, which must be sublated through class-struggle on its way to universal self-determination.

This schematic version of a logic of difference and excess internal to capitalism is framed by a larger difference articulated by the narrative of history. Not all areas of the globe have traveled the logical path to capital/ism. How can such a difference, such a transgression of the logical by the historico-geographical, be explained? The AMP is a descriptive/historical, not a logical explanation, a heteronomous and determinant judgment that still allows the autonomous reflexive judgment that Kant performed to do its bit surreptitiously. In the famous section of the *Grundrisse* on pre-capitalist formations, Marx revives the notion of nature as man's body without organs, encountered over a decade ago in the early manuscripts.[105] To be the member of a community without property in land, "as in most of the *Asiatic* land forms," is to have property "appear . . . mediated *for* him *through* a cession *by* the total unity . . . *realized in the form of* the despot." The heavily philosophical language (I have emphasized certain words to bring this out) here accounts for how "property" appears to an individual who is still only defined in terms of Species-Life rather than Species-Being. For "property" for this individual is "the relation of the individual to the *natural* conditions of labour and of reproduction as belonging to him as the objective, nature-given body without organs of his subjectivity."

It is almost as if Species-Life has not yet differentiated itself into Species-Being. There is something like a relationship, across the very different philosophical projects, between this "individual" and the para-subjective raw man of the Third Critique, and the arena of the unconscious symbolic in Hegel. With a bit of Freudian hindsight, one can even imagine this child in the lap of the earth as being the mother's phallus rather than having a phallus for itself. For the mediator, according to Marx, is the despot as "father."

By the second and third forms—Roman and Germanic respec-

---

105. Marx, *Grundrisse*, p. 472–479. All the quotations from the *Grundrisse* in this section are from these pages. I have not given separate references.

tively—the language has become less noticeably philosophical. The second form still has vestiges of the relationship to nature represented as Species-Life in the manuscripts: "the earth in itself . . . offers no resistance to [attempts to] relate to it as the nature without organs of the living individual." It is with the Germanic that we are into the European Middle Ages and European feudalism and therefore "Asiatic history is a kind of indifferent unity of town and countryside . . . the Middle Ages (Germanic period) begins with the land as the seat of history, whose further development then moves forward in the contradiction between town and countryside; the modern is the urbanization of the countryside." This is not an explanation but an attempt to fit historical presuppositions into a logical mold. The earlier notion, that the human can be seen in two ways—natural (part of nature without *human* organ-specificity—Species-*Life*) and human (self-exemplifying individual—Species-*Being*) is now being re-cast as a sequential (historical) story as well as a spacing (geography). (As I have pointed out in note 86, Williams and Balibar continue the relay.)

In the spirit of deconstructive reading (unaccusing, unexcusing, attentive, situationally productive through dismantling), it must be said that the vision of time here—an ordered series of chunks of present—is what permitted this effort to undergo a complete reversal of intention when the "different" parts of the globe wanted to enter the predictive stream (history as the inevitable consequence of past chunks of present leading to future chunks of present) of "the same". Marx's cautions to himself—"the condition that the capitalist, in order to posit himself as capital must bring . . . excepting only already available, previous wage labor—belongs among the antediluvian conditions of capital, belongs to its *historic presuppositions* . . . but in no way to its *contemporary* history"—can work both ways.[106] It could have happened otherwise, but this is the only path to the modern that we have. An effort to fit historical *presuppositions* (the "first form"—mediated by the "oriental despot"—has little specificity) into philosophy turns around into an attempt to make philosophical morphology give its seal of approval upon the historical status of "the present" of a Russia or China.

---

106. Marx, *Capital*, 3:459.

Some scholars have seen the Asiatic Mode as one version of the first form: primitive communism.[107] This may be read as Marx's narrativization of the difference at the origin. It is already asymmetrical, interested. The first is a version of the selfsame, man in nature as species-being, one foot into history. The second marks the place of the other, locked into species-life, forever caught back in a deviation that cannot be normative. In my estimation, both are theoretical fictions, a methodological presupposition without which the internal coherence of an argument cannot be secured. In order to secure the argument laying out the logical narrative of the self-determination of capital, Marx has recourse to the "first form." Primitive communism, safely remote in time, has not created significant problems within the generally realist undertaking to treat Marx's speculative morphology as an adequate blueprint for social justice. The Asiatic Mode of Production has revealed itself to be neither historico-geographically "Asiatic" nor logically a "mode of production."

It is well known that such "revelations" are by no means universally accepted. Marx's followers in the political as well as the disciplinary sphere have labored mightily to account for this para-historical and para-logical theoretical fiction in order to provide adequate or approximate justification for state planning and social engineering. These are the labors that broadly determine discussions of colonialism. The uneasy coexistence of marxism and nationalism with nationalism and anti-marxism—and woman's asymmetrical insertion within it—is often sustained by the decision to read a theoretical fiction as grounds for adequate justification of political action, even when the actual name and lineaments of the "Asiatic Mode" are forgotten.[108] In the rather more limited sphere of literary criticism, as we have seen, both theoretical fictions can be offered as grounding, if only for a literary taxonomy. But even literary taxonomies are not unrelated to politics.

---

107. Umberto Mellotti, "The Primitive Commune and Its Various Forms of Dissolution," in *Marx and the Third World*, tr. Pat Ransford (London: Macmillan, 1977), p. 28f is a representative example.

108. The complex interplay between "earlier" texts such as Henri Grimal, *Decolonization: the British, French and Dutch Empires 1919–1963*, tr. Stephan De Vos (London: Routledge, 1978) and James Blaut, *The National Question* (London: Zed,

The Asiatic Mode and Primitive Communism, then, are names that inhabit the pre-historical or para-geographical space/time that mark the outside of the feudalism-capitalism circuit. The implementation of marxism into socialism/communism entails the persistent sublation or différance of capitalism. Without capitalism the specifically marxian practical dialectic cannot operate.

The question of revolution is situated within this broader require-ment. Strictly speaking, a revolution brings in a new mode of produc-tion. The relationship between the previous mode and the new one, however, must in actual fact be consonant with the feudalism-capital-ism-communism/socialism series. This is one of the reasons why it was imperative to establish that Russia was already inserted into a developed capitalist economy on the eve of the Revolution. Gramsci introduces unequal development by way of "The Southern Question."[109] And, in a bold move, Mao Zedong had seen the need for a prescriptive *cultural* revolution, in the cultural coding of the production of value, as it were, because the mode of economic production of value did not fit. In the context of the multinational Russian empire, Lenin thinks State; Stalin, Nation. In the context of monolithic hierarchical mandarin China, Mao thinks Culture. A formula perhaps, with the attendant problems; but, as a matter of emphasis, plausible.

Capitalism is thus the *pharmakon* of Marxism.[110] It produces the pos-sibility of the operation of the dialectic that will produce socialism, but left to its own resources it is also that which blocks that operation.

As in most theoretically ambivalent situations, there is an asymmetry here. In the first instance, while capitalism—with its maximization of social productivity—allows the marxian dialectic to play, one is speak-

1987) on the one hand and Benedict Anderson, *Imagined Communities: Reflections on the Origin and Spread of Nationalism* (London: Verso, 1983) and Partha Chatterjee, *Nationalist Thought and the Colonial World: A Derivative Discourse?* (London: Zed, 1986) on the other deploy the old debate in new forms. Its most interesting dis-placement is in the justification for development.

109. Gramsci, *The Southern Question*, tr. Pasquale Verdicchio (West Lafayette, Ind.: Bordighera, 1995).

110. For *pharmakon*, poison that is medicinal when knowingly administered, see Derrida, "Plato's Pharmacy," in *Disseminations*, tr. Barbara Johnson (Chicago: Univ. of Chicago Press, 1981), pp. 61–172.

ing only of the economic sphere. If, on the other hand, we are speaking of the entire social fabric, Marxism can only ever be a *critical* approach. Marx was writing before the advent of post-industrial capitalism and the transformation of labor union movements within it. Passages like the following would bear no large-scale moral suasion today:

> Even where a man without means obtains credit as an industrialist or merchant, it is given in the expectation that he will function as a capitalist, will use the capital borrowed to appropriate unpaid labor. He is given credit as a potential capitalist. And this fact is so very much admired by the economic apologists, that a man without wealth but with energy, determination, ability and business acumen can transform himself into a capitalist this way . . . actually reinforces the rule of capital itself, widens its basis and enables it to recruit ever new forces from the lower strata of society. The way that the Catholic Church of the Middle Ages built its hierarchy out of the best brains of the nation, without regard to status, birth or wealth, was likewise a major means of reinforcing the rule of the priests and suppressing the laity. The more a dominant class is able to absorb the best people from the dominated classes, the more solid and dangerous is its rule.[111]

There is no state on the globe today that is not part of the capitalist economic system or can want to eschew it fully. In fact, within the economic sphere, Marxism—at its best as a speculative morphology, devised by an activist-philosopher who had taught himself contemporary economics enough to see it as a *human* (because social) science, and through this perception launched a thoroughgoing critique of political economy—can operate in today's world only as a persistent critique of a system—micro-electronic post-industrial world capitalism—that a polity cannot not want to inhabit, for that is the "real" of the situation. To treat what is powerfully speculative as predictive social engineering, assuming a fully rational human subject conscious of rights as well as impersonal responsibility, can only have violent and violating consequences. It goes without saying that a literary taxonomy that bases itself

---

111. Marx, *Capital* 3:735–736.

on the predictive framework, however subtle in its maneuvers, can be violent and violating in its own restricted sphere.

In the second instance, capitalism left to its own resources blocks the operations of marxism by the logic of unequal development. Here the heritage of colonialism and the operation of neocolonialism can only be confronted by systems of collective responsibility-based ethics, although battered by gendering, that belong to the sphere of the native informant; the European Enlightenment, followed by the bourgeois revolution, can only ever give us ideas of social redress through the notion of rights. Marx is a peculiar critical phenomenon that appeared in the latter sphere. The push and pull of rights and responsibilities unevenly agonize the field of différance between capitalism and socialism. One of the theaters of that agon is global resistance spelled out "as responses to local micro problems . . . [that] gradually . . . began to relate . . . to macro-policies of economic development and the market-economy led linear development agencies and international financial institutions like the World Bank."[112] This is the theater where today's "native informants" collectively attempt to make their own history as they act (in the most robust sense of agency) a part they have not chosen, in a script that has as its task to keep them silent and invisible.[113]

We are aware of the familiar and indulgent treatments of Marx's gaffe about the "Asiatic Mode." As I have already indicated, I do not think that the entire problem is solved by filling up the gaps in the knowledge available to Marx in order to prove that the AMP is or is not empirically and/or theoretically valid. I have therefore made no attempt to present a digest of the voluminous literature produced on the subject and instead concentrate on three easily available secondary texts.[114] They seem, moreover, to confront the wider-ranging issues involved in Marx's proposal of an "Asiatic" mode, soon to lose any connection with

---

112. Raghavan, *Recolonization: GATT, the Uruguay Round & the Third World* (London: Zed, 1990), p. 34.

113. Marx, "Eighteenth Brumaire," p. 143.

114. For a general account, see Stephen P. Dunn, *The Fall and Rise of the Asiatic Mode of Production* (New York: Routledge, 1982). I am of course hampered by the fact that I know no Russian.

any "real" Asia: Ranajit Guha's *A Rule of Property for Bengal* (1963), Perry Anderson's appendix to the *Lineages of the Absolutist State* (1974), and Samir Amin's *Unequal Development* (published in French in 1973).[115] The hope for the best is, of course, that the transnationally *literate* student and teacher of literature—who is, by definition, not an *expert* in transnational affairs—will consult such general sources analytically to piece together an approach. A book such as this must be prepared for the worst: appropriation or hostility based on the sanctioned ignorance of both elite theorist and self-styled activist, in different spheres.

A Rule of Property for Bengal allows us to see the operation of the "Asiatic Mode" in India, admittedly Marx's prime "source" for it. Guha focuses on Bengal, because Bengal was the area where the British first acquired territory.

A century before Marx, Philip Francis, an officer of the East India Company in East India (basically Bihar and Bengal) had already assumed that land tenure in that region was nothing like what was going to be Marx's sweeping generalization: no private property in land, ground rent and state tax identical. "[T]he basic assumption of the official line 'that the ruling power was proprietor of the soil' . . . was considered by Francis as 'not less false in fact than absurd in theory and dangerous in practice' . . ."[116] Guha gives a detailed analysis of the politico-economic presuppositions of the group of the company's officers who regularized the prevalent system of land tenure into a colonial framework. He places the most visionary of these men, particularly Philip Francis, as swinging between physiocracy and mercantilism. (These are the two schools that political economy, the object of Marx's critique, superseded.) From such a position, what Francis in particular seemed to be attempting was to make it easier for that corner of India, the first British possession on the subcontinent, to operate within a

---

115. Ranajit Guha, *A Rule of Property for Bengal: An Essay on the Idea of Permanent Settlement,* 2d ed. (New York: Apt Books, 1982). See also Samir Amin, *Unequal Development: An Essay on the Social Formations of Peripheral Capitalism,* tr. Brian Pearce (New York: Monthly Review Press, 1976).

116. Guha, *Rule of Property,* p. 98.

unilinear logic of landed property already being played out in Europe: thus the effacement of difference.

(The time to call it a preparation for the capitalist mode of production was yet to come. These protagonists saw the case of Bengal as a laboratory experiment of insertion, rather, into free trade. Marx shows us nearly a century later that the capitalization of land looks forward to industrial capitalism, without much interest in theorizing the capitalizing of land by its own logic. A specifically marxist critique of political economy has not yet theorized the ecological imperative.)[117]

This early experiment—the first workings of monopoly capitalist colonialism—did not take something resembling "the Asiatic Mode of Production" as its presupposition because it did not need to. Involvement with learning the tedious detail of the previous system soon made such tremendous generalizations irrelevant. Marx's sources were, of course, documents written by people who were less directly related to the hands-on work of the transition.

At any rate, according to one group of historians the experiment, as envisioned by the most enlightened of the colonizers, to make the native landowners free agents in the development of agri-capitalism, did not succeed. I have not the primary scholarship to make a judgment here, although my "personal experience," as granddaughter of an absentee landowner's manager, wants to give assent to it:

He [Thomas Law, one of the "leading champions" of this policy] expected the mechanism of sales to operate in such a way that in course of time all but those who had the necessary entrepreneurial abilities would be eliminated from proprietorship, and "a class of na-

---

117. Vandana Shiva's *Ecology and the Politics of Survival: Conflicts over Natural Resources in India* (New Delhi: Sage, 1991), the essays included in Shiva and Ingunn Moser, eds., *Biopolitics: A Feminist and Ecological Reader on Biotechnology* (London: Zed, 1995), as well as essays in *The Ecologist* and other publications of the environmentalist movement certainly elaborate the problem within a generally Marxist paradigm. But they rethink neither Marx's urbanist teleology nor the place of the agency of labor power in the specifically ecological argument. James O'Connor's new book *Natural Causes: Essays in Ecological Marxism* (New York: Guilford, 1998) promises great things in this area but has arrived too late for me to incorporate a reading into this book.

tive gentlemen proprietors" would emerge to take their place. . . . He was blissfully unaware that during the thirty-two years since it was launched the Permanent Settlement had gone off the orbit he had so neatly calculated for it, and that his "gentleman proprietors," *nouveaux riches* though they mostly were with no claim to noble descent, had proved themselves to be exceeedingly fond of the traditional ways of estate management: far from imitating the model landlords of Arthur Young, they were happy to be living off the fat of the land, but comfortably away from it.[118]

I will let the reader decide how she wants to put the story together, including the asymmetrical insertion of female landowners like Rani Bhabani into the narrative.[119] The entire discourse of accounting for colonialism as well as the deployment of gendering in nationalism is imbricated there. All I need to emphasize is that the "Asiatic Mode of production" as a "real" description of "actual practices" is not an issue in its ostensibly appropriate place and time. It will come to be needed as the crucial theoretical fiction to set the machinery of the emancipatory transformation of Hegelianism presenting itself as a general system. (It is possible for Wittfogel in the fifties to call the soviet system a despotic state on the Asiatic or oriental model to distinguish it from Western democracy; in the nineties businesspeople looking to "modernize" the Eastern bloc define socialism as "the State is your customer" to distinguish it from possessive individualism.) And, when it performs that function, its very invocation is therefore its foreclosure.

But then the "Asiatic Mode of Production" has no very serious or precise empirical pretensions any more, only an interesting history as a political gambit. Perry Anderson comments on the problem of measuring the great imperial systems of China and the Islamic world by way of a presupposition paradoxically devised to shore up the possibility of a systemic description of the North Atlantic as the "West": "Any serious theoretical explanation of the historical field outside of feudal Europe will have to supersede traditional and generic contrasts with it, and

---

118. Guha, *Rule of Property*, pp. 179, 182. See also Victor Kiernan, *Marxism and Imperialism* (New York: St. Martin's, 1975), p. 191.

119. Guha, *Rule of Property*, pp. 57–58.

proceed to a concrete and accurate typology of social formations and state systems in their own right, which respects their very great differences of structure and development. It is merely in the night of our ignorance that all alien shapes take on the same hue."[120]

To continue this brief tabulation of basic speculative/empirical secondary sources, I propose that Samir Amin's *Unequal Development*, first published in 1973, was just such an effort. Amin does not reject the AMP out of hand. He merely readjusts the perspective. His interest is not in the "correction" of the AMP. He asks us to focus on the fact that the main resource of this mode of production is "tribute." Thus the great shifting currents of global imperialism rather than the teleological narrative of capitalism (inaugurating the possibility of socialism as *différance*/sublation into communism) becomes the logic of his analysis. This would allow for the possibility of making the full grid of dominations as well as exploitation, our analytical tool kit, rather than consider domination as merely the subtext of the economic as the most abstract logical instance. (And now that, in the current stage of "capitalism [being] transformed into imperialism,"—globalization in trade and finance capital—the native informant's foreclosed perspective is located in woman's global subalternity, the computing of the great narrative of history by the shifting currents of global imperialism seem more apposite.)[121]

From this perspective, where the crucial focus is not how to provide an adequate reason for (a) the transformation of land into capital, the issue is not (b) the so-called identity of state tax and ground rent. Scholars of the non-Western world often come up against the problem that words (signs) and therefore concepts that do not have a field of play there are applied to signify absences. Items (a) and (b) are such complex concept/signifiers. Imagining a more encompassing feature of global history, Amin invites us to read the "same phenomenon" not as failed capitalism but as successful imperialism—tribute-paying economic formations. These are successful or "strong" examples of feudalism. If the definition of feudalism is not kept confined to the European example,

120. Anderson, *Lineages*, p. 549.
121. V. I. Lenin, *Imperialism: The Highest Stage of Capitalism: A Popular Outline* (New York: International Publishers, 1939), p. 22.

then that very example can be seen as a case of weak or failed feudalism. (Amin goes into considerable detail over this.) It can be conjectured that the European case is the one scenario where a *generally* less "advanced" civilization (a big, difficult adjective that we have no problem applying to the recipients of imperialism from above) conquered a more "advanced" one. Capitalism developed as a "dangerous supplement" to the "weak" moment in European feudalism because the conquerors could not establish a resilient state.[122]

Plenty of conclusions can be drawn from this bold re-inscription. For our purposes, the following can immediately be advanced:

First, to posit the AMP as historically static, and therefore socially inferior was to confuse insusceptibility to the motion of a *philosophical* morphology, the dialectic, conceived in one narrative instantiation, with *historical* stasis; and draw a *social* conclusion—and, inevitably, *moral* inferiority—from it. That Marx was not free from this "confusion" is not merely due to his being a nineteenth-century European, the reason generally advanced. I think one might consider that Marx's self-position as the agent of *Aufhebung* was precisely by virtue of breaking *mere* philosophy open by re-constellating it in the sphere of political economy—"confusing" philosophy with "history"—and pursuing the question of difference into the narrative of history. Such strong methodological "confusion" runs the risk of a restoration of the same hierarchy—philosophy (science) on top, being "applied" to history (matter or *hyle*)—dialectical as well as historical materialism.

Thus we cannot excuse Marx's tremendous shifting of paradigms

---

122. I am, of course, comparing styles of argument rather than voting for the "correct" alternative. Even with this proviso, I am not quite sure why Jan Nederveen Pieterse thinks military enterprise contradicts the argument from "weak feudalism": "The interpretation of the rise of Europe out of the dialectic of backwardness overlooks the gigantic military and imperialist effort of the Crusades. . . . Where European commerce was weak, force of arms was called in to make up for European backwardness. It is the weakness of imperial formations *outside* of Europe then which was part of the conditions of Europe's rise" (Pieterse, *Empire and Emancipation: Power & Liberation on a World Scale* [London: Pluto Press, 1990], p. 91). The rise of capitalism, and capitalist imperialism, cannot be argued in terms of the push-and-pull of weak commerce against weak imperialism; not that it can be argued successfully in terms of anything. Again, it is the style of argument, the politics of the production of knowledge and validity claims, that is at issue.

from the violent consequences of the first wave of global marxisms which, under the myriad overdeterminations of military and political pressure, read the paradigm shift within the realist assumption that a speculative morphology was an *adequate* blueprint for social justice. It does not, on the other hand, call for academic accusations against Marxism as such, offering alternatives based on similar presuppositions about deconstructive themes as immediately translatable into socialist hegemony.[123] I am making an attempt here to work at the deconstructive "new politics of reading," which involves an effort to enter the protocols of Marx's text in order to re-inscribe it for use.[124]

If we can think of Amin's re-inscription as taking the historical account as point of entry, then we can think difference as arising from strength (successful feudalisms, the great tributary systems) blocking transformation and weakness (weak feudalism, the European serf mode of production) reterritorializing itself as history. This makes us aware that, in the argument for the AMP, the extraordinary achievements of the pre-capitalist imperial civilizations are generally ignored, whereas, over against them, the dynamic social achievements of capitalism are always intoned, in spite of the price paid for them. (I am not, of course, writing in support of imperialism. I am pointing at Eurocentric strategies of narrativizing history, so that Europe can congratulate itself for progress, even if by default.) The second conclusion that can be advanced is that Amin's re-inscription allows us to think of religion, culture (as necessarily inadequate mode of giving assent), and variants of "nationalism," not necessarily adequately coded on a fully developed European model nation-state—and not only capitalism—as powerful/dangerous and productive/repressive *pharmakoi*. The first three have long histories of being used by dominant groups to consolidate oppression, as well as by subordinate groups to consolidate dissent, the line between the two forever shifting precisely because of the *phar-*

---

123. I am referring, of course, to Ernesto Laclau and Chantal Mouffe's provocative and learned book *Hegemony and Socialist Strategy*, tr. Winston Moore and Paul Cammack (London: Verso, 1985).

124. Protocol is not logic, but pre-comprehended procedural priority; backing out of the room in front of royalty rather than taking the quickest way; giving "the public use of reason" the priority, rather than taking the more realistic way: that (the hu)man is (not only) a rational animal; that you cannot compute the limits of reason by *rational* expectations theory.

makon-character of the signs. They are still running interference, for better and for worse, in the re-coding of capitalism into democracy in the post-Soviet world order.

The greatest gift of *Unequal Development*, for the general reader, was its attention to the social materiality of sub-Saharan Africa. Against the later Jamesonian assertion that all of Africa can be seen as relating from "the tribal mode of production" to world-system capitalism, one can place an unemphatic paragraph such as the following:

> In order to obtain [a] proletariat quickly, the colonialists dispossessed the African rural communities by force and deliberately drove them back into confined, poor regions, with no means of modernizing and intensifying their farming. They thus compelled the traditional society to become a supplier of temporary or permanent migrants. . . . Henceforth we can no longer speak of a traditional society in this part of the continent [Kenya, Uganda, Tanzania, Rwanda, Burundi, Zambia, Malawi, Angola, Mozambique, Zimbabwe, Botswana, Lesotho, Swaziland, and South Africa].[125]

Guha's *Rule of Property* shows that any assumption of something resembling the AMP was irrelevant in the place and time appropriate for it. Anderson's *Absolutist State* cautions that at issue is not just the question of whether history is uni- or multi-linear (the usual terms of the political debate), but a radical perspectivism. Amin's *Unequal Development* attempts such a shift in perspective from within the discipline of historical sociology and reconstellates the mis-named "Asiatic" mode. I have discussed these three secondary sources because they seem, in their different ways, to outlines routes of taking a distance from the debate.

The "Asiatic Mode of Production" can indeed operate as a kind of deconstructive lever to open up Marx's text in a de-*con*structive way.

---

125. Amin, *Unequal Development*, pp. 327–328. Mahmood Mamdani has added new cultural material to this argument, by showing how the British constructed African "custom" and gave "chiefs" the power to rule by such colonially outlined "custom" (Mamdani, *Citizen and Subject: Contemporary Africa and the Legacy of Late Colonialism* [Princeton: Princeton Univ. Press, 1996]). That argument belongs to my Chapter 3.

First, the concept-metaphor of the AMP makes visible the site-specific limits of Modes of Production as an explanatory category.[126] In the current state of the art, Anderson opts for "civilization," a term that is being revised by cultural studies and being used by some sociologists in the more "Western" parts of the former Soviet bloc as a passport into the culture of capitalism.[127] He still looks forward to a time when, with the appropriate non-Eurocentric research methods, "*real* mode of production" analyses of these other spaces will be possible.[128] Amin, given his bolder theoretical re-distribution of emphasis in terms of the dominant instance, re-formulates the terms of analysis if the globe rather than the European exception is to be taken as premise:

[A]ll the peripheral societies of the tribute-paying mode [among them Northwestern Europe] g[a]ve birth to capitalism. . . . [By contrast, t]he historical duration of the fully developed tribute-paying mode was . . . , in principle, very long. Nevertheless, this compatibility with progress meant relatively blocked development, in relation, that is, to the progress possible in less advanced, less developed formations, in which the conflict between production relations and productive forces manifests itself sooner, compelling an advance beyond precapitalist relations.[129]

Barry Hindess and Paul Q. Hirst deal with the transgressive potential of the AMP in two steps. In *Pre-Capitalist Modes of Production*, the two authors felt that the Asiatic Mode was the only one that did not qualify

---

126. Barry Hindess and Paul Q. Hirst, "The 'Asiatic' Mode of Production," *Pre-Capitalist Modes of Production* (London: Routledge, 1987).

127. I have discussed this in Spivak, *Thinking Academic Freedom in Gendered Postcoloniality* (Cape Town: Univ. of Cape Town Press, 1992).

128. Anderson, *Lineages*, p. 548.

129. Amin, *Unequal Development*, pp. 56, 54. I am not suggesting that this is the correct or "real" narrative. I am not even suggesting that there can be a possible correct narrative. I am simply remarking on the reversal and displacement of the received narrative values here. By comparison, *Eurocentrism*, tr. Russell Moore (New York: Monthly Review, 1989) is both more topical and more pallid. K. N. Chaudhuri's *Asia before Europe: Economy and Civilization of the Indian Ocean from the Rise of Islam to 1750* (Cambridge: Cambridge Univ. Press, 1990) is perhaps further displaced, but it does not reverse the received doxa with as much panache.

as a mode of production. *Mode of Production and Social Formation* "rejects the pertinence of the concept of the mode of production."[130] This is an elegant and intelligent book, and it is not to dispraise it to say that it has not moved far from proving, with Marx, that the analysis of capital must presuppose capital, use its reductive method, and see the past as capital's prehistory. "As the concept of mode of production is displaced, so the concepts of relations of production and social formations gain in theoretical importance" (*MP* 6). Reducing, they conclude that "[p]*ossession in separation* is . . . the crucial concept for the analysis of classes" (*MP* 64). Criticizing the notion that knowledge appropriates or corresponds to its object, they write

> Concepts are deployed in ordered successions to produce [the] effects [of analysis and solutions]. This order is the order created *by the practice of theoretical work itself:* it is guaranteed by no necessary "logic" or "dialectic" nor by any necessary mechanism of correspondence with the real itself. . . . [D]iscourse is interminable . . . because the forms of closure promised in epistemological criteria of validity do not work. (*MP* 7–8)

One can question their all-or-nothing stance, of course, although in general their new positions seem admirable. By the logical consequence of their own terms, however, it is the Asiatic Mode of Production that, by its mode of existence, should be their major didactic example. The social relations entailed by the authoritative discursive theoretical systems, possessing the clue to systemic knowledge, must create, in something called "Asia," an exception. Because Asia cannot allow its local (European) concatenations to close and be universalized, it must be defined as separate; yet this separation reveals the absurdity of the possessive and possessed system. This is still a "possession *in* separation," not the radical racist separation reserved for Africa.

The AMP does not have this privileged didactic place in Hindess and Hirst's auto-critique. They merely repeat that they "did not deny the possibility of existence of the forms of social relations posited in the

---

130. Hindess and Hirst, *Mode of Production and Social Formation: An Auto-Critique of Pre-Capitalist Modes of Production* (Atlantic Highlands, N.J.: Humanities Press, 1977), p. 2. Hereafter *MP*.

tax/rent couple" (MP 43). By thus not denying the relations internal to the AMP, they denegate the relations between (their own complicity with) the very theoretical discourse they are at last rejecting—and the AMP. "[I]t does not contain the means"—separation from the means, in other words—"to subordinate the labour process." The recapitulation ends in two reiterations: that the AMP could not qualify as a mode of production (with no reference to the changed status of this apparent "fact" now that the latter concept is being rejected); and that the tired cliché of the AMP's emptiness (rather than the non-possession) of the means could not lead to the production of capitalism.

Better for our purposes to call the glass half full, as does Amin. Better so to reverse "nonpossession of the means" to "the strength of the tributary mode of production," that the very sense of "mode" is displaced, the terms of analysis shifted to the millennial movement of peoples. Amin's book cannot predict what will have happened by the internal logic of capital, vindicating his critique of that very logic as the major model of explanation (almost the exact structural opposite of the critical predicament of Hindess and Hirst): in the post-Soviet financialization of the globe, something like an irrational tributary system being foisted as "the free market" by the Bretton Woods organizations upon a fantasmatic and monstrous global "state," with its "economic citizens," operating together with and separately from socalled nation-states, so that indigenous Southern capital cannot flourish by its own untrammeled logic.[131]

---

131. The task of an expanded "literary" criticism, which considers the making of the social "textile" as well, here overflows its borders. The ethics of reading (J. Hillis Miller, *The Ethics of Reading: Kant, de Man, Eliot, Trollope, James, and Benjamin* [New York: Columbia University Press, 1987]; Wayne C. Booth, *The Company We Keep: An Ethics of Fiction* [Berkeley: University of California Press, 1988]) here takes the study of the representation of the self-consolidating other (Edward W. Said, *Orientalism* [New York: Pantheon, 1978]) on board and risks noticing that to stop at accusing the equally self-consolidating essentialized Colonizer or Imperialist is to legitimize colonialism/imperialism by reversal. At the time of first writing, an acknowledgment of the "enabling violation" of imperialism was the result of that risk. This was a reterritorialization of Marx's confidence in the transitional benefits of imperialism: "When a great social revolution shall have mastered the results of the bourgeois epoch, the market of the world and the modern powers of production, and subjected them to the common control of the most advanced peoples, then only will human progress cease to resemble that

Serious consideration of the Asiatic Mode also leads scholars to the notion of the norm as aberration. We have already seen this in Samir Amin's argument about the central question to which the AMP was supposed to provide an answer: why did capitalism develop only in Europe? In the Soviet debate of the 1960s, some Soviet scholars, questioning the Marxian five-part model and starting from "the semantically confused concept of 'slave,'" were "inevitably . . . led to the conclusion that the 'classical' social order, as defined by Marx and Engels, is an aberrant phenomenon."[132] If we consider the Soviet argument and Amin's thesis together—the first stemming directly from a consideration of the AMP and the second from the related question of multilinearity—the passage from antiquity to feudalism in Europe, as well as the transition from feudalism to capitalism, can be read as having happened along a chain of weakness and aberration. A deconstructive glance would not see a non-European norm standing over against this dynamic of aberrations that wrote history. It would rather suggest that this other perspective undoes the strict opposition between norm and aberration and makes post-revolutionary social engineering, on the basis of a proven authentic (European, not Asiatic) origin, as fraught as any positivization of the indeterminate. Between first writing and current revision, this last sentence has found its own vindication. "Authentic" Asiatic (and, mutatis mutandis, African) models of social engineering have led to Islamist, Hindu, or yet ethnic nationalisms that, often exacerbated by racist misapprehensions, cannot bode well.

The Asiatic Mode of Production then, in new and variously globalized politics of reading, makes visible the fault lines within the account of history as (European) modes of production. It can supplement the

---

hideous pagan idol, who would not drink the nectar but from the skulls of the slain ("The Future Results of the British Rule in India," *New York Daily Tribune*, 8 Aug. 1853, in *Surveys from Exile*, p. 325). Now the pursuit of alternative development rather than class-fixed culturalist nativism seems to be the consequence of the risk. In this second take, "literary" or "cultural" study becomes discontinuous with the terrain of the specific risktaking. And the refusal of the "Asia" of "the Asiatic Mode"—in the name of the alternative socialization of land "held" loosely in common; the refusal of the "Africa" of the tribal mode, in the name of post-Apartheid, comes more to the fore.

132. Dunn, *Fall and Rise*, pp. 102, 97.

lacuna within the dominant account in such a way that the self-identity of dominance begins to waver. Yet, in its orthodox formulation, it is precisely the name of a gulf across which above (the State) and below (the peasant community) cannot engage in the dialectic of revolution. According to this account, Europe was obliged not to supplement but to supervene, in order to provide a (colonial/capitalist) state with which the dialectic of resistance might become possible. That this normalizing vision of imperialism was far too simple in its outlines has been abundantly demonstrated. What I want now to suggest is that, even if the substantive content and explanatory and predictive potential of the Asiatic Mode of Production is and has been discredited, the ruse of declaring the dangerous supplement a stasis that must be interrupted in its own interest is still with us. In that sense, Jameson's essay has great symbolic importance. At the inception of global cultural studies in the United States, it sutures the two struggles together.

This may then be the moment to acknowledge that, as Derrida has argued about Nietzsche and Nazism, it is futile to excuse away the connections between the texts of Marx and the possibility of reading them so as to support totalitarianism or modernization.[133] No possible

---

133. It is worth quoting three short bits from Derrida, "Otobiographies," if only to suggest that the reader consult Derrida's entire text in order to institute corresponding procedures with Marx. This will also indicate the care entailed by deconstructive reading. Let this footnote serve as a control for any *seeming* attempt on my part to "consider the biography of [Marx] as a corpus of empirical accidents that leaves both a name and a signature outside a system which would itself be offered up to an immanent philosophical reading" (p. 5) or "to illuminate the 'youthful' with a teleological insight in the form of a 'lesson'" (p. 23). Here are the Derrida bits: "One may wonder how and why what is so naïvely called a falsification was possible (one can't falsify just anything), how and why the 'same' words and the 'same' statements—if they are indeed the same—might several times be made to serve certain meanings and certain contexts that are said to be different, even incompatible. One may wonder why the only teaching institution or the only beginning of a teaching instituion that ever succeeded in taking as its model the teaching of Nietzsche on teaching will have been a Nazi one" (p. 24). Yet Nietzsche has not the hindsight that you do. "[H]e is dead—a trivial piece of evidence, but incredible enough when you get right down to it and when the name's genius or genie is still there to make us forget the fact of his death. At the very least, to be dead means that no profit or deficit, no good or evil, whether calculated or not, can *ever* return again to the bearer of the name. Only the name can inherit" (p. 7).

reading is a *mis*-reading. The spirit of refutation and de-fetishization is a homo-erotic adventure that simply gives the game to the best arguer, the best manipulator of power. The challenge of deconstruction is not to excuse, but to suspend accusation to examine with painstaking care if the protocols of the text contains a moment that can produce something that will generate a new and useful reading. In an earlier discussion, Derrida had used a different concept-metaphor, of a "name X as a *lever of intervention*, in order to maintain a grasp on the previous organization, which is to be transformed effectively," for new uses, as it were.[134] Such a lever—to move into other bits of vocabulary—can be perceived as a moment of transgression in the text—or a moment of bafflement that discloses not only limits but also possibilities to a new politics of reading. Roland Barthes set off a good deal of pious polemic on both sides by choosing the violent metaphor of the *death* of the author to describe a related phenomenon, as Nietzsche chose the *death* of God.[135] The deconstructive figure is one of complicity as well as (and therefore fully neither/nor) deicide-parricide. Barthes's closing passage carries only the conviction of the latter: "It is derisory to condemn the new writing in the name of a humanism hypocritically turned champion of the reader's rights. . . . The birth of the reader must be at the cost of the death of the Author." Even if we question the authority of Marx, his ghost keeps (us) going; only, as in the case of Kant, the ghost for the "native informant" is rather different from the messianic illegal immigrant who emerges at the end of *Specters of Marx*. We say rather: *bhindeshi . . .*[136]

At any rate, the altered politics of reading proposed by Derrida is more circumspect in the interest of Barthes's "newly-born reader."[137]

"Nevertheless, let's remember that he 'swore' not to publish these lectures [*Future of Our Educational Institutions*]" (p. 22).

134. Derrida, "Interview with Jean-Louis Houdebine and Guy Scarpetta," in *Positions*, tr. Alan Bass (Chicago: Univ. of Chicago Press, 1981), p. 71.

135. Roland Barthes, "The Death of the Author," in *Image-Music-Text*, tr. Stephen Heath (New York: Hill and Wang, 1977), p. 148.

136. See epigraph to Spivak, "Ghostwriting."

137. This is of course the English title of Hélène Cixous and Catherine Clément, *The Newly-Born Woman*, tr. Betsy Wing (Minneapolis: University of Minnesota Press, 1986). I use this phrase in my text because I want to emphasize the connection between the woman as reader as model, and a general new politics of reading.

And it is in the spirit of such circum-spection, (ex)orbitant to the pro- and contra- of received readings, that one may ask: where in Marx is that lever to turn the text, to de-con-struct it for use, where that moment of transgression or bafflement? In my reading of Marx in the last decade, that lever and moment (concept-metaphors necessarily mixed) is in Value.

Whereas in economic theory there has been a lively controversy around the usefulness of the notion of value, Marxist cultural critique has remained strangely silent about it. Neither Raymond Williams nor Stuart Hall in Britain, nor Critical Theory in Western Germany or the United States, nor yet Fredric Jameson or the Social Text group in the United States, or the Althusserians or the post-Althusserians in France, ever work with its implications. I think there is a text for historians of consciousness here that I leave aside in order to mark first a passage where Marx warns that an analysis based on the labor theory of value restricted to the narrative of the development of its forms of appearance in Britain will encounter its limits as a general explanatory model and yield results in the interest of Britain. It is the section entitled "Foreign Trade" in *Capital* 3. The entire section is worth reading to appreciate Marx's demonstration of how the interested representation of foreign trade seems to annul the validity of his own analysis of political economy, especially its insistence that the rate of profit has a tendency to fall. Here a couple of cryptic sentences will have to serve as place markers: "Is the general rate of profit raised by the higher profit rate made by capital invested in foreign trade, and colonial trade in particular? . . . . As soon as we take our leave of the money form, however, this semblance vanishes." A sentence such as the following, therefore, takes on far more than incidental significance: "In comparing the English rate of interest with the Indian, for example, we must not take the Bank of England's interest rate but rather that charged, for instance, by people lending small machines to petty producers in domestic industry."[138] This suggestion will travel intact into the relationship between global and (post-colonial) national cultural studies.

Let us pause a moment on the adverbial clause "as soon as we take our leave of the money form."

---

138. Marx *Capital* 3:344–347, 732.

In *Capital* II, Marx defines industrial capital as

the capital that, in the course of its total circuit, assumes and again throws off these forms [of money capital, productive capital, and commodity capital], and fulfils in each of them the corresponding [*entsprechende*] function. . . . [N]ot only does every particular circuit (implicitly) presuppose the others, but also . . . the repetition of the circuit in one form include[s] the specifications of the circuit [*Beschreibung des Kreislaufs*] in the other forms. Thus the entire distinction represents itself [*stellt sich dar*] as purely formal [*bloss formaler*] . . . The circuit of capital is a constant process of interruption; . . . each of these stages not only conditions the other, but at the same time excludes it.[139]

Thus to understand industrial capital by way of only one of its circuits is not so much incorrect as incomplete. Let us keep this in mind as we say a few words about the circuit of money capital.

The entire chapter on that particular circuit emphasizes the fact that money and money capital are not identical. But since both are in the money-form, it is easy for the bourgeois economist to cover over this fact and represent industrial capital as nothing but the mysterious reproduction of money.[140] If this is true in the case of industrial capital because of its rational complexity, in the case of "foreign trade," although Marx keeps his case confined to the value-magnitude of labor-power, such passages as "foreign trade cheapens . . . the necessary means of subsistence into which variable capital [laborpower] is converted," and "the use of slaves and coolies, etc.," allows us to supplement Marx's analysis by suggesting that, especially in that branch of foreign trade which is "colonial trade," one of the reasons why the

---

139. Marx, *Capital* 2:133, 181, 182; translation modified.

140. It remains surprising to me that Derrida insists on sticking to this view. (I keep thinking that there must be some ulterior philosophical point I am missing, like those who think Derrida is insulting the great oral culture by emphasizing graphematics.) See, for example, his discussion of chrematistics in Aristotle and its earlier counterpart in Plato as serious and complete economic explanations in *Given Time: I. Counterfeit Money*, tr. Peggy Kamuf (Chicago: Univ. of Chicago Press, 1992), pp. 157–159.

"money-form" as explanatory model is particularly misleading is because, relative to the social productivity of "the privileged country," the "total or expanded form of value" is still operative in the colonies. As I have discussed elsewhere, this form, comprised of "chain[s] . . . [or] endless series . . . of disparate and unconnected expressions of value," is particularly rich for the analysis of expressions of the value-form in appearances other than economic.[141] In the second passage I have quoted from *Capital* 3, however, Marx appears to carry the disparity even in the bourgeois explanation of capital as money-generation: the "disparity and unconnectedness" between the Bank of England and indigenous moneylending.

In order to limn our native informant's perspective in this space where the money-form of value is letting in the total or expanded form surreptitiously, we must unmoor the march of the forms of value from a historically evolutionary storyline. The heterogeneous and uneven social texture of what was given the convenient nomenclature of "the Asiatic Mode of Production" can then be seen, by Samir Amin's grid of imperial formations, as differentiated sites of similar conflicts between the general and the total or expanded forms of value. Upon these sites a weak variety gets on the way to capitalism: the serf-to-bourgeois story that Marx gives as a normative advance in the *Communist Manifesto*. Capital, the result of a weakness in the imperial body politic, is a poison that can become medicine. Because of the much broader script of imperial formations within which capitalism plays its role, the latter's seeming advance is caught back into its transformation into imperialism by way precisely of the money-circuit: finance capital. We are living such a transformation today. The possibility of its differantial transformation into socialism is halted, as it is thickened in its minute particularity by the incessant push and pull of self and other, rights and responsibility.[142] In its current configuration, with debt-bondage and tribute-system practiced by foreign aid (International Monetary Fund and the International Bank for Reconstruction and Development) and foreign trade

---

141. Marx, *Capital* 1:154; Spivak, *Outside*, pp. 75–76.

142. "After" the originary irreducible cut of a "self" from/to the other, this is the second session, the self/other (capitalism/socialism) tug-of-war of our everyday, the différance of our temporizing.

(General Agreement on Tariffs and Trade and World Trade Organization) in the continuing narrative of shifting imperialist formations, it is the new gendered subaltern who shoulders the system.[143] It is not just a coincidence that, when she remains in subalternity, she is epistemically violated by longstanding cultural formations that have bound her mind in unreasoned responsibility. And, although this last point takes us clear out of this book's argument, it is worth mentioning that, when she is in the collective resistance to aid-trade imperialism that is developing globally at the grassroots level, she is in an arena where movements for local self-manangement, each with its value chain, as it were, immediately run interference for the global. Reverting to Marx's language in "Foreign Trade," it is as if "domestic industry" should question the Bank of England. By contrast, and paradoxically, self-consciously "global" efforts at multicultural justice in the North still remain bound by the civil structure of the Northern nation-state.

In Marx's account of "Foreign Trade," it is an analysis based on the money form that is shown to be inadequate or misleading in the context of colonial trade. But bourgeois economics has always explained capital by the money-form. And for the capitalist, it is the circuit of production (of value as capital—*but expressed in the money-form*—not goods and services) that has been the best explanatory model. Combining these two in the post-Soviet world, when the financialization of the globe seems at last possible, the capitalist solution of this problem is to "develop" and restructure the "colony" in such a way that the analysis fits. Marx too thought that capitalist colonialism would shock the Asiatic Mode of Production into normative historical evolution so that unilinear resistance could begin. It is not surprising, therefore, that Marx found the total or expanded form of value "defective."[144]

---

143. This phrase is much used by enthusiasts. I simply mean a person at the ground level of society who is already a victim of patriarchal practices. As long as we think of World Trade, we can cite homeworking, sweated labor, child labor, things that are easy to oppose. As we move into globalization as financialization, global universalist feminism works for imperialism by an unexamined enthusiasm for credit-baiting of the gendered subaltern: so-called women's micro-enterprise.

144. Marx, *Capital* 1:156–157.

The total or expanded form of value is no doubt defective for an analysis of the logic of capital. But for readings of cognitive, cultural, political, or affective value-production, this is the form that we have tacitly come to acknowledge. (If I were writing this section today, I would draw out the suggestion in note 117 and point at the usefulness of this form in the "multiculture"—in Shiva's sense, close to the word's Latin roots, where "root" itself is as much "metaphorical" as "literal"— of global resistance to "Development" from below: the native informant's perspective that so-called radical critique is foreclosing today. I continue, here, with a modification of the earlier text:) If we dissociate the total or expanded form from a necessarily *economic* coding, we can see the family resemblance, the structural similarity, indeed the discursive continuity, of the two concept-metaphors: "value" (or "worth," *Wert* in Marx), "power" in Foucault, and "desire" in the Deleuze and Guattari of *Anti-Oedipus*. Other examples can no doubt be found. In the total or expanded form, it is the myriad and heterogeneous possibilities of value-coding that constitute the field. Chains of value-coding become meaningful, constitute exchange, and disperse, even as poles of resistance articulate themselves in or as the socius. The so-called phenomenality of resistances has its being by virtue of discursive formations as much as value is expressed as different substantive contents by different forms of appearance.

In the same chapter of the *History of Sexuality*, Foucault suggests that a study of local foci [*foyers*] alone will not suffice for power/knowledge analysis. The larger lines of overall strategies must be tracked at the same time. We know that Foucault warns us against studying power in terms of the Law. As he questions Marx, he seems also to put himself against broad-stroke analyses in terms of modes of production. In the context of the European Enlightenment and post-Enlightenment, however, his own analyses seem to take for granted the relationship between modes of production and social formations in a general way.[145]

---

145. This tendency is most notable in *Discipline and Punish*, tr. Alan Sheridan (New York: Pantheon, 1977), and also in the underlying argument about modernity in "Periodization," in *History of Sexuality*, vol. 1, tr. Robert Hurley (New York: Vintage, 1990), pp. 115–131.

If we attempt to read Marx and Foucault together by using "value" as a lever, then it might be possible to suggest that, in the analysis of overall strategies, the coding of the economic as the most important impersonal motor of the strategies of power and the organization of knowledge is not in fact dispensable.[146] The economic is the last instance in the sense that it is the most abstract. Lyotard has warned against "the idea that thinking is able to build a system of total knowledge about clouds of thoughts by passing from one site to another and accumulating the views it produces at each site" as *"par excellence* the sin, the arrogance of the mind."[147] Yet, if one allows thinking other than the historian's or philosopher's, what is most astonishing about the thinking of economist/capitalist (rational expectations in ethics *and* planning) is that the "sin" succeeds, indeed seductively so, in its own terms, even as it provides alibis for the new imperialism.

Thus the Foucauldian notion of the double-fronted analysis is particularly appropriate to transnational cultural studies if it is articulated with a deconstructive reading of Marx by way of "value." And, as I will continue to insist, vice versa. In the broad stroke, the economic is the most abstract and rational instance. It is among the visible aggregative apparatuses whose irreducible constituents are the heterogeneous *pouvoir/savoir* field, where the total or expanded form of value is incessantly coded, affectively, cognitively, and in ways that, by being named, are as much effaced as disclosed.

I suggest above that these two foci are deployed in subaltern women's economic resistance today: local confronting global, diversified knowledge confronting monoculture. Although, strictly speaking, they do not share the native informant's perspective, underclass diasporic women's exilic predicament can also be examined in terms of these two foci. For if the economic is among the most important in the field of overall strategy, gendering is one of the most important in the expanded form of the local. The human being cannot be proper to itself without as-

146. The notion of the economic "under erasure" has been developed in Spivak, "Scattered Speculations on the Question of Value,' in *In Other Worlds*, p. 168.
147. Lyotard, *Peregrinations: Law, Form, Event* (New York: Columbia Univ. Press, 1988), pp. 6–7.

suming sexual difference appearing in the value-form of "sex/gender systems."[148] Although *Anti-Oedipus* never actually picks up the notion of the value-form, it comes closest to working with the possibilities of the theory of value as the contentless immediately codable in Marx. This for the authors is "desiring-production." Just as "value" itself is a misleading word because, strictly speaking, it is catachrestic, so is "desire" misleading because of its paleonymic burden of an originary phenomenal passion—from philosophical intentionality on the one hand to psychoanalytic definitive lack on the other. The authors attempt to bypass the catachrestic by positing the machine as the definitive predication of the human. This may be compared to Marx's insistence on abstract average labor whenever magnitude of value is measured, whether in use or exchange, a point counterintuitive to most readers.

An extended discussion of Deleuze and Guattari's re-reading of Marx would be out of place here. Briefly, their suggestion is, first, that (production of) code is more important than (production of) exchange. In my estimation, this is because the abstract computations of exchange are most feasible and important only in the economic. Second, they keep the relationship between desiring-production and social-production uncomputable (though unavoidable for analysis) and give priority to both. Third, they think of the naming of a body without organs as part of the mechanics of desiring-production emerging into a code.

---

148. Gayle Rubin, "The Traffic in Women: On the 'Political Economy' of Sex," in Rayna R. Reiter, ed., *Toward an Anthropology of Women* (New York: Monthly Review, 1975), pp. 157–210. For a discussion of Luce Irigaray's development of an ethics of sexual difference, which takes this insistence beyond mere conviction, see Spivak, "French Feminism Revisited" in *Outside*, pp. 163–171. However inconvenient it might be, a serious study of the assumption of sexual difference will involve knowing a language, at least (see Ellen Rooney's comments on this position in "What Is to Be Done," in Elizabeth Weed, ed., *Coming to Terms: Feminism, Theory, Politics,* [New York: Routledge, 1989], pp. 230–239). There just is no way to sponsor global cultural studies of gendering made easy without falling into neo-colonialism. Otherwise, a Marx can diagnose "no social change" when he has nothing with which to grasp a society changing. And today, in the more restricted literary-critical field, a Jameson can diagnose "denied" access to "psychologism and private subjectivity" without benefit of a feel for the nooks and crannies of language where alone such access can be barred.

Thus in their book not only Capital but Nature as such a name is also "produced."

Writing within a coding of desiring- and social-production where the second is definitely assumed to be prior to the first, Marx bases his entire critique of ideology on "Capital [being] the body without organs of . . . the capitalist being."[149] But the opposite pole, the limits of being human, the Realm of Freedom, species-life, where "Nature is the great body without organ of man," is just as interpretable for Deleuze and Guattari: "The full body . . . may be the body of the earth, that of the despotic body, or capital."[150] By the time one gets to call the effects of all the desiring-machines everywhere *anything*—capital, or nature, or despot—a good deal of inaccessible coding has already taken place. To quote Derrida, this inaccessible is the undecidable through which all decisions must cut.[151] For there is of course a tremendous political difference between the name being capital, or despot, or yet nature.

In French the main title of *Anti-Oedipus* is "Capitalism and Schizophrenia." Its critique of institutional psychoanalysis is at least as important as the re-reading of Marx. Briefly, that critique can be stated in the following way: taking the total or expanded field of value-coding (later to be called rhizome-like) which is desiring-production/social-production imbricated in para-phenomenal ways, psychoanalysis subjects it to the general form of value, which leads to a system of general (universal) equivalence of affective/cognitive coding.

Is there something like a relationship between this urge and the

---

149. Deleuze and Guattari, *Anti-Oedipus*, p. 10.

150. The Marx passage, quoted in note 104, is from *Early Writings*, p. 328. The Deleuze and Guattari fragment is in *Ibid.*, p. 10.

151. "Force of Law," pp. 963–965. This acknowledgment of the undecidable in judging human guilt after death produced unease and sanctimoniousness in supporter and adversary in the unusually protracted exchanges over Paul de Man's wartime writings and Heidegger's politics (see Derrida, *Mémoires for Paul de Man*, tr. Cecile Lindsay et al. [New York: Columbia Univ. Press, 1986]; and *Of Spirit: Heidegger and the Question*, tr. Geoffrey Bennington and Rachel Bowlby [Chicago: Univ. of Chicago Press, 1989]; as also my comment on the latter in "Responsibility," in *boundary 2* 21.3 [Fall 1994]: 19–49). That Derrida should do what he says, even under duress, is striking in these texts.

bourgeois economists' desire to explain all economic phenomena by way of the money-form? Is the seduction of psychoanalysis similar to the seduction of the money-form: a "non-defective" decoding apparatus? The possibility becomes particularly troubling when applied to colonial, post-colonial, migrant, and post-emancipation discourses. For when we use psychoanalysis in the production of taxonomic descriptives in literary and cultural critique, what disappears is the arena of practice, which persistently norms the presuppositions of psychoanalysis in responsible action. Put another way, the shifting dynamics of the ethical moment in psychoanalysis, which is lodged in the shuttling of transference and counter-transference, is emptied out in such theoretical activity. The subaltern does not take a step toward the theorist in the hope of a "cure." What, apart from intelligibility, is the ethico-political agenda of psychoanalysis as a collective taxonomic descriptive in cultural critique?

In keeping with their massive re-constellative project, Deleuze and Guattari's brief remarks on the Asiatic Mode are startlingly innovative for the non-specialist. I tabulate some of the high points below.

The freshness of their reading is all the more surprising because they unquestioningly accept the Morgan-Engels division of the history of the world into Savage, Barbarian, Civil. Describing the barbarian formation, they gently rewrite Marx by ascribing to the marxian AMP a locus of change and a fluidity of rhythm that is precisely what is lacking in its received version: "It is exactly in this way that Marx defines Asiatic production: a higher unity of the State establishes itself on the foundations of the primitive rural communities, which keep their ownership of the soil, while the State becomes the true owner in conformity with the apparent objective movement that assigns the productive forces to it in the great projects undertaken, and makes it appear as the cause of the collective conditions of appropriation."[152]

Thus, because they see the socius as a surface of re-coding (re-territorializing), they are able to subvert evolutionist models and read Despot-or-State-as-cause   as   one-naming-of-the-full-body-as-cause,   as

---

152. Deleuze and Guattari, *Anti-Oedipus*, p. 194.

much as capital or nature. From the point of view of the average member of society, the evolutionary model is ideological in the simplest sense.

Again, because Deleuze and Guattari see desiring/social production (or the other way around, at the same time) as the coding and re-coding of the everyday in collusion with the miraculating great narratives, they can see the Asiatic Mode as a place of constant connections rather than an unbridged and unbridgeable gulf. Both sides are involved there because both sides are fragmentarily and disjunctively woven of machines coupled in bits and pieces, among them the "human" machine:

> The despotic State . . . forms a new deterriorialized full body; on the other hand it maintains the old territorialities, integrates them as parts or organs of production in the new machine . . . The State is the original abstract essence that is not to be confused with a beginning. . . . As for the subaggregates themselves, the primitive territorial machines, they are the concrete itself . . . but their segments here enter into relationships corresponding to the essence.[153]

Deleuze and Guattari are not specialists of Asia. Yet, because they have, in my judgment, applied a broad intuition of value-production and coding to a study of globality, they are able to hint at an approach to a "third world" full of "agents" of coding. A far cry indeed from Marx's "no economic, only political change," where agency is given over to the colonizer for brutal insertion into the circuit of the same. Thus it is possible for them to drop this quiet bombshell, in parentheses: "There is no great change, *from this point of view*, when the State no longer does anything more than guarantee the private property of a ruling class that becomes distinct from the State."[154] No great change, *from this point of view*, between the AMP and European feudalism, since the issue or telos, for Deleuze and Guattari, is not simply the emergence of capitalism. There is a difference, an orchestration of differences. But "the despotic machine holds this in common with the

---

153. Ibid., pp. 198–199. For a discussion of the Ottoman "despotic" state as a place of constant connections, see Spivak, "Scattered Speculations on the Question of Cultural Studies," *Outside*, pp. 263–266.

154. Deleuze and Guattari, *Anti-Oedipus*, p. 196.

primitive machine . . . the dread of decoded flows."[155] We have seen that, by this argument, capitalism dreads that as well, and psychoanalysis arises to appease that dread.

In the case of Gayle Rubin, it is the conviction of the heterogeneous construction of the female in society that leads to an appreciation of what we are calling, after Marx, the total or expanded form of value. This is all the more impressive because she has a good deal of faith in psychoanalysis and structuralist anthropology—both systems of general (universal) equivalence—as explanatory models.

Rubin calls the multiform coding of sex/gender systems a "political economy." Since the economic coding of value has such a dominant position of abstraction in value-theory, a position that questions abstraction and univocity might want to stay away from that name. An essay such as Rubin's, coming when it did, made a whole generation of U.S. and Atlantic feminists aware of sex/gender as the condition and effect of heterogeneous coding systems. It can certainly be said therefore that, although she remains within the outlines and presuppositions of humanist individualism, Gayle Rubin must be counted among the thinkers pushing Marx's value-thought into a new politics of reading. If I point at a rather symptomatic problem in her essay, it is in the spirit of a common struggle.

As I have already indicated, Rubin has confidence in psychoanalysis and structural anthropology. It is with these new tools (transformed by feminism) that she wants to open up Engels's articulation of herstory with history. It is her choice of the appropriate field of action for the two new disciplines that seems to me somewhat interpretable within the anti-imperialist argument. It is an unacknowledged version of what is most problematic in Jameson's "Third World Literature." Psychoanalysis (such as it is), for us. Anthropology (as, in Jameson, nationalism), for them. As Johannes Fabian has pointed out, for the anthropologist, "[d]ispersal in space [can] reflect . . . directly . . . sequence in Time."[156] (In Chapter 3, I will suggest investigations of regulative psychobiography.) In her assignment of functions to psychoanaly-

---

155. Ibid., p. 197.
156. Johannes Fabian, *Time and the Other: How Anthropology Makes Its Object* (New York: Columbia Univ. Press, 1983), p. 12.

sis and anthropology, Rubin shares with Jean-François Lyotard, Robert Morris, a certain Lévi-Strauss (all of whom I shall discuss in the last chapter), and indeed most of us in the position of writing books such as this one the tendency to assign a static ethnicity to the Other in order to locate critique or confirmation of the most sophisticated thought or act of the West. I think it is necessary for all of us to watch out against the curious politics of this all-too-seductive move. I have elsewhere called this vigilance "a persistent critique of what we cannot not want." Again, in a spirit of solidarity, I would suggest that this is the reason why, although we can get a feminist critique of Engels in Rubin, we cannot get the ingredients for a critique of "the Asiatic Mode of Production," which *The Origin of the Family* takes as given.[157]

At the end of her essay, Rubin promises that feminism will be able to cure masculism of its Oedipus complex if it uses her method of analyzing its own complicity in the fabrication of sex/gender systems. A deconstructive approach, paradoxically more "realistic" about great outcomes, would put it in the language of persistent effort and deferred fulfillment, in a "future" that is not simply a future "present." If *Anti-Oedipus* cannot break into feminism, Gayle Rubin cannot break with Oedipus. This way of working, half in and half out of what is at hand, negotiating with pre-existing structures of violence, is the way that works, the way things work, says deconstruction, whatever the purist claim.

In this chapter, I have tried to read two moments in Kant and Hegel to disclose how the native informant perspective is foreclosed in some of the backbone thinking of the modern Atlantic tradition, in the figuration of ethics and history. Since Marx has remained a contemporary to contend with, I have assembled a dossier around the "Asiatic Mode of Production" and "Value"; suggesting, I suppose, that the symptomaticity of the one concept can be kept persistently in check by the use of the conceptual scheme of the other; and that, in different ways, both can be used as deconstructive levers for a new politics of reading this philosopher who wished to insert history into ethics. My general effort

---

157. Engels, *The Origin of the Family, Private Property and the State* (New York: International Publishers, 1942).

has been to make visible the peculiar usefulness of deconstruction in uncovering these tracks.

These are the last Three Wise Men of the Continental (European) tradition. I have used them to track a foreclosure: the native informant. The next remaining chapters are on women's texts, bits of women's lives, the representation of women. As the historical narrative moves from colony to postcolony to globality, the native informant is thrown out—to use the Freudian concept-metaphor of *Verwerfung*—into the discursive world as a cryptonym, inhabiting us so that we cannot claim the credit of our proper name.

CHAPTER TWO

Literature

I

As promised, this chapter will pick at the vicissitudes of the native informant as figure in literary representation. I am working here with rather an old-fashioned binary opposition between philosophy and literature; that the first concatenates arguments and the second figures the impossible. For both the native informant seems unavoidable. Let us hold on to this opposition, if only as a *différance*, one pushing at the other so that our discourse may live.

I wrote in the last chapter that when the Woman is put outside of Philosophy by the Master Subject, she is argued into that dismissal, not foreclosed as a casual rhetorical gesture; and that the ruses against the racial other are different. Such textual tendencies are the condition and effect of received ideas. Resistance and the object of resistance often find their best articulation in such available tendencies as a picking field for interpellations given and taken. I can grasp the fierce energies of nineteenth-century bourgeois feminism in Northwestern Europe, whose inheritors we, as women publishing within the international book trade, at least partially are, as having been interpellated as resistance within that picking field. Such narratives are "true" because they mobilize. As in all instituting, however unsystematic, the subject of feminism is produced by the performative of a declaration of independence, which must necessarily state itself as already given, in a constative statement of women's identity and/or solidarity, natural, historical, social, psychological. When such solidarity is in the triumphalist mode, it must want "to celebrate the female rather than deconstruct the male."[1] But what female is the subject of such a celebration, such a declaration of independence? If it entails an unacknowledged complicity with the very males we refuse to deconstruct, a persistent critique may be in order.[2] It is a truism to say that the law is constituted by its own transgression; that trivial intimacy is the relationship between nineteenth-century feminism and the axiomatics of imperialism.

Reading women writing, men celebrating the female, men and women critiquing imperialism in the substance and rhetoric of their text, I seem to have done little more than reiterate a well-known narrative: Northwestern European male philosophers foreclosed the "native informant" in order to establish the Northwestern European subject as "the same," whether from above or from below. Women publishing are not-quite-not-native informants, even for feminist scholars. When publishing women are from the dominant "culture," they sometimes share, with male authors, the tendency to create an inchoate "other" (often female), who is not even a native informant but a piece of material evidence once again establishing the Northwestern European subject as "the same." Such textual tendencies are the condition and effect of received ideeas. Yet, against all straws in the wind, one must write in the hope that it is not a deal done forever, that it is possible to resist from within.

In order to resist, we must remind ourselves that it should not be possible, in principle, to read nineteenth-century British literature without remembering that imperialism, understood as England's social mission, was a crucial part of the cultural representation of England to the English. The rôle of literature in the production of cultural representation should not be ignored. When I first wrote these words, these two obvious "facts" were certainly disregarded in the reading of nineteenth-century British literature. By contrast today, a section of so-

---

1. Review of Shari Benstock, *Women of the Left Bank*, in *News from Nowhere* 6 (Spring 1989): 64.

2. For a similar caution, see Ifi Amadiume, *Male Daughters, Female Husbands* (London: Zed, 1987), p. 9.

called postcolonialist feminism insists upon these facts with a certain narcissism. This itself attests to the continuing success of the imperialist project, displaced and dispersed into more modern forms.

Again at the time of the first writing of this chapter, some of us had hoped that, if these "facts" were remembered, not only in the study of British literature but also in the study of the literatures of the European colonizing cultures of the great age of imperialism, we would produce a narrative, in literary history, of the "worlding" of what could once be called "the Third World," and now increasingly, taking the second World into uneven account, is called "the South." In the event, the current conjuncture produces a "culturalist" dominant that seems altogether bent to foster the consideration of the old Third World as distant cultures, exploited but with rich intact literary heritages waiting to be recovered, interpreted, and curricularized in English/French/German/Dutch translation; delivering the emergence of a "South" that provides proof of transnational cultural exchange.

It seems particularly unfortunate when the emergent perspective of feminist criticism reproduces the axioms of imperialism. An isolationist admiration for the literature of the female subject in Europe and Anglo-America establishes the high feminist norm. It is supported and operated by an information-retrieval approach to "Third World" (the term is increasingly, and insultingly, "emergent") literature, which often employs a deliberately "non-theoretical" methodology with self-conscious rectitude.

I have written at length on this phenomenon in the post-Soviet world. In this chapter I examine its prefiguration in the literature of the nineteenth century. I consider two twentieth-century texts that undertake to alter the case, to refigure earlier texts with critical intimacy. There is an asymmetrical glimpse of a postcolonial writer who is exorbitant to this itinerary.

First a most celebrated text of feminism: *Jane Eyre*.[3] Let us plot the novel's reach and grasp, and locate its structural motors. Let us then read *Wide Sargasso Sea* as *Jane Eyre*'s reinscription and *Frankenstein* as an analysis—even a deconstruction—of a "worlding" such as *Jane*

---

3. Charlotte Brontë, *Jane Eyre* (New York: n.p., 1960); hereafter *JE*, followed by page numbers.

Eyre's.[4] Rhys and Shelley critique the axiomatics of imperialism in substance and rhetoric. Mahasweta Devi's "Pterodactyl, Puran Sahay, and Pirtha" displaces those axiomatics into postcolonial discourse.

I need hardly mention that the object of my investigation is the printed book, not its "author." To make such a distinction is, of course, to ignore the lessons of deconstruction. As I have indicated in the previous chapter, one kind of deconstructive critical approach would loosen the binding of the book, undo the opposition between verbal text and the bio-graphy of the named subject "Charlotte Brontë," and see the two as each other's "scene of writing." In such a reading, the life that writes itself as "my life" is as much a production in psychosocial space (other names can be found) as the book that is written by the holder of the named life—a book that is then consigned to what is most often recognized as genuinely "social": the world of publication and distribution.[5] To touch Brontë's "life" in such a way, however, would be too risky here.[6] We must rather take shelter in a more conservative

---

4. Jean Rhys, *Wide Sargasso Sea* (Harmondsworth: Penguin, 1966); all further references to this work, abbreviated *WSS*, will be included in the text. Mary Shelley, *Frankenstein; or, The Modern Prometheus* (New York: New American Library, 1965); all further references to this work, abbreviated *F*, will be included in the text. Mahasweta Devi, "Pterodactyl, Puran Sahay, and Pirtha," in *Imaginary Maps*, tr. Spivak (New York: Routledge, 1994), pp. 95–196 (references to this work, abbreviated *IM*, will be included in the text). For "worlding," see Martin Heidegger, "The Origin of the Work of Art," in David Farrell Krell, ed., *Basic Works: From Being and Time (1927) to the Task of Thinking (1964)* (San Francisco: Harper, 1993), pp. 137–212. Heidegger's idea, that the lineaments of the conflict in the making of the text are set or posited in it insofar as it is a *work* of art, is useful here. What I am doing with these texts is obviously influenced by my sense of how the setting-to-work mode of deconstruction is a reinscription of Heidegger's privileging of art (see Appendix).

5. I have tried to do this in my essay "Unmaking and Making in *To the Lighthouse*," in Spivak, *In Other Worlds*, pp. 30–45.

6. In the previous chapter, the deconstructive approach to "a life," to the "credit of a proper name" has been discussed (see note 94). Brontë's life has been and continues to be worked over with rather different presuppositions. In addition to Rebecca Fraser, *Charlotte Brontë* (London: Methuen, 1988), and *The Brontës: Charlotte Brontë and Her Family* (New York: Crown, 1988); Lyndall Gordon, *Charlotte Brontë: A Passionate Life* (New York: W. W. Norton, 1995); Elizabeth Cleghorn Gaskell (1810–1865), *The Life of Charlotte Brontë*, a lovely femi-erotic contempo-

approach which, not wishing to lose the important advantages won by U.S. feminism, will continue to honor the suspect binary oppositions—book and author, individual and history—and start with an assurance of the following sort: my readings here do not seek to undermine the excellence of the individual artist. If even minimally successful, the readings will incite a degree of rage against the imperialist narrativization of history, precisely because it produces so abject a script for a female we would rather celebrate. I provide these assurances to allow myself some room to situate feminist individualism in its historical determination rather than simply to canonize it as feminism as such.

Sympathetic U.S. feminists have remarked that I do not do justice to Jane Eyre's subjectivity. A word of explanation is perhaps in order. The broad strokes of my presuppositions are that what is at stake, for feminist individualism in the age of imperialism, is precisely the making of human beings, the constitution and "interpellation" of the subject not only as individual but also as "individualist."[7] This stake is represented on two registers: childrearing and soul-making. The first is domestic-society-through-sexual-reproduction cathected as "companionate love"; the second is the imperialist project cathected as civil-society-through-social-mission. As the female individualist, not-quite-not-male, articulates herself in shifting relationship to what is at stake, the

---

rary biography, ed. Alan Shelston (Harmondsworth: Penguin, 1975); Margot Peters, *Unquiet Soul: A Biography of Charlotte Brontë* (Garden City, N.Y.: Doubleday, 1975); and Tom Winnifrith, *A New Life of Charlotte Brontë* (Basingstoke, Hampshire: Macmillan, 1988); there is the considerable correspondence and *The Life and Works of Charlotte Brontë and Her Sisters* (London: John Murray, 1920–1922), started in 1899 by the indefatigable Mrs. Humphrey Ward, and continuing on to 1929. All we can do is to point at the structure of foreclosure in the novel in the pages that follow.

7. As always, I take my formula from Louis Althusser, "Ideology and Ideological State Apparatuses (Notes Towards an Investigation)," in *"Lenin and Philosophy" and Other Essays*, tr. Ben Brewster (New York: Monthly Review Press, 1971), pp. 127–186. For an acute differentiation between the individual and individualism, see V. N. Volosinov, *Marxism and the Philosophy of Language*, tr. Ladislav Matejka and I. R. Titunik (New York: Studies in Language, 1973), pp. 93–94, 152–153. For a "straight" analysis of the roots and ramifications of English "individualism," see C. B. MacPherson, *The Political Theory of Possessive Individualism: Hobbes to Locke* (Oxford: Oxford Univ. Press, 1962).

"native subaltern female" (*within* discourse, *as* a signifier) is excluded from any share in this emerging norm.[8] If we read this account from an isolationist perspective in a "metropolitan" context, we see nothing there but the psychobiography of the militant female subject. In a reading such as mine, by contrast, the effort is to wrench oneself away from the mesmerizing focus of the "subject-constitution" of the female individualist.

To develop further the notion that my stance need not be an accusing one, I will refer to a passage from Roberto Fernandez Retamar's "Caliban," although, as I hope will be clear by the end of this book, I myself do not think that the postcolonial should take Calibán as an inescapable model.[9] José Enriqué Rodó had argued in 1900 that the model for the Latin American intellectual in relationship to Europe could be Shakespeare's Ariel.[10] In 1971 Retamar, denying the possibility of an identifiable "Latin American Culture," recast the model as Caliban. Not surprisingly, this powerful exchange still excludes any specific consideration of the civilizations of the Maya, the Aztecs, the Incas, or the smaller nations of what is now called Latin America.[11] Let

---

8. I am constructing an analogy with Homi Bhabha's powerful notion of "not-quite/not-white" in his "Of Mimicry and Man: The Ambiguity of Colonial Discourse," *October* 28 (Spring 1984): 132. I should also add that I use the word "native" here in reaction to the term "Third World Woman." It cannot, of course, apply with equal historical justice to both the West Indian and the Indian contexts nor to contexts of imperialism by transportation. The subaltern will be defined in the next chapter. Here suffice it to say that she is seen over against the emergent bourgeoisie of the colonies, whose share in female emancipation is another story. Bertha Mason in *Jane Eyre* is not, in that sense, a subaltern. As I will argue later, she is removed from bourgeois class mobility by her madness; the mad are subaltern of a special sort. It should also be added that the category of subalternity, like the category of exile, works differently for women.

9. Roberto Fernandez Retamar, "Caliban: Notes towards a Discussion of Culture in Our America," tr. Lynn Garafola et al., in *Massachusetts Review* 15 (Winter–Spring 1974): 7–72; all further references to this work, abbreviated *C*, will be included in the text.

10. José Enrique Rodó, *Ariel*, ed. Gordon Brotherston (Cambridge: Cambridge Univ. Press, 1967).

11. Gordon Brotherston, the editor of *Ariel*, went on to write *The Book of the Fourth World: Reading the Native Americas through Their Literature* (Cambridge:

us note carefully that, at this stage of my argument, this "conversation" between Europe and Latin America (without a specific consideration of the political economy of the "worlding" of the "native") provides a sufficient thematic description of our attempt to confront the ethnocentric and reverse-ethnocentric benevolent double bind (that is, considering the "native" as object for enthusiastic information-retrieval and thus denying its own "worlding") that I sketched in my opening paragraphs.

In a moving passage in "Calibán," Retamar locates both Caliban and Ariel in the intellectual in neo-colonialism:

> There is no real Ariel-Caliban polarity: both are slaves in the hands of Prospero, the foreign magician. But Caliban is the rude and unconquerable master of the island, while Ariel, a creature of the air, although also a child of the isle, is the intellectual. The deformed Caliban—enslaved, robbed of his island, and taught the language by Prospero—rebukes him thus: "You taught me language, and my profit on't/Is, I know how to curse." (*C* 28)

As we attempt to unlearn our so-called privilege as Ariel and "seek from [a certain] Caliban the honor of a place in his rebellious and glorious ranks," we do not ask that our students and colleagues should emulate us but that they should attend to us (*C* 72). If, however, we are driven by a nostalgia for lost origins, we too run the risk of effacing the "native" and stepping forth as "the real Caliban," of forgetting that he is a name in a play, an inaccessible blankness circumscribed by an interpretable text.[12] The stagings of Caliban work alongside the narrativization of history: claiming to *be* Caliban legitimizes the very individualism that we must persistently attempt to undermine from within.

Elizabeth Fox-Genovese, in an article on history and women's history, shows us how to define the historical moment of feminism in the

---

Cambridge Univ. Press, 1992), a book inspired by a sense of the effective foreclosure of the native Americas in the debate over the question of Latin American identity.

12. For an elaboration of "an inaccessible blankness circumscribed by an interpretable text," see Chapter 3.

West in terms of female access to individualism.[13] The battle for female individualism plays itself out within the larger theater of the establishment of meritocratic individualism, indexed in the aesthetic field by the ideology of "the creative imagination." Fox-Genovese's presupposition will guide us into the beautifully orchestrated opening of *Jane Eyre*.

It is a scene of the marginalization and privatization of the protagonist: "There was no possibility of taking a walk that day. . . . Out-door exercise was now out of the question. I was glad of it" (*JE* 9). The movement continues as Jane breaks the rules of the appropriate topography of withdrawal. The family at the center withdraws into the sanctioned architectural space of the withdrawing room or drawing room; Jane inserts herself—"I slipped in"—into the margin—"A small breakfast-room *adjoined* the drawing room" (*JE* 9; emphasis mine).

The manipulation of the domestic inscription of space within the upwardly mobilizing currents of the eighteenth- and nineteenth-century bourgeoisie in England and France is well known. It seems fitting that the place to which Jane withdraws is not only not the withdrawing room but also not the dining room, the sanctioned place of family meals. Nor is it the library, the appropriate place for reading. The breakfast room "contained a book-case" (*JE* 9). As Rudolph Ackerman wrote in his *Repository* (1823), one of the many manuals of taste in circulation in nineteenth-century England, these low bookcases and stands were designed to "contain all the books that may be desired for a sitting-room without reference to the library."[14] Even in this already triply off-center place, "having drawn the red moreen curtain nearly close, I [Jane] was shrined in double retirement" (*JE* 9–10).

Here in Jane's self-marginalized uniqueness, the reader becomes her accomplice: the reader and Jane are united—both are reading. Yet Jane still preserves her odd privilege, for she continues never quite doing the

---

13. Elizabeth Fox-Genovese, "Placing Women's History in History," *New Left Review* 133 (May–June 1982): 5–29. I should perhaps add here that I find it increasingly difficult to resonate with the consequences that Fox-Genovese has drawn from this insight in the intervening decades.

14. Rudolph Ackermann, *The Repository of Arts, Literature, Commerce, Manufactures, Fashions, and Politics* (London: R. Ackermann, 1823), p. 310.

proper thing in its proper place. She cares little for reading what is *meant* to be read: the "letter-press." She reads the pictures. The power of this singular hermeneutics is precisely that it can make the outside inside. "At intervals, while turning over the leaves of my book, I studied the aspect of that winter afternoon." Under the clear panes of glass, the rain no longer penetrates, "the drear November day" is rather a one-dimensional "aspect" to be "studied," not decoded like the "letter-press" but, like pictures, deciphered by the unique creative imagination of the marginal individualist (*JE* 10).

Before following the track of this unique imagination, let us consider the suggestion that the progress of Jane Eyre can be charted through a sequential arrangement of the family/counter-family dyad. In the novel, we encounter, first, the Reeds as the legal family and Jane, the late Mr. Reed's sister's daughter, as the representative of a near incestuous counter-family; second, the Brocklehursts, who run the school to which Jane is sent, as the legal family and Jane, Miss Temple, and Helen Burns as a counter-family that falls short because it is only a community of women; third, Rochester and the mad Mrs. Rochester as the legal family and Jane and Rochester as the illicit counter-family. Other items may be added to the thematic chain in this sequence: Rochester and Celine Varens as structually functional counter-family; Rochester and Blanche Ingram as dissimulation of legality—and so on. It is during this sequence that Jane is moved from the counter-family to the family-in-law. In the next sequence, it is Jane who restores full family status to the as-yet-incomplete community of siblings, the Riverses. The final sequence of the book is a *community of families*, with Jane, Rochester, and their children at the center.

In terms of the narrative energy of the novel, how is Jane moved from the place of the counter-family to the family-in-law? It is the active *pouvoir-savoir* or making-sense-ability of imperialism that provides the discursive field.[15]

(My working definition of "discursive field" must assume the existence of discrete "systems of signs" at hand in the socius, each related to

---

15. For an explanation of *pouvoir-savoir* as making-sense-ability, see Spivak, "More on Power/Knowledge," in *Outside*, pp. 34–36.

a specific axiomatics. I have explained in detail elsewhere in what way such a definition would be at a greater level of social instantiation than the ground-level sub-individual or pre-ontic "murmur" or network of *pouvoir* [to be able to] and *savoir* [to know] reduced to force and utterance as theorized by Foucault. I am identifying these systems as discursive fields. "Imperialism as social mission" generates the possibility of one such axiomatics. I hope to demonstrate through the following example how the individual artist taps the discursive field at hand with a sure touch, if not with transhistorical clairvoyance, in order to make the narrative structure move. It is crucial that we extend our analysis of this example beyond the minimal diagnosis of "racism.")[16]

Let us consider the figure of Bertha Mason, a figure produced by the axiomatics of imperialism. Through Bertha Mason, the white Jamaican Creole, Brontë renders the human/animal frontier as acceptably indeterminate, so that a good greater than the letter of the Law can be broached. Here is the famous passage, in the voice of Jane: "In the deep shade, at the further end of the room, a figure ran backwards and forwards. What it was, whether beast or human being, one could not . . . tell: it grovelled, seemingly, on all fours; it snatched and growled like some strange wild animal: but it was covered with clothing, and a quantity of dark, grizzled hair, wild as a mane, hid its head and face" (*JE* 295).

In a matching passage, given in the voice of Rochester speaking *to* Jane, Brontë presents the imperative for a shift beyond the Law: pro-

---

16. This precaution seems to be particularly important. That "racism" is an immensely complex issue is evident. (One can begin to sense its theoretical complexity by consulting the work of Anthony Appiah, Kimberle Crenshaw, Kendall Thomas, and Patricia Williams, among others.) But its dismissive and diagnostic use is another matter. Since its first publication in 1985, the essay version of this chapter has been reprinted at least eleven times and continues to be at an alarming rate. In its original version, the essay arose out of the shock of the discovery of the axiomatics of imperialism in a text well known since childhood in immediately post-Independence India. Thus the essay bore no mark of the awareness of class-bound complicity that has slowly developed thereafter. A simple invocation of race and gender, with no bridle of auto-critique, covers exploitation over successfully. This, I believe, is the source of the popularity of the earlier version.

pelled as if by divine injunction rather than human motive. In the terms of my argument in this chapter, we might say that this is the register not of mere marriage or sexual reproduction but of Europe and its not-yet-human Other, of soul-making. The field of imperial conquest is here inscribed as Hell:

> "One night I had been awakened by her yells . . . it was a fiery West Indian night. . . .
>
> "'This life,' said I at last, 'is hell!—this is the air—those are the sounds of the bottomless pit! *I have a right* to deliver myself from it if I can. . . . Let me break away, and go home to God!' . . .
>
> "A wind fresh from Europe blew over the ocean and rushed through the open casement: the storm broke, streamed, thundered, blazed, and the air grew pure . . . . It was true Wisdom that consoled me in that hour, and showed me the right path. . . .
>
> "The sweet wind from Europe was still whispering in the refreshed leaves, and the Atlantic was thundering in glorious liberty. . . .
>
> "'Go,' said Hope, 'and live again in Europe. . . . You have done all that God and Humanity require of you.'" (*JE* 310–311; emphasis mine)

It is the unquestioned *pouvoir-savoir* of imperialist axiomatics, then, that conditions Jane's move from the counter-family set to the set of the family-in-law. Marxist critics such as Terry Eagleton have seen this only in terms of the ambiguous *class* position of the governess.[17] Sandra Gilbert and Susan Gubar, on the other hand, have seen Bertha Mason only in psychological terms, as Jane's dark double.[18]

I will not enter the critical debates that offer themselves here. I will simply develop the suggestion that nineteenth-century feminist indi-vidualism could conceive of a "greater" project than access to the closed circle of the nuclear family. This is the project of soul making beyond

---

17. Terry Eagleton, *Myths of Power: A Marxist Study of the Brontës* (New York: Barnes & Noble, 1975); this is one of the general propositions of the book.

18. Sandra M. Gilbert and Susan Gubar, *The Madwoman in the Attic: The Woman Writer and the Nineteenth-Century Literary Imagination* (New Haven: Yale Univ. Press, 1979), pp. 360–362.

"mere" sexual reproduction. Here the native "subject" is not almost an animal but rather the object of what might be termed violation, in the name of the categorical imperative.[19]

I am using "Kant" in this essay as a metonym for that most flexible ethical moment in the European eighteenth century that I have read in the previous chapter. Kant words the categorical imperative, conceived as the universal moral law given in pure reason and "prescribe[d by practical reason] to practical thought (to empirical will) [as] . . . actualize me," in the following way: "Everything in creation which he [man] wishes and over which he has power can be used merely as a means; only man, and, it with him, every rational creature, is an end in itself."[20] It is thus a moving displacement of Christian ethics from religion to philosophy.[21] As Kant writes: "The possibility of such a command as, 'Love God above all and thy neighbor as thyself,' resonates well [*stimmt zusammen*] with this. For, as a command, it requires attention [*Achtung*] to a law which orders love and does not leave it to arbitrary choice to make love the principle."

The "categorical" in Kant cannot be adequately represented in determinately grounded action. Indeed, it is Jean-Luc Nancy's central argument in *L'impératif catégorique* that the categorical imperative is the mark of alterity (love does not depend on the freedom of choice, as the text quoted would imply) in the ethical. The dangerous transformative power of philosophy, however, is that its formal subtlety can be travestied in the service of the state. Such a travesty in the case of the categorical imperative can justify the imperialist project by producing the following formula: make the heathen into a human so that he can be treated as an end in himself; in the interest of admitting the raw man

---

19. In the context of the female of unspecified race, Derrida sees Kant as the "categorical pornographer" (*Glas* [Lincoln: Univ. Of Nebraska Press, 1986], p. 128).

20. Lyotard, *Lessons*, p. 175, and Kant, *Critique of Practical Reason*, tr. Lewis White Beck (New York: Macmillan, 1993), p. 90. The next passage quoted from Kant is from p. 86.

21. For a comparison with the unavailability of this *historical* conjuncture for Islam, see Spivak, "Reading *The Satanic Verses*," in *Outside*, pp. 238–240.

into the noumenon; yesterday's imperialism, today's "Development."[22] This project is presented as a sort of tangent in *Jane Eyre*, a tangent that escapes the closed circle of the narrative conclusion. This tangent is the story of St. John Rivers, who is granted the important task of concluding the text.

At the novel's end, the allegorical language of Christian psychobiography—rather than the textually constituted and seemingly private grammar of the creative imagination that I noted in the novel's opening—marks the inaccessibility of the imperialist project as such to the nascent "feminist" scenario. The concluding passage of *Jane Eyre* places St. John Rivers within the fold of *Pilgrim's Progress*. Eagleton pays no attention to this but accepts the novel's ideological lexicon, which establishes St. John Rivers's heroism by equating a life in Calcutta with an unquestioning choice of death. Gilbert and Gubar, by calling *Jane Eyre* "Plain Jane's Progress," see the novel as simply replacing the male protagonist with the female. They do not notice the distance between sexual reproduction and soul making, both actualized by the unquestioned idiom of imperialist presuppositions evident in the last part of *Jane Eyre:* "Firm, faithful, and devoted, full of energy, and zeal, and truth [St. John Rivers] labours for his race. . . . His is the sternness of the warrior Greatheart, who guards his pilgrim convoy from the onslaught of Apollyon. . . . His is the ambition of the high master-spirit[s] . . . who stand without fault before the throne of God; who share the last mighty victories of the Lamb; who are called, and chosen, and faithful" (*JE* 455).

Earlier in the novel, St. John Rivers himself justifies the project: "My vocation? My great work? . . . My hopes of being numbered in the band

---

22. I have tried to justify the reduction of sociohistorical problems to formulas or propositions in Chapter 3. The "travesty" I speak of does not befall the Kantian ethic in its purity, as an accident, but rather exists within its lineaments as a possible supplement, as I argue in Chapter 1. On the register of the human being as child rather than heathen, my formula can be found, for example, in "What Is Enlightenment?" in Kant, *"Foundations of the Metaphysics of Morals," "What Is Enlightenment?" and a Passage from "The Metaphysics of Morals,"* tr. and ed. Lewis White Beck (Indianapolis: Bobbs-Merrill, 1959). Dan Rather spoke of the Haitians as "children" during a September 1994 *CBS Evening News* report of the U.S. occupation of Haiti. See also Spivak, "Academic Freedom," in *Pretexts* 5.1–2 (1995): 117–156.

who have merged all ambitions in the glorious one of bettering their race—of carrying knowledge into the realms of ignorance—of substituting peace for war—freedom for bondage—religion for superstition—the hope of heaven for the fear of hell? (*JE* 376)." Imperialism and its territorial and subject-constituting project attempt a violent deconstruction of the oppositions insisted upon in this passage.

When Jean Rhys, born on the Caribbean island of Dominica, read *Jane Eyre* as a child, she was moved by Bertha Mason: "I thought I'd try to write her a life."[23] *Wide Sargasso Sea*, the slim novel published in 1965, at the end of Rhys's long career, is that "life."

I have suggested that Bertha's function in *Jane Eyre* is to render indeterminate the boundary between human and animal and thereby to weaken her entitlement under the spirit if not the letter of the Law. When Rhys rewrites the scene in *Jane Eyre* where Jane hears "a snarling, snatching sound, almost like a dog quarrelling" and then encounters a bleeding Richard Mason (*JE* 210), she keeps Bertha's humanity intact. Grace Poole, another character originally in *Jane Eyre*, describes the incident to Bertha in *Wide Sargasso Sea:* "So you don't remember that you attacked this gentleman with a knife? . . . I didn't hear all he said except 'I cannot interfere legally between yourself and your husband'. It was when he said 'legally' that you flew at him'" (*WSS* 150). In Rhys's retelling, it is the duplicity in Richard that Bertha picks out in the word "legally"—not a mere bestiality in herself—that prompts her violent *re*action.

In the figure of Antoinette, whom in *Wide Sargasso Sea* Rochester violently renames Bertha, Rhys suggests that so intimate a thing as a personal and human identity might be determined by the politics of

---

23. Jean Rhys, in an interview with Elizabeth Vreeland, quoted in Nancy Harrison, *Jean Rhys and the Novel as Women's Text* (Chapel Hill: Univ. of North Carolina Press, 1988), p. 128. Maggie Humm (*Border Traffic: Strategies of Contemporary Women Writers* [New York: Manchester Univ. Press, 1991], pp. 62–93) and others have subsequently fleshed out the West Indian background much more thoroughly than I have been able to. Humm's excellent essay unaccountably thinks I "downplay" Christophine. To repeat: I think it is one of the strengths of Rhys's novel that it stages the non-containment of Christophine. Of course she is a powerful mother-figure, but in the end and textually, she's let go.

imperialism. Antoinette, as a white Creole child growing up at the time of emancipation in Jamaica, is caught between the English imperialist and the black native. In recounting Antoinette's development, Rhys reinscribes some thematics of Narcissus.

There are, noticeably, many images of mirroring in the text. I will quote one from the first section. In this passage, Tia is the little black servant girl who is Antoinette's closest companion: "We had eaten the same food, slept side by side, bathed in the same river. As I ran, I thought, I will live with Tia and I will be like her. . . . When I was close I saw the jagged stone in her hand but I did not see her throw it. . . . We stared at each other, blood on my face, tears on hers. It was as if I saw myself. Like in a looking glass" (*WSS* 38).

A progressive sequence of dreams reinforces the mirror imagery. In its second occurrence, the dream is partially set in a *hortus conclusus*, an "enclosed garden"—Rhys uses the phrase (*WSS* 50)—a Romance re-writing of the Narcissus topos as the place of encounter with Love.[24] In the enclosed garden, Antoinette encounters not Love but a strange threatening voice that says merely "in here," inviting her into a prison that masquerades as the legalization of love (*WSS* 50).

In Ovid's *Metamorphoses*, Narcissus's madness is disclosed when he recognizes his other as his self: "Iste ego sum."[25] Rhys makes Antoinette see herself as her other, Brontë's Bertha. In the last section of *Wide Sargasso Sea*, Antoinette acts out *Jane Eyre*'s conclusion and recognizes herself as the so-called ghost in Thornfield Hall: "I went into the hall again with the tall candle in my hand. It was then that I saw her—the ghost. The woman with the streaming hair. She was surrounded by a gilt frame but I knew her" (*WSS* 154). The gilt frame encloses a mirror: as Narcissus's pool reflects the selfed other, so this "pool" reflects the othered self. Here the dream sequence ends, with an invocation of none

24. See Louise Vinge, *The Narcissus Theme in Western European Literature up to the Early Nineteenth Century*, tr. Robert Dewsnap et al. (Lund, Sweden: Gleepers, 1967), chap. 5.

25. For a detailed study of this text, see John Brenkman, "Narcissus in the Text," *Georgia Review* 30 (Summer 1976): 293–327; and Spivak, "Echo," in Donna Landry and Gerald McLean, eds., *The Spivak Reader* (New York: Routledge, 1995), pp. 126–202.

other than Tia, the other that could not be selfed, because the fracture of imperialism rather than the Ovidian pool intervened. (I will return to this difficult point.) "That was the third time I had my dream, and it ended. . . . I called 'Tia' and jumped and woke" (*WSS* 155). It is now, at the very end of the book, that Antoinette/Bertha can say: "Now at last I know why I was brought here and what I have to do" (*WSS* 155–156). We can read this as her having been brought into the England of Brontë's novel: "This cardboard house"—a book between cardboard covers—"where I walk at night is not England" (*WSS* 148). In this fictive England, she must play out her rôle, act out the transformation of her "self" into that fictive Other, set fire to the house and kill herself, so that Jane Eyre can become the feminist individualist heroine of British fiction. I must read this as an allegory of the general epistemic violence of imperialism, the construction of a self-immolating colonial subject for the glorification of the social mission of the colonizer.[26] Rhys sees to it that the woman from the colonies is not sacrificed as an insane animal for her sister's consolation.

Critics have remarked that the *Wide Sargasso Sea* treats Rochester with understanding and sympathy.[27] Indeed, he narrates the entire middle section of the book. Rhys makes it clear that he is a victim of the patriarchal inheritance law of entailment rather than of a father's natural preference for the firstborn: in *Wide Sargasso Sea*, Rochester's situation is clearly that of a younger son dispatched to the colonies to buy an heiress.

If in the case of Antoinette and her identity, Rhys utilizes the thematics of Narcissus, in the case of Rochester and his patrimony, she touches on the thematics of Oedipus. (In this she has her finger on our "historical moment." If, in the nineteenth century, subject-constitution is rep-

26. I must assure Arun P. Mukherjee that I do not think this is the *only* violence perpetrated by imperialism ("Interrogating Postcolonialism: Some Uneasy Conjunctures," in Harish Trivedi and Meenakshi Mukherjee, eds., *Interrogating Post-Colonialism: Theory, Text and Context* [Shimla: Indian Inst. of Advanced Study, 1996], p. 19). It is just that people like her and me may be affected by it unwittingly, so it's worth pointing out.

27. See, e.g., Thomas F. Staley, *Jean Rhys: A Critical Study* (Austin: Univ. of Texas Press, 1979), pp. 108–116. It is interesting to note Staley's discomfort with this and his consequent dissatisfaction with the novel.

resented as childbearing and soul making, in the twentieth century psychoanalysis allows Northwestern Europe to plot the itinerary of the subject from Narcissus [the "imaginary"] to Oedipus [the "symbolic"].[28] This subject, however, is the normative male subject. In Rhys's reinscription of these themes, divided between the female and the male protagonist, feminism and a critique of imperialism come together.)

In place of the "wind from Europe" scene, Rhys writes in the scenario of a suppressed letter to a father, a letter that would be the "correct" explanation of the tragedy of the book.[29] "I thought about the letter which should have been written to England a week ago. Dear Father . . ." (WSS 57).

This is the first instance: the letter not written. Shortly afterward:

> Dear Father. The thirty thousand pounds have been paid to me without question or condition. No provision made for her (that must be seen to). . . . I will never be a disgrace to you or to my dear brother the son you love. No begging letters, no mean requests. None of the furtive shabby manoeuvres of a younger son. I have sold my soul or you have sold it, and after all is it such a bad bargain? The girl is thought to be beautiful, she is beautiful. And yet . . . (WSS 59)

This is the second instance: the letter not sent. The formal letter is uninteresting; I will quote only a part of it:

> Dear Father, we have arrived from Jamaica after an uncomfortable few days. This little estate in the Windward Islands is part of the family property and Antoinette is much attached to it. . . . All is well and has gone according to your plans and wishes. I dealt of course with Richard Mason . . . He seemed to become attached to me and trusted me completely. This place is very beautiful but my illness has

---

28. Of course this is a crude summary of Lacan's purging the Freudian scenario of its narrative content. All use of "theory" in this book is either reconstellative or scrupulously "mistaken." For the reconstellative use of psychoanalysis, see pp. 283–286. It continues to fascinate me how critics swear by the universal applicability of the meager ground of evidence used by Freud and Lacan.

29. I have tried to relate castration and suppressed letters in my "The Letter As Cutting Edge," in In Other Worlds, pp. 3–14.

left me too exhausted to appreciate it fully. I will write again in a few days' time. (*WSS* 63)

And so on.

Rhys's version of the Oedipal exchange is ironic, not a closed circle. We cannot know if the letter actually reaches its destination. "I wondered how they got their letters posted," Rochester muses. "I folded mine and put it into a drawer of the desk. . . . There are blanks in my mind that cannot be filled up" (*WSS* 64). It is as if the text presses us to note the analogy between letter and mind.

Rhys denies to Brontë's Rochester the one thing that is supposed to be secured in the Oedipal relay: the Name of the Father, or the patronymic. In *Wide Sargasso Sea*, the character corresponding to Rochester has no name. His writing of the final version of the letter to his father is supervised, in the strictest possible sense, by an image of the *loss* of the patronymic: "There was a crude bookshelf made of three shingles strung together *over the desk* and I looked at the books, Byron's poems, novels by Sir Walter Scott, *Confessions of an Opium Eater.* . . . and on the last shelf, *Life and Letters of . . .* The rest was eaten away" (*WSS* 63; emphasis mine).

It is one of the strengths of *Wide Sargasso Sea* that it can mark, with uncanny clarity, the limits of its own discourse; in Christophine, Antoinette's black nurse. We may perhaps surmise the distance between *Jane Eyre* and *Wide Sargasso Sea* by remarking that Christophine's unfinished story is the tangent to the latter narrative, as St. John Rivers's story is to the former. Christophine is not a native of Jamaica; she is from Martinique. Taxonomically, she belongs to the category of the good servant rather than that of the pure native. But within these borders, Rhys creates a powerfully suggestive figure.

Christophine is the first interpreter and named speaking subject in the text. "The Jamaican ladies had never approved of my mother, 'because she pretty like pretty self' Christophine said" (*WSS* 18). Although she is a commodified person ("'she was your father's wedding present to me,'" explains Antoinette's mother, "'one of his presents'" [*WSS* 18]), Rhys assigns her some crucial functions in the text. It is Christophine who judges that black ritual practices are culture specific and cannot be used by whites as cheap remedies for social evils such as Rochester's lack of love for Antoinette. Most important, it is Christophine alone whom Rhys allows to offer a hard analysis of Rochester's actions, to challenge him in a face-to-face encounter. The entire extended passage is worthy of comment. I quote a brief extract:

> She is Creole girl, and she have the sun in her. Tell the truth now. She don't come to your house in this place England they tell me about, she don't come to your beautiful house to beg you to marry with her. No, it's you come all the long way to her house it's you beg her to marry. And she love you and she give you all she have. Now you say you don't love her and you break up. What you do with her money, eh?" [And then Rochester, the white man, comments silently to himself:] Her voice was still quiet but with a hiss in it when she said "money." (*WSS* 130)

Rhys does not, however, romanticize individual heroics on the part of the oppressed. When the Man refers to the forces of Law and Order, Christophine recognizes their power. This exposure of civil inequality is emphasized by the fact that, just before the Man's successful threat, Christophine had invoked the emancipation of slaves in Jamaica by proclaiming: "No chain gang, no tread machine, no dark jail either. This is free country and I am free woman" (*WSS* 131).

As I mentioned above, Christophine is tangential to this narrative. Rhys's text will not attempt to contain her in a novel that rewrites a canonical English book within the European novelistic tradition in the interest of the white Creole rather than the native. No perspective *critical* of imperialism can turn the other into a self, because the project of imperialism has always already historically refracted what might have been an incommensurable and discontinuous other into a domesticated other that consolidates the imperialist self. (I will continue to emphasize this point in the book.) The Caliban of Retamar, caught between Europe and Latin America, reflects this predicament. We can read Rhys's inscription of Narcissus as a thematization of the same problematic.

Of course, we cannot know Jean Rhys's feelings about the matter. We can, however, look at the scene of Christophine's inscription in the text. Immediately after the exchange between her and the Man, well before the conclusion, she is quietly placed out of the story, with neither narrative nor characterological justification: "'Read and write I don't know. Other things I know.' She walked away without looking back" (*WSS*, p. 133). A proud message of textual—"read and write"—abdication. In my estimation, the staging of the abdication is a singular strength, not a weakness, of *Wide Sargasso Sea*.[30]

Indeed, if Rhys rewrites the madwoman's attack on the Man by underlining the abuse of "legality," she still cannot deal with the passage that corresponds to St. John Rivers's own justification of his martyrdom, for those justifications have been displaced into the current idiom of modernization and development. Attempts to construct the "Third World Woman" as a signifier remind us that the hegemonic definition of literature is itself caught within the history of imperialism. A full literary reinscription cannot easily flourish in the imperialist fracture or discontinuity, covered over by an alien legal system operating as Law as such, an alien ideology established as only Truth, and a set of human sciences busy establishing the "native" as a self-consolidating other.

In the Indian case at least, it would be difficult to find an ideological clue to the planned epistemic violence of imperialism merely by rearranging curricula or syllabi within existing norms of literary pedagogy. For a later period of imperialism—when the constituted colonial subject has firmly taken hold—straightforward experiments of comparison can be undertaken, say, between the functionally witless India of *Mrs. Dalloway*, on the one hand, and literary and cultural production in India in the 1920s, on the other. But the first half of the nineteenth century resists questioning through literary history or criticism in the narrow sense as defined by the axiomatics for (and against) colonial disciplinary production because both are implicated in the project of producing Ariel. To reopen the fracture without succumbing to a nostalgia for lost

30. Mary Lou Emery's contextually richer opinion is somewhat different (in *Jean Rhys at "World's End": Novels of Colonial and Sexual Exile* [Austin: Univ. of Texas Press, 1990]). I cannot, of course, be "responsible" within Christophine's text (in terms of available psychobiographies), as I have tried to be with Bhubaneswari Bhaduri in the next chapter. And one would need to be thus "responsible" in order to venture a judgment about the representation of Christophine. These are the limits and openings of a non-locationist cultural studies, one that does not keep itself confined to national origin.

origins, the literary critic must turn to the archives of imperial governance.[31]

Mary Lou Emery (see note 30) makes a case that Jean Rhys uses specifically Caribbean stylistic strategies that enrich the reading of the book. I find most persuasive her explication of such details as "being marooned." Her bolder suggestion—that the textual practices of *Wide Sargasso Sea* borrow from and enact the technique of the obeah—complicates my conviction that the other cannot be fully selfed. I can only see this as a mark of the limits of the desire to self the other, a desire that is reflected in Rhys's own poem "Obeah Night," the last two lines of which are a subscript: *"Edward Rochester or Raworth / Written in Spring 1842."*[32] As in the case of Friday in *Foe*, a novel I read later in this chapter, I must see the staging of the departure of Christophine as a move to guard the margin.

Mary Shelley's *Frankenstein* emerges out of a different conjuncture of British class history. A text of nascent feminism, it remains cryptic, I think, simply because it does not speak the language of feminist individualism that we have come to hail as the language of high feminism within English literature. Barbara Johnson's brief study tries to rescue this recalcitrant text for the service of feminist autobiography.[33] Alternatively, George Levine reads *Frankenstein* in the context of the creative imagination and the nature of the hero. He sees the novel as a book about its own writing and about writing itself, a Romantic allegory of reading within which Jane Eyre as unself-conscious critic would fit quite nicely.[34]

---

31. Gauri Viswanathan's work in progress is an excellent example of this turn.

32. Jean Rhys, "Obeah Night," in *The Penguin Book of Caribbean Verse in English*, ed. Paula Burnett (Harmondsworth: Penguin, 1986). It is interesting that in the novel, Rhys performs a gesture undermining the superscript. She does not allow Rochester a name.

33. Barbara Johnson, "My Monster / My Self," *Diacritics* 12 (Summer 1982): 2–10.

34. Mary Poovey, "My Hideous Progeny: Mary Shelley and the Feminization of Romanticism," *PMLA* 5.95.3 (May 1980): 332–347. See also George Levine, *The Realistic Imagination: English Fiction from Frankenstein to Lady Chatterley* (Chicago: Univ. of Chicago Press, 1981), pp. 23–35.

I propose to take *Frankenstein* out of this arena and focus on it in terms of that sense of English cultural identity that I invoked at the opening of this essay. Within that focus we are obliged to admit that, although *Frankenstein* is ostensibly about the origin and evolution of man in society, it does not deploy the axiomatics of imperialism for crucial textual functions.

Let me say at once that there is plenty of incidental imperialist sentiment in *Frankenstein*. My point, within the argument of this essay, is that the discursive field of imperialism does not produce unquestioned ideological correlatives for the narrative structuring of the book. The discourse of imperialism surfaces in a curiously powerful way in Shelley's novel, and I will later discuss the moment at which it emerges. *Frankenstein*, however, is not a battleground of male and female individualism articulated in terms of sexual reproduction (family and female) and social subject-production (race and male). That binary opposition is undone in Victor Frankenstein's laboratory—an artificial womb where both projects are undertaken simultaneously, though the terms are never openly spelled out. Frankenstein's apparent antagonist is God himself as Maker of Man, but his real competitor is also woman as the maker of children. It is not just that his dream of the death of mother and bride and the actual death of his bride are associated with the visit of his monstrous homoerotic "corpse," unnatural because bereft of a determinable childhood: "No father had watched my infant days, no mother had blessed me with smiles and caresses; or if they had, all my past was now a blot, a blind vacancy in which I distinguished nothing" (*F* 115). It is Frankenstein's own ambiguous and miscued understanding of the real motive for the monster's vengefulness that reveals his competition with woman as maker: "I created a rational creature and was bound towards him to assure, as far as was in my power, his happiness and well-being. This was my duty, but there was another still paramount to that. My duties towards the beings of my own species had greater claims to my attention because they included a greater proportion of happiness or misery. Urged by this view, I refused, and I did right in refusing, to create a companion for the first creature" (*F* 206).

It is impossible not to notice the accents of transgression inflecting Frankenstein's demolition of his experiment to create the future Eve. Even in the laboratory, the woman-in-the-making is not a bodied corpse but "a human being." The (il)logic of the metaphor bestows on her a prior existence that Frankenstein aborts, rather than an anterior death that he reembodies: "The remains of the half-finished creature, whom I had destroyed, lay scattered on the floor, and I almost felt as if I had mangled the living flesh of a human being" (F 163).

In Shelley's view, man's hubris as soul maker both usurps the place of God and attempts—vainly—to sublate woman's physiological prerogative.[35] Indeed, indulging a Freudian fantasy here, I could urge that, if to give and withhold to/from the mother a phallus is *the* male fetish, then to give and withhold to/from the man a womb might be the female fetish in an impossible world of psychoanalytic equilibrium.[36] The icon of the sublimated womb in man is surely his productive brain, the box in the head.

In the judgment of classical psychoanalysis, the phallic mother exists only by virtue of the castration-anxious son; in *Frankenstein*'s judgment, the hysteric father (Victor Frankenstein gifted with his laboratory—the womb of theoretical reason) cannot produce a daughter. Here the language of racism—the dark side of imperialism understood as social mission—combines with the hysteria of masculism into the idiom of (the withdrawal of) sexual reproduction rather than subject-constitution; and is judged by the text. The rôles of masculine and feminine

---

35. In the late 1980s, I had suggested that the reader consult the publications of the Feminist International Network for the best overview of the current debate on reproductive technology. In the mid-1990s, I would suggest following, on the one hand, UN publications, and on the other FINRRAGE. In the final analysis, there is no substitute for field reports by local women. This book ends with a tiny bit of that with respect to child labor.

36. For the male fetish, see Freud, "Fetishism," *SE* 21: 152–157. For a more "serious" Freudian study of *Frankenstein*, see Mary Jacobus, "Is There a Woman in This Text?" *New Literary History* 14 (Autumn 1982): 117–141. My "fantasy" would of course be disproved by the "fact" that the opposition male/female is asymmetrical, and that it is more difficult for a woman to assume the position of fetishist than for a man; see Mary Ann Doane, "Film and the Masquerade: Theorising the Female Spectator," *Screen* 23 (Sept.–Oct. 1982): 74–87. Again, a category "mistake." I had written the above before undertaking a study of Melanie Klein. I should do without the apology now. I have expanded this point of view in Spivak, "'Circumfession': My Story as the (M)other's Story," forthcoming.

individualists are hence reversed and displaced. Frankenstein cannot produce a "daughter" because "she might become ten thousand times more malignant than her mate . . . [and because] one of the first results of those sympathies for which the demon thirsted would be children, and a race of devils would be propagated upon the earth who might make the very existence of the species of man a condition precarious and full of terror" (*F* 158).

This particular narrative strand also launches a thoroughgoing critique of the eighteenth-century European discourses on the origin of society through (Western Christian) man. Should it be mentioned that, much like Jean-Jacques Rousseau in his *Confessions*, Frankenstein declares himself to be "by birth a Genevese" (*F* 31)?

In this overtly didactic text, Shelley's point is that social planning should not be based on pure, theoretical, or natural-scientific reason alone, which is her implicit critique of the utilitarian vision of an engineered society. To this end, she presents in the first part of her deliberately schematic story three characters, childhood friends, who seem to represent Kant's three-part conception of the human subject: Victor Frankenstein, the forces of theoretical reason or "natural philosophy"; Henry Clerval, the forces of practical reason or "the moral relation of things"; and Elizabeth Lavenza, that aesthetic judgment—"the aerial creation of the poets"—which, according to Kant, is "a suitable mediating link connecting the realm of the concept of nature and that of the concept of freedom . . . (which) promotes . . . *moral* feeling" (*F* 37, 36; *CJ* 39).

(In Chapter 1, I have tried to show that, in the unplanned place of the sublime in the planned section reserved for the aesthetic—as structurally withdrawn as Jane Eyre's curtained retreat—it is the foreclosure of the native informant that permits Kant's text to bridge nature and freedom. I will here try to show that Mary Shelley's text attempts to foreground a version of the native informant in the Monster. In my estimation, then, it may be argued that Shelley's text is in an aporetic relationship with the narrative support of philosophical resources it must use [do I resonate with *Frankenstein* because my relationship with deconstruction may be similar?]; to ask the Monster's questions toward

Kant's solution of the antinomy would be to destroy the permissible narrative that allows the system to stand.[37] And indeed, the system does not stand, also because, as in Kant, the male subject seeks to operate it alone.)

The three-part subject does not operate harmoniously. That Henry Clerval, associated as he is with practical reason, should have as his "design . . . to visit India, in the belief that he had in his knowledge of its various languages, and in the views he had taken of its society, the means of materially assisting the progress of European colonization and trade" is proof of this, as well as part of the incidental imperialist sentiment that I speak of above (F 151–152). It should be pointed out that the language here is entrepreneurial rather than missionary: "He came to the university with the design of making himself complete master of the Oriental languages, as thus he should open a field for the plan of life he had marked out for himself. Resolved to pursue no inglorious career, he turned his eyes towards the East as affording scope for his spirit of enterprise. The Persian, Arabic, and Sanskrit languages engaged his attention" (F 66–67).

But it is of course Victor Frankenstein, with his strange itinerary of obsession with natural philosophy, who offers the strongest demonstration that the multiple perspectives of the three-part Kantian subject cannot co-operate harmoniously if woman and native informant are allowed into the enclosure. Frankenstein creates a putative human subject out of natural philosophy alone. According to his own miscued summation: "In a fit of enthusiastic madness I created a rational creature" (F 206). It is not at all farfetched to say that Kant's categorical imperative can most easily be mistaken for the hypothetical imperative—a command to ground in cognitive comprehension what can be apprehended only by moral will—by putting natural philosophy in the place of practical reason.

I should hasten to add here that just as readings such as this one do not necessarily accuse Charlotte Brontë the named individual of har-

---

37. For the notion of permissible narratives, see Melanie Klein, "Love, Guilt and Reparation," in *Love, Guilt and Reparation and Other Works* (London: Hogarth, 1975), pp. 317, 328.

boring imperialist sentiments, so also they do not necessarily commend Mary Shelley the named individual for writing a successful Kantian allegory. The most I can say is that it is possible to read these texts, within the frame of imperialism and the Kantian ethical moment, in a politically useful way. Such an approach must naïvely presuppose that a "disinterested" reading attempts to render transparent the interests of the hegemonic readership. (Other "political" readings—for instance, that the monster is the nascent working class—can also be advanced.)

Frankenstein is built in the established epistolary tradition of multiple frames. At the heart of the multiple frames, the narrative of the monster (as reported by Frankenstein to Robert Walton, who then recounts it in a letter to his sister) is of his almost learning, clandestinely, to be human. It is invariably noticed that the monster reads *Paradise Lost* as true history. What is not so often noticed is that he also reads Plutarch's *Lives*, "the histories of the first founders of the ancient republics," which he compares to the "patriarchal lives of my protectors" (*F* 123, 124). And his *education* comes through "Volney's *Ruins of Empires*," which purported to be a prefiguration of the French Revolution, published after the event and after the author had rounded off his theory with practice (*F* 113). Volney's book is an attempt at an enlightened universal secular, rather than a Eurocentric Christian, history, written from the perspective of a narrator "from below."[38]

This Caliban's education in (universal secular) humanity takes place through the monster's eavesdropping on the instruction of an Ariel—Safie, the Christianized "Arabian" to whom "a residence in Turkey was abhorrent" (*F* 121). In depicting Safie, Shelley uses some commonplaces of eighteenth-century liberalism that are shared by many today: Safie's Muslim father was a victim of (bad) Christian religious prejudice

---

38. [Constantin François Chasseboeuf de Volney], *The Ruins; or, Meditations on the Revolutions of Empires*, tr. pub. (London: n.p., 1811). In *Time and the Other*, Johannes Fabian has showed us the manipulation of time in "new" secular histories of a similar kind. The most striking ignoring of the monster's education through Volney is in Sandra Gilbert's otherwise brilliant "Horror's Twin: Mary Shelley's Monstrous Eve," *Feminist Studies* 4 (June 1980). Her subsequent work has most convincingly filled in such lacunae; see, e.g., her piece on H. Rider Haggard's *She* ("Rider Haggard's Heart of Darkness," *Partisan Review* 50.3 [1983]: 444–453).

and yet was himself a wily and ungrateful man not as morally refined as her (good) Christian mother. Having tasted the emancipation of woman, Safie could not go home. The confusion between "Turk" and "Arab" also has its counterpart today.

Although we are a far cry here from the unexamined and covert axiomatics of imperialism in *Jane Eyre*, we will gain nothing by celebrating the time-bound pieties that Shelley, the daughter of two anti-evangelicals, produces. It is more interesting for us that Shelley differentiates the Other, works at the Caliban/Ariel distinction, and *cannot* make the monster identical with the proper recipient of these lessons. To me, the scrupulous distancing is a mark of the book's political importance. Although he had "heard of the discovery of the American hemisphere and *wept with Safie* over the helpless fate of its original inhabitants," Safie cannot reciprocate his attachment. When she first catches sight of him, "Safie, unable to attend to her friend [Agatha], rushed out of the cottage" (*F* 114 [emphasis mine], 129).

In the taxonomy of characters, the Muslim-Christian Safie belongs with Rhys's Antoinette/Bertha. And indeed, like Christophine the good servant, the subject created by the fiat of natural philosophy is the tangential unresolved moment in *Frankenstein*. The simple suggestion that the monster is human inside but monstrous outside and only provoked into vengefulness is clearly not enough to bear the burden of so great a historical dilemma.

At one moment, in fact, Shelley's Frankenstein does try to tame the monster, to humanize him by bringing him within the circuit of the Law. He "repair[s] to a criminal judge in the town and . . . relate[s his] history briefly but with firmness"—the first and disinterested version of the narrative of Frankenstein—"marking the dates with accuracy and never deviating into invective or exclamation. . . . When I had concluded my narration I said, 'This is the being whom I accuse and for whose seizure and punishment I call upon you to exert your whole power. It is your duty as a magistrate'" (*F* 189, 190).

The sheer social reasonableness of the mundane voice of Shelley's "Genevan magistrate" reminds us that the radically other cannot be selfed, that the monster has "properties" that will not be contained by "proper" measures: "I will exert myself," he says, "and if it is in my power to seize the monster, be assured that he shall suffer punishment proportionate to his crimes. But I fear, from what you have yourself described to be his properties, that this will prove impracticable; and thus, while every proper measure is pursued, you should make up your mind to disappointment" (*F* 190).

In the end, as is obvious to most readers, distinctions of human individuality seem to fall away from the novel. Monster, Frankenstein, and Walton seem to become each other's relays. Frankenstein's story comes to an end in death; Walton concludes his own story within the frame of his function as letter writer. In the *narrative* conclusion, he is the natural philosopher who learns from Frankenstein's example. At the end of the *text*, the monster, having confessed his guilt toward his maker and ostensibly intending to immolate himself, is borne away on an ice raft. We do not see the conflagration of his funeral pile—the self-immolation is not consummated in the text: he too cannot be contained by the text. And to stage that non-containment is, I insist, one of *Frankenstein*'s strengths. In terms of narrative logic, he is "lost in darkness and distance" (*F* 211)—these are the last words of the novel—into an existential temporality that is coherent with neither the territorializing individual imagination (as in the opening of *Jane Eyre*) nor the authoritative scenario of Christian psychobiography (as at the end of Brontë's work). The very relationship between sexual reproduction and social subject-production—the dynamic nineteenth-century topos of feminism-in-imperialism—remains problematic within the limits of Shelley's text and, paradoxically, constitutes its strength.

Earlier, I offered a reading of woman as womb holder in *Frankenstein*. I would now suggest that there is a framing woman in the book who is neither tangential, nor encircled, nor yet encircling. "Mrs. Saville," "excellent Margaret," "beloved Sister" are her address and kinship inscription (*F* 15, 17, 22). She is the occasion, though not the protagonist, of the novel. She is the feminine *subject* rather than the female individualist: she is the irreducible *recipient*-function of the letters that make up *Frankenstein*. I have commented on the singular appropriative hermeneutics of the reader reading with Jane in the opening pages of *Jane Eyre*. Here the reader must read with Margaret Saville in the crucial sense that she must *intercept* the recipient-function, read the letters *as* recipient, in order for the novel to exist.[39] Margaret Saville does not

---

39. "A letter is always and *a priori* intercepted, . . . the 'subjects' are neither the senders nor the receivers of messages. . . . The letter is constituted by its interception" (Jacques Derrida, "Discussion," after Claude Rabant, "Il n'a aucune chance

respond to close the text as a frame. The frame is thus simultaneously not a frame, and the monster can step "beyond the text" and be "lost in darkness." Within the allegory of our reading, the place of both the English lady and the unnamable monster are left open by this great flawed text. It is satisfying for a postcolonial reader to consider this a noble resolution for a nineteenth-century English novel. Shelley herself abundantly "identifies" with Victor Frankenstein.[40]

Shelley's emancipatory vision cannot extend beyond the speculary situation of the colonial enterprise, where the master alone has a history, master and subject locked up in the cracked mirror of the present, and the subject's future, although indefinite, is vectored specifically toward and away from the master. Within this restricted vision, Shelley gives to the monster the right to refuse the withholding of the master's returned gaze—to refuse an *apartheid* of speculation, as it were: "'I will not be tempted to set myself in opposition to thee. . . . How can I move thee?' . . . [He] placed his hated hands before my [Frankenstein's] eyes, which I flung from me with violence; 'thus I take from thee a sight which you abhor. Still thou canst listen to me'" (*F*, 95, 96).

His request, not granted, is, as we have seen, for a gendered future, for the colonial female subject.

I want now to advance the argument just a bit further, and make a contrastive point. The task of the postcolonial writer, the descendant of the colonial female subject that history did in fact produce, cannot be restrained within the specular master-slave enclosure so powerfully staged in *Frankenstein*. I turn to Mahasweta Devi's "Pterodactyl, Pirtha, and Puran Sahay" to measure out some of the differences between the

---

de l'entendre," in *Affranchissement du transfert et de la lettre*, ed. René Major [Paris: Confrontation, 1981], p. 106; my translation). Margaret Saville is made to appropriate the reader's "subject" into the signature of her own "individuality."

40. The most striking internal evidence is the "Author's Introduction" that, after dreaming of the yet-unnamed Victor Frankenstein figure and being terrified (through, yet not yet quite through, him) by the monster in a scene she later reproduced in Frankenstein's story, Shelley began her tale "on the morrow . . . with the words 'It was on a dreary night of November'" (*F* xi). Those are the opening words of chapter 5 of the finished book, where Frankenstein begins to recount the actual making of his monster (*F* 56).

sympathetic and supportive colonial staging of the situation of the refusal of the withholding of specular exchange in favor of the monstrous
colonial subject; and the postcolonial performance of the construction
of the constitutional subject of the new nation, in subalternity rather
than, as most often by renaming the colonial subject, as citizen.[41] In the
process, the native informant advances into the contemporary context
described in the last section of the previous chapter.

Devi's work is focused on the so-called original inhabitants or
ādivāsis (and the formerly untouchable lowest Hindu castes) in India,
over 80 million at last count, and massively underreported in colonial
and postcolonial studies.[42] There are 300-odd divisions, most with its
individual language, divided into four large language groups. I have
frequently made the obvious point that, in the interest of placing the
subaltern into hegemony—citizenship of the postcolonial state, constitutional subjectship—the movement Devi is associated with imposes a
structural unity upon this vast group. This is an ab-use of the Enlightenment rather than divisive identitarianism.

In "Pterodactyl," Devi foregrounds this ab-usive (or catachrestic—
there is no literal referent for the concept "original Indian nation" or
ādim bhāratiya jāti) spirit of aboriginal unity in her postscript: "[In this
place no name—such as Madhya Pradesh or Nagesia—has been used
literally. Madhya Pradesh is here India, Nagesia village the entire tribal
society. I have deliberately conflated the ways—rules and customs of
different *Austric* tribes and groups, and the idea of the ancestral soul is
also my own. I have merely tried to express my estimation, born of
experience, of Indian aboriginal society, through the *myth* of the pterodactyl.]—Mahasweta Devi."[43]

---

41. It should be mentioned that Mahasweta Devi's work is by no means
represntative of contemporary Bengali (or Indian) fiction and therefore cannot
serve as an example of Jamesonian "third world literature."
42. Dhirendranath Baske, *Paschimbanger Adibasi Samaj* (Calcutta: Shubar-
norekha, 1987), vol. 1., projected from p. 17.
43. *IM* 196; translation modified. The catachresis involved in "original Indian
nation" is not just that there is no one "tribe" including all aboriginals resident in
what is now "India." It is also that the concept "India" is itself not "Indian," and
further, not identical with the concept *Bhārata*, just as "nation" and *jāti* have
different histories. Furthermore, the sentiment of an entire nation as place of origin

At the end of *Remembrance of Things Past*, Proust writes lengthily of the task before him, the writing, presumably, of the many-volumed book that we have just finished. Devi's gesture belongs to this topos. After the experience of the entire novella, the author tells us that the only authority in the story is rhetorical. She hands us the gift of a small but crucial aporia, the truth-value of the story, as an interpolation within square brackets, "the severe economy of a writing holding back declaration within a discipline of severely observed markers."[44] This truth is not exactitude. We cannot "learn about" the subaltern only by reading literary texts, or, mutatis mutandis, sociohistorical documents. "It is just that there be law, but law is not justice."[45] It is responsible to read books, but book learning is not responsibility.

The native informant is not a catachresis here, but quite literally the person who feeds anthropology. The closing note of the novella tells us that the author will not be one. In the story itself there are at least two powerful figures who cannot be appropriated into that perspective. Part of that immunity to appropriation comes through the theme of the resistance to Development (hinted at in the interstices of my reading of Marx) as aboriginal resistance. The most extreme case is that of Shankar, who could rather easily have filled the bill for an authentic native informant, but to whom the very suggestion would be irrelevant: "'I can't see you. But I say to you in great humility, you can't do anything for us. We became unclean as soon as you entered our lives. No more roads, no more relief—what will you give to a people in exchange for the vanished land, home field, burial-ground?' Shankar comes up close and says, 'Can you move far away? Very far? Very, very far?'" (*IM 120*).

---

is not a statement within aboriginal discursive formations, where locality is of much greater importance. I point this out in some detail because, first, the word "catachresis" is one of the worst offenders in the general crime of inaccessibility; second, even the most hegemonic identity would show itself to be catachrestic under close scrutiny; and, finally, the (ab-)use of the Enlightenment in the interest of building a civil society brings the subaltern discursive formation into crisis, makes it deconstruct. It should also be mentioned that the word "tribal," although no longer internationally favored because of the African situation, may still be found in domestic usage in India, where the word is used over against "caste."

44. Derrida, *Of Spirit*, p. 32.
45. Derrida, "Force of Law," p. 947.

Devi stages the workings of the postcolonial state with minute knowledge, anger, and loving despair.[46] There are suppressed dissident radicals, there is the national government seeking electoral publicity, there are systemic bureaucrats beneath good and evil, subaltern state functionaries to whom the so-called Enlightenment principles of democracy are counter-intuitive. Then there is the worst product of postcoloniality, the Indian who uses the alibis of Development to exploit the tribals and destroy their lifesystem. Over against him is the handful of conscientious and understanding government workers who operate through a system of official sabotage and small compromises. The central figure is Puran Sahay, a journalist. (Devi herself, in addition to being an ecology-health-literacy activist and a fiction writer, is also an indefatigable interventionist journalist. I have been scrupulous about not accusing authors. There is no such tax on praise.)

The conception of Puran's private life, delicately inscribed within the gender-emancipation of domestic society among the committed section of the metropolitan and urban lower-middle-class, would merit a separate discussion. In the novella he leaves this frame scenario to climb the Pirtha hills and descend into the Pirtha valley, aboriginal terrain in development. (This "unframing" of Puran may also be a "liminalizing.") The fruit of his travels is the kind of organizing reportage that Devi herself undertakes, in the form of a report for his ally Harisharan. We do not see the more public report he will write for the newspaper *Dibasjyoti*. There is also a report not (to be) sent, but "sent" to the extent that it is available in the literary space of the novella, that challenges each claim of the decolonizing state with a vignette from these hills.

Like the monster in *Frankenstein*, Puran too steps away from the narrative of this tale, but into action within the postcolonial new nation: "A *truck* comes by. Puran raises his hand, steps up."

---

46. Devi joined the legendary undivided Communist Party of India in 1942. She has been as much a part of the anti-colonial struggles as she has been witness to the failure of decolonization. There is little "colonial discourse" writing in her fiction. In "Choli ka pichhe" [Behind the bodice], in Devi, *The Breast Stories*, tr. Spivak (Calcutta: Seagull, 1997), p. 140, there is a brilliantly ironic moment against putting all the ills of contemporary society at the door of British colonialism.

I have so far summarized a story involving subaltern freedom in the new nation. But that story is also a frame. Before I proceed to disclose the curious heart of the story, let me remind the reader that the indigenous caste-Hindu non-elite self-"free"ing women, Saraswati, Puran's woman-friend, and the wives of the other committed workers, wait in the frame outside this frame. The narrative of subaltern freedom and even middle-level indigenous female (self-)emancipation cannot yet be continuous.[47]

The heart, then: a story of funeral rites, and through it the initiation of Puran, the interventionist journalist, into a subaltern responsibility that is at odds (asymptotic, asymmetrical, aporetic, out of discursivity, *différend*) with the fight for rights. An aboriginal boy has drawn the picture of a pterodactyl on the cave wall. Puran and a "good" government officer do not allow this to become public. No native informant, again. Through his unintentionally successful "prediction" of rain, Puran becomes part of the group's ongoing historical record. He sees the pterodactyl. Or, perhaps, the pterodactyl reveals itself to him in the peculiar corporeality of the specter.[48]

If the exchange between the nameless monster (without history) and Victor Frankenstein is a finally futile refusal of withheld specularity, the situation of the gaze between pterodactyl (before history) and a "national" history that holds aboriginal and non-aboriginal together is somewhat different. There can be no speculation here; in a textual space rhetorically separated from the counter-factual funeral, the aboriginal and the non-aboriginal must pull together. Here is Puran as the pterodactyl looks, perhaps at him:

> You are moveless with your wings folded, I do not wish to touch you, you are outside my wisdom, reason, and feelings, who can place his hand on the axial moment of the end of the third phase of the Mesozoic and the beginnings of the Kenozoic geological ages? . . . What do

---

47. A small moment in the text which contributes to Puran's liminalization. But it is the denegation of such differences that can give rise to the global sisterhood required for the financialization of the globe. Who is silenced by the female hero? (See pages 353–421, the last movement of the book.)

48. Derrida, *Specters*, p. 6 and *passim*.

its eyes want to tell Puran? . . . There is no communication between eyes. Only a dusky waiting, without end. What does it want to tell: We are extinct by the inevitable natural geological evolution. You too are endangered. You too will become extinct in nuclear explosions, or in war, or in the aggressive advance of the strong as it obliterates the weak, . . . think if you are going forward or back. . . . What will you finally grow in the soil, having murdered nature in the application of man-imposed substitutes? . . . The dusky lidless eyes remain unresponsive. (*IM* 156–157)

For the modern Indian the pterodactyl is an empirical impossibility. For the modern aboriginal Indian the pterodactyl may be the soul of the ancestors, as imagined by the author, who has placed her signature outside the frame.[49] The fiction does not judge between the registers of truth and exactitude, simply stages them in separate spaces. This is not science fiction. And the pterodactyl is not a symbol.

The pterodactyl dies and Bikhia, the boy struck dumb—withdrawn from communication by becoming the pterodactyl's "guardian," its "priest"—buries it in the underground caverns of the river, walls resplendent with "undiscovered" cave paintings, perhaps ancient, perhaps contemporary. The aboriginal is not museumized in this text. He allows Puran to accompany him. The burial itself is unlike current practice. Now, Shankar says, they burn bodies, like Hindus. "We bury the ash and receive a stone. I've heard that we buried the bodies in the old days." And this memory is contained, of course, within the imagination of an imagined identity, fictive practices. This mourning is not anthropological but ethico-political. (Puran has situated his study of anthropology, transcodings of the native informant's speech, as useful but unequal to these encounters.)

Puran, a caste-Hindu, remote stranger in a now Hindu-majority land, earns the right to assist at the laying to rest of a previous aboriginal civilization, itself catachrestic when imagined as a unity, in a rhe-

---

49. For the labyrinthine dynamics of the author's signature promising that (the gift of) the text is factually counterfeit, see Derrida, *Given Time*, pp. 107–172. The interest here is not merely "speculative." It has something like a relationship with the fact that, reading literature, we learn to learn from the singular and the unverifiable.

torical space that is textually separate from a frame narrative that may as well be the central narrative, of the separate agendas of tribal and journalistic resistances to Development, each aporetic to the other, the site of a dilemma.

The funeral lament, the unreal elegy that must accompany all beginnings, is placed at the end of the narrative, just before Puran hops on the truck, and the postscript signed by the author begins. The subject of the elegy is suspended between journalist-character and author-figure:

> Puran's amazed heart discovers what love for Pirtha there is in his heart, perhaps he cannot remain a distant spectator anywhere in life. Pterodactyl's eyes. Bikhiya's eyes. Oh ancient civilization, the foundation and ground of the civilization of India, oh first sustaining civilization, we are in truth defeated. A continent! We destroyed it undiscovered, as we are destroying the primordial forest, water, living beings, the human. A *truck* comes by. Puran raises his hand, steps up. (*IM* 196)

In my estimation, and in spite of strong critical objections, the *Wide Sargasso Sea* is necessarily bound by the reach of the European novel. So is "Pterodactyl." It too invokes aboriginal narrativity, as Rhys does obeah. We have no choice but to allow the literary imagination its promiscuities. But if, as critics, we wish to reopen the epistemic fracture of imperialism without succumbing to the nostalgia for lost origins, we must turn to the archives of imperialist governance. I have not made that move in this chapter. In the next chapter, by way of a modest and inexpert "reading" of "archives," I try to extend, outside of the reach of the European novelistic tradition, the most powerful suggestion in *Wide Sargasso Sea*: that *Jane Eyre* can be read as the orchestration and staging of the self-immolation of Bertha Mason as a "good wife." The power of that suggestion remains unclear if we remain insufficiently knowledgeable about the history of the legal manipulation of widow-sacrifice in the entitlement of the British government in India. In that sense, my efforts in the next chapter may be considered a step in one direction of a less restricted practice of cultural studies.

It is by way of such moves, rather than merely by *deciding* to celebrate the female, that feminist criticism can be a force in changing the discipline. To do so, however, it must recognize that it is complicitous with the institution within which it seeks its space. That slow labor might transform it from opposition to critique.

Let me describe a certain area of this complicity in a theoretical and a historical way:

A restricted use of a critical or resistant approach may lead to the discovery that the basis of a truth-claim is no more than a trope. In the case of academic feminism the discovery is that to take the privileged male of the white race as a norm for universal humanity is no more than a politically interested figuration. It is a trope that passes itself off as truth and claims that woman or the racial other is merely a kind of troping of that truth of man—in the sense that they must be understood *as* unlike (non-identical with) it and yet *with* reference to it. In so far as it participates in this discovery, even the most "essentialist" feminism or race-analysis may be engaged in a tropological deconstruction. As it establishes the truth of this discovery, however, it begins to perform the problems inherent in the institution of epistemological production, of the production, in other words, of any "truth" at all. By this logic, varieties of feminist theory and practice must reckon with the possibility that, like any other discursive practice, they are marked and constituted by, even as they constitute, the field of their production. If much of what I write here seems to apply as much to the general operations of imperialist disciplinary practice as to feminism, it is because I wish to point at the dangers of not acknowledging the connections between the two.

(These problems—that "truths" can only be shored up by strategic exclusions, by declaring opposition where there is complicity, by denying the possibility of randomness, by proclaiming a provisional origin or point of departure as ground—are the substance of deconstructive concerns. The price of the insight into the tropological nature of a truth-claim is the blindness of truth-telling.)[50]

My historical caveat is, in sum, that feminism within the social rela-

---

50. The references to these concerns are to be found pervasively in Paul de Man's later and Jacques Derrida's earlier work. For specific references, see de Man, *Allegories of Reading: Figural Language in Rousseau, Nietzsche, Rilke, Proust* (New Haven: Yale Univ. Press, 1979), pp. 205, 208–209, 236, 253; and Derrida, "Limited inc: abc," *Glyph* 2 (1977).

tions and institutions of the metropolis has something like a relationship with the fight for individualism in the upwardly class-mobile bourgeois cultural politics of the European nineteenth century. Thus, even as we feminist critics discover the troping error of the masculist truth-claim to universality or academic objectivity, we perform the lie of constituting a truth of global sisterhood where the mesmerizing model remains male and female sparring partners of generalizable or universalizable sexuality who are the chief protagonists in that European contest. In order to claim sexual difference where it makes a difference, global sisterhood must receive this articulation even if the sisters in question are Asian, African, Arab.[51] Or so some of us had thought. In today's atmosphere of triumphalist globalization, where the old slogan of "Women in Development" has been blithely changed into "Gender and Development," and a hard-hatted white woman points the way to a smiling Arab woman in ethnic dress upon a World Bank publicity pamphlet, such utopianism is consigned to the future anterior.

II

I will attempt to consolidate my general points by way of reading three masculist texts: "Le Cygne" by Baudelaire, "William the Conqueror" by Kipling, and a discussion paper laid before a secret meeting of the court of directors of the East India Company. The first two—a subtle lyric and a classic "popular" narrative of imperialist sentiments—can both be made to offer us a mirror of our performance of certain imperialist ideological structures even as we deconstruct the tropological error of masculism celebrating the female. The third, mere minutes of a meeting, shows the affinity between those structures and some of racism's crude presuppositions.

Baudelaire's stunning poem begins "Andromaque, je pense à vous" (Andromache, I am thinking of you). The poet transforms the "truth" of the memory of a cityscape to the allegorical troping of literary history and a metaphor for his consuming melancholy. The woman in the

---

51. Because the Latin American countries have had a more direct and long-standing relationship with U.S. imperialism, the relationship and demands are more informed and specific even when oppressive. Rigoberta Menchú can be sidearilized by the Latin American Studies Association.

case, Queen Andromache, is no more than the poet's object, not only brought forth into textual existence by the magisterial "I am thinking of you," not only celebrated as Homer's good heroine beside the erring Helen, not only used to establish the classic continuity of the brotherhood of European poetry—celebrating women from Homer through Virgil and Racine now to Baudelaire—but also utilized thus by way of the careful invocation of a woman mourning a husband.[52] As if this is not enough, the boldly obvious pun in the title (in French *cygne* and *signe* sound the same) gives her the status of sign rather than subject from the start. Yet this emptying out—by phonocentric convention a sign means something other than itself whereas a person is self-proximate, even self-identical—is accompanied by the usual gestures of hyperbolic admiration. By the time the "real" swan appears, its figuration as sign is not secure precisely because the word *cygne* happens, properly or literally, to mean "swan." It is as if, by being the sign of the poet's prowess, Queen Andromache is more of a swan than the swan itself. It now begins to seem possible that, in the world of Baudelaire's poem, sign-status is not necessarily less ontologically felicitous than personstatus, or indeed that, in "Le Cygne," personhood might not be operated by the laws of everyday phonocentrism—the privileging of voice-consciousness over any system of mere signs.[53] Yet, as I have argued elsewhere, at whatever remove from phonocentrism we throw the dice, and however phonocentrism is critiqued, the ontic differential between the poet-operating-as-controlling-subject and the womanmanipulated-as-sign will not disappear.[54]

Once this is granted, we are free to notice the power of Andromache

---

52. I have attempted to show another example of the invocation of the brotherhood of European poets in "Finding Feminist Readings: Dante-Yeats," in Spivak, *In Other Worlds.* I have already cited Genevieve Lloyd, *The Man of Reason* more than once. Derrida has staged the homo-eroticity of European philosophy in the lefthand column of *Glas.*

53. For the dubious (unknown) of the truth of personhood in Baudelaire, see de Man, *Blindness and Insight: Essays in the Rhetoric of Contemporary Criticism,* 2d ed. (Minneapolis: Univ. of Minnesota Press, 1983), p. 35, and *The Rhetoric of Romanticism* (New York: Columbia Univ. Press, 1984), p. 243.

54. Spivak, "Displacement and the Discourse of Woman," in Mark Krupnick, ed., *Displacement: Derrida and After* (Bloomington: Indiana Univ. Press, 1983), pp. 184–186.

within the syntactic and metaphoric logic of the poem. The memory of the real city (given in the simple declarative of reportage) is put under the spell of the reflection of the mythic Andromache (metonymically represented by her griefs) in the false river of her own tears (representation at four removes) by the force of the *jadis* (once), repeated strategically:

> Ce petit fleuve
> pauvre et triste miroir ou *jadis* resplendit
> L'immense majesté de vos douleurs de veuve
>
> (That narrow stream,
> poor and sad mirror that *once* resplended
> with the immense majesty of your widow's grief)[55]
> (1–3; emphasis mine)

and, "Là s'étalait *jadis* une ménagerie" (a menagerie *once* sprawled just there; l. 13, emphasis mine). If Andromache is forever present in every reading of the poem by the poet's act of thought, the real swan, as it is introduced after the spell-binding *jadis*, is controlled by the absolute past, stronger than the preterite in English: "je vis" (I saw, l. 14).

Thus Andromache is the condition of the emergence of the image of the swan. But she is also its effect, for when the poet most specifies her by her kinship inscriptions, she is compared metonymically to the swan in the words "vil bétail" (vile cattle; the word has connotations of breeding-cattle that would relate interestingly in making Andromache the condition and effect of the fertilization of Baudelaire's memory as well). Unlike the description of the predicament of the Woman as Queen in the Great Tradition, that of the poet's predicament is not made to shuttle rhetorically between the status of condition and effect. Lines 29–33 ("Paris change . . . une image m'opprime"—Paris is changing . . . an image oppresses me) stand on their own. In fact we cannot be sure what image oppresses the poet; he guards the secret. Here the poet's "self" is made to remain hermetically other to the reader. The delicate paratactic gesture of the colon with which the next movement opens:

---

55. Charles Baudelaire, *Baudelaire*, tr. Francis Scarfe (Baltimore: Penguin, 1961), p. 209. Line numbers are indicated in the text.

"Je pense à mon grand cygne" (I think of my great swan, l. 34) certainly draws the reader into thinking that the image is that of the swan. But is it not possible that this obsessed, oppressed, and melancholic speaker should turn to a dear memory to escape from the oppression of an image? Certainly a T. S. Eliot would claim affinity with Baudelaire on the issue of an "escape from Personality" into "a medium . . . in which impressions and experiences combine in peculiar and unexpected ways."[56] Since parataxis, even more than the rhetorical question, will allow such indeterminacy, it seems fair to expect the deliberate syntactic logic of the poem to harbor it.

The point I am making, then, is that, whatever the spectacular manipulative mechanics of Andromache as fertilizing agent might be, in "Le Cygne" the poet-speaker retains a syntactically impregnable house and a rhetorically enigmatic "subjectivity."

At the end of the poem, the "à" of "penser à" (think of) seems to change function and become a dedicatory "to" toward many crowded lonely people until the text seems to disappear in the vague inconsequence of "bien d'autres encore" (and many others). Although Andromache does not appear, her singular control (as a memory-sign framed by the poet's apostrophe) over the production of the poem is reasserted by force of contrast. She remains the only "thou" in the apostrophe that is not quite one: "I *am thinking* of you." The poet's self-deconstruction seems to be made possible by the metaphor of the powerful woman.

This is the outline of a reading that shows that not only the power but even the self-undermining of the man may be operated by the troping of the woman. We should certainly consider it an important moment in our education when we learn to read the homoerotic Great Tradition in this way.[57] This kind of reading may be a not insignificant supplement to theorizing about feminine subjectivity and retrieving woman as object of investigation, two justifiably important activities within feminist literary criticism in the Northwestern European mode. The price of learning such a tropological deconstruction of masculism,

---

56. T. S. Eliot, "Tradition and the Individual Talent," in *The Sacred Woode: Essays on Poetry and Criticism*, 7th ed. (London: Methuen, 1967), pp. 58, 56.
57. As in Spivak, "Finding Feminist Readings," note 4.

however, was the performance of a blindness to the *other woman* in the text.

Introducing the list of nameless people at the end of the poem, there stands a nameless woman moving her feet in the mud, who is distinguished by nothing but color, a derisive name for her ethnicity: "Je pense à la négresse" (I think of the negress; l. 42). Here the object of thought is clearly in the third person. Indeed, this vague figure with her fixed and haggard eye is almost "naturalized" or "de-personified." (By contrast, the "natural" swan, looking up, as per Ovid only man does, may be seen as "personified.") The negress is an image not of semiosis but of what de Man has called "the stutter, the *piétinement*" (her only named action in the poem) "of aimless enumeration."[58] The swan is gifted with speech. "Eau, quand donc pleuvras-tu? quand tonneras-tu, foudre?" (O water, when will you rain down? O lightning, when will you rage? ll. 23–24) the poet had heard him say. This woman is mute. Andromache begins the poem and usurps the first half of the second section, which Baudelaire brings to an end by addressing her again by name, and specifying her, through intricate echoes of Virgil, as Hector's widow and Helenus's wife. Andromache's geography is not only implicit in her history. In a metaphoric gender-switch, the *false* river Simois created by *her* tears had, to begin with, fertilized *his* memory of the intricate cartography of the changeful city of Paris, itself implausibly shadowed by the name of Homer's hero: "Ce Simoïs menteur qui par vos pleurs grandit, / A fécondé ma mémoire fertile" (That lying Simoïs that grew from your tears, has suddenly enriched my fertile memory; ll. 4–5). Against all this labyrinthine specificity and exchange between male and female is juxtaposed the immense vagueness of

---

58. I will consider later the question of Jeanne Duval, Baudelaire's Afro-European mistress. Here let me say that I am concerned with the staging of the figure of the negress in the text. Of Duval, Baudelaire had written in his suicide note at age twenty-four: she "is the only woman I have ever loved—she has nothing" (Baudelaire, *Correspondance générale*, ed. Jacques Crépet, Paris: Louis Conrad, 1947, vol. 1. p. 72; translation mine). Even if one were to read the poem as no more than a direct biographical transcript, one might wonder at the historical irony that produces such a hierarchized presentation of the only beloved woman.

the negress' space, etched in no more than three words: "la superbe Afrique" (superb Africa; l. 44).

Indeed, if Andromache is the over-specified condition of emergence of the title-image (the swan), the only possible function of the negress would be to mark the indeterminate moment when specificity is dissolved at poem's end. Baudelaire does not stage her non-containment by the text (as does Rhys with Christophine and Shelley with Frankenstein), but rather keeps her contained to release the "many others" who are the posterity of the poem.

Let us recall the idea of reading by interception of the text as it flies from implied reader to implied receiver by animating the perspective of the native informant: denial of access to autobiography as recognized by the Euroteleological tradition; "autobiographies" mediated by dominant investigator or field worker, used as "objective evidence" for the "sciences" of anthropology and ethnolinguistics; followed by the curious "objectified" subject-positioning of this other in "oral history" politicized by exceptionalized "testimony."

Such a reading, as I have pointed out, is a "mistake," inappropriate to the text. Yet deconstructive approaches have suggested that every reading may be an upheaval parasitical to the text. Here I use the resources of deconstruction "in the service of reading" to develop a strategy (rather than a theory) of reading matching the situation of reading that might lead to a literary critique of imperialism, although its very inclusion in the covers of a book courts its effacement or neutralization as strategy. A reading that, *in a certain way*, falls prey to its own critique, perhaps.

If to develop such a perspective we look at the naming of the negress, we uncover a curious tale. She might of course "be" Jeanne Duval, Baudelaire's famous Afro-European mistress. But there is another, textual, clue as well. Lines 41–44 of "Le Cygne" use two lines from another poem by Baudelaire titled "A Une malabaraise" (To a Malabar woman):[59] "L'oeil pensif, et suivant, dans nos sales brouillard, / Des cocotiers absents les fantômes épars" (Eyes pensive, pursuing in our dirty fogs, the vanished ghosts of absent palm trees, ll. 27–28). The

---

59. Baudelaire, *Les Fleurs du mal*, ed. Antoine Adam (Paris: Garnier, 1961), p. 382.

"original" of the negress in "Le Cygne" is a textual palimpsest of the
"original" of the agonist of "A Une malabaraise," one of two women
Baudelaire encountered in Mauritius and the island of Reunion respectively. Who are these "malabarians"? Malabar is the name of the south-
ernmost stretch of the southwest coast of India. The islands of
Mauritius and Reunion, terrains of military colonial exchange between
France and Britain, have a sizeable population of Indian origin as a
result of the British import of Indian indentured labor. These people
are not necessarily, not even largely, from India's Malabar coast. Their
naming is like "American Indian" or "turkey cock," products of
hegemonic false cartography. At the time of Baudelaire's writing, the
French colonists treated these unfortunate people so harshly that the
British imperial authorities finally prohibited further emigration of la-
borers from India (1882). It is also this vague woman, encountered on
either one of the two colonial possessions, mis-named by white convention, that Baudelaire shifts and mis-places, for the *poem's* requirements,
on an imagined native place as generalized as "Africa." Literary history
recovers her as the Europeanized class-mobile immigrant mulatta. It is
as if the staging of Safie/Frankenstein, Antoinette/Christophine is here
in the undisclosed margins of the text.[60]

Under the principles of New Criticism, it is not permitted to introduce such "extraneous" considerations into a reading of the poem. The
reader will recall my invocation of the deconstructive approach to the
text of "life" on page 73. In this book I have used this allowance spar-
ingly—for Marx and now for Baudelaire. I should mention here that,
unlike psychobiographical criticism, deconstructive reading does not
privilege the text of life as an obligatory object of investigation. It is part
of the text being read, written otherwise and elsewhere.[61] I am attempting to read a bit of that part of the text to suggest here that, whereas
Baudelaire, inscribing himself as a poet within the tradition of Euro-

---

60. For important distinctions betwen Orientalism and discourse on Africa, see
Christopher Miller, *Blank Darkness: Africanist Discourse in French* (Chicago: Univ. of
Chicago Press, 1985), pp. 14–23.

61. See Derrida's strategy of reading Hegel in *Glas* and Freud in *The Post Card:
From Socrates to Freud and Beyond,* tr. Alan Bass (Chicago: Univ. of Chicago Press,
1987).

pean poetry, is meticulous about the specificity of that tradition, the inscription of himself as an admirer of negresses can only be deciphered by guesswork outside of the boundaries of the poem. Such disclosures are seemingly irrelevant to the poem's proper functioning. And they are mired in a conventionally sanctioned carelessness about ethnic identities, which has rather little to do with the obvious "fact" that all identities are irreducibly hybrid, inevitably instituted by the representation of performance as statement.[62] I am suggesting further that, if we recognize the lineaments of domination in the first case and ignore the foreclosure of the second, we are, in part, Baudelaire's accomplice.

Indeed, there are at least three ways of ignoring the inscription of the "negress." First, by asserting, as did a U.S. woman student in my class, that perhaps Baudelaire meant to focus on her predicament as being exiled without history or geography. Without attention to developing the native informant perspective, such an assertion can unfortunately collapse into what Lisa Jardine has called "recovering some concealed radical message from ostensibly reactionary writing."[63] The second way of ignoring the negress is to bring in precisely the details about Jeanne Duval or the elusive *malabaraise*, without attending to the way the negress is displayed in the poem. Third, and this troubles me most, is by suggesting, as Edward Ahearn has done, that the negress is somehow Baudelaire's dark double.[64] We are, of course, reminded of Jane and

---

62. For the latter point see Derrida, "Declarations of Independence," in *New Political Science* 15 (1982), pp. 7–15.

63. This acute sentence, delivered at the 1985 Sexual Difference Conference at Southampton, disappears in the published version, but is certainly consonant with its general argument. See Lisa Jardine, "Girl Talk (for Boys on the Left), or Marginalising Feminist Critical Praxis," *Oxford Literary Review* 8.1–2 (1986): 208–217.

64. Edward Ahearn, "Black Woman, White Poet: Exile and Exploitation in Baudelaire's Jeanne Duval Poems," *French Review* 51 (1977): 212–220. Andrew Bush, focusing on Baudelaire's own oedipal problems, reduces the asymmetrical deployment of the two women through a continuist approach that ignores the rhetorical texture of the poem ("'Le cygne' or 'El cisne': the History of a Misreading," *Comparative Literature Studies* 17.4 [Dec. 1980]: 419, 423). Edward W. Kaplan takes the desire to appropriate the womb and the feminine in general as fulfilled in the declaration ("Baudelaire's Portrait of the Poet as Widow: Three Poèmes en Prose and 'Le Cygne,'" *Symposium* 34.3 [Fall 1980]: 245, 246). Christopher Miller

156

Bertha. These readings, as they deconstruct an error, themselves perform a lie.

The transnationally literate teacher of the literature of Northwestern Europe does not have to fetch far to find material for investigation. It was an element of chance that brought together Baudelaire, Kipling, and the East India Company for this reader. I discovered the scandal in

---

offers a sympathetic reading of the poem as "alterity without prejudice" (*Blank Darkness*, p. 136); although he does, of course, see that "[t]here is one element that prevents total equality: the poetic subject" (p. 138). As his subtitle indicates, his research focuses on specifically French Africanism, and as such supplements my more generalist reading. A small point about the usefulness of de Man's notion of allegory. Miller's source seems to be "The Rhetoric of Temporality," included in the second edition of *Blindness and Insight*, ed. Wlad Godzich (Minneapolis: Univ. of Minnesota Press, 1983), pp. 187–228. Even in that text, to postulate "no possibility of . . . identity" in a void of "temporal difference" is not to postulate "*pure difference* [which] *becomes pure identity.*" To "renounce" nostalgia (de Man) is precisely not to "nullify" it (Miller, *Blank Darkness*, p. 131). However, as I have silently indicated in Chapter 1, the source for de Man's definition of allegory is *Allegories of Reading*, which leads us on to an encompassing "irony" where the definition of allegory is sublated: permanent parabasis, persistent interruption. Miller refers to a conversation in n. 47 (p. 134), to say that de Man "'disavow[ed] the article ["Rhetoric of Temporality"] completely.'" In 1970, in the crowded English department lounge at the University of Iowa, in the moments after the adjournment of a lecture and discussion, de Man responded to my compliment on the recently published "Rhetoric" with the disarming words: "I had not read Derrida yet." When Miller writes "if the word 'allegory' is taken in its broadest sense, as designating *a distance between discourse and its object*, all Africanist utterances are allegorical" (p. 136; emphasis mine); we would recommend de Man's deconstructive definition of allegory as it overflows into "irony"—I consistently turn de Man around thus—which takes the activism of "speaking otherwise" into account; and suggest that the point now is to change distance into persistent interruption, where the agency of *allegorein*—located in an unlocatable alterity presupposed by a responsible and minimal identitarianism—is seen thus to be sited in the *other* of otherwise. There is something like a relationship between this and Marx's insistence that, unless the *tendency* of the rate of profit to fall were effortfully changed into a *crisis*, socialism could not become—in this activist sense—an ironic allegory of capitalism (Marx, *Capital* 3: 317–375; he does not, of course, use the word "allegory," he only knew the received sense). If Miller's argument relates to race, Marx's imperative relates to class. I have used this notion of allegory in the context of gender in "Acting Bits: Identity Talk," in Dennis Crow, ed., *Geography and Identity: Exploring and Living Geopolitics of Identity* (Washington: Maisonneuve, 1996).

Baudelaire's poem because I wanted to teach an author on whom Walter Benjamin had written on in a course combining theory and history in practical criticism: varieties of reaction to the "age of [European] revolution" could not be bypassed. The story by Kipling I discovered in a volume loaned by a radical white South African friend in response to a desperate need for bedtime reading. A certain historical irony in *The Penguin Book of English Short Stories* passing between a South African and an Indian as a text to lull her into sleep? The East India Company minutes I found at the India Office Library in London while "looking for something else." And deconstructive cautions, looking for complicity where only an oppositional euphoria is felt, made such a random trio of texts yield the troubling double standard operating under the auspices of feminist literary criticism in the workplace. The moving present—also a text written otherwise and elsewhere—does indeed become interminable fieldwork for the student of cultural politics. If the successful colonial subject, related to but not identical with the native informant, is himself (or indeed, herself) a "wild anthropologist" who succeeds in becoming a simulacrum ("mimic [wo]man") of his (or her) imposed object of study as s/he gains in "civilizational competence," the postcolonial subject, in order to resist a mere celebration of global hybridity, must turn that savage training to account and anthropologize the heritage of the Euro–United States more deliberately.

Writing in the 1880s, Kipling is attempting to create a species of New Woman in his short story "William the Conqueror"; and, in the attempt, he reveals most of the shortcomings of a benevolent masculism.[65] William is the name of the female protagonist. By implying archly that her conquest of the heart of the male protagonist is to be compared to the Norman Conquest of England, is Kipling producing a proleptic parody of "the personal is political"? We cannot know. If, however, in pondering this question we overlook the fact that, under cover of the romance, the conquest of India is being effaced and reinscribed as a historically appropriate event rather than anything that

---

65. I hope the reader will tolerate this word. I like the faint echo of "muscling" in there. "Masculinism" seems to be about being masculine; the corresponding word, relating to being feminine, would be "femininism."

could in fact be called a "conquest," we are, once again, applying the dark double standard.

Kipling's New Woman is distinctly unbeautiful. "Her face was white as bone, and in the centre of her forehead was a big silvery scar the size of a shilling—the mark of a Delhi sore."[66] She does that most un-feminine thing: travel by dreadful train across horrid India in the company of men to tend the poor bestial Indians in the throes of the Madras famine of 1876–1878. Kipling is no doubt ironic (again, somewhat archly, but that is his habitual tone) about the traffic of British girls in the colonies. In recompense, to treat "William" differently, he makes her almost a man. She "look[s] more like a boy than ever" (*WC* 229), and her brother admits that "she's as clever as a man, confound her" (*WC* 235). In the end, however, Kipling shows that a woman's a woman for all that, and she conquers, as women will, through love. "Life with men who had a great deal of work to do, and very little time to do it in, had taught her the wisdom of effacing as well as of fending for herself" (*WC* 236). And she nurtures sentiments appropriate to a true "man's woman": "That[to make fun of a girl]'s different. . . . She was only a girl, and she hadn't done anything except walk like a quail, and she *does*. But it isn't fair to make fun of a man" (*WC* 257).

Kipling does not write about sexual difference subtly. I will point at one more detail to indicate the kind of function it performs in his text. In the interest of creating a "different" kind of romance, Kipling gives to his hero some soft and "feminine" qualities. The protagonists come together in love when he teaches her how to milk goats to feed starving Indian babies. But this possible effeminacy is forestalled by a proper objective correlative from classical pastoral with Biblical overtones:

---

66. Rudyard Kipling, *The Writings in Prose and Verse* (New York: Scribner's, 1913), vol. 31, no. 1, p. 227. Hereafter cited in text as *WC*. "It was a story about 'a new sort of woman,' wrote Carrie [Rudyard's wife], and 'she turned out stunningly' . . . She is presented in the round, as no earlier of Kipling's heroines had been" (Charles Carrington, *Rudyard Kipling: His Life and Work* [London: Macmillan, 1955], pp. 276, 277). But even such a temperate "feminist" gesture was quickly misunderstood. The protagonist has been described as "a hard-riding young lady with a preference for men of action" (Stephen Lucius Gwynn, "The Madness of Mr. Kipling," in *Kipling: The Critical Heritage*, ed. Roger Lancelot Green [London: Routledge, 1971], p. 213).

"One waiting at the tent door beheld with new eyes a young man, beautiful as Paris, a god in a halo of golden dust, walking slowly at the head of his flocks, while at his knee ran small naked Cupids" (*WC* 249).[67] Before we dismiss this as Victorian kitsch—some critics find this passage admirable—we should note that this is the story's icon for imperialism *in loco parentis*.[68] It is made painfully clear a few pages later: "She dreamed for the twentieth time of the god in the golden dust, and woke refreshed to feed loathsome black children" (*WC* 261; "Kipling's attitude to children, with its special tenderness and understanding").[69] At any rate, love flourishes and, at the end of the story, at the festival of Christmas, "drawing closer to Scott . . . it was William who wiped her eyes," even as some men of the Club sang "Glad tidings of great joy I bring / To you and all mankind" (*WC* 274). It is one of the clichés of imperialism that the settlement of the colonies—the liberation of Kuwait?—is part of these glad tidings.

There is a lot of self-conscious "local color" in the story. At first glance, then, it might seem as if the complaint about Baudelaire, that he denies the negress her proper and specific space, cannot be entertained here. And it is of course correct that Kipling is a chronicler of "Indian life." Let us therefore pause a moment on Kipling's technique of specifying India.

"Is it officially declared yet?" are the first words of the text. Narrative logic throws a good deal of weight on the answer to this question.

---

67. I cannot resist the temptation to include here a comparable bit of Orientalism, transforming the actual Indian scene into a biblical Orient, to be found in J. W. Kaye's contemporary *History of the Sepoy War in India, 1857–58* (London: W. H. Allen, 1880–88). Kaye is describing British women taken out to grind corn by insurgent Indian soldiers during the so-called Indian Mutiny: "As they sat there on the ground, these Christian captives must have had some glimmering recollection of their biblical studies, and remembered how in *the East* the grinding of corn was ever regarded as a symbol of subjection." (Kaye, *History*, 2:355, emphasis mine; cited in Rudrangshu Mukherjee, "'Satan Let Loose upon Earth': The Massacres in Kanpur in the Revolt of 1847 in India," paper delivered at Subaltern Studies Conference, Calcutta, Dec. 23, 1989).

68. For favorable assessments of this passage, see Green, *Kipling*, p. 213 and Carrington, *Rudyard Kipling*, p. 224.

69. Kingsley Amis, *Rudyard Kipling and His World* (New York: Scribner's, 1975), p. 25.

Indeed, the first movement of narrative energy in "William the Conqueror" seems to be a demonstration of how an affirmative answer to this question might be shaped. Slowly the reader comes to sense that the "it" in question is the precise descriptive substantive "Famine," and that the affirmative answer to the initial question is coded in benevolent imperialism: "the operation of the Famine Code" (*WC* 223)—the exasperated yet heroic British tending the incompetent, unreasonable, and childish South Indians. The panoramic heterogeneity of the people and landscape of southern India is offered in declaration of and apposition to the monolithic rubric: Famine.

The narrative purpose of "Famine"—the container of the specificity of South India—is instrumental. When it has served to promote love between the two human (that is, British) actors, the rubric is dissolved, the declaration undone: "And so Love ran about the camp unrebuked in broad daylight, while men picked up the pieces and put them neatly away of the Famine in the Eight Districts" (*WC* 204).[70]

The action moves back to Northwest India, where it began. Here is an account of that move: "The large open names of the home towns were good to listen to. Umballa, Ludhiana, Phillour, Jullundur, they rang like marriage-bells in her ears, and William felt deeply and truly sorry for all strangers and outsiders—visitors, tourists, and those fresh caught for the service of the country" (*WC* 273).

These sonorous place-names are in Punjab. We have left Madras

---

70. I am not considering the contentious question of Kipling's "imperialism" here. I am looking rather at the fact that sexual difference becomes relevant in this text only in terms of the colonizer. It is, however, worth pointing at a poignant piece of evidence of the effects of imperialism. Almost all the Western critics I have read, many of them (such as T. S. Eliot, George Orwell, Lionel Trilling, Randall Jarrell) conveniently collected in Green, *Kipling*, and Eliot L. Gilbert, ed., *Kipling and the Critics* (New York: New York Univ. Press, 1965), speak of the formative impact of Kipling's stories and novels upon their boyhood. Compare the following remark by a Bengali writer to that collective testimony: "I read Kipling's *Jungle Book* first at the age of ten in an East Bengal village, but never read anything else by him for fear of being hurt by his racial arrogance" (Nirad C. Chaudhuri, "The Wolf without a Pack," *TLS* [Oct. 6, 1978]); the above is a memory; it is followed in Chaudhuri's piece by a judgment, reflecting so-called decolonization and the disavowal of the economic, with which I cannot agree.

behind as we have left "Famine" behind. The mention of "home" and "outside" is not a specification of India at all, but rather the disappearance of India if defined as the habitation of Indians. The description of William and Scott's "homecoming" to the North leaves the distinct impression that the North is more British—India has receded here. This is how the roll of names I quote above is introduced:

> The South of Pagodas and palm-trees, the over-populated Hindu South, was done with. Here was the land she knew, and before her lay the good life she understood, among folk of her own caste and mind. They were picking them up at almost every station now—men and women coming in for the Christmas Week, with racquets, with fox-terriers and saddles. . . . Scott would stroll up to William's window, and murmur: "Good enough, isn't it?" and William would answer with sighs of pure delight: "Good enough, indeed." (*WC* 272)

Thus the incantation of the names, far from being a composition of place, is precisely the combination of effacement of specificity and appropriation that one might call violation. It starts early on in a benign way, as we encounter the hero putting on evening clothes: "Scott moved leisurely to his room, and changed into *the evening-dress of the season and the country;* spotless white linen from head to foot, with a broad silk cummerbund" (*WC* 225; emphasis mine). "The dress of the season and country" sutures nature and culture and inscribes nature appropriately. Thus "home" and "outside" become terms of a distinction between the old and the new British in India. The words "Punjabi" and "Madrassi" are consistently used for the British who "serve" in those parts of India. The word "native," which is supposed to mean "autocthonous," is paradoxically recoded as an unindividuated para-humanity that cannot aspire to a proper habitation.[71]

---

71. This appropriation of the place-name is much more striking in the American case. For the "failed parallel" between India and the United States, see Spivak, "Scattered Speculations on the Question of Cultural Studies," *Outside*, p. 262. When epistemic violation succeeds, these re-codings are internalized. This need not necessarily be a dead end. Such internalizations can be de-hegemonized, the oppressor's name charged with a resistant meaning, conducive to strategic unification. For comments on such a move in the Indian tribal context, see Spivak,

Kipling uses many Hindusthani words in his text—pidgin Hindusthani, barbaric to the native speaker, devoid of syntactic connections, always infelicitous, almost always incorrect. The narrative practice sanctions this usage and establishes it as "correct," without, of course, any translation. This is British pidgin, originating in a decision that Hindusthani is a language of servants not worth mastering "correctly"; this is the version of the language that is established textually as "correct."[72] By contrast, the Hindusthani speech of the Indian servants is painstakingly translated into archaic and awkward English. The servants' occasional forays into English are mocked in phonetic transcription. Let us call this set of moves—in effect a mark of perceiving a language as subordinate—translation-as-violation. And let us contrast this to a high European moment in the discussion of translation as such.

Walter Benjamin wrote as follows on the topic of translation from classical Greek into German: "Instead of making itself similar to the meaning . . . the translation must rather, lovingly and in detail, in its own language, form itself according to the manner of meaning in the original, to make both recognizable as broken parts of the greater language." This passage quite logically assumes that the language one translates from is structurally the language of authority rather than subordination. Commenting on this passage de Man writes, "The faithful translation, which is always literal, how can it also be free? It can only be free if it reveals the instability of the original, and if it reveals that instability as the linguistic tension between trope and meaning. Pure language is perhaps more present in the translation than in the original, but in the mode of trope."[73]

The distant model of this high discourse on translation is the European Renaissance, when a tremendous activity of translation from texts

"Woman in Difference: Mahasweta Devi's 'Douloti the Bountiful,'" in *Outside*, pp. 77–95.

72. I am not speaking, of course, of British scholarship in Indian languages, generally in grammar-establishment and philology. That specialized work takes its place in the history of the constitution of disciplines and as such in the epistemic project of imperialism. I have commented on it briefly in the next chapter.

73. De Man, "'Conclusions': Walter Benjamin's 'The Task of the Translator,'" in *The Resistance to Theory* (Minneapolis: Univ. of Minnesota Press, 1986), pp. 91–92.

of classical antiquity helped shape hegemonic Europe's cultural self-representation. (German cultural self-representation, in the eighteenth and nineteenth centuries, of non-participation in the Renaissance, which I have invoked in Chapter 1, gives the specifically German speculations on the problem of translation a particular character.) When, however, the violence of imperialism straddles a subjected language, translation can become a species of violation as well. Freedom-in-troping arguments from the European Renaissance do not apply directly to the translation-as-violation in Kipling's text.[74]

Just as they do not deny the irreducible hybridity of all language. When Mahasweta constructs a unique underclass hybrid language of Eastern India and uses it skillfully to contrast passages in Sanskritized Bengali, the politics of her technique is quite different from Kipling's.

I have been arguing that the tropological deconstruction of masculism does not exempt us from performing the lie of imperialism. Let us consider David Arnold's essay on the Madras famine in that frame. (Some of the documentation provided by Arnold puts the noble-whites-helping-imcompetent-blacks scenario into question.)[75] In my experience, most classroom discussions of Kipling's story are taken up by the analysis of the taming-of-the-tomboy routine between the two white protagonists. Toward the end of such a class hour I deflected the discussion to a quotation in Arnold's essay of a Tamil sexual-rôle-reversal doggerel sung by peasant women in order to make the drought end: "A wonder has taken place, O Lord! The male is grinding millet and the female is ploughing fields. / Is not your heart moved with pity, O God! / The widow Brahmani is ploughing the field." In order to think this folk-ritual as potentially efficacious by way of a reminder of chaos in a universe that should be divinely ordered, the women must take seriously a patriarchal division of sexual labor. What little time was left in the class was taken up with a young woman's insistence that the

---

74. I have developed this argument at greater length in "The Politics of Translation," in *Outside*, pp. 179–200.

75. David Arnold, "Famine in Peasant Consciousness and Peasant Action: Madras 1876–78," in Ranajit Guha, ed., *Subaltern Studies: Writings on South Asian History and Society*, vol. 3 (Delhi: Oxford Univ. Press, 1984), pp. 62–115. The passage quoted is from p. 73.

peasant women must have been singing the doggerel ironically. This is of course one possibility among many. But when we are ignorant of the historical frame, of the *pouvoir-savoir* mechanisms by which a subject is constituted and interpellated within that frame, insistence on this sort of pop-psych irony most often springs from the imposition of our own historical and voluntarist constitution within the second wave of U.S. academic feminism as a "universal" model of the "natural" reactions of the female mind.[76] This may also be called an example of translation-as-violation.

The structure of translation-as-violation describes certain tendencies within third-worldist literary pedagogy more directly. It is of course part of my general argument that, unless third-worldist feminism develops a vigilance against such tendencies, it cannot help but participate in them. Our own mania for "third world literature" anthologies, when the teacher or critic often has no sense of the original languages, or of the subject-constitution of the social and gendered agents in question (and when therefore the student cannot sense this as a loss), participates more in the logic of translation-as-violation than in the ideal of translation as freedom-in-troping. What is at play there is a phenomenon that can be called "sanctioned ignorance," now sanctioned more than ever by an invocation of "globality"—a word serving to hide the financialization of the globe, or "hybridity"—a word serving to obliterate the irreducible hybridity of all language.

Let us look briefly at the document from the East India Company. (Although a commercial company, between the end of the eighteenth and the middle of the nineteenth centuries the East India Company governed its possessions in India. This is referred to in greater detail in the next chapter. Here suffice it to remind ourselves that we are reading about the employment of Indians in their own governance.) The language here is so explicit that not much analytical effort is required. Let me tabulate the points I would emphasize. This document reflects an attempt, in the interests of efficiency, to revise racial discrimination based on chromatism, the visible difference in skin color. (Chromatism

---

76. The last chapter of Carolyn G. Heilbrun's moving book *Writing a Woman's Life* (New York: Norton, 1988), pp. 124–131, is also an example of this.

seems to have something like a hold on the official philosophy of U.S. anti-racist feminism. When it is not "third world women," the buzz-word is "women of color." This leads to absurdities. Japanese women, for instance, have to be coded as "third world women!" Hispanics must be seen as "women of color," and postcolonial female subjects, even when they are women of the indigenous elite of Asia and Africa, obvi-ous examples of the production of Ariel's mate, are invited to masquer-ade as Caliban in the margins. This nomenclature is based on the implicit acceptance of "white" as "transparent" or "no-color," and is therefore reactive upon the self-representation of the white.)

The standards being applied in the document to legitimate racial discrimination show that both the native male and the native female are clearly inferior to the European female. Indeed, as in "William the Conqueror" and the classroom reaction to it, sexual difference comes into play only in the white arena. The concept of legitimacy in the union of the sexes only comes into being with the introduction of the European. And, even as Caliban is defined out, it is only the produced Ariel who is allowed into the arena; the final requirement for the ac-ceptable half-caste is a "European liberal education."[77] "Here, then, are extracts from the document itself:

> The chairman laid before [a Secret Court of the Directors of the Hon'ble Company Held on 6th March, 1822] a Paper signed by Him-self and the Deputy Chairman submitting several suggestions in view to an exposition and practical illustration of the Standing Order of 1791 which provides "That no person the son of a Native Indian shall be appointed to employment in the Civil, Military, or Marine Service of the Company."[78]

Here are the passages on chromatism and the acceptability of the Euro-pean female:

---

77. For a comparable screening and a selective Christianization of slaves in South Africa, see Robert Shell, *Children of Bondage: A Social History of the Slave Society at the Cape of Good Hope, 1652–1838* (Hanover, N.H.: Univ. Press of New England, 1994).
78. L/P & S/1/2, Minutes of the Secret Court of Directors, 1784–1858.

It may be *fairly* deduced, that the *complexion* of those Persons was in view of the Court a serious objection to their admission. . . . The next object of consideration is the offspring of a connection between a European and a half-caste; and *it appears a matter of indifference whether the European blood be on the Male or the Female side.* The Candidates for admission to the company's service, who have been of this class of persons, have since 1791 been subjected to the examination of one of the Committees of the Direction; and if they have exhibited signs of native origin in their colour or otherwise, have been accepted or rejected by the Committee according to the degree in which their hue appeared objectionable or unobjectionable. These rejections . . . have produced some anomalies. One Brother has been accepted, another rejected. Europeans whose parents were both European, have been on the brink of Rejection for their dark complexion. . . . Discrepancies have arisen from the different views entertained by the Committee. (emphasis mine.)

In the interest of the efficient management of these anomalies and absurdities, the following criteria are offered. Here we will encounter native intercourse implicitly placed outside of legitimacy as such; and the clinching requirement of a "European liberal education."

It is submitted
That the Sons of aboriginal Natives of India and of the Countries to the Eastward of Native Portugese Indians, of Native West Indians, and of Africans of either sex, who are the Offspring of a connection of such Natives with Europeans, be invariably held ineligible. . . . That the Descendants from aboriginal Native Indians in the second and succeeding generations shall be held eligible . . . on production of certain Certificates . . . that the grandfather or grandmother of the Candidate . . . was bona fide an European . . . that the father or mother of the Candidate was bona fide an European. A Certificate of Marriage of the father and mother of the candidate. The Baptismal Certificate of the Candidate. A certificate from the Master or Masters of some reputable seminary or seminaries in the United Kingdom of Great Britain and Ireland that the Candidate has had the benefit of a liberal Education under his or her tuition for a period of six years. . . . The inconveniences which might arise from the indiscriminate or unconditional admission into the Company's service of the Descendants of aboriginal Native Indians in the second or succeeding gen-

erations will be obviated . . . by the stipulated qualification of *legitimate birth* and liberal European education. (emphasis mine.)

To repeat, this document describes the efficient articulation of the right of access to a white world administering the black.[79] Because I think that this point cannot be too strongly made, I have put it forth as Exhibit C in my argument that much so-called cross-cultural disciplinary practice, even when "feminist," reproduces and forecloses colonialist structures: sanctioned ignorance, and a refusal of subject-status and therefore human-ness; that an unexamined chromatism is not only no solution but belongs to the repertory of colonialist axiomatics. On the face of it, the document seems infinitely more brutal than anything that might happen in the house of feminist criticism.[80] But mere benevolent intentions will not remove the possibility that the *structural* effect of limited access to the norm can be shared by two such disparate phenomena.

When versions of this general argument are presented to academic women's resource groups and the like, sympathy seems instantaneous.

---

79. "Aboriginal" is being used here to mean full-blooded subcontinentals.

80. More than a decade after first writing, I take comfort in the fact that Colette Guillaumin was already speaking of this in 1977. Guilaumin, *Racism, Sexism, Power and Ideology*, tr. Robert Miles (London: Routledge, 1995), pp. 141–142 and *passim*. How is one to read religiosity and nationalism in the production of U.S. protest? Consider "grave suspicions concerning the prominence of regressive tendencies in the political culture of the Federal Republic" (Richard Wolin, "Introduction," in Jürgen Habermas, *The New Conservatism: Cultural Criticism and the Historians' Debate*, tr. Shierry Weber Nicholsen [Cambridge: MIT Press, 1989], p. xxxi). Consider World War II, and you have John Okada's *No-No Boys* (Seattle: Univ. of Washington Press, 1957), see Sanda Lwin, Columbia Univ. dissertation in progress. Consider globalization, and you come to realize that what Guillaumin calls "the *idea* of race" is in the domain of sex, not the "idea of sex," but gender; and it can be "transformed" that much more easily at the end "of the present century into a means for [global capital; she is, as a European and in the middle of the Cold War, still talking 'state'] to achieve their goals of domination, exploitation and extermination. This is a matter of simple fact" (p. 99). Population control policy as gynocide is part of Malini Karkal's thesis. The transformation of "Women in Development" to "Gender and Development" (acknowledged World Bank/UN policy) for achieving the financialization of the globe is part of that current work of mine that constantly threatens to unhinge this book.

Yet, because of the presence of the double standard, the difference in the quality or level of generosity of discourse and allocation for the matter of the first and third worlds remains striking. This discrepancy is also to be observed within curricular planning. In the distribution of resources, feminist literary criticism celebrates the heroines of the North Atlantic tradition in a singular and individualist way, and the collective presence of women elsewhere in a pluralized and inchoate fashion. These tendencies are not covered over by our campus battles for affirmative action on behalf of "women of color," or by "international conferences" using non-repeatable funds (soft money) as substitutes for curricular change. Such battles should of course be fought with our full participation, such conferences arranged when they replace white boys talking postcoloniality. But they are ad hoc anti-sexist and anti-racist activities that should be distinguished from a specifically feminist revolution in habits of thought and intervention through a persistently critical classroom presence. In the absence of persistent vigilance, there is no guarantee that an upwardly mobile woman of color in the U.S. academy would not participate in the structure I have outlined—at least to the extent of conflating the problems of ethnic domination in the United States with the problems of exploitation across the international division of labor; just as many in Britain tend to confuse it with problems of Immigration Law. It may be painful to reckon that this, too, is a case of the certified half-caste's limited access to the norm. It is almost as if the problem of racism within feminism can qualify as such only when resident or aspiring to be resident in the North.

Indeed, those of us who ask for these standards are becoming marginalized within mainstream feminism. We are deeply interested in the tropological deconstruction of masculist universalism. But when questions of the inscription of feminine subject effects arise, we do not want to be caught within the institutional performance of the imperialist lie. We know the "correction" of a performative deconstruction is to point at another troping, and thus to another errant performance, that the critique must be persistent. We want the chance of an entry into that vertiginous process. And this can perhaps begin to happen if, in terms of disciplinary standards, you grant the thoroughly stratified larger theatre of the South, the stage of so-called de-colonization, equal rights of historical, geographical, linguistic specificity and theoretical agency.

If Feminism takes its place with ethnic studies as American studies, or postcolonialism as migrant hybridism, the South is once again in shadow, the diasporic stands in for the native informant.

III

It is well to remember this when we quite correctly congratulate ourselves on today's literary criticism in the United States, attentive to the representation and selfrepresentation of margins. So much so, indeed, that the President's Forum at the Modern Language Association annual convention almost routinely addresses questions of marginality. The American Comparative Literature Association took note of multiculturalism in a recent autocritical document.[81] Such congratulations are altogether appropriate because it is also true that, perhaps as a result of these efforts, a strong demand to keep U.S. culture purely "Western" has also been consolidated.[82] But this confrontation, important as it is,

---

81. The results have since been collected in Charles Bernheimer, ed., *Comparative Literature in the Age of Multiculturalism* (Baltimore: Johns Hopkins Univ. Press, 1995).

82. Some of the initial texts were Allan Bloom, *The Closing of the American Mind: How Higher Education Has Failed Democracy and Impoverished the Souls of Today's Students* (New York: Simon and Schuster, 1987); and E. D. Hirsch, *Cultural Literacy: What Every American Needs to Know* (New York: Vintage, 1988). It is interesting to compare these with, say, Nathan Glazer, *Beyond the Melting Pot: The Negroes, Puerto Ricans, Jews, Italians, and Irish of New York City* (Cambridge: MIT Press, 1963). So far at first writing. But the field shifts fast here. At the time of revision, the plot has thickened. Arthur Schlesinger, Jr., *The Disuniting of America* (New York: Norton, 1992), exhorts the new multiculturalism to embrace the pluralist American dream in the approved American way. Daniel Patrick Moynihan, *Pandaemonium: Ethnicity in International Politics* (New York: Oxford Univ. Press, 1993) and Zbigniew K. Brzezinski, *Out of Control: Global Turmoil on the Eve of the Twenty-First Century* (New York: Scribner, 1993) appropriate some of the slogans of the other side. Charles Taylor, *Multiculturalism and "The Politics of Recognition"* (Princeton: Princeton Univ. Press, 1992) Bruce Ackerman, *The Future of Liberal Revolution* (New Haven: Yale Univ. Press, 1992), and John Rawls, *Political Liberalism* (New York: Columbia Univ. Press, 1993) come to terms with multiculturalism in the post-Soviet conjuncture in more sophisticated ways. Their treatment signals toward my work in progress. I return now to the original footnote. I have not updated the original in collecting ugly arguments for reverse discrimination: "Leftist teach-

does not amount to granting equal representation to the South; it testifies to the internal transformation of the North in response to global trends. Under pressure of this internal debate, we often conflate the two; and we tend to monumentalize something we call "margins," where the distinction between North and South is domesticated. Yet, for the sake of the daily work at the ground level, we must still raise the persistent voice of autocritique, lest we unwittingly fill the now unrecognizably displaced subject-position of the native informant.

As we try to shore up our defenses, we tend to leave untouched the politics of the specialists of the margin—area studies, anthropology, and the like. Third World studies, including Third World feminist studies in English, become so diluted that all linguistic specificity or scholarly depth in the study of culture is often ignored. Indeed, works in often indifferent English translation or works written in English or the European languages in the recently decolonized areas of the globe or written by people of so-called ethnic origin in First World space are beginning to constitute something called "Third World literature." Within this arena of tertiary education in literature, the upwardly mobile exmarginal, *justifiably* searching for validation, can help commodify marginality. Sometimes, with the best of intentions and in the name of convenience, an institutionalized double standard tends to get established: one standard of preparation and testing for our own kind and quite another for the rest of the world. Even as we join in the struggle

---

ers have created an atmosphere in which those who question the value of women's studies and ethnic studies are labelled sexist, racist or 'cold warriors'" (Lawrence W. Hyman, "The Culture Battle," *On Campus* 8 (Apr. 1989): 5; see also Lee Dembert, "Left Censorship at Stanford," *New York Times* 5 May 1989, p. A35. Roger Kimball, *Tenured Radicals: How Politics Has Corrupted Our Higher Education* (New York: Harper, 1990) remains a dubious classic. I cannot resist the temptation of marking two recent skirmishes: Governor Pete Wilson, in his capacity as trustee of the University of California, obliges that system to drop affirmative action; Yale University returns $20 million—donated for teaching "Western Civilization" courses—to alumnus Lee Bass. This note could easily invaginate this book, for here the native informant changes as fast as the national debt. My "Teaching for the Times," in Jan Nederveen Pieterse and Bhikhu Parekh, eds., *The Decolonizing of the Imagination* (London: Zed, 1995), pp. 177–202, is still pertinent, I think. But one must reconcile oneself to writing for an anthropology of the future.

to establish the institutional study of marginality we must still go on saying "And yet . . ."

Consider Sartre, speaking his commitment just after World War II:

> And, diverse though man's projects [*projets*—this word has the general existentialist sense of undertaking to construct a life] may be, at least none of them is wholly foreign to me. . . . Every project, even that of a Chinese, an Indian or a Negro, can be understood by a European. . . . The European of 1945 can throw himself [pro-ject] out of a situation which he conceives towards his limits [*se jeter à partir d'une situation qu'il conçoit vers ses limites*] in the same way, and . . . he may redo [*refaire*] in himself the project of the Chinese, of the Indian or the African . . . There is always some way of understanding an idiot, a child, a primitive man or a foreigner *if one has sufficient information*.[83]

Sartre's personal and political good faith cannot be doubted. Yet, commenting on Sartre's anthropologizing of Heidegger, Derrida wrote in 1968: "Everything occurs as if the sign 'man' had no origin, no historical, cultural, or linguistic limit."[84] Indeed, if one looks at the rhetorical trace of Rome in "none of [man's projects] is wholly alien to me" [*humani nil a me alienum puto* (Terence via the *philosophes*)], one realizes that the history obliterated here is that of the arrogance of the radical European humanist conscience, which will consolidate it*self* by imagining the other, or, as Sartre puts it, "redo in himself the other's project," through the collection of information. Much of our literary critical globalism or Third Worldism cannot even qualify to the conscientiousness of this arrogance.

The opposite point of view, although its political importance cannot be denied, that only the marginal can speak for the margin, can, in its institutional consequences, legitimize such an arrogance of conscience. Faced with this double bind, let us consider a few methodological suggestions:

---

83. Sartre, *Existentialism and Humanism*, tr. Philip Mairet (New York: Haskell House, 1948), pp. 46–47. Translation modified.

84. Derrida, "The Ends of Man," in *Margins*, p. 116. He has since written on Heidegger's philosophical complicity with Nazism in *Of Spirit*.

1. Let us learn to distinguish between "internal colonization"—the patterns of exploitation and domination of disenfranchised groups within a metropolitan country like the United States or Britain—and the colonization of other spaces, of which Robinson Crusoe's island is a "pure" example.[85]
2. Let us learn to discriminate the terms *colonialism*—in the European formation stretching from the mid-eighteenth to the mid-twentieth centuries *neocolonialism*—dominant economic, political, and culturalist maneuvers emerging in our century after the uneven dissolution of the territorial empires—and *postcoloniality*—the contemporary global condition, since the first term is supposed to have passed or be passing into the second.
3. Let us take seriously the possibility that systems of representation come to hand when we secure our *own* culture—our own cultural explanations. Consider the following set:
   a. The making of an American is defined by at least a desire to enter the "We the People" of the Constitution. One cannot dismiss this as mere "essentialism" and take a position against civil rights, the Equal Rights Amendment, or the transformative opinions in favor of women's reproductive rights. We in the United States cannot not want to inhabit this rational abstraction.
   b. Traditionally, this desire for the abstract collective American "We the People" has been recoded by the fabrication of ethnic enclaves, affectively bonded subcultures, simulacra for survival that, claiming to preserve the ethnos of origin, move further and further away from the vicissitudes and transformations of the nation or group of origin. "How seriously can we [Africans] take . . . [Alice Walker's] Africa, which reads like an overlay of South Africa over a vaguely realized Nigeria?"[86]

---

85. For internal colonization, see Amin, *Unequal Development* p. 369; Philip S. Foner and George E. Walker, *Proceedings of the Black National and State Conventions, 1865–1900* (Philadelphia: Temple Univ. Press, 1986); Cherríe Moraga, *The Last Generation* (Boston: South End Press, 1993).

86. J. M. Coetzee, "The Beginnings of (Wo)man in Africa," *New York Times Book Review*, 30 Apr. 1989.

c. Our current tendency to obliterate the difference between U.S. internal colonization and the transformations and vicissitudes in decolonized space in the name of the pure native invests this already established ethnocultural agenda. At worst, it secures the "They" of development or aggression against the Constitutional "We." At best, it suits our institutional convenience, bringing the Third World home. The double standard can then begin to operate.[87]

In the face of the double bind of Eurocentric arrogance or unexamined nativism, the suggestions above are substantive. Deconstructive cautions would put a critical frame almost around them (we can never be fully critical) and in between them, so that we do not compound the problem by imagining the double bind too easily resolved. In fact, and in the most practical way, double binds are less dangerously enabling than the unilaterality of dilemmas solved. Thus, if we keep in mind only the substantive suggestions, we might want to help ourselves by a greater effort at historical contextualization. Yet this too, if unaccompanied by the habit of critical reading, may feed the Eurocentric arrogance in Sartre's declaration: "there is always some way of understanding [the other] if one has sufficient information." The necessarily open critical frame reminds us that the institutional organization of historical context is no more than *our* unavoidable starting point. The question remains: With this necessary preparation, to quote Sartre again, *how* does "the European"—or, in the neocolonial context, the U.S. critic and teacher of the humanities—"redo *in himself* [or herself] the project of the Chinese, of the Indian or the African?"

In the face of *this* question, deconstruction might propose a double gesture: Begin where you are; but, when in search of absolute justifications, remember that the margin as such is the impossible boundary marking off the wholly other, and the encounter with the wholly other, as it may be figured, has an unpredictable relationship to our ethical rules. The named marginal is as much a concealment as a disclosure of the margin, and where s/he discloses, s/he is singular. This double

87. The last few paragraphs are a self-citation from "Scattered Speculations on the Question of Cultural Studies," in Spivak, *Outside*, pp. 278–279.

gesture informs the remark made in 1968 at a philosophical colloquium: "I was thinking, first of all, of all those places—cultural, linguistic, political, etc.—where the organization of a philosophical
colloquium simply would have no meaning, where it would be no more
meaningful to instigate it than to prohibit it."[88]

To meditate on the figuration of the wholly other as margin, I will
look at a novel in English, *Foe*, by a white South African, J. M.
Coetzee.[89] This novel reopens two English texts in which the early
eighteenth century tried to constitute marginality: Daniel Defoe's *Robinson Crusoe* (1719) and *Roxana* (1724).[90] In *Crusoe*, the white man marginalized in the forest encounters Friday the savage in the margin. In
Roxana, the individualist female infiltrates nascent bourgeois society. In
Coetzee's novel, a double gesture is performed. In the narrative, Roxana begins her construction of the marginal where she is, but when her
project approaches fulfillment, the text steps in and reminds us that
Friday is in the margin as such, the placeholder (*lieutenant*) of the
wholly other, the figure that makes impossibility visible.

I use the novel as a didactic aid to share with my students some of the
problems of which I have been writing. For the substantive provision of
what may be called a historical context, I use Derek Attridge's "Oppressive Silence: J. M. Coetzee's *Foe* and the Politics of the Canon."[91] My
reading attempts to supplement his. It attends to the rhetorical conduct
of the text as the latter stages writing and reading. It is my hope that
such attention would point out that the traditional historically contex-
tualized interpretation might produce closures that are as problematic
as they are reasonable and satisfactory, that "the danger to which the
sovereign decision [of the traditional historical critic] responds is un-

---

88. Derrida, "Ends of Man," pp. 112–113.
89. J. M. Coetzee, *Foe* (New York: Viking, 1987).
90. Daniel Defoe, *Robinson Crusoe: An Authoritative Text/Backgrounds/Sources/
Criticism*, ed. Michael Shinagel (New York: Norton, 1975), hereafter cited in text as
RC; and Daniel Defoe, *Roxana: The Fortunate Mistress*, ed. Jane Jack (Oxford: Oxford Univ. Press, 1964), hereafter cited in text as *R*.
91. In Karen R. Lawrence, ed., *Decolonizing Tradition: New Views of Twentieth-
Century "British" Literary Canons* (Urbana: Univ. of Illinois Press, 1992), pp. 212–
238.

decidability."[92] Notwithstanding all the legalistic efforts of literary criticism, literature remains singular and unverifiable.

Coetzee's novel figures the singular and unverifiable margin, the refracting barrier over against the wholly other that one assumes in the dark.[93] The native informant disappears in that shelter.[94]

If we want to start something, we must ignore that our starting point is, *all efforts taken,* shaky. If we want to get something done, we must ignore that, *all provisions made,* the end will be inconclusive. This ignoring is not an active forgetfulness; it is, rather, an active *marginalizing* of the marshiness, the swampiness, the lack of firm grounding in the margins, at beginning and end. Those of us who "know" this also know that it is in those margins that philosophy philosophizes. These necessarily and actively marginalized margins haunt what we start and get done, as curious guardians. Paradoxically, if we do not marginalize them but make them the center of our attention, they slip away and nothing gets done. Perhaps *some* of the problems with *some* of what is recognizably deconstructive has been a seeming fixation with the stalled origin and the stalled end; many names for *différance* and *aporia.* Derrida's work on the ethical, on justice and the gift, faces those problems.[95] Here let me say a cruder thing: if we forget the productive unease that what we do with the utmost care is judged in the margins, in the political field one

---

92. Werner Hamacher, "Journals, Politics: Notes on Paul de Man's Wartime Journalism," in *Responses: On Paul de Man's Wartime Journalism,* ed. Werner Hamacher et al. (Lincoln: Univ. of Nebraska Press, 1989), p. 439.

93. In 1972, Derrida published his *Marges: De la philosophie* (Paris: Minuit). I was taken by the caesura (here represented by the conventional colon) in his title. In *De la grammatologie,* Derrida let the title stand by itself. Five years later, a cannier Derrida stuck the word "margins" before a comparably structured title: *de la philosophie.* The obvious conjectures: I, the philosopher, philosophize in the margins; philosophy has its curious being in the margins; here I philosophize in an unauthorized way, attending to margins; and others, crowd the mind. The absent word is "margin" in the singular.

94. In 1987–88, at the English Institute presentation, I had taken shelter in the crudely non-philosophical outskirts of what seemed the deconstructive enclosure. With exquisite detail, deconstruction overtook me.

95. In "Force of Law," *Given Time, Gift of Death, Aporias* and *passim* (as they say); see Appendix.

gets the liberal pluralism of repressive tolerance and sanctioned ignorance, and varieties of fundamentalism, totaliarianism, and cultural
revolution; and in the field of writing about and teaching literature, one
gets the benign or resentful conservatism of the establishment *and* the
multiculturalist masquerade of the privileged as the disenfranchised, or
their liberator, both anchored in a lack of respect for the singularity and
unverifiability of "literature as such."

This is marginal in the general sense, no more and no less than a
formula for doing things: the active and necessary marginalization of
the strange guardians in the margin who keep us from vanguardism.
The marginal in the narrow sense are the victims of the best-known
history of centralization: the emergence of the straight white christian
man of property as the ethical subject. Because there is something like a
relationship between the general and the narrow sense, the problem of
making a margin in the house of feminism can be stated in another way.
In her influential and by now classic essay "The Laugh of the Medusa,"
Hélène Cixous writes: "As subject *for* history, woman occurs simultaneously in several places."[96] This can be taken to mean that, in a historical
narrative in which single male figures or groups of men are definitive,
woman or women as such cannot fit neatly into the established periodizing rubrics or categories. Maximally, as Cixous goes on to point out,
this might also mean that the feminist woman becomes part of every
struggle, *in a certain way*.

Academic U.S. feminism has not really been part of every struggle.
But today's increasing interest in multiculturalist or postcolonial marginality, in marginality in the narrow sense, is a straw in the globalizing
wind within feminism in the academy. The exuberance of this interest
sometimes overlooks a problem: that a concern with women, *and* men,
who have not been written in the *same* cultural inscription (a working
hypothesis that works well in colonial situations), cannot be mobilized
in the same way as the investigation of gendering in one's own. It is not
impossible, but new ways have to be learned and taught, and attention
to the margin in general must be persistently renewed. We understand

---

96. Hélène Cixous, "The Laugh of the Medusa," in Elaine Marks and Isabelle de
Courtivron, eds., *New French Feminisms: An Anthology* (Amherst: Univ. of Massachusetts Press, 1980), p. 252.

it more easily when folks of the other *gender* inscription wish to join in our struggle. For example, given the history of centuries of patriarchal privilege—including malevolence *and* benevolence toward women—I confess to a certain unease—not prohibitive obviously—celebrating a man's text about a woman. Yet, when we want to intervene in the heritage of colonialism or the practice of neocolonialism, we take our goodwill for our guarantee.

On the threshold of Coetzee's reading of *The Life and Adventures of Robinson Crusoe* stands Marx's paragraph on Defoe's novel.[97] It is usually taken to be about capitalism, but this is in fact not so. The main drift of Marx's chapter in which the paragraph occurs is that in generalized commodity production, the commodity has a fetish character. It represents the relationship between persons as a relationship between things. In modes of production other than capitalist, this fetish character disappears. Marx chooses four examples, three precapitalist and one post. Of the three precapitalist examples, Robinson is the first and most interesting because the other two are situations of exchange, although not of generalized commodity exchange. Robinson's example is the production of use-values.

Romantic anti-capitalism produces cozy axiomatics: use good, exchange bad; use concrete, exchange abstract; et cetera. But in fact use-value and exchange-value are, for Marx, forms of appearance [*Erscheinungsformen*]. And, if the magnitude of value is to be measured, whether in use or exchange, the only way to do it is by abstract average labor. The empirical fact that one usually does not need to measure the magnitude of value of a thing one is going to use immediately makes no difference here: "A use-value, or good [*Gut*], therefore, has value only because abstract human labor is objectified [*vergegenständlicht*] or materialized in it."[98] Marx's great example of this is Robinson. His critique of political economists including Ricardo is that they read it as literary commentators on *Robinson Crusoe* think Marx read it; applying capitalist standards.

---

97. Marx, *Capital*, 1:169–170. Unless otherwise indicated, all passages from Marx are taken from these two pages.
98. Ibid., p. 129.

Marx is not interested in the novel, and all the English translations hide this by rendering his introduction of Robinson as: "Let us first look at Robinson on his island." Rather is the character of Robinson for Marx a form of appearance of man in nature, able to calculate abstract average labor because the labor is all his own: "Let Robinson first appear on his island," writes Marx. In his situation, of man in nature, Robinson already of "necessity" thinks abstract labor. Marx is teaching the worker the counter-intuitive lesson that the complicity of use- and exchange-*value* shows that the private is measured by and contains within it the possibility of the social. The seemingly concrete individual is predicated by the possibility of abstraction:[99] "He knows that . . . the activity of one and the same Robinson . . . consists of nothing but different modes of human labor . . . all the relations between Robinson and the objects . . . of his own creation, are here . . . simple and clear . . . and yet . . . contain all the essential determinants of value." Time, rather than money, is Robinson's general equivalent. I touch this base before I enter *Foe* because, in my reading, Coetzee's book seems interested in space rather than time, as it stages the difficulties of a timekeeping investigation before a space that will not yield its inscription.[100]

Marx does not (perhaps cannot) use Robinson in his form of appearance as a simple colonist, as Coetzee must. *Foe* is more about spacing and displacement than about the timing of labor. Just as the Jamaican white Jean Rhys's rewriting of the nineteenth-century English classic *Jane Eyre* does not find Jane useful as the paradigm of the feminist norm, so does the South African white's rewriting of an eighteenth-century classic not find Crusoe useful as the normative man in nature making visible a constitutive chronometry. This Crusoe bequeathes a lightly

---

99. I have discussed this at much greater length in Spivak, "Scattered Speculations on the Question of Value," in *In Other Worlds*, pp. 154–175, and "Limits and Openings of Marx in Derrida," in *Outside*, pp. 97–119.

100. Reading *Robinson* as a book for Europe, one could not do better than Pierre Macherey's study in *Theory of Literary Production*, tr. Geoffrey Wall (New York: Methuen, 1978); and Michel de Certeau, *Heterologies: Discourse on the Other*, tr. Brian Massumi (Minneapolis: Univ. of Minnesota Press, 1986). Both of these studies emphasize timing.

inscribed space to an indefinite future: "'The planting is not for us,' said he. 'We have nothing to plant—that is our misfortune. . . . The planting is reserved for those who come after us and have the foresight to bring seed. I only clear the ground for them'" (F 33). The theme of the transition from land to landed capital is, after all, only *one* important strand of the mission of imperialism.

Foe's Crusoe has no interest in keeping time. Indeed, the narrator of *Foe*, who is *not* Crusoe, "search[es] the poles . . . but [finds] no carvings, not even notches to indicate that he counted the years of his banishment or the cycles of the moon" (*Foe* 16). She begs him to keep a record, but he resolutely refuses. Although produced by merchant capitalism, Crusoe has no interest in being its agent, not even to the extent of saving tools. Coetzee's focus is on gender and empire, rather than the story of capital.

Who is this female narrator of *Robinson Crusoe?* We know that the original had no room for women. There was the typecast mother, the benevolent widow whose rôle it was to play the benevolent widow, the nameless wife who was married and died in the conditional mode in one sentence so that Crusoe could leave for the East Indies in the very year of the founding of the Bank of England; and last but not least, the "seven women" he sent at the end of the story, "being such as I found proper for service, or for wives to such as would take them," together with "five cows, three of them being big with calf" (*RC* 237). So who is this female narrator? It is time to tabulate some of the ways in which Coetzee alters Defoe as he cites him.

First, consider the title. We know of course that Foe is Defoe's proper patronymic. He was born the son of James and Ann Foe. But in restoring this proper name—and, therefore, by implication the *real* book by the *real* author—Coetzee also makes it a common noun. Whose Foe is Mr. Foe? Let the question hang for now.

The narrator of *Foe* is an Englishwoman named Susan Barton, who wants to "father" her story into history, with Mr. Foe's help. Coetzee has trouble negotiating a gendered position; he and the text strain to make the trouble noticeable. This text will not defend itself against the undecidability and discomfort of imagining a woman. Is that authoritative word *father* being turned into a false but useful analogy (catachresis) here? Or is Coetzee's Susan being made to operate that traditional masculist topos of reversal (that we have seen in *Frankenstein*) and making Foe "gestate"? We cannot know. As Attridge points out, there is talk of "free choice" in *Foe*.

At any rate, Susan Barton has written a title, *The Female Castaway*, as well as a memoir and many letters, and sent them to Mr. Foe, not all of which have arrived at their destination.[101] "More is at stake in the history you write, I will admit, for it must not only tell the truth about us but please the readers too. Will you not bear in mind, however, that my life is drearily suspended till your writing is done?" (*Foe* 63). What happens to *The Female Castaway?* Susan Barton begins the novel with quotation marks, a self-citation: "At last I could row no further" (*Foe* 5). This first part—the story of the discovery of Crusoe and Friday, Crusoe's death on board ship on the trip back to England, and her arrival in England with Friday—is her memoirs. As for her history, it is either the book *Robinson Crusoe* or the book *Foe*, we cannot know now. At this point, it is simply the mark of the citation and alteration that is every reading, an allegory of the guardian that watches over all claims to demonstrate the truth of a text by quotation. At the beginning of the text is a quotation with no fixed origin.

Before the story of fathering can go any further, a strange sequence intervenes. It is as if the margins of bound books are themselves dissolved into a general textuality. Coetzee makes the final episode of Defoe's novel *Roxana* flow into this citation of *Robinson Crusoe*. Coetzee's Susan Barton is also Defoe's Roxana, whose first name is Susan. (There are other incidental similarities.)

Because Crusoe and Susan/Roxana are made to inhabit the same text, we are obliged to ask a further question: What happens when the unequal balance of gender determination in the representation of the marginal is allowed to tip?

The male marginal in the early eighteenth-century imagination can be the solitary contemplative christian, earning the right to imperialist soul-making even as he is framed by the dynamic narrative of mercantile capitalism elsewhere. The female marginal is the *exceptional* entrepreneurial woman for whom the marriage contract is an inconvenience

---

101. To thicken the thematics of sexual difference here, one might look at Derrida, "The Purveyor of Truth," in *The Post Card*, pp. 411–496. What happens when letters do not arrive at their destination?

when the man is a fool. (A century and a half later, Tillie Olsen wrote the poignant tragedy of an exceptional revolutionary woman married to a bewildered, merely "normally" patriarchal man.)[102] Not only because of Defoe's own patriarchal production but also because of the conventions of the picaresque, his heroine must be a rogue—a social marginal finally centralizing herself through marriage. In this enterprise, she *uses* the money *held* by men as aristocrats, *made* by men as merchants; *and* she uses her sexuality as labor power.

In the presentation of this narrative, Defoe has at least two predictable problems that raise important questions about principles and the dissimulation of principle as well as about the negotiability of all commitments through the production and coding of value.

First: the relationship between principles and the *dissimulation* of principles. Defoe cannot make his Roxana utter her passion for woman's freedom except as a ruse for her real desire to own, control, and manage money:

> tho' I could give up my Virtue . . . yet I wou'd not give up my Money, which, tho' it was true, yet was really too gross for me to acknowledge . . . I was oblig'd to give a new Turn to it, and talk upon a kind of an elevated strain . . . as follows: I told him, I had, perhaps, differing Notions of Matrimony, from what the receiv'd Custom had given us of it; that I thought a Woman was a free Agent, as well as a Man, and was born free, and cou'd she manage herself suitably, may enjoy that Liberty to as much purpose as Men do. (*RC* 147)

Second: the representation of the affective value of mothering when contrasted with the destiny of female individualism. Susan Suleiman has recently discussed the immense ramifications of this binary opposition in "Writing and Motherhood."[103] I will add a theoretical explanation of Defoe's problem of representation: Sexuality used as labor power outside of the institution of marriage (not only in the British early eighteenth century, and not only among the bourgeoisie) pro-

---

102. Tillie Olsen, *Tell Me a Riddle* (New York: Peter Smith, 1986).
103. In Shirley Nelson Gamer et al., eds., *The (M)other Tongue: Essays in Feminist Psychoanalytic Interpretation* (Ithaca: Cornell Univ. Press, 1985), pp. 352–377.

duces children as commodities that cannot be legitimately exchanged and may produce an affective value that cannot be fully coded. Surrogacy has made this visible in our time.

I think it is for rather an important reason that none of these issues is quite relevant for Coetzee: *He* is involved in a historically implausible but politically provocative revision. He attempts to represent the bourgeois individualist woman in early capitalism as the *agent* of *other-directed* ethics rather than as a combatant in the preferential ethics of self-interest; as the counterfigure to Jane Eyre, as a strictured complication of Kipling's William. She is a subject *for* history. It is therefore she who is involved in the construction of the marginal—both Cruso (Coetzee's spelling) and Friday, *and* herself as character—as object of knowledge. The rhetoric of *Foe*, especially the last section, shows that as such an agent, she is also the instrument of defense against undecidability. This is the liability of the peculiarly European "sense of responsibility for the human conscience."[104]

Thus, for Coetzee, the basic theme of marriage and sexuality, freed on the island from heavy historical determination, becomes a radical counterfactual: the woman giving pleasure, without the usual affective charge, *as* use-value, *in* need. Thus also, Defoe's problem of the dissimulation of the desire for liberty as a ruse for control of money is ennobled in *Foe* into the *full* if unrecognized, unacknowledged, and undeveloped capitalist agency that we have already noticed: Susan's longing for "freedom of choice in writing her history," Susan's desire to use *time* as the general equivalent, begging Cruso to mark time, dating her own section of the book meticulously, indeed, at first living on Clock Lane; and, the problem of representation of the affective value of mothering as opposed to the ambitions of possessive female individualism is dismissed by Coetzee's Susan Barton as Mr. Foe's ideas of a woman's dilemma, as merely "father-born."

If we take the open-ended double-value or abyssality of *Father* under advisement here, a decision is not easy to make. "Without venturing up to that perilous necessity," let us decide that the problem is recast from

---

104. Zbigniew Herbert, cited in Shula Marks, ed., *Not Either an Experimental Doll: The Separate Lives of Three South African Women* (Bloomington: Indiana Univ. Press, 1987), epigraph.

the point of view of the feminist as agent, trying at once to rescue mothering from the European patriarchal coding and the "native" from the colonial account.[105] From the point of view of an other-directed ethico-politics, in this mother-daughter subplot, Coetzee marks an aporia.

Susan Barton had gone to Bahia Blanca to search for her daughter and had been shipwrecked on Crusoe's island on her way back. (Although Defoe's Roxana is a great traveler in the Northwest European world looking forward to the turmoil of the transition from mercantile and commercial capital, she does not venture into the new cartography of the space of conquest.) Now a woman who claims to be her daughter haunts her footsteps and wants to be reclaimed. Susan Barton cannot recognize her as her lost daughter, however, and tries to get rid of her in many ways. She is convinced that this encounter and pursuit are Foe's fabrication. (Attridge clues us into the "historical" Defoe's contribution to this scenario.) We cannot be convinced of this explanation. By everyday common sense, Susan Barton's credibility or sanity would here be thrown in doubt. But what place does credibility or verifiability have in this book (or in "literature"), a real or imagined citation of Defoe's real book and Barton's unreal one, in a way that resembles the dream's "citation" of waking reality? I am suggesting that here the book may be gesturing toward the impossibility of restoring the history of empire and recovering the lost text of mothering *in the same register of language*. It is true that we are each of us overdetermined, part historian, part mother, and many other determinations besides. But overdetermination can itself be disclosed when the condensed rebus in the dream has been straightened out in analytical prose. Because of this dislocation, there can be no politics founded on a continuous overdetermined multiplicity of agencies. It is merely defensive to dress up the strategic desirability of alliance politics and conscientious pluralism in the continuous space opened up by socialized capital in the language of undecidability and plurality. In the middle of *Foe*, the mysterious expul-

---

105. To be aware of perilous necessities and not to venture up to them is an early version of the active marginalization of the margin. See Derrida, *Grammatology*, pp. 74–75 and Appendix.

sion of the daughter can be read as marking this aporia. (In "Shibboleth," Derrida takes Paul Celan's citation of the cry from February 1936, the eve of the Spanish Civil war—*No pasaran*—and translates it, strictly, as *aporia*.)[106] One cannot pass through an aporia. Yet Franco did pass through. Celan's poem stands guardian, marking the date, 13 February 1936, reminder of a history that did not happen. The main narrative of *Foe* passes through this obstinate sequence—bits of fiction that cannot articulate as a story.) Susan Barton lures her strange daughter into the heart of Epping Forest and tells her, "You are father-born. What you know of your parentage comes to you in the form of stories, and the stories have but a single source" (*Foe* 91). Yet this too could be a dream. "What do I mean by it, father-born?" Susan asks herself in the letter in which she recounts this to Foe. "I wake in the grey of a London dawn with the word still faintly in my eyes . . . Have I expelled her, lost her at last in the forest?" But is a dream contained in a dream citation a loss of authority? This first severing is not neat. Susan writes Foe again: "I must tell you of a dead stillborn girl-child" she unwraps in a ditch some miles out of Marlborough: "Try though I might, I could not put from my thoughts the little sleeper who would never awake, the pinched eyes that would never see the sky, the curled fingers that would never open. Who was the child but I, in another life?" (*Foe* 105). I read "in another life" as, also, another story, another register, and pass on to more plausible explanations offered by this text, where plausibility is plural.

We could ourselves "explain" this curious sequence in various ways. We could fault Coetzee for not letting a woman have free access to both authorship and motherhood. We could praise him for not presuming to speak a completed text on motherhood. I would rather save the book, call it the mark of *aporia* in the center, and teach my students something about the impossibility of a political program founded on overdetermination.[107]

---

106. Derrida, "Shibboleth," in Attridge, ed., *Acts*, p. 399f. See also the somewhat different earlier version, as translated in *Midrash and Literature*, ed. Geoffrey H. Hartman and Sanford Budick (New Haven: Yale Univ. Press, 1986), pp. 307–347.

107. Although this phrase is not coined by them, the enablement for this program is generally sought in Laclau and Mouffe, *Hegemony and Socialist Strategy*. By contrast, Louis Althusser's "Contradiction and Overdetermination," in *For Marx*, tr. Ben Brewster (New York: Vintage, 1969), is more about theory than strategy.

In the frame of this peculiar aporia, the decision to keep or reject the mother-daughter story is presented in terms of the making of narratives. First, Susan is imagined as imagining Foe imagining the history of *The Female Castaway*. In my reading, these imaginings may signify no more than Defoe's idea of a woman's dilemma, here thematized as Foe's problem in writing the story. At first, Susan Barton imagines a rejection: "I write my letters, I seal them, I drop them in the box. One day when we are departed you will tip them out and glance through them. 'Better had there been only Cruso and Friday.' You will murmur to yourself: 'Better without the woman.' Yet where would you be without woman? . . . Could you have made up Cruso and Friday and the island . . . ? I think not. Many strengths you have, but invention is not one of them" (*Foe* 71–72).

These musings describe Daniel Defoe's *Robinson Crusoe* as we have it today, without the woman as inventor and progenitor. Yet in Coetzee's story, it is described as a road not taken. The actual is presented as the counterfactual. Defoe's *Robinson Crusoe*, which engenders *Foe*, does not exist.

Next, when Susan meets Foe, he tries to question her on the details of the plot. It is a long series of questions, and Foe supplies the answers himself and tells her the structure of his storying of *The Female Castaway*:

> "We therefore have five parts in all: The loss of the daughter; the quest for the daughter in Brazil; abandonment of the quest, and the adventure of the island; assumption of the quest by the daughter; and reunion of the daughter with the mother. It is thus that we make up a book: loss, then quest, then recovery; beginning, then middle, then end. As to novelty, this is lent by the island episode—which is properly the second part of the middle—and by the reversal in which the daughter takes up the quest abandoned by her mother. . . . the island is not a story in itself," said Foe gently. (*Foe* 117)

We do not read this projected novel in *Foe*. I should like to think that, in terms of *textual* strategy, Coetzee's text makes (De)foe's book share its own concerns. My previous remarks on the formal peculiarities of the mother-daughter subplot carried the implication that feminism (within "the same" cultural inscription) and anticolonialism (for or against racial "others") cannot occupy a continuous (narrative) space.

Here, Mr. Foe is made to take a similar decision within his framework of *structural* strategy. The island is the central story of both the real *Robinson Crusoe* and this fictive projected *Female Castaway*. In the former, the frame narrative is capitalism and colony. In the latter, it would be the mother-daughter story. The two cannot occupy a continuous space. Susan Barton tries to break the binary opposition by broaching the real margin that has been haunting the text since its first page. The stalling of that breaching or broaching *is* the story of *Foe:* "'In the letters that you did not read,' I said, 'I told you of my conviction that, if the story seems stupid, that is becuse it so doggedly holds its silence. The shadow whose lack you feel is there: it is the loss of Friday's tongue'" (*Foe* 117).

In *Foe*, Friday's tongue has been cut off—by slavers, says Robinson. (Attridge provides the "real" detail of Coetzee's answer to this in an interview, a genre that is generated to bring undecidability under control.) Susan wants to know him, to give him speech, to learn from him, to father his story, which will also be her story: the account of her anguish as Friday grows dull in London; her longing for Friday's desire and her exasperation at herself; the orchestration of her desire to construct Friday as subject so that he can be her informant, cannot be summarized. She asks Friday to explain the origin of his loss through a few pictures. She must recognize with chagrin that her picture of Robinson possibly cutting out his tongue, "might also be taken to show Cruso as a beneficent father putting a lump of fish into the mouth of child Friday" (*Foe* 68–69). Each picture fails this way. The unrepeatability of the unique event can only be repeated imperfectly. And then, "who was to say there do not exist entire tribes in Africa among whom the men are mute and speech is reserved to women?" (*Foe* 69). Who, indeed? Susan is at her wit's end. That too is a margin. When she "begins to turn in Friday's dance," it is not a *con*-versation—a turning together—for "Friday is sluggishly asleep on a hurdle behind the door" (*Foe* 104). But her project remains to "give a voice" to Friday: "The story of Friday's tongue is a story unable to be told, or unable to be told by me. That is to say, many stories can be told of Friday's tongue, but the true story is buried within Friday, who is mute. The true story will not be heard till by art we have found a means of giving voice to Friday" (*Foe* 118). Where is the guarantee of this techno-scientific vision? ("Art" is also "artifice," "prosthesis.") Where indeed is the guarantee of

Attridge's conviction that Friday is a metaphor for the work of art? Even by old-fashioned rules of reading, is Susan Barton the voice of the book?

Contrast this to Defoe's text. It was noticed rather quickly, after the first publication of *Robinson Crusoe*, that Defoe kept Friday's language acquisition skills at a low level. It is also noticeable that, at their first encounter, "I began to speak to him, and teach him to speak to me" (*RC* 161). Like us, Crusoe does not need to learn to speak to the racial inferior. Of course Crusoe knows the savages have a language. And it is a longstanding topos that barbarians by definition do not speak language. But the contrast here is also between the colonialist—who gives the native speech—and the metropolitan anti-imperialist—who wants to give the native voice. (In the interview cited by Attridge, Coetzee provides the racial difference between Crusoe's and his own Friday. I ask my students to note it, not to make it the way to an unproductive closure.) The last scene in Susan's narrative stands as a warning to both. Before I read it I want to remind ourselves of the last scene involving Friday in *Robinson Crusoe*. Friday is not only the "domesticated anti-type," as John Richetti calls him;[108] he is also the prototype of the successful colonial subject. He learns his master's speech, does his master's work, happily swears loyalty, believes the culture of the master is better, and kills his other self to enter the shady plains of Northwestern Europe: Eurocentric economic migrant. The footsore company have just escaped from wolves. It is bitter cold, the night is advancing. At this point Friday offers to amuse the company with a huge threatening bear, and Robinson quite surprisingly allows him to do so. Friday speaks to the bear *in English*. The bear understands his tone and gestures. Like two blood brothers, they dance in the trees. Finally, Friday kills the bear with a gun in his ear. He has reinscribed his savagery. This is an amusement available to the natives. He makes his masters his spectators and replaces the arrow with the gun. He is on his way out of the margin. If Bertha Mason had to occupy the indeterminate space between human and animal, Crusoe's Friday crosses that space.

Now let us look at the last scene of Friday in Susan's narrative. Foe

---

108. John Richetti, *Defoe's Narratives: Situation and Structures* (Oxford: Clarendon Press, 1975), p. 56.

asks Susan to teach Friday to write. The discussion of speech and writing between these two European principals is of great interest. Susan thinks it is a poor idea but agrees because she "find[s] it thankless to argue" (*Foe* 144). The staging of this errant scene of writing should be examined fully in a classroom reading.

One of the words Barton tries to teach Friday is *Africa*. This effort is rich in meaning and its limits. The metropolitan anti-imperialist cannot teach the native the proper name of his nation or continent. And "[i]t is impossible to distinguish a continent from an island, a peninsula, or a large land mass."[109] *Africa*, a Roman name for what the Greeks called "Libya," itself perhaps a latinization of the name of the Berber tribe Aourigha (perhaps pronounced "Afarika"), is a metonym that points to a great indeterminacy: the mysteriousness of the space upon which we are born. *Africa* is only a timebound naming; like all proper names it is a mark with an arbitrary connection to its referent, a catachresis.[110] The earth as temporary dwelling has no foundational name. Nationalism can only ever be a crucial political agenda against oppression. All longings to the contrary, it cannot provide the absolute guarantee of identity.

This scene of writing may also be an unfinished thematizing of dissemination, where words are losing their mode of existence as semes. "Friday wrote the four letters *h-o-u-s*, or four shapes passably like them: whether they were truly the four letters, and stood truly for the word *house* and the picture I had drawn, and the thing itself, only he knew" (*Foe* 145–146).

At this stage the only letter he seems to be able to reproduce is *h*. *H* is a strange letter in this book—it is the letter of muteness itself. When Crusoe had first shown Friday's loss to Susan,

"La-la-la," said Cruso, and motioned to Friday to repeat. "Ha-ha-ha," said Friday from the back of his throat. "He has no tongue," said

---

109. Chaudhuri, *Asia before Europe*, p. 23. Earlier in the same paragraph we read, "[i]t is easily seen that the identity and the totality of the 'excluded set,' Asia [and, *mutatis mutandis*, Africa], will hold over time only as long as the identity of the 'set of sets,' Europe, is intact."

110. For a brief account of the violence of the timebound naming, see Miller, *Blank Darkness*, pp. 6–14.

Cruso. Gripping Friday by the hair, he brought his face close to mine. "Do you see?" he said. "It is too dark," said I. "La-la-la," said Cruso. "Ha-ha-ha," said Friday. I drew away, and Cruso released Friday's hair. (*Foe* 22–23)

H is the failed echolalia of the mute. All through the book the letter *H* is typographically raised and separated from the line in vague mimicry of eighteenth-century typeface. It is noticeable because no other letter of the alphabet is treated in this way. Is it also a reminder of the alterity of history, a line we cannot cross?

The next day Friday dresses up in Foe's clothes and proceeds to write: a packed series of *os*. "'It is a beginning,' sa[ys] Foe. 'Tomorrow you must teach him *a*'" (*Foe* 152). This is where Susan's narrative ends, with the injunction of a continued writing lesson that never happens. One can of course say that Foe is wrong. It is not a beginning unless one forgets the previous forgetting; and *o* could conceivably be *omega*, the end.

We also remember that in *Robinson Crusoe* "saying *O*" is Friday's pidgin translation of his native word for prayer; and it is around the accounts of praying practices that Robinson shares with us the two negatives of reason. Within natural law what negates reason is *un*reason. Its example is Friday and his tribe's saying "*O*." Within divine law, reason is sublimely negated by revelation. Its example is the inconstancies of Christian doctrine, naively pointed out by Friday. As Susan confesses that she is not a good writing teacher, so does Robinson confess that he is not a good religious instructor, for he cannot make revelation accessible to the merely reasonable savage (*RC* 169–173). In the light of this, it is particularly interesting to notice what Coetzee stages between the inside margins of the first and second days of the writing lesson: "While Foe and I spoke, Friday filled his slate with open eyes, each set upon a human foot: row upon row of eyes: walking eyes. . . . 'Give! Give me the slate, Friday!' I commanded. Whereupon, instead of obeying me, Friday put three fingers into his mouth and wet them with spittle and rubbed the slate clean" (*Foe* 147).

Here is the guardian of the margin. Neither narrative nor text gives pride of place to this bit; miming the active marginalizing of the margin perhaps; but where would such abyssal speculations end? This event changes the course of Foe's and Susan's conversation only to the extent that Susan finally says: "How can Friday know what freedom means when he barely knows his name?" The answers may be in that margin that we cannot penetrate, that we must indeed ignore to go forward.

Are those walking eyes rebuses, hieroglyphs, ideograms, or is their secret that they hold no secret at all? Each scrupulous effort at decoding or deciphering will bring its own rewards; but there is a structural possibility that they are nothing. Even then it would be writing, but that argument has no place here.[111]

It is the withholding that is of interest in terms of Susan Barton's narrative. The night before, Susan had said to Foe: "it is still in my power to guide and amend. Above all, to withhold. By such means do I still endeavor to be father of my story" (*Foe* 123). After this Foe and Susan Barton copulate for the first time.

Yet it is Friday rather than Susan who is the unemphatic agent of withholding in the text. For every territorial space that is value coded by colonialism *and* every command of metropolitan anticolonialism for the native to yield his "voice," there is a space of withholding, marked by a secret that may not be a secret but cannot be unlocked. "The native," whatever that might mean, is not only a victim, but also an agent. The curious guardian at the margin who will not inform.

Benita Parry has criticized Homi Bhabha, Abdul JanMohammed, and Gayatri Spivak for being so enamored of deconstruction that they will not let the native speak.[112] She has forgotten that we are natives too. We talk like Defoe's Friday, only much better. Nearly three hundred years have, after all, passed since Defoe's fabrication of Friday. Territorial imperialism, in the offing then, has given place to neocolonialism and now globalization. Within the broad taxonomy that I am proposing here, and at the time of writing, the murderous project of apartheid kept South Africa caught in that earlier dispensation.[113] It has now

---

111. See Derrida, *Spurs*, tr. Barbara Harlow (Chicago: Univ. of Chicago Press, 1979), pp. 125–128.

112. Benita Parry, "Problems in Current Theories of Colonial Discourse," *Oxford Literary Review* 9 (1987): 27–58.

113. Negotiations with the current conjuncture have led to various internal maneuvers that are beyond the scope of this chapter. David Atwell of the University of Pietermaritzberg has pointed out to me the existence of the notion of a "colonialism of a special type" in South Africa, a colonialism that did not, by and large, export surplus value. He makes the interesting suggestion that this, too, might

entered the decolonized context. I have no doubt that, among the migrant population in metropolitan space, the resistant postcolonial South African will become equally a scandal if s/he seems not to celebrate the native voice with reverent abandon.

Postcolonial persons from formerly colonized countries are able to communicate to each other (and to metropolitans), to exchange, to establish sociality, because we have had access to the so-called culture of imperialism. Shall we then assign to that culture a measure of "moral luck"?[114] I think there can be no doubt that the answer is "no." This impossible "no" to a structure that one critiques yet inhabits intimately is the deconstructive position, of which postcoloniality is a historical case. The neocolonial anticolonialist still longs for the object of a conscientious ethnography, sometimes gender marked for feminism: "where women inscribed themselves as healers, ascetics, singers of sacred songs, artizans and artists."[115]

I have no objection to conscientious ethnography, although I am forewarned by its relationship to the history of the discipline of anthropology. But my particular word to Parry is that her efforts (to give voice to the native) as well as mine (to give warning of the attendant problem) are judged by the strange margins of which Friday with his withholding slate is only a fictive mark. That arbitrary name—Friday—may be "the name of the possibility . . . of keeping a secret that is visible inside [à l'intérieure] but not outside [à l'extérieure]."[116]

Does the book *Foe* recuperate this margin? The last section, narrated by a reader of unspecified gender and date, is a sort of reading lesson that would suggest the opposite. To recover this suggestion, let us turn to Barton and Foe's copulation.

Coetzee plays the register of legible banality with panache. This is

---

explain Coetzee's Cruso's noncommittal attitude toward classic metropolitan interests. I keep to my much less finetuned point of territorial presence—though even there, the difference between settler colonies like South Africa, Australia, Canada, and the United States, and territorial imperialisms on the model of Sub-Saharan Africa, Algeria, India and the like, must be kept in mind.

114. Bernard Williams, *Moral Luck: Philosophical Papers 1973–1980* (Cambridge: Cambridge Univ. Press, 1981), pp. 20–39.

115. Parry, "Problems," p. 35.

116. Derrida, *Gift of Death*, p. 108.

the second take on the misfiring of the mother-daughter story. Susan's supposed daughter is present earlier in the evening. The scene is put to rest by these noticeably unremarkable words: "Her appearances, or apparitions, or whatever they were, disturbed me less now that I knew her better" (*Foe* 136). Foe detains Barton with a seducer's touch. In bed she claims "'a privilege that comes with the first night.' . . . Then I drew off my shift and straddled him (which he did not seem easy with, in a woman). 'This is the manner of the Muse when she visits her poets,' I whispered" (*Foe* 139).

In the pleasant pause after this musing-cum-fathering, an act that is also a deliberately staged scene of (future) writing (rather different from Friday's withheld writing), Susan grows drowsy, and Foe speaks, unexpectedly, of sea monsters; and resumes, "to us [Friday] leaves the task of descending into that eye [across which he rows and is safe]" (*Foe* 141).

It is this sea monster, an image engendered in the representation of the primal scene of writing but also dredged up from *The Tempest*, a play repeatedly read as a representation of the colonizer-colonized dialectic, that allows the indeterminate reader, the central character of this last section, to descend into "Friday's home."[117] In other words, this reading knits itself into Susan's scene of strange fathering, leaving Friday's writing lesson apart.

"At one corner of the house, above head-height, a plaque is bolted to the wall. *Daniel Defoe, Author*, are the words, white on blue, and then more writing too small to read" (*F* 155). We have seen these plaques in London. Defoe is dead and memorialized, but the dates are too small to read.

Under the name of the dead father, we enter and discover Susan Barton's book, unpublished. The topmost leaf crumbles. Then the reader reads the self-quotation that opens *Foe*, now properly addressed: "Dear Mr. Foe." Clear textual signals for a controlled reading.

The quotation marks disappear, and the reader is staged as filling the subject position, for Barton's text continues. This is easy reading. Nothing is cited, everything is at once real and fantastic, all the permis-

---

117. Attridge points at many echoes of *The Tempest* in *Foe*. See also Rob Nixon, "Caribbean and African Appropriations of *The Tempest*," in Robert von Hallenberg, ed., *Politics and Poetic Value* (Chicago: Univ. of Chicago Press, 1987), pp. 185–206.

sive indulgences of narrative fiction in the narrow sense are available to the reader, who is the sole shifter on this trip. The ride is smooth, the trip leads not to Crusoe's island but to the second wreck, where Susan Barton lies fat and dead. *Robinson Crusoe* has not been written, and *Foe* is annulled, for now Barton will not reach Crusoe's island. Friday is affirmed to be there, the margin caught in the empire of signs. "This is a place where bodies are their own signs. It is the home of Friday" (*Foe* 157). We must deny all that has come before in the book not to ask: What is the guarantee of this confidence?

For *this* end, texts are porous. They go through to wish fulfillment. Yet we also know that Coetzee's entire book warns that Friday's body is not its own sign. In this end, which I can read as the staging of the wish to invade the margin, the seaweeds seem to sigh: if only there were no texts. The end is written lovingly, and we will not give it up. But we cannot hold together, in a continuous narrative space, the voyage of reading at the end of the book, Susan Barton's narrative, and the withheld slate of the native who will not be an informant.

Perhaps that is the novel's message: the impossible politics of overdetermination (mothering, authoring, giving voice to the native "in" the text; a white male South African writer engaging in such inscriptions "outside" the text) should not be regularized into a blithe continuity, where the European redoes the primitive's project in herself. It can, however, lead to a scrupulously differentiated politics, depending on "where you are." Coetzee's text can be taught as:

1. correcting Defoe's imagination of the marginal, in comradeship
2. reinscribing the white woman as agent, as the asymmetrical double of the author. (Perhaps the problems with the figure of "fathering" mark this asymmetry)
3. situating the politics of overdetermination as aporia
4. halting before Friday, since for Coetzee, here, now, *and* for Susan Barton, *and* for Daniel Foe, that is the arbitrary name of the withheld limit.

At first I had wanted to end with the following sentence: Mr. Foe is everyone's Foe, the enabling violator, for without him there is nothing to cite. A month after finishing with writing, I heard Derrida's paper on friendship.[118] I want to say now that this *Foe*, in history, is the site where the line between friend and foe is undone. When one wants to be a friend to the other, it withdraws its graphematic space. Foe allows that story to be told.

It is no doubt because I heard and read Derrida's pieces on friendhsip and margins and read Bernard Williams's "Moral Luck" that I could work out this didactic exercise. I know that Stanley Fish has no objections to accepting the consequences of *reading* theory.[119] Theory itself has no *con*-sequence. It is autosequential rather than automatic. Theory is the production of theory, lost in its setting to work. It is always withdrawn from that open end, as it is from that which it wants to theorize. Theory is a bit like Mr. Foe, always off the mark, yet it is what we undo in work. Without it, nothing but the wished-for inarticulation of the natural body: "a slow stream, without breath, without interruption," betrayed by the spacing of the words that wish it (*Foe* 157).

I should hope that my students would keep this duplicitous agent of active marginalizing—theory, our friend Foe—in mind as they read interventionist writing ("fiction" and "nonfiction") with informed sympathy. Mongane Serote's *To Every Birth Its Blood* is an example of interventionist fiction not "necessarily directed at the elite international readership"—ourselves—"addressed by South African writers such as J. M. Coetzee and Nadine Gordimer." *Not Either an Experimental Doll: The Separate Lives of Three South African Women* is the "nonfiction" account of the unavoidable thwarting (in the middle of our century, by a metropolitan white anticolonialist activist woman and a successful black colonial female subject, both anxious to help) of the native seeking (rather than withholding) agency, Lily Moya, a poor Christian orphan "Bantu" woman in her teens.[120]

---

118. Derrida, "The Politics of Friendship," tr. Gabriel Motzkin and Michael Syrotinski, *American Imago* 50.3 (fall 1993): 353–391. It has subsequently been expanded and published in book form as *The Politics of Friendship*, tr. George Collins (New York: Verso, 1997). I am referring to my experience of hearing the oral presentation of the first. There is a good footnote on the "modern rehabilitation of the word *foe*" on p. 109 (n. 13) of the published book.

119. Stanley Fish, "Consequences," in *Doing What Comes Naturally* (Durham: Duke Univ. Press, 1989), pp. 315–341.

120. Mongane Serote, *To Every Birth Its Blood* (New York: Thunder's Mouth

In a letter to Mabel Palmer, the white anticolonialist activist, Lily wrote her conviction : "We make people believe that civilization came with evil." Less than two years later, after Palmer sent her a message "of total emotional rejection coupled with her act of generosity in funding Lily to an alternative school," Lily undid that conviction and wrote: "I was never meant to be a stone but a human feelings not either an experimental doll."[121] The stone is (in the) margin.

At a recent conference, Coetzee juxtaposed passages from Mothobi Mutloatse and Nadine Gordimer and commented: "The white writer in South Africa is in an impossible position."[122] Deconstruction would see the experience of the impossible as the type case of experience. Yet, that common human grain is made visible only in extremis, in the exceptional:[123] here by the responsible white writer in South Africa. Coetzee stages the range of that experience by claiming corrective comradeship and complicity with Foe, with Susan Barton. The novel is a staging of the emergence of the experience of the impossible when the historical or national elite does not abdicate responsibility upon the

---

Press, 1989). The quoted passage is from William Finnegan, "A Distant Rumbling in the Township," *New York Times Book Review*, 7 May 1989, p. 38; Shula Marks, *Experimental Doll*. Moya's diagnosis of "schizophrenia" (p. 201) is an uncanny demonstration of Deleuze and Guattari's argument in *Anti-Oedipus*, pp. 166–184.

121. Marks, *Experimental Doll*, pp. 89, 42. I have rearranged parts of the sentence in the interest of coherence.

122. Conference on "Re-defining Marginality," Univ. of Tulsa, 30 March 1989. This is the position he has described elsewhere as "generated by the concerns of people no longer European, not yet African" (*White Writing: On the Culture of Letters in South Africa* [New Haven: Yale Univ. Press, 1988], p. 11). Coetzee juxtaposed Mutloatse, "Editor's Introduction," in *Reconstruction*, ed. Mothobi Mutolatse (Johannesburg: Ravan Press, 1981), p. 6, and as quoted in N. Ndebele, "The English Language and Social Change in South Africa," *Tri-Quarterly* 69 (1987): 235, n. 17; and Nadine Gordimer, "Living in the Interregnum," in *The Essential Gesture: Writing, Politics and Places* (New York: Knopf, 1988), pp. 275–276.

123. Derrida comments, for example, after an interminably detailed speculative "reading" of Paul Celan's "Ash-Glory Behind . . .," that we do not need the Holocaust to experience the paradoxes of witnessing and bearing witness that the poem sets to work. They are available to us in the precomprehended presuppositions of the possibility of everyday communication (Day 2, Seminar on the Secret and Testimony, New York Univ., Fall 1994). This is the paradox of "the universal exception," Derrida, *Gift of Death*, pp. 82–85.

easy road of a call to arms by way of a vanguardism that must, of course, never be acknowledged.

A colleague unnerved me by suggesting that this book, like all transactions among men, left the women anonymous. I should like to discount the suggestion: I would rather use it to repeat my opening cautions. Does "the sign 'woman' have no origin, no historical, cultural, or linguistic limit"? We have seen the women in *Robinson Crusoe.* In *Foe* the good white woman's anguish is stumped by an ignorance that seems removable only by anthropology: "who was to say there do not exist entire tribes in Africa among whom the men are mute and speech is reserved to women?" Traveling around the United States, advising aspiring culture studies programs, I encounter a good deal of resistance to research among faculty, which silences me when, from the other side, I hear the criticism that culture studies undermines the rigor of literary scholarship. What relationship is there between this resistance to research and the demand that Coetzee put in place some Woman Friday so that we can then criticize him for insufficient representation? I would rather have the moment of anguish, which fantasizes a woman-power society somewhere in subaltern alterity; a romanticization also often encountered in the academy.

Further, said my colleague: "Coetzee has read a lot of theory, and it shows. But . . ." But what? "Theory should lead to practice." (So much for theory having no consequences.)[124] What should the practice have

---

124. In my judgment, Aristotle, whom criticism by hearsay dismisses simply as valorizing theory, is rather more careful about separating the object of theory (concentrated attention) from practice (good action). Since the object of theory is invariables [ἀΐδια] that are "birthless" [αγέντα—the ecological circle, or $e = mc^2$ would qualify] and [directly] un-phrasable [αφραςτα; *Nicomachean Ethics* 6.3.3; as in Chapter 1, my translation is so clumsy to avoid the heavy Christianization of "what is eternal does not come into existence or perish," *Ethics*, tr. H. Rackham (Cambridge: Harvard Univ. Press, 1956), p. 333. Aristotle bluntly states that thought [διάνοια] by itself moves nothing (*Ethics* 6.2.5) and, when, taking the precaution of the *découpage* of a theorem, he begins simply to assume that there are five ways in the psyche of getting to truth by way of stating or denying, he places at the head of the list τέχνη—"a truth-attaining rational quality concerned with practice that leads to good and bad for human beings" (Ethics 6.5.4; Rackham, p. 337).

been in this case? A book that did not show the reading of theory, resembling more "what a [feminist or political] novel should be," giving a call to arms that satisfies the academic but never touches the policy-makers? Should my colleague have known that her nice notion of the relationship between theory and practice has caused and is causing a good deal of suffering in the world? If figuration is seen as a *case* of theoretical production (one practice among many), or as making visible the impossible that is the condition of possibility of all setting of theory to work, could another politics of reading have led her to the conclusion that her desire to help racially differentiated colonial others had a threshold and a limit? "I quite like metafiction, but . . . ," she added. For what sort of patafiction of concrete experience must we reserve our seal of approval? The field of work is a broken and uneven place. The conventional highway of a politically correct single issue is merely the shortest distance between two signposted exits.

CHAPTER THREE

History

If by our old-fashioned reckoning philosophy concatenates and literature figures, feminist historiography often excavates. What is the fate of
the historians' informant? As every undergraduate historian knows, historical knowledge cannot be established on single cases. Thus this
chapter is not historical work, as much as Chapter 1 was not philoso-
phizing. The anxiety of so-called interdisciplinary work is that one
computes with the methodological training of one discipline, however
transformed. This chapter is two stories about the informant in history.

In the previous chapter, I have tried to argue that a critical intimacy
with deconstruction might help metropolitan feminist celebration of
the female to acknowledge a responsibility toward the trace of the
other, not to mention toward other struggles. That acknowledgment is
as much a recovery as it is a loss of the wholly other.[1] The excavation,

---

1. Melanie Klein's work on reparation is pertinent here. The infant conjures
with part objects. As the child grows it begins to construct whole persons, a situation that marks the loss of the scene of original difference, marked by an inchoate
subject space and a part object—generally the breast. When the shuttling scenario
of responsibility as reparation to whole parental persons (imago and "real") catches
hold, it is in a certain sense a commemoration of that initial loss *as loss*. This is
obviously not the moment to digest Klein's incredibly careful work with children. I
hope to elaborate its suggestions and possibilites in the future. The idea of reparation is most famously launched in "Love, Guilt and Reparation," in *Love, Guilt and
Reparation and Other Works* (London: Hogarth Press, 1975), pp. 306–343.

retrieval, and celebration of the historical individual, the effort of bringing her within accessibility, is written within that double bind at which we begin. But a just world must entail normalization; the promise of justice must attend not only to the seduction of power, but also to the anguish that knowledge must suppress difference as well as differance, that a fully just world is impossible, forever deferred and different from our projections, the undecidable in the face of which we must risk the decision that we can hear the other.

In 1982, a conference with the title "Europe and Its Others" was proposed by the sociology of literature group at Essex. I suggested an alternative title: "Europe as an Other."[2] It is a sign of the amount of work done in the last decade and a half that this title would be perfectly appropriate today, although it was ill-considered then, in at least three ways. First, the effort to present Europe as an Other involves careful disciplinary preparation in the matter of the Other, as well as political impatience with the matter of Europe. We were not yet such a group. The task of discussing the representation of Europe by other cultures should require a preparation broad and deep enough to check superficial enthusiasm and condemnation. (V. Y. Mudimbe's *The Invention of Africa* remains a model of such breadth and depth.)[3] It is to be hoped that the sociology of academic politics will not stop the expert from considering, mutatis mutandis, our own theoretical contributions.

Second, that alternative title, as it was proposed a decade and a half ago, ignored the fact that the history and the theory that such a conference would, indeed should, want to expose are precisely those of how Europe had consolidated itself as sovereign subject by defining its colonies as "Others," even as it constituted them, for purposes of administration and the expansion of markets, into programmed near-images of that very sovereign self. Third, the proposed revision nostalgically assumed that a critique of imperialism would restore a sovereignty for the lost self of the colonies so that Europe could, once and for all, be put in

2. The proceedings of this conference have since been published as Francis Barker, ed., *Europe and Its Others* (Colchester: Univ. of Essex Press, 1985), in 2 vols.

3. Valentin Y. Mudimbe, *The Invention of Africa: Gnosis, Philosophy, and the Order of Knowledge* (Bloomington: Indiana University Press, 1988).

the place of the other that it always was. That would indeed be a disavowal, of a trace of that other, "Europe" by vague proper name, in our own hybrid history—a Europe that is today called upon to acknowledge its own hybrid past.[4]

If instead, people of our disciplinary outlines or *découpages* concentrated on documenting and theorizing the itinerary of the consolidation of Europe as sovereign subject, indeed sovereign and Subject, then we would point at an alternative geography of the "worlding" of today's global South. When this book was started, "the Third World" offered an entire privileged discursive *field* within metropolitan radical criticism. In that field, "The Third World *Woman*" was a particularly privileged signifier.[5] As I have already mentioned, today, in the interest of the financialization of the globe, "Women in Development" has changed to "Gender and Development."[6] The result is an altogether speeded up cultural studies exchange between North and South, where national identities must be preserved intact.[7] (The red herring of nationalist-racist opposition, rather than globalizing-imperialist benevolence, to cultural studies makes auto-critique particularly difficult.) Upon the terrain of that exchange, the Woman from the South is a particularly privileged signifier, as object and mediator; as she is, in the market, the favored agent-as-instrument of transnational capital's glo-

---

4. For Europe's hybrid past, see Derrida, "The Other Heading," p. 83, and Chapter 1, note 28. It is one of the many virtues of Homi Bhabha's work that he has never lost sight of the hybridity of the colonized.

5. At one end she is the ethnic minority student of any class at a privileged U.S. institute of tertiary education. At the other end, she is the exquisite parodic heroine of Clarice Lispector's "The Smallest Woman in the World," in Lispector, *Family Ties*, tr. Giovanni Pontiero (Austin: Univ. of Texas Press, 1972), pp. 88–95.

6. This change is no doubt reflected in various papers of the World Bank, although it does not merit an entry on the World Bank website at the time of writing. I am reporting from the experience of the Fourth World Women's Conference (Beijing, 1995). The World Bank job description for "Director for Gender and Development" may be of interest (*The Economist*, 22 Mar. 1997). As of April 1997, the World Bank has set up a Gender Home Page "to promote dialogue between the Bank, its partners and organizations and individuals worldwide who are concerned with *gender and development*; and once the system has been fully tested, most of the material will be available externally at this site" (emphasis mine).

7. See "Translator's Preface," *IM* xxiii–xxix.

balizing reach.[8] I will refer to the current incarnation of the class-privileged instrument of transnational capital later in this chapter. But first let us look at the Rani of Sirmur, an earlier incarnation of the class-privileged woman from elsewhere, as the agent/instrument of industrial capitalism's nascent empire.[9]

One of the major difficulties with consolidating a figure from the British nineteenth century in India as an object of knowledge is that, over the last decade and a half, British India has been painstakingly constructed as a cultural commodity with a dubious function. The deepening of the international division of labor as a result of the new micro-eletronic capitalism, the proliferation of worldwide neocolonial aggression, the possibility of nuclear holocaust, and now the exigencies of globalization encroach upon the constitution of the everyday life of the Anglo–United States. The era of *Pax Britannica*, caught in a super-realistic lyrical grandeur on television, film, and paperback, provides that audience at the same time with a justification of imperialism dissimulated under the lineaments of a manageable and benevolent self-

---

8. For a particularly incisive analysis, see Farida Akhter, "Eugenic and Racist Premise of Reproductive Rights and Population Control," in *Depopulating Bangladesh: Essays on the Politics of Fertility* (Dhaka: Narigrantha Prabartana, 1992), pp. 41–56. I should say at once that the apparent tendentiousness of some of the positions, a result of the embattled bitterness of the activist, is nothing as compared to the cultural stereotyped and sanctioned ignorance at our end.

9. Questions of subalternity and of subaltern speech will be raised later in this chapter. Harish Trivedi is correct in suggesting that we should not "look for the subaltern in a queen" but incorrect in thinking that that is my project here ("India and Post-Colonial Discourse," in Harish Trivedi and Meenakshi Mukherjee, eds., *Interrogating Post-Colonialism: Theory, Text and Context* (Shimla: Indian Inst. of Advanced Study, 1996), p. 240. Two riders: First, it may be somewhat precipitous to translate "Rani" as "queen" (I propose no alternative), with all the British or European paraphernalia that the word calls forth (see considerations of African "philosophy" in Paulin Hountondji, *African Philosophy: Myth and Reality*, tr. Henri Evans (London: Hutchinson, 1983); and the problem of translating *dharma* as "religion," *nyāya* as "logic" and the like, discussed in Spivak and Matilal, *Epic as Ethic*. Second: when I visited the Sirmur "palace" in Nahan in 1986, it was striking that archival records began *after* the Rani. The question of colonial and pre-colonial and the use of well-placed women are as much the common threads in this chapter as the issue of the woman's attempted speech act, Sati for the Rani, counter-Sati for Bhubaneswari, neither heeded as such.

criticism. It is in history and so-called archivist postcolonial criticism that this is, alas, most evident.

The contemptuous spuriousness of the project can be glimpsed on the most superficial level, if we contrast it, for example, to that of the U.S. "nostalgia film," which Fredric Jameson has described as a "well-nigh libidinal historicism." Jameson finds "the 1950's" to be "the privileged lost object of desire . . . for Americans," at least partly because they signify "the stability and prosperity of a pax Americana." Speaking of "the insensible colonization of the present by the nostalgia mode" in a film such as *Body Heat*, Jameson observes, "the setting has been strategically framed, with great ingenuity, to eschew most of the signals that normally convey the contemporaneity of the United States in its mutlinational era . . . as though [the narrative] were set in some eternal thirties, beyond real historical time."[10] No such ingenuity is needed in the case of the spurious simulacrum of imperial India or colonial Africa. The rural landscape of *Gandhi* or *Out of Africa*, comfortably masquerading as the backdrop of Raj or colony, is in fact the un-retouched landscape of rural India or Africa today. The different resonance of *Home and the World* in India and in Northwest Europe is a case in point.

It is against these disciplinary and cultural tendencies of representation that I proposed, in the mid-eighties, a "reading" of a handful of archival material, bits of "the unprocessed *historical record*."[11] At that stage, the point was to reconcile such a reading with the fact that, within the discipline of history, influential figures like Dominick La-Capra and Hayden White were questioning a privileging of the archives:

> That language . . . is the *instrument of mediation* between the consciousness and the world that consciousness inhabits [White writes with some derision] . . . will not be news to literary theorists, but it has not yet reached the historians buried in the archives hoping, by what

---

10. Fredric Jameson, *Postmodernism; or, The Cultural Logic of Late Capitalism* (Durham: Duke Univ. Press, 1991), pp. 20–21.

11. Hayden White, *Metahistory: The Historical Imagination in Nineteenth-Century Europe* (Baltimore: Johns Hopkins Univ. Press, 1973), p. 5.

they call a "sifting of the facts" or "the manipulation of the data," to find the form of the reality that will serve as the object of representation in the account that they will write "when all the facts are known" and they have finally "got the story straight."[12]

In that a hegemonic nineteenth-century European historiography had designated the archives as a repository of "facts," and I proposed that they should be "read," my position could be consonant with White's. The records I read showed the soldiers and administrators of the East India Company constructing the object of representations that becomes a reality of India. This is "literature" in the general sense—the archives selectively preserving the changeover of the episteme—as its condition; with "literature" in the narrow sense—all the genres—as its effect. The distinction—between archive and literature—blurs a bit later. To grasp the distinction, the literary critic must turn to the archives. On a somewhat precious register of literary theory, it is possible to say that this was the construction of a fiction whose task was to produce a whole collection of "effects of the real," and that the "misreading" of this "fiction" produced the proper name "India." The colonizer constructs himself as he constructs the colony. The relationship is intimate, an open secret that cannot be part of official knowledge.

As a disciplinary literary critic, I was thus skeptical of White's privileging of literary criticism. To reveal the irreducibly tropological nature of historical work no doubt redresses the balance of the discipline of history. Such a suggestion would carry weight, however, if it were made from a perspective equally knowledgeable about the specificity of the study of history *and* the study of literature as institutionalized disciplines. Alongside the careful (narrative) history of history, historiography, and philosophy of history *within the disciplinarization* of history in "The Absurdist Moment in Contemporary Literary Theory," White presented a loose-knit taxonomy of the development of recent literary criticism, quite outside of the history of its institutionalization. He seemed to take at face value the American New Critics, whose ideologi-

12. White, *Tropics of Discourse: Essays in Cultural Criticism* (Baltimore: Johns Hopkins Univ. Press, 1987), pp. 125–126.

cal effigy still rules our discipline. This allowed him to arrive at a point where he could speak of the "moral" and the "aesthetic" as if they were a matter of mere preference as to choice of ground.[13]

Perhaps because he profited from White's pathbreaking work and a more benign exposure to Derrida, Foucault, and Lacan, Dominick La-Capra's position seems at once bolder and more tempered. He too "urges the intellectual historian to learn of developments in . . . literary criticism and philosophy." But he is also aware that

> at present, more experimental forms of literary criticism, when they do not replace older types of formal or "new" criticism, threaten to remain on the level of delicate miniatures. . . . "History" itself may be invoked as an extremely abstract, indeed intemporal, category either to defend or to reproach more formal and micrological methods of criticism. Or the "context"s that are called upon to flesh out an inter-pretation may be the outgrowth of wild speculation rather than care-ful research.[14]

Yet LaCapra also cautions against enthusiastic and uncritical "archiv-ism," its

> indiscriminate mystique . . . which is bound up with hegemonic pre-tensions. . . . The archive as fetish is a literal substitute for the "real-ity" of the past which is "always already" lost for the historian. When it is fetishized, the archive is more than the repository of traces of the past which may be used in its inferential reconstruction. It is a stand-in for the past that brings the mystified experience of the thing itself— an experience that is always open to question when one deals with writing or other inscriptions.[15]

I find these admonitions just, although I remain troubled about the ontological status of a "past" in a wildly speculative way. LaCapra pro-

---

13. White, *Metahistory*, pp. xi–xii.

14. Dominick LaCapra, *Rethinking Intellectual History: Texts, Contexts, Language* (Ithaca: Cornell Univ. Press, 1983), p. 344.

15. LaCapra, *History and Criticism* (Ithaca: Cornell Univ. Press, 1985), p. 92, n. 17.

duces them, however, in defense of the (Western) historian's consideration of "great works." But, as I have suggested in the previous chapter, at a time of an epistemic makeover and the establishment of an intimate relationship between the "literary" and the "colonial," the reading of literature can directly supplement the writing of history with suspicious ease.[16] In Chapter 2, I have suggested that great works of literature cannot easily flourish in the fracture or discontinuity that is covered over by an alien legal system masquerading as law as such, an alien ideology established as the only truth, and a set of human sciences busy establishing the "native" as self-consolidating other ("epistemic violence"). For the early part of the nineteenth century in India, the literary critic must turn to the archives of imperial governance to supplement the consolidation of what will come to be recognized as "nationalist" literature. Again, the introduction of the thematics of imperialism alters the radical arguments. "Often the dimensions of the document that make it a text of a certain sort with its own historicity and its relations to sociopolitical processes (for example, relations of power)," LaCapra writes, "are filtered out when it is used purely and simply as a quarry for facts in the reconstruction of the past."[17] Even so modest a consideration of the construction of the object of imperialism as the present essay cannot be guilty of that error.

Perhaps my intent is to displace (not transcend) the mere reversal of the literary and the archival implicit in much of LaCapra's work. To me, literature and the archives seem complicit in that they are both a crosshatching of condensations, a traffic in telescoped symbols, that can only too easily be read as each other's repetition-with-a-displacement. The authority of the author is there matched by the control of the archon, the official custodian of truth.[18] It is archivization that interests us, naturally.

---

16. This ease is reflected in Benedict Anderson's conjuring with the novel in the production of an influential theory of nationalism in *Imagined Communities*. For the makeover of the term "literature" in the Bengali case, see Sumanta Banerjee, *The Parlour and the Streets: Elite and Popular Culture in Nineteenth Century Calcutta* (Calcutta: Seagull Books, 1989).

17. LaCapra, *Rethinking*, p. 31.

18. Derrida, "Archive-Fever," *Diacritics* 25 (Summer 1995): 9–63.

In a slightly different context, rethinking intellectual history, La-Capra proposes that the "relation between practices in the past and historical accounts of them" is "transferential"; and adds, "I use 'transference' in the modified psychoanalytic sense of a repetition-displacement of the past into the present as it necessarily bears on the future."

The transference-situation in analysis is one where the tug-of-war of desire is at work on *both* sides—on the part of both the analysand and the analyst, with the emphasis inevitably on the analysand. Both come to occupy the subject position in the uneven progressive-regressive exchange. The task of the "construction" of a "history" devolves on both. To wish to replicate this in disciplinary historiography might simply mark the site of a radical version of the academic intellectual's desire for power. This desire can be located in the slippage between the suggestion that the relation between past practices and historical accounts is transferential, and, as LaCapra goes on to say in four paragraphs—the suggestion that, however difficult it might be—a "transferential relation" must be "negotiate[d] critically."[19] In the first position, the historian uneasily occupies the couch. In the second, the logic of the analogy would make the historian share the responsibility of the analyst. The distance covered by the slippage between these two positions is precisely the metaphor of the "cure." Although I am generally sympathetic with LaCapra's use of the transference-model in disciplinary critique and the critique of the *mentalité*-school of historiography, I cannot overlook the fact that to dissimulate the space of the "cure" disqualifies any methodolgical analogy taken from transference. I have argued elsewhere, writing directly on psychoanalytic

---

19. Ibid., 72–73. When it uses the Lacanian explanatory model to understand the law (resolutely lower case), its consequences, and its scope, Slavoj Zizek's work remains an exception to the hermeneutic circle described in the text. See especially *Tarrying with the Negative: Kant, Hegel, and the Critique of Ideology* (Durham: Duke University Press, 1993). This may well be related to the fact that, having served and being active in the upper reaches of the government, Zizek is "responsible" within the political calculus in ways that few academic cultural critics can be. If Freud set the tone for institutionalizing the reading of narrative as ethical instantiation, Zizek's use of Lacan offers readings of narrative as political instantiation, minimizing the usual problem of reading plot summary as unmediated representation of the psychoanalytic morphology.

literary criticism, that this disqualification is perhaps irreducible.[20] Chapter 1 considers Deleuze and Guattari's more serious criticism of psychoanalysis itself as the production of a general equivalent that manages the crisis of capitalism. The psychoanalytic metaphor for transformative disciplinary practice in the human sciences will always remain a catachresis, for there can be no distinction between transference-neuroses and rememoration outside of clinical practice: not to mention the fact that, at least by Freud's account, transference-neuroses are the source of science.[21]

LaCapra is too sophisticated a thinker not to suspect this. In the place of this catachresis he offers us a "fiction": "It is a useful critical fiction to believe that the texts of phenomena to be interpreted may answer one back and even be convincing enough to lead one to change one's mind."[22] If the "past" is quite "other," this "useful fiction" might track the mechanics of the construction of the *self-consolidating* other, the past as a past present—a history that is in some sense a genealogy of the historian. What is marked is the site of desire. I need not belabor the point.

I should have liked to establish a transferential relationship with the Rani of Sirmur. I pray instead to be haunted by her slight ghost, bypassing the arrogance of the cure. There is not much text in her name in the archives. And of course there is no pretense of continuity of cultural inscription between her soul and the mental theater of the archivists. To establish something like a simulacrum of continuity is that "epistemic violation" that I invoked in my more turgid phase. It started in the Rani's son's generation. She was only the instrumental agent of the settlement.

---

20. Spivak, "The Letter as Cutting Edge," in *In Other Worlds*, pp. 3–14. See also Spivak, "Woman in Difference," *Outside*, p. 77–95. Ronald Inden has an interesting idea of the material of history as "dream" in *Imagining India* (London: Blackwell, 1990), pp. 55–56, 40–41; Inden does not suggest, of course, that the critic can work a transference here. For a superreal counterfactual dream account, see Bhudeb Mukhopadhyay, "Swapnalabdha Bharatbarsher Itihash," in *Bhudeb Rachana Sambhar*, ed. Pramathanath Bisi (Calcutta: Mitra and Ghosh, 1969), pp. 341–374.

21. Freud, "Beyond the Pleasure Principle," *SE* 18, 18, 50–51. I am of course not taking into account the viability of psychoanalysis as cure.

22. LaCapra, *History and Criticism*, p. 73.

To be haunted is also to lay to rest any hope of "detecting the traces of [an] uninterrupted narrative, in restoring to the surface of the text the repressed and buried reality of [a] fundamental history, [in which] the doctrine of a political unconscious finds its function and its necessity," which was Fredric Jameson's project some years ago.[23] If for us the assurance of transference gives way to the possibility of haunting, it is also true that for us the only figure of the unconscious is that of a radical series of discontinuous interruptions. In a mere miming of that figure, one might say that the epistemic story of imperialism is the story of a series of interruptions, a repeated tearing of time that cannot be sutured. As I have urged in the previous chapter, today's cultural studies should think at least twice before acting on a wish to achieve that impossible seam, endorsing Sartre's imperial conviction: "There is always some way of understanding an idiot, a child, a primitive man or a foreigner *if one has sufficient information.*"

But if in today's world, one ventures into the arena of exploitation (I will write of it in the last chapter), in globalization the Masters and Mistresses try as little to neutralize epistemic discontinuity with the woman or girl of the rank and file as did the Company's functionaries with the Rani. And, although references to (post)colonialism have become more frequent than when these chapters were first written, the story of reference remains unchanged—the willed (auto)biography of the West still masquerades as disinterested history, even when the critic presumes to touch its unconscious.[24]

---

23. Fredric Jameson, *The Political Unconscious: Narrative as a Socially Symbolic Act* (Ithaca: Cornell Univ. Press, 1981), p. 20.

24. Hayden White has his version of an uninterrupted narrative whose fundamental history must be restored: it is the history of consciouness itself, "the deep [tropologically progressivist] structure of the historical imagination," "the single tradition of historical thinking" (*Metahistory*, pp. ix–x). Everything proceeds here as if the sign "consciousness" has no history, no geopolitical specificity. In order to put together his theory of the "political unconscious" as the vast container of the uninterrupted narrative of fundamental history, Fredric Jameson also taps psychoanalysis. He constructs an adequate analogy between the Lacanian subject-model/discursive-orders of the Imaginary, symbolic, and Real on the one hand, and the functioning of text and history on the other. It is Dominick LaCapra who has, in my view, successfully analyzed this problematic maneuver, suggesting that this is to misappropriate Lacan in rather a serious way (*Rethinking*, pp. 245–251).

Haunting for transference, the unconscious as interruption. I must confess that I have not been able to stop tinkering with bits of Freudian terminology. As far as I am able to understand my own practice, I do so in order to borrow a seductive and risky interpretive vocabulary and a powerful metaphorics, not to construct a collective socioplitical Subject, nor yet to find an analogy for reading in the analytic situation. More about this later. The field of Third World criticism has become so quickly fraught that I must repeat another version of the methodological caution that I advanced in my reading of Hegel's reference to the *Gītā*: In the United States the Third Worldism currently afloat in humanistic disciplines is often openly ethnicist or primitivist. In reading that bit of Hegel I was entering that rôle to offer a subversive message. There is no such clear subversion here. I was born in India and received my primary, secondary, and tertiary education there, including two years of graduate work. My Indian example could thus be seen as a nostalgic investigation of the lost roots of my own identity. Yet even as I know that one cannot freely enter the thickets of "motivations," I would maintain that my chief project is to be wary of such nostalgia entertained by academics in the self-imposed exile of eurocentric economic migration; for I feel it myself. I turn to Indian material because, in the absence of advanced disciplinary training, that accident of birth and education had provided me with a *sense* of the historical canvas, a hold on some of the pertinent languages that are useful tools for a *bricoleur*—especially when she is armed with the Marxist skepticism of "concrete experience" as the final arbiter and with a critique of disciplinary formations. The Indian case cannot be taken as representative of all countries, nations, cultures, and the like that may be invoked as the Other of Europe as Self. This caution seems all the more necessary because, at the other end, studies of the English, French, and German eighteenth century are still repeatedly adduced as *representative* of the emergence of *the* ethical consensus—and studies of Emerson, Thoreau, and Henry Adams advanced as a study of the *American* mind. I use Mahasweta because I am bilingual in Bengali and English and she is literally a postcolonial case.

To set the stage for the Rani of Sirmur, let us consider three examples from the collections of "Proceedings"—dispatches, letters, consultations moving at the slow pace of horse, foot, ships laboriously rounding the Cape, and the quill pens of writers and copyists—surrounding the half-forgotten maneuvers of the "Settlement" of the many states of the Shimla hills in the first two decades of the nineteenth century.[25] This is the Highland scrub country of the lower Himalayas between Punjab proper on the West, Nepal and Sikkim on the East, and what was to be named the Northwest Provinces—today's Uttar Pradesh—in the South. The country lies between the two great rivers Sutlej and Yamuna, and there are thus two valleys tucked in between the scrub, the Kaardah and the Dehra valleys, or doons. The many kings of these hills had lived out a heterogeneous and precarious equilibrium surrounded by the militarily and politically energetic Sikhs of the Punjab and Gurk-

---

25. To orient the literary reader, it should be pointed out that the time is over a century earlier than the fictional time of *A Passage to India* (1924). The fictional space of that novel is a rather well-settled Native State, feeling the first rumbles of national liberation. Forster's personal experience was in lusher and less remote Central India. The states I am speaking of, being in the foothills of the northwestern Himalayas, were part of another game altogether. (See Peter Hopkirk, *The Great Game* [New York: Kodansha, 1994] and Spivak, "Foucault and Najibullah," in Kathy Komar and Ross Schidler, eds., *Lyrical Symbols and Narrative Transformations: Essays in Honor of Ralph Freedman* [Columbia, S.C.: Camden House, 1997]). Giving both of these games a lie, there is now an interest in finding in these states a "Hindu India" as opposed to the "British India," which is the basis of the independent Republic of India. This can then open the way to a theocracy operating with an apparently democratic structure. See, for example, an unmediated "documentary" directed by a scion of one of these states, which stages a "modern" English-speaking, electioneering Rani who gives cultural training to the next generation, a training that includes support of widow suicide as free choice in a moment of exaltation that transcends ordinary common sense ("A Zenana: Scenes and Recollections," independent video by Roger Sandall and Jayasinhji Jhala, 1982). This view is legitimized by reversal by the superficially "feminist" position that the women were always coerced. I will write at length about widow-suicide later in this chapter. Compare the unmediated "modernization" of a film like *Diganta* by the bourgeois feminist, fiercely "individualist" Indian filmmaker Aparna Sen, which attempts to claim abortion as an unexamined metonym for a crudely understood "reproductive right" as right to ownership, where an infantilized pregnant wife with a guitar-playing husband gets an abortion in a fit of pique because she was "not allowed" to pursue her career by giving a dance recital in a distant city. For the construction of classical dance as a terrain of female careers and, in postcolonial discourse, as "feminist performance," see my "How to Teach a 'Culturally Different' Book," in Francis Barker et al., eds., *Colonial Discourse / Postcolonial Theory* (Manchester: Univ. of Manchester Press, 1994), p. 131.

has of Nepal and by those relatively distant "paramount powers," the Mughal Emperor and the Pathan King of Delhi, the latter through his proxy the Nazim of Sirhind. It is a centuries-old scene of the constant dispersal of the space of power, with representations of representation operating successfully though not taking anyone in as the representation of truth—and above all, animated by no desire to compete with those four greater surrounding powers. When therefore, on August 2, 1784, David Ochterlony writes in secret consultation to the governor-general-in-council: "The aggression of the Goorkahs compelled us to have recourse to arms *in vindication of our insulted honour,*" most of the hill states were not, indeed could not be, particularly forthcoming in partisanship.[26] This provided the East India Company with the right to claim entitlement to the settlement of the states.

This minimal account is necessary to introduce my first example, which comes from the pen of Captain Geoffrey Birch (an assistant agent of the governor) writing to Charles Metcalfe, the resident at Delhi. Metcalfe sends a copy to John Adam, the governor's secretary at Fort William in Calcutta. The time is the end of 1815. The copy of the letter from young Geoffrey Birch (born in a petty merchant's family in Middlesex just before the French Revolution, he is twenty-nine at this point) is taking its time traveling five hundred miles across the Indo-Gangetic plains from resident in Delhi to governor's secretary in Calcutta. Birch in the meantime is advancing his career, riding about in the hills with a single native escort—a slight romantic figure if encountered in the pages of a novel or on the screen. He is actually engaged in consolidating the Self of Europe by obliging the native to cathect the space of the Other on his home ground. We have seen the achieved version in "William the Conqueror" in Chapter 2. He is worlding *their own world,* which is far from mere uninscribed earth, anew, by obliging *them* to domesticate the alien as Master. Much "thicker" descriptions of this are, of course, to be found in settler colonies—a worlding visited upon "native" Americans, Black South Africans, Australian Aborigines, the Suomis of Northern Europe . . .

As mentioned in the previous chapter, the worlding of a world on

---

26. Board's Collections, 1819–1820, extract Bengal Secret Consultations, n.d. All archival sources consulted are at the India Office Library in London.

uninscribed earth alludes to Heidegger's "The Origin of the Work of Art." Again, Heidegger suggests that the strife between thrusting world and settling earth—it is a violent concept-metaphor of violation—is strifed—realized or posited as strife—in the work of art as work. Many of Heidegger's examples in that piece are spatial. If the Heideggerian concept-metaphor of earth and world is used to describe the imperialist project, what emerges out of the violence of the rift (*Riss* in Heidegger has the violent implication of a fracture—"fighting of the battle," "the intimacy of opponents"—rather than the relatively "cool" connotation of a gap) is the multifarious thingliness (*Dinglichkeit*) of a represented world on a map, not merely "the materiality of oil paint affirmed and foregrounded in its own right" as in some masterwork of European art, being endlessly commented on by philosopher and literary critic.[27] The agents of this cartographic transformation in the narrow sense are not only great names like Vincent Van Gogh, but also small unimportant folk like Geoffrey Birch, as well as policy makers. The technique is the great anonymous technique of capital—understood, as we have seen in Ranajit Guha's discussion in *A Rule of Property*—as physiocracy, mercantilism, free trade, or even civilizing mission (social productivity). I am also suggesting that the necessary yet contradictory assumption of an uninscribed earth that is the condition of possibility of the worlding of a world generates the force to make the "native" see himself as "other." The setting-to-work mode of deconstruction would, I think, find the Heideggerian theory judged in the force of doing and undoing

---

27. Heidegger, "Origin," pp. 174, 188; Jameson, "Postmodernism," p. 59. Heidegger's attitude toward this "struggle" in 1935, when the essay was first written, may be far from benign. Compare, for example, the orchestration of the word *Streit* (conflict/strife) in the German sentences from which my two phrases are cited. The first is from the section entitled "The Work and Truth," and the second from "Truth and Art": "Das Werksein des Werkes besteht in der Be*streit*ung des *Streit*es zwischen Welt und Erde"; "der *Streit* ist kein Riss als das Aufreissen einer blossen Kluft, sondern der *Streit* ist die Innigkeit des Sichzugehörens der *Streiten*den." It is not okay to fill these outlines with the story of imperial settlement, although Heidegger flirts with it constantly. We are back with de Man's Kant-Schiller argument. With a little help from Derrida (he interminabilizes "The Origin" in *The Truth in Painting*), I play Schiller to Heidegger's Kant.

the worlded world in the work (here of imperial settlement). The telling of this story here is a tiny part of that interminable force field.

George III required of his Cadet only that "he [be] well-grounded in Vulgar Fractions, write . . . a good Hand, and [have] gone through the Latin Grammar."[28] The Military Committee of the East India Company went by the same rules. With this intellectual preparation and thirteen years of soldiering (he joined when he was sixteen) Captain Birch is effectively and violently sliding one discourse under another. His letter carries these words, by no means singular in that era and in those contexts: "[I have undertaken this journey] to acquaint the people who they are subject to, for as I suspected they were not properly informed of it and seem only to have heard of our existence from conquering the Goorkah and from having seen a few Europeans passing thro' the country."[29]

Birch on horseback passing through the country sees himself as a representative image. By his sight and utterance rumor is being replaced by information, the figure of the European on the hills is being reinscribed from stranger to Master, to the sovereign as Subject with a capital *S*, even as the native shrinks into the consolidating subjected subject in the lower case. The truth value of the stranger is being established as the reference point for the true (insertion into) history of these wild regions.

Let Captain Birch as agent of determination remain a reminder that the "Colonizing Power" is far from monolithic—that its class-composition and social positionality are necessarily heterogeneous.

My second example is from a letter in secret consultation from Major General Sir David Ochterlony, superintendent and agent to the governor-general-in-council, written to John Adam, the governor's secretary. By contrast to Birch, General Ochterlony was a gentleman and cordially hated the hill people. He is the kind of person one imagines in the first flush of enthusiasm against Imperialism. His letter contains these memorable words, again not unusual from a man of his station. The nice antithetical balance reminds one in fact of certain nineteenth-

28. "Regulations for the Admission of Gentlemen Cadets into the Royal Military Academy at Woolwich," *Service Army List: Bengal*, vol. 2, military records, n.d.
29. Board's Collections, 1819–1820, extract Bengal Secret Consultations, n.d.

century novels on the topic of imperialism as social mission, *Jane Eyre*'s St. John Rivers: "Mr. Fraser . . . considers these Highlanders as having the germs of all virtue, and I see them only possessing all the brutality and purfidy [sic] of the rudest times without the courage and all the depravity and treachery of the modern days without the knowledge or refinement." My particular example comes from the last paragraph of the letter: "I do not think," Ochterlony writes, "the restoration will be received so much as an obligation as a right, and I look forward to discontent and murmurs, if not turbulence . . . to any play which does not give back the Territory unalienated, and the revenue undiminished in all its feudal relations."[30] Perhaps considering that the stake for the East India Company was the establishment and extension of its trading rights and its market, an enlightened analysis would have seen the so-called restoration as a right of native kings. But I think it would be historically unsound to credit the syphilitic Rajah Kurrum Perkash [sic] of Sirmoor, of whom Ochterlony is writing, with such an enlightened perspective. What is more interesting to us is that, although the Territory was not given back unalienated, and the revenue was more than halved, once again the "native" (King's) subject-position rewrote itself as the position of the object of Imperialism. What was at first perceived as a right came to be accepted as obligation—as being obliged. This is now quite often the enlightened viewpoint: that the victims of imperialism must feel *nothing but an obligation* in the long run. There is no need for the concept of a sociopolitical unconscious here. If we want to continue within the Freudian fantasy, we can say that this is the moment of secondary revision.

My third example concerns some deletions made in a letter to the Marquess of Hastings, Lord Moira, governor-general-in-council, by the board of control of the East India Company, drafted by its committee on correspondence in the Company's offices in Leadenhall Street in the city of London. If from Geoffrey Birch to David Ochterlony was a step up in class, from the governor-general's superintendent to the world where the board of the Company corrects the court as it reprimands the governor-general is a leap into the stratosphere. This serves

---

30. Bengal Secret Correspondence, 27 Sept. 1815.

to re-emphasize the heterogeneity of the "Colonial Powers." We are once again witnessing the production of othering. Here the native states are being distinguished from "our [colonial] governments."

The minimal context is as follows: The governor-general was allowing half-pay subalterns to serve with regular troops in Native governments. The court of directors drafted a letter to reprimand him. I find this passage interesting because it makes brutally visible the policy that is more often noticed in the more general arenas of ideological production like education, religious conversion, or accessibility to common law.

If the project of Imperialism is violently to put together the episteme that will "mean" (for others) and "know" (for the self) the colonial subject as history's nearly-selved other, the example of these deletions indicate explicitly what is always implicit: that meaning/knowledge intersects power. These deletions, disclosing the withdrawal of military training, are just as operative in fabricating an answer to the question: "Who is the native?" as my other examples. The narrative of imperialism-as-history is especially intelligible because planned; and here, contrary to Foucault's suggestion, the "model of language [*langue*] and signs" is complicit with "that of war and battle."[31]

The passage cited below was drafted by the court of directors, and later expunged by the board of control of the East India Company. The actual letter received by the governor, to be found in the National Archives in New Delhi, does not contain this passage:

> The first and main point in which you have erred has been in permitting Europeans not in the Company's service to remain in India. [This practice] would lead to an implicit improvement of the Discipline of the Troops of Native Powers, and that too through the Agency of Officers who, as they are not subject to Martial Law, could not be adequately controlled by the Indian Governments [the East India Company's Governments in Bengal, Bombay, and Madras Presidencies]. The limited degree of science which it may be consistent with good policy to impart to the troops of native powers in

---

31. Michel Foucault, *Power/Knowledge: Selected Interviews and Other Writings: 1972–1977*, tr. Colin Gordon et al. (New York: Pantheon, 1980), p. 114.

alliance with the British government, should be imparted by officers in our own service: because from those officers only have we a sure guarantee that our intentions shall not be overstepped.[32]

The bold frankness of the passage comes through in the first reading. We must not forget that the Court of Directors at this time contained those very "saintly chairs," Charles Grant, Edward Parry, and others, whose obsession with the Christianizing of India is too well known to belabor. I am not so much concerned here with the policy of giving Christianity with one hand and ensuring military superiority with the other in this absolutely overt way, as with the strategy of the planned representation of master and native (an opposition with a different nuance from the more familiar master-servant). The master is the subject of science or knowledge. The science in question here is the "interested" science of war rather than "disinterested" knowledge as such. The manipulation of the pedagogy of this science is also in the "interest" of creating what will come to be perceived as a "natural" difference between the "master" and the "native"—a difference in human or racial material.

The committee of correspondence of the Company let this bold passage pass. The board of control deleted it and simply ordered that the hiring out of subalterns be stopped. In the place of the deleted passages that I just read, they substituted the following: "whatever may be your opinion upon the propriety of these orders, we desire that they may be implicitly obeyed: and we desire also that we may not again be placed in the painful alternative of either doing an act of apparent harshness or of acquiescing in an arrangement, not only made without our consent, but such as beforehand it must have been known that we should disapprove."

Continuing our Freudian or rather wild-psychoanalytical fantasy, we see here something approaching the plan to produce the image of the European Master as a (paranoid-schizophrenic) super-ego—a fearful figure where desire and the law *must* coincide: our desire is your law if

---

32. Despatches to Bengal, vol. 82, collections 13,990–14,004, Draft Military Bengal, 8 Dec. 1819.

you govern in our name, even before that desire has been articulated as a law to be obeyed.[33]

My three examples announce, in various modes, (a) the installment of the glimpsed stranger as the sovereign subject of information—the agent an instrument: Captain Geoffrey Birch; (b) the reinscription of right as being-obliged—the agent the stereotype of the imperialist villain: Major-General Sir David Ochterlony; and (c) the divided master in the metropolis issuing desire proleptically as law: the agent anonymous because incorporated. All three are engaged in producing an "other" text—the "true" history of the native Hill States.

Of the three great European critics of ideology and rationality—Marx, Nietzsche, and Freud—Freud is the only one who worked within an institution, and indeed worked to shape an institutional science. The conflict between the critique of the intending subject and the work of instituting a "science" animates the detail of Freud's text. There we can find a monitory model on a rather larger scale, for our own desire to practice and produce an "interested" critique *within academic disciplines*.[34] By contrast, merely to locate a diagnostic taxonomy in psychoanalysis or to counter it by another is to ignore the fact that Freud problematizes any statement of method that would begin, putatively, "I choose because . . ."

---

33. Again Melanie Klein is more useful here. See esp. Klein, *The Psycho-Analysis of Children*, tr. Alix Strachey (New York: Free Press, 1984). When the paranoid-schizophrenic super-ego becomes the depressive super-ego, it is much more gentle. This is the colonial subject. Klein is up front about the role of violence in the formation of conscience. We can use her insights to see how today's postcolonial critic is produced. I call this enabling violation. Benita Parry would like to deny this, and Deleuze and Guattari reject it. I have discussed Parry in the previous chapter. For Deleuze and Guattari's admiration and critique of Klein, see the scattered references in *Anti-Oedipus*. To be sure, Klein is descriptive and curative rather than analytic and revolutionary. The authors may, however, be misjudging her by suggesting that the part object in Klein is *textually* committed to "a lost unity or a totality to come" (p. 324). To develop this objection here would be out of place.

34. Laclau's brilliant "Deconstruction, Pragmatism," welcomes this conflict as a solution rather than a monitory aporia that must always betray you into errancy even as something comes to be in the future anterior, the future as past.

In the classic chapters on the dream-work in *The Interpretation of Dreams*, Freud develops the notion of "over-determination" as the principle of fabrication of the images in the dream-text. When one reads a dream-text one cannot hold to a simple theory of a text as expression, where the cause of the expression is the fully self-present deliberative consciousness of the subject. It can therefore be suggested that in extending the notion of "determination" Freud is working within the philosophical tendency that focuses on determination—*Bestimmung*, tuning—rather than causality. When we are attempting to deal with as heterogeneous a fabrication as the imperialist representation of the empire, the notion of determinate representations is much more useful than that of deliberate or deliberate(d) cause. It is in this spirit that I turn briefly to Freud's discourse here, *not* because I wish to compare the text produced by imperialism to a dream.[35]

Freud customarily speaks of the over-determination of images in a dream-text as a telescoping of many determinations: *mehrfach determiniert*. In the section on "Means of Representation," however, Freud, still speaking of overdetermination, uses the phrase *anders determiniert* (determined otherwise). The *quality* of the images in the dream-text is determined *otherwise* "by two independent moments [*Momente*]." Is Freud using the philosophically charged word "Moment," rendered into the more colloquial "factor" in the *Standard Edition*, with any precision? We cannot know.[36] If we give Freud the stylist the benefit of the doubt, however, the two independent moments that determine the dream-text otherwise seem akin to different philosophical moments of appearance of consciousness. The first is our old friend "wish-fulfillment," where the psychic agency seems close to the deliberative consciousness that we colloquially identify as our "self." With respect to

---

35. If there is a designated "wish" operating this statement, it would be trivially interpretable.

36. Freud, *SE* 4:330. The next three Freudian passages are from the same page. It is worth remarking that in Hegel "determinate being [*Dasein*] is determinate being [what escapes the English translation, is the 'name' of determinate being determined in German]; its determinateness is determinateness-in-being [*seiende Bestimmtheit*], quality" (Hegel, *Science of Logic*, tr. A. V. Miller [New York: Humanities Press, 1976], p. 109; italics author's). A discussion of the play between the Freudian *determinieren* and the Hegelian *bestimmen* would take us too far afield.

the second moment, Freud uses the word that covers for him when he wants to finesse the question of agency: "work." Let us note the hesitation and the economic metaphor in his language: "We shall not be altering the sense of this empirically based assertion if we put it in these terms: the greatest intensity is shown by those elements in a dream on whose imaging [*Bildung*] the fullest amount of condensation-work has been made use of [*die ausgiebigste Verdichtungsarbeit in Anspruch genommen wurde*]." Who knows if Freud is correct? All we notice is that he is marking the site of a desire similar to ours: the desire to hold in *one* thought something like a wish *and* an economy. In the text being read, a desire not to assign blame to some monolithic near-deliberative "British" or "colonial power," and yet not to pretend that to understand is to forgive. "We may expect," writes Freud, "that it will eventually turn out to be possible to express this condition [*Bedingung*] and the other (namely relation to the wish-fulfilment) in a single formula." He is not speaking of the type of image that constitutes the dream-text, but rather of the "transvaluation of all psychic value" in this otherwise-determination. What better concept-metaphor could one find for the transvaluing discursive shifts I have looked at in those little bits of archival material that I have quoted?

Using the Freudian concept-metaphor as a formal rather than methodological model, then, I am going to suggest that to disclose only the race-class-gender determinations of social practices is to see overdetermination as only many determinations.[37] If we notice that explanations and discourses are irreducibly fractured by the epistemic violence of monopoly imperialism, we begin to entertain the possibility of a determination whose ground is itself a figuration: a "determination otherwise." Of course Freud never speaks of imperialism. But the notion of figuration at the ground (rather different from *non*-foundationalism) surfaces in the pervasive Freudian discourse of *Entstellung*, or displacement as grounding in the emergence of significance.

Let us first consider the narrative of the modes of production, our object of investigation in the last section of Chapter 1. The historical

---

37. This is the basis of the pluralism of the New Social Movements. See Laclau and Mouffe, *Hegemony*, p. 198.

moment in our story would qualify as a not quite correct transitional space from semi-feudalism to capitalism, since the correct configurations are usually taken to be found only in Europe.

It is easily surmised that the company of United Merchants trading in the East Indies, otherwise known as the East India Company, prefigured the shifting relationship between state-formation and economic crisis-management within which we live today. The interest of the Company did not change by accident from a commercial to a territorial one. (It cannot be repeated often enough that in financial globalization the wheel has come full circle. Today, the interest of finance capital requires the de-authorization of the state. If we keep ourselves confined to questions of world trade alone, we do not appreciate the full extent of the textual knotting, and the use of women within it.)[38]

As the first great transnational company before the fact, the East India Company followed what seemed a necessary law and engaged in the business of state-formation. It produced the scandal of a misshapen and monstrous state that, although by definition chartered by the state of Britain, burst the boundaries of the metropolitan or mother-state. The governments of India were the *Company's* governments, the army the *Company's* army, attempts at legal re-inscription the *Company's*. Indeed, the new cartography and the systemic normalization of India, of which the "settlement" of these hill states forms a part, were undertaken and established by the *Company*. These undertakings found new

---

38. Chandra Talpade Mohanty, basing herself on the rich scholarship of the last two decades, rightly observes the crucial role of women in holding up world trade. (See Mohanty, "Women Workers," esp. pp. 5 and 7). In financialization, however, women's micro-enterprise—credit-baiting without infrastructural involvement—opens the poorest rural women into direct commercial exploitation by the international commercial sector through the alliances between Women's World Banking and unexamined universalist feminism. We cannot dismiss finance capital and notice only the exacerbation of wage labor as the result of globalization. Then credit-baiting can be offered as a "solution." The exacerbation of wage labor for women—the feminization of labor—happened as capital was on the way to globalization through the computerization of stock exchanges and postfordist homeworking, and so-called free trade initiatives. World trade is now the second in command of the full financialization of the globe possible after "the revolution of 1989." More of this unravels as my text progresses.

vigor precisely when, beginning with the renewal of the Company's charter in 1813, its strictly commercial monopoly was whittled away.

It is true, of course, that the British Parliament took a much greater interest in education after 1813. To follow that narrative is to track the uneven emancipation and constitution of the male and female bourgeoisie. In these hill states, outlying what will come to be the Empire, that narrative begins late and remains more insistently male for a longer time. This is a different story, an inconsequential fragment from the haphazard process of state-formation by focusing on the strategy of limning the frontier. It is no doubt less important than the story of the serpentine relationship between the regulation of British *domestic* enterprise by the Crown and political parties on the one hand, and *foreign* trade on the other. I focus on the necessary but almost clandestine *state*-formation that accompanied this process. My argument is thus also distinct from the official narrative of India's accession to nationhood through inclusion in the British Empire.[39] It is by the law of supplementarity (what seems a rupture is also a repetition), then, that we are confronted, not by the Company's empire, but by the Company's *state*, formed ad hoc, British by national adjective, not by proper name. Here the explanatory power of economics in the last instance was

---

39. For the relationship between mercantilism and imperialism presented by disciplinary historiography, see Bernard Semmel, *The Rise of Free Trade Imperialism: Classical Political Economy: The Empire of Free Trade Imperialism, 1750–1850* (Cambridge: Cambridge Univ. Press, 1970). The standard view is well enough summarized as follows: "The subject [of Protectionism] is therefore essentially connected with England, and is only incidentally connected with India" (Parakunnel Joseph Thomas, *Mercantilism and the East India Trade* [London: Frank Cass, 1963], p. v). When, in "The East India Company—Its History and Results" (1853), Marx comments on the conflict between the British Parliament and the Company, he too sees it as a version of the conflict of mercantilism. Necessarily lacking familiarity with late capitalist conflict between nation-states and multi- and transnationals, he describes the conflict as one between commerce and industry, between domestic and colonial manufacture: "Thus India became the battlefield in the contest of the industrial interest on the one side, and of the moneyocracy and oligarchy on the other. The manufacturers, conscious of their ascendancy in England, ask now for the annihilation of these antagonistic powers in India, for the destruction of the whole ancient fabric of Indian government, and for the final eclipse of the East India Company" (Marx, *Surveys*, p. 315).

made crudely visible, even as the relative autonomy of the political led to improvised statecraft, to the monstrously invaginated state-within-a-state where the part was larger than the whole.[40] Unless we take this account, we cannot understand the textual emergence of the Rani. I am not simply intoning a potted history of the company; and feminism here cannot simply be confined to gender relations.

The standard historian of India analyzes this ad hoc state-formation simply from the point of view of India's lack of nationhood, and the standard oppositional texts do not necessarily disagree.[41] This is, once again, to assume the growth-pattern in Europe, more particularly Britain, as the unquestioned norm, considering the problems only in the domestic context, emphasizing the colonial as the normative. Here what is one narrativization of history is seen not only "as it really was," but implicitly "as it ought to be."

As must be eminently clear, I am no historian. For the literary person interested in Colonial discourse (as at that far away conference in Essex), and without mature disciplinary judgment, it is the standard rather than the innovative historian who is more important. She has not the scholarship to get into the disciplinary debate. Therefore I choose Percival Spear, who looks at the vigorous cartographic re-inscription after 1813 as partly due to the fact that "a victory of an Indian leader was a victory for himself; a victory of an English general was a victory for England." From this it is not difficult to write unproblematically about the years 1813–1818: "The time was thus ripe for a new start in India."[42] Here, in a "non-theoretical" context, a phrase as seemingly un-

---

40. I have discussed invagination in Chapter 1.

41. As "standard oppositional texts," I am thinking, of course, of Partha Chatterjee, *Nationalist Thought*, and *The Nation and Its Fragments: Colonial and Postcolonial Histories* (Princeton: Princeton Univ. Press, 1993).

42. Percival Spear, *India: A Modern History* (Ann Arbor: Univ. of Michigan Press, 1972), pp. 229, 235. Any extended consideration would "read" the "archives" in order to problematize common "factual" generalizations such as "exhaustion of the countryside," "general stagnation of life," and "social diseases" and raise the question of this overdetermined production, a strategy beyond the reach of the specializing undergraduate, the active unit of ideological production for whom such authoritative texts are written. The undoubtedly well-meant love and gratitude for "India" and "Indians," like all proper names, are "effects of the real," "repre-

problematic as "new start" firmly covers over the contradiction between a mission to restore and a project to "world" a "world" that we
have noticed earlier. (This contradiction is displaced into our own
moral dilemma between "tradition" and "development.") In fact, even
if the focus is England rather than India, it is possible to argue that the
part (Indian administration) began to alter the nature of the whole (the
home government) rather than necessarily vice versa.[43]

Let us return to the suggestion that the invaginated state makes
crudely visible the "economic in the last instance." Here is a passage
from another standard textbook, C. H. Philips's *The East India Company
(1784–1834)*:

> Any person who bought shares in the capital stock of the East India
> Company was denominated a Proprietor, and was permitted to attend
> the meetings of the General Court of Proprietors. The possession of
> £500 stock entitled the holder to vote "in a show of hands"; possession
> of £1,000 stock gave the Proprietor one vote in a ballot, £3,000 two

---

sentations," and should be read as such. Spear, dealing only in realities and facts,
begins with a factual teleological narrative core, which he proceeds to expand in his
book: "The purpose of this book is to portray the transformation of India under the
impact of the West into a modern nation state" (Spear, *India*, pp. 231–233, p. vii).
Indeed, I choose Spear rather than an up-to-date research historian because he is
much closer to the general view, certainly in the United States. To lend the name
"transformation" to this tremendous and uneven clash of discursive formations is to
exclude all else in the history of the colony and the postcolony but the itinerary:
native informant / colonial subject / postcolonial subject / globalized subject—that
this book is trying to trace. In the wake of the Cold War, there is a mood of
triumphalist Americanism in the United States. "Democratization," code name for
the transformation of (efficient through inefficient to wild) state capitalisms and
their colonies to tributary economies of rationalized global financialization—
carries with it the aura of the civilizing mission of earlier colonialisms. Again, the
talk is of "transformation." And it is now more specifically in terms of gender than
anything else. This is the globalized subject. The rationalization of sexuality, the
invasive restructuring of gender relations, poor women's credit-baiting without
infrastructural involvement in the name of women's micro-enterprise, the revision
of women-in-development (modernization) to gender-and-development (New
World Economic Order)—all this is seen as global sisterhood. The Rani of Sirmur
is a remote harbinger.
    43. See for instance, Christopher Hill, *Pelican Economic History of Britain*, vol. 2
(New York: Penguin, 1969), pp. 216–220.

votes, £6,000 three votes, and £10,000 and upwards four votes, which was the maximum. A contemporary writer maliciously described the General Court as "a popular senate; no distinction as to citizenship— the Englishman, the Frenchman, the American; no difference as to religion—the Jew, the Turk, the Pagan; no impediment as to sex—the old women of both sexes."

It is interesting to note that "Thackeray's *mulatto* heiress in *Vanity Fair* had three starts (or votes) to her name in the East India Proprietors' List."[44] *This* scenario is what the-Company-protecting-a-woman-protecting-a-child will ensure, in the colony. This is also a question of representation—as portrait and as proxy.[45]

India did not become an *imperial* possession until the second half of the nineteenth century. By then the foundations of what we call "colonial production" were firmly in place. The East India Company was dissolved in 1858, a year *after* the Indian Mutiny.

The protracted history of the growing conflict between Their Majesties' governments and the Company seems familiar to the non-specialist, then, in the context of current struggles between nations and transnationals, even as the specialist reminds us that the conflict emerged as a belated supplement to the earlier domestic conflict between the administrative machinery of mercantile interests on the one hand and the state on the other. By the India Act of 1784, Pitt sought to curb the Company. One of his chief achievements was the institution of the Board of Control, which would exercise a controlling influence on the Company. My last example in Section 2 illustrates this. The Court of Directors of the Company had written to its Governor-General: "The first and main point in which you have erred has been in permitting Europeans not in the *Company*'s service to remain in India;" and the Board of Control, the part of the Company that stood for the putative whole, the British state, had substituted: "Whatever . . . the

44. C. H. Philips, *The East India Company (1784–1834)* (Manchester: Manchester Univ. Press, 1961), p. 2.
45. On the contemporary representation of third-world women as victims, see Chandra Talpade Mohanty, "Under Western Eyes: Feminist Scholarship and Colonial Discourses," in Chandra Talpade Mohanty et al., eds., *Third World Women and the Politics of Feminism* (Bloomington: Indiana Univ. Press, 1991), pp. 51–80.

propriety of the orders we desire that they may be implicitly obeyed." Here the conflict between politics (the State) and economics (the Company), in that historical conjuncture, becomes abundantly clear. The East India Company is a paranational entity establishing its own political domain in an ad hoc way. Its indirect sphere of influence extends beyond Britain and India, into, for example, the fledgling United States.[46] The nation-state, the proper repository of centralized political power, aims at, and finally succeeds in, bringing the Company under its will. It is a prefiguration of the murderous, changeful, and productive contradictions between politics and economics within which we live today. To define colonialism as *either* rupture *or* continuity alone might thus be to reduce overdetermination to a species of determinism.

Of course the political discourse available to the individual agents of the Company came from yet elsewhere. Although the ideologues of the Company could theorize the Permanent Settlement in economic terms by way of physiocracy, mercantilism, and free trade—in power/knowledge terms, especially in the case of "protected" native states like the Hill States, it was the discourse of feudalism that was at hand.[47] Ochterlony in secret consultation writes to the governor-general: "If there be a native government established it appears to his lordship that it ought to possess all the *visible* signs of sovereignty compatible with its feudal relation towards the British government, which may give it responsibility in the eyes of subjects."[48]

An exquisite amalgam of the imagery of feudalism, mercantilism, and militarism, shadowily prefiguring the discourse of neocolonialism, is to be found in a letter from John Adam to Ochterlony:

> You will remember that it was proposed to occupy the Kaardah Doon permanently for the Hon'bl Company. This possession besides its eventual importance in a military point of view might contribute to the general reimbursement of the expense which the British Govern-

---

46. For an account of the Company's American trade, see Philips, *East India Company*, pp. 106–107, 156–158. Mutatis mutandis, elite cultural studies today can become a minute part of the trade in intellectual property along this route.
47. See Spivak, "More on Power/Knowledge," in *Outside*, pp. 25–51.
48. Bengal Secret Correspondence, 2 Aug. 1815.

ment must necessarily incur . . . and generally, to perform all the duties resulting from the feudatory relation in which they will stand towards us and to secure the free passage of our merchants and their goods through their respective territories, or else to guarantee in a proclamation to be published throughout the territories under consideration.[49]

We have already commented upon the thematics of obligation and duty. The publication of a proclamation authenticates the factual bases of these pseudo-ethical requirements. The facts are seen as based on feudal axiomatics, even as the metropolitan literature of this period can be shown to draw from imperialist axiomatics. It is now possible to suggest that these mechanics of the constitution of "facts" are dissimulated in the official historical record—the book of facts—institutionally represented on the level of general education by a book like Spear's *India*.

The resort to feudal discourse can equally be supported by an inability or refusal to recognize the principle of commercial monopoly by territorial infringement when it was operated by the natives as a localized version of *their* so-called entitlement. Thus Geoffrey Birch to John Adam:

I shall also beg leave to mention one species of oppression which I see no remedy for without putting government to some expense. Kalsee is the Mart for all the country lying between the Jumna and Tonse, and Merchandize is also frequently bought from Gurwal and Bussahir. As there is no place of shelter for the Traders to resort to, the Mahajens and Bunneahs of the town invite them to their houses, and I learn there is an understanding amongst them, that another shall not interfere with them in bidding for the merchandize in his house, consequently the trader is at his mercy as to the price, independent, of which he charges for the accommodation and for weighting or counting the goods.[50]

---

49. Ibid., 22 May 1815.
50. Board's Collections, 1819–1820, extract Bengal Secret Consultations, 12 Nov. 1815.

Birch "remedies" this oppression by introducing supervised and equitable weights and measures. Here indeed for a moment the discourse of classical Marxism seems to take on explanatory importance. For, even as a new cartography is being written on this disputed terrain, what is being introduced is exploitation with no extra-economic coercion. Labor power is, as it were, being freed. Arrived here, however, the analysis must be complicated. For, to control the field of an indiscriminate "freeing" of labor power—as a preliminary prefiguration of the international division of labor—something happens that Western Marxist apologists for imperialism have not been able to account for: a phantasmatic discourse of *race* is deployed. Here my argument is, of course, that imperialism is *not* racial determinism in the last instance. The burning question of the nineteenth century was not just the color line. The usefulness of the Rani-with-prince-separate-from-husband in this feudal-capitalist textualizing of the limits of the colony is a complex deployment of gender.

In order to construct the Rani of Sirmur as an object of knowledge, then, it should be grasped that she emerges in the archives because of the commercial/territorial interests of the East India Company. We have brought the discussion in the previous section to the point where it can be argued that the colonial context did not allow the emergence of the clean contours of a "working class."[51] This section will discuss briefly the deployment of the discourse of race in view of the appropriation of a role in gendering.

On my way to the Rani, I must therefore stop for a moment on Robert Ross. He maps the hill country cognitively.

He was born in Perth in 1789. He arrived in India at age sixteen. He was truly a vulgar-fraction lad. He was a bit free-spirited in his dealings with the Company, and, when he died on the Cape in 1854, he was in some disfavor. What is important for us is that *this* was the boy who, between the ages of twenty-three and twenty-five, compiled a brief

---

51. For a discussion of this in the context of Bengal but with considerably wider application, see Dipesh Chakrabarty, *Rethinking Working-Class History: Bengal, 1890–1940* (Princeton: Princeton Univ. Press, 1989).

"Statistical and Geographical Memoir of the Hill Countries Situated between the Rivers Tamas and Sutlej." *This* was the "authoritative" document constructed out of hearsay and interpreted conversations that, by the Court of Director's own admission in a dispatch to Bengal, obtained approval of the "restoration" of the ancient kingdoms in the hills.[52] And the Rani became an instrument. Thus the lines of restoring (a) woman's history according to Western definitions of historicity were laid down.

Ross's brief demographic analysis of the hills is that the *people* there are all "aboriginals of various kinds"; that the Sikhs, the Gurkhas, and the Moguls are varieties of "foreign yoke"; and that the rightful lords of the land are the Hindu chiefs about whose provenance or origin he is silent. This naive and phantasmatic race-differentiated historical demography is, curiously enough, identical in its broad outlines with the Aryanist version of ancient India that historians like Romila Thapar question.[53] What is at stake is a "worlding," the reinscription of a cartography that must (re)present itself as impeccable. I have written above of the contradiction involved in the necessary colonialist presupposition of an uninscribed earth. That uneasy contradiction is made visible in the Court's simultaneous acceptance as "evidence" of Ross's race-divisive unauthorized historical demography with a mild "suggestion," in the event ignored, "that he should give references to the authorities on which he founds his details, particularly the historical statements which he deduced from remote ages"; and their guarded refusal of such status to a "native" map. "This map, although being of Native hands,

---

52. Despatches to Bengal, vol. 22, collections 13,990–14,004, Bengal Political Department, answers to letters, 10, 12 and 28 Dec. 1816; and quotation from Service Army List: Bengal, vol. 2, Military Records.

53. In *Ancient India: A Textbook of History for Middle Schools* (New Delhi: NCERT, 1975), and *Medieval India: A Textbook of History for Middle Schools* (New Delhi: NCERT, 1978), Professor Thapar attempted to control the production of this narrative at the level of secondary education. (See also Thapar, *Interpreting Early India* [New York: Oxford Univ. Press, 1992]). Forces of national and global politics and political economy have used what we here see in Ross to mobilize large-scale Hindu nationalist violence, which justifies itself as reactive and restorative. To see this narrative in action globally, see Biju Mathew et al., "Vasudhaiva Kutumbakam: The Hindu in the World," forthcoming in *Diasporas*.

Sir David Ochterlony does not venture to rely on it, would have served
to give us some idea."[54]

Even as Ross and Birch are hoping that it is the "aboriginal subjects"
who will be transformed by the "extraction and appropriation of surplus-value with no extra-economic coercions" (free wage-labor) and by
what today we would call "training in consumerism" (quite different
from "raising the standard of living"—their phrase is "introducing imperceptibly a gradual improvement in the habits and manners of the
people"),[55] it is the Hindu chiefs whose claims they endorse and autho-
rize. The full ideological flowering of this authorization—the divisive
deployment of the discourse of race—is to be seen in the correct but
aesthetically indifferent verses composed by Sir Monier Monier-
Williams seventy years later and inscribed on the doorway of the Indian
Institute at Oxford, the last line of which runs: May the mutual friendship of the land of the Aryans and the land of the Anglos constantly
increase.

Even this racialized appropriation of caste-Hinduism was, of course,
asymmetrical. One effect of establishing a version of the British system
was the development of an uneasy separation between disciplinary formation in institutional studies and the native, now alternative, tradition
of "high culture." Within the former, the cultural explanations generated by authoritative scholars began to match the planned epistemic
violence in the fields of education and the law.[56]

I locate here not only the founding of the Indian Institute at Oxford
in 1883, but also of the Asiatic Society of Bengal in 1784, and the
immense analytic and taxonomic work undertaken by scholars such as
Arthur Macdonnell and Arthur Berriedale Keith, who were both colonial administrators and organizers of the matter of Sanskrit. From their
confident utilitarian-hegemonic plans for students and scholars of Sanskrit, it is impossible to guess at either the aggressive repression of

54. Despatches to Bengal, Answer to Political Letter of 11 Dec. 1816; dated 1
Dec. 1819.
55. Board's Collection, 1819–1820, Extract Bengal Secret Consultations, 27
Oct. 1815.
56. Gauri Viswanathan, *The Masks of Conquest* (New York: Columbia Univ.
Press, 1989), offers a documented narrative of this phenomenon.

Sanskrit in the general educational framework, or the increasing "feudalization" of the performative use of Sanskrit in the everyday life of Brahminical-hegemonic India. A version of history was gradually established in which the Brahmin was shown to have the same intentions toward the Hindu code as the codifying British: "In order to preserve Hindu society intact [the] successors [of the original Brahmins] had to reduce everything to writing and make them more and more rigid. And that is what has preserved Hindu society in spite of a succession of political upheavals and foreign invasions."[57]

This is the 1925 verdict of Mahāmahopadhyāya Haraprasad Shastri, learned Indianist, brilliant representative of the indigenous elite within colonial production. To signal the asymmetry in the relationship between authority and explanation (depending on the race-class of the authority) compare this 1928 remark by Edward Thompson, English intellectual: "Hinduism was what it seemed to be. . . . It was a higher civilization that won [against it], both with Akbar and the English."[58] And add this, from a letter by an English soldier-scholar in the last decade of the last century: "The study of Sanskrit, 'the language of the gods' has afforded me intense enjoyment during the last 25 years of my life in India, but it has not, I am thankful to say, led me, *as it has some*, to give up a hearty belief in our own grand religion."[59]

Let us return to the case of Sirmur. Under the auspices of a race-divisive historiography, Robert Ross gives to each hill state an "original" outdated outline, and then a second dated outline, generally marked with a seventeenth- or eighteenth-century date. The project is to restore to each state the lineaments of this second origin. Yet, just as the

---

57. Mahāmahopādhyāya Haraprasad Shastri, *A Descriptive Catalogue of Sanskrit Manuscripts in the Government Collection under the Care of the Asiatic Society of Bengal,* vol. 3 (Calcutta: Asiatic Society, 1925), p. viii.

58. Edward Thompson, *Suttee: A Historical and Philosophical Enquiry into the Hindu Rite of Widow-Burning* (London: 1925), pp. 130, 47.

59. Holograph letter (from G. A. Jacob to an unnamed correspondent) attached to inside front cover of the Sterling Memorial Library (Yale) copy of *The Mahanarayana-Upanishad of the Atharva-Veda with the Dipika of Narayana,* ed. Colonel G. A. Jacob (Bombay: Govt. Central Book Depot, 1888). Emphasis mine. Invocations of the peculiar dangers of this knowledge are a topos that belongs to the race differentiation that I am discussing in this chapter.

argument for class-formation cannot be sufficient in this context, the argument from race-division will also be seen not to be so.

The project of the restoration of origin did not apply to Sirmur. As we approach Sirmur, we move from the discourses of class and race into gender—and we are in the shadow of shadows. The Raja of Sirmur, Karam Prakash, was deposed by the British. The ostensible reason given was that he was barbaric and dissolute. Since the accusation of barbarism was brought in the secret correspondence against many of these chiefs, that does not seem sufficient grounds for removal from the throne. The only remaining reason, then, was that he had syphilis, which I take to be his "loathsome disease." The Rani is established as the immediate guardian of the minor king Fatteh Prakash, her son, because there are no trustworthy male relatives in the royal house. This, too, seems somewhat implausible, since Geoffrey Birch rides around with a man from the House of Sirmur, Duleep Singh by name, whose astuteness he elaborately praises. It would seem that it was necessary to hold Sirmur under a child guarded by a woman, because the "dismemberment of Sirmoor" (as spelled out in a secret communication) was in the cards. The entire eastern half of Sirmur had to be annexed immediately, and all of it eventually, to secure the Company's trade routes and frontier against Nepal, to investigate the efficacy of "opening a commercial communication through Bussaher with the country beyond the snowy mountains."[60]

This, then, is why the Rani surfaces briefly, as an individual, in the archives; because she is a king's wife and a weaker vessel, on the chessboard of the Great Game. We are not sure of her name. She is once referred to as Rani Gulani and once as Gulari. In general she is referred to, properly, as the Ranee by the higher officers of the Company, and "this Ranny" by Geoffrey Birch and Robert Ross.

Since woman is not a genitalist category, and because the women of royal houses have a special place, I must once again quote a bit of colonial discourse from Edward Thompson's *Suttee.*

The most detailed record of women's names in early colonial India is

60. Despatches to Bengal, Answer to Political Letter, 11 Dec. 1816, dated 1 Dec. 1819. Here we are in "the great game" mentioned in note 25.

in the context of widow self-immolation. There are many lists of pathetically misspelled names of the satis of the artisanal, peasant, village-priestly, money-lender, clerical, and comparable social groups from Bengal, where *Satis* were most common. Consider in that frame Edward Thompson's words of praise for General Charles Hervey's appreciation of the problem of *Sati:* "Hervey has a passage which brings out the pity of a system which looked only for prettiness and constancy in woman. He obtained the names of satis who had died on the pyres of Bikanir Rajas; they were such names as: 'Ray Queen, Sun-ray, Love's Delight, Garland, Virtue Found, Echo, Soft Eye, Comfort, Moonbeam, Love-lorn, Dear Heart, Eye-play, Arbour-born, Smile, Love-bud, Glad Omen, Mist-clad, or Cloud-sprung—the last a favourite name.'"[61]

There is no more dangerous pastime than transposing proper names into common nouns, translating them, and using them as sociological evidence. I attempt to reconstruct the names on that list and begin to feel Hervey-Thompson's arrogance. What, for instance, might "Comfort" have been. Was it "Shanti"? Readers are reminded of the last line of T. S. Eliot's *The Waste Land.* There the word bears the mark of one kind of stereotyping of India—the grandeur of the ecumenical *Upanisads.* Or was it "Swasti"? Readers are reminded of the *swastika,* the brahmanic ritual mark of domestic comfort (as in "God Bless Our Home") stereotyped into a criminal parody of Aryan hegemony. Between these two appropriations, where is our pretty and constant burnt widow? The aura of the names owes more to writers like Edward Fitzgerald, the "translator" of the *Rubayyat of Omar Khayyam,* who helped to construct a certain picture of the oriental woman through the supposed "objectivity" of translation, than to sociological exactitude.[62] By this sort of reckoning, the translated proper names of a random

---

61. Thompson, *Suttee,* p. 132.

62. Edward W. Said, *Orientalism* (New York: Pantheon, 1978) remains the authoritative text here. It is not that names are unimportant. In 1996, Megawati Sukarnoputri is mobilizing for power in Indonesia. She has discarded her married name and chosen a last name which means "daughter of [former President] Sukarno," for obvious reasons. Her first name, meaning "Cloudsprung," celebrates the rainy day of her birth, says her father. Barbara Crossette, writing in *The New*

collection of contemporary French philosophers, or board of directors of prestigious southern U.S. corporations, would give evidence of a ferocious investment in an archangelic and hagiocentric theocracy.

Against such olympian violations of women's names we have the meticulously preserved baptismal records of each and every cadet in the Company's service. Where no baptismal certificate could be located, there is an impressive array of legal attestations to establish identity. A title and a vaguely sketched first name will suffice for the king of Sirmur's wife because of the specific purpose she is made to serve. According to the first charter, "the executive authority was to be in the Ranee and the Constitutive Officers of the Government subject to the control and direction of Captain Birch acting under the orders of Sir David Ochterlony on the part of the British Government, [and] the Military Defence of the Country was to devolve on the British Government."

Only two specific acts of hers are recorded. As soon as she is strictly separated from her deposed and banished husband, his other two wives, who had been parceled off to yet another place for fear of intrigue, ask to come back to her household and are received. Soon after, she remembers a great-aunt with whom her husband had long ago quarrelled and re-institutes a pension for her. She is astute. She allocates Rs. 900, but promises Rs. 700 at first because she knows that Auntie will ask for more. These events are recorded because they cost money. "It has been necessary for Captain Birch," Ochterlony writes, "occasionally to interfere with her authoritatively to counteract the facility of the Ranee's disposition."[63] We imagine her in her crumbling palace, separated from the authority of her no doubt patriarchal and dissolute husband, sud-

---

York Times, identifies her as one of a number of dynastic female leaders in Asia ("Enthralled by Asia's Ruling Women? Look Again," 10 Nov. 1996, sec. 4, p. 3, col. 1). Female leaders in Europe—Margaret Thatcher or Pamela Harriman—are identified with capital. How does one choose between capitalism and patriarchy? The once and current socialist countries have not been well known for feminism. All of this has to be pondered if we decide to work at Sukarnoputri's naming; not to mention, given Indonesian politics, its Sanskrit rather than Arabic provenance. My schoolfriend Hasi (Smile) has been a doctor at a hospital in San Antonio for nearly twenty years.

63. Board's Collections, 1819–1820, extract Bengal Secret Consultations, Adani to Ochterlony, 22 May 1815.

denly managed by a young white man in her own household. Such examples must be accommodated within the epistemic violence of the worlding of worlds that I have described above. For this too is the sudden appearance of an alien agent of "true" history in native space. There is no romance to be found here. Caught thus between patriarchy and imperialism, she is in a representative predicament, a woman whose "exchange," from "feudal" to "modern," as the agent of her subject-child, will establish historicity.

And then the Rani suddenly declares her intention to be a *Sati*. One cannot accuse Geoffrey Birch of reporting on the Rani too leniently. Therefore it is particularly noticeable that he is obliged to use the language of affect when he does report this to the Resident in Delhi:

> This Ranny appears to be completely devoted to her husband, of which you may greatly judge by the following conversation which took place in a conference I had with her sometime ago [sic] she observed, that "her life and the Rajah's are one" which I consequently concluded to allude to her intention of burning herself at his death, so I replied, she should now relinquish all thoughts of doing so, and devote herself to the love of her son and live for him. She said to the effect, that it was so decreed and she must not attend to advice deviating from it: so I conclude, she has resolved upon sacrificing herself.[64]

Now begins the tale of a singular manipulation of her private life (I am aware of the problems with introducing a notion of "private life" into this context. Let us assume it as a name for whatever it is that is being maneuvered in the "separation of interests" between indigenous patriarchy and colonial government.): "I should consider a very grateful office, if Government may think proper to authorize my interference to prevent the Ranny fulfilling her intention. The best mode of effecting it would probably present itself on the occasion, but I should feel great satisfaction by being honored with any regulation from government for my conduct upon it."

This chapter will end with an analysis of the Brahmanical discourse

---

64. Board's Collections, 1819–1820, extract Bengal Secret Consultations, copy of a letter from Birch to Metcalfe included in Metcalfe to Adam, 5 Mar. 1816.

of widow sacrifice: beginning with moments from its so-called authority in the *Ṛg-Veda*, through the admonitory texts of the *Dharmaśāstra*, the legal sanctions of the sixteenth century and after. I will work toward the conclusion that widow-sacrifice was a manipulation of female *subject*-formation by way of a constructed counter-narrative of woman's consciousness, thus woman's being, thus woman's being-good, thus the good woman's desire, thus woman's desire; so that, since *Sati* was not the invariable rule for widows, this sanctioned suicide could paradoxically become the signifier of woman as exception. I will suggest that the British ignore the space of *Sati* as an ideological battleground, and construct the woman as an *object* of slaughter, the saving of which can mark the moment when not only a civil but a good society is born out of domestic chaos. Between patriarchal subject-formation and imperialist object-constitution, it is the place of the free will or agency of the sexed subject as female that is successfully effaced.[65]

For the female "subject," a sanctioned self-immolation within Hindu patriarchal discourse, even as it takes away the effect of "fall" attached to an unsanctioned suicide, brings praise for the act of choice on another register. By the inexorable ideological production of the sexed subject, such a death can be understood by the female subject as an *exceptional* signifier of her own desire, exceeding the general rule of a widow's conduct. The self-immolation of widows was not *invariable* ritual prescription. *If, however, the widow did decide thus to exceed the letter of ritual*, to turn back was a transgression for which a particular type of penance is prescribed. When before the era of abolition, a petty British police officer was obliged to be present at each widow-sacrifice to ascertain its "legality," to be dissuaded by him after a decision was, by contrast, read as a mark of real free choice, a choice of freedom. Within the two contending versions of freedom, the constitution of the female subject *in life* was thoroughly undermined.

These years were also the time when the British were assiduously

---

65. For further distinctions between subject and agent, see Spivak, "Reading *The Satanic Verses*" and "Scattered Speculations on the Question of Culture Studies," *Outside*, pp. 217–241, 255–284; and "A Dialogue on Democracy," in David Trend, ed., *Radical Democracy: Identity, Citizenship, and the State* (New York: Routledge, 1995), p. 218.

checking out the legality of *Sati*s by consulting pundits and priests. (In the event, when the law abolishing *Sati* was written, the discourse was once again the race-divisive one of the bestial Hindu versus the noble Hindu, the latter being represented as equally outraged by the practice as the British.)

For obvious reasons, the Rani was not susceptible to these general moves toward *Sati*. Saving *her* could not provide the topos of the founding of a good society. As we have argued, restoration of Aryan authority combined in contradiction with the proto-proletarianization of the Aborigine had already filled that requirement. She could not be offered the choice to choose freedom. She was asked to live for her son; and she responded from within her patriarchal formation. She must not be allowed to perform even a "legal" *sati*, and, therefore, for her, pundits could not be consulted to produce the proper patriarchal legal sanction. In her case, the pundits must be coerced to produce *expedient* advice. Here discursive representation almost assumes the status of analysis, although, if one begins to wonder what "every means of influence and persuasion" might mean, that confidence begins to waver.

Here is the governor's secretary's letter to the resident:

> The question referred is one of great delicacy and has attracted a proportionate share of the attention of the Governor General in Council. The general practice of the British Government of abstaining from authoritative interference in matters so closely allied to the religious prejudice of natives among its own subjects, must be considered to be peculiarly incumbent on it with reference to persons of the Ranee's condition in life . . . The considerations which in all cases must influence the Government . . . are powerfully aided by the peculiar circumstances of the Ranee's situation and *the political importance of the continued exercise by her of the administration of the Raj of Sirmore during the minority of Rajah Futteh Perkash.* While, therefore, the Governor General in Council cannot direct any authoritative or compulsory interference in this case, His Lordship in Council is ardently desirous, that every means of influence and persuasion should be employed to induce the Ranee to forgoe her supposed determination. His Lordship in Council is induced to hope, that the circumstance of her being actually engaged in the administration of the Government of her Son, the acknowledged importance of her continuing to perform the public functions of belonging to that situation, together with

the actual *separation of interests* which must now be deemed to subsist between her and her husband, may, if explained and represented with suitable skill and address to the Pundits and Brahmins whose authority is likely to sway the Ranee's opinion, lead to such a declaration on their part as would satisfy her mind and lead her to adopt a different resolution. . . . The Governor General in Council authorises Captain Birch to refuse to convey any message from Kurram Pergash [her husband] to the Ranee [to the effect that she should accompany him to a more distant place of banishment], and to signify to him as well as to the Ranee herself . . . that the paramount duty of watching over the interests of the minor Rajah and his subjects must supersede any obligation of duty toward her husband which under other circumstances might render her complying with his wishes expedient and proper.

(I should mention here that "paramount" is an epithet invariably associated with imperial power.) In that last sentence of the letter, authority annuls itself most strongly by vesting the agent: "Captain Birch will accordingly interpose to prevent the Rannee's removal from Sirmore without the consent of the Governor General in Council."[66] "Separation of interest from her husband." This is one of the major wedges of contemporary credit-baiting; credit extended to wives alone. It is an overdetermined script of cultural intervention: capital versus patriarchy as well as capital colluding with patriarchy.

But had Captain Birch read the Rani right? Did she after all merely want to be with her husband and leave her colonized prison palace? If Birch is reading her motive and desire wrong, it is an example of critical subject-predication being practiced in a crude though successfully oppressive way. The next few letters in the secret consultation merely defer the Rajah's further banishment, almost as if not to test the Rani's resolution.

And there the matter is dropped.

The present provisional end of the story will be familiar to anyone who has researched in collections of records. Yet I do want to dwell on this all too familiar phenomenon to note the pattern of exclusions that makes the familiar function as such. As the historical record is made up,

---

66. Board's Collections, 1819–1820, Adam to Metcalfe, 22 May 1815.

who is dropped out, when, and why? We remind ourselves of the meticulously tabulated cadets whose existence is considered "reasonable" enough for the production of the account of history. The Rani emerges only when she is needed in the space of imperial production.

I have no training in or aptitude for archival research. I looked at a broader spread of the political and secret correspondence with India, at the Crown Representative Records, at the Residency Records, at a set of Privy Council Appeals, and at Bengal Proceedings in general. The Rani is not in any of these things. In the era of the abolition, a Royal Sati would have been a minor embarrassment.

The end of the story is, in an academic sense, uneventful. I found out, to a fair degree of certainty, that she had died a natural death. The steps to the discovery would not seem terribly out-of-the-way to a regular investigative colonial historian. But I want to dwell on this very ordinariness. I want to ask what is not considered important enough by the hidden parts of the discipline, hidden only because they are too well known in their typicality to be of any interest to anyone engaged in the retrieval of knowledge. I want to dwell on it because work with deconstructive approaches to the subject and with the ethical concerns of the final Foucault have made me more and more aware of the importance of the neglected details of the everyday. (In the central part of this chapter, I will keep undisturbed an earlier dissatisfaction with Foucault's itinerary before he made his final move.)

Of what is history made as it happens? Of the differed-deferred "identity" of people in the deferred-differed "unity" of actions. When we speak on this level of sophistication, attempting to grasp the inaccessible intimacy of the least sophisticated, least self-conscious way of being, it is the bits and pieces found unspectacular by the search for the Rani that are most rich in educative promise. I am not speaking of a history-writing that concentrates on the object-details of everyday life rather than merely on narrative or intellectual analysis of great events, although that is, indeed, a great gain. I am speaking of a history that can attend to the details of the putting together of a continuous-seeming self for everyday life. This may well be the limit of history-*writing*. In Heidegger, a version of this would be the "historial" rather than the historical. In pursuit of this, Foucault finally took a distance from history as chronology. And Derrida remains interested in the chanciness that must be reined in in the necessary production of this continuity.

These are not just problems of writing the history of the Rani of Sirmur, but the writing of history in general. Paradoxically, the retrieval of the history of the margin can be a lesson not only to the writing of woman's history triumphant, but also to the writing of the most hegemonic historical accounts. This is not merely a rhetorical device until enough research has been done. Or, if so, this is the strongest sense of rhetoric, which works at the silences between bits of language to see what will work as meaning, to ward off a silence filled with nothing but noise. And the "until" signals a logical rather than a chronological future, logic marking a point beyond which systematic research cannot capture what the everyday sense of self shores up. It is to emphasize these limits that I will briefly mention the fadeout points in the unspectacular retrieval routine of the news of the Rani's death. It must be kept in mind that by the account of these fadeout points, I represent the rhetorical limits of logic, which in turn disclose, by cor-doning off, the violent limits of rhetoricity. No one can "present" them, or to present (them) is to represent. It must also be kept in mind that, given a different structure of authority and policing in the sub-Himala-yan rural areas of India in the late eighteenth and nineteenth centuries, in trying to locate the Rani we may be groping in the margins of official Western history, but we are not among marginal women in their con-text. (This difference might not necessarily be an earlier stage in evolu-tionary progression; it may have a relationship with a different ethic, consideration of which would take us too far afield.)

The first step was to go to Nahan, the county seat of the modern district of Sirmur. Unlike the archives, where the past is already di-gested as the raw material for history writing, the past here is a past of memory, which constitutes itself differently in different subjects inter-connecting. This is a fadeout that literature has tried to capture rhetori-cally, and that regular "historical fiction" tries to deny.[67] One of the most fascinating aspects of postcoloniality in a former colony is the palimpsest of precolonial and postcolonial continuity ruptured by the imperfect imposition of an Enlightenment episteme, itself traves-

---

67. I would cite here two texts as different as Rainer Maria Rilke, *The Notebooks of Malte Laurids Brigge*, tr. Stephen Mitchell (New York: Random House, 1983) and Devi, "Pterodactyl."

tied in the metropolitan social formations of the eighteenth and nine-teenth centuries. The ordinary rural folk of the remote hill district of Sirmur, outside of British India proper, were re-coded by the rupture more in the breach than in the commission. Independent India has put the mark of electoral politics as well as the economic re-composition of the rural landowning class upon this "backward" area of the modern state of Himachal Pradesh, of which Sirmur is a part. Legally, the so-called royal house of Sirmur no longer exists. Yet, by a rather com-mon paradox, the house had come to feel its "royal"-ness rather more strongly under colonial influence, writing its accoutrements on a Euro-pean model, or even perhaps a European conception of a "native" King. The history of this re-territorialized self-representation begins from the reign of Fateh Prakash, and I found the usual ledgers, portraits, photographs, by showing interest to the last secretary of the last "King," who died in 1948. From the end of the century one began to see photographs of the Ranis, models for emancipated ladies in Raj films or Satyajit Ray's *The Home and the World* and now mobilizable into Hindu nationalism (see note 25). The old "retainer"'s (no other word seems right) nostalgia was for this pre-telematic colonial "hyper-real." The current occupant of the palace is an elected member of the state legislative assembly and seems as thoroughly involved in the post-colonial re-coding and re-territorializing of "democracy" as his great-great-grandfather had been in a similar project around the cultural-political signifier "aristocracy"; both relating catachrestically to European social formations. My Rani stands, liminally, on the shadow-border of the prehistory of this colonial/postcolonial (dis)con-tinuity. She can be invoked, for she is Fateh Prakash's mother, and he is in history, when history is understood on the Western model. But she cannot be commemorated.

On my many visits to Nahan, I had to play the lines of favor in a network reminiscent of a litigious rather than military *Prisoner of Zenda*. Fateh Prakash's line ended in female issue, now the younger queen of Jaipur. The male descendant of the younger male line occupies the vanished throne. But the seat is being contested by the Maharani of Jaipur.

Jaipur, one of the beauty spots of Northwest India, and home of the famous pink stone palace hotel, is one of the best-known former native principalities of British India. Here we must think of constant international travel, indeed of the global cosmopolitan elite. Here the border between migrant and indigenous has shifted from above, although popular Hindu nationalism today is to be found here too. Any attempt to think of Rani Gulari in the context of contemporary India would produce the cosmopolitan litigious elite Maharani of Jaipur. My account can at best mark rupture, fadeout, colonial discontinuity.

In fact, as a result of the litigation, the fortified old palace is under lock and key. By favor of Jaipur's representative, I spent a night in this palace, where the Rani had lived under Geoffrey Birch's surveillance. I was locked in as night fell, for the presence of any party involved in the litigation would have prejudiced the case. The palace as space is thoroughly inscribed into the British Civil Code and what the British had codified as Hindu Law (legitimacy and inheritance). Spacious outer quarters reminiscent of some macabre stage set for *Great Expectations*, low-ceilinged, cage-like inner quarters with the inevitable stucco network in front.

The narrative pathos of this unscholarly account is at a great remove from the austere practice of critical philosophy. Yet, the differantial contaminations of absolute alterity (even to utter the words is to differentiate them from some other thing, which should of course be impossible) that allow us to mime responsibility to the other, cannot allow this pathos merely to be faded out. As I approached her house after a long series of detective maneuvers, I was miming the route of an unknowing, a progressive différance, an "experience" of how I could not know her. Nothing unusual here, and therefore never considered worthy of mention, of notice.

The palace was a legend of this deferment and difference. On the south, past the open terrace and directly below it, stretched the peaks and waves of the foothills of the Himalayas as far as the eye could see. I was halted by the discourse of the European sublime and, percolated through it, Kalidāsa, the fifth-century Sanskrit court-poet beloved of Goethe, both out of the Rani's reach. To the East, the less lofty two-storied Mughal wing of the women's quarters, with the stucco jalousies, now permanently locked, undoubtedly the Rani's habitation. I was lodged in the men's wing, added on in the nineteenth century, with its floor-to-ceiling tarnished mirrors and life-size portraits of indifferent quality. In between a Kali temple totally embraced by a giant *ashwathva* tree. Here I was halted by my own ideological formation as child of a

Kali-worshipping sect, an East Indian phenomenon imbricated with the so-called Bengal Renaissance, as clearly out of the Rani's reach.[68] There were no papers, the ostensible reason for my visit, and of course, no trace of the Rani. Again, a reaching and an un-grasping.

I made five visits in all. This was the last. On the very first try, in search of the palace, I had walked about in the hills where buses did not go. Shy hardy women gathered leaves and vegetation from the hillside to feed their goats. They could not have had a historical memory of the Rani. And they are, have been historically, at a distance from the culture of imperialism, and from the relay between princely state and nation-state that swept the Rani's descendants into its currents and whirlpools. They were the rural subaltern, the real constituency of feminism, accepting their lot as the norm, quite different from the urban female sub-proletarian in crisis and resistance. If I wanted to touch their everyday without the epistemic transcoding of anthropological field work, the effort would be a much greater undoing, indeed, of life's goals, than the effort to catch the Rani in vain, in history. These are the familiar limits of knowing; why do we resist it when deconstruction points at them?

Development studies of Indian women tell us that this group of women, unorganized landless female labor, is one of the targets of super-exploitation where local, national, and international capital intersect.[69] I must look into the available statistics to see if Himachal Pradesh falls into this category.[70] By that route of super-exploitation these women are brought into capital logic, into the possibility of crisis and

---

68. For "Bengal Renaissance," see Atulchandra Gupta, ed., *Studies in the Bengal Renaissance* (Calcutta: National Council of Education, 1977). The Rani's son had visited the Brahmo Samaj.

69. See Kalpana Bardhan, "Women, Work, Welfare and Status: Forces of Tradition and Change in India," in *South Asia Bulletin* 6.1 (Spring 1986).

70. Here is the notched mark of another invagination. This sentence was written in 1990. All it would have taken is checking *The Economic and Political Weekly* or a bit of computer-surfing in the library catalogues. But the author of this book is literary by inclination, drawn to the singular and unverifiable text, and sufficiently influenced by deconstruction to think that lives are woven or text-ile as well. (This is, after all, the argument that I have been making about literary authors.) For her the "looking into" came to involve developing critical intimacy with (the situation of) these women. And she realized once again that the text of lives, like the verbal

resistance and, paradoxically, the questioning becomes easier. This much is true. They are not part of any unified "third world women's resistance," an idea based on capital logic. Here is the parody of the "moral luck" of imperialism, by virtue of which I became a feminist. There are cement factories where the bus travels. Again, the Rani recedes.

I caught the Rani in an "alternative" record, a minimal thanatography for the priests' convenience. The priests of the House of Sirmur are in Hardwar. In the priests' house the past is not a past of memory. Indeed there is no past. The "books" are long scrolls, each resembling the other, a kind of "living present," released by death as simple punctuation.[71] Where does this stream of parchment begin? You could construct a disciplinary "historical" answer by consulting the right sources, or becoming a source yourself. But in fact it begins nowhere, for the

---

text, is caught, not even in language, but in idiom. (This is the argument I have been making about what falls out of the Ariel-Calibán debate.) She respects "curative" problem-solving crisis-work with an interpreter; but all she can do is the "preventive" work of the texture of subaltern teaching. And therefore she will be permitted to find it curious that little is said, in radical feminist writing in India, about the country's forbidding heteroglossia as a limit to "the secret encounter" (see Spivak, "Translator's Preface," *IM*, xxv; and "Scattered Speculations on the Question of Linguisticulture," in *Proceedings of the International Symposium on Linguisticulture* [Osaka: Univ. of Osaka Press, 1996], pp. i–viii). Following her "I must look into . . ." she retreated into areas where she could not only speak and teach the language, but with enough facility that she could shift idiom. Shamefacedly, forever a critic of Bengali chauvinism (about which the implied reader of this book will know little), she was obliged to locate her "looking into" in West Bengal and Bangladesh. Some mark of that move will surface in Chapter 4. Here suffice it to say that even in that retreat, Purulia and Chittagong stop her with indigenous languages and Arakan-Burmese hybrid idiom. This book is not yet ready to stop at those limits. On the other hand, and upon the register of great apparatuses, as World Trade becomes secondary to finance capital, the peculiar phenomenon of credit-baiting without infrastructural involvement or involvement in social redistribution (see note 41) creates a general subaltern will for the financialization of the globe. This is the new globalized subject, rather different from the visible violence of super-exploitation. This book now hems me in from that other text, as the Rani's trajectory did then.

71. Derrida's analysis of Husserl's "living present" as only accessible if the subject thinks its own death is to be found in *Speech and Phenomena: And Other Essays on Husserl's Theory of Signs*, tr. David B. Allison (Evanston: Northwestern Univ. Press, 1973), pp. 53–54.

first available scrolls are in medias res. The Rani was not a *Sati*. She died in 1837, and the list of ingredients for her funeral indicate that her death was "normal."

Theoreticist friends in Britain and the United States have found in my tracking of the Rani too much concern with "historical realism," too little with "theory." I remain perplexed by this critique. I hope a second reading will persuade them that my concern has been with the fabrication of representations of so-called historical reality.

At the other end of the spectrum, custodians of Critical Thought ask "what sort of society could ever be grounded in" what their cursory and "interested" reading reduces to "the linguistic nihilism" associated with deconstruction.[72] A careful deconstructive method, displacing rather than only reversing oppositions (such as between colonizer and colonized) by taking the investigator's own complicity into account—I remind the reader of my use of Freud as monitory model—does not wish to officiate at the grounding of societies, but rather to be the gadfly who alone may hope to take the distance accorded to a "critical" "thought," as she marks the distance between the "writing" and writing of history. "Germany" may have taught us to think the ethical subject, but imperialism used Woman, "freeing" her to legitimize itself.

We are proceeding, then, on the assumption that women outside of the mode of production narrative mark the points of fadeout in the writing of disciplinary history even as they mime "writing as such," footprints of the trace (of someone? something?—we are obliged mistakenly to ask) that efface as they disclose. If, as Jameson suggests, the mode of production narrative is the final reference, these women are insufficiently represented or representable in that narration. We can docket them, but we cannot grasp them at all. The possibility of possession, of being haunted, is cut by the imposition of the tough reasonableness of capital's mode of exploitation. Or, to tease out Marx rather than follow Jameson, the mode of production narrative is so efficient because it is constructed in terms of the most efficient and abstract coding of

---

72. Kenneth Asher, "Deconstruction's Use and Abuse of Nietzsche," *Telos* 62 (Winter 1984–85): 175.

value, the economic. Thus, to repeat an earlier intuition, the ground-level value-codings that write these women's lives elude us. These codes are measurable only in the (ebb and flow) mode of the total or expanded form, which is "defective" from a rationalist point of view. We pay the price of epistemically fractured transcoding when we explain them as general exemplars of anthropological descriptions.[73]

As a feminist literary critic pulling deconstruction into the service of reading, I am more attentive to these elusive figures, although of course deeply interested in the accounts of women who are in step with the mode of production narrative, as participants/resisters/victims. If indeed the relationship between capitalism and socialism is that of a *pharmakon* (medicine in *différance* with poison), these elusive figures mark moments where neither medicine nor poison quite catches. Indeed, it is only in their death that they enter a narrative *for us*, they become figurable. In the rhythm of their daily living, the elusion is familiarly performed or (un)performed, since to elude constatation in the act is not necessarily a performance. I attend to these figures because they continue to impose the highest standards on our technniques of re-

---

73. Therefore the UN must first rationalize "woman" before they can develop her. Yet the Rani of Sirmur and Bhubaneswari Bhaduri (*vide infra*), indeed Lily Moya and Rigoberta Menchú (see Shula Marks, ed., *Not Either an Experimental Doll* [Bloomington: Indiana Univ. Press, 1987]; and *I, Rigoberta Menchú: An Indian Woman in Guatemala*, tr. Ann Wright [London: Verso, 1984]), will be instructive if they remain singular and secretive (for "secret," see *IM* xxv). They must exceed the system to come to us, in the mode of the literary. Capital remains the accessible abstract in general—the matheme still contaminated by the human. Psychocultural *systems*—regulative psychobiographies, psychoanalysis included—tend toward it. In search of the discursive abstractions that are the condition and effect of the concrete singular, Foucault was smart to choose the rarefied rather than the "thick" (for documentation, see Spivak, "More on Power/Knowledge," *Outside*, pp. 25–51). But we must also attend to Menchú, reading her too against the grain of her necessarily identity-political idiom, borrowing from a much older collective tactic against colonial conquest: "Of course, I'd need a lot of time to tell you about all my people, because it's not easy to understand just like that. And I think I've given some idea of that in my account. Nevertheless, I'm still keeping my Indian identity a secret. I'm still keeping secret what I think no-one should know. Not even anthropologists or intellectuals, no matter how many books they have, can find out all our secrets" (p. 247). That text is not in books, and the secret keeps us, not the other way around.

trieval, even as they judge them, not in our rationalist mode. In fact, since they are outside of our efforts, their judgment is not intended. Following a certain statement of Derrida's, perhaps we should rather say: they are the figures of justice as the experience of the impossible.[74]

In this section I will focus on a figure who intended to be retrieved, who wrote with her body. It is as if she attempted to "speak" across death, by rendering her body graphematic.[75] In the archives, Rani Gulari emerges only on call, when needed, as coerced agent/instrument/witness for the colonialism of capital. She is the "purer" figure of

---

74. Since this writing, the textualist study of history has taken on a life of its own. For the U.S. literary critic, the pages of the journal *Representations* would yield the richest harvest. Other prominent texts are Carlo Ginzburg, *Myths, Emblems, Clues*, tr. John and Anne C. Tedeschi (London: Hutchinson, 1990); and Martin Jay, *Force Fields: Between Intellectual History and Cultural Critique* (New York: Routledge, 1993). Peter de Bolla gives an account of poststructuralist history in "Disfiguring History," *Diacritics* 16 (Winter 1986): 49–58. The list could go on. Joan Wallach Scott has productively unpacked LaCapra's transferential analogy by "historiciz[ing] both sides of [the relationship between the power of the historian's analytic frame and the events that are the object of his or her study] by denying the fixity and transcendence of anything that appears to operate as a foundation" ("Experience," in Judith Butler and Joan W. Scott, eds., *Feminists Theorize the Political* [New York: Routledge, 1992], p. 37). Scott's model can get "responsibility" going—asymmetrically. But with the Rani the asymmetry is so great that "responsibility" cannot catch. On the cusp of colonialism, she is pre-emergent for colonial discourse. In the pre-colonial dominant "Hindu" discourse she is absent except as a corpse by way of a funerary list. Indeed that dominant discourse goes underground by her living, precisely as (wife and mother) woman. There is no possibility of provincializing Europe here, as Dipesh Chakrabarty would have it, no possibility of catching at semes, as Jay Smith would like (Chakrabarty, "Postcoloniality and the Artifice of History: Who Speaks for 'Indian' Pasts?" *Representations* 37 [Winter 1992]: 1–26; Smith, "No More Language Games: Words, Beliefs, and the Political Culture of Early Modern France," *American Historical Review* 102.5 [Dec. 1997]: 1416). What emerges on the figure of the Rani is interpretation as such; any genealogy of that history can see her as no more than an insubstantial languaged instrument. She is as unverifiable as literature, and yet she is written in, indeed permits the writing of, history as coloniality—so that the postcolonial can come to see his "historical self-location" as a problem (Vivek Dhareshwar, "'Our Time': History, Sovereignty, Politics," *Economic and Political Weekly*, 11 Feb. 1995, pp. 317–324).

75. For the argument that all Speech Acts are graphematic, see Derrida, "Signature Event Context," *Margins*, pp. 307–330.

fadeout. This woman tried to join uncoerced intending (male) agents of anti-colonialism. She was born in Calcutta a hundred years later and understood "nationalism," another efficient coding.[76] Anticipating her production world-historically though not in intent, Gulari had been a letter in the alphabet of the discursive transformation that remotely set in motion the definition of "India" as a modern nation—miraculating site of state-as-intention—a word that could find enunciative comple-tion only as object of "liberation" in order, then, to constitute "iden-tity." The woman in this section tried to be decisive in extremis, yet lost herself in the undecidable womanspace of justice. She "spoke," but women did not, do not, "hear" her. Before I come to her, I will lay out, in a long digression, some of the decisive judgments that I risked, some years ago, in order to attend to her mystery.

Whatever power these meditations may command has been earned by a politically interested refusal to acknowledge the undecidable, to push to the limit the founding presuppositions of my desires, as far as they are within my grasp. This three-stroke formula, applied both to the most resolutely committed and to the most ironic discourse, keeps track of what Althusser so aptly named "philosophies of denegation," and Derrida, before psychoanalysis, "desistance."[77] Calling the place of the investigator into question remains a meaningless piety in many

---

76. Understood and exceeded, keeping her secret, as we shall see in the rest of this chapter, in spite of the most tremendous effort to "speak." Benedict Anderson (*Imagined Communities: Reflections on the Origin and Spread of Nationalism* [London: Verso, 1983], and Partha Chatterjee, in books I have already cited, together offer us an exhaustive gloss on the mechanics of this coding but, as Homi K. Bhabha points out in "DissemiNation" (*Nation and Narration* [New York: Routledge, 1990], pp. 291–322) with reference to Anderson in particular, accounts of coding cannot account for excess or "incommensurability." Bhabha's argument relates specifically to the unresolvability of the minority; mine, here, as Irigaray's in "The Necessity for Sexuate Rights" (Margaret Whitford, ed. *The Irigaray Reader* [Cambridge: Blackwell, 1991], pp. 204–211) to the excess of the "sexuate." It is in the excess of the sexuate, forever escaping formalization (for the connection to Derrida, see Appendix) that Bhubaneswari speaks, keeps her secret, and is silenced. The rest of the text circles around this enigma, by way of the psychocultural *system* of Sati.

77. Louis Althusser, *Lenin and Philosophy and Other Essays*, tr. Ben Brewster (New York: Monthly Review Press, 1971), p. 66. Derrida, "Desistance," in Philippe Lacoue-Labarthe, *Typography: Mimesis, Philosophy, Politics*, tr. Christopher Fynsk (Cambridge: Harvard Univ. Press, 1989), pp. 1–42.

recent critiques of the sovereign subject. Although I attempt to sound the precariousness of my position throughout, I know such gestures can never suffice.

Some of the most radical criticism coming out of the West in the eighties was the result of an interested desire to conserve the subject of the West, or the West as Subject. The theory of pluralized "subject-effects" often provided a cover for this subject of knowledge. Although the history of Europe as Subject was narrativized by the law, political economy, and ideology of the West, this concealed Subject pretended it had "no geo-political determinations." The much-publicized critique of the sovereign subject thus actually inaugurated a Subject. I will argue for this conclusion by considering a text by two great practitioners of the critique: "Intellectuals and Power: A Conversation between Michel Foucault and Gilles Deleuze."[78] In the event, just as some "third world women's" critique romanticize the united struggle of working-class women, these hegemonic radicals also allow undivided subjectivity to workers' struggles. My example is outside both circuits. I must therefore spend some time with the hegemonic radicals.

I have chosen this friendly exchange between two activist philosophers of history because it undoes the opposition between authoritative

---

78. Michel Foucault, *Language, Counter-Memory, Practice: Selected Essays and Interviews*, tr. Donald Bouchard and Sherry Simon (Ithaca: Cornell University Press, 1977), pp. 205–217 (hereafter *FD*). I have modified the English version of this, as of other English translations, where faithfulness to the original seemed to demand it. It is important to note that the greatest "influence" of Western European intellectuals upon U.S. professors and students happens through collections of essays rather than long books in translation. And, in those collections, it is understandably the more topical pieces that gain a greater currency. (Derrida's "Structure, Sign and Play in the Discourse of the Human Sciences," in Richard Macksey and Eugenio Donato, eds., *The Structuralist Controversy: The Languages of Criticism and the Sciences of Man* [Baltimore: Johns Hopkins Univ. Press, 1972], is a case in point.) From the perspective of theoretical production and ideological reproduction, therefore, the conversation under consideration has not necessarily been superseded. In my own meagre production, interviews, the least considered genre, have proved embarrassingly popular. It goes without saying that one does not produce a Samuel P. Huntington (*The Clash of Civilizations and the Remaking of World Order* [New York: Simon & Schuster, 1996]) to counter this. More about Huntington later.

theoretical production and the unguarded practice of conversation, enabling one to glimpse the track of ideology. (Like the conference, the interview is a site of betrayal.) Earlier and elsewhere I have considered their theoretical brilliance. This is a chapter of another disciplinary mistake: telling life stories in the name of history.

The participants in this conversation emphasize the most important contributions of French poststructuralist theory: first, that the networks of power/desire/interest are so heterogeneous that their reduction to a coherent narrative is counterproductive—a persistent critique is needed; and second, that intellectuals must attempt to disclose and know the discourse of society's other. Yet the two systematically and surprisingly ignore the question of ideology and their own implication in intellectual and economic history.

Although one of its chief presuppositions is the critique of the sovereign subject, the conversation between Foucault and Deleuze is framed by two monolithic and anonymous subjects-in-revolution: "A Maoist" (*FD* 205) and "the workers' struggle" (*FD* 217). Intellectuals, however, are named and differentiated; moreover, a Chinese Maoism is nowhere operative. Maoism here simply creates an aura of narrative specificity, which would be a harmless rhetorical banality were it not that the innocent appropriation of the proper name "Maoism" for the eccentric phenomenon of French intellectual "Maoism" and subsequent "New Philosophy" symptomatically renders "Asia" transparent.[79]

Deleuze's reference to the workers' struggle is equally problematic; it is obviously a genuflection: "We are unable to touch [power] in any point of its application without finding ourselves confronted by this diffuse mass, so that we are necessarily led . . . to the desire to blow it up completely. Every partial revolutionary attack or defense is linked in

---

79. There is an implicit reference here to the post-1968 wave of Maoism in France. See Michel Foucault, "On Popular Justice: A Discussion with Maoists," *Power/Knowledge*, p. 134 (hereafter *PK*). Explication of the reference strengthens my point by laying bare the mechanics of appropriation. The status of China in this discussion is exemplary. If Foucault persistently clears himself by saying "I know nothing about China," his interlocutors show toward China what Derrida calls the "Chinese prejudice."

this way to the workers' struggle" (*FD* 217). The apparent banality signals a disavaowal. The statement ignores the international division of labor, a gesture that often marks poststructuralist political theory. (Today's post-Soviet universalist feminist—"gender and development," United Nation style—dissimulates it; its rôle will come clear at the very end of the chapter, as it leads into the next.)[80]

The invocation of *the* workers' struggle is baleful in its very innocence; it is incapable of dealing with global capitalism: the subject-production of worker and unemployed within nation-state ideologies in its Center; the increasing subtraction of the working class in the periphery from the realization of surplus value and thus from "humanistic" training in consumerism; and the large-scale presence of paracapitalist labor as well as the heterogeneous structural status of agriculture in the periphery. Ignoring the international division of labor, rendering "Asia" (and on occasion "Africa") transparent (unless the subject is ostensibly the "Third World"); reestablishing the legal subject of socialized capital—these are problems as common to much poststructuralist as to "regular" theory. (The invocation of "woman" is as problematic in the current conjuncture.) Why should such occlusions be sanctioned in precisely those intellectuals who are our best prophets of heterogeneity and the Other?

The link to the workers' struggle is located in the desire to blow up power at any point of its application. It reads too much like a valorization of *any* desire destructive of *any* power. Walter Benjamin comments on Baudelaire's comparable politics by way of quotations from Marx:

> Marx continues in his description of the *conspirateurs de profession* as follows: ". . . They have no other aim but the immediate one of overthrowing the existing government, and they profoundly despise the more theoretical enlightenment of the workers as to their class intersts. Thus their anger—not proletarian but plebeian—at the *habits noirs* (black coats), the more or less educated people who represent [*vertreten*] that side of the movement and of whom they can never become entirely independent, as they cannot of the official representatives [*Repräsentanten*] of the party. Baudelaire's political insights

---

80. This is part of a much broader symptom, as Eric Wolf discusses in *Europe and the People without History* (Berkeley: University of California Press, 1982).

do not go fundamentally beyond the insights of these professional conspirators. . . ." He could perhaps have made Flaubert's statement, "Of all of politics I understand only one thing: the revolt," his own.[81]

This, too, is a rewriting of accountable responsibility as narcissism, lower case; perhaps we cannot do otherwise, but one can tend. Or else, why speak of "the gift" at all?[82]

The link to the workers' struggle is located, simply, in desire. This is not the "desire" of *Anti-Oedipus*, which is a deliberate mis-name for a general flow (where the "subject" is a residuum), for which no adequate name can be found: a nominalist catachresis. I have admiration for that bold effort, especially for the ways in which it is linked with that other nominalist catachresis: value. To check psychologism, *Anti-Oedipus* uses the concept-metaphor of machines: Desire does not lack anything; it does not lack its object. It is, rather, the subject that is lacking in desire, or desire that lacks a fixed subject; there is no fixed subject except by repression. Desire and its object are a unity: it is the machine, as a machine of a machine. Desire is machine, the object of desire also a connected machine, so that the product is lifted from the process of producing, and something detaches itself from producing to product and gives a leftover to the vagabond, nomad subject.[83]

One of the canniest moments in deconstruction is its caution, from early days to the latest, that the catachrestic is bound to the "empirical."[84] In the absence of such a practical caution, the philosopher oscil-

---

81. Walter Benjamin, *Charles Baudelaire: A Lyric Poet in the Era of High Capitalism*, tr. Harry Zohn (London: Verso, 1983), p. 12. Foucault finds in Baudelaire the typecase of modernity (Foucault, "What Is Enlightenment?" in Paul Rabinow, ed., *The Foucault Reader* [New York: Pantheon, 1984], pp. 39–42).

82. "Even if the gift were never anything but a simulacrum, one must still *render an account* of the possibility of this simulacrum. And one must also render an account of the desire to render an account. This cannot be done against or without the *principle of reason* (*principium reddendae rationis*), even if the latter finds there its limit as well as its resource" (Derrida, *Given Time*, p. 31).

83. Deleuze and Guattari, *Anti-Oedipus*, pp. 40–41 and *passim*, p. 26.

84. "What is writing? How can it be identified? What certitude of essence must guide the empirical investigation? . . . Without venturing up to the perilous necessity of the question or the arche-question 'what is,' let us take shelter in the field of grammatological knowledge" (*OG* 75). In "Desistance," Derrida points out that the

lates between theoretical catachresis and practical naive realism as a contradiction that *may* be harmless in a context, where much goodwill may perhaps be taken for granted. As we see daily, such a contradiction between theory and its judgment is dire if "applied" globally.

Thus desire as catachresis in *Anti-Oedipus* does not alter the specificity of the desiring subject (or leftover subject-effect) that attaches to specific instances of "empirical" desire. The subject-effect that surreptitiously emerges is much like the generalized ideological subject of the theorist. This may be the legal subject of socialized capital, neither labor nor management, holding a "strong" passport, using a "strong" or "hard" currency, with supposedly unquestioned access to due process. Again, the lineaments of the UN-style feminist *aparatchik* are almost identical; her struggles against patriarchal measures are altogether admirable in her location; but dire when "applied" globally. In the era of globalizing capital, the catachreses "desire" and "globe"—the global crust as body-without-organs—are contaminated by empirical paleonymy in particular ways. It is a (Euro-U.S.) cut in a (Group of Seven) flow.

Deleuze and Guattari consider the relations between desire, power, and subjectivity on the "empirical" or constituted level in a slightly off-sync mode: against the family, and against colonialism. This renders them incapable of articulating a general or global theory of interests textualized to the conjuncture. In this context, their indifference to ideology (a theory of which is necessary for an understanding of constituted interests within systems of representation) is striking but consistent. Foucault's work cannot work on the subject-constituting register of ideology because of its tenacious committment to the sub-individual and, at the other end, the great aggregative apparatuses *(dispositifs)*. Yet, as this conversational register shows, the empirical subject, the intending subject, the self even, must be constantly assumed in radical calculations. Thus in his influential essay "Ideology and Ideological State Apparatuses (Notes towards an Investigation)," Louis Althusser must inhabit that unavoidable middle ground, and assume a subject even as

---

critical is always contaminated by the dogmatic and thus makes Kant's distinction "speculative." In *Glas* philosophemes are typographically mimed, rather than "acted out" in intended behavior, as in the conversation we are discussing. For the emergence of the category of experience in the later work, see Appendix.

he uses "a more scientific language" to describe abstract average labor or labor-power: "The reproduction of labour power requires not only a reproduction of its skills, but also at the same time, a reproduction of its submission to the ruling ideology for the workers, and a reproduction of the ability to manipulate the ruling ideology correctly for the agents of exploitation and repression, so that they, too, will provide for the domination of the ruling class 'in and by words' [*par la parole*]."[85]

When Foucault considers the pervasive heterogeneity of power, he does not ignore the immense institutional heterogeneity that Althusser here attempts to schematize. Similarly, in speaking of alliances and systems of signs, the state and war-machines, in *A Thousand Plateaus*, Deleuze and Guattari open up that very field.[86] Foucault cannot, however, admit that a developed theory of ideology *can* recognize its own material production in institutionality, as well as in the "effective instruments for the formation and accumulation of knowledge" (*PK* 102).[87] Because these philosophers seem obliged to reject all arguments naming the concept of ideology as *only* schematic rather than textual, they are equally obliged to produce a mechanically schematic opposition between interest and desire, when their catachreses inevitably bleed into the "empirical" field. Thus they unwittingly align themselves with bourgeois sociologists who fill the place of ideology with a continuistic "unconscious" or a parasubjective "culture" (or Bretton Woods activists who speak of "culture" alone). The mechanical relation between desire and interest is clear in such sentences as: "We never desire against our interests, because interest always follows and finds itself where desire has placed it" (*FD* 215). An undifferentiated desire is the agent, and power slips in to create the effects of desire: "power . . . produces positive effects at the level of desire—and also at the level of knowledge" (*PK* 59).[88]

This parasubjective matrix, cross-hatched with heterogeneity, sur-

---

85. Althusser, *Lenin and Philosophy*, pp. 132–133; translation modified.

86. Deleuze and Guattari, *A Thousand Plateaus: Capitalism and Schizophrenia*, tr. Brian Massumi (Minneapolis: Univ. of Minnesota Press, 1987), pp. 351–423.

87. On this see also Stuart Hall, "The Problem of Ideology—Marxism without Guarantees," in Betty Matthews, ed., *Marx: A Hundred Years On* (London: Lawrence and Wishart, 1983), pp. 57–84.

88. For a more appreciative interpretation that attempts to bypass this risk, though never, of course, fully, see Spivak, "More on Power/Knowledge."

reptitiously ushers in the unnamed Subject, at least for those intellectual workers influenced by the new hegemony of pure catachresis. The race for "the last instance" is now between economics and power. Because, by the unacknowledged inevitable empirical contamination of catachreses, desire is tacitly and repeatedly "defined" on an orthodox model, it can be unitarily opposed to "being deceived." Ideology as "false consciousness" (being deceived) has been called into question by Althusser. Even Reich implied notions of collective will rather than a dichotomy of deception and undeceived desire: "We must accept the screams of Reich: no, the masses were not deceived; at a particular moment, they actually desired a fascist regime" (FD 215).

These philosophers will not entertain the thought of constitutive contradiction—that is where they admittedly part company from the Left. In the name of desire, they tacitly reintroduce the undivided subject into the discourse of power. On the register of practice, Foucault often seems to conflate "individual" and "subject";[89] and the impact on his own concept-metaphors is perhaps intensified in his followers. Because of the power of the word "power," Foucault admits to using the "metaphor of the point which progressively irradiates its surroundings." Such slips become the rule rather than the exception in less careful hands. And that radiating point, animating an effectively heliocentric discourse, fills the empty place of the agent with the historical sun of theory, the Subject of Europe.[90]

It is not surprising, therefore, that upon the empirical register of

---

89. For one example among many see PK 98.

90. It is not surprising, then, that Foucault's work, early and late, is supported by too simple a notion of repression. Here the antagonist is Freud, not Marx. "I have the impression that [the notion of repression] is wholly inadequate to the analysis of the mechanisms and effects of power that it is so pervasively used to characterize today" (PK 92). The delicacy and subtlety of Freud's suggestion—that under repression the phenomenal identity of affects is indeterminate because an unpleasure can be desired as pleasure, thus radically reinscribing the relationship between desire and "interest"—seems quite deflated here. For an elaboration of this notion of repression, see OG 88, 333–334 and Derrida, Limited inc. abc (Evanston: Northwestern Univ. Press, 1988), pp. 74–75. Again, the problem is the refusal to take on board the level of the constituted subject—in the name of uncontaminated catachreses.

resistance-talk, Foucault articulates another corollary of the disavowal of the rôle of ideology in reproducing the social relations of production: an unquestioned valorization of the oppressed as subject, the "object being," as Deleuze admiringly remarks, "to establish conditions where the prisoners themselves would be able to speak." Foucault adds that "the masses know perfectly well, clearly"—once again the thematics of being undeceived—"they know far better than [the intellectual] and they certainly say it very well" (*FD* 206, 207). The ventriloquism of the speaking subaltern is the left intellectual's stock-in-trade.

What happens to the critique of the sovereign subject in these pronouncements? The limits of this representationalist realism are reached with Deleuze: "Reality is what actually happens in a factory, in a school, in barracks, in a prison, in a police station" (*FD* 212). This foreclosing of the necessity of the difficult task of counterhegemonic ideological production has not been salutary. It has helped positivist empiricism— the justifying foundation of advanced capitalist neocolonialism—to define its own arena as "concrete experience," "what actually happens." (As in the case of capitalist colonialism, and mutatis mutandis, of exploitation-as-"Development." Evidence is daily produced by computing the national subject of the global South in this unproblematic way. And an alibi for globalization is produced by calling on the testimony of the credit-baited female.) Indeed, the concrete experience that is the guarantor of the political appeal of prisoners, soldiers, and schoolchildren is disclosed through the concrete experience of the intellectual, the one who diagnoses the episteme.[91] Neither Deleuze nor Foucault seems aware that the intellectual within globalizing capital, brandishing concrete experience, can help consolidate the international division of la-

---

91. Althusser's version of this particular situation may be too schematic, but it nevertheless seems more careful in its program than the argument under study. "Class *instinct*," Althusser writes, "is subjective and spontaneous. Class *position* is objective and rational. To arrive at proletarian class positions, the class instinct of proletarians only needs to be *educated*, the class instinct of the petty bourgeoisie, *and hence of intellectuals*, has, on the contrary, to be *revolutionized*" (*Lenin and Philosophy*, p. 13). It is the effortful double bind, the always already crossed aporia, of this careful program that may be one reading of Derrida's current insistence upon justice as an experience of the impossible, upon decisions being always categorically insufficient to their supposed premises (see Appendix).

bor by making one model of "concrete experience" *the* model. We are witnessing this in our discipline daily as we see the postcolonial *migrant* become the norm, thus occluding the native once again.[92]

The unrecognized contradiction within a position that valorizes the concrete experience of the oppressed, while being so uncritical about the historical rôle of the intellectual, is maintained by a verbal slippage. Deleuze makes this remarkable pronouncement: "A theory is like a box of tools. Nothing to do with the signifier" (*FD* 208). Considering that the verbalism of the theoretical world and its access to any work defined against it as "practical" is irreducible, such a declaration (referring *only* to an in-house contretemps with hermeneutics), helps *only* the intellectual anxious to prove that intellectual labor is just like manual labor.

It is when signifiers are left to look after themselves that verbal slippages happen. The signifier "representation" is a case in point. In the same dismissive tone that severs theory's link to the signifier, Deleuze declares, "There is no more representation; there's nothing but action"—"action of theory and action of practice which relate to each other as relays and form networks" (*FD* 206–207).

An important point is being made here: the production of theory is also a practice; the opposition between abstract "pure" theory and concrete "applied" practice is too quick and easy.[93] But Deleuze's articulation of the argument is problematic. Two senses of representation are being run together: representation as "speaking for," as in politics, and representation as "re-presentation," as in art or philosophy. Since the-

---

92. "Is the repetition really useful here?" my anonymous reader asks. I cite one among a hundred random examples: a conference on "Disciplinary and Interdisciplinary: Negotiating the Margin" at Columbia University on 7 November 1997. The entire conference turned on amity among various minorities in the United States (read New York) as the end of radical feminism, an end that seemed altogether salutary in the face of the vicious identitarian conflict raging under the surface. A strengthened multicultural U.S. subject, the newest face of postcoloniality, still does nothing for globality and may do harm. The point remains worth repeating, alas.

93. Foucault's subsequent explanation (*PK* 145) of this Deleuzian statement comes closer to Derrida's notion that theory cannot be an exhaustive taxonomy and is always normed by practice.

ory is also only "action," the theoretician does not represent (speak for) the oppressed group. Indeed, the subject is not seen as a representative consciousness (one re-presenting reality adequately). These two senses of representation—within state formation and the law, on the one hand, and in subject-predication, on the other—are related but irreducibly discontinuous. To cover over the discontinuity with an analogy that is presented as a proof reflects again a paradoxical subject-privileging.[94] *Because* "the person who speaks and acts . . . is always a multiplicity," no "theorizing intellectual . . . [or] party or . . . union" can represent "those who act and struggle" (*FD* 206). Are those who act and *struggle* mute, as opposed to those who act and *speak* (*FD* 206)? These immense problems are buried in the differences between the "same" words: consciousness and conscience (both *conscience* in French), representation and re-presentation. The critique of ideological subject-constitution within state formations and systems of political economy can now be effaced, as can the active theoretical practice of the "transformation of consciousness." The banality of leftist intellectuals' lists of self-knowing, politically canny subalterns stands revealed; representing them, the intellectuals represent themselves as transparent.

If such a critique and such a project are not to be given up, the shifting distinctions between representation within the state and political economy, on the one hand, and within the theory of the Subject, on the other, must not be obliterated. Let us consider the play of *vertreten* ("represent" in the first sense) and *darstellen* ("re-present" in the second sense) in a famous passage in *The Eighteenth Brumaire of Louis Bonaparte*, where Marx touches on "class" as a descriptive and transformative concept in a manner somewhat more complex than Althusser's distinction between class instinct and class position would allow. This is important

94. Cf. the suprisingly uncritical notions of representation entertained in *PK* 141, 188. My remarks concluding this paragraph, criticizing intellectuals' representations of subaltern groups, should be rigorously distinguished from a coalition politics that takes into account its framing within socialized capital and unites people not because they are oppressed but because they are exploited. This model works best within a parliamentary democracy, where representation is not only not banished but elaborately staged.

in the context of the argument from the working class both from our two philosophers and "political" third-world feminism from the metropolis.

Marx's contention here is that the descriptive definition of a class can be a differential one—its cutting off and difference from all other classes: "in so far as millions of families live under economic conditions of existence that cut off their mode of life, their interest, and their formation from those of the other classes and place them in inimical confrontation [*feindlich gegenüberstellen*], they form a class."[95] There is no such thing as a "class instinct" at work here. In fact, the collectivity of familial existence, which might be considered the arena of "instinct," is discontinuous with, though operated by, the differential isolation of classes. In this context, one far more pertinent to the France of the 1970s than it can be to the international periphery, the formation of a class is *artificial* and economic, and the economic agency or *interest* is impersonal because it is systematic and heterogeneous. This agency or interest is tied to the Hegelian critique of the individual subject, for it marks the subject's empty place in that process without a subject which is history and political economy. Here the capitalist is defined as "the conscious bearer [*Träger*] of the limitless movement of capital." My point is that Marx is not working to create an undivided subject where desire and interest coincide. Class consciousness does not operate toward that goal. Both in the economic area (capitalist) and in the political (world-historical agent), Marx is obliged to construct models of a divided and dislocated subject whose parts are not continuous or coherent with each other. A celebrated passage like the description of capital as the Faustian monster brings this home vividly.[96]

The following passage, continuing the quotation from *The Eighteenth Brumaire*, is also working on the structural principle of a dispersed and dislocated class subject: the (absent collective) consciousness of the small peasant proprietor class finds its "bearer" in a "representative" who appears to work in another's interest. "Representative" here does not derive from *darstellen;* this sharpens the contrast Foucault and Deleuze slide over, the contrast, say, between a proxy and a portrait. There is, of course, a relationship between them, one that has received

---

95. Marx, *Surveys from Exile*, p. 239.
96. Marx, *Capital* 1: 254, 302.

political and ideological exacerbation in the European tradition at least since the poet and the sophist, the actor and the orator, have both been seen as harmful. In the guise of a post-Marxist decription of the scene of power, we thus encounter a much older debate: between representation or rhetoric as tropology and as persuasion. *Darstellen* belongs to the first constellation, *vertreten*—with stronger suggestions of substitution—to the second. Again, they are related, but running them together, especially in order to say that beyond both is where oppressed subjects speak, act, and know *for themselves*, leads to an essentialist, utopian politics that can, when transferred to single-issue gender rather than class, give unquestioning support to the financialization of the globe, which ruthlessly constructs a general will in the credit-baited rural woman even as it "format"s her through UN Plans of Action so that she can be "developed." Beyond this concatenation, transparent as rhetoric in the service of "truth" has always made itself out to be, is the much-invoked oppressed subject (as Woman), speaking, acting, and knowing that gender in development is best for her. It is in the shadow of this unfortunate marionette that the history of the unheeded subaltern must unfold.

Here is Marx's passage, using *vertreten* where the English uses "represent," discussing a social "subject" whose consciousness is dislocated and incoherent with its *Vertretung* (as much a substitution as a representation). The small peasant proprietors

cannot represent themselves; they must be represented. Their representative must appear simultaneously as their master, as an authority over them, as unrestricted governmental power that protects them from the other classes and sends them rain and sunshine from above. The political influence [in the place of the class interest, since there is no unified class subject] of the small peasant proprietors therefore finds its last expression [the implication of a chain of substitutions—*Vertretungen*—is strong here] in the executive force [*Exekutivegewalt*—less personal in German; Derrida translates *Gewalt* as violence in another context in "Force of Law"] subordinating society to itself.[97]

***

97. This is a highly ironic passage in Marx, written in the context of the fraudulent "representation" by Louis Napoleon and the regular suppression of the "revolutionary peasants" by bourgeois interests (*Surveys*, p. 239). Many hasty readers think Marx is advancing this as his own opinion about all peasantry!

Such a model of social incoherence—necessary gaps between the source of "influence" (in this case the small peasant proprietors), the "representative" (Louis Napoleon), and the historical-political phenomenon (executive control)—implies not only a critique of the subject as *individual* agent but even a critique of the subjectivity of a *collective* agency. The necessarily dislocated machine of history moves because "the identity of the *interests*" of these proprietors "fails to produce a feeling of community, national links, or a political organization." The event of representation as *Vertretung* (in the constellation of rhetoric-as-persuasion) behaves like a *Darstellung* (or rhetoric-as-trope), taking its place in the gap between the formation of a (descriptive) class and the nonformation of a (transformative) class: "In so far as millions of families live under economic conditions of existence that separate their mode of life . . . *they form a class*. In so far as . . . the identity of their interests fails to produce a feeling of community . . . *they do not form a class*."[98] The complicity of *vertreten* and *darstellen*, their identity-in-difference as the place of practice—since this complicity is precisely what Marxists must expose, as Marx does in *The Eighteenth Brumaire*—can only be appreciated if they are not conflated by a sleight of word.

It would be merely tendentious to argue that this textualizes Marx too much, making him inaccessible to the common "man," who, a victim of common sense, is so deeply placed in a heritage of positivism that Marx's irreducible emphasis on the work of the negative, on the necessity for defetishizing the concrete, is persistently wrested from him by the strongest adversary, "the historical tradition" in the air.[99] I have been trying to point out that the uncommon "man," the contemporary philosopher of practice, and the uncommon woman, the metropolitan enthusiast of "third world resistance," sometimes exhibit the same positivism.

The gravity of the problem is apparent if one agrees that the devel-

---

98. Marx, *Surveys from Exile*, p. 239. Emphasis mine.

99. See the excellent short definition and discussion of common sense in Errol Lawrence, "Just Plain Common Sense: The 'Roots' of Racism," in Hazel V. Carby, et al., *The Empire Strikes Back: Race and Racism in 70s Britain* (London: Hutchinson, 1982), p. 48. The Gramscian notions of "common sense" and "good sense" are extensively discussed in Marcia Landy, *Film, Politics, and Gramsci* (Minneapolis: Univ. of Minnesota Press, 1994), pp. 73–98.

opment of a transformative class "consciousness" from a descriptive class "position" is not in Marx a task engaging the ground level of consciousness. Class consciousness remains with the feeling of community that belongs to national links and political organizations, not with that other feeling of community whose structural model is the family. Although *not* identified with nature, the family here is constellated with what Marx calls "natural exchange," which is, philosophically speaking, a "placeholder" for use value.[100] "Natural exchange" is contrasted to "intercourse with society," where the word "intercourse" (*Verkehr*) is Marx's usual word for "commerce." This "intercourse" thus holds the place of the exchange leading to the production of surplus value, and it is in the area of this intercourse that the feeling of community leading to class agency must be developed. Full class agency (if there were such a thing) is not an ideological transformation of consciousness on the ground level, a desiring identity of the agents and their interest—the identity whose absence troubles Foucault and Deleuze. It is a contestatory *replacement* as well as an *appropriation* (a *supplementation*) of something that is "artificial" to begin with—"economic conditions of existence that separate their mode of life." Marx's formulations show a cautious respect for the nascent critique of individual and collective subjective agency. The projects of class consciousness and of the transformation of consciousness are discontinuous issues for him. Today's analogue would be "transnational literacy" as opposed to the mobilizing potential of unexamined culturalism.[101] Conversely, contemporary invocations of "libidinal economy" and desire as the determining interest, combined with the practical politics of the oppressed (under socialized capital) "speaking for themselves," restore the category of the sovereign subject within the theory that seems most to question it.

No doubt the exclusion of the family, albeit a family belonging to a

---

100. "Use value" in Marx can be shown to be a "theoretical fiction"—as much of a potential oxymoron as "natural exchange." I have attempted to develop this in "Scattered Speculations on the Question of Value," in *In Other Worlds*, pp. 154–175.

101. Developed in Spivak, "Teaching for the Times," in Bhikhu Parekh and Jan Nederveen Pieterse, eds., *The Decolonization of the Imagination* (London: Zed, 1995), pp. 177–202; "Diasporas Old & New: Women in a Transnational World," in *Textual Practice* 10.2 (1996): 245–269; and, with specific reference to India, in Biju Mathews et al., "Vasudhaiva."

specific class formation, is part of the masculine frame within which Marxism marks its birth.[102] Historically as well as in today's global political economy, the family's rôle in patriarchal social relations is so heterogeneous and contested that merely replacing the family in this problematic is not going to break the frame. Nor does the solution lie in the positivist inclusion of a monolithic collectivity of "women" in the list of the oppressed whose unfractured subjectivity allows them to speak for themselves against an equally monolithic "same system."

In the context of the development of a strategic, artificial, and second-level "consciousness," Marx uses the concept of the patronymic, always keeping within the broader concept of representation as *Vertretung:* The small peasant proprietors "are therefore incapable of making their class interest valid in their proper name [*im eigenen Namen*], whether through a parliament or through a convention." The absence of the nonfamilial artificial collective proper name is supplied by the only proper name "historical tradition" can offer—the patronymic itself—the Name of the Father (in a not dissimilar spirit Jean Rhys had denied that name to her fictional [Rochester] character): "Historical tradition produced the French peasants' belief that a miracle would occur, that a man *named* Napoleon would restore all their glory. And an individual turned up"—the untranslatable *es fand sich* (there found itself an individual?) demolishes all questions of agency or the agent's connection with his interest—"who gave himself out to be that man" (this pretense is, by contrast, his only proper agency) "because he carried [*trägt*-the word used for the capitalist's relationship to capital] the Napoleonic Code, which commands" that "inquiry into paternity is forbidden." While Marx here seems to be working within a patriarchal metaphorics, one should note the textual subtlety of the passage. It is the Law of the Father (the Napoleonic Code) that paradoxically prohibits the search for the natural father. Thus, it is according to a strict observance of the historical Law of the Father that the formed yet unformed class's faith in the natural father is gainsaid.

I have dwelt so long on this passage in Marx because it spells out the inner dynamics of *Vertretung*, or representation in the political context.

---

102. Derrida's "Linguistic Circle of Geneva" (in *Margins*), especially pp. 143–144, can provide a method for assessing the irreducible place of the family in Marx's morphology of class formation.

Representation in the economic context is *Darstellung*, the philosophical concept of representation as staging or, indeed, signification, which relates to the divided subject in an indirect way. The most obvious passage is well known: "In the exchange relationship [*Austauschverhält-nis*] of commodities their exchange-value appeared to us totally independent of their use value. But if we subtract their use-value from the product of labour, we obtain their value, as it was just determined [*bestimmt*]. The common element that represents itself [*sich darstellt*] in the exchange relation, or the exchange value of the commodity, is thus its value."[103]

According to Marx, under capitalism, value, as produced in necessary and surplus labor, is computed as the representation/sign of objectified labor (which is rigorously distinguished from human activity). Conversely, in the absence of a theory of exploitation as the extraction (production), appropriation, and realization of (surplus) value *as representation of labor power*, capitalist exploitation must be seen as a variety of domination (the mechanics of power as such). "The thrust of Marxism," Deleuze suggests, "was to determine the problem [that power is more diffuse than the structure of exploitation and state formation] essentially in terms of interests (power is held by a ruling class defined by its interests)" (*FD* 214).

One cannot object to this minimalist summary of Marx's project, just as one cannot ignore that, in parts of the *Anti-Oedipus*, Deleuze and Guattari build their case on a brilliant if "poetic" grasp of Marx's *theory* of the money form. Yet we might consolidate our critique in the following way: the relationship between global capitalism (exploitation in economics) and nation-state alliances (domination in geopolitics) is so macrological that it cannot account for the micrological texture of power.[104] Sub-individual micrologies cannot grasp the "empirical" field. To move toward such an accounting one must move toward theories of

---

103. Marx, *Capital*, 1:128. This is common sense. Marx then goes beyond this to show that value means abstraction in both use and exchange. To develop that reading is beside the point here.

104. The situation has changed in the New World Order. Let us call the World Bank / IMF / World Trade Organization "the economic"; and the United Nations "the political." The relationship between them is being negotiated in the name of gender ("the cultural"), which is, perhaps, micrology as such.

ideology—of subject formations that micrologically and often erratically operate the interests that congeal the micrologies and are congealed in macrologies. Such theories cannot afford to overlook that this line *is* erratic, and that the category of representation in its *two* senses is crucial. They must note how the staging of the world in representation—its scene of writing, its *Darstellung*—dissimulates the choice of and need for "heroes," paternal proxies, agents of power—*Vertretung*.

My view is that radical practice should attend to this double session of representations rather than reintroduce the individual subject through totalizing concepts of power and desire. It is also my view that, in keeping the area of class practice on a second level of abstraction, Marx was in effect keeping open the (Kantian and) Hegelian critique of the individual subject as agent.[105] This view does not oblige me to ignore that, by implicitly defining the family and the mother tongue as the ground level where culture and convention seem nature's own way of organizing "her" own subversion, Marx himself rehearses an ancient subterfuge.[106] In the context of poststructuralist claims to critical practice, however, Marx seems more recuperable than the clandestine restoration of subjective essentialism.

The reduction of Marx to a benevolent but dated figure most often serves the interest of launching a new theory of interpretation. In the Foucault-Deleuze conversation, the issue seems to be that there is no representation, no signifier (Is it to be presumed that the signifier has already been dispatched? There is, then, no sign-structure operating experience, and thus might one lay semiotics to rest?); theory is a relay of practice (thus laying problems of theoretical practice to rest); and the oppressed can know and speak for themselves. This reintroduces the constitutive subject on at least two levels: the Subject of desire and

---

105. I am aware that the relationship between Marxism and neo-Kantianism is a politically fraught one. I do not myself see how a continuous line can be established between Marx's own texts and the Kantian ethical moment. It does seem to me, however, that Marx's questioning of the individual as agent of history should be read in the context of the breaking up of the individual subject inaugurated by Kant's critique of Descartes.

106. Marx, *Grundrisse*, pp. 162–163.

power as an irreducible methodological presupposition; and the self-proximate, if not self-identical, subject of the oppressed. Further, the intellectuals, who are neither of these S/subjects, become transparent in the relay race, for they merely report on the nonrepresented subject and analyze (without analyzing) the workings of (the unnamed Subject irreducibly presupposed by) power and desire. The produced "transparency" marks the place of "interest"; it is maintained by vehement denegation: "Now this rôle of referee, judge and universal witness is one which I *absolutely refuse* to adopt." One responsibility of the critic might be to read and write so that the impossibility of such interested individualistic refusals of the institutional privileges of power bestowed on the subject is taken seriously. The refusal of sign-system blocks the way to a developed theory of ideology in the "empirical." Here, too, the peculiar tone of denegation is heard. To Jacques-Alain Miller's suggestion that "the institution is itself discursive," Foucault responds, "Yes, if you like, but it doesn't much matter for my notion of the apparatus to be able to say that this is discursive and that isn't . . . given that my problem isn't a linguistic one" (*PK* 198). Why this conflation of language and discourse from the master of discourse analysis?

Edward W. Said's critique of power in Foucault as a captivating and mystifying category that allows him "to obliterate the rôle of classes, the rôle of economics, the rôle of insurgency and rebellion," is pertinent here, although the importance of the name of "power" in the sub-individual is not to be ignored.[107] I add to Said's analysis the notion of the surreptitious subject of power and desire marked by the transparency of the intellectual.

This S/subject, curiously sewn together into a transparency by denegations, belongs to the exploiters' side of the international division of labor. It is impossible for contemporary French intellectuals to imagine the kind of Power and Desire that would inhabit the unnamed subject of the Other of Europe. It is not only that everything they read, critical or uncritical, is caught within the debate of the production of that Other, supporting or critiquing the constitution of the Subject as Europe. It is also that, in the constitution of that Other of Europe, great

---

107. Edward W. Said, *The World, the Text, and the Critic* (Cambridge: Harvard Univ. Press, 1983), p. 243.

care was taken to obliterate the textual ingredients with which such a subject could cathect, could occupy (invest?) its itinerary—not only by ideological and scientific production, but also by the institution of the law. However reductionistic an economic analysis might seem, the French intellectuals forget at their peril that this entire overdetermined enterprise was in the interest of a dynamic economic situation requiring that interests, motives (desires), and power (of knowledge) be ruthlessly dislocated. To invoke that dislocation now as a radical discovery that should make us diagnose the economic (conditions of existence that separate out "classes" descriptively) as a piece of dated analytic machinery may well be to continue the work of that dislocation and unwittingly to help in securing "a new balance of hegemonic relations."[108] In the face of the possibility that the intellectual is complicit in the persistent constitution of the Other as the Self's shadow, a possibility of political practice for the intellectual would be to put the economic "under erasure," to see the economic factor as irreducible as it reinscribes the social text, even as it is erased, however imperfectly, when it claims to be the final determinant or the transcendental signified.[109]

Until very recently, the clearest available example of such epistemic violence was the remotely orchestrated, far-flung, and heterogeneous project to constitute the colonial subject as Other. This project is also the asymmetrical obliteration of the trace of that Other in its precarious Subject-ivity. It is well known that Foucault locates one case of epistemic violence, a complete overhaul of the episteme, in the redefinition of madness at the end of the European eighteenth century.[110] But what if that particular redefinition was only a part of the narrative of history in Europe as well as in the colonies? What if the two projects of epistemic overhaul worked as dislocated and unacknowledged parts

108. Carby, *Empire*, p. 34.

109. This argument is developed further in Spivak, "Scattered Speculations." Once again, the *Anti-Oedipus* did not ignore the economic text, although the treatment was perhaps too allegorical. In this respect, the move from schizo- to rhyzo-analysis in *A Thousand Plateaus* was not, perhaps, salutary.

110. See Foucault, *Madness and Civilization: A History of Insanity in the Age of Reason*, tr. Richard Howard (New York: Pantheon, 1965), pp. 251, 262, 269.

of a vast two-handed engine? Perhaps it is no more than to ask that the subtext of the palimpsestic narrative of imperialism be recognized as "subjugated knowledge," "a whole set of knowledges that have been disqualified as inadequate to their task or insufficiently elaborated: naive knowledges, located low down on the hierarchy, beneath the required level of cognition or scientificity" (*PK* 82).

This is not to describe "the way things really were" or to privilege the narrative of history as imperialism as the best version of history.[111] It is, rather, to continue the account of how *one* explanation and narrative of reality was established as the normative one. A comparable account in the case(s) of Central and Eastern Europe is soon to be launched. To elaborate on this, let us consider for the moment and briefly the underpinnings of the British codification of Hindu Law.

Once again, I am not a South Asianist. I turn to Indian material because I have some accident-of-birth facility there.

Here, then, is a schematic summary of the epistemic violence of the codification of Hindu Law. If it clarifies the notion of epistemic violence, my final discussion of widow-sacrifice may gain added significance.

At the end of the eighteenth century, Hindu Law, insofar as it can be described as a unitary system, operated in terms of four texts that "staged" a four-part episteme defined by the subject's use of memory: *sruti* (the heard), *smriti* (the remembered), *sastra* (the calculus), and *vyavahāra* (the performance).[112] The origins of what had been heard and what was remembered were not necessarily continuous or identical. Every invocation of *sruti* technically recited (or reopened) the event of originary "hearing" or revelation. The second two texts—the learned and the performed—were seen as dialectically continuous. Legal theo-

---

111. Although I consider Fredric Jameson's *Political Unconscious: Narrative as a Socially Symbolic Act* (Ithaca: Cornell Univ. Press, 1981) to be a text of great critical weight, or perhaps *because* I do so, I would like my program here to be distinguished from one of restoring the relics of a privileged narrative: "It is in detecting the traces of that uninterrupted narrative, in restoring to the surface of the text the repressed and buried reality of this fundamental history, that the doctrine of a political unconscious finds its function and its necessity" (p. 20).

112. For a detailed account of this transformation in the case of temple dancers, see Kunal Parker's forthcoming work.

rists and practitioners were not in any given case certain if this structure described the body of law or four ways of settling a dispute. The legitimation, through a binary vision, of the polymorphous structure of legal performance, "internally" noncoherent and open at both ends, is the narrative of codification I offer as an example of epistemic violence.

Consider the often-quoted programmatic lines from Macaulay's infamous "Minute on Indian Education" (1835):

> We must at present do our best to form a class who may be interpreters between us and the millions whom we govern; a class of persons, Indian in blood and colour, but English in taste, in opinions, in morals, and in intellect. To that class we may leave it to refine the vernacular dialects of the country, to enrich those dialects with terms of science borrowed from the Western nomenclature, and to render them by degrees fit vehicles for conveying knowledge to the great mass of the population.[113]

The education of colonial subjects complements their production in law. One effect of establishing a version of the British system was the development of an uneasy separation between disciplinary formation in Sanskrit studies and the native, now alternative, tradition of Sanskrit "high culture." In the first section, I have suggested that within the former, the cultural explanations generated by authoritative scholars matched the epistemic violence of the legal project.

Those authorities would be *the very best* of the sources for the non-specialist French intellectual's entry into the civilization of the Other.[114] I am, however, not referring to intellectuals and scholars of colonial production, like Shastri, when I say that the Other as Subject is inaccessible to Foucault and Deleuze. I am thinking of the general nonspecialist, nonacademic population across the class spectrum, for whom the episteme operates its silent programming function. Without consider-

---

113. Thomas Babington Macaulay, "Minute on Indian Education," in *Selected Writings*, John Clive and Thomas Pinney, eds. (Chicago: Univ. of Chicago Press, 1972), p. 249.

114. I have discussed this issue in greater detail with reference to Julia Kristeva's *About Chinese Women*, tr. Anita Barrows (London: Marion Boyars, 1977), in "French Feminism in an International Frame," in *In Other Worlds*, pp. 136–141.

ing the map of exploitation, on what grid of "oppression" would they place this motley crew?

Let us now move to consider the margins (one can just as well say the silent, silenced center) of the circuit marked out by this epistemic violence, men and women among the illiterate peasantry, Aboriginals, and the lowest strata of the urban subproletariat. According to Foucault and Deleuze (in the First World, under the standardization and regimentation of socialized capital, though they do not seem to recognize this) and mutatis mutandis the metropolitan "third world feminist" only interested in resistance within capital logic, the oppressed, if given the chance (the problem of representation cannot be bypassed here), and on the way to solidarity through alliance politics (a Marxist thematic is at work here) *can speak and know their conditions*. We must now confront the following question: On the other side of the international division of labor from socialized capital, inside *and* outside the circuit of the epistemic violence of imperialist law and education supplementing an earlier economic text, *can the subaltern speak?*

We have already considered the possibility that, given the exigencies of the inauguration of colonial records, the instrumental woman (the Rani of Sirmur) is not fully written.

Antonio Gramsci's work on the "subaltern classes" extends the class-position/class-consciousness argument isolated in *The Eighteenth Brumaire*. Perhaps because Gramsci criticizes the vanguardistic position of the Leninist intellectual, he is concerned with the intellectual's rôle in the subaltern's cultural and political movement into the hegemony. This movement must be made to determine the production of history as narrative (of truth). In texts such as *The Southern Question*, Gramsci considers the movement of historical-political economy in Italy within what can be seen as an allegory of reading taken from or prefiguring an international division of labor.[115] Yet an account of the phased development of the subaltern is thrown out of joint when his cultural macrology is operated, however remotely, by the epistemic interference with

---

115. Antonio Gramsci, *The Southern Question*, tr. Pasquale Verdicchio (West Lafayette, Ind.: Bordighera, Inc., 1995). As usual, I am using "allegory of reading" in the sense suggested by Paul de Man.

legal and disciplinary definitions accompanying the imperialist project. When I move, at the end of this essay, to the question of woman as subaltern, I will suggest that the possibility of collectivity itself is persistently foreclosed through the manipulation of female agency.

The first part of my proposition—that the phased development of the subaltern is complicated by the imperialist project—is confronted by the "Subaltern Studies" group. They *must* ask, Can the subaltern speak? Here we are within Foucault's own discipline of history and with people who acknowledge his influence. Their project is to rethink Indian colonial historiography from the perspective of the discontinuous chain of peasant insurgencies during the colonial occupation. This is indeed the problem of "the permission to narrate" discussed by Said.[116] As Ranajit Guha, the founding editor of the collective, argues,

> The historiography of Indian nationalism has for a long time been dominated by elitism—colonialist elitism and bourgeois-nationalist elitism . . . shar[ing] the prejudice that the making of the Indian nation and the development of the consciousness—nationalism—which confirmed this process were exclusively or predominantly elite achievements. In the colonialist and neo-colonialist historiographies these achievements are credited to British colonial rulers, administrators, policies, institutions, and culture; in the nationalist and neo-nationalist writings—to Indian elite personalities, institutions, activities and ideas.[117]

Certain members of the Indian elite are of course native informants for first-world intellectuals interested in the voice of the Other. But one must nevertheless insist that the colonized subaltern *subject* is irretrievably heterogeneous.

Against the indigenous elite we may set what Guha calls "the *politics of the people*," both outside ("this was an *autonomous* domain, for it neither originated from elite politics nor did its existence depend on the latter") and inside ("it continued to operate vigorously in spite of [colonialism], adjusting itself to the conditions prevailing under the Raj and

---

116. Edward W. Said, "Permission to Narrate," *London Review of Books* (16 Feb. 1984).

117. Guha, *Subaltern Studies*, (Delhi: Oxford Univ. Press, 1982), 1:1.

in many respects developing entirely new strains in both form and content") the circuit of colonial production. I cannot entirely endorse this insistence of determinate vigor and full autonomy, for practical historiographic exigencies will not allow such endorsements to privilege subaltern consciousness. Against the possible charge that his approach is essentialist, Guha constructs a definition of the people (the place of that essence) that can be only an identity-in-differential. He proposes a dynamic stratification grid describing colonial social production at large. Even the third group on the list, the buffer group, as it were, between the people and the great macro-structural dominant groups, is itself defined as a place of in-betweenness. The classification falls into: "dominant foreign groups," and "dominant indigenous groups at the all-India and at the regional and local levels" representing the elite; and "[t]he social groups and elements included in [the terms "people" and "subaltern classes"] represent[ing] *the demographic difference between the total Indian population and all those whom we have described as the "elite."*[118]

"The task of research" projected here is "to investigate, identify and measure the *specific* nature and degree of the *deviation* of [the] elements [constituting item 3] from the ideal and situate it historically." "Investigate, identify, and measure the specific": a program could hardly be more essentialist and taxonomic. Yet a curious methodological imperative is at work. I have argued that, in the Foucault-Deleuze conversation, a postrepresentationalist vocabulary hides an essenialist agenda. In subaltern studies, because of the violence of imperialist epistemic, social, and disciplinary inscription, a project understood in essentialist terms must traffic in a radical textual practice of differences. The object

---

118. Ibid., pp. 4, 8. The usefulness of this tightly defined term was largely lost when *Selected Subaltern Studies* was launched in the United States under Spivak's initiative (New York: Oxford Univ. Press, 1988). Guha, ed., *A Subaltern Studies Reader* (Minneapolis: Univ. of Minnesota Press, 1997) is now a corrective. In the now generalized usage, it is precisely this notion of the subaltern inhabiting a space of difference that is lost in statements such as the following: "The subaltern is force-fed into appropriating the master's culture" (Emily Apter, "French Colonial Studies and Postcolonial Theory," *Sub-Stance* 76/77, vol. 24, nos. 1–2 [1995]: 178); or worse still, Jameson's curious definition of subalternity as "the experience of inferiority" ("Marx's Purloined Letter," *New Left Review* 209 [1994]: 95).

of the group's investigation, in this case not even of the people as such but of the floating buffer zone of the regional elite—is a *deviation* from an *ideal*—the people or subaltern—which is itself defined as a difference from the elite. It is toward this structure that the research is oriented, a predicament rather different from the self-diagnosed transparency of the first-world radical intellectual. What taxonomy can fix such a space? Whether or not they themselves perceive it—in fact Guha sees his definition of "the people" within the master-slave dialectic—their text articulates the difficult task of rewriting its own conditions of impossibility as the conditions of its possibility. "At the regional and local levels [the dominant indigenous groups] . . . if belonging to social strata hierarchically inferior to those of the dominant all-Indian groups *acted in the interests of the latter and not in conformity to interests corresponding truly to their own social being.*"[119] When these writers speak, in their essentializing language, of a gap between interest and action in the intermediate group, their conclusions are closer to Marx than to the self-conscious naivete of Deleuze's pronouncement on the issue. Guha, like Marx, speaks of interest in terms of the social rather than the libidinal being. The Name-of-the-Father imagery in *The Eighteenth Brumaire* can help to emphasize that, on the level of class or group action, "true correspondence to own being" is as artificial or social as the patronymic.

It is to this intermediate group that the second woman in this chapter belongs. The pattern of domination is here determined mainly by gender rather than class. The subordinated gender following the dominant within the challenge of nationalism while remaining caught within gender oppression is not an unknown story.

For the (gender-unspecified) "true" subaltern group, whose identity is its difference, there is no unrepresentable subaltern subject that can know and speak itself; the intellectual's solution is not to abstain from representation. The problem is that the subject's itinerary has not been left traced so as to offer an object of seduction to the representing intellectual. In the slightly dated language of the Indian group, the question becomes, How can we touch the consciousness of the people,

---

119. Guha, *Subaltern Studies*, 1: 1.

even as we investigate their politics? With what voice-consciousness can the subaltern speak?

My question about how to earn the "secret encounter" with the contemporary hill women of Sirmur is a practical version of this. The woman of whom I will speak in this section was not a "true" subaltern, but a metropolitan middle-class girl. Further, the effort she made to write or speak her body was in the accents of accountable reason, the instrument of self-conscious responsibility. Still her Speech Act was refused. She was made to unspeak herself posthumously, by other women. In an earlier version of this chapter, I had summarized this historical indifference and its results as: the subaltern cannot speak.

The critique by Ajit K. Chaudhury, a West Bengali Marxist, of Guha's search for the subaltern consciousness can be taken as representative of a moment of the production process that includes the subaltern.[120] Chaudhury's perception that the Marxist view of the transformation of consciousness involves the knowledge of social relations seems, in principle, astute. Yet the heritage of the positivist ideology that has appropriated orthodox Marxism obliges him to add this rider: "This is not to belittle the importance of understanding peasants' consciousness or workers' consciousness *in its pure form*. This enriches our knowledge of the peasant and the worker and, possibly, throws light on how a particular mode takes on different forms in different regions, *which is considered a problem of second order importance in classical Marxism*."[121]

This variety of "internationalist Marxism," which believes in a pure, retrievable form of consciousness only to dismiss it, thus closing off what in Marx remain moments of productive bafflement, can at once be the occasion for Foucault's and Deleuze's rejection of Marxism *and* the

---

120. Since then, in the disciplinary fallout after the serious electoral and terrorist augmentation of Hindu nationalism in India, more alarming charges have been leveled at the group. See Aijaz Ahmad, *In Theory: Classes, Nations, Literatures* (New York: Verso, 1992), pp. 68, 194, 207–211; and Sumit Sarkar, "The Fascism of the Sangh Parivar," *Economic and Political Weekly*, 30 Jan. 1993, pp. 163–167.

121. Ajit K. Chaudhury, "New Wave Social Science," *Frontier* 16–24 (28 Jan. 1984), p. 10. Emphasis mine.

source of the critical motivation of the subaltern studies groups. All three are united in the assumption that there *is* a pure form of consciousness. On the French scene, there is a shuffling of signifiers: "the unconscious" or "the subject-in-oppression" clandestinely fills the space of "the pure form of consciousness." In orthodox "internationalist" intellectual Marxism, whether in the First World or the Third, the pure form of consciousness remains, paradoxically, a material effect, and therefore a second-order problem. This often earns it the reputation of racism and sexism. In the subaltern studies group it needs development according to the unacknowledged terms of its own articulation.

Within the effaced itinerary of the subaltern subject, the track of sexual difference is doubly effaced.[122] The question is not of female participation in insurgency, or the ground rules of the sexual division of labor, for both of which there is "evidence." It is, rather, that, both as object of colonialist historiography and as subject of insurgency, the ideological construction of gender keeps the male dominant. If, in the contest of colonial production, the subaltern has no history and cannot speak, the subaltern as female is even more deeply in shadow.

In the first part of this chapter we meditate upon an elusive female figure called into the service of colonialism. In the last part we will look at a comparable figure in anti-colonialist nationalism. The regulative psychobiography of widow self-immolation will be pertinent in both cases. In the interest of the invaginated spaces of this book, let us remind ourselves of the gradual emergence of the new subaltern in the New World Order.

The contemporary international division of labor is a displacement of the divided field of nineteenth-century territorial imperialism. Put in the abstractions of capital logic, in the wake of industrial capitalism and mercantile conquest, a group of countries, generally first-world, were in the position of investing capital; another group, generally third-world, provided the field for investment, both through the subordinate indigenous capitalists and through their ill-protected and shifting labor force. In the interest of maintaining the circulation and growth of industrial capital (and of the concomitant task of administration within

---

122. I do not believe that the recent trend of romanticizing anything written by the Aboriginal or outcaste ("dalit" = oppressed) intellectual has lifted the effacement.

nineteenth-century territorial imperialism), transportation, law, and standardized education systems were developed—even as local industries were destroyed or restructured, land distribution was rearranged, and raw material was transferred to the colonizing country. With so-called decolonization, the growth of multinational capital, and the relief of the administrative charge, "development" did not now involve wholesale state-level legislation and establishing education *systems* in a comparable way. This impedes the growth of consumerism in the former colonies. With modern telecommunications and the emergence of advanced capitalist economies at the two edges of Asia, maintaining the international division of labor serves to keep the supply of cheap labor in the periphery. The implosion of the Soviet Union in 1989 has smoothed a way to the financialization of the globe. Already in the mid-seventies, the newly electronified stock exchanges added to the growth of telecommunication, which allowed global capitalism to emerge through export-based subcontracting and postfordism. "Under this strategy, manufacturers based in developed countries subcontract the most labor intensive stages of production, for example, sewing or assembly, to the Third World nations where labor is cheap. Once assembled, the multinational re-imports the goods—under generous tariff exemptions—to the developed country *instead of selling them to the local market.*" Here the link to training in consumerism is almost snapped. "While global recession has markedly slowed trade and investment worldwide since 1979, international subcontracting has boomed. . . . In these cases, multinationals are freer to resist militant workers, revolutionary upheavals, and even economic downturns."[123]

Human labor is not, of course, intrinsically "cheap" or "expensive." An absence of labor laws (or a discriminatory enforcement of them), a totalitarian state (often entailed by development and modernization in the periphery), and minimal subsistence requirements on the part of the worker will ensure "cheapness." To keep this crucial item intact, the urban proletariat in what is now called the "developing" nations must not be systematically trained in the ideology of consumerism (parading as the philosophy of a classless society) that, against all odds, prepares

---

123. "Contracting Poverty," *Multinational Monitor* 4.8 (Aug. 1983):8. This report was contributed by John Cavanagh and Joy Hackel, who work on the International Corporations Project at the Institute for Policy Studies. Emphasis mine.

the ground for resistance through the coalition politics Foucault mentions (*FD* 216). This separation from the ideology of consumerism is increasingly exacerbated by the proliferating phenomena of international subcontracting.

In the post-Soviet world, the Bretton Woods organizations, together with the United Nations, are beginning to legislate for a monstrous North/South global state, which is coming into being as micrologically as the trade-controlled colonial state that was mentioned earlier. If Macaulay had spoken of a class of persons, Indian in blood and colour, but English in taste, in opinions, in morals, and in intellect; and Marx of the capitalist as *Faust*'s "mechanical man," there is now an impersonal "Economic Citizen," site of authority and legitimation, lodged in finance capital markets and transnational companies.[124] And if under postfordism and international subcontracting, unorganized or permanently casual female labor was already becoming the mainstay of world trade, in contemporary globalization, the mechanism of "aid" is supported by the poorest women of the South, who form the base of what I have elsewhere called globe-girdling struggles (ecology, resistance to "population *control*"), where the boundary between global and local becomes indeterminate. This is the ground of the emergence of the new subaltern—rather different from the nationalist example we will consider later. To confront this group is not only to represent (*vertreten*) them globally in the absence of infrastructural support, but also to learn to represent (*darstellen*) ourselves. This argument would take us into a critique of a disciplinary anthropology and the relationship between elementary pedagogy and disciplinary formation. It would also question the implicit demand, made by intellectuals who choose the "naturally articulate" subject of oppression, that such a subject come through a history that is a foreshortened mode-of-production narrative.

Not surprisingly, some members of *indigenous dominant* groups in the "developing" countries, members of the local bourgeoisie, find the language of alliance politics attractive. Identifying with forms of resistance plausible in advanced capitalist countries is often of a piece with that elitist bent of bourgeois historiography described by Ranajit Guha.

---

124. Saskia Sassen, "On Economic Citizenship," in *Losing Control? Sovereignty in An Age of Globalization* (New York: Columbia Univ. Press, 1996), pp. 31–58.

Belief in the plausibility of global alliance politics is increasingly prevalent among women of dominant social groups interested in "international feminism" in the "developing" nations as well as among well-placed Southern diasporics in the North. At the other end of the scale, those most separated from any possibility of an alliance among "women, prisoners, conscripted soldiers, hospital patients, and homosexuals" (*FD* 216) are the females of the urban subproletariat. In their case, the denial and withholding of consumerism and the structure of exploitation is compounded by patriarchal social relations.

That Deleuze and Foucault ignored both the epistemic violence of imperialism and the international division of labor would matter less if they did not, in closing, touch on third-world issues. In France it is impossible to ignore the problem of their *tiers monde*, the inhabitants of the erstwhile French African colonies. Deleuze limits his consideration of the Third World to these old local and regional indigenous elite who are, ideally, subaltern. In this context, references to the maintenance of the surplus army of labor fall into reverse-ethnic sentimentality. Since he is speaking of the heritage of nineteenth-century territorial imperialism, his reference is to the nation-state rather than the globalizing center:

> French capitalism needs greatly a floating signifier of unemployment. In this perspective, we begin to see the unity of the forms of repression: restrictions on immigration, once it is acknowledged that the most difficult and thankless jobs go to immigrant workers; repression in the factories, because the French must reacquire the "taste" for increasingly harder work; the struggle against youth and the repression of the educational system. (*FD* 211–212)

This is certainly an acceptable analysis. Yet it shows again that the Third World can enter the resistance program of an alliance politics directed against a *"unified* repression" only when it is confined to the third-world groups that are directly accessible to the First World.[125]

---

125. The mechanics of the invention of the Third World as signifier are susceptible to the type of analysis directed at the constitution of race as a signifier in Carby, *Empire*. In the contemprary conjuncture, in response to the augmentation of Eurocentric migration as the demographic fallout of postcoloniality, neocolonialism, end of the Soviet Union, and global financialization, the South (the Third

This benevolent first-world appropriation and reinscription of the Third World as an Other is the founding characteristic of much third-worldism in the U.S. human sciences today.

Foucault continues the critique of Marxism by invoking geographical discontinuity. The real mark of "geographical (geopolitcal) discontinuity" is the international division of labor. But Foucault uses the term to distinguish between exploitation (extraction and appropriation of surplus value; read, the field of Marxist analysis) and domination ("power" studies) and to suggest the latter's greater potential for resistance based on alliance politics. He cannot acknowledge that such a monist and unified access to a conception of "power" (methodologically presupposing a Subject-of-power) is made possible by a certain stage in exploitation, for his vision of geographical discontinuity is geopolitically specific to the First World:

> This geographical discontinuity of which you speak might mean perhaps the following: as soon as we struggle against *exploitation*, the proletariat not only leads the struggle but also defines its targets, its methods, its places and its instruments; and to ally oneself with the proletariat is to consolidate with its positions, its ideology, it is to take up again the motives for their combat. This means total immersion [in the Marxist project]. But if it is against *power* that one struggles, then all those who acknowledge it as intolerable can begin the struggle wherever they find themselves and in terms of their own activity (or passivity). In engaging in this struggle that is *their own*, whose objectives they clearly understand and whose methods they can determine, they enter into the revolutionary process. As allies of the proletariat, to be sure, because power is exercised the way it is in order to maintain capitalist exploitation. They genuinely serve the cause of the proletariat by fighting in those places where they find themselves oppressed. Women, prisoners, conscripted soldiers, hospital patients, and homosexuals have now begun a specific struggle against the particular form of power, the constraints and controls, that are exercised over them. (*FD* 216)

World of yore, with shifting bits of the old Second World thrown in) is being reinvented as the South-in-the-North. Even so brilliant a book as Etienne Balibar and Immanuel Wallerstein, *Race, Nation, Class: Ambiguous Identities*, tr. Chris Turner (New York: Verso, 1991) starts from this invention as unquestioned premise.

This is an admirable program of localized resistance. Where possible, this model of resistance is not an alternative to, but can complement, macrological struggles along "Marxist" lines. Yet if its situation is universalized, it accomodates unacknowledged privileging of the subject. Without a theory of ideology, it can lead to a dangerous utopianism. And, if confined to migrant struggles in Northern countries, it can work against global social justice.

The topographical reinscription of imperialism never specifically informed Foucault's presuppositions. Notice the omission of the fact, in the following passage, that the new mechanism of power in the seventeenth and eighteenth centuries (the extraction of surplus value without extra-economic coercion is its marxist description) is secured *by means of* territorial imperialism—the Earth and its products—"elsewhere." The representation of sovereignty is crucial in these theaters: "In the seventeenth and eighteenth centuries, we have the production of an important phenomenon, the emergence, or rather the invention, of a new mechanism of power possessed of highly specific procedural techniques . . . which is also, I believe, absolutely incompatible with the relations of sovereignty. This new mechanism of power is more dependent upon bodies and what they do than the Earth and its products" (*PK* 104).

Sometimes it seems as if the very brilliance of Foucault's analysis of the centuries of European imperialism produces a miniature version of that heterogeneous phenomenon: management of space—but by doctors; development of administrations—but in asylums; considerations of the periphery—but in terms of the insane, prisoners, and children. The clinic, the asylum, the prison, the university—all seem to be screen-allegories that foreclose a reading of the broader narratives of imperialism. (One could open a similar discussion of the ferocious motif of "deterritorialization" in Deleuze and Guattari.) "One can perfectly well not talk about something because one doesn't know about it," Foucault might murmur (*PK* 66). Yet we have already spoken of the sanctioned ignorance that every critic of imperialism must chart.

By contrast, the early Derrida seemed aware of ethnocentrism in the production of knowledge.[126] (We have seen this in his comments on

---

126. Subsequently, as I indicate at length elsewhere (*Outside*, pp. 113–115; "Ghostwriting," pp. 69–71, 82) his work in these areas has speculated with the

Kant quoted in Chapter 1. Like "empirical investigation, . . . tak[ing] shelter in the field of grammatological knowledge" obliges "operat[ing] through 'examples,'" *OG* 75.)

The examples Derrida lays out—to show the limits of grammatology as a positive science—come from the appropriate ideological self-justification of an imperialist project. In the European seventeenth century, he writes, there were three kinds of "prejudices" operating in histories of writing which constituted a "symptom of the crisis of European consciousness" (*OG* 75): the "theological prejudice," the "Chinese prejudice," and the "hieroglyphist prejudice." The first can be indexed as: God wrote a primordial or natural script: Hebrew or Greek. The second: Chinese is a perfect *blueprint* for philosophical writing, but it is only a blueprint. True philosophical writing is "independen[t] with regard to history" (*OG* 79) and will sublate Chinese into an easy-to-learn script that will supersede actual Chinese. The third: that the Egyptian script is too sublime to be deciphered.

The first prejudice preserves the "actuality" of Hebrew or Greek; the last two ("rational" and "mystical," respectively) collude to support the first, where the center of the logos is seen as the Judaeo-Christian God (the appropriation of the Hellenic Other through assimilation is an earlier story)—a "prejudice" still sustained in efforts to give the cartography of the Judaeo-Christian myth the status of geopolitical history:

> The concept of Chinese writing thus functioned as a sort of *European hallucination*. . . . This functioning obeyed a rigorous necessity. . . . It was not disturbed by the knowledge of Chinese script . . . which was

---

tendencies of computing migrancy or displacement as an origin (see page 17); in the figure of the absolute *arrivant*, of the marrano, and, most recently, in his seminars, hospitality. He would figure the indigenous subaltern, from the perspective of the metropolitan hybrid, as a correlative of cultural conservatism, topological archaism, ontopological nostalgia (*Specters*, p. 82). Here, too, he speculates with already existing tendencies. Just as pedigreed Marxists have been told, by Derrida among others, that Marx must be read in Marx's way, *as if* the reader were haunted by Marx's ghost; so might one deconstruct deconstruction (as Klein Freuded Freud): do not accuse, do not excuse, make it "your own," turn it around and use—with no guarantees—except that this formula too will become useless tomorrow—or in the moment of its saying: "each time that ethnocentrism is precipitately and ostentatiously reversed, some effort silently hides behind all the spectacular effects to consolidate an inside and to draw from it some domestic benefit."

then available. . . . A *"hieroglyphist prejudice"* had produced the same effect of *interested blindness*. Far from proceeding . . . from ethnocentric scorn, the occultation takes the form of an hyperbolical admiration. We have not finished demonstrating the necessity of this pattern. Our century is not free from it; each time that ethnocentrism is precipitately and ostentatiously reversed, some effort silently hides behind all the spectacular effects to *consolidate an inside* and to draw from it some domestic benefit. (*OG* 80; Derrida italicizes only "hieroglyphist prejudice")

This pattern operates the culturalist excuse for Development encountered, for example, in John Rawls's *Political Liberalism*, as it does all unexamined metropolitan hybridism.[127]

Derrida closes the chapter by showing again that the project of grammatology is obliged to develop *within* the discourse of presence. It is not just a critique of presence but an awareness of the itinerary of the discourse of presence in one's *own* critique, a vigilance precisely against too great a claim for transparency. The word "writing" as the name of the object and model of grammatology is a practice "only within the *historical* closure, that is to say within the limits of science and philosophy" (*OG* 93).

Derrida calls the ethnocentrism of the European science of writing in the late seventeenth and early eighteenth centuries a symptom of the general crisis of European consciousness. It is, of course, part of a larger symptom, or perhaps the crisis itself, the slow turn from feudalism to capitalism via the first waves of capitalist imperialism. The itinerary of recognition through assimilation of the Other can be more interestingly traced, it seems to me, in the imperialist constitution of the colonial subject and the foreclosure of the figure of the "native informant."

Can the subaltern speak? What might the elite do to watch out for the continuing construction of the subaltern? The question of "woman" seems most problematic in this context. Confronted by the ferocious standardizing benevolence of most U.S. and Western European human-scientific radicalism (recognition by assimilation) today, and the exclusion of the margins of even the center-periphery articulation (the

---

127. John Rawls, *Political Liberalism* (New York: Columbia Univ. Press, 1993).

"true and differential subaltern"), the analogue of class-consciousness rather than race-consciousness in this area seems historically, disciplinarily, and practically forbidden by Right and Left alike.

In so fraught a field, it is not easy to ask the question of the subaltern woman as subject; it is thus all the more necessary to remind pragmatic radicals that such a question is not an idealist red herring. Though all feminist or antisexist projects cannot be reduced to this one, to ignore it is an unacknowledged political gesture that has a long history and collaborates with a masculist radicalism that operates by strategic exclusions, equating "nationalist" and "people" (as counterproductive as the equation of "feminist" and "woman").

If I ask myself, How is it possible to want to die by fire to mourn a husband ritually? I am asking the question of the (gendered) subaltern woman as subject, not, as my friend Jonathan Culler somewhat tendentiously suggests, trying to "produce difference by differing" or to "appeal . . . to a sexual identity defined as essential and privileg[ing] experiences associated with that identity."[128] Culler is here a part of that mainstream project of Western feminism that both continues and displaces the battle over the right to individualism between women and men in situations of upward class mobility. One suspects that the debate between U.S. feminism and European "theory" (as theory is generally represented by women from the United States or Britain) occupies a significant corner of that very terrain. I am generally sympathetic with the call to make U.S. feminism more "theoretical." It seems, however, that the problem of the muted subject of the subaltern woman, though not solved by an "essentialist" search for lost origins, cannot be served by the call for more theory in Anglo-America either.

That call is often given in the name of a critique of "positivism," which is seen here as identical with "essentialism." Yet Hegel, the modern inaugurator of "the work of the negative," was not a stranger to the notion of essences. For Marx, the curious persistence of essentialism within the dialectic was a profound and productive problem. Thus, the stringent binary opposition between positivism/essentialism (read,

---

128. Jonathan Culler, *On Deconstruction: Theory and Criticism after Structuralism* (Ithaca: Cornell Univ. Press, 1982), p. 48.

U.S.) and "theory" (read, French or Franco-German via Anglo-American) may be spurious. Apart from repressing the ambiguous complicity between essentialism and critiques of positivism (acknowledged by Derrida in "Of Grammatology as a Positive Science"), it also errs by implying that positivism is not a theory. This move allows the emergence of a proper name, a positive essence, Theory. And once again, the position of the investigator remains unquestioned. If and when this territorial debate turns toward the Third World, no change in the question of method is to be discerned. This debate cannot take into account that, in the case of the woman as subaltern, rather few ingredients for the constitution of the itinerary of the trace of a sexed subject (rather than an anthropological object) can be gathered to locate the possibility of dissemination.

Yet I remain generally sympathetic to aligning feminism with the critique of positivism and the defetishization of the concrete. I am also far from averse to learning from the work of Western theorists, though I have learned to insist on marking their positionality as investigating subjects. Given these conditions, and as a literary critic, I tactically confronted the immense problem of the consciousness of the woman as subaltern. I reinvented the problem in a sentence and transformed it into the object of a simple semiosis. What can such a transformation mean?

This gesture of transformation marks the fact that knowledge of the other subject is theoretically impossible. Empirical work in the discipline constantly performs this transformation tacitly. It is a transformation from a first-second person performance to the constatation in the third person. It is, in other words, at once a gesture of control and an acknowledgment of limits. Freud provides a homology for such positional hazards.

Sarah Kofman has suggested that the deep ambiguity of Freud's use of women as a scapegoat may be read as a reaction-formation to an initial and continuing desire to give the hysteric a voice, to transform her into the *subject* of hysteria.[129] The masculine-imperialist ideological

---

129. Sarah Kofman, *The Enigma of Woman: Woman in Freud's Writings*, tr. Catherine Porter (Ithaca: Cornell Univ. Press, 1985).

formation that shaped that desire into "the daughter's seduction" is part of the same formation that constructs the monolithic "third-world woman." No contemporary metropolitan investigator is not influenced by that formation. Part of our "unlearning" project is to articulate our participation in that formation—by *measuring* silences, if necessary—into the *object* of investigation. Thus, when confronted with the questions, Can the subaltern speak? and Can the subaltern (as woman) speak? our efforts to give the subaltern a voice in history will be doubly open to the dangers run by Freud's discourse. It is in acknowledgment of these dangers rather than as solution to a problem that I put together the sentence "White men are saving brown women from brown men," a sentence that runs like a red thread through today's "gender and development." My impulse is not unlike the one to be encountered in Freud's investigation of the sentence "A child is being beaten."[130]

The use of Freud here does not imply an isomorphic analogy between subject-formation and the behavior of social collectives, a frequent practice, often accompanied by a reference to Reich, in the conversation between Deleuze and Foucault. I am, in other words, not suggesting that "White men are saving brown women from brown men" is a sentence indicating a *collective* fantasy symptomatic of a *collective* itinerary of sadomasochistic repression in a *collective* imperialist enterprise. There is a satisfying symmetry in such an allegory, but I would rather invite the reader to consider it a problem in "wild psychoanalysis" than a clinching solution.[131] Just as Freud's insistence on making the woman the scapegoat in "A child is being beaten" and elsewhere discloses his political interests, however imperfectly, so my insistence on imperialist subject-production as the occasion for this sentence discloses a politics that I cannot step around.

---

130. Freud, "'A Child Is Being Beaten': A Contribution to the Study of the Origin of Sexual Perversion," *SE* 17. For a list of ways in which Western criticism constructs "third world woman," see Chandra Talpade Mohanty, "Under Western Eyes: Feminist Scholarship and Colonial Discourses," in Mohanty et al., eds., *Third World Women and the Politics of Feminism* (Bloomington: Indiana Univ. Press, 1991), pp. 51–80.

131. Freud, "'Wild' Psycho-Analysis," *SE* vol. 11, pp. 221–227. A good deal of psychoanalytic social critique would fit this description.

Further, I am attempting to borrow the general methodological aura of Freud's strategy toward the sentence he constructed *as a sentence* out of the many similar substantive accounts his patients gave him. This does not mean I will offer a case of transference-in-analysis as an iso-morphic model for the transaction between reader and text (here the constructed sentence). As I repeat in this chapter, the analogy between transference and literary criticism or historiography is no more than a productive catachresis. To say that the subject is a text does not autho-rize the converse pronouncement: that the verbal text is a subject.

I am fascinated, rather, by how Freud predicates a *history* of repres-sion that produces the final sentence. It is a history with a double origin, one hidden in the amnesia of the infant, the other lodged in our archaic past, assuming by implication a preoriginary space where human and animal were not yet differentiated.[132] We are driven to impose a homol-ogy of this Freudian strategy on the Marxist narrative to explain the ideological dissimulation of imperialist political economy and outline a history of repression that produces a sentence like the one I have sketched: "White men are saving brown women from brown men"— giving honorary whiteness to the colonial subject on precisely this issue. This history also has a double origin, one hidden in the maneuverings behind the British abolition of widow sacrifice in 1829,[133] the other

---

132. Freud, "'A Child Is Being Beaten,'" p. 188.

133. For a brilliant account of how the "reality" of widow-sacrificing was consti-tuted or "textualized" during the colonial period, see Lata Mani, "Contentious Traditions: The Debate on *Sati* in Colonial India," in *Recasting Women: Essays in Colonial History* (Delhi: Kāli for Women, 1989), pp. 88–126. I profited from discus-sion with Dr. Mani at the inception of this project. Here I present some of my differences from her position. The "printing mistake in the Bengali translation" (p. 109) that she cites is not the same as the mistake I discuss, which is in the ancient Sanskrit. It is of course altogether interesting that there should be all these erran-cies in the justification of the practice. A regulative psychobiography is not identical with "textual hegemony" (p. 96). I agree with Mani that the latter mode of explana-tion cannot take "regional variations" into account. A regulative psychobiography is another mode of "textualist oppression" when it produces not only "women's con-sciousness" but a "gendered episteme" (mechanics of the construction of objects of knowledge together with validity-criteria for statements of knowledge). You do not have to "read verbal texts" here. It is something comparable to Gramsci's "inven-

lodged in the classical and Vedic past of "Hindu" India, the *Rg-Veda* and the *Dharmasāstra*. An undifferentiated transcendental preoriginary space can only too easily be predicated for this other history.

The sentence I have constructed is one among many displacements describing the relationship between brown and white men (sometimes brown and white women worked in).[134] It takes its place among some sentences of "hyperbolic admiration" or of pious guilt that Derrida speaks of in connection with the "hieroglyphist prejudice." The relationship between the imperialist subject and the subject of imperialism is at least ambiguous.

---

tory without traces" (Antonio Gramsci, *Selections from the Prison Notebooks*, tr. Quintin Hoare and Geoffrey Nowell Smith [New York: International Publishers, 1971], p. 324). Like Mani (p. 125, n. 90), I too wish to "add" to Kosambi's "strategies." To the "supplement[ation of the linguistic study of problems of ancient Indian culture] by intelligent use of archaeology, anthropology, sociology and a suitable historical perspective" (Kosambi, "Combined Methods in Indology," *Indo-Iranian Journal* 6 [1963]: 177), I would add the insights of psychoanalysis, though not the regulative psychobiography of its choice. Alas, in spite of our factualist fetish, "facts" alone may account for women's oppression, but they will never allow us to approach gendering, a net where we ourselves are enmeshed, as we decide what (the) facts are. Because of epistemic prejudice, Kosambi's bold and plain speech can and has been misunderstood; but his word "live" can take on board a more complex notion of the mental theater as Mani cannot: "Indian peasants in villages far from any city *live* in a manner closer to the days when the Purānas were written than do the descendants of the brahmins who wrote the Purānas" (emphasis mine). Precisely. The self-representation in gendering is regulated by the Puranic psychobiography, with the Brahmin as the model. In the last chapter I will consider what Kosambi mentions in the next sentence: "A stage further back are the pitiful fragments of tribal groups, usually sunk to the level of marginal castes; they rely heavily upon food-gathering and have the corresponding mentality." Kosambi's somewhat doctrinaire Marxism would not allow him to think of the tribal episteme as anything but only backward, of course. After the *sati* of Rup Kanwar in September 1987, a body of literature on the contemporary situation has emerged. That requires quite a different engagement (see Radha Kumar, "Agitation against Sati, 1987–88," in *The History of Doing* [Delhi: Kāli for Women, 1993], pp. 172–181.)

134. See Kumari Jayawardena, *The White Woman's Other Burden: Western Women and South Asia during British Colonial Rule* (New York: Routledge, 1995). Envy, backlash, reaction-formation; these are the routes by which such efforts may, in the absence of ethical responsibility, lead to opposite results. I have repeatedly invoked Melanie Klein and Assia Djebar in this context. See also Spivak, "Psychoanalysis in Left Field," pp. 66–69.

The Hindu widow ascends the pyre of the dead husband and immolates herself upon it. This is widow sacrifice. (The conventional transcription of the Sanskrit word for the widow would be *sati*. The early colonial British transcribed it *suttee*.) The rite was not practiced universally and was not caste- or class-fixed. The abolition of this rite by the British has been generally understood as a case of "White men saving brown women from brown men." White women—from the nineteenth-century British Missionary Registers to Mary Daly—have not produced an alternative understanding. Against this is the Indian nativist statement, a parody of the nostalgia for lost origins: "The women wanted to die," still being advanced (see note 25).[135]

The two sentences go a long way to legitimize each other. One never encounters the testimony of the women's voice consciousness. Such a testimony would not be ideology-transcendent or "fully" subjective, of course, but it would constitute the ingredients for producing a countersentence. As one goes down the grotesquely mistranscibed names of these women, the sacrificed widows, in the police reports included in the records of the East India Company, one cannot put together a "voice." The most one can sense is the immense heterogeneity breaking through even such a skeletal and ignorant account (castes, for example, are regularly described as tribes). Faced with the dialectically interlocking sentences that are constructible as "White men are saving brown women from brown men" and "The women wanted to die," the metropolitan feminist migrant (removed from the actual theater of decolonization) asks the question of simple semiosis—What does this signify?—and begins to plot a history.

As I have suggested in the previous chapter, to mark the moment when not only a civil but a good society is born out of domestic confusion, singular events that break the letter of the law to institute its spirit

135. The examples of female ventriloquist complicity, quoted by Lata Mani in her brilliant article "Production of an Official Discourse on *Sati* in early Nineteenth Century Bengal," *Economic and Political Weekly* 21.17 (26 Apr. 1986), women's studies supp., p. 36, proves my point. The point is not that a refusal would not be ventriloquism for Women's Rights. One is not suggesting that only the latter is correct free will. One is suggesting that the freedom of the will is negotiable, and it is not on the grounds of a disinterested free will that we will be able to justify an action, in this case against the burning of widows, to the adequate satisfaction of all. The ethical aporia is not negotiable. We must act in view of this.

are often invoked. The protection of women by men often provides such an event. If we remember that the British boasted of their absolute equity toward and noninterference with native custom/law, an invocation of this sanctioned transgression of the letter for the sake of the spirit may be read in J. D. M. Derrett's remark: "The very first legislation upon Hindu Law was carried through without the assent of a single Hindu." The legislation is not named here. The next sentence, where the measure is named, is equally interesting if one considers the implications of the survival of a colonially established "good" society after decolonization: "The recurrence of *sati* in independent India is probably an obscurantist revival which cannot long survive even in a very backward part of the country."[136]

Whether this observation is correct or not, what interests me is that the protection of woman (today the "third-world woman") becomes a signifier for the establishment of a *good* society (now a good planet) which must, at such inaugurative moments, transgress mere legality, or equity of legal policy. In this particular case, the process also allowed the redefinition as a crime of what had been tolerated, known, or adulated as ritual. In other words, this one item in Hindu law jumped the frontier between the private and the public domain.

Although Foucault's *historical narrative*, focusing solely on Western Europe, sees merely a tolerance for the criminal antedating the development of criminology in the late eighteenth century (*PK* 41), his *theoretical description* of the "episteme" is pertinent here: "The *episteme* is the 'apparatus' which makes possible the separation not of the true from the false, but of what may not be characterized as scientific" (*PK* 197)— ritual as opposed to crime, the one fixed by superstition, the other by legal science.[137]

The leap of *suttee* from private to public has a clear but complex

---

136. J. D. M. Derrett, *Hindu Law Past and Present: Being an Account of the Controversy Which Preceded the Enactment of the Hindu Code, and Text of the Code as Enacted, and Some Comments Thereon* (Calcutta: A. Mukherjee and Co., 1957), p. 46.

137. Kosambi comments on such shifts as a matter of course. Of the much admired widow remarriage reform, e.g., he writes: "[t]hat he [R. G. Bhāndārkar] spoke for a very narrow class in the attempt to speak for the whole of India never struck him, nor for that matter other contemporary 'reformers'. Still, *the silent change of emphasis from caste to class was a necessary advance*" (D. D. Kosambi, *Myth and Reality: Studies in the Formation of Indian Culture* [Bombay: Popular Prakashan,

relationship with the changeover from a mercantile and commercial to a territorial and administrative British presence; it can be followed in correspondence among the police stations, the lower and higher courts, the courts of directors, the prince regent's court, and the like.[138] (It is interesting to note that, from the point of view of the native "colonial subject," also emergent from the "feudalism-capitalism" transition— necessarily askew because "colonial"—*sati* is a signifier with the reverse social charge: "Groups rendered psychologically marginal by their exposure to Western impact . . . had come under pressure to demonstrate, to others as well as to themselves, their ritual purity and allegiance to traditional high culture. To many of them *sati* became an important proof of their conformity to older norms at a time when these norms had become shaky within.")[139]

If the mercantile-territorial/feudal-capitalist transitions provide a first historical origin for my sentence—"white men are saving brown women from brown men"—that origin is evidently lost in the more general history of humankind as work, its origin placed by Marx in the material exchange or "metabolism" between the human being and Na-

---

1962], p. 38, n. 2; emphasis mine). We would say "shift" rather than "advance"; for it is this silent century-old epistemic shift that allows today's Hindu nationalism to proclaim itself anti-casteist, nationalist—even "secular." Incidentally, to confine the construction of *Sati* to colonial negotiations, and finally to the Ram Mohun Roy– Lord William Bentinck exchange, is also to avoid the question of "subaltern consciousness." For further commentary on the differences between Mani and Spivak, see Sumit Sarkar, "Orientalism Revisited: Saidian Frameworks in the Writing of Modern Indian History," *Oxford Literary Review* 16 (1994): 223. I remain grateful to Professor Sarkar for noticing that "Mani's article stands in marked contrast to the much more substantive discussion of pre-colonial and colonial discourses on sati in Spivak, 'Can the Subaltern Speak?'" To claim that caste or clitoridectomy is no more than a colonial construction advances nothing today. Romila Thapar tells me that the seventh-century historian Bāṇabhaṭṭa objected to *Sati*. There may be something Eurocentric about assuming that imperialism began with Europe.

138. Today, interference in women's cultural privacy remains a project of making rural women available for micro-enterprise in the economic sphere, and a project of bettering women's lives in the political. Demands for a more responsible tempo—woman's time—so that the violence of the change does not scar the episteme, are often impatiently rejected as cultural conservatism.

139. Ashis Nandy, "Sati: A Nineteenth Century Tale of Women, Violence and Protest," *Rammohun Roy and the Process of Modernization in India*, ed. V. C. Joshi (Delhi: Vikas Publishing House, 1975), p. 68.

ture, the story of capitalist expansion, the slow freeing of labor power as commodity, the narrative of the modes of production, the transition from feudalism via mercantilism to capitalism.[140] As my first chapter has argued, even the precarious normativity of this narrative is sustained by the putatively changeless stopgap of the "Asiatic" mode of production, which steps in to sustain it whenever it might become apparent that the story of capital logic is the story of the West, that only imperialism can aggressively insist upon the universality of the mode of production narrative, that to ignore or invade the subaltern today is, willy-nilly, to continue the imperialist project; in the name of modernization, in the interest of globalization. The origin of my sentence is thus lost in the shuffle between other, more powerful discourses. Given that the abolition of *sati* was in itself admirable, is it still possible to wonder if a perception of the origin of my sentence might contain interventionist possibilities?

I will later place the mobilizing of woman into *Sati* with the place of the epic instance of "heroism"—suicide in the name of "nation"; "martyrdom"—suicide in the name of "God"; and other species of self-"sacrifice." These are transcendental figurations of the (agent of the) gift of time. The feminist project is not simply to stage the woman as victim, but to ask: Why does "husband" become an appropriate name for *radical* alterity? Why is "to be" equal to "to be wife"? This may even lead to such questions as the contemporary equation of "to be" with "to be gainfully employed."[141] Let us stop this line of questioning, for it will no longer allow the general reader to keep *sati* contained within the particularisms of "cultural difference"—that allowed imperialism to give itself yet another legitimation in its "civilizing mission," today recoded, it bears repetition, as the more tolerable phrase "gender and development," the copula "and" (with its concealed charge of supplementation) replacing the more transparent earlier phrase "woman in development."[142]

---

140. *Capital*, 3:958–959.

141. Spivak, "Diasporas," p. 248.

142. In "The Supplement of Copula: Philosophy Before Linguistics" (*Margins*, pp. 175–205), Derrida argues that every copula is a supplement. In his own work, he has reopened the copula by working on the ethical (see Appendix). The copula in

Imperialism's (or globalization's) image as the establisher of the good society is marked by the espousal of the woman as *object* of protection from her own kind. How should one examine this dissimulation of patriarchal strategy, which apparently grants the woman free choice as *subject?* In other words, how does one make the move from "Britain" to "Hinduism"? Even the attempt shows that, like "Development," "Imperialism" is not identical with chromatism, or mere prejudice against people of color. To approach this question, I will touch briefly on the *Dharmasāstra* and the *Rg-Veda*. Although two vastly different kinds of texts, they can represent "the archaic origin" in my homology from Freud. My readings are an interested and inexpert examination, by a female expatriate, of the fabrication of repression, a constructed counternarrative of woman's consciousness, thus woman's being, thus woman's being good, thus the good woman's desire, thus woman's desire. Paradoxically, these same moves allow us to witness the unfixed place of woman as a signifier in the inscription of the social individual. Thus "woman" is caught between the interested "normalization" of capital and the regressive "envy" of the colonized male.[143] The "enlightened" colonial subject moves toward the former, without asking the less "practical" question of psychobiography. *Sati* returns—once again grasped as victimage versus cultural heroism—in the rift of the failure of decolonization. It is the somewhat fanatical Melanie Klein who has given this writer the confidence to suggest that to ignore the rôle of violence in the development of conscience is to court the repetition of suicide as accountability.[144]

What is it to ask the question of psychobiography? I should need much greater learning to be a real player here. But it is part of the tragic

---

this sentence may mean that the relationship between men and women is patriarchal until rationalized. Not very far from either consciousness-raising or classical Marxism. These suggestions call for a mourning-work hinted at in "Foucault and Najibullah."

143. I am using "Envy" in the sense established by Melanie Klein in "Envy and Gratitude," in *Envy and Gratitude and Other Works* (New York: Free Press, 1975), pp. 176–235.

144. Klein, "The Early Development of Conscience in the Child," in *Love, Guilt and Reparation and Other Works (1921–1945)*, p. 257.

narrative of the atrophy of classical learning that the scholar cannot ask the radical questions.[145]

The two moments in the *Dharmasāstra* that I am interested in are the discourse on sanctioned suicides and the nature of the rites for the dead.[146] Framed in these two discourses, the self-immolation of widows seems an exception to the rule. The general scriptural doctrine is that suicide is reprehensible. Room is made, however, for certain forms of suicide that, as formulaic performance, lose the phenomenal identity of being suicide. The first category of sanctioned suicides arises out of *tatvajnāna*, or the knowledge of right principles. Here the knowing subject comprehends the insubstantiality or mere phenomenality (which may be the same thing as nonphenomenality) of its identity. At a certain point in time, *tat tva* was interpreted as "that you," but even without that, *tatva* is thatness or quiddity. Thus, this enlightened self truly knows the "that"-ness of its identity. Its demolition of that identity is not *ātmaghāta* (a killing of the self). The paradox of knowing the limits of knowledge is that the strongest assertion of agency, to negate the possibility of agency, cannot be an example of itself. Curiously enough, the self-*sacrifice* of gods is sanctioned by natural ecology, useful for the working of the economy of Nature and the Universe, rather than by self-knowledge. In this *logically* anterior stage, inhabited by gods rather than human beings, of this particular chain of displacements, suicide and sacrifice (*ātmaghāta* and *ātmadāna*) seem as little distinct as an "interior" (self-knowledge) and an "exterior" (ecology) sanction.

This philosophical space, however, does not accommodate the self-immolating woman. For her we look where room is made to sanction

---

145. It is in this spirit that Assia Djebar asked the help of an Arabic scholar to allow her to read certain Arabic chronicles imaginatively in order to write *Far from Medina*, tr. Dorothy Blair (London: Quartet, 1994). I have been energized by Peter van de Veer's approbation in "Sati and Sanskrit: The Move from Orientalism to Hinduism," in Mieke Bal and Inge E. Boer, eds., *The Point of Theory: Practices of Cultural Analysis* (New York: Continuum, 1994), pp. 251–259.

146. Since I am no expert, the following account leans heavily on Pandurang Vaman Kane, *History of the Dharmasastra* (Poona: Bhandarkar Oriental Institute, 1963) (hereafter *HD*, with volume, part, and page numbers).

suicides that cannot claim truth-knowledge as a state that is, at any rate, easily verifiable and belongs in the area of *sruti* (what was heard) rather than *smriti* (what is remembered). This third exception to the general rule about suicide annuls the phenomenal identity or irrationality of self-immolation if performed in certain places rather than in a certain state of enlightenment. Thus we move from an interior sanction (truth-knowledge) to an exterior one (place of pilgrimage). It is possible for a woman to perform *this* type of (non)suicide.[147]

Yet even this is not the *proper* place for the woman to annul the proper name of suicide through the destruction of her proper self. For her alone is sanctioned self-immolation on a dead spouse's pyre. (The few male examples cited in Hindu antiquity of self-immolation on another's pyre, being proofs of enthusiasm and devotion to a master or superior, reveal the structure of domination within the rite).

This suicide that is not suicide may be read as a simulacrum of both truth-knowledge and piety of place. If the former, it is as if the knowledge *in a subject* of its own insubstantiality and mere phenomenality is dramatized so that the dead husband becomes the exteriorized example and place of the extinguished subject and the widow becomes the (non)agent who "acts it out": the logical consequence of placing agency in alterity: transforming ethics into an institutional calculus that supposedly codes the absent agent's intention. If the latter, it is as if the metonym for all sacred places is now that burning bed of wood, constructed by elaborate ritual, where the woman's subject, legally displaced from herself, is being consumed. It is in terms of this profound ideology of the displaced place of the female subject that the paradox of free choice comes into play. For the male subject, it is the felicity of the suicide, a felicity that will annul rather than establish its status as such, that is noted. For the female subject, a sanctioned self-immolation, even as it takes away the effect of "fall" (*pātaka*) attached to an unsanctioned suicide, brings praise for the act of choice on another register. By

---

147. Upendra Thakur, *The History of Suicide in India: An Introduction* (Delhi: Munshi Ram Manohar Lal, 1963), p. 9, has a useful list of Sanskrit primary sources on sacred places. This laboriously decent book betrays all the signs of the schizophrenia of the colonial subject, such as bourgeois nationalism, patriarchal communalism, and an "enlightened reasonableness."

the inexorable ideological production of the sexed subject, such a death can be understood by the female subject as an *exceptional* signifier of her own desire, exceeding the general rule for a widow's conduct.

In certain periods and areas this exceptional rule became the general rule in a class-specific way. Ashis Nandy relates its marked prevalence in eighteenth- and early nineteenth-century Bengal to factors ranging from population control to communal misogyny.[148] Certainly its prevalence there in the previous centuries was because in Bengal, unlike elsewhere in India, widows could inherit property. Thus, what the British see as poor victimized women going to the slaughter is in fact an ideological battleground. As P. V. Kane, the great historian of the *Dharmaśāstra*, has correctly observed: "In Bengal, [the fact that] the widow of a sonless member even in a joint Hindu family is entitled to practically the same rights over joint family property which her deceased husband would have had . . . must have frequently induced the surviving members to get rid of the widow by appealing at a most distressing hour to her devotion to and love for her husband" (*HD* II.2, 635).

Yet benevolent and enlightened males were and are sympathetic with the "courage" of the woman's free choice in the matter. They thus often accept the production of the sexed subaltern subject: "Modern India does not justify the practice of *sati*, but it is a warped mentality that rebukes modern Indians for expressing admiration and reverence for the cool and unfaltering courage of Indian women in becoming *satis* or performing the *jauhar* for cherishing their ideals of womanly conduct" (*HD*, II.2, 636).

This patriarchal admiration is consonant with the logic of the practice. By contrast, the relationship between British benevolence and that logic is in fact "a case of conflict . . . that cannot be equitably resolved for lack of a rule of judgment applicable to both arguments. One side's legitimacy does not imply the other's lack of legitimacy."[149] Historically, legitimacy was of course established by virtue of abstract institu-

---

148. Nandy, "Sati."
149. Jean-François Lyotard, *The Differend: Phrases in Dispute*, tr. Georges Van Den Abbeele (Minneapolis: Univ. of Minnesota Press, 1988), p. xi.

tional power. Who in nineteenth-century India could have waited for the women's time here?

> In the differend, something "asks" to be put into phrases, and suffers from the wrong of not being able to be put into phrases right away. This is when the human beings who thought they could use language as an instrument of communication learn through the feeling of pain which accompanies silence (and of pleasure which accompanies the invention of a new idiom), that they are summoned by language, not to augment to their profit the quantity of information communicable through existing idioms, but to recognize that what remains to be phrased exceeds what they can presently phrase, and that they must be allowed to institute idioms which do not yet exist.[150]

It is of course unthinkable that such an allowance could ever be made or seized for or through the agency of nonbourgeois women in British India, as it is unthinkable in globalization in the name of feminism today. In the event, as the discourse of what the reformers perceived as heathen ritual or superstition was recoded as crime, one diagnosis of female free will was substituted for another. In the last movement of this chapter we will bear witness to what may have been an effort to institute an idiomatic moment in the scripting of the reproductive body. It was not read or heard; it remained in the space of the differend.

It must be remembered that the self-immolation of widows was not *invariable* ritual prescription. If, however, the widow does decide thus to exceed the letter of ritual, to turn back is a transgression for which a particular type of penance is prescribed.[151] With the local British police

---

150. Ibid., p. 13.

151. *HD*, II.2, p. 633. There are suggestions that this "prescribed penance" was far exceeded by social practice. In the passage later, published in 1938, notice the Hindu patristic assumptions about the freedom of female will at work in phrases like "courage" and "strength of character." The unexamined presuppositions of the passage might be that the complete objectification of the widow-concubine was just punishment for abdication of the right to courage, signifying subject status: "Some widows, however, had not the courage to go through the fiery ordeal; nor had they sufficient strength of mind and character to live up to the high ascetic ideal prescribed for them [*brahmacarya*]. It is sad to record that they were driven to lead the

officer supervising the immolation, to be dissuaded after a decision was, by contrast, a mark of real free choice, a choice of freedom. The ambiguity of the position of the indigenous colonial elite is disclosed in the nationalistic romanticization of the purity, strength, and love of these self-sacrificing women. The two set pieces are Rabindranath Tagore's paean to the "self-renouncing paternal grandmothers of Bengal," and Ananda Coomaraswamy's eulogy of *suttee* as "this last proof of the perfect unity of body and soul."[152]

Obviously I am not advocating the killing of widows. I am suggesting that, within the two contending versions of freedom, the constitution of the female subject in *life* is the place of the *différend*. In the case of widow self-immolation, ritual is not being redefined as patriarchy but as *crime*.[153] The gravity of *sati* was that it was ideologically cathected as "reward," just as the gravity of imperialism was that it was ideologically cathected as "social mission." Between patriarchy and Development, this is the subaltern woman's situation today. Thompson's understanding of *sati* as "punishment" is thus far off the mark:

> It may seem unjust and illogical that the Moguls, who freely impaled and flayed alive, or nationals of Europe, whose countries had such ferocious penal codes and had known, scarcely a century before suttee began to shock the English conscience, orgies of witch-burning and religious persecution, should have felt as they did about suttee. But the differences seemed to them this—the victims of their cruelties were tortured by a law which considered them offenders, whereas the victims of suttee were punished for no offense but the physical weakness which had placed them at man's mercy. The rite seemed to prove a depravity and arrogance such as no other human offense had brought to light.[154]

No. As in the case of war, martyrdom, "terrorism"—self-sacrifice in general—the "felicitous" *sati* may have (been imagined to have) thought

life of a concubine or *avaruddha stri* [incarcerated wife]." A. S. Altekar, *The Position of Women in Hindu Civilization: From Prehistoric Times to the Present Day* (Delhi: Motilal Banarsidass, 1938), p. 156.

152. Quoted in Dineshchandra Sen, *Brhat-Banga* (Calcutta: Univ. of Calcutta Press, 1935), vol. 2: 913–914.

153. In *The Gift of Death*, Derrida has suggested how an Abrahamic sacrifice today would be docketed as crime (pp. 85–86).

154. Thompson, *Suttee*, p. 132.

she was exceeding and transcending the ethical. That is its danger. Not all soldiers die unwillingly. And there are female suicide bombers.

All through the mid- and late-eighteenth century, in the spirit of the codification of the law, the British in India collaborated and consulted with learned Brahmans to judge whether *suttee* was legal by their homogenized version of Hindu law. *Sati* was still contained within the interested use of cultural relativism. The collaboration was often idiosyncratic, as in the case of the significance of being dissuaded. Sometimes, as in the general Sastric prohibition against the immolation of widows with small children, the British collaboration seems confused.[155] In the beginning of the nineteenth century, the British authorities, and especially the British in England, repeatedly suggested that collaboration made it appear as if the British condoned this practice. When the law was finally written, the history of the long period of collaboration was effaced, and the language celebrated the noble Hindu who was against the bad Hindu, the latter given to savage atrocities:

> The practice of Suttee . . . is revolting to the feeling of human nature. . . . In many instances, acts of atrocity have been perpetrated, which have been shocking to the Hindoos themselves. . . . Actuated by these considerations of the Governor-General in Council, without intending to depart from one of the first and most important principles of the system of British Government in India that all classes of the people be secure in the observance of their religious usages, so long as that system can be adhered to without violation of the paramount dictates of justice and humanity, has deemed it right to establish the following rules. . . . (*HD*, II.2, 624–625)

(Topically, it is a celebration of Safie over the Monster in *Frankenstein*.)

That this was an alternative ideology of the graded sanctioning of varieties of suicide as exception, rather than its inscription as "sin," was of course not understood. *Sati* could not, of course, be read with Christian female martyrdom, with the defunct husband standing in for the transcendental One; or with war, with the husband standing in for sovereign or state, for whose sake an intoxicating ideology of self-

---

155. Here, as well as for the Brahman debate over *sati*, see Mani, "Production," p. 71f.

sacrifice can be mobilized. It had to be categorized with murder, infanticide, and the lethal exposure of the very old. The agency was always male; the woman was always the victim. The dubious place of the free will of the constituted sexed subject as female was successfully effaced. There is no itinerary we can retrace here. Since the other sanctioned suicides did not involve the scene of this constitution, they entered neither the ideological battleground at the archaic origin—the tradition of the *Dharmaśāstra*—nor the scene of the reinscription of ritual as crime—the British abolition. The only related transformation was Mahatma Gandhi's reinscription of the notion of *satyāgraha*, or hunger strike, as resistance. But this is not the place to discuss the details of that sea change. I would merely invite the reader to compare the auras of widow sacrifice and Gandhian resistance. The root in the first part of *satyāgraha* and *sati* are the same.

Since the beginning of the Puranic era (the earliest *Purāṇas* date from the 4th century B.C.), learned Brahmans debated the doctrinal appropriateness of *sati* as of sanctioned suicides in sacred places in general. (This debate still continues in an academic way.) Sometimes the caste provenance of the practice was in question. The general law for widows, that they should observe *brahmacarya*, was, however, hardly ever debated. It is not enough to translate *brahmacarya* as "celibacy." It should be recognized that, of the four ages of being in Hindu (or Brahmanical) *regulative* psychobiography, *brahmacarya* is the social practice anterior to the kinship inscription of marriage. The man—widower or husband—graduates through *vānaprastha* (forest life) into the mature celibacy and renunciation of *samnyāsa* (laying aside).[156] The woman as wife is indispensable for *gārhasthya*, or householdership, and may accompany her husband into forest life. She has no access (according to Brahmanical sanction) to the final celibacy of asceticism, or *samnyāsa*. The woman as widow, by the general law of sacred doctrine, must regress to an anteriority transformed into stasis. The institutional evils attendant upon this law are well known; I am considering its asymmetrical effect on the ideological formation of the sexed subject. It is thus of much greater

---

156. We are speaking here of the regulative norms of Brahmanism, rather than "things as they were." See Robert Lingat, *The Classical Law of India*, tr. J. D. M. Derrett (Berkeley: University of California Press, 1973), p. 46.

significance that there was no debate on this nonexceptional fate of widows—either among Hindus or between Hindus and British—than that the *exceptional* prescription of self-immolation was actively contested.[157] Here the possibility of recovering a (sexually) subaltern subject is once again lost and overdetermined.

This legally programmed asymmetry in the status of the subject, which effectively defines the woman as object of *one* husband, obviously operates in the interest of the legally symmetrical subject-status of the male. The self-immolation of the widow thereby becomes the extreme case of the general law rather than an exception to it. It is not surprising, then, to read of heavenly rewards for the *sati*, where the quality of being the object of a unique possessor is emphasized by way of rivalry with other females, those ecstatic heavenly dancers, paragons of female beauty and male pleasure who sing her praise: "In heaven she, being solely devoted to her husband, and praised by groups of *apsarās* [heavenly dancers], sports with her husband as long as fourteen Indras rule" (*HD*, II.2, 631).

The profound irony in locating the woman's free will in self-immolation is once again revealed in a verse accompanying the earlier passage: "As long as the woman [as wife: *stri*] does not burn herself in fire on the death of her husband, she is never released [*mucyate*] from her female body [*strisarir*—i.e., in the cycle of births]." Even as it operates the most subtle general release from individual agency, the sanctioned suicide peculiar to woman draws its ideological strength by *identifying* individual agency with the supraindividual: kill yourself on your husband's pyre now, and you may kill your female body in the entire cycle of birth.

In a further twist of the paradox, this emphasis on free will establishes the peculiar misfortune of holding a female body. The word for the self that is actually burned is the standard word for spirit in the noblest

---

157. Both the vestigial possibility of widow remarriage in ancient India and the legal institution of widow remarriage in 1856 are transactions among men. Widow remarriage is very much an exception, perhaps because it left the program of subject-formation untouched. In all the "lore" of widow remarriage, it is the father and the husband who are applauded for their reformist courage and selflessness. As Kosambi would remind us, we are only considering caste-Hindu India here.

impersonal sense *(ātman)*, while the verb "release," through the root of salvation in the noblest sense *(muc → mokṣa)* is in the passive, and the word for that which is annulled in the cycle of birth is the everyday word for the body. The ideological message writes itself in the benevolent twentieth-century male historian's admiration: "The Jauhar [group self-immolation of aristocratic Rajput war-widows or imminent war-widows] practiced by the Rajput ladies of Chitor and other places for saving themselves from unspeakable atrocities at the hands of the victorious Moslems are too well known to need any lengthy notice" *(HD* II.2, 629).[158]

Although *jauhar* is not, strictly speaking, an act of *sati*, and although I do not wish to speak for the sanctioned sexual violence of conquering male armies, "Moslem" or otherwise, female self-immolation in the face of it is a legitimation of rape as "natural" and works, in the long run, in the interest of unique genital possession of the female. The group rape perpetrated by the conquerors is a metonymic celebration of territorial acquisition. Just as the general law for widows was unquestioned, so this act of female heroism persists among the patriotic tales told to children, thus operating on the crudest level of ideological reproduction. It has also played a tremendous rôle, precisely as an overdetermined signifier, in acting out Hindu communalism. (The Internet produced spurious statistics on Hindu "genocide" in Bangladesh.)[159] Simultaneously, the broader question of the constitution of the sexed subject is hidden by foregrounding the visible violence of *sati*. The task of recovering a (sexually) subaltern subject is lost in an institutional textuality at the archaic origin.

As I mentioned above, when the status of the legal subject as property-holder could be temporarily bestowed on the *female* relict, the self-immolation of widows was stringently enforced. Raghunandana, the late fifteenth/sixteenth-century legalist whose interpretations are supposed to lend the greatest authority to such enforcement, takes as

---

158. Middle-class Bengali children of my generation received this indoctrination through Abanindranath Tagore, *Raj-Kahini* (Calcutta: Signet, 1968), a lovely imaginative reconstruction of the famous *Annals and Antiquities of Rajasthan* (London: Oxford Univ. Press, 1920) by James Tod (1782–1835).

159. Mathews et al., "Vasudhaiva."

his text a curious passage from the *Rg-Veda*, the most ancient of the Hindu sacred texts, the first of the *Srutis*. In doing so, he is following a centuries-old tradition commemorating a peculiar and transparent misreading at the very place of sanction. Here is the verse outlining certain steps within the rites for the dead. Even at a simple reading it is clear that it is "not addressed to widows at all, but to ladies of the deceased man's household whose husbands were living." Why then was it taken as authoritative? This, the unemphatic transposition of the dead for the living husband, is a different order of mystery at the archaic origin from the ones we have been discussing: "Let these whose husbands are worthy and are living enter the house, tearless, healthy, and well adorned" (*HD* II.2, 634).

But this crucial transposition is not the only mistake here. The authority is lodged in a disputed passage and an alternate reading. In the second line, here translated "Let these wives first step into the house," the word for first is *agré*. Some have read it as *agné*, "O fire." As Kane makes clear, however, "even without this change Aparārka and others rely for the practice of *Sati* on this verse" (*HD* IV.2, 199). Here is another screen around one origin of the history of the subaltern female subject. Is it a historical oneirocritique that one should perform on a statement such as: "Therefore it must be admitted that either the MSS are corrupt or Raghunandana committed an innocent slip" (*HD* II.2, 634)? It should be mentioned that the rest of the poem is either about that general law of *brahmacarya*-in-stasis for widows, to which *sati* is an exception, or about *niyoga*—"appointing a brother or any near kinsman to raise up issue to a deceased husband by marrying his widow."[160]

If P. V. Kane is the authority on the history of the *Dharmaśāstra*,

---

160. Sir Monier Monier-Williams, *Sanskrit-English Dictionary* (Oxford: Clarendon, 1989), p. 552. Historians are often impatient if modernists seem to be attempting to import "feministic" judgments into ancient patriarchies. The real question is, of course, why structures of patriarchal domination should be unquestioningly recorded. Historical sanctions for collective action toward social justice can only be developed if people outside of the discipline question standards of "objectivity" preserved as such by the hegemonic tradition. It does not seem inappropriate to notice that so "objective" an instrument as a dictionary can use the deeply sexist-partisan explanatory expression: "raise up issue to a deceased husband"!

Mulla's *Principles of Hindu Law* is the practical guide. It is part of the historical text of what Freud calls "kettle logic" that we are unraveling here, that Mulla's textbook adduces, just as definitively, that the *Rg-Vedic* verse under consideration was proof that "remarriage of widows and divorce are recognized in some of the old texts."[161]

One cannot help wondering about the rôle of the word *yoni*. In context, with the localizing adverb *agré* (in front), the word means "dwelling-place." But that does not efface its primary sense of "genital" (not yet perhaps specifically *female* genital). How can we take as the authority for the choice of a widow's self-immolation a passage celebrating the entry of adorned wives into a dwelling place invoked on this occasion by its *yoni*-name, so that the extracontextual icon is almost one of entry into civic production or birth? Paradoxically, the imagic relationship of vagina and fire lends a kind of strength to the authority-claim.[162] This paradox is strengthened by Raghunandana's modification of the verse so as to read, "Let them first ascend the *fluid* abode [or origin, with, of course, the *yoni*-name—*ā rohantu jalayōnimagné*], O fire [or of fire]." Why should one accept that this "probably mean[s] 'may fire be to them as cool as water'" (*HD* II.2, 634)? The fluid genital of fire, a corrupt phrasing, might figure a sexual indeterminacy providing a simulacrum for the intellectual indeterminacy of *tattvajnāna* (truth-knowledge), that I have discussed on pp. 292–293. These speculations are certainly no more absurd than the ones I have cited. Scriptural sanction, in other words, is a gesture of evidence, rather than rational textual support.

I have written above of a constructed counternarrative of woman's consciousness, thus woman's being, thus woman's being good, thus the good woman's desire, thus woman's desire. This slippage can be seen in the fracture inscribed in the very word *sati*, the feminine form of *sat*. *Sat* transcends any gender-specific notion of masculinity and moves up into

---

161. Sunderlal T. Desai, *Mulla: Principles of Hindu Law* (Bombay: N. M. Tripathi, 1982), p. 184.

162. I am grateful to Professor Alison Finley of Trinity College (Hartford, Conn.) for discussing the passage with me. Professor Finley is an expert on the *Rg-Veda*. I hasten to add that she would find my readings as irresponsibly "literary-critical" as the ancient historian would find it "modernist".

not only human but also spiritual universality. It is the present participle of the verb "to be" and as such means not only being but the True, the Good, the Right. In the sacred texts it is essence, universal spirit. Even as a prefix it indicates appropriate, felicitous, fit. It is noble enough to have entered the most privileged discourse of modern Western philosophy: Heidegger's meditation on Being.[163] *Sati*, the feminine of this word, simply means "good wife."

In fact, *sati* or *suttee* as the proper name of the rite of widow self-immolation commemorates a grammatical error on the part of the British, quite as the nomenclature "American Indian" commemorates a factual error on the part of Columbus. The word in the various Indian languages is "the burning of the *sati*" or the good wife, who thus escapes the regressive stasis of the widow in *brahmacarya*. This exemplifies the race-class-gender overdeterminations of the situation. It can perhaps be caught even when it is flattened out: white men, seeking to save brown women from brown men, imposed upon those women a greater ideological construction by absolutely identifying, *within discursive practice*, good-wifehood and self-immolation on the husband's pyre by an ignorant (but sanctioned) synecdoche. On the other side of thus constituting the *object*, the abolition (or removal) of which will provide the occasion for establishing a good, as distinguished from merely civil, society, is the Hindu manipulation of female *subject*-constitution, which I have tried to discuss.

(I have already mentioned Edward Thompson's *Suttee*, published in 1928. I cannot do justice here to this perfect specimen of the justification of imperialism as a civilizing mission. Nowhere in his book, written by someone who avowedly "loved India," is there any questioning of the "beneficial ruthlessness" of the British in India as motivated by territorial expansionism or management of industrial capital. The problem with his book is, indeed, a problem of representation, the construction of a continuous and homogeneous "India" in terms of heads of state and British administrators, from the perspective of "a man of good sense" who would be the transparent voice of reasonable humanity. "India" can then be represented, in the other sense, by its

---

163. Martin Heidegger, *An Introduction to Metaphysics*, tr. Ralph Manheim (New York: Doubleday Anchor, 1961), p. 58.

imperial masters. My reason for referring to *suttee* here is Thompson's finessing of the word *sati* as "faithful" in the very first sentence of his book, an inaccurate translation that is nonetheless an English permit for the insertion of the female subject into twentieth-century discourse.[164] After such a taming of the subject, Thompson can write, under the heading "The Psychology of the '*Sati*'," "I had intended to try to examine this; but the truth is, it has ceased to puzzle me.")[165]

Between patriarchy and imperialism, subject-constitution and object-formation, the figure of the woman disappears, not into a pristine nothingness, but into a violent shuttling that is the displaced figuration of the "third-world woman" caught between tradition and modernization, culturalism and development. These considerations would revise every detail of judgments that seem valid for a history of sexuality in the West: "Such would be the property of repression, that which distinguishes it from the prohibitions maintained by simple penal law: repression functions well as a sentence to disappear, but also as an injunction to silence, affirmation of non-existence; and consequently states that of all this there is nothing to say, to see, to know."[166] The case of *suttee* as exemplum of the woman-in-imperialism would challenge and deconstruct this opposition between subject (law) and object-of-knowledge (repression) and mark the place of "disappearance" with something other than silence and nonexistence, a violent aporia between subject and object status.[167]

---

164. Thompson, *Suttee*, pp. 37, 15. For the status of the proper name as "mark," see Derrida, "My Chances/*Mes Chances:* A Rendezvous with some Epicurean Stereophonies," in Joseph H. Smith and William Kerrigan, eds., *Taking Chances: Derrida, Psychoanalysis, and Literature,* (Baltimore: Johns Hopkins Univ. Press, 1984), pp. 1–32.

165. Thompson, *Suttee*, p. 137.

166. Michel Foucault, *History of Sexuality*, 1:4.

167. The European context is different here. In the monotheist tradition, as it has been argued by Derrida in his discussions specifically of Kierkegaard in *The Gift of Death*, the moment of sacrifice—Abraham ready to kill his son—turns love into hate and displaces the ethical. What is it to introduce woman into this narrative, Derrida has asked, and John Caputo has attempted to construct a benevolent American-feminist answer by speaking in various voices, as provided by the historically male imagining of women; he has even attempted to acknowledge "[t]he name of Sarah . . . [as] the name of violence. In order to protect the heritage of her son, Isaac, Sarah had Abraham take Hagar, Abraham's concubine and the Egyptian slave

Sati as a woman's proper name is in fairly widespread use in India today. Naming a female infant "a good wife" has its own proleptic irony, and the irony is all the greater because this sense of the common noun is not the primary operator in the proper name.[168] Behind the naming of the infant is *the* Sati of Hindu mythology, Durga in her manifestation as a good wife.[169] In part of the story, Sati—she is already called that—arrives at her father's court uninvited, in the absence, even, of an invitation for her divine husband Siva. Her father starts to abuse Siva and Sati dies in pain. Siva arrives in a fury and dances over the universe with Sati's corpse on his shoulder. Visnu dismembers her body

---

of Sarah, and Ishmael, the illegitimate son of Abraham and Hagar, out to the desert and abandon them. The descendants of Ishmael, the 'Ishmaelites,' became a wandering tribe of nomads, the outcasts" (John Caputo, *Against Ethics: Contributions to a Poetics of Obligation With Constant Reference to Deconstruction* [Bloomington: Indiana Univ. Press, 1993], pp. 145–146). But if, for the sake of time, we remember no more than Freud's intuition, the maternal sacrifice must perhaps invoke not merely the peoples of the Book, but also the pre- and para-monotheistic world (Freud, "Moses and Monotheism," *SE* 22: 83). It is not only Abraham who can be imagined—as he is by Caputo's "Johanna de Silentio" (feminine of Kierkegaard's Johannes)—"in a world without others, a world without the law" (Caputo, *Against Ethics*, p. 141). In *Beloved* Toni Morrison gives us maternal sacrifice, Sethe, the slave about to be freed (neither African nor American), historically in that world without the law. History asks for the maternal sacrifice on the impossible passage, and does not stay the mother's hand. The ring of the covenant—the brand on Sethe's nameless mother's breast—does not ensure continuity. Historiality is not changed into genealogy. The matrilineality of slavery is ruptured on the underground railroad. Sethe does not understand her mother's tongue. On the cusp of the violent change from animisim to dehegemonised Christianity is the maternal sacrifice. It marks an obstinate refusal to rational allegorization. It is only after this shedding of blood that the first African-American is born—Denver, named after the white woman who assisted at her birth. U.S. civil society (and, of course, culture—Morrison's next book is *Jazz*) has domesticated the cusp. And *Beloved* remains a story not to pass on, the beloved ghost laid to rest. In spite of the Latin American Indian (what a multiple errant history in that naming) topos of claiming secrecy in the face of the conquistador, I remain somewhat persuaded by Doris Sommers's placing of the theme of secrecy in Morrison and Menchú together (Doris Sommers, "No Secrets," in Georg M. Gugelberger, ed., *The Real Thing: Testimonial Discourse and Latin America* [Durham: Duke Univ. Press, 1996], pp.130–157).

168. The fact that the word was also used as a form of address for a well-born woman ("lady") complicates matters.

169. It should be remembered that this account does not exhaust her many manifestations within the pantheon.

and bits are strewn over the earth. Around each such relic bit is a great place of pilgrimage.

Figures like the goddess Athena—"fathers' daughters self-professedly uncontaminated by the womb"—are useful for establishing women's ideological self-debasement, which is to be distinguished from a deconstructive attitude toward the essentialist subject. The story of the mythic Sati, reversing every narrateme of the rite, performs a similar function: the living husband avenges the wife's death, a transaction between great male gods fulfills the destruction of the female body and thus inscribes the earth as sacred geography. To see this as proof of the feminism of classical Hinduism or of Indian culture as goddess-centered and therefore feminist is as ideologically contaminated by nativism or reverse ethnocentrism as it was imperialist to erase the image of the luminous fighting Mother Durga and invest the proper noun Sati with no significance other than the ritual burning of the helpless widow as a sacrificial offering who can then be saved. May the empowering voice of so-called superstition (Durga) not be a better starting point for transformation than the belittling or punitive befriending of the white mythology of "reasonableness" (British police)? The interested do-gooding of corporate philanthropy keeps the question worth asking.[170]

If the oppressed under postmodern capital have no necessarily unmediated access to "correct" resistance, can the ideology of *sati*, coming from the history of the periphery, be sublated into any model of interventionist practice? Since this essay operates on the notion that all such clear-cut nostalgias for lost origins are suspect, especially as grounds for counterhegemonic ideological production, I must proceed by way of an example.[171]

A young woman of sixteen or seventeen, Bhubaneswari Bhaduri, hanged herself in her father's modest apartment in North Calcutta in

---

170. I have taken this question further, in an analysis of metropolitan multiculturalism, in "Moving Devi," essay for an exhibition on the Great Goddess at the Arthur M. Sackler gallery at the Smithsonian, in March 1999.

171. A position against nostalgia as a basis of counterhegemonic ideological production does not endorse its negative use. Within the complexity of contemporary political economy, it would, for example, be highly questionable to urge that

1926. The suicide was a puzzle since, as Bhubaneswari was menstruating at the time, it was clearly not a case of illicit pregnancy. Nearly a decade later, it was discovered, in a letter she had left for her elder sister, that she was a member of one of the many groups involved in the armed struggle for Indian independence. She had been entrusted with a political assassination. Unable to confront the task and yet aware of the practical need for trust, she killed herself.

Bhubaneswari had known that her death would be diagnosed as the outcome of illegitimate passion. She had therefore waited for the onset of menstruation. While waiting, Bhubaneswari, the *brahmacārini* who was no doubt looking forward to good wifehood, perhaps rewrote the social text of *sati*-suicide in an interventionist way. (One tentative explanation of her inexplicable act had been a possible melancholia brought on by her father's death and her brother-in-law's repeated taunts that she was too old to be not-yet-a-wife.) She generalized the sanctioned motive for female suicide by taking immense trouble to displace (not merely deny), in the physiological inscription of her body, its imprisonment within legitimate passion by a single male. In the immediate context, her act became absurd, a case of delirium rather than sanity. The displacing gesture—waiting for menstruation—is at first a reversal of the interdict against a menstruating widow's right to immolate herself; the unclean widow must wait, publicly, until the cleansing bath of the fourth day, when she is no longer menstruating, in order to claim her dubious privilege.

In this reading, Bhubaneswari Bhaduri's suicide is an unemphatic, ad hoc, subaltern rewriting of the social text of *sati*-suicide as much as the hegemonic account of the blazing, fighting, familial Durga. The emergent dissenting possibilities of that hegemonic account of the fighting mother are well documented and popularly well remembered through

---

the current Indian working-class crime of burning brides who bring insufficient dowries and of subsequently disguising the murder as suicide is either a *use* or *abuse* of the tradition of *sati*-suicide. The most that can be claimed is that it is a displacement on a chain of semiosis with the female subject as signifier, which would lead us back into the narrative we have been unraveling. Clearly, one must work to stop the crime of bride burning *in every way*. If, however, that work is accomplished by unexamined nostalgia or its opposite, it will assist actively in the substitution of race/ethnos or sheer genitalism as a signifier in the place of the female subject.

the discourse of the male leaders and participants in the Independence movement. The subaltern as female cannot be heard or read.

I know of Bhubaneswari's life and death through family connections. Before investigating them more thoroughly, I asked a Bengali woman, a philosopher and Sanskritist whose early intellectual production is almost identical to mine, to start the process. Two responses: (a) Why, when her two sisters, Saileswari and Raseswari, led such full and wonderful lives, are you interested in the hapless Bhubaneswari? (b) I asked her nieces. It appears that it was a case of illicit love.

I was so unnerved by this failure of communication that, in the first version of this text, I wrote, in the accents of passionate lament: the subaltern cannot speak! It was an inadvisable remark.

In the intervening years between the publication of the second part of this chapter in essay form and this revision, I have profited greatly from the many published responses to it. I will refer to two of them here: "Can the Subaltern Vote?" and "Silencing Sycorax."[172]

As I have been insisting, Bhubaneswari Bhaduri was not a "true" subaltern. She was a woman of the middle class, with access, however clandestine, to the bourgeois movement for Independence. Indeed the Rani of Sirmur, with her claim to elevated birth, was not a subaltern at all. Part of what I seem to have argued in this chapter is that woman's interception of the claim to subalternity can be staked out across strict lines of definition by virtue of their muting by heterogeneous circumstances. Gulari cannot speak to us because indigenous patriarchal "history" would only keep a record of her funeral and colonial history only needed her as an incidental instrument. Bhubaneswari attempted to "speak" by turning her body into a text of woman/writing. The immediate passion of my declaration "the subaltern cannot speak," came from the despair that, in her own family, among women, in no more than fifty years, her attempt had failed. I am not laying the blame for

---

172. Leerom Medovoi et al., "Can the Subaltern Vote?" *Socialist Review* 20.3 (July–Sept. 1990):133–149; and Abena Busia, "Silencing Sycorax: On African Colonial Discourse and the Unvoiced Female," *Cultural Critique* 14 (Winter 1989–90): 81–104.

the muting on the *colonial* authorities here, as Busia seems to think: "Gayatri Spivak's 'Can the Subaltern Speak?'—section 4 of which is a compelling explication of this role of disappearing in the case of Indian women in British legal history."[173]

I am pointing, rather, at her silencing by her own more emancipated granddaughters: a new mainstream. To this can be added two newer groups: one, the liberal multiculturalist metropolitan academy, Susan Barton's great-granddaughters; as follows:

As I have been saying all along, I think it is important to acknowledge our complicity in the muting, in order precisely to be more effective in the long run. Our work cannot succeed if we always have a scapegoat. The postcolonial migrant investigator is touched by the colonial social formations. Busia strikes a positive note for further work when she points out that, after all, I am able to read Bhubaneswari's case, and therefore she *has* spoken in some way. Busia is right, of course. All speaking, even seemingly the most immediate, entails a distanced decipherment by another, which is, at best, an interception. That is what speaking is.

I acknowledge this theoretical point, and also acknowledge the practical importance, for oneself and others, of being upbeat about future work. Yet the moot decipherment by another in an academic institution (willy-nilly a knowledge-production factory) many years later must not be too quickly identified with the "speaking" of the subaltern. It is not a mere tautology to say that the colonial or postcolonial subaltern is defined as the being on the other side of difference, or an epistemic fracture, even from other groupings among the colonized. What is at stake when we insist that the subaltern speaks?

In "Can the Subaltern Vote?" the three authors apply the question of stakes to "political speaking." This seems to me to be a fruitful way of extending my reading of subaltern speech into a collective arena. Access to "citizenship" (civil society) by becoming a voter (in the nation) is indeed the symbolic circuit of the mobilizing of subalternity into hegemony. This terrain, ever negotiating between national liberation and

---

173. Busia, "Silencing," p. 102.

globalization, allows for examining the casting of the vote itself as a performative convention given as constative "speech" of the subaltern subject. It is part of my current concerns to see how this set is manipulated to legitimize globalization; but it is beyond the scope of this book. Here let us remain confined to the field of academic prose, and advance three points:

1. Simply by being postcolonial or the member of an ethnic minority, we are not "subaltern." That word is reserved for the sheer heterogeneity of decolonized space.
2. When a line of communication is established between a member of subaltern groups and the circuits of citizenship or institutionality, the subaltern has been inserted into the long road to hegemony. Unless we want to be romantic purists or primitivists about "preserving subalternity"—a contradiction in terms—this is absolutely to be desired. (It goes without saying that museumized or curricularized access to ethnic origin—another battle that must be fought—is not identical with preserving subalternity.) Remembering this allows us to take pride in our work without making missionary claims.
3. This trace-structure (effacement in disclosure) surfaces as the tragic emotions of the political activist, springing not out of superficial utopianism, but out of the depths of what Bimal Krishna Matilal has called "moral love." Mahasweta Devi, herself an indefatigable activist, documents this emotion with exquisite care in "Pterodactyl, Puran Sahay, and Pirtha."

And finally, the third group: Bhubaneswari's elder sister's eldest daughter's eldest daughter's eldest daughter is a new U.S. immigrant and was recently promoted to an executive position in a U.S.-based transnational. She will be helpful in the emerging South Asian market precisely because she is a well-placed Southern diasporic.

For Europe, the time when the new capitalism *definitely* superseded the old can be established with fair precision: it was the beginning of the twentieth century. . . . [With t]he boom at the end of the nineteenth centtury and the crisis of 1900-03 . . . [c]artels become one of the foundations of the whole of economic life. Capitalism has been transformed into imperialism.[174]

Today's program of global financialization carries on that relay. Bhubaneswari had fought for national liberation. Her great-grandniece works for the New Empire. This too is a historical silencing of the subaltern. When the news of this young woman's promotion was broadcast in the family amidst general jubilation I could not help remarking to the eldest surviving female member: "Bhubaneswari"—her nickname had been Talu—"hanged herself in vain," but not too loudly. Is it any wonder that this young woman is a staunch multiculturalist, believes in natural childbirth, and wears only cotton?

---

174. V. I. Lenin, *Imperialism: The Highest Stage of Capitalism: A Popular Outline* (London: Pluto Press, 1996), pp. 15, 17.

CHAPTER FOUR

Culture

In the last three chapters we have considered how things were. Now let us consider the history of the present as differantiating event: code name "our culture." Let us enter by way of a major controversial text of the eighties, Fredric Jameson on Postmodernism.[1]

The tendency to conflate poststructuralism and postmodernism was a result of Jürgen Habermas's spirited interviews of the 1980s that claimed that the poststructuralists could be viewed as "Young Conservatives" who, on the basis of modernistic attitudes . . . justify an irreconcilable anti-modernism.[2] The subsequent debate, between Habermas and Lyotard, is not directly to the point here, but it did contribute to the ease with which the conflation could be performed.[3] Here, then, we have an example of the fabrication of the master narratives of cultural history as cultural explanation. This narrativization has been at work in

---

1. The initial discussion was in terms of "Postmodernism; or, The Cultural Logic of Late Capitalism," as it appeared in *New Left Review* 146 (July–Aug. 1984):59–92. The article itself had much more influence by itself than as the first chapter of the book of the same name, published in 1995. Further, its presuppositions are elaborated, not contradicted, in the book. I have therefore kept the discussion confined to it, although the page references have been changed.

2. These interviews are collected in Jürgen Habermas, *Autonomy and Solidarity: Interviews*, ed. Peter Dews (London: Verso, 1986).

3. For the itinerary of those debates, see *Les Cahiers de philosophie* 5 (Spring 1988).

the last twenty years in putting to rest the productive and justifiable unease among the practitioners in the field. It is obvious that the producers of the authoritative and continuous narrative of cultural history cannot accept the proposition that the conflation of poststructuralism and postmodernism might be an *incident* in the metacritical production of a narrative of cultural history as cultural production rather than a disinterested account of such a history. In other words, why was it structurally necessary—since one must not subscribe to conspiracy theories one cannot fault intellectual interest groups—to neutralize the potential for a critique of modernization in poststructural thinking? In the field of critical theory, the sheer possibility of such a question is being managed by placing poststructuralism within the logic of the avant-garde of the earlier part of this century.[4]

For the general context in the U.S. literary academy, perhaps the most brilliant example of the conflation of postmodernism and poststructuralism has been performed by Jameson in "Postmodernism, or the Cultural Logic of Late Capitalism." I share the contradictions in this text.

First contradiction: a desire to obliterate the subject-position implied by our everyday as we speak about "our world." For Jameson's text to make sense, the reader must fill a subject-position referring at least to State, Institution, Hero-ritual, construction of the object of investigation: distinguished U.S. professor of the humanities with a considerable radical reputation commenting on the postmodern cultural dominant: one of the new "nomads." This is to be borne in mind particularly when we invoke the empirical, even if it vitiates the generality of our argument. Let us now read this sentence: "it is at least empirically arguable that *our* daily life, *our* psychic experience, *our* cultural languages, are today dominated by space rather than by categories of time, as in the preceding period of high modernism proper."[5]

Indeed, a theory of "cultural dominants" must exercise caution about the specificity of subject-positions most particularly, because it is

---

4. Peter Bürger, *Theory of the Avant-Garde*, tr. Michael Shaw (Minneapolis: Univ. of Minnesota Press, 1984), followed by *The Decline of Modernism*, tr. Nicholas Walker (Cambridge: Polity Press, 1992).

5. Jameson, *Postmodernism*, p. 16; hereafter *PM*, followed by page reference.

caught in a double bind: a power-analysis of cultural dominants is bound to make visible the repression of emergent heterogeneity: unless careful, the analysis can itself collaborate in that repression by refusing it access to the status of the idiom of cultural description. The double bind is reflected in Jameson's desire to keep heterogeneity at bay:

> I am very far from feeling that all cultural production today is "post-modern" in the broad sense I will be conferring on this term. The postmodern is however the force field in which very different kinds of cultural impulses—what Raymond Williams has usefully termed "re-sidual" and "emergent" forms of cultural production—must make their way. If we do not achieve some general sense of a cultural domi-nant, then we fall back into a view of present history as sheer hetero-geneity, random difference, a coexistence of a host of distinct forces whose effectivity is undecidable. (*PM* 6)

It is not immediately clear why these are the only alternatives open to a cultural critic, although I am quite in agreement with the idea that the emergent or residual must make its way in the dominant. But if we only concentrate on the dominant, we forget that the difference between varieties of the emergent and residual *may* be the difference between radical and conservative resistance to the dominant, although this is by no means certain. Williams distinguishes scrupulously and insistently between the "alternative" and the "oppositional" in the "emergent."[6] And, in order to gain a measure of risky certitude, we must keep focus-ing on the traces of the heterogeneous. As Williams writes, "[a]gain and again what we have to observe is in effect a *pre-emergence*, active and pressing but not yet fully articulated, rather than the evident emer-gence which could be more confidently named."

This proviso is perhaps irrelevant for Jameson. For the code words in the last sentence of the passage by him quoted above make it clear that it is the battle between marxism and deconstruction that is being re-played on this terrain. I should like to point at some of the conse-

---

6. Raymond Williams, "Base and Superstructure in Marxist Cultural Theory," in *Problems in Materialism and Culture* (London: Verso, 1980), pp. 40–42; *Marxism and Literature* (Oxford: Oxford Univ. Press, 1977), pp. 121–127. The next quoted passage is from p. 126 of the latter.

quences of this skirmish as it relates to the production of "postmodernism" as descriptive of a cultural dominant.[7]

In describing postmodernism as a *force*-field, Jameson is obliged to
neutralize marxism as an analysis of *power*. Related to the latter, marxist
practice must take the risk of an axio-teleology (a value-system that has
an end in view). This is what Jameson dismisses with the damning word
"moralism": "Of some positive moral evaluation of postmodernism little needs to be said. . . . But in that case it is only consequent to reject
moralizing condemnations of the postmodern and of its essential trivi-
ality when juxtaposed against the Utopian 'high seriousness' of the
great modernisms: judgments one finds both on the Left and on the
radical Right" (*PM* 46).

One must of course be in sympathy with the general good sense of
this passage. It leads, however, to the second set of contradictions, as
Jameson outlines a "whole new" mindset, "a *genuinely* dialectical attempt to think our present of time in History."[8]

Transnational literacy keeps the abstract as such, the economic, visible under erasure. Yet it cannot afford to ignore the irreducible heterogeneity of the cultural in the name of a "cultural dominant" simply
because it is dominant. Jameson imagines that the semi-autonomy
(Herbert Marcuse) and therefore, necessarily, the relative autonomy
(Louis Althusser) of the cultural has "been destroyed by the logic of late
capitalism" and then goes on to say that "everything in our social life
. . . can be said to have become 'cultural' in some original and as yet
untheorized sense" (*PM* 48).

Let us rather put it this way. It is perhaps because there is a semi- or
relative autonomy to the discursivity of cultural explanations that it can
recode the abstract in general; and the transnational dominant can
write "everything in *our* social life," and theirs, as "cultural." For us, the

---

7. I hope it is clear by now that I am not writing about contemporary Indian art.
For a learned position on its periodization, see Geeta Kapur, "The Centre-Periph-
ery Model; or, How Are We Placed? Contemporary Cultural Practice in India,"
Third Text 16/17 (Autumn/Winter 1991): 9–17; and "Globalization and Culture,"
Third Text 39 (Summer 1997): 21–38.

8. *PM* 46, emphasis mine. The announcement of "whole new" things gives to
Jameson's work a certain charming energy.

dominant culture; for them heterogeneity and cultural relativism. I will suggest below that the nominalist theoretical practice in the use of the word "culture" is to be learnt from underclass multiculturalism in metropolitan civil societies. The "dialectic" may be a philosophical dominant that disqualifies and excludes the inconvenient as its other and vice versa. We are reminded of Hindess and Hirst's canny comment: "Concepts are deployed in ordered successions to produce [the] effects [of analysis and solutions]. This order is the order created *by the practice of theoretical work itself*: it is guaranteed by no necessary 'logic' or 'dialectic' nor by any necessary mechanism of correspondence with the real itself" (see p. 94).

Thus, although Jameson seems to be against a mere periodizing view of history, there are examples of a stolidly isomorphic theory of the relationship between modes of production and styles and their concomitant cultural explanations that Jameson himself recognizes as crucial to his argument: "[M]y own cultural periodization of the stages of realism, modernism and postmodernism is both inspired and confirmed by [Ernest] Mandel's tripartite scheme" (*PM* 36).

Are we to think that, although postmodernism is linked to "multinational capital" in the same isomorphic way as earlier styles (or cultural dominants?) to earlier modes of production of value, the nature of "our" world of multinational capital is such that postmodernism is a whole new thing? If so, the contrast between Van Gogh's "Peasant Shoes" and Andy Warhol's "Diamond Dust Shoes" does not theorize this difference persuasively.

Van Gogh's "content, those initial raw materials"—are they identical?—are "to be grasped simply as the whole object world of agricultural misery" (*PM* 7). Again, a pretty down-to-earth theory of the relationship between art and society. The next step is to see this "glorious materialization of pure color in oil paint . . . as an act of compensation . . . producing a whole new Utopian realm . . . which . . . now reconstitutes [the visual] as . . . some new division of labor in the body of capital, some new fragmentation of the emergent new sensorium which replicates the specializations and divisions of capitalist life at the same time that it seeks in precisely such fragmentation a desperate Utopian compensation for them" (*PM* 7).

This utopia-from-realization of capitalism is not *morphologically* ("theoretically") dissimilar from the euphoria-in-derealization (which of course is the paradoxical *realization* of the spirit of "multinational capital") that we are offered later in the essay as the whole new untheorized thing about postmodernism (see note 33). And, if we stick to the example of Warhol's shoes, offered immediately as representing the contrast between modernism and postmodernism we find that, just as Van Gogh's shoes were the object world of peasant misery, Warhol's shoes are commodity fetishism, "dead objects hanging together" (*PM* 8). And, it may be argued that the "compensatory, decorative exhilaration" (*PM* 10) in Warhol is not morphologically dissimilar to the Utopian moment in Van Gogh. This is not a theoretical but a substantive difference. Indeed, Jameson sccs this when he calls Warhol's use of "the photographic negative . . . the inversion of Van Gogh's Utopian gesture" (*PM* 9). An inversion (like a reversal) belongs to the same theoretical space; it is not the as yet untheorized. Although there is a desire to claim "postmodernism" as a rupture, it is also a repetition. This is part of the mechanics of the production of the term, and part of the object of my investigation, and I will draw a political lesson from it.

Why for example is the photographic negative seen as "the object world . . . becom[ing] a set of texts or simulacra?" (*PM* 9). Are texts identical with simulacra? Never mind. *If* the artist is filling this signifier—the photographic negative—with this particular signification, he shares the critic's desire for a claim to radical discontinuity or rupture. For the photo-graph—the writing of the sun—is also a guarantee of the existence of the object-world. Indeed, if one wanted to extend the concept-metaphor, one could locate a break between film (the photographic negative) and video (electronic virtual space), and extend Jameson's isomorphic practice to say that postmodernism (and postmodernization as postfordism) is related to micro-electronic transnational capitalism rather than multinational late capitalism. And then the International Ladies Garment Workers' Union can reveal to us that hi-tech postfordism is supported, in the lower ranks, by labor practices that would fit right into old-style industrial capitalism.[9]

This contradiction between desire (for rupture) and performance (of repetition) becomes most productive where Jameson is most brilliant,

---

9. Jan Borowy, *Designing the Future for Garment Workers* (Toronto: International Ladies Garment Workers' Union, 1995).

in the analysis of the Bonaventure hotel in Los Angeles. Jameson's thesis about this hotel is that it is "a dialectical intensification of the auto-referentiality of all modern culture" (*PM* 42). Yet he interprets it as an "allegorical signifier of . . . [an] older promenade" (*PM* 42), and, of course, a "miniature city" (*PM* 38), as script is supposed to be a miniaturization of an absent speech. It is a tribute to the lyrical persuasiveness of Jameson's prose and our justified confidence in his political position that we tend not to notice it when this contradiction reduces itself to absurdity: "Here the narrative stroll has been underscored, reified, and replaced by a transportation machine which becomes the *allegorical signifier of* that older promenade we are no longer allowed to conduct on our own; and this is a dialectical intensification of the *autoreferentiality* of all modern culture, which tends to turn upon itself and designate its own cultural production as its content" (*PM* 42; emphasis mine). Nothing that is *auto*-referential can of course be an *allegorical* signifier of something older.

In fact, with the analytical ingredients that Jameson has provided, one could, rightly or wrongly, construct the opposite interpretation: that the hotel, being a miniature of the city outside, refers to it constantly, for the analyst or participant to get its drift. Most utopias forget that utopia is nowhere and make the empirically representational move (a gesture not confined to postmodernity or even modernity). In certain conjunctures, they can be productive. That this dystopia became a nuisance, referring without bringing to crisis (without a shift in the discursive production), and that the local merchants could no longer ply their trade satisfactorily or effectively, should perhaps be related to varieties of the cultural politics of self-representation.[10]

———

10. For a "responsible" fit, see Dolores Hayden, *Seven American Utopias: The Architecture of Communitarian Socialism* (Cambridge: MIT Press, 1976). For a located self-ethnicizing postcolonial culturally self-representing "misfit"-producing spectacular public-built space, consider the argument advanced in Charles Correa, "The Public, the Private, and the Sacred," *Daedalus* 118.4 (Fall 1989): 93–114. This is an appropriation of the "sacred" for a golden-agist culturally conservative view of the majority religion, of course arguing that it is not really religious: "by *sacred* one does not mean only the religious, but the primordial as well," for presentation in an upmarket universalist U.S. journal with an appropriately nostalgic Greek name (duly reprinted in an Indian journal of a similar type—*Architecture and Design* 8.5

I have taken such pains with Jameson's theorization of the postmodern ostensibly as rupture but effectively as repetition because I believe the persuasive power of his essay lies elsewhere. In fact he bases his argument on the deduced experience of a general U.S. ideological subject when faced with Van Gogh, Warhol, Munch (that bravura description, for example, is full of philosophical muddle about expression and indication, but why worry?), when placed in the Bonaventure. Rather

---

[1991]: 91–99. Contrast this to my discussion below of the "sacred" as a name for nature as radical alterity in our attempt to understand Aboriginal cultural conform ity. Our problem is that quick-fix, class-based secularists mistake us as advancing Correa's nostalgic argument and withdraw support, whereas the U.S. culturalist moral imperialism finds such self-ethnicized nostalgia altogether useful. An unexamined cultural studies internationally, joins hands with an unexamined ethnic studies stateside, to oil the wheels of what can only be called the ideological state apparatus. "Plenty of everyday architects," writes Vikramaditya Prakash of the University of Washington School of Architecture, "[in India], doing small commissions around the country, especially houses, use *vastu-parusha mandala* [Correa's subject-matter, Hindu scriptural architectonics]"—as an imitative model without, of course, the complex astronomical calculations made for the temples in the earlier practice. "It has also," Prakash continues, "I believe, become commonplace to advertise this on their visiting cards" (unpublished communication). Here is epistemic violation of the neo-colonial kind, ethnic self-makeover on the level of everyday urban life, going hand in hand with the Tommy Hilfiger jackets cannily mentioned in footnote 56. Small-time Delhi tailors advertise "ethenic [sic] clothing" on handwritten signs stuck to lampposts. Architecture and clothing, how we house and write our lives and our bodies, our furnishings. The point I am making is that it is not some longing for originary purity that refuses to consider this as a variety of postnational hybrid resistance. It is in fact the benign rusing face of what allows the United States to "export democracy" to "older cultures" even as the globetrotting self-ethnicizers dine out on difference. And, as the editor of *Foreign Affairs*—the journal of the Council on Foreign Affairs of the United States government—argues, only countries with at least a $6,000 per capita income can practice democracy; therefore, first promote "economic growth by permanent involvement in the country's affairs through foreign aid as well as computerizing their police forces, as in the case of Tanzania, *then* think of exporting democracy." (Paper presented at Conference on "Does America Have a Democratic Mission?" University of Virginia, 19–21 Mar. 1998; the portion in quotation marks is a close paraphrase. The marks have been used to signify the codic value of each word. That code invaginates this book as well, from above. A sanctioned ignorance and, alas, ignoring, of the code allows triumphalist hybridism as well as nostalgic nativism to function. Business as usual.)

than prove that the subject has disappeared in postmodernism, the entire analysis hangs on the presence of a subject in a postmodern hyperspace where it *feels* that old-fashioned thing: a loss of identity. The postmodern, as an inversion of the modern, repeats its discourse.

One of the most interesting maneuvers by which Jameson secures postmodernism as rupture is his appropriation of deconstruction. For Jameson it is Derrida (*écriture*, textuality, decentered subject) who is the exemplary postmodern theorist. I have already pointed at the passage where he de-moralizes the Left anti-postmodernist stance in the interest of keeping what may be generally described as deconstruction (heterogeneity, undecidability) at bay.[11] In the rest of the essay, however, he shows us how a deconstructive vocabulary can be put to political use if it is employed to describe the postmodern phenomenon. To do this, he must transform a philosopheme into a narrateme, transform what is logical into chronology.[12] Jameson's superb stylistic panache makes him perform this in an offhand parenthesis:

> (Of the two possible formulations of this notion [the "death" or *decentering* of the subject]—the historicist one, that a once-existing centered subject, in the period of classical capitalism and the nuclear family, has today in the world of organizational bureaucracy dissolved; and the more radical poststructuralist position, for which a subject never existed in the first place but constituted something like an ideological mirage—I obviously incline towards the former; the latter must in any case take into account something like a "reality of the appearance"). (*PM* 15)

Now this is not just a casual choice or declaration among many. I have commented elsewhere on the significance of the relationship be-

---

11. Jameson himself might not admit that the list of concepts seem to point to Derrida. But "undecidability"?

12. Since its first writing, Laclau and Mouffe's *Hegemony* has pointed the way toward the most efficient transcoding of deconstructive themes into political description. See also Laclau, "Deconstruction, Pragmatism, Hegemony" in Chantal Mouffe, ed., *Deconstruction and Pragmatism* (New York: Routledge, 1996), pp. 47–67.

tween philosopheme and narrateme in Hegel and Marx.[13] Here I should like to comment on the implications of performing this operation on Derrida, since he is the "radical poststructuralist" who has most elaborately accounted for the "reality of the appearance." These implications are not without significance for an understanding of the theory of practice in Marx.

The early Derrida spends a good deal of time defining the graphematic structure. The word is used because writing is historically fixed as the structure that operates in the absence of its origin, the sender. Derrida points out that no code can operate without this *structural* necessity. It is therefore theoretically impossible to privilege speech on the ground of the subject's self-presence. Any practice based on such a theory will lead to the investment of hegemonic access to self-assertion of the subject of theory with the value of the subject as such.[14]

In a related but not identical move, Derrida suggests that the inauguration of any argument must assume unified origins for its founding terms in order to get started. If, however, one examines the mechanics of this assumption, one sees that a structure of repetition, which cannot be posited as deriving from something existing as prior, has been suppressed or finessed in the process. This is a complicated point, and nearly all of Derrida's writing has been a discussion of such suppressions or finessing (sometimes defined as mere counter-examples or difficulties), *managed in different ways in different texts.* In this brief summary, let us call this the suppression of a graphematic structure, the trace of something irreducibly non-self-present, different from that which is begun, at the origin. The decision to call it that, however, is a methodologically necessary step that cannot be endorsed by deconstructive theory. The graphematic structure that seems to inhabit the inauguration of all thought and action is a structure *like* writing, it is not writing commonly conceived. Although one calls it graphematic, one cannot read it as the mark of an absent *presence.* This is the double bind

---

13. "Subaltern Studies: Deconstructing Historiography," in *In Other Worlds*, pp. 200–201.

14. The graphematic structure is described in "Signature Event Context" as the name of a structure that resembles the *logocentric* predication of writing, which is of course interested with human interest as such and is, in a trivial sense, wrong.

that founds all deconstructive theoretical practice. It has made its appearance repeatedly at moments of strategy-suggestion in this book. The "graph" (writing) of "graphematic," like all concept-metaphors in deconstruction, is a catachresis, a (conceptually) false metaphor, and/or a (metaphorically) compromised concept.

It is in this sense that the individual's sense of the "subject" is graphematic, catachrestic. Human beings think their own selves by thus finessing the assumption of a graphematic structure. There is no way to get hold of a subject before the two-step outlined in the paragraph above. Of course to represent any complex speculation in a few sentences does it injustice. Nevertheless, it is not too fanciful to say that what I have summarized here is an account of the famous de-centered (by no means dead) subject.[15] It is my suspicion that Anglo-U.S. critics such as Jameson, Terry Eagleton, and Frank Lentricchia insist so specifically on the de-centering, and on a narrative of de-centering, because the first and last Derrida they read *carefully* was "Structure, Sign, and Play" and the first chapter of *Of Grammatology*, where there is some invocation of "our epoch," meaning, specifically, an "epoch" that privileges language and thinks in structures. In fact, to consider the idea, that the subject can only be thought by the finessing of a graphematic structure at the origin, as a continuous alternative to the subject becoming decentered with multinational capitalism or the passing of the preSocratics is to make an "interested" misreading of it.[16]

---

15. Indeed, it can be shown by textual analysis that all the so-called poststructuralists, at their most theoretical, situate subjecting rather than kill the subject or pronounce it dead. Humanism names man (at best the human being) as the master of an unexamined subjective agency. To question this conviction is not to "kill the subject."

16. In a curious early essay, where Wlad Godzich correctly points out that I should have altered the extant translation of a passage from Rousseau ("The Domestication of Derrida," in Jonathan Arac et al., eds., *The Yale Critics: Deconstruction in America* [Minneapolis: Univ. of Minnesota Press, 1983], p. 40, n. 10), he writes that "[t]ruth as manifestation . . . pre-supposes the occurrence of instances of epiphany which can be recorded. . . . Derrida's dilemma is that to make logocentrism manifest, he must tell its history. . . . Derrida's double dependence upon narrative permits the contamination of his deconstruction by logocentrism" (p. 34). But for the title of the piece, the reader cannot guess, I think, that Godzich might be chiding de Man for the "domestication of Derrida," in finding in this "contami-

Read in this way, the argument about the subject entailed by decon-struction could be this: The subject is always centered. Deconstruction persistently notices—unavoidably centering itself in order to notice—that this centering is an "effect-structure" entailing indeterminate boundaries that can only be deciphered as determining. No politics can occupy itself with only this question. But when a political analysis or program forgets this it runs the risk of declaring ruptures in place of repetition—a risk that can congeal into varieties of totalitarianism, often irrespective of ostensible political positions. It is dangerous and foolish to imagine that decisions are taken by the selfpresent subject: "'[C]risis' is derived from the Greek, *Kríno*, *Krísis* (to decide) and refers to a *moment of decisive intervention*, a moment of transformation, a mo-ment of rupture. Crisis, as Kosselleck notes, is a moment of objective contradiction yet subjective intervention."[17] In deconstructive lan-guage, the interminable auto-critical enabling moment appears: "Even if time and prudence, the patience of knowledge and the mastery of conditions were hypothetically unlimited, the decision would be struc-turally finite, however late it came, decision of urgency and precipita-tion, acting in the night of non-knowledge and non-rule."[18] Deconstruction can neither allow that there was "once" a centered subject nor that there should be a "deconstructive" politics whose sub-ject should be de-centered. It is only a certain "interest" that can claim deconstructive arguments about the subject for postmodernism by sug-gesting that "high-modernist conception[s] . . . stand or fall along with that older notion *(or experience)* of the so-called centered subject" (*PM* 15). And again, the interest of the critic is marked in parentheses.

(In the later Derrida, the "experience of the impossible" has come to play an important rôle [see Appendix]. And the impossibility of decen-

nation" an "inconsistency," a "blindness"? There is no such hesitation in most critics, who diagnose a recognition of this irreducible aporia as a problem of various sorts, moral, political, logical, and the like. Giles Gunn, *The Culture of Criticism and the Criticism of Culture* (New York: Oxford Univ. Press, 1987), pp. 60–61, is a representative sample. It was with irritation at this tendency, in the particular case in John Searle, to diagnose as a failing what was claimed as a theoretical subtlety, that Derrida coined the expression *sec* in "Signature Event Context."

17. Colin Hay, "Rethinking Crisis: Narratives of the New Right and Construc-tions of Crisis," *Rethinking Marxism* 8.2 (Summer 1995): 63.

18. Derrida, "Force of Law," p. 967.

tered agency has come to inhabit the argument from accountable reason. Before we pursue the critique further, it might therefore be pertinent to quote a statement of it in a speech given by Derrida himself at Columbia University, where he spoke of the responsibility of the academic in a modern university, necessarily imbricated with the structures of a post-industrial managerial society: "One can doubtless decenter the subject, as is easily said, without retesting the bond between, on the one hand, responsibility, and, on the other, freedom of subjective consciousness or purity of intentionality."[19] Heidegger, in using *Destruktion* as if he could control it, bypasses this challenge with murderous consequences. The armchair deconstructor, decentering his or her subject at will "denies the [prior] axiomatics *en bloc* and keeps it going as a survivor, with minor adjustments *de rigeur* and daily compromises lacking in rigor. So coping, so operating at top speed, one accounts and becomes accountable for nothing: not for what happens, not for the reasons to continue assuming responsibilities without a concept."

Jameson wishes to claim a whole new "experience" for the postmodern, and forget Marxist moralism: become accountable for nothing. I am suggesting that a theory that proposes that artists are celebrating this experience of derealization that entails the decentered subject in a postmodern society, even if correct, would be talking about how the *individual* is left without a sense of control in a high-tech society. It is because of this that it is quite appropriate for Jameson to claim that, if the *individual subject* were taught how to read the allegory of the postmodern in art and architecture, he (or she?) might know his place in the world system.

I am not altogether certain of this and to such uncertainties I will come at the end. Here let me say that this subject, unlike the subject of which a Kant, a Hegel, a Heidegger, or a Derrida speaks, is not an "it"

---

19. Derrida, "Mochlos: or, The Conflict of the Faculties," in Richard Rand, ed., *Logomachia: The Conflict of the Faculties* (Lincoln: Univ. of Nebraska Press, 1993), p. 11. The next quoted passage is from the same page. This passage is also worth considering because, three pages earlier, Derrida brings up Heidegger's Rectorate Address, offers a short analysis, and remarks: "I cannot explore this path today" (p. 8). I believe the exploration in *Of Spirit* leads him to a different conclusion from the one offered in "Mochlos."

(Derrida has offered repeated critiques of the implicit gendering of this subject, but that is beside the point here), s/he is a "he or she." As long as Jameson is actually talking about the already individuated subject, he is most instructive, and it is here that his account of the "postmodern sublime" would fit. And here he resonates with the Williams who sees "the notion of intention" as "the key emphasis" in the question of the dominant.[20]

By this account, technology seems as fearfully unrepresentable as the sublime did to Kant. To cope with this the "common man" (the individual subject? one is never sure, for the question "who goes to museums" is never asked when the museum is invoked on page 76) tries to connect himself to the global computer hook-up. (The Internet has since then domesticated the sublime, somewhat like the cultivated ruins and wildernesses two centuries ago.) Postmodern art, as in Nam June Paik's multiple video screens or Portman's Bonaventure hotel, allegorizes this fearful unrepresentability so that the individual subject can presumably act it out. What he should learn (Jameson's last instance is correctly pedagogic) to do however is to work with something that seems equally fearfully unrepresentable but can be mapped: "that enormous and threatening . . . other reality of economic and social institutions" (*PM* 38).

It should be clear by now that I am in general agreement with this plan. It should, however, also be clear that Jameson's fable about unrepresentable technology leading to (a generally unsatisfactory) paranoid social practice, (a satisfactory if correctly understood) schizophrenic aesthetic practice, and cognitive (not "moral") political practice, is not a complete rupture with Kant's Analytic of the Sublime. It is as much a psychologized appropriation as Schiller's in an earlier age, in the name of politics rather than aesthetics. Jameson is of course correct in pointing out that the phenomenon of technology as alterity was not available to Kant. But this, as in the case of Van Gogh and Warhol, is a substantive historical difference. The morphology Jameson acts out as correct cognitive practice in the face of the postmodern technological sublime is a kind of pre-critical displacement, on the individual level, of that two-step that Kant described two centuries

---

20. Williams, *Problems*, p. 36.

ago: "I cannot comprehend, but I have the rational will." Kant warns us that this self-reassurance of the subject of ethics cannot be cognitive, although it must represent the singular as universalizable. Jameson, taking a certain marxist line (the principles of which he repudiates in his rejection of moralism), must insist on the rational as cognitive. Thus, in the manner of the subject of the teleological judgment, he must propose a historical purpose for the world that is *almost* natural, a final author who holds the mysterious name "History" whose predication is simply "what hurts."[21] The unexamined contradictions within that postion (we recall the vigilance in Kant's "only in practical reason") are made visible in the claim that the following position is the "genuinely dialectical" philosophy of history:

> Marx powerfully urges us to do the impossible, namely, to think this development positively *and* negatively all at once; to achieve, in other words, a type of thinking that would be capable of grasping the demonstrably baleful features of capitalism along with its extraordinary and liberating dynamism simultaneously within a single thought, and without attenuating any of the force of either judgement. (*PM* 47)

"Holding the positive and negative within a single thought without attenuating any of the force of either judgement" resembles an aporia more than a cognitive mapping: But an aporia discloses itself only as a crossing. And anyone programmed into this civil society has already crossed over. The dynamics of the dialectic, as the entire first sections of the *Grundrisse* show, will not allow the work of the negative to stand still "within a single thought." It is interesting to see how, under the influence of British neo-Hegelianism, the domestication of the dialectic in a desire to map the world was expressed by a poet of reaction to modernism who was rather far from being a Marxist. "[T]he system['s] . . . stylistic arrangements of experience . . . have helped me to hold in a

---

21. Jameson, *The Political Unconscious: Narrative as a Socially Symbolic Act* (Ithaca: Cornell Univ. Press, 1981), p. 102. It is the genius of deconstruction to speculate with this "inexorable *form* of events," to unmoor "the experience of Necessity" into a necessary experience of the impossible. "History" as a name of radical alterity is not "what refuses desire" but what—by rusing temporizing as prior to, indeed, transcending, temporalization—keeps desire going.

single thought reality and justice"[22] The Sartre who formulates the theory of the compulsion to be free might be a connection between these two positions to which Jameson's prescription or desire bears something like a relation.

Let us rather turn to *Capital* 3 in search of an aporia (de Man) out of a difference (Derrida). I here refer back to my suggestion that a quick transformation of the deconstructive morphology to the narrative of a Fall has implications for a marxist theory of practice.

In this passage Marx is indeed speaking of "one of the civilizing aspects of capital."[23] The language is one of movement:

> it *leads towards* a stage at which compulsion and the monopolization of social development (with its material and intellectual advantages) by one section of society at the expense of another disappears; on the other hand it creates the material means and the seed for structures [*Verhältnissen*] that permit, *in a higher form of society*, this surplus labour to be combined, . . . (Emphasis mine.)

Immediately following this passage, where Marx points out, not how to *think* well and ill of capitalism at the same time, but that one must work to sublate the good things *in* capitalism *out of* capitalism, he broaches, somewhat abruptly, a figure that I will call "graphematic," following the description I have laid down on page 322: "The realm of freedom."

"The realm of necessity," according to this passage, embraces "all forms of society . . . under all possible modes of production." "Freedom

---

22. W. B. Yeats, *A Vision* (New York: Macmillan, 1961), p. 25.

23. *Capital*, 3:958. The rest of the passage is from pp. 958–959. My translation of *Verhältnis* as "structure" is permittd by Marx's sustained use of this word as more systemic than *Beziehung*. (See Hegel, *Science of Logic*, tr. A. V. Miller [New York: Humanities Press, 1969], p. 554. The word "Relation" is *Verhältnis* in the German.) The analogy would be to the relationship between *Revolution* and *Umwälzung* (upheaval). In the German, the anterior placing of the phrase I have emphasized makes the more beneficial combination of surplus labor dependent upon the higher form of society to a greater degree, and tones down the admiration of mere capitalism. For a critique of the notion of the germination of structures in Marx, see Derrida, *Positions*, tr. Alan Bass (Chicago: Univ. of Chicago Press, 1981), p. 78. That makes no difference to my point here, of course.

in this sphere . . . always remains [within] a sphere of necessity. The true realm of freedom, the development of human powers as an end in itself, begins beyond it."

As it is articulated here, the realm of freedom is a telos that is free of the realm of necessity, except insofar as the latter can form a basis for it. Some thirty years before this, a realm that was more origin than end was imagincd as a dubious realm of freedom (actually describing what would later be called the realm of necessity) that imposed a limit on all planned practice: "Nature is man's *body without organs*, that is to say nature in so far as it is not the human body. Man *lives* from Nature."[24] The secret of estranged labor as instrument of resistance, when rationalized through the measuring stick of value, had not yet been unlocked.

The realm of necessity or material production is contained within that dubious *arche* and this serene *telos*. These two spaces contain the possibility of naming what is radically other to all efforts for social justice. The earlier passage seems to describe what is only natural (with the human as an almost obliterated moment in it) and the later the only human (with all references to nature appropriated). The inside of these two outsides is described in this passage in *Capital* 3 as "governing the human metabolism with nature in a rational way . . . instead of being dominated by it as a blind power." This larger drama between nature and humanity, with pure nature and pure humanity as limits to rational planning at either side, subsumes the narrative of capital itself as one of its moments. Although Marx wrote that at a certain moment in the production of relative surplus-value the machine begins to determine the self-articulation of the worker, the fearful alterity of the technological sublime would still remain written, in Marx, *within* the drama of the natural and the human. Here Jameson should remain obliged to "historicize" Marx quite in the same way as he does Kant. This is no doubt why he invokes Late Capitalism.

What is more interesting to me here is the way in which Marx attempts to break into that pure outside—pre-originary and post-teleological—of pure nature and humanity. The concept of "metabolism

24. Marx, *Early Writings*, p. 328. Translation modified.

with" allows a break into the former, the "with" slipping the "subject"-position of the metabolism from nature to man, even while keeping it within "materialist" outlines.[25]

And because, via the same concept-metaphor, the "development of human powers as an end in itself" retains an odor of the body (the predication of the human as such remains "materialist") building itself after proper waste disposal, Marx can claim a relationship with that which "lies beyond," "begins beyond": "The pure realm of freedom . . . can only flourish with this realm of necessity as its basis." (As is well known, the concept-metaphor of "metabolism" is an important one in the Marxian text and argument. The famous passage on the cell in the preamble to *Capital* 1 belongs within this discursive logic.)[26] Such a supplementary relationship, breaching the limits of planned (*Capital* 3) or revolutionary (*Economic and Philosophical Manuscripts*) action is possible only because there is something already dividing the apparently pure formulations at origin and end, the trace of the human in the natural and the trace of nature in the human, and of course the paleonymy of "metabolism" as concept-metaphor. The pre-originary and the post-teleological are inscribed by the trace of the other and thus, as pure pre- or post- they are effaced in their articulation.

This might seem a mere making-esoteric of a political text. Let me say at once that, because (or in spite) of this graphematic traffic at either end of theoretical practice (planned economy or revolution), it can be demonstrated that the place of practice remains un-totalizable in Marx. Because, in spite of (perhaps unacknowledged or clandestine) efforts at encroaching its boundaries, the arena of practice, identical with the arena of necessity, remains bounded by these two realms of "freedom," it can never be adequate to all of human/natural reality, never be abso-

---

25. I am indebted to the documentation in Alfred Schmidt's rich study *The Concept of Nature in Marx*, tr. Ben Fowkes (London: New Left Books, 1971), pp. 76–93 and 127–163. It will be obvious that my notions of limits are not Schmidt's.

26. Marx, as a considerable Hellenist, could not have missed the fact that μεταβολή was regularly used of a change of government, just as σύμβολή for a skirmish as well as a contract.

lutely justified. When Jameson reads the passage in its entirety as "wrestling a realm of freedom from the realm of necessity," he is in fact doing what the passage will not allow, that is to say an expansion of the forever self-differed and self-deferred arena of theoretical practice, the story of "freedom, in this sphere [of necessity]" into the whole story. The arena of practice, as staged in the Marxian passage, would rather imply that the subject of this practice, belonging to the bound narrative of modes of production, must be centered in rational management; it is however bounded by possibly indeterminate boundaries that Marx necessarily deciphers as determining (see page 323). A deconstructive approach that is not immediately rewritten into a narrative of the modes of production can work at these graphematic moments in Marx and develop them into the persistent asymmetry between theory and practice without transforming the dialectic into an aporetic doublethink, or dismissing the irreducible ethico-political moment in Marx as moralism.[27] It is possible for such an approach to appreciate rather than strategically exclude the last line of the paragraph where Marx outlines an appropriately matter-of-fact project, within the arena recognized as no more than the realm of necessity and irreducibly situational: "The reduction of the working day is the basic prerequisite."

The level of reading that can find an alibi in Marx for *thinking capitalism as both positive and negative at once* does not match Jameson's usual sophistication. It marks the management of a contradiction, the covering-over of a foreclosure. Reduced to its most trivial form, this reading of Marx is where the absolute justifications for state capitalism begin to merge into the absolute justifications for development, and, in a curious homology, a plea for understanding postmodernism begins to use the axiomatics of imperialism to manipulate a crisis in, and thus to operate, an argument: the residual and emergent must make their way in the dominant. In Jameson there is the magical invocation of multinational capitalism without attention to its multinational consequences and the discussion of a poem that "seems to have adopted schizophrenic frag-

---

27. Since I first wrote these words, Derrida's *Specters of Marx* has proved at least the second half of this sentence correct. I look forward to Etienne Balibar's forthcoming commentary on "Messianism" in that text.

mentation as its fundamental aesthetic," whose annunciatory first line just happens to be "china."

> Perelman's poem . . . turns out to have little enough to do with that referent called China. The author has, in fact, related how, strolling through Chinatown, he came across a book of photographs whose idiogrammatic captions remained a dead letter to him (or perhaps, one should say, a material signifier). The sentences of the poem in question are then Perelman's *own* captions to those pictures, their referents another image, another absent text; and the unity of the poem is no longer to be found within its language but outside itself, in the bound unity of another, absent book. (*PM* 30; emphasis mine)

This is a striking allegorical narrative of the production of postmodernism as a descriptive term for aesthetic practice. Its use here can be contrasted to its use in the context of architectural practice.

When postmodern architectural "historicism" borrows architectural idioms from far-flung periods without any regard for idiomatic coherence or reproduction of appropriate context, this, unlike mock Gothic, or British Palladian, or Federal Georgian, can be seen as a foregrounding of radical citationality, of the suggestion that the "aura" of the original cannot be structurally privileged. Far from being an "effacement" of the past (*PM* 18), it can be read as a questioning of the identification of continuist narratives of history with History as such, perhaps even a reminder to the necessarily class-mixed users of public space that at the limit, History, rather than being a transcendental signifier for the weight of authority (or the authoritative explanation) is a catachresis, a metaphor that has no literal referent.[28] Here the position of the architect-subject is defined by a distancing and differentiation from (rather than an effacement of) a dominant narrative of history.

One of the peculiar imperatives of deconstructive practice is to fix the

---

28. This is of course not to say that nothing ever happens. This particular bit is what Derrida shares with Rorty and a deliberately down-home pragmatic explanation can be found in *AF*. My differences with this position will be explained later in the chapter.

critical glance not specifically at the putative identity of the two poles in a binary opposition, but at the hidden ethico-political agenda that drives the differentiation between the two.[29] This in fact is how deconstructive practice is ever mindful of the eventuating "historical moment."[30] Such an imperative would make us notice that the self-differentiation of postmodern architecture from a recognizable historical narrative and that of a poem such as Perelman's (in Jameson's reading) from China, or indeed Jameson's own self-differentiation from Marxist moralism by strategic invocations of "multinational capitalism" are not politically equivalent gestures, because these gestures are constituted by fairly clearly assigned subject- and object-positions: the narrative the architect cites and fragments is hegemonic and immensely well documented; the "moralism" Jameson dismisses is *also* an object of red-baiting by the contemporary political dominant, including those who systematically operate "multinationalist capitalism"; the obliteration and appropriation of the rich signifying practice of the Chinese in Chinatowns by the white *flâneur*, however *personally* innocent, does not belong to the carefully documented dominant historical narrative that is part of the compulsory curriculum for every first-year college student in the United States. In other words, "China" as referent hides the hybrid of Chinatown, hidden in its turn from the culturally unmarked Anglo.

A book of photographs in Chinatown refers to China through the heterogeneous relief-mapping of marginal migration, where Perelman has his own place. How does he, as hybrid (because American), force China into American idiom? How does he make his text "mean," with holes in the place of poems?[31] The cultural politics of the poem depends

---

29. The metaphor of hiding is perhaps inappropriate, for this concealment may be necessary to the disclosure. Call it a palimpsest or a rebus spelling out complicity.

30. The event—*événement* or *Ereignis* (Heidegger)—is a heavy philosophical theme that I have not the training to tackle. In a more vulgar way, I submit here my conviction that *événement* in Derrida's writing is a name for the indefinitely differentiating "present"—*eine differente Beziehung* (Hegel).

31. Here is another bit of "proof" that Derrida is not a postmodernist. His notion of irreducible iterability ("citation" is inevitable) entails the wounding effect of a constant gouging by différance of the irreducible supposition of an "original."

on his force vector within this mapping, not on the question of reference. To reduce it to that, is mere "modernism." Every declared rupture is an undeclared repetition.

The conflation of the "outsider" in Euramerican space with the global outsider or the white *flâneur* in Taiwan, Hong Kong, the People's Republic—are these homogeneous spaces?—has something, then, like a cultural politics. The emptying out (or denial) of signifying possibility and the imposition of one's own caption on a geopolitical other seen as uninscribed earth relies on the axiomatics of imperialism, to be sure; but, and this is my point, the case is different within the map of marginality in the metropolis; either better or worse, but different, for the Chinese in Chinatown are American. Reading Jameson's Perelman's gesture, however "postmodern" it might seem in its imagic prac-

---

Thus even the text-ile or weaving metaphor—since Freud "naturalized" it by suggesting that women "wove" their pubic hair to cover their lack of a phallus ("Femininity," *SE* 22: 132; I must say, if I may break decorum yet once again, that the idea of a Viennese gentleman proposing this "scientifically" and millions of men and women considering this seriously, while a woman dismisses Farida Akhter as "essentialist," stupifies me)—is suspect. "Iterability" is cutting and pasting—here cutting and sewing on (*couture et coupure*), and the cuts bleed. (The necessary yet impossible first "cut" is différance from the "original," the primordial wound of living-in-time, for example. "All the examples stand out, are cut out [*se découpent*] in this way. Regard the holes if you can. . . . Here again I do nothing other, could [*puis*] do nothing other, than cite, as perhaps you have just seen [or, as perhaps you have come to see—*comme vous venez peut-être de voir*—the lesson of *Glas*, as it were]: only displace the syntactic arrangement around a physical wound, real or feigned [*feinte*], that points at [*signale*] and makes the other be forgotten" (Derrida, *Glas*, pp. 208b, 210b, 215b; translation modified). Those Chinese photos and ideographic captions, mentioned in conversation by Perelman, are the "examples." (This is comparable to all that biographical material about "Negresses" in Baudelaire.) Displacing the syntactic arrangement from hybrid ideogram to hybrid phonetic script to draw attention and make be forgotten (cross out? put under erasure?) is rather more complicated than absent reference. The problem of migrancy, if you like, for which Perelman may be taking the responsibility in the poem. You must decide if the residual(s) (Chinese as well as U.S. nostalgia) being dragged into an emergent by way of the social intent of the dominant is here alternative or oppositional; mess with the preemergent. At any rate, for a Derridian figure, the wounds of all this cutting would bleed. For Spivak, it would be a shift from masculist (the absent reference in the patronym) to a feminist (the bleeding of preemergence) model of explanation.

tice, and indeed however innocent in its personal poetics, cannot be simply equated with (a) Derrida's remark about France in 1968 either: "What I will call 'France,' then, . . . will be the nonempirical site of a movement, a structure and an articulation of the question of 'man'"; or (b) postmodernist architecture's "historicism" in the eighties, or yet opposed to (c) Keats's yearning for the referent to the carving on the Grecian urn.[32] Reading it, we must remember that the ideograms are a "material signifier" either because of the "normal" Western subject's ignorance of "Chinese," or because multicultural solidarity in the United States cannot depend on national-identity sharing—that there is no play between knowledge and its abdication here, as in Portman's (non)promenade in the Bonaventura. *Either*, it is complicitous, however unwittingly, with the production of the "postmodern"-ist debate as well as the postmodern, like other Western terms of periodization since the late eighteenth century, in being produced by way of a dissimulation of the geopolitical other. *Or*, it takes a stand in the residual and emergent making their way in the dominant, as it wanders, like Baudelaire in "The Swan." Our task as reader is to take a risky decision in the "night of non-knowledge," not just to learn to *think* plus and minus at the same time. Otherwise, the discourse of postmodernism here functions to suggest that the *cultural* (not merely the economic) logic of micro-electronic capitalism is universal, that the *cultural* logic that holds for London and Paris and Liverpool and Nevada City also holds for Hong Kong or Bankura or Beirut. This apparently descriptive gesture is, alas, a performative: the thing is done with words; culture is cultural explanation; to say everything is cultural is to make everything *merely* cultural. Radical multiculturalism thinks of "culture" as the name of a complex strategic situation in a particular society—residual moving into the dominant as emergent.

(As it is, some of the singular sentences in Perelman's poem remind one of Brecht; and others refer this reader to the innocent aura of the great Midwestern Poetry Workshop in the '70s [where and when it was her good fortune to make the poet's acquaintance]. It is a marvelous

---

32. Derrida, "Ends of Man," p. 114.

unemphatic ending, where two sentences, by making sense together, blow the poem's cover in a fake fortune-cookie message: "Time to wake up. / But better get used to dreams.")[33]

It is not now difficult to understand that, in search of a pluralized "paralogical politics" that will fit the postmodern condition, Jean-

---

33. "I wrote the poem after looking, not at a book of photographs as Jameson writes, but at some sort of Chinese primer containing simple four-color pictures of 'the world': family, kitchen, school, rivers, airports, and village festivals" (Bob Perelman, *The Marginalization of Poetry: Language Writing and Literary History* [Princeton: Princeton Univ. Press, 1996], p. 176, n. 37; all Perelman quotations in this note are from this book). Here is a way in to a choice, informed by all the asymmetrical interests of the book you are holding in your hand, and considering "Perelman" as a textual figure, weaving poetry and/as criticism, not conflating the two. The primer is a hyphenated American (child)'s entry into the (m)other tongue. The complicity of ontogeny and the larger economies of colony/postcolony/migrancy is marked in "Attention," a poem by Rae Armantrout that Perelman quotes earlier. Like most theoretically inclined literary critics, Perelman is unaware of Lacan's largely unacknowledged debt to Melanie Klein. "'Ventriloquy / is the mother tongue,'" Perelman writes, "articulates a model of how linguistic subjects are formed through a complex of imitation, control, rebellion that leaves all selves multiple masters and puppets of one another; it is a Lacanian lecture condensed into one memorable sentence" (pp. 22–23). A reading of Melanie Klein takes the subject on the other side of language into trace structures recalling the gift of time, if there is any; as well as forward from the mother tongue into the broad ethical economies of temporizing a life, in this case a hybrid life of cultural collision. Perelman modestly writes of the "seventies [as a time when] faith in the rebirth of modernist ambition and of the cultural centrality of poetry was easier to maintain than in the nineties. Today parataxis can seem symptomatic of late capitalism rather than oppositional" (p. 62)—Raymond Williams's word. But parataxis demands syntax, and can operate a sustained parabasis, as "a code by which . . . [the] reader . . . [is] signified throughout the narrative" (Barthes, "The Structural Analysis of Narrative," in *Image/Music/Text*, tr. Stephen Heath [New York: Hill and Wang, 1977], p. 110), and thus leave the way open for opposition, bind the subject in the unilaterality that responsibly doublebinds every opposition for the sake of "freedom from" that is haunted by the terrible prospect of "freedom to." The distinction between Pound and Derrida in Perelman's opening poem can be read with this in mind: "Is it [*Glas*] really that different / from, say *The Cantos*? (Yes. *The Cantos*'s growing incoherence reflects Pound's free-fall / writing situation; Derrida's institutional address is central. Unlike Pound's, Derrida's cut threads always reappear farther along)" (p. 9).

François Lyotard should invent the "pagan," as Perelman "invents" "China" and Barthes "Japan."[34]

I have often departed from accepted scholarly or critical practice in this book. I have attempted to imagine or construct (im)possible practices, re-constellated classics into implausible and impertinent readings for the sake of disciplinary critique, applauded gestures that could not lead to a model for action, made an effort, indeed, to take a distance from the principle of reason from within, without inclining toward irrationalism: obtuse angling. In this chapter, too, I will try something out of the way. Having considered a major figure in the literary-critical postmodernist debate, I will move to the space where the word has become a diagnostic name for recognizable phenomena.

When this chapter was first written, I opened with the idea that every rupture is a repetition, that so-called postmodernism entailed epistemic practices that would fit right into the modern.

In the intervening years, the word "postmodern" has become as generalized as the word "subaltern."[35] One has it from a reliable source that two famous ecological and feminist activists have taken out a contract for a book demolishing postmodernism, with a British radical press rather notorious for bending with the wind; the newest entry in the subsection entitled "Postmodernism, against" in any self-respecting library operating in the abstract name of "practice." To situate this bit of come-lately self-righteousness, I will look at what was defined as *not* postmodern in metropolitan hip culture more than a decade ago, and try to suggest that, like most periodizing and culturally descriptive or explanatory terms in the pre- and post-imperialist West, what is *not* postmodern shares with the postmodern a manipulation of the geopo-

---

34. Lyotard, *Instructions païennes* (Paris: Galilée, 1977); *Rudiments païens: Genre dissertatif* (Paris: Union Générale d'Editions, 1977). Wilde and Barthes's Japan differs from Heidegger's Greece, Derrida's France. In the latter "the cut threads always reappear farther along," and *you* make a *jamdani* with them, "good" or "bad."

35. Whether the two terms are linked (positively or negatively), delinked, or used selectively, would indicate cultural politics. The word "postcolonial" often mediates between the two, in various ways.

litical other in its production; as the Southern "star" does with the Northern in serving up sanctioned ignorance to a constituency mistaking polemic for its own sake for resistance as such.

Cut threads. I now attempt to enter the web of text-ility, as it is woven into the social text as vanishing present.

Architecture and clothing, both inscribing nature within culture, are privileged arenas of inscription. In the field of architecture, the discourse of postmodernism is particularly self-conscious. Postmodern architecture—originally challenging the assumptions of modernist architecture—can be situated as one movement among many.[36] But fashion in clothing is in the most obvious sense ephemeral, in the most obvious sense more tied to market turnover (and therefore able, for example, to take direct advantage of electronic communication systems to move into postfordist fax-determined small-is-beautiful freedom-of-choice), and therefore its language has long been wedded to the "aesthetic as such," the "conceptless" hyperreal. This, too, may explain the unexplained "Allegories" in Ackerman—alluding to a lexicon and thus producing a portentous reference—or rather knowledge-effect.[37] Here the metropolitan interventionist tabloid, with its restricted commitment to urban welfare and race/gender issues, spins into an unquestioned (and, indeed, if theorized, aporetic) space of contradiction. The constitution of a radical elite alibi for political practice can dress cool. The comprehension of cultural signifiers such as "postmodernism" or "minimalism" is taken as given there. This is of course one of the ways to perpetrate a kind of "wild" cultural pedagogy that establishes these

---

36. Peter Brooker, ed., *Modernism/Post-Modernism* (London: Longman, 1992) and Mark Wigley, *The Architecture of Deconstruction: Derrida's Haunt* (Cambridge: MIT Press, 1993) will give a sense of the march of time. Jameson's specifically architectural claims for the definitiveness of postmodernism in the eighties is now as out of date as this book's first take on colonial discourse or McLuhan's prediction for the Third World.

37. Under the influence of Walter Benjamin and Paul de Man, I had cottoned on to this in the field of literary production some time ago, it seems. See Spivak, "Allégorie et histoire de la poésie: Hypothèse de travail," *Poétique* 8 (1971): 427–444; and "Thoughts on the Principle of Allegory," *Genre* (Dec. 1972): 327–352.

terms as quick diagnostic fixes within whatever functions as a general elite culture (which also produces the unnamed subject of Jameson's postmodern cultural dominant).

Here are some excerpts from a piece entitled "Like the Boys" that appeared in *Village Voice* in 1984:

> The designer is Japan's Rei Kawakubo . . . a woman with a total aesthetic, a world view. . . . She's a tough independent lady with a genius for design, a brilliant sense of marketing and business, a lust for control, and her very specific idea of what women need in 1984. . . . Rei Kawakubo, it is said, started Comme des Garçons so she could have total control over her life and answer to no one. In all, this is a very feminist story. . . . There's no postmodernist flip to her minimalist aesthetic. . . . While New York blossoms with a postmodernist pallette . . . Japanese architects hunker down in oriental high tech. . . . Is Rei a feminist? It's hard to determine. She seldom speaks to the press. In photographs she has a strong handsome serious face that needs no makeup. Johanne Siff, who spent two years in Japan on a Watson Fellowship studying the emergence of women in the contemporary arts, explains that there is no organized feminist movement to parallel what American women experienced in the '70s. . . . Everyone who works for Rei believes in her idea. . . . Something about everything for the simplest and purest life. . . . Rei seems to be getting at something more political [than fashion]: feminist; free; revolutionary.[38]

---

38. Carol Troy, "Like the Boys," *Village Voice*, 14 Feb. 1984, pp. 37, 41. All the bits are from these two pages. As an example of orientalist feminist capitalist cultural supremacist stereotyping, the entire piece is worth reading. I am using the piece as an example. I do not think Carol Troy is necessarily particularly foolish or knavish; this *is* radical chic tabloid journalism. I do not know Ms. Kawakubo, and have no interest in saying good or ill about her. I am interested in her representation and self-representation as discursive productions in available discursive fields, history and discourse as condition and effect of the economic under erasure. Also, I am treating her as an example of something. I could, now, use a spectacular example of a Bangladeshi female designer and the Parisian glossy *Elle*, but I think there I will not be able to preserve the distance of exemplification. A propos of architecture, the facile contrast drawn between Japan and New York would be exploded, for example, by taking a look at Bernard Tschumi, *Event-Cities (Praxis)* (Cambridge: MIT Press, 1994). A propos Japanese feminism, Japanese women's participation in the globe-girdling resistance movements is impressive; I am holding in my hand a book on childbirth written in Bengali (not translated into Bengali)

This is not transnationalization in the way in which the Bangladeshi example in note 136 would be; Japan and the United States are *inter pares*. But "[a]ll the main points" nonetheless "boiled down to the biggest legal issue: under which country's law is this?" It looks like, in 1984, the buildings were Bank of New York and the merchandise Tokyo's Fuji Bank.[39] And I repeat, it is my last movement in this chapter that moves to strictly transnational capital; not this one.

I have argued that the privileged inhabitant of neo-colonial space is often bestowed a subject-position as geo-political other by the dominant radical. (One is most struck by this when planning or attending international conferences.)

Rei Kawakubo has caught on so well—she designs costumes for Merce Cunningham—and gone through so many transmogrifications that this account of her launching will seem hopelessly dated to the chic. But that is part of my point.

By now, we can recognize the strategy. How very different she is, how *Japanese*. Yet, the authoritative cultural discourse that defines her and indeed defines Japan is placed in Euramerican cultural history. Over against this is her reported self-description, freeing herself from this very history, the appropriate answer conditioned by a question we can almost hear in the background, produced for one of the most important consumer guides in metropolitan New York by canny "Rei Kawakubo, 41, an extraordinary Japanese businesswoman/designer . . . born in Tokyo in 1943 . . . either three or four when the atom bombs exploded at Nagasaki" and: "I have always felt it important," she says, "not to be confined by tradition or custom or geography." How does a 1943-born Japanese buy such freedom? We will see one earlier postwar attempt below. Today through electronic capitalism, of course. And what do the Euramerican fashion ideologues think about this? I want to put together some ingredients for an answer in the following pages, hoping that, as with the rest of the book, this will give the reader a sense

---

by a Japanese activist (Mugiko Nishikawa, *Japaner Motoichi Gramer Janmo-poddhotir Poriborton o Adhunik Dai* [Dhaka: Narigrantha, 1992]). Yayori Matsui's *Women's Asia* (London: Zed, 1989) also tells a different story.

39. These are the laws that, as the morning news in New York City reports on 12 Mar. 1998, are making Japanese entrepreneurs hang themselves. We cannot keep up with the vanishing present. Readers will remember that time as the era when finance capital came crashing down in the Asia-Pacific.

of the axiomatics of imperialism at work. Why are they operative? Because the lines of contact between imperialism and de-colonization on the one hand, and the march of world capitalism on the other, constitute the most encompassing crisis of narrative today—the problem of producing plausible stories so business can go on as usual. There is no doubt that one cannot get to "the truth of culture" this way. But the "truth of culture," in my view, *is* the battle for the production of legitimizing cultural explanations.

The writer of the *Voice* piece thinks Rei thinks that she can get freedom from tradition or locale by removing class markers from the clothing she designs: "(I think by [her] two references to mobility she means no indications of social class)". This argument can of course be quickly dismissed. At Christmas sales in 1986, the cheapest T-shirt in her New York store cost $135, the cheapest cotton shirt, $195.

Let us rather step back into a debate specifically concerning the emergence of Japan in the text of cultural identity and cultural difference (the-same-yet-not-the-same, different-but-not-different), the weave of which is so specific to "our spacetime." Let us look at a passage from a rather interesting document in Japanese cultural history, "Takeuchi Yoshimi['s] . . . long meditation on the wartime symposium . . . 'Overcoming the Modern.'"[40]

It is a meditation on identity and difference: "independent" (rather than for an imperialist master) participation in World War II and subsequent subjection to U.S. occupation:

> Because of Japan's post-war postion, she sees herself as capable of leading the Asian revolution. But the post-imperialist countries of Asia are not convinced of this. To them, Japan must therefore present herself as part of the advanced West. Japan must present herself as Asian in order to convince the West that she is the best representative of Asia. This leads the Japanese political-cultural consciousness into an aporia. And thus the Japanese intellectual today must persist in creating endless tensions.[41]

---

40. H. D. Harootunian, "Visible Discourses / Invisible Ideologies," *South Atlantic Quarterly* 87.3 (Summer 1988): 453–454.

41. Takeuchi Yoshimi, "Kindai no chokoku," in Takaaki Yoshimoto, ed., *Gendai Nihon shiso taike*, vol. 4: *Nashonarizumu shoshū* (Tokyo: Chikuma Shōbo, 1964),

Programs of cultural self-representation are never correct or incorrect. They are the substance of cultural inscriptions. The point is not that Kawakubo and indeed Japan's present situation in the Asia Pacific have not fulfilled Takeuchi's predictions. It is that Kawakubo's avowal is inscribed on a chain of displacements that accommodates it. "I have always felt it important not to be confined by tradition or custom or geography" legitimates its opposite: "To the West Japan must present herself as Asian," as Samuel Huntington legitimates McLuhan. What neither statement allows is that the subject-position in them is class-fixed. In fact, the emergence of Japan as a cultural signifier in the service of politics in the present century is as much of a struggle between identity and difference as was that of India in the last.

To define Kawakubo, Troy appropriates her within the geography of a New York cityscape, in direct contravention of her expressed wish to be "free of geography." And the copywriter for *Vogue* (cited by Troy) keeps to the art-historical patter where "postmodernism" is a term of diagnosis like any other, inscribes her as the Other of Europe: "Kawakubo is not a postmodernist, she is a minimalist and a conceptualist and therefore not interested in the European concepts of dress." Even as U.S. newsmedia intermittently comment on Japan's suicidal samurai spirit as its secret to economic growth, the United States electronic industry (among others) is obliged to deal with Japan as an "equal" (a version of identity).[42] Meanwhile Kawakubo's clothes, minimalist or not, are worn precisely by the crowd that goes to museums and hotels and takes hi-tech for its plaything, the recognizable global subject who is a candidate for learning cognitive mapping. Those unwilling masters of multinationalism can shuttle between Nam June Paik (identity—no mention of his postcolonial provenance) and Perelman's China book (difference—no mention of the diasporic nature of the Chinese in Chinatown). The "alternative" discourse of fashion remains as asymptotic to radical theory as is the garment industry to fashion design. The informed goodwill of the well-dressed radical sutures the asymptote in an aporetic crossing, an impossible chiasmus. The spec-

---

p. 402. Cited in Noguchi Takehiko, "The Reappearance of Nationalism in Literature and the End of the 'Postwar Period," tr. Betsey Scheiner and Yoko Woodson, paper delivered at University of California (San Diego), 12 May 1983.

42. I have not attempted to bring this up to date.

tacular in-house journal called *Six*, in its own way as uncategorizable as *Glas*, inhabits this suture. Published in Tokyo for Comme des garçons, Inc., these handsome, heavy, oversize journals commission celebrated photographers, designers, and celebrated members of the high cultural Euro-U.S. world—with the occasional Japanese—to produce a species of pre-theoretical witnessing with an aura of theory, as shy of serious scholarship as it is of fashion patter. I hope to study this phenomenon elsewhere.

If I seem to be insisting too much here, it is because the thoroughly transmogrified (im)possible perspective of the native informant (a Japanese *worker*, an inhabitant of Chinatown, the implied reader of the book of Chinese photographs) would see, if it could, nothing but the appropriation of its trace in the interstices of the powerful texts of the master's radical discourse. (The situation is not helped by the fact that these generalized native informants sometimes appear in the Sunday supplements of national journals, mouthing for us the answers that we want to hear as confirmation of our view of the world). Such appropriations seem to be common to texts that are postmodernist, modernist, or, since Kawakubo was, for a season or two in the mid-eighties supposedly a minimalist, minimalist.

Consider, for example, the opening page of Roland Barthes's *Empire of Signs*, a text of high modernist spirit that deliberately expands on Baudelaire's "Invitation to a Voyage":

> Mon enfant, ma soeur,
> songe à la douceur
> d'aller *là-bas* vivre ensemble . . .
> là tout n'est qu'ordre et beauté
> luxe, calme, et volupté

How lovingly commentators have fixed a real name to Baudelaire's "là-bas!" The consensus is Belgium.[43]

Barthes forestalls the pedant by spelling out the problem in the very first sentences of the first section (entitled "là-bas") of his book. This is the later Barthes who, in the name of going beyond semiotics, reinstates the geo-politically differentiated confessional subject. His text

---

43. Baudelaire, *Oeuvres* (Paris: Pleiade, 1944), pp. 66–67.

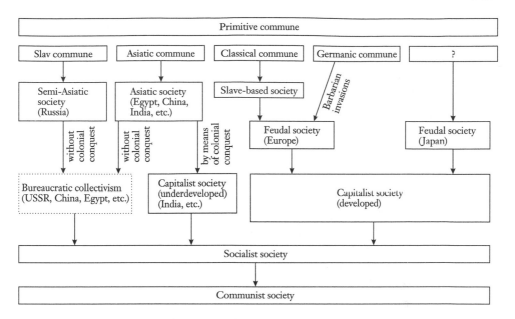

A reconstruction of Marx's concept of historical development. From Umberto Melotti, *Marx and the Third World*, tr. Pat Ransford (London: Macmillan, 1977), p. 26.

can therefore begin: "*If I want* to imagine a fictive nation, *I can* give it an invented name. . . . I can also . . . isolate away there [*là-bas*] a certain number of features . . . and . . . deliberately form a system that I *will call:* Japan."[44]

I want, I can, I will. Throughout this book, my point has been that the subject-position of this I is historically constructed and produced so that it can become transparent at will (even when belonging to the indigenous postcolonial elite turned diasporic like the present writer). This is not altogether overlooked by Barthes, of course. There is a certain slippage working in the construction of his object. When speaking of the fictive nation with the invented name, he is aware that "it is then that fantasy itself I compromise by the sign of literature." There is no invocation of the compromise involved in taking a historically

44. Barthes, *Empire of Signs*, tr. Richard Howard (New York: Hill and Wang, 1982), p. 3, emphasis mine.

named place to be the ground of an "invented game." I am of course not claiming that history is real and fiction unreal. I am simply asking that the binary differential created by Barthes himself make its claims both ways. The historical sedimentation of the name Japan as "the other place"—neither the China or the Near East that is the object of hyperbolic admiration and curiosity of the European seventeenth and eighteenth centuries, nor the India that is the inverted ground of identity-and-difference in the British and German eighteenth and nineteenth; but precisely that Japan, an "other place" in Marx's project of the Asiatic Mode (see figure), inheritor of an investment of the fictive as such that we have come to recognize through the symbolist-imagist idiom of Yeats and Pound via Fenellosa, next rendered through the U.S. occupation, itself contesting in that play (Asia to the West—Western to postimperialist Asia), the Empire of Signs. Just as in the eighteenth century the *Neuholländer-Feuerländer* is not an accidental choice as the example for the parergonal subject (although its specificity may be delivered by the poetic function), and in the nineteenth the classical Indian for an arrested aesthetic historicity, so might Japan not be altogether accidental in 1970. (Examples are "situated.") It is as if, in the European imaginary, Narcissus at his pool had escaped from the Hegelian trajectory of Oedipus, and guarded in Japan the fantasmatic place of the specular. As Malcolm McLaren, "purveyor of the Sex Pistols and Adam Ant," opined: "Japan was for so long an isolated island that it has never got over its hunger for the status of ideas."[45]

Even if history is a grand narrative, my point is that the subject-position of the native informant, crucial yet foreclosed, is also historically and therefore geopolitically inscribed. However you docket *The Empire of Signs*, from the historically (im)possible yet historial perspective of the native informant, the signs of a different periodization disappear before a generic resemblance between Barthes and, say, Perelman. "The sentences of [*The Empire of Signs*] are then," a Jameson may write, "[Barthes's] *own* captions to those features, their referents another image, another absent text; and the unity of the [book] is . . . to be found . . . in the bound unity of another absent book" (see page 331). The

---

45. Quoted in Troy, "Like the Boys," p. 41.

disavowals then strike all the more: "To me the Orient is a matter of indifference"—again, from the (im)possible perspective of the native informant it would be the common tone across the great theoretical difference between the later Barthes and the Hindess and Hirst of the middle period (see page 94) that would ring out—

> merely providing a reserve of features whose manipulation—whose invented play—allows me to "entertain" the idea of an unheard-of symbolic system, one altogether detached from our own. What can be addressed, in the consideration of the Orient, are not . . . another metaphysics, another wisdom (though the latter might appear thoroughly desirable), it is the possibility of a difference, of a mutation.[46]

The clear-headed innocent arrogance of this assumption of a subject-position that claims the other as grounds for difference might seem to some to be preferable to ostensible benevolence. One notices something of a similar confidence in Richard Rorty's argument: the project of the Enlightenment is considered altogether defensible if only taken not as objectively and universally valid but as the cherished values of a historically definable group, one's own.[47]

There is a photograph of a handsome Japanese head dressed in what can be identified as "traditional Japanese dress" gracing the frontispiece of *The Empire of Signs*. If "[i]n the most radical form of Brecht's epic

---

46. Barthes, *Empire*, p. 3.

47. One can, of course, neither accuse nor excuse Barthes but make use of his material as I hope I do Derrida's. Here is the abstract of a dissertation, written under the supervision of Greg Ulmer (*Applied Grammatology: Post(e)-Pedagogy from Jacques Derrida to Joseph Beuys* [Baltimore: Johns Hopkins Univ. Press, 1985]), another practical deconstructionist: "This dissertation extrapolates a method primarily from Roland Barthes's *Empire of Signs*. . . . In terms of pedagogical applications, tourism is an oft repeated term for the new attitude required by the electronic classroom. Cultivating access and links among bits of information requires one to move through information as a tourist; informatics and generative assignments supplement memory in invention tourism" (Craig Jonathan Saper, *Tourism and Invention: Roland Barthes's "Empire of Signs,"* [Ann Arbor: Univ. of Michigan Press, 1994], n.p.). Will the electronic classroom supplement electronic capitalism by emptying the rest of the world of "real" detail? The reader must decide.

theater . . . [t]he erasure of the face is the emblematic signature of . . . [the] undermin[ing of] a bourgeois concept of subjectivity in order to make *tabula rasa* for a radically different form of subjectivity," here the placing of the face "under erasure," keeping it abundantly visible though crossed out by a draining of affect, keeps any form of assigned subjectivity, however abyssal, from emerging at all.[48] On the model of those nineteenth-century "allegorical" appropriations of the fabrication of fabric into a fashion system, the native informant's (im)possible perspective might put together an "allegory" here as well. The trick is to place, beside that impenetrable "Japanese" face, the faces and bodies of the 1983 *French* catalogue of Kawakubo's boutique *Comme des garçons*.[49] (*Six* did not start until 1989.) The faces and the clothes in the catalogue are also recognizably "Japanese" without "real" Japanese specificity, comparable, let us say, to the "India" in that by now mythical art-object, George Harrison's "My Sweet Lord," or contemporary "Indy-pop" in Britain, or indeed Perelman's "China."[50] Although there are captions in the catalogue, as in Ackerman's book (see page 410), orienting the individual subject into cognitive consumership, there is for us yet another level of text that is perhaps more productive of allegorical excess. In Ackerman's volumes the "allegories" were invariably framed by undistinguished figures of British Palladian representations of architectural support, as unmarked yet as ideologically charged a signal as Barthes's Japanese. In Kawakubo's catalogue the frame—perhaps masquerading as mere background—consists of photographic representations of architecture. These are recognizable monuments, testifying to history in a way that opposes yet legitimizes Ackerman's mute Palladians. If Britain sucks Empire from Rome, *Comme des garçons* sucks style from France. And France is to fashion what Japan is to

---

48. Rainer Nägele, "Puppet Play and Trauerspiel," *Qui Parle* 3.1 (Spring 1989): 40; word order rearranged.

49. *Comme des garçons* 81 (5 July 1983).

50. Under the auspices of the New World Order, the production of such authoritative hybrids as representations and representatives of an unmarked origin is the name of the game, especially in the field of ideology as culture in the service of the political calculus that manages the abstract economic machine.

otherness. The subject remains Europe, in *Six* the nuanced Euro-clone, whatever the markings of the auteur.

But Rei Kawakubo is neither postmodernist nor Barthesian. We are told repeatedly that she is a "minimalist." Looking at the clothing she designs (the reader might find it quite difficult to believe that I am moved by its powerful and luxurious whimsy), I would guess that this description owes a good deal to the bunkerlike designs of her show-rooms, and her preference for dull black, dull gold, grey. Be that as it may, I should like now to glance at a famous definitive text of minimalism, Robert Morris's "Aligned with Nazca."[51]

Morris, a practicing artist, lacks the lucid arrogance of a Barthes or a Rorty. And *Artforum* is somewhere between *Village Voice* and *The New Left Review*—where Jameson's essay was first published. Today it dominates the emergent biennales of Johannesburg or Kwangju, trying to manage the crisis of electronic capitalism in those areas with the digital narcissism of virtual art. In the mid-seventies—the Euro-U.S. recession has just begun—Morris's is a careful, sophisticated and humane piece, deeply marked by subject-object talk, just right for the loosely academic curator. It dovetails miraculously with Jameson's "Postmodernism." Each author claims for his movement space rather than time as the proper stuff not only of art, but indeed of a "cultural dominant." This is not Morris's phrase, of course, but he is as deeply aware of the march of time in movements. Keeping in mind that Jameson claims the importance of space for postmodernism in the name of the death or decentering of the subject, its emptying of affect and the attendant euphoria; and that Morris emphasizes the importance of the freeing of space from (for example Beckett's) interiority in the *interest* of a perceiving self more coordinated with its body, let us note the latter's insistence upon distinguishing Minimalism in its various phases from "the art of the '60s":

The art of the '60s was, by and large, open and had an impulse for public scale, was informal by a logic in its structure, sustained by a . . .

---

51. *Artforum* 14.7 (Oct. 1975): 26–39; hereafter *AN*, with page numbers following.

belief in a historical unfolding of formal modes which was very close to a belief in progress. The art of that decade was one of dialogue: the power of the individual artist to contribute to public, relatively stable formats which critical strategies, until late in the decade, did not crumble. Mid-way into the '70s one energetic part of the art horizon has a completely different profile. Here the private replaces the public impulse. Space itself has come to have another meaning. . . . Deeply skeptical of experiences beyond the reach of the body, the more formal aspect of the work in question provides a place in which the perceiving self might take measure of certain aspects of its own physical existence. (*AN* 39)

Equally skeptical of participating in any public art enterprise, the other side of Minimalism does, by this explanation, expose a single individual's limit in examining, testing, and ultimately shaping the interior space of the self.

Both Morris and Jameson are phonocentric. For one writing is the mark of man's exploitation of man. For the other, *écriture* is the mark of the subject's death under late capitalism. For Morris to treat space as "real" space rather than the flat space of writing would be "to channel the powers of *nature* into human design. Nature's power flows through the artist's marks." (There is no rap on the knuckles as in Petchesky on Akhter [see page 386].) For Jameson, to see *écriture* as the product of a cultural dominant allows the placing of the individual in line with *history* rather than Nature. And, even as Morris's artist will "have both terms: the flat *and* the spatial . . . the abstract figure *and* the concrete existent," so will Jameson's individual subject retain a "dialectical" view in realizing that to entertain the question of the subject is to regress. No ideas of the graphematic structure of the concept-metaphor Nature or History, no consideration of human metabolism or the limiting realm of Freedom can disturb these presuppositions.

Morris draws attention to the possible theoretical kinship between some mysterious geometric stonework in Peru and these principles of Minimalist art. Ostensibly, he is most careful to point out that no one knows the "real" significance of the Peruvian earth graphics. Toward the middle of his essay he writes:

One can speculate that the lines in the desert were spiritual irrigation systems connecting certain places of power in the surrounding sierra to the lower plains. . . . *It is possible to imagine* that the Nazcans . . . made a trek into the crystalline highlands to attempt a record long line towards one of the peaks invested with special powers. *Whatever the intentions of these forms* on the desert, they are *morphically* related to certain arts we see today. If *Nazca* purposes were lost in the past, they can nevertheless throw our present context into a helpful relief. *(AN 33)*

One cannot help admiring the scruple with which the passage above tries to avoid any pretense at a correct interpretation of what the Nazcans were about. The binary opposition that supports the scruple is between intention and form. As in the case of Barthes's opposition between fantasy and reality, the seemingly disinterested dyad allows the operation of an interested narrative. For us, the Nazcas *still* have the form (a concept whose pure outlines are unwittingly borrowed at least from Plato), the undifferentiated "we" have *both* form and intent. As in the case of Jameson, who explains the subject's need not to focus on the subject, what is being explained here is not the morphic behavior of Minimalism, but its intentional history, because "*all* twentieth-century art seems compelled by a type of Cartesian projection" *(AN 33)*. As a result of this, the minute historical specificity of the Minimalist move-ment can express its *intent* in terms of a form that resembles the Nazca. It is in fact the Nazca's intentions that are finally explained, for who can deny that the Nazcans were close to Nature?

First, the intentional burden of Minimalism itself: "Perhaps the most compelling aspect of Minimalism was that it was the only art of objects . . . which ever attempted to mediate between the notational knowledge of flat concerns (systems, the diagrammatic, the logically constructed and placed, the preconceived) and the concerns of objects (the relativity of perception in depth)."[52] Then the intentions of a slightly later period: "The tendency of later work involved with enclosed spaces for the self has a complex relation to Minimalist esthetics in that it accentuates certain attitudes about reflexiveness and the conditions of perception which were only acknowledged by the earlier work." Now the true explanation of the Nazca lines, *much* earlier work, of course; effectively,

---

52. This passage and the two following passages from Morris are from *AN* 38.

in cultural politics, outside of history, "our" history. The direction of the metaphor of what throws light on what has been reversed: "In the light of these remarks on the nature of the surface and the spatial, the lines of Nazca take on a deeper meaning. For here, as in Minimalism, the flat and spatial are mediated." In other words, the intending subject *either* has no history, *or* its only history is that of the contemporary Euro-American, who, though contaminated and thus condemned, by the intervention of writing to a Cartesian twentieth century, still seems able, through the power of Art, to recapture the Nazcan preventive pre-originary attitude toward a writing that is yet to come. Whatever the initial apologies, it is this intending subject who reveals the "deeper meaning" of the Nazcan lines.[53]

One could perhaps overlook this ignoring of the implied historical narrative by invoking the notorious a-historicity of the subjectivist artist. Let us consider how the text would make such a decision problematic.

The beginning of the essay is in the form of a short "Prologue-Diary." This is followed by a "Log" where the traveler's diary imperceptibly flows into an authoritative commentary. This is followed by an untitled section that contains the interpretation proper, from which most of my quotations have so far been taken.

Derrida has written at length about the eighteenth-century antecedents of the travelogue (*OG* 117). Let us simply note here that this "Diary" begins with rather a brutal indication of difference: "Peru . . . Military junta of the left. Communized haciendas, nationalized utilities. Attempting to avoid Allende's unworkable democracy. In six years Pizarro got it all with 200 men and 80 horses."[54] There is too much political subtext telescoped here for a full-scale commentary. Let us simply note again that the general suggestion of the essay is a common one; that the art of the "free world" is more able to get to the core of humanity of the precolonial paradise than any rational planning by postcolonials.

Some powerful phallocentric imagery is used to convey this natural sympathy in the "Diary": "Erotic pottery. Ripe and rotting fruit.

---

53. This strategy is laid bare in Derrida, "From and Meaning: A Note on the Phenomenology of Language," in *Margins*, pp. 155–173.
54. This and the next two passages are from *AN* 26.

Bought avocados. Skeleton water pots with erections. . . . Glistening brown nude boys in the irrigation ditches. Remembering the female mummy in the Herrera museum. . . . Twinges of necrophilia in the groin. Mud pots with erections. She was from Paracas. The mummy. About three thousand years ago." This is followed by the description of an actual woman seen at a distance. Then, interspersed with paratactic sentences on Peruvian standards of female beauty now and then: "Hand cut peeling an avocado. . . . Herrera female mummy. Perfect set of teeth. Hand sticky with blood and avocado." Then a description of trepanning and various civilizational generalizations. Finally, "water pots with erections for spouts. Impregnating the desert. Long lines of irrigation slits and trenches. Glistening nude boys bathing. Brown erections in the muddy water."

D. H. Lawrence has made this an easy phallic code to break. In this species of blood-identification through tumescence, a civilization presumably cannot be "othered." The artist-explorer from another world cannot find what he is looking for. So, at the end of this brief section, "No lines. Missed them completely in the fading light. Try tomorrow." The next section opens in the everyday language of the sober travelogue: "At 7:30 the next morning I returned to the Pampa Colorado in search of the lines I had missed the day before" (*AN* 26). After this staged antithesis of body and mind, we are on our way to the interpretative sublation of the Nazcas.

The phallocentric sexual imagery works a certain slippage here. The female sexual object is clearly a figure for the long-dead but beautifully preserved civilization, the latter connoted by the erect-spouted pots. But it is also a "real" lust, a "real" stirring in the artist's loins, accompanied by a communion with Nature as his "real" blood mingles with the "real" avocado. It is this transhistorical, and transpolitical, possibility of male bonding that allows Minimalism to uncover the "deeper meaning" of the Nazcas: "For here, *as in Minimalism*, the flat and spatial are mediated. At least in relation to my proposed theory of their functions, the lines work toward this mediation."[55]

I have proposed in this book that a different standard of literary evaluation, necessarily provisional, can emerge if we work at the

---

55. Ibid., p. 38. Morris is careful: "At least according to . . ." But there is no mistaking what is logically though not chronologically prior.

(im)possible perspective of the native informant as a reminder of alterity, rather than remain caught in some identity forever. The minute particulars of a hegemonic art-critical or literary-historical periodization, dependent generally on descriptive diagnoses expressively associated with a collective mindset, foreclose moments of the axiomatics of imperialism that can only be irregularly systematized. This alternate historical narrative discloses the irregular commonality of the foreclosure, where the lines between art and fashion become indeterminate, rather than the neat constructed periods of the "true" accounts of history.

In Chapter 2, we have seen that the indigenous population of the Americas escaped the Ariel-Calibán debate. And here we notice, similarly, that the Nazca can be explained by way of an enlightened Minimalism. The East-West aporia-talk in the "Overcoming Modernity" debate in Japan, following homologous structural lines, thus says nothing of Japan's indigenous minorities. (Indeed, given that the Aboriginals of the East Kimberley region of Australia displace the oppositions of liberal/radical multiculturalism [see page 404], it is at least interesting that the Aboriginal Ainu of Okinawa have looked to Australia for models of emancipatory legislation.)

In Chapters 2 and 3 I have suggested that a plangent female individualist such as Rei Kawakubo, emerging as the favored subject/object of feminism/masculism, often allows an other woman to disappear.[56] Who

---

56. But fashion, to coin a phrase, is fickle, and we are talking postindustrial tempo here. In all fairness, I should note that Kawakubo is no longer interpellated as "feminist" (no makeup) and "minimalist." Whatever her personal cosmetic style, she is now assimilated within the hybridist discourse of New York "turning Japanese" (Lynn Yaeger, "Material World: Pacific Overtures: Turning Japanese," *Village Voice*, 3 Sept. 1996, p. 34. All the quotations are from this page). Not minimalist—"Commodity fetishism has me poised, Sandy Pittman–like, on a veritable Everest of desire—teetering between a pale velvet, puffed muslin Comme dress [no longer exotic, recognizable by a nickname, whereas the title of the earlier Troy piece had been an English translation of the French phrase *comme des garçons*. She is as non-classless as earlier:] I want both these items with all my heart, but will, in all likelihood, end up with neither—the dress costs $1785." But the tabloid writer is now savvy to these Marie-Antoinette-playing-at-milkmaids-structures, although she too must draw the obligatory contrast between there *(là-bas!)* and here: "Though the situation in their native land is no doubt different (probably everyone's walking around in Burberry or Hilfiger), in New York City . . . All four

might she be in the context of postmodernism? To attempt an answer to this question, I will open the hatch, jump off into the space of capital, let go of the line of a singular argument, until I am caught in the web of textile once again.

In the multiculturalist struggle, the use of the word "culture" is comparable to Foucault's use of "power." It is a name that one lends to a complex strategic situation in a particular society.[57] "Our culture," with its claim to a pattern of behavior beyond reason alone, is opposed to the claim of the culture of the European Enlightenment to Reason as such. In its paleonymic—as a name with a history, in other words—and in its idiomatic strength, multiculturalism—as long as it does not code mimicry as resistance—performs a critique, however inchoate, of the limits of the rational structures of civil society.

In an article entitled "An Anthropologist Looks at Ballet as a Form of Ethnic Dance," Joann Kealiinohomoku writes:

> Western dance scholars have not used the word *ethnic* in its objective sense; they have used it as a euphemism for such old fashioned terms as "heathen," "pagan," "savage," or the more recent term "exotic." . . . [D]ue to the social climate which rejects the connotations with which our former words for "they" were invested, and because of a certain sophistication assumed by the apologists for the "they," English-speaking scholars were hard-pressed to find designations for the kinds of non-Western dance which they wished to discuss.[58]

---

of [these Japanese designers] are expensive. . . . so repeat after me: I'm using these stores as a lab! I'm adapting these ideas! I can go to a thrift shop and copy this stuff! I'm getting a sewing machine. . . . Comme, especially this season, is exquisite beyond the dreams of even the most style-obsessed mortals—a group of spectacular velveteen clothes that manage to combine the grace of ceremonial court robes with the winsome oh-is-the-lining-hanging-out? appeal of the grungiest thrift shop outfit." Yes, Kawakubo is no more than an example. The general argument stands. The photo on the *Voice* page is of a sultry Anglo head swathed in a hybrid kimono.

57. In the *History of Sexuality*, Michel Foucault describes his use of the word "power" in the following way: "One needs to be nominalistic, no doubt: power is not an institution, and not a structure; neither is it a certain strength we are endowed with; *it is the name that one lends [prêter] to a complex strategical situation in a particular society*" (p. 93; emphasis mine).

58. Roger Copeland and Marshall Cohen, eds., *What Is Dance? Readings in Theory and Criticism* (New York: Oxford Univ. Press, 1983), pp. 546, 547–548.

If the multiculturalists use the word "culture" as Foucault uses "power," the liberal strand of benevolent Euro-American supporters might be using the word according to the strategy Kealiinohomoku points out. Here too providing learned definitions of culture will not cut much ice. Richard Rorty, always smart enough to notice the poverty of the Emperor's wardrobe, trumps Kealiinohomoku by suggesting that "the rhetoric that we Westerners use in trying to get everybody to be more like us would be improved if we were more frankly ethnocentric, and less professedly universalist."[59] The battle lines are drawn openly here.

---

59. Rorty, "Justice as a Larger Loyalty," in Ron Bontekoe and Marietta Stepaniants, eds., *Justice and Democracy: Cross-Cultural Perspectives* (Honolulu: Univ. of Hawai'i Press, 1997), pp. 9–22. See also "Solidarity or Objectivity," in John Rajchman and Cornel West, eds., *Post-Analytic Philosophy* (New York: Columbia Univ. Press, 1985), pp. 3–19; and "Solidarity," in Rorty, *Contingency, Irony, and Solidarity* (Cambridge: Cambridge Univ. Press, 1989), pp. 189–198. It is, however, in the piece cited in the text and in "Does Academic Freedom Have Philosophical Presuppositions?" *Academe* 80.6 (Nov.–Dec. 1994):52–63; hereafter *AH*) that his point of view discloses its political implications, its kinship with more reactionary and less intelligent texts such as Samuel P. Huntington's *The Clash of Civilizations and the Remaking of World Order* (New York: Simon and Schuster, 1996). Neither author mentions the narrative history of international capital. Therefore, when Rorty writes "the only difference between desirable objectivity and undesirable politicization is the difference between the social practice carried out in the name of each" (*AH* 55), we agree and point out that it is because of the social practices recoding capitalism as civilizing mission (imperialism), as development (neo-colonialism) and as democracy (post-Soviet globalization) that we examine a particular heritage of the Enlightenment, and the "culture" of multiculturalism questions its "heirs," when they "urg[e] . . . that we Westerners [be] more frankly ethnocentric . . . [and] peel apart Enlightenment liberalism from Enlightenment rationalism" ("Justice," pp. 19, 20). The mystery of claiming a heritage by peeling it from rationalism is indeed what radical metropolitan multiculturalism seems to confront through complicity. Rorty claims that the presuppositions do not matter, the practices they explain do; thus seeming to write off culture as explanation. This is disingenuous, for he obviously cannot argue that the "emptiness" of "correspondence" in "truth corresponds to reality" is "optional." He must therefore draw on distinctions such as public (practice) versus private (belief—academic or theological); or short-run (beliefs do not matter) versus long-run ("in the long run physicists whose rhetoric is pragmatist rather than Western Rationalist might be better citizens of a better academic community," *AH* 58). It is in the interest of the long run, then, that we would support supplementing rather than jettisoning Kant. In Chap-

If the multiculturalists' many cultures cannot be captured by some textbook definition, nor can Rorty's Enlightenment culture. Simply put, culture alive is always on the run, always changeful. Our task is to look at the two strategies: culture as a battle cry against one culture's claim to Reason as such, by insider as well as outsider; and culture as a nice name for the exoticism of the outsiders.

For those who speak from the liberal-democratic position, as for the

---

ter 1 we have seen how Kant may be read as suggesting that the human being is programmed to supplement rational morality by the name of God. Working through the Kierkegaard-Levinas-Derrida rather than the Dewey-Rorty line, this name may be seen as *a* name of the radical alterity that the self as "the narrative center of gravity" is programmed to imagine in an ethics of responsibility. The agency of the call to responsibility that is the program of being is then placed in a wholly other that makes (no = all the) difference. It is not only that different presuppositions may lead to the same practice. It is also that the same presuppositions may lead to different practices. Rather than have "dinosaurs" and "mountains" as the name of radical alterity (what discourse cannot touch, *AH* 63, n. 21), let us, as the postcolonial subject is being appropriated into globality, follow the impossible perspective of the native informant and place an always prior agency there instead of in the self. This may move capital toward socialism. That persistent effort (disclosing responsibility toward the other-as-beneficiary by effacing radical alterity) is micrological, always halfway, but not therefore *only* a "muddling through . . . [with] no rules" at all (*AH* 55). Rorty regularly condescends to "nonspecialists" when speaking of philosophical arguments (e.g., *AH* 54). Glass houses. Where he is himself a nonspecialist, he is taken in by such specious arguments that multinationals relocate in the South for global social justice. No, the CEO is not a Kantian. He knows that the "just" thing would be to allow the price of labor to rise equally and is therefore against unions and the welfare state; just as, if the professor had thought through the practical meaning of "economic social justice," he would not have presupposed that it necessarily required "sacrific[ing] the blessing of political liberty" ("Justice," p. 22). He can look in the Anglo tradition if he likes. This may, for example, be what Percy Shelley meant when he suggested that the poetry (connecting to the other, and to general humanity through metaphor and figuration in general) of the new economic systems would not lead to the "exasperation of the inequality of mankind [sic]" as it did in 1818 because there was infoglut and "we want the creative faculty to imagine that which we know" (Percy Bysshe Shelley, "A Defence of Poetry," in Bruce R. McElderry, Jr., ed., *Shelley's Critical Prose*, [Lincoln: Univ. Of Nebraska Press, 1967], p. 29). Choose, if you can, between Shelley's unacknowledged primitivism and Rorty's "frank ethnocentrism." But let us not anticipate ourselves, although anticipating Rorty is beyond the scope of this book. The peculiar patriotism of *Achieving Our Country: Leftist Thought in Twentieth-Century America* (Cambridge: Harvard Univ. Press, 1998) will have to wait.

multiculturalist activists, culture is invaginated in civil society, and neither side can openly acknowledge it. The Son-of-Enlightenments' claim to the felicitous subjectship of civil society as such is too massive and obvious to belabor: it is the claim "to certain fundamental intuitive ideas viewed as latent in the public political culture of a democratic society."[60]

For the activists the "particular society" in Foucault's sentence is the civil society in the metropolis, rather than the hyperreal "international civil society" that bypasses the state in globality. And "the complex strategic situation" is not merely to bring down the European Enlightenment's claim to its felicitous subjectship (what Althusser used to call the Ideological Subject), but also to wish insertion into it in the place of the agent: the citizen. The demands go from civil acknowledgement of culturally diverse practices, through gaining mainstream education with a culturally inclusive curriculum, to referencing cultural themes in art, literature, film, video; and, in a slightly different move, *bi*-lingualism, which never quite graduates into multilingualism. This too is invagination, but the vector is critical rather than conservative.

In the previous chapters, we dealt with some texts of philosophy, history, and literature even as they were imbricated in the social text that produced anyone who can read this book. Here we seem more directly figured in the textile of the social, and in the social folds of textile. There is a quick march of names: colonial, postcolonial, New Immigrant, hybrid, transnational; postmodern, subaltern. "Our culture." It is therefore altogether salutary to remember, again, that "culture" is also a regulator of how one knows: Foucault's famous capacity-to-know doublet: *pouvoir/savoir* as the ability to know is "culture" at ground level. (Of course Foucault uses other words, most noticeably "discourse.") From this point of view, taxonomies of culture are possible and useful. But any "culture" at work is a play of differences (if you can separate work and play) from these taxonomies. This is not a poststructuralist pronouncement. Simply put, it is how language use is a play of differences from dictionaries. Yet dictionaries are possible and useful. No *langue-parole* or system-process distinction can catch this

---

60. John Rawls, as quoted in Rajeswari Sunder Rajan, "Politics of Equal Dignity," *Book Review* (Dec. 1995): 23.

play, culture at work. Culture alive is always on the run, always changeful. There is no reason to throw up one's hands over this. We do our
work with this limit to the power of vanguardism of theory in view.

I am therefore a student of cultural politics. In what interest are
differences defined? When the process-people correct the systems-
people, what may be the agenda? As I work at this at the end of a book
that has run away from me, I am of course open to your view. You will
judge my agenda in the process.

As far as I can understand it, my agenda remains an old-fashioned
Marxist one. Marx attempted to make the factory workers rethink
themselves as agents of production, not as victims of capitalism. They
advanced their labor, the capitalist repaid them only partially. Their
claim to the rest was their claim to socialism (tone it down: the welfare
state; dress it up: civil society). Today in the old metropolitan countries,
the capitalist is the benefactor "creating jobs," and the worker is systematically deprived of welfare because it is a "free" gift. Suppose we
analogized globally. Today in the post-Soviet world, privatization is the
kingpin of economic restructuring for globalization. It means a broad-
stroke change in the global economic pattern—"a new attempt to impose unification on the world by and through the 'market.'" It is now
more than ever impossible for the new or developing states—the newly
decolonizing or the old decolonized nations—to escape the orthodox
constraints of a "neo-liberal" world economic system that, in the name
of Development, and now, "sustainable development," removes all barriers between itself and fragile national economies, so that any possibility of social redistribution is severely damaged. In this new
transnationality, "the new diaspora," the new scattering of the seeds of
"developing" nations so that they can take root on developed ground,
means: Eurocentric migration, labor export both male and female, border crossings, the seeking of political asylum, and the haunting in-place
uprooting of "comfort women" in Asia and Africa. By analogy with the
Marxian project above, the hyphenated Americans belonging loosely to
the first and the fourth groups might rethink themselves as *possible*
agents of exploitation, not its victims; then the idea that the nation-state
that they now call home gives "aid" to the nation-state that they still
call culture, in order to consolidate the new unification for international capital, might lead to what I call "transnational literacy." Then
our multiculturalism, or our use of the word "culture," will name a

different strategic situation from *only* our own desire to be the agent of a developed civil society. Which we need not give up; but let us want a different agency, shift the position a bit. I have been consistent in my insistence that the economic be kept visible under erasure.[61] What good will it do? Who knows? Marx's books were not enough and the text of his doing remained caught in the squabbles of preparty formation and the vicissitudes of personal life. You work my agenda out.

One of the alarming developments of the recent past is the wave of academico-cultural "postcolonialism" that seems to be hitting the elite migrants in Europe. In the summer of 1996, this writer was invited to grace a goodly number of European podiums on the occasion of "post-colonialism." In France I earned the ire of a well-placed Franco-Maghrebian and an Indian-French teacher of English because I warned that much of U.S. academic postcolonialism was bogus, an argument I am making more responsibly here. (It was noticeable that the Algerians spoke altogether differently; they were confronting their difference from the failure of decolonization in Algeria. And in February I had shared a podium with the Algerian militant Khaleda Messaoudi, whose awareness of transnational capitalism in the face of religious violence was exemplary.)[62] In Germany I earned derision from an Indian-German teacher of English because I spoke on Derrida, Djebar, Klein, and Diamela Eltit rather than on my Indian hybrid soul. There is not enough time to develop all the permutations and combinations.

In the broad strokes of cultural-political narrativizing, I will risk a generalization here. Elite "postcolonialism" seems to be as much a strategy of differentiating oneself from the racial underclass as it is to speak in its name.

Let me offer an explanation from an earlier conjuncture, by a person whose work had not yet been invaginated by the local as it confronts the

---

61. Spivak, "Scattered Speculations on the Question of Value," *In Other Worlds*, p. 168.

62. Conference on "Resistance and Silence," LiteraturWerkstatt (Berlin), 17–21 Feb. 1996. On the failure of decolonization, see Wole Soyinka, *The Open Sore of a Continent: A Personal Narrative of the Nigerian Crisis* (New York: Oxford Univ. Press, 1996).

global.[63] This chapter is, after all, one woman teetering on the *socle mouvant* of the history of the vanishing present, running after "culture" on the run, failure guaranteed. In parentheses, I have indicated how this earlier version can be updated, for the moment.

The period of capitalist territorial colonialism and imperialism, which began at the end of the eighteenth century, supposedly ended in the mid-forties, when neo-colonialism began. During that earlier period, a class was produced of indigenous functionary-intelligentsia who were not-quite-not-white and acted as buffers between the foreign rulers and the native ruled. This is the most accessible and abstract account of the making of the so-called colonial subject. It is the narrative that supports the master narrative of the dominant European subject.

As we thus stalk the postcolonial briskly, we may indeed ask: what was the cultural-political fate of this indigenous elite as the great territorial imperialisms began to be dismantled, and the period of decolonization began? In the new nations, they had a strong hand in fashioning a new cultural identity. This did not always dovetail with the cultural-political situation in the metropolis. For the indigenous elite did not have an established new informant position. They did not gain a foothold in the inception of "national" cultural studies in Britain in the '60s, for that movement was working-class-based and oriented toward mi-

---

63. In 1989, for example, I was on well-meaning metropolitan lists of good feminist users of postmodernism, grouped with people whose work is in some cases absurdly different from mine: "It would be reckless not to cite the central role of Feminist writings for a reading of postmodernism. . . . In *Art after Modernism*, for example, there are three contributions in the section titled 'Gender/Difference/Power.' Laura Mulvey's 'Visual Pleasure and Narrative Cinema,' Constance Penley's '"A Certain Refusal of Difference": Feminist Film Theory,' and Kate Linker's 'Representation and Sexuality.' Yet there are powerful contributions besides these: Jacqueline Rose's *Sexuality in the Field of Vision*; Roszika Parker and Griselda Pollock's *Framing Feminism*; Abigail Solomon-Godeau's essay in *Sexual Difference: Both Sides of the Camera*; the essays that appear in the journal *Camera Obscura* (by Constance Penley, Jane Weinstock, Meaghan Morris, and others); Annette Kuhn's *The Power of the Image: Essays on Representation and Sexuality*; Gayatri Spivak's *In Other Worlds*; and, more recently, Meaghan Morris's *The Pirate's Fiancée: Feminism, Reading Postmodernism*. All these essays contribute integrally to the continuing discussion of the postmodern as a struggle to value otherness" (Timothy Druckery, "Reading Postmodernism," *Camerawork* 16.1 [Spring 1989]: 20–21).

grant culture almost from the start. The area studies disciplines that sprang up during the Cold War years and gave support to the American self-representation as the custodian of decolonization absorbed some members of this class. It was not until the '70s and the computerization of the great stock exchanges and the dismantling of nationally based capital that a benevolent third-worldist cultural studies impulse began to infect the U.S. academy.[64]

This impulse, with its immense potential for crisis management through production of knowledge, housed the colonial subject as *post* colonial turned informant. This position is generally so beleaguered by the pervasive hostility of the traditional humanist authorities toward any disturbance of the Euramerican canon that its own cultural-political provenance can hardly be discussed without the uneasy feeling of divided loyalties. There is so much room for real misunderstanding here that I must also hasten to add that I am not speaking about the slow change from colonial to postcolonial in the "new" nation.[65] I am only trying to account for the sudden prominence of the postcolonial informant on the stage of U.S. English studies.

The postcolonial informant has rather little to say about the oppressed minorities *in* the decolonized nation as such, except, at best, as especially well-prepared investigator. Yet the aura of identification with those distant objects of oppression clings to these informants as, again at best, they identify with the other racial and ethnic minorities in metropolitan space. At worst, they take advantage of the aura and play the native informant uncontaminated by disavowed involvement with the machinery of the production of knowledge. Thus this last group either undermines the struggle by simulating an effect of a new third world, by piecing together great legitimizing narratives of cultural and ethnic specificity and continuity, and of national identity—a species of "retrospective hallucination."[66] Or, and more recently, the more stellar level predicates upward class-mobility as resistance, confining the de-

64. For area studies see Carl Pletsch, "The Three Worlds."

65. Geeta Kapur, "When Was Modernism in Indian / Third World Art?" *South Atlantic Quarterly* 92.3 (Summer 1993): 473–514, tabulates this change in the context of the periodization of Indian art.

66. Jean Baudrillard, "The Precession of Simulacra," in *Simulations*, tr. Paul Foss et al. (New York: Semiotext(e), 1983), p. 22.

stabilization of the metropole merely to the changes in the ethnic composition of the population. The continuous and varied product of this dissimulation is an "other" or "ground level activity," "emergent discourses" for postmodernity, a kind of built-in critical moment. Both the racial underclass and the subaltern South step back into the penumbra.

This activity generates a kind of formula: colonialism was modernization/ism :: postcolonialism is resistance to postmodernism; *or,* the "true" postmodernism; now, only the postmodern postcolonialist is the triumphalist self-declared hybrid. The actual postcolonial areas have a class-specific and internationally controlled limited access to a telematic society of information command, which is often also the indigenous contact-point or source of the discourse of cultural specificity and difference. My suggestion is that academic assertions of this difference, supporting the simulated specificity of a radical position, often dissimulate the implicit collaboration of the postcolonial in the service of *neo*-colonialism. (Today this has been displaced into hybridist postnational talk, celebrating globalization as Americanization.) This simulation-dissimulation two-step can take the discourse of feminism on board. As Kalpana Bardhan writes, in postcoloniality

> women hardly constitute a collectivity with shared interests and needs. They are [as] stratified as men are. . . . In such a context, gender politics can hardly be a surrogate for class politics. . . . If the wage-and-access differentials follow the lines of traditional privilege, then attention gets conveniently deflected from the adaptive dexterity of capitalist exploitation process to the stubbornness of feudal values [national-cultural-ethnic specificity?] when it is actually a symbiotic relationship between the two.[67]

(Today UN-style universalist feminism simulates a women's collectivity, unwittingly, one hopes, to use the needs of the needy in the interests of the greedy, so to speak. The gendered "postcolonial" plays rather an important rôle here.) I prefer to call this relationship complicitous (folded together) rather than symbiotic (living on/off one another). Folded together, we live on/off whatever lies on the other side, in the minute particulars of our living as in the broadest structures of

---

67. Bardhan, "Women, Work," pp. 3, 5.

policy. My own text could not have been written or read without that folding together. It is an absurd denial of history simply to ask for its prohibition. A caution, a vigilance, a persistent taking of distance always out of step with total involvement, a desire for permanent parabasis, is all that responsible academic criticism can aspire to. Any bigger claim within the academic enclosure is a trick.[68]

It was the eruption of Hindu nationalism in India in December 1992, resulting in the destruction of a mosque in Ayodhya, that taught us a

---

68. Both metropolitan postcolonialist and Southern academic critics of post-colonialism have objected to my call for vigilance (Robert Young, Review of Spivak, *Outside*, in *Textual Practice* 10.1 [Spring 1996]:238; and Harish Trivedi in Trivedi and Meenakshee Mukherjee, *Interrogating Postcolonialism: Theory, Text and Context* [Shimla: Indian Institute of Advanced Study, 1996], p. 240.) I generally quote Farhad Mazhar, as knowledgable in the textuality of literature as in the textuality of "activism," differently. He writes ironically about what kind of "Third World Literature" is rewarded internationally. He rages at the complicity between capitalism and religion:

> Okay, Notebook. Are you going to get the Philipps Prize this time?
> Try, try, Allah is your hope.
> Achtung. Take care. Be vigilant. Watch it.
> I am copying down the crawling of the grass.
> I am taking down the paw of the jaguar.
> I am slipping. My foot is losing its hold.
> I am taking down with my heel the problems of my footing.
> Watch it. Watch it. Attention.
> In the old days you had to fight on the other side of the barbed wire,

A suggestion, I think of the national liberation struggle, of frontiers and jails. But in postcoloniality, in the failure of decolonization—

> Now on both sides: right and left, above and below, in water and dry land.
> Go to the crocodile and get your teeth fixed.
> From the snake, a rubber spine,
> Go to the bat and suckle yourself
> My Chum, my untimely Notebook, these are very bad times.
> Watch your step on all sides, my friend

lesson about the failure of decolonization in India, the remote motor of the exodus of those of us who became the globe-trotting postcolonials, ready for entanglements in new global complicities.

For it is not only the political power brokers on the right in the nation who mobilized the forces of fundamentalism in the name of historically authoritative national identity; there is an isolationist counter-nationalism among the ideologues of the left parties as well. Some professed anti-nationalists of the diasporic left, taking a passionate stand against religious nationalism in the country of origin, betrayed the power of the reactive nationalism of the ex-patriate. Nationalism, like culture, is a moving base—a *socle mouvant* (to quote Foucault again)—of differences, as dangerous as it is powerful, always ahead or deferred by definitions, pro or contra, upon which it relies. Against this, globality—or post-nationalist talk—is a representation—

And then the last words, in English but in Bengali script:

Be careful!!

("Ashomoyer Noteboi," in *Ashomoyer Noteboi* [Dhaka: Protipokkho, 1994], p. 42; translation mine)

One cannot read a poem like a manifesto, of course. But the poem does urge vigilance because, in postcoloniality, you can't recognize your friends anymore. (It is of course "true" that the counting of friends as any collectivity is fraught. "How many are we?" Derrida asks, as he iterates Montaigne iterating Aristotle: "O my friends, there is no friend" (Derrida, *The Politics of Friendship*, tr. George Collins [New York: Verso, 1997], p. x and *passim*). Yet the friend must be addressed, and even that seems perilous today when we move out of the NGO or the classroom.) This poem is written after the elections, after various summits and various UN conferences. Its writer runs a large ecological agriculture collective and therefore does independent practical research on the exploitation of biodiversity. The question of globalization, clinched by cultural writers in terms of the outlines of domestic justice for underclass Eurocentric migration, quite often not even touching the narcissism of the well-placed, so-called postcolonial intellectuals who then identify themselves as precisely aligned with that underclass, bypasses the fact that the local in the South directly engages global greed. Once again, then, a glimpse of the sources of my feeling for the need to be vigilant. The unpopular position, then, is not just a single consensus breaker's position but rather reflects what this writer learns from her contact with workers in counterglobalist resistance.

both as *Darstellung* or theatre and as *Vertretung* or delegation as functionary—of the financialization of the globe, or globalization. What I had earlier seen as the upwardly class-mobile metropolitan ruse of recoding mimicry as resistance, comes into its own in this dispensation.[69] Fundamentalist nationalism arises in the loosened hyphen between nation and state as the latter is mortgaged further and further by the forces of financialization, although the determinations are never clear. The first items in the following couples are fuzzy, the second abstract: nation-state, subject-agency (institutionally validated action), identity-citizenship. Much manipulation, maneuvering, and mobilization can take place in the interest of the latter in the name of its fuzzy partner.[70] Experience gained in the interim suggested another way of conjuring with nationalism, in the name not of the globe but of a global girdling.

Globality is invoked in the interest of the financialization of the globe, or globalization. To think globality is to think the politics of thinking globality. How are the loose outlines of popular politics inscribed? Marshall McLuhan is rather a minor example of a "watershed intellectual." Yet his *Global Village* does provide something like deep background for the history of our present, for the backlash of underclass multiculturalism.[71] I couple McLuhan's book with Jean-François Lyotard's *The Postmodern Condition*, which offers a different though related

---

69. See, for example, Arjun Appadurai, "Patriotism and Its Futures," *Public Culture* 5.3 (Spring 1993): 411–429.

70. Information on the progressive mortgaging of the South to the forces of financialization is ceaselessly proliferating on all fronts. For a brief introduction to the principle, see Cheryl Payer, *Lent and Lost: Foreign Credit and Third World Development* (London: Zed, 1991). An interesting development is to be found in Roger C. Altman, "The Nuke of the 90's," *Sunday New York Times Magazine*, 8 Mar. 1998, pp. 34–35. The author, as the *Magazine* informs us, is "an investment banker, [who] served in the United States Treasury Department under Presidents Carter and Clinton." As for agency, when the poor are thoroughly disenfranchised, such ancient "institutions" as religion and gendering, reducible to seeming formulaic abstractions, kick in their validating mechanism.

71. Marshall McLuhan, *The Global Village: Transformations in World Life Media in the 21st Century* (New York: Oxford Univ. Press, 1989); hereafter *GV*.

riff on Jameson's topic, and has had something like a watershed effect in those very sections of the academy that spawn "theory."[72] Although McLuhan belongs to the mad scientist phase of the '60s, and Lyotard leans on the critique of the paradigms of modernist science produced by philosophers of science such as Thomas Kuhn, Paul Feyerabend, Roy Bhaskar, Nancy Cartwright, and the like, the two share a common and stated presupposition.[73] Namely, that the advances in electronic technology have made it possible for "the West" (McLuhan) or "telematic society" (Lyotard) to go back to the possibility of precapitalist spiritual riches without their attendant discomforts. This will turn out to be a legitimation of the only apparently decentered postfordist postmodern capitalism, and global telecommunication. McLuhan launches the argument in terms of the activities of the left brain—rational and visual— that the West has so far been engaged in—over against the activities of the right brain—holistic and acoustic—that the West is graduating to, thanks to electronic technology. To prove this he proposes to rewrite the history of scientific discoveries through the rationalist model of the tetrad, which he passes off as no more than a metaphor.[74]

According to McLuhan, although the Third World has so far oper-

---

72. Jean-François Lyotard, *The Postmodern Condition: A Report on Knowledge*, tr. Geoff Bennington and Brian Massumi (Minneapolis: Univ. of Minnesota Press, 1984).

73. Thomas S. Kuhn, *The Structure of Scientific Revolutions* (Chicago: Univ. of Chicago Press, 1970); Paul K. Feyerabend, *Against Method: Outline of an Anarchistic Theory of Knowledge* (New York: Schocken, 1978); Roy Bhaskar, *A Realist Theory of Science* (Hassocks, Sussex: Harvester, 1978); and Nancy Cartwright, *How the Laws of Physics Lie* (Oxford: Clarendon, 1983).

74. To read this move would involve us in the history of the interested differentiation between concept and metaphor, for which there is no time. I refer you to Derrida's essays "White Mythology"—white does also mean "white people" in the essay, White Mythology being reason—and "The Retreat of the Metaphor" ("White Mythology: Metaphor in the Text of Philosophy," in *Margins*, pp. 207–271; "The *Retrait* of Metaphor," *Enclitic* 2.2 [1978]: 5–33.) McLuhan's initiative is also a profound denial of language, which, assuming this model of the brain to be correct, an assumption by no means unquestioned, negotiates the gap between the so-called two sides of the brain in diversified ways that might as well be called "cultural."

ated through the holistic right brain, it is now coming more and more towards the left side. How McLuhan manages to draw this absurd conclusion from the hegemonic Moorish, Arabic, Persian, Indian, Korean, Chinese, and Japanese traditions is alas, only too easily explained, but would involve analytical polemics that have no place here. The point is that,

> certainly by the turn of the century, the Third World will implode upon itself for different reasons: too many people and too little food . . . the tetrad of the cancer cell reveals, in small, the immediate hereafter of the world: cancer enhances cell reproduction, retrieves primitive cell evolution, and transforms itself into self-consumption. . . . The new technologic man . . . must become his brother's keeper, in spite of himself. . . . Ecology shifts the "White Man's Burden" on to the shoulders of the "Man-in-the-Street".[75]

So much for tradition and modernity—Enlightenment and communitarianism. This offers a general justification for "Development," the civilizing (modernizing/democratizing) mission of the new Imperialism. "The West" is now the New World, we must take the old New World upon our shoulders. And what is going to be the model?

"EFTS (Electronic Funds Transfer System) . . . may be considered the working prototype of all . . . planetary data bases. . . . When an organization becomes the largest economic grouping in the nation, it *is* the social structure" (*GV* 108, 124). And, we might add, such financialization *is* the secret of globalization, and it can proceed unimpeded in the post-Soviet era. The rest of the book is an impassioned song of

---

75. *GV* 110, 93. The same sort of Western cultural supremacist position, supporting globalization, produces the opposite argument today: "Thanks to the interconnected world which the West has created, . . . slowing the diffusion of technology to other civilizations is increasingly difficult. . . . The diffusion of technology and the economic development of non-Western societies in the second half of the twentieth century are now producing a return to the historical pattern. . . . [B]y the middle of the twenty-first century, if not before, the distribution of economic product and manufacturing output among the leading civilizations is likely to resemble that of 1800 [China as the world's largest economy]. The two-hundred-year Western 'blip' on the world economy will be over" (Huntington, *Clash*, pp. 87–88).

praise for the Bell Telephone System and AT&T.[76] We are not surprised that the book ends on a particular nationalist/imperialist note: "Canadians and Americans share something very precious: a sense of the last frontier. The Canadian North has replaced the American West" (*GV* 147).

Of course Lyotard doesn't mess with theories of right brain consciousness. The entire argument is muted in his book. He advances the idea that each (social? historical? libidinal?—all of the above, perhaps) "condition" offers or is produced by—one cannot be sure—language

---

76. In the previous footnote, we have remarked that, in thirty years, the Western supremacist prophets of technology are making the opposite prediction, implicitly in support of not merely an economic but a political ("cultural") globalization: "[T]hese [Non-Western] societies *should* adopt recent Western ways by, for example, abandoning slavery, practicing religious toleration, educating women, permitting mixed marriages, tolerating homosexuality and conscientious objection to war, and so on. As a loyal Westerner, I think they should indeed do all these things. I agree with Rawls about what it takes to count as reasonable, and about what kind of societies we Westerners should accept as members of a global moral community. But I think the rhetoric we Westerners use in trying to get everybody to be more like us would be improved if we were more frankly ethnocentric" (Rorty, "Justice," emphasis author's). One is obliged to point out that this passage, which we have already quoted once, can undoubtedly offer an even more convenient excuse for military activity and exploitation than the argument from universalist rationality. Let us give McLuhan the benefit of the doubt as well, but nonetheless point out that his predictions about the global benevolence of AT&T have misfired. It was in response precisely to the exceptionally massive downsizing at AT&T that the former U.S. Secretary of Labor uttered the words that I quote on page 392. On the age-old binary principle that truth may be stranger than fiction, let us recall here an incident that will be lost in the annals of coincidences. At the 1995 Atlanta Olympics, celebrated on television with a nationalist triumphalism whose imagery and rhetoric strongly resembled National Socialist monumental triumphalism, and close upon the downsizng at AT&T, it was precisely the hi-tech communications compound of AT&T, predictably christened "The Global Village," that was bombed. Rorty and Huntington's new hotpeace (rather than Cold War) move would, by contrast, scrap the civilizing-mission-cum-global-villagizing alibi altogether, short-circuit the global secessionist community of high-tech managers as Macaulay's colonial subjects come full circle. To note this no longer anticipates my argument in this chapter. It transforms books such as this one, narrative footnotes and all, into the memorabilia of a previous conjuncture, attempting to catch a vanishing present.

games used for legitimization. He suggests that in the telematic or electronic world, neither the narrative of social justice (Marx), nor the narrative of development (capital), provides legitimation.[77] *Now* legitimacy is offered according to a model that generates forms—otherwise identified as short tales—without an end in view: morphogenetic, innovative, but non-teleological. Although there is no unsophisticated faith in a raised consciousness here, the acquisition of a new language-game to match the telematic or electronic condition shows a naive faith (that many share) that minds change collectively at the same speed as world structures.

Lyotard gets his model of legitimation by short tale from the oral formulaic epic tradition. The argument is itself a hidden great narrative that might go like this: under the pressure of the slow historical movement that finally led to modernity, the great oral epics such as the *Iliad*, the *Odyssey*, the *Mahābhārata*, the *Rāmāyana*, and, of course, the epics of the Nordic tradition, received narrative closure. They became long stories with beginnings, middles, and ends. When the pre-modern singer of tales actually performed the epics, however, *his* legitimization came from how many new episodes or tales he could spin, through his memory of the oral formula. We fully telematic societies, with our vast impersonal "virtual" memories, are supposed to have acceded to the pre-modern pre-capitalist condition, with none of its problems, and we can now proceed like the old singer of tales. Lyotard's model is the singer of tales from the Native American ethnic group Kashinahua. Incidentally, the old episodic epic tradition, through long historical transmogrification, is alive and well not only among the Aboriginal subaltern, but also—appropriated and re-constellated—in counter-global revolutionary theater (indeed it is the most stylized end of all politics of counter-discourse, which is theater for political mobilization), not necessarily in the hegemonic language, owing little or noth-

---

77. The narrative of Lyotard's own poignant but thoroughly Western European disaffection from Marxism is laid out in "A Memorial of Marxism: for Pierre Souyri," *Peregrinations: Law, Form, Event* (New York: Columbia Univ. Press, 1988), pp. 45–75. Incidentally, a rather astute remark about bourgeois national liberation movements and the attendant failure of decolonization is to be found on p. 27 of that book.

ing to the European novelistic tradition, about which Benedict Anderson et al. go on endlessly.[78] This phenomenon falls out of benevolent definitions of World Literature, produced in the North. Cultural politics.

It is not surprising that both Lyotard and McLuhan end on the pious

---

78. Anderson, *Imagined Communities*, pp. 28–40. The conservative and liberal, literary and political, influence of this received idea is vast in its range and scope and far pre-dates Anderson. Margaret Doody's compendious effort at breaking this modernist parochialism in *The True Story of the Novel* (New Brunswick: Rutgers Univ. Press, 1996) gives me hope that similar research can be undertaken for other great ancient traditions. There are disciplinary-historical, indeed disciplinary-historiographical, determinants why such research has not been forthcoming. In the absence of sufficient consideration of counter-examples, there is surely a degree of question-begging in the transformation into scholarly premise of what is otherwise a cliché? It must, however, be added that such scholarly investigation may soon be dismissed as "nationalist," "parochial." In the Indian case, a recent "Indian" issue of the *New Yorker* (23 and 30 June 1997), firmly founded on what I have defined as "sanctioned ignorance," has dismissed all Indian regional literatures, some with millennial histories and active contemporary scenes—Jacques Derrida opened the 1997 Calcutta Book Fair, where most of the books presented were in Bengali and other Indian languages—as a mere curiosity. I understand that *The Vintage Book of Indian Writing*, edited by Salman Rushdie, devotes itself entirely to Indian writing in English. It is sadly evident that, in the global village, the same system of (linguistic) exchange must operate; it must complete the work of imperialism. The well-known words bear repeating: "I have no knowledge of either Sanscrit or Arabic . . . I have never found one among them [the Orientalists] who could deny that a single shelf of a good European library was worth the whole native literature of India and Arabia. . . . In India, English is the language spoken by the ruling class. It is spoken by the higher class of natives at the seats of Government. It is likely to become the language of commerce throughout the seas of the East. It is the language of two great European communities which are rising, the one in the south of Africa, the other in Australasia. . . . We must at present do our best to form a class who may be interpreters between us and the millions whom we govern; a class of persons, Indian in blood and colour, but English in taste, in opinions, in morals, and in intellect" (Thomas Babington Macaulay, "Minute on Indian Education," in John Clive and Thomas Pinney, eds., *Selected Writings* [Chicago: Univ. of Chicago Press, 1972], pp. 241, 242, 249). This regrettable politics of the production of dominant "history," dominant "knowledge," is matched by the passage from the *Encyclopedia of Life Support Systems* projected by UNESCO that I have quoted in the Preface, which "defines" the Aboriginal period of human history as the "timescale of the *far past* . . . associated with *inactive* approaches in which there is no concern for envi-

note that "what knowledge there is will [McLuhan] or should [Lyotard] be available to all." Hail to thee, *pax electronica*. On the way to the "level playing field" of the World Trade Organization through the distribution of "free telecommunication" to all. The USAID logo for the Global Knowledge 1997 conference was an African woman, wearing cloth, holding a cell phone to her ear.[79]

It is also no surprise that, in the hot peace following the Cold War, it is in fact the great UN conferences that legitimate themselves, mostly in the name of woman, innovatively and morphogenetically, proliferating bureaucratic forms that seem international activism to women who will forever remain protected from subaltern *pouvoir/savoir*. But Lyotard may be wrong also in estimating that the ancient singer of tales legitimized himself by a simple and acknowledged absence of the teleologic. The thinking of the binary opposition between "linear" and "layered" or "cyclical" time is peculiarly "modern." Another version of that same uncritical assumption: that the collective subject is isomorphic with social structures of cultural explanation.[80] These self-legiti-

---

ronmental degradation and sustainability" (*Encyclopedia of Life Support Systems: Conceptual Framework* [Whitstable: Oyster Press, 1997], p. 13). I think the argument that I merely advanced in the Preface is worth repeating here, for the text will give it substance. It was of course as impossible for the Aboriginal to think sustainability as it was for Aristotle to "decipher . . . the secret of the expression of value," because of "the historical limitation inherent in the society in which [they] lived" (Marx, *Capital: a Critique of Political Economy*, tr. Ben Fowkes, vol. 1 [New York: Vintage, 1976], p. 152). Yet the practical philosophy of living in the rhythm of the ecobiome is hardly to be dismissed as "no concern"! In the age of informatics, the Native Informant, abandoned by the Postcolonial Subject, is being reconstituted for (epistemic) exploitation.

79. For a compelling account of the workings of the scam, see Najma Sadeque, *How "They" Run the World* (Lahore: Shirkat Gah, 1996), pp. 28–30. My only objection to this brilliant pamphlet is that it does not emphasize the production of the colonial subject in imperialism and thus cannot emphasize our complicity, which we must acknowledge in order to act.

80. "What if there was no other concept of time than the one that Heidegger calls 'vulgar'?" asks the Derrida from whom I learn. However peoples theorized time, the idea that the theory reflected a naturalized mindset may be a modernist mistake. As much as it is for us, for them too, a theory of time may have been a site of conflict with the "vulgar" experience of time. "What if the exoteric aporia therefore remained in a certain way irreducible, calling for an endurance, or shall we rather say an *experience* other than that consisting in opposing, from both sides

mizing modern(ization) conferences are in fact non-teleological only in terms of the telos that they so abundantly proclaim: the End of Woman as the End of Man.

For the great narrative of Development is not dead. The cultural politics of books like *Global Village* and *Postmodern Condition* and the well-meaning raps upon raps upon the global electronic future that we often hear is to provide the narrative of development(globalization)-democratization (U.S. mission) an alibi. My generation in India, born before Independence, realizes only too well that many of the functionaries of the civilizing mission of imperialism were well-meaning.[81] The point here is not personal accusations. And in fact what these functionaries gave was often what I call an enabling violation—a rape that produces a healthy child, whose existence cannot be advanced as a justification for the rape. Imperialism cannot be justified by the fact that India has railways and I speak English well. Many of the functionaries of the civilizing mission were well-meaning; but alas, you can do good with contempt or paternal-maternal-sororal benevolence in your heart. And today, you can knife the poor nation in the back and offer band-aids for a photo opportunity. Scapegoating colonialism in the direst possible way shields the new imperialism of exploitation as development.

A crude theory of national identity—we were asked by Indians, we were asked by the Somalis, we were asked by Africans—is used to legitimize this narrative and silence opposition.[82] Alternative development

---

of an indivisible line, an other concept, a nonvulgar concept, to the so-called vulgar concept?" (Derrida, *Aporias*, tr. Thomas Dutoit [Stanford: Stanford Univ. Press, 1993], p. 14).

81. "The hearts of innumerable men and women responded with idealistic fervor to [Cecil Rhodes's] clarion, because it went without saying that it would be good for Africa, or for anywhere else, to be made British. At this point it might be useful to wonder which of the idealisms that make our hearts beat faster will seem wrong-headed to people a hundred years from now" (Doris Lessing, *African Laughter: Four Visits to Zimbabwe* [New York: Harper, 1992], p. 3).

82. This monolithic notion of identity quite ignores the critical diversity within a country. I will tax your patience with a single and random example: the "Telecom Revolution" issue of *Seminar* 404 (Apr. 1993), a Delhi-based journal. (All references in this note are from this issue of *Seminar*.) The editorial politics of the journal are critical of "Development." Yet in this issue, as in others, the journal allows all sides to speak around a topic. The industry-affiliated and management-affiliated "Indi-

collectives, national-local health care, ecology, and literacy collectives have been in place for a long time, and play a critical role at the grassroots level. Why are they seldom heard? These oppositional structures are indigenous NGOs (Non-Governmental Organizations). The governments of developing nations are, with the disappearance of the possibility of nonalignment in the post-Soviet world, heavily mortgaged to international development organizations. The relationship between the government and the spectrum of indigenous non-governmental organizations is at least as ambiguous and complex as the glibly invoked "identity of the nation."[83] The NGOs that surface at the "NGO Forum"s of the UN conferences have been so thoroughly vetted by the donor countries, and the content of their presentations so organized by categories furnished by the UN, that neither subject nor object bears much resemblance to the "real thing," if you will pardon the expression.

The main funding and co-ordinating agency of the great narrative of development is the World Bank. The phrase "sustainable development" has entered the discourse of all the bodies that manage globality.

---

ans" were of course in favor of versions of the "Development" perspective. One writer, arguing for gradual privatization, writes: "One aspect of the socialistic pattern ethos was the tendency to make a sacred cow of distributive justice and the needs of the poor rural populace. . . . Even when sincere, it was the wrong priority. The rural and urban poor need food, shelter, drinking water, literacy, health care and many other basic things before they need a telephone" (M. B. Athreya, "Managing Telecoms," p. 35). Another invokes the "global village" and recommends out-and-out "foreign . . . direct . . . large-scale investment" on the model of Indonesia (N. Vittal, "Shaping a New Future," p. 39). One sole voice, from Applied Electronics Research at the Indian Institute of Technology, points at the rise of paper consumption (contrary to all predictions), to infoglut, to the fact that "the market by itself is likely to worsen rather than improve certain grievous distortions in our economy," and diagnoses "the real worry today" to be "the distortion caused by the large rent-seeking opportunities offered by technology imports" (P. K. Indiresan, "Social and Economic Implications," pp. 14, 17). Will the "real Indian" please stand up? He will be called a "consensus breaker."

83. Feminists know that every generalization is set askew if you bring in the question of woman. Think of this twist: There is a comparatively innocent pastime in a poor country of wrenching a salary-structure from international funds by establishing an NGO. Even in such cases, there is a difference between the men in, say, the large village or small town, who actually put together this local NGO, and the far less well-paid selfless rural woman workers, who often use this structure to break out of family restriction and work in the countryside.

Development to sustain what? The general ideology of global development is racist paternalism (and alas, increasingly, sororalism); its general
economics capital-intensive investment; its broad politics the silencing
of resistance and of the subaltern as the rhetoric of their protest is
constantly appropriated.

Certain European cultural and educational organizations seem in the
grip of academic "postcolonialism" on the U.S. model. Its condition
and effect are the general social refusal to the waves of asylum-seeking
economic migrants. I choose Sweden because I spoke a version of the
last few pages there, at a conference on the global village. It seems
particularly apposite for considerations of the history of the present
because Sweden is a generally "enlightened" donor country; responsible in the context of globality and global postcoloniality. It is in its
domestic treatment of the great waves of migration generated by the
so-called end of the Cold War that its enlightenment begins to crumble: postcolonial migrancy. This book forages in the crease between
global postcoloniality and postcolonial migrancy. Thus it is important
for us to note that although whenever we were cornered in arguments
by liberals of the right who brought up Cuba, Sweden was cited as the
model for the Sandinista; and whatever its image in the field of global
aid, the Swedish state was closing off welfare for the detritus of globality. It seemed to be the final demise of Second International Socialism.
I say final because we used to think it died in 1914 when the German
Social Democrats voted in war credits. As Immanuel Wallerstein and
others have pointed out, the benefits of the Second International can,
however, be felt in the state structures of Northwestern European
countries. It was these benefits that were being regulated and withdrawn by way of a 1976 amendment to the Aliens Act that introduced
"special reasons for denial." Under pressure of economic restructuring
and the New World Order, socialism in one country was crumbling in
the North as well.
　　As I have imagined, in the New World Order—or hot peace—the
hyphen between nation and state comes looser than usual; and that in
that gap fundamentalisms fester. Even Sweden could offer an example
of this. In that dreadful winter of mosque-breaking, I mused upon
Hindu nationalism: India too used to be a "socialist country with a
mixed economy." We have our King Rāma (the mythic Hindu king who
is the hero of the Hindu nationalists), and Sweden, it turned out, had

Karl XII.[84] Swedish protest against the outrage of November 30, 1992 (when a group of young Swedish racists marched under the banner of the King), was strong. Yet, unless one believed (and many do) that faith in human equality is simply a natural characteristic of the Swedish nation (it is against such convictions that underclass multiculturalism fights) I am obliged to point out that we non-sectarian Hindus had thought, until the massacre of December 6, 1992, "it can't happen here."

Although we must work to elect public officials who must soldier to shore up the benefits of the Welfare State, that alone is not the kingpin of the global future.

Let us now place cultural studies at the academic end of a spectrum that, traversing the political, vanishes at last into the necessary impossibility of the ethical.[85] Thus: cultural studies; "radical" art; mainstreaming; globegirdling movements. I explain each of the first three by way of

---

84. A footnote for non-Swedish readers: Karl XII (1682–1718) is the national hero for romantic Swedish nationalists. The last of the absolutist kings, this young militarist, masculist, charismatic monarch fought for eighteen years—valiantly, tragically, and in vain—to hold together the extensive Swedish empire. Defeated and bereft, he rode back with one companion over a thousand miles in three days to continue fighting on the home front and was mysteriously shot while inspecting the military situation from the ramparts. It may seem surprising that the man who lost the empire should be a national hero. But identity politics often attempts to renegotiate the state in the name of the nation by way of a promise of the return of the glorious repressed of history. For such "wild" psychoanalyses of the "discontent" of a "nation," an object lost can produce much more politico-ideological momentum. It should perhaps be recalled that in the narrativization of the career of King Rāmā in the epic *Rāmāyana*, it is his filial, martial, and racist heroism in unjust banishment that feeds the "national" imaginary; his actual reign is not foregrounded. Indeed, the Sanskrit denomination for India chosen for "contemporary" designation is *Bhārātā*, the kingdom of Bharata, Rāmā's younger stepbrother, who governed "in his name." "Carrying on Charles XII's task," or "re-establishing a nation to govern in Rāma's name," are better projects for psychological mobilization.

85. I have written at length of the ethical moment and the secret encounter in *IM* 197–205. Friends have asked me what I meant by writing: "'Culture' is an alibi for 'Development,' which is an alibi for the financialization of the globe. The new subject of 'culture' is the witting or unwitting spokesperson for economic restructuring" (*Travesia* 3.1–2 [1994]:286). I suppose this section is an indirect amplification of that idea.

somewhat singular cases in order to get to the last. I repeat: I remain a literary critic by training; disciplinarizing the singular. Perhaps this is also the problem with all radical interventions within firmly established conventions—academy or art—insufficiently canny not only about globality but also about their own unwitting place and rôle in globalization. Part of what I include in the next few pages is an extract from a speech addressed to Indian cultural studies academics a week before the conference in Sweden (see *IM*, xxiii–xxxi). I mention this because my elite involvement in the history of the present is as an itinerant subject of the new "Conference Culture," and I am still scratching at the rift between global postcoloniality and metropolitan migrancy.[86] Jameson's immense influence in Taiwan and China, combined with his typically U.S. confusion between China and "China"—as in his reading of Bob Perelman's poem, which I discuss above—similarly figures the trajectory of contemporary cultural studies exchange.[87]

The initial attempt in the Bandung conference (1955), to establish a third way, neither with the Eastern nor within the Western bloc in the World-System, in response to the seemingly New World Order established after World War II, was not accompanied by commensurate intellectual effort. The only idioms deployed for the nurturing of that nascent Third World in the cultural field belonged to positions emerging from resistance within the supposedly Old World Order, anti-imperialism, and/or nationalism. The idioms that are coming in to fill that space in this New World Order ascertain perhaps that the cultural lobby be once again of no help in producing a transnationally literate actor. These idioms are: national origin, subnationalism, nationalism, cultural-nativism or relativism, religion, and/or—in Northern radical chic—hybridism, postnationalism. It is this last group that produces

---

86. "Setting to Work (Transnational Ccultural Studies)," in Peter Osborne, ed., *A Critical Sense: Interviews with Intellectuals* (New York: Routledge, 1996), pp. 170–172.

87. See Zhang Longxi, "Western Theory and Chinese Reality," *Critical Inquiry* (Autumn 1992):108–109; Xiaobing Tang, "Orientalism and the Question of Universality: The Language of Contemporary Chinese Literary Theory," *positions* 1.2 (1993): 410, n. 2; and Jing Wang, *High Culture Fever: Politics, Aesthetics, and Ideology in Deng's China* (Berkeley: Univ. of California Press, 1996), p. 245. I am grateful to Steven Venturino for bringing these to my attention.

most of the cultural studies talk. Speaking to this Indian audience, full of many people who are finished in the United States as in a finishing school, I quoted Antonio Gramsci. Necessarily without a detailed awareness of the rich history of the African-American struggle, Gramsci was somewhat off the mark when he presented the hypothesis that American expansionism would use African-Americans to conquer the African market and the extension of American civilization (although the case of South Africa and the use of African-Americans in U.S. military aggression seem to support Gramsci).[88] But if his hypothesis is applied to the New Immigrant intellectuals and their countries of national origin, it seems particularly apposite today. The partners are of course, cultural studies, liberal multiculturalism, post-Fordist transnational capitalism in aid of export-based foreign capital investment, and so-called Free Trade. Globalization deconstructs the difference between this set and Development as such. (The newest entrant, the financializing female diasporic, was not to be found in the activist/academic audience in Hyderabad. She is in Cairo, in Beijing, in Women's World Banking. Madeleine Albright, weeping in Prague as she pushes NATO, one sentence in Czech and one in English, speaking as a diasporic come home at last, on July 14, 1997, dislodges the Bastille Day party at the French Embassy.)

Perhaps because of the partnership in globalization, the same students in the United States spend much time and money (fellowships abroad, recommendation letters, etc.) to get hegemonic languages just right to catch Lacan or Negri—not to mention Heidegger or Marx—but think a proposal to learn the language of a migrant group elitist. Whereas international affairs, development economics, business administration merrily traffic in transnationality, cultural studies—talking interdisciplinary, even postdisciplinary talk, will not walk the walk for transnational *literacy* (not expertise); too intimidating![89] Against such a

---

88. Antonio Gramsci, "The Intellectuals," in Quintin Hoare and Geoffrey Nowell Smith, tr., *Selections from the Prison Notebooks* (New York: International Publishers, 1971), p. 21.

89. For pedagogic suggestions see Spivak, "Teaching for the Times," in Jan Nederveen Pieterse, ed., *Decolonizing the Imagination* (London: Zed, 1995), pp. 177–202.

tough group, what I say below may seem peculiarly fragile. But, although every victory is a warning, we cannot afford to forget that the people did push the World Bank out of the Narmada Valley in India in March 1993.

In the interest of transnational literacy, then, the writer of this chapter circulates. Southern nationalism, Northern welfare state. Let us now move to the old master in his (her) benevolent mode: a site-specific art show on a migrant community in London. Unexamined culturalism represented by a roving solidaritarian artist often representing Amnesty International. When I proposed that we show evidence of the fact that ethnic entrepreneurs were pimping for the transnationals and selling their women into sweated labor (lowering wages without legal control), that collaborating artist's response was that he did not want to show sexist exploitation within the community. He wanted to show just white racism. Cultural politics. Abdication of responsibility. The migrant is all good. The whites are all bad. Legitimation by reversal. Reverse racism.

Rather than continue to celebrate the essentializing moralism of Colonizer/Colonized, White/Black, it had seemed necessary to me to make visible to the viewing public what the activists in the field knew. That the keeping apart of migrancy and development allowed the setting of thousands of unskilled female Bangladeshi homeworkers in London's East End in unwitting competition with thousands of unskilled female workers in the export-based garment industry in Bangladesh proper. The latter were "winning" because they cost £500 less per head a year and could bear witness to "women in development." (We are now approaching the women who disappear as we celebrate the hybrid feminist/individualist designer [see page 352].) Ethnicization of female super-exploitation is a global story, an episode in the same large-scale story that generates our demand for cross-culturalism: successful pimping requires it. In the event, the ignorance of artist and journalist in the pages of the *Guardian* were written up as deconstruction waylaying political art, because I had used the word "invisible" for women's sweated labor.

This kind of competition—among located women without agency— is part of the broad competition between Northern and Southern trades union as well as Northern and Southern industry in the New World Order that is an obstacle to any non-hyphenated international solidarity, cultural or economic, indeed on any front. Here is an example, but they can be indefinitely multiplied, on diverse and discontinuous levels: "In applying preferential liberalizing measures to Bangladesh, Canada may have to extend similar facilities to all other LDCs [Least Developed Countries], including Vietnam and Haiti. Vietnam in particular is a potentially serious threat to Bangladesh, though currently its privileges are restrained by the on-going trade embargo, thereby giving Bangladesh a short head-start in rationalizing its garment export activities."[90] This is what is usually described as "the free market." The World Bank and the World Trade Organization are major manipulators of such competition.[91] And you cannot work to undo the aporia between migrancy-in-racism and Development with a capital D if you are not transnationally literate, if you do not take forced competition into account. It seems interesting that the same artist now has a show called "a cemetery of images" on Rwanda (where he spent twelve days recently), which celebrates international NGOs as the only correct access route to the images of Rwandan suffering. I do not doubt the seriousness of his shock, or the sophistication of his innovations within modernist aesthetic conventions. But history is larger than personal goodwill, and we must learn to be responsible as we must study to be political. "The world has abandoned Africa," the artist said to *The Chicago Tribune* (19 Feb. 1995, p. 27). Such would not have been his feeling if he had attended one of the seminars at my university, or read the regular World Bank bulletins, on "emergent" stock markets. In the absence of global analysis, sensationalism ostentatiously withheld—his photographs were in sealed boxes, a technique I have already seen copied—repeats the tongue-clucking horror of sensationalism abundantly purveyed.[92]

---

90. "Impact Study of the Multi-Fibre Arrangement (MFA) on Bangladesh" (unpublished document prepared by Econolynx International, Ltd., Nepean, Ont., 1992), p. i.

91. For a fascinating prehistory of this conflict, see Colleen Lye, "Model Modernity: Writing the Far East" (Columbia Univ. dissertation in progress), chap. 1.

92. There seems to be an attempt at singularizing a statistic in his most recent work, focusing on the eyes of a woman witnessing horror (although for this viewer there was too much time to read the artist's pathetic text, too little time to make eye contact, the first gesture of the ethical face to face. Over against it is *Rwanda Not So*

From our academic or "cultural work" niches, we can supplement the globe-girdling movements with "mainstreaming," somewhere between moonlighting and educating public opinion. My example is an economics professor, so the intervention might seem too cut and dried. It is not without significance, I think, that a literary or artistic example of *global* mainstreaming (neither romantic anticapitalism, nor grandiose anti-imperialism) is hard to find. Aesthetics and politics? Think it through, although nostalgic U.S. nationalism does not. My example for the moment is Amartya Sen, whose defense of support for higher education in the South, in the face of the World Bank's insistence that higher education in the developing countries should be de-emphasized because it is unproductive, is a case in point.[93] At the same time, my own university has won a competition, and opened a program funded by the World Bank, where the eligible students are middle-level bureaucrats from developing countries. High-level indoctrination in Columbia University, but no higher education in Dhaka or Delhi.

In the contemporary context, when the world is broadly divided simply into North and South, the World Bank and other international agencies can divide the world into maps that make visible the irreducibly abstract quality of geo-graphy. One of the guiding principles of geography—"nation"—being inextricably tangled with the mysterious phenomena of language (synthesis with the absolute other) and birth (susceptible to both species-life [gestation] and species-being [Law])—

Innocent: When Women Become Killers (London: African Rights, 1995), arguing large-scale women's involvement in the genocide. I have heard the latter discredited on the argument that Rakiya Omaar, one of the co-directors of African Rights, is a Tutsi sympathizer. It is difficult to step from transnational literacy to a perusal of "assigned subject-positions." I thank Mahmood Mamdani for providing the material for a historical assessment in *Citizen and Subject*, and then continuing on to present an account in "From Conquest to Consent as the Basis of State Formation: Reflections on Rwanda," *New Left Review* 216 (Mar./Apr. 1996): 3–36.

93. For the defense, see *Education and Training in the 1990s: Developing Countries' Needs and Strategies* (New York: UN Development Program, 1989). For the World Bank argument, see George Psacharopoulos, *Higher Education in Developing Countries: A Cost-Benefit Analysis*, World Bank Staff Working Paper 440 (Washington: World Bank, 1980); and *Education for Development: An Analysis of Investment Choices* (New York: Oxford Univ. Press for the World Bank, 1985).

380

both discloses and effaces this abstract character.[94] But the boundaries crosshatching these new maps or "information systems" are hardly ever national or "natural." They are investment boundaries that change constantly because the dynamics of international capital are fast-moving. One of the not inconsiderable motive forces in the drawing up of these maps is the appropriation of the Fourth World's ecosystems in the name of Development. You wheel now to the "native informant" as such, increasingly appropriated in globalization.

The pre-national is now globalized, after an uneven insertion into the nation form of appearance.

A kinship in exploitation may be mobilized through the land-grabbing and reforestation practiced against the First Nations of the Americas, the destruction of the reindeer forests of the Suomis of Scandinavia, Finland, and Russia, the tree-felling and the large-scale eucalyptus planting against the original nations in India, and the so-called Flood Action Plan against the fisher folk and landless peasants of Bangladesh, honorary Fourth Worlders. Indeed such a kinship exists potentially between all the early civilizations that have been pushed back and away to make way for more traditional geographical elements of the map and the world today.

Upon the body of this North/South world, and to maintain the fantastic cartography of the World Bank map, yet another kind of unification is being practiced. As I have mentioned earlier, the barriers between fragile national economies and international capital are being removed, the possibility of social redistribution in the so-called developing states, uncertain at best, are disappearing even further. What we have to notice here is that the developing national states are not only linked by the common thread of profound ecological loss, the loss of forest and river as foundation of life, but also plagued by the complicity, however apparently remote, of the power lines of local developers with the forces of global capital. That this complicity is, at best, unknown to the glib theorists of globality-talk or those who still whinge on about old-style imperialism is no secret to the initiative for a global movement for non-Eurocentric ecological justice.

---

94. See Spivak, *Outside*, p. 69.

Why non-Eurocentric? Theorists who used to define New Social Movements as anti-systemic now say that the future lies with these movements.[95] But they are skeptical because, taking the European Economic Community as model, they see these movements as wanting state power. But if the focus is shifted from the EEC, the predicament of the developing state, in spite of the fact that it negotiates with nationalism and is still the site of justice and redistribution, is such that it is no longer the main theater for these movements that must aspire to global reach. These globe-girdling movements have to stand behind the state, plagued as it is from the inside by the forces of internal colonization and the local bourgeoisie and plagued from the outside by these increasingly orthodox economic constraints under global economic re-structuring. Therefore, there is no interest in grabbing state power as a main program in the non-Eurocentric global movement for ecological justice. Indeed, the electoral left parties often see them as insufficiently political. This instrumentality of what can only be called nationalism or even nationalist localism in the interior of a strategy-driven rather than crisis-driven globalization is certainly beyond the benevolent study of "other cultures" in the North. Upon this ground, it is easy to cultivate "postnationalism" in the interest of global financialization by way of the "international civil society" of private business, bypassing the individual states, where powerful non-governmental organizations (NGOs) collaborate with the Bretton Woods organizations with the mediation of the new UN.

And here a strong connection, indeed a complicity, between the bourgeoisie of the Third World and migrants in the First cannot be ignored. However important it is to acknowledge the affective sub-

95. If the former secretary of state Lawrence Eagleburger is a representative example, U.S. policymakers do not even know the term. On March 21, Secretary Eagleburger specified correctly that the policy areas for the twenty-first century were weapons of mass destruction, the environment, and global finance; if the United States did not develop real policy in these areas, it would soon have to be the reluctant and embarrassed policeman of the world. Is it heartening that he did not know of the detail-oriented persistent resistance of the non-Eurocentric New Social Movements? On the same occasion, the editor of *Foreign Affairs*—a South Asian diasporic—made the suggestion mentioned in note 10. He certainly knew of the existence of these movements and showed the appropriate contempt.

space in which migrants, especially the underclass, must endure racism, *if* we are talking globality, it is one of the painful imperatives of the impossible within the ethical situation that we have to admit that the interest of the migrant, however remote, is in dominant global capital. The migrant is in First World space. I am altogether in support of metropolitan activism against the race- gender- class-exploitation of the migrant underclass, but we are talking globality here. There are some severe lessons that one must learn. We have to keep this particularly in mind because this is also the export/import line from religious national parties in the South to cultural studies folk in the North. (The division is further exacerbated by the Trade Union movement in the North being asked to circumvent even the General Agreement on Tariffs and Trade by invoking "human rights violations" at the same time as, as part of economic restructuring, the World Bank demands privatization and the decimation of trade unions in the South—unions that can otherwise agitate for more humane labor laws. More about this later.)

Having seen the powerful and risky rôle played by Christian liberation theology, some of us have dreamed of animist liberation theologies to girdle the perhaps impossible vision of an ecologically just world.[96] Indeed, the name theology is alien to this thinking. Nature is also super-nature in this way of thinking and knowing. (Please be sure that I am not positing some generalized tribal mind.) Even super, as in supernatural, is out of the way. For nature, the sacred other of the human community, is in this thinking also bound by the structure of ethical responsibility. No individual transcendence theology, of being just in this world in view of the next, however the next is underplayed, can bring us to this.

Indeed, it is my conviction that the internationality of ecological justice in that impossible, undivided world of which one must dream, in view of the impossibility of which one must work, obsessively, cannot be reached by invoking any of the so-called great religions of the world because the history of their greatness is too deeply imbricated in the

---

96. For a critique of the risks of Latin American liberation theologies, see Ofelia Schutte, *Cultural Identity and Social Liberation in Latin American Thought* (Albany: State Univ. Of New York Press, 1993), pp. 175–205.

narrative of the ebb and flow of power. In the case of Hindu India, a phrase as terrifying to us as "Christian Europe," no amount of reinventing the nature poetry of the *Rg-Veda* will in this view suffice to undo that history. I have no doubt that we must learn to learn from the original practical ecological philosophies of the world. Again, I am not romanticizing, liberation theology does not romanticize every Christian. We are talking about using the strongest mobilizing discourse in the world in a certain way, for the globe, not merely for Fourth World uplift. I say this again because it is so easy to dismiss this as quixotic moralism. This learning can only be attempted through the supplementation of collective effort by love. What deserves the name of love is an effort—over which one has no control yet at which one must not strain—which is slow, attentive on both sides—how does one win the attention of the subaltern without coercion or crisis?—mindchanging on both sides, at the possibility of an unascertainable ethical singularity that is not ever a sustainable condition. The necessary collective efforts are to change laws, relations of production, systems of education, and health care. But without the mind-changing one-on-one responsible contact, nothing will stick.[97]

---

97. After I spoke of the destruction of a centuries-old ecological culture in Bangladesh through the transformation of common property and the substitution of learning by information command and the subsequent transformation of the country into the raw material for maps of investment, Andrew Steer, deputy director of the Department of Environment at the World Bank, remarked that I had been "giving a sermon" (European Parliament, 28 Apr. 1993). And yet, under the new intellectual capital agreements of the GATT, it is precisely the traditional knowledge of indigenous and rural peoples of the South that is being appropriated, patented, and "sold" back to them by the South, without any attempt at learning the attendant biorhythms that persistently deconstruct the opposition between human and natural. I am not "responsible" enough in a sacrificial tradition to be able to guess, without anthropologistic contamination, how this transfers to human/animal. It is because Derrida is not "responsible" on this terrain that his "New International" is so pretentious and feeble (see Spivak, "Ghostwriting," for extended discusssion), and he writes on *aimance* (loveness? "loveance" seems comical) in so obscure and prolix a way that it remains forever protected from setting to work (Derrida, *Politics of Friendship*, p. 8).UN conferences provide alibis for derailing these efforts in the interest of capital rather than the social in the name of an

One word on ethical singularity, not a fancy name for mass contact or for engagement with the common sense of the people. It is something that may be described by way of the following situation, as long as we keep in mind that we are (a) phenomenalizing figures and (b) *not* speaking of radical alterity:

We all know that when we engage profoundly with *one* person, the responses—the answers—come from both sides. Let us call this responsibility, as well as "answer"ability or accountability. We also know, and if we don't we have been unfortunate, that in such engagements, we want to reveal and reveal, conceal nothing. Yet on both sides, there is always a sense that something has not got across. This is what we call the secret, not something that one wants to conceal, but something that one wants desperately to reveal in this relationship of singularity and responsibility and accountability. (It would be more philosophical to say that "secret" is the name lent to the fact or possibility that everything does not go across. Never mind.) In this sense, ethical singularity can be called a secret encounter. (Please note that I am not talking about meeting in secret.)[98] Ethical singularity is approached when responses flow from both sides. Otherwise, the idea, that if the person I am doing good to resembles me and has my rights, he or she will be better off, does not begin to disclose-efface the (im)possible ethical relation. (Nor of course does an attitude of unqualified admiration for the person as an example of his or her culture.)

Among Indian Aboriginals, I know a very small percentage of a small

---

ethics about the achievement of which they know little. The worst offenders, precisely because they dare to witness, are so-called U.S. feminists whose "activism" is merely organizing these conferences with a ferocious leadership complex and an insatiable hunger for publicity. I use these violent adjectives advisedly, to warn against every achievement-of-solidarity claim coming from these quarters, to "work at the screen" of the production of the attendant images. I understand that there are plans at the United Nations for setting up a body to oversee the protection of indigenous rights to intellectual property. Such a project, now perhaps necessary, comes into being in the violence of a violation of the originary "communism" of the Aboriginal, and yoking her/him into an object of imperial protection.

98. This discussion is indebted to Derrida's scattered writings on responsibility, my understanding of which I have tried to set to work in "Responsibility." The theme of the secret is my vulgarization of a moment in Derrida, "Passions," in David Wood, ed., *Derrida: A Critical Reader* (Cambridge: Blackwell, 1992).

percentage that was "denotified" in 1952. These forest-dwelling tribals, defined by the British as "criminal tribes," had been left alone not just by the British, but also by the Hindu and Muslim civilizations of India. They are not "radicals." But because they (unlike the larger ethnic groups) were left alone, they conform to certain cultural norms, thinking, like us, that culture is nature, and instantiate certain attitudes that can be extremely useful for us, who have lost them, in our global predicament. Their active cultural script is as much on the unravel, as ungraspable, as anyone else's. We are not proposing to catch their culture, but using some residues to fight the dominant, which have irreducibly changed us. They are themselves interested in changing their life pattern, and, as far as we can, we too should be interested in following into this desire. (We will consider the Australian aboriginals' notion of a "loss of language" below.) But must that part of their cultural habit that internalizes the techniques of their pre-national ecological sanity be irretrievably lost to planetary justice in the urgently needed process of integration, as a minority, into the modern state?

In search of "our culture" in the history of the present, we encounter another "pre-national" group thrust into the dubious "unity" of a statistical collective: subaltern women. From this angle, if the non-Eurocentric ecological movement offers us one vision of an undivided world, the women's movement against population control and reproductive engineering offers us another. Here too, the rôle of the state is interpretable. Mortgaged as it is to the forces of the New World Economic Order, it bows to the dictates of international population control. When McLuhan writes that "[e]cology shifts the 'White Man's Burden' on to the shoulders of the 'Man-in-the-street'" (see page 366), he anticipates the kettle logic of today's international population control policies exactly. The blame for the exhaustion of the world's resources is placed on Southern population explosion. And hence, upon the poorest women of the South. This in turn—making women an issue—is taken as a justification for so-called aid, and deflects attention from Northern over-consumption: the two faces of globalization. McLuhan himself, did not, of course, think of women at all. But today, in the post-Soviet world, when globalization is the name of the game, a much older topos is activated. I stated in Chapter 3 that to mark the moment when not only a civil but a good society is born out of domestic confusion, singular events that break the letter of the law to instill its spirit are often invoked, and that the protection of women by men often provides such an event. In this phase of capitalism/feminism, it is capitalist women saving the female subaltern. WID—Women in Development—is a subsidiary of USAid, and WEDO—Women in Environment and Development Organization, is a generally North-controlled international nongovernmental organization with illustrious Southern spokeswomen. This matronizing and sororizing of women in development is also a way of silencing the subaltern and should be placed with the single example that is offered in Chapter 3.[99]

The academic diasporic or minority woman thinking transnationality must be literate enough to ask: *cui bono*, working *for* whom, in what interest? In "The Body as Property: A Feminist Re-Vision," Rosalind Pollack Petchesky almost quotes Farida Akhter, a Bangladeshi activist, for a few lines, only to substitute Carole Pateman, whose "critique" seems to her to have an "affinity" with Akhter but to be "more systematic and encompassing." Not content with silencing Akhter by substitution, she then proceeds to provide a "feminist" alternative to such "essentialism" by way of ethnography (New Guinea tribal women cannot be different from women exploited by postfordism in Bangladesh!), sixteenth-century Paris, "the early-modern European origins of ideas about owning one's own body" among the women of the British Levellers, and, finally, the work of Patricia Williams, the African-American legal theorist. Here is her version of Akhter:

> Farida Akhter, a women's health activist and researcher in Bangladesh, condemns "the individual right of woman over her own body" as an "unconscious mirroring of the capitalist-patriarchal ideology . . . premised on the logic of bourgeois individualism and inner urge of private property." According to Akhter, the idea that a woman owns her body turns it into a "reproductive factory," objectifies it, and denies that reproductive capacity is a "natural power we carry within ourselves." Behind her call for a "new social relationship" with regard

---

99. For a more detailed position paper on International Population Control, see Spivak, "A Reply to Gro Harlem Bruntland," *Environment* 37.1 (Jan.–Feb. 1995): 2–3.

to this "natural power" of woman lies a split between "the natural" woman and "the social" woman that brings Akhter closer to the essentialized embrace of "difference" by radical feminists than her Marxist framework might suggest.[100]

In *Capital* 1, Marx writes that the pivot of socialist resistance is to understand that labor *power* is the only commodity that is the site of a dynamic struggle (*Zwieschlächtigkeit*) between the private and the socializable. If the worker gets beyond thinking of work as *Privatarbeit* or individual work, and perceives it as a potential commodity (laborpower) of which s/he is the part-subject (since laborpower is an abstract average), s/he can begin to resist the appropriation of surplus value and turn capital toward social redistribution. As a person who is daily organizing struggles against transnationalization, Akhter expects familiarity with this first lesson of training for resistance. The trivial meaning of the proletarian is that s/he possesses nothing but the body and is therefore "free." If one remains stuck on that, there is no possibility of socialism, but only employment on the factory floor. This *Zwieschlägtigkeit* between "private" and "social" (labor and laborpower) is Akhter's "split between the 'natural' and the 'social.'" Notice that, in keeping with Marx, she uses "power," where Petechesky substitutes "woman." And indeed, there is a bit of a paradox here: that the "natural" in the human body should be susceptible to "socialization"! Why is Akhter speaking of a "reproductive *power*"? Because, as a person working against the depredations of capitalist/individualist reproductive engineering, she is daily aware that reproductive laborpower has been socialized. When she calls for a "new social relationship," she is using it in the strict Marxist sense of "social relations of production." New because the Marxist distinction between all other commodities and laborpower will not hold here. The produced commodities are children, also coded within the affective value form, not things. U.S. personalism cannot think Marx's risky formulation of the resistant use of socialized laborpower, just as it reduces Freud's risky metapsychology to ego psycho-

---

100. In Faye Ginsburg and Rayna Rapp, eds., *Conceiving the New World Order* (Berkeley: Univ. of California Press, 1995), pp. 394–395. See also Carole Pateman, *The Sexual Contract* (London: Polity Press, 1988).

analysis. Further, since its implied subject is the agent of rights-based bourgeois liberalism, it cannot think of the owned body from the proletarian perspective, as a dead end road. It can only be the bearer of the "abstract" legal body coded as "concrete." (It is of course also true that U.S.-based UN feminism works in the interest of global financialization, a.k.a. development. Here I should say of Petchesky what I have said of Brontë and Freud in Chapters 2 and 3. Akhter expresses similar sentiments more simply in "unconscious mirroring.") Incidentally, it is also possible that the split between "natural" and "social" is that split between species-life and species-being that the young Marx brings forward and displaces into his later work as that between the realm of freedom and the realm of necessity: the limit to planning. We have already touched upon this in our discussion of Jameson earlier in this chapter.

It takes the tempo of classroom teaching to show how U.S.-based feminism cannot recognize theoretical sophistication in the South, which for the former can only be the repository of an ethnographic "cultural difference." Here suffice it to say that Carole Pateman, with respect, is certainly not a more "systematic and encompassing" version of Akhter. In her excellent discussion of marriage and prostitution, Pateman extends the discussion of the transition from feudalism to capitalism; Akhter is in touch with transnational capital, which sees the body as script; you cannot answer the demand for a new social relation of production in the New World Order (post-Soviet financialization, patenting of the DNA of the subaltern body for pharmaceutical speculation, etc.) by citing anthropology and early modern Europe.[101] In-

---

101. As the reader is repeatedly informed, in this book the hidden agenda, as far as the writer can know it, is to track the "native informant." DNA patenting ("the U.S. claim to broad chunks of the human 'genome'") is the dead end road of the native informant as "new proletarian," owning nothing but his/her body, while the high road of postcolonialism accedes to bourgeois feminism. For a summary of the debates—a starting point, not a final authority—see *People, Plants, and Patents: The Impact of Intellectual Property on Trade, Plant Biodiversity, and Rural Society* (Ottawa: International Development Research Centre, 1994). The quoted passage is from p. 116. I am grateful to Farhad Mazhar for giving me this book. As I print out final copy, I come across "The Biotech Century: Human Life as Intellectual Property,"

deed, it is not a question of citing colored folk against colored folk, but understanding the analysis. But perhaps the worst moment is the use of Patricia Williams. I cannot comment on the ethico-political agenda of silencing the critical voice of the South by way of a woman of color in the North. It should at least be obvious that the abusive constitution of the body in chattel slavery is not the socialization of the body in exploitation. The matrilineality of slavery cannot be used as an affective alibi for the commodification of reproductive labor power. Williams herself makes it quite clear that today's underclass African-American wants to *feel* ownership of the body in reaction against her specific history and situation. And that situation is the contradiction of the use of chattel slavery to advance industrial capitalism. Patricia Williams writes of this use, this passage, within the U.S. juridico-legal system. She cannot be further used to "disprove" the conjunctural predicament of the South. Women in a transnational world—notice Petchesky's use of artistic representation as evidence through the diasporic artists Mira Nair and Meena Alexander, both of Indian origin; not to mention the fact that, in transnationalization, the cases of Bangladesh and India are alto-

---

by Jeremy Rifkin, in *The Nation* (13 Apr. 1998): 11–19. It is a fine fact-filled piece and, because it addresses the *Nation* readership, it speaks of "[o]ur very sense of self and society *will* likely change" in the future, and calls upon comforting parallels in European history: "as it did when the early Renaissance spirit swept over medieval Europe more than 600 years ago" (p. 11; emphasis mine). I am arguing that when someone from the Southern hemisphere exhibits this changed sense, we cannot recognize it. Although the passage quoted above has a strangely upbeat ring, by the end of the piece Mr. Rifkin is appropriately apprehensive. "What might it mean for subsequent generations to grow up in a world where . . . life itself [is reduced] to an objectified status" he asks (p. 19). The post-Nietzschean ethical move of deconstruction, where the body's metapsychological script—Derrida mentions specifically genetic script as early as the *Grammatology*—is a figure of the alterity that defines the human as being called by the other—to responsibility—rather than as a repository of an "unique and essential quality" that can only clamor for rights. Within the politico-legal calculus, "Genetic rights" is indeed "likely to emerge as the seminal issue of the coming era" (p. 19). And given the exploitation of the human genome of the Southern hemisphere, it should. We write in the hope that it will not lose its ethical overshadow, the sense of the written body as an experience of the impossible.

gether dissimilar—must beware of the politics of the appropriation of theory.

The globe-girdlers have neither time nor money for fanfare. "Links between individual women, *critical* grassroots investigation." These unemphatic phrases in the publicity leaflet of FINRRAGE (Feminist International Network of Resistance to Reproductive and Genetic Engineering), when seen in action, are signposts to that two-way road, with the compromised other as teacher when needed.

If in globe-girdling ecology, one confronts the World Bank on one side and on the other side learns to earn an (im)possible secret encounter, in this sort of feminist initiative against population control and genetic engineering, the movement faces the multinational pharmaceutical on one side, but on the other side there is, again, that slow supplementing tempo of the secret encounter. Otherwise, the metropolitan feminist too often asks all women to become like herself: citizen of a dead-end world. The recoding of the *pouvoir/savoir* of women in globality is an immense field of study. Abortion as right or murder, queerness as preference or sin, surrogacy as fulfillment or trade are only three items within it. A consideration of this epistemic upheaval cannot be launched here.

Yet another item on this necessary and impossible task of globe-girdling, resistance to Development as a strategy of alternative development: organizing homeworkers—women who work at home under conditions of "sweating."

This type of woman's labor dates from before capitalism and thus is prior in a linear trajectory. It is the exacerbation, in globality, of a residual phenomenon already accompanying industrial capitalism. Under international subcontracting and now post-Fordist capitalism, it extends from Aran Islands sweaters to high-tech computer terminal work at home. Now women all over the world are in this abstract catachrestic unity—this "common fate"—absorbing many of the costs of management, of health care, of workplace safety and the like by working at home. We must therefore learn not to treat homeworking as a peripheral phenomenon, as if it is no more than a continuation of unpaid service in the home. We must keep trying to deconstruct the breach between home and work in the ideology of our global struggle to reach this female grounding (and crowning—gendering uses class alliances by showcasing the latter) layer that holds up contemporary global capital.[102] We have to face this difficult truth: that internalized gendering by women, perceived as ethical choice within "cultural" inscription, accepts exploitation as it accepts sexism in the name of a willing conviction that this is how one is good as a woman, even ethical as a woman. We must fight to pass laws, and be vigilant that they are implemented. But the real force of the struggle comes from the actual players contemplating the possibility that to organize against homeworking is not to stop being a good woman, a responsible woman, a real woman (therefore with husband and home), a woman; and only then walk with us in a two-way response structure toward the possibility of a presupposition that is more than a task merely of thinking on both sides: that there are more than one ways of being a good woman.[103] Here "culture" constricts, and we have to join those from within the cultural inscription who join to lift the stricture.

Although no account of contemporary globe-girdling movements is complete without mentioning the struggle for justice to homeworkers, homeworking is, strictly speaking, largely an urban phenomenon. It relates to the "global village" insofar as that expression carries the tenor of the McLuhan-Lyotard claim to the appropriations of the rural. In the movements for ecological, environmental, and reproductive justice, the rural-local directly fronts the global, and "the village" is a concept-metaphor contaminated by the empirical.

The village must teach us to make the globe a world. We must learn to learn. Cultural studies is otherwise only a symptom. Electronification of biodiversity is colonialism's newest trick. When we move from learning to learn ecological sanity from "primitive communism" in the secret encounter to the computerized database, we have moved so far in degree that we have moved in kind. From the infinite care and passion

---

102. See Swasti Mitter, *Common Fate, Common Bond* (London: Pluto Press, 1986), and Carol Wolkowitz and Sheila Allen, *Homeworking: Myth and Reality* (London: Macmillian, 1987).

103. "The solution is not in the courts but in an awake, aware people" (Mumia Abu-Jamal, *Live from Death Row*, [Reading, Mass.: Addison-Wesley, 1995], p. 102).

of learning we have bypassed knowledge (which is obsolete now) into the telematic postmodern culture of information command.[104]

Robert Reich, the former U.S. secretary of labor, tells us that

> electronic capitalism . . . enables the most successful to secede from the rest of society. It is now possible for top level managers, professionals and technicians to communicate directly with their counterparts around the world to generate new products and services for other counterparts around the world without depending economically upon the productivity of lower-wage and less-skilled people. . . . The word "community" right now . . . connotes very appealing images.

---

104. What does it mean to say: "Based on this publication, UNDP will begin a process of consultations with indigenous people's organizations in Latin and Central America, Asia and the Pacific and, possibly, Africa. What we will seek is their view of the most appropriate strategies for preserving traditional knowledge and garnering acknowledgment for their innovations and contributions"? (Sarah L. Timpson and Luis Gomez-Echeverri, "Foreword," in *Conserving Indigenous Knowledge: Integrating Two Systems of Innovation*, UNDP, n.p., p. iv). You do not learn mindsets, "epistemes" if you can think υποκειμενα, by "consulting organizations." For better or for worse, by the time these people have formed organizations to consult with a UN body, the discursive formation has already been ruptured. The words "conserving" and "integrating" in the title of the pamphlet tell their own tale. For better or for worse, we are confronting an aporia here. When the work of the rupture is more or less complete—colonization through privatization securely in place—then these conservative integrations will acquire a high degree of convenience. This is the mechanism by which they will have stood the test of time. It is predicated upon the success of imperialist social transformation. This is not a Luddite position, but rather the opposite. I accept the consequences of the technicity of so-called natural intelligence. It cannot be upgraded as so-called artificial intelligence can. Prosthetic arguments for computer-aided education and theories of virtual reality seem by comparison naive. P. Cloke et al., *Writing the Rural: Five Cultural Geographies* (London: Paul Chapman, 1994) attempts to unmoor the rural from more positivistic geographies and, especially in the case of Martin Phillips, "Habermas, Rural Studies and Critical Social Theory," succeeds in rethinking the rural by public-private divisions that would be rather different from the usual. Yet, keeping themselves confined to the Euro-U.S. landscape, they are quite unable to imagine how the binary opposition between the rural-local and the virtual-global is now undone, and how new forms of resistance in the former directly impinge upon the latter, although the (non)relationship of differends, discussed in the previous chapter, remain in the cultural sphere.

But in reality, very few people live in socioeconomically diverse town-ships.[105]

This is the part of "the telematic society of information command" that drives the whole. Strictly speaking, the rubric "postcolonial" belonged to an earlier discursive formation. The "hyperreal" community of "very appealing images" coexisting with a secessionist global network is the dream of the New Immigrant.[106] The community of images can be provided by the Internet.[107] The real-time hard-copy life-style wants to enter the white or white-clone cultural enclave, the pool that largely supplies the "top level managers, professionals, and technicians" who can "secede from the rest of society . . . and communicate directly with their counterparts around the world," of whom Robert Reich speaks. This, in other words, is the spawning bed of the potential global sub-ject. This enclave can—depending upon its class connections—contain the impulse toward cultural museumization as part of its sensitivity training. The New Immigrant humanities teacher will relate to the institutionalization of this impulse.

---

105. Conversation between Robert Reich and David Bennahum on "Into the Matrix" (http://www.reach.com/matrix/meme2–02.html) (24 Jan. 1996).

106. As always, by New Immigrant I mean the continuing influx of immigrants since, by "[t]he Immigration and Nationality Act of October 1, 1965," Lyndon Johnson "swept away both the national-origin system and the Asia-Pacific Trian-gle," precisely the groups escaping decolonization, one way or another. "That the Act would, for example, create a massive brain drain from developing countries and increase Asian immigration 500 per cent was entirely unexpected" (Maldwyn Allen Jones, *American Immigration*, 2d ed. Chicago: Univ. of Chicago Press, 1992], pp. 266, 267). For purposes of definition, I have repeated this footnote in other writing. It goes without saying that, in the post-Soviet phase, the patterns of this "new" immigration have a fast-changing dynamic. The increasing legislative and electoral rage against immigrants should strengthen the argument in my essay. A superficial understanding of this rage has, however, exacerbated the unexamined culturalist competition that is my target.

107. In "Vasudhaiva," the Internet image of the "global Hindu" has been dis-cussed. There is no doubt that other "cultural origins" in new immigrancy consoli-date themselves in American hyphenation mutatis mutandis, in comparable ways. Kwame Anthony Appiah and Henry Louis Gates, Jr., eds., *The Dictionary of Global Culture* (New York: Knopf, 1997), an admirable undertaking, provides a possibility of bridging the gaps between the various groups.

The New Immigrant is as much the name of a figure as the Native Informant, or indeed, the Postcolonial—a figure woven in the folds of a text. If a figure makes visible the impossible, it also invites the imagination to transform the impossible into an experience, a rôle.[108] And, given the difference between mercantile capitalism (dependent upon exploration and conquest) and transnational financialization (the mode of production that determines "postcolonial → new immigrant"), the rôle is now experienced in real-time hard-copy. The Fuegan and the New Hollander could not read Kant. (The fact that Kant could not "read" them was considered a mark of excellence by default.) The person from Burkina Faso or Albania can refuse Fukuyama by playing the New Immigrant—liberally or critically.[109] Those are the stakes in this chapter; they will relate, let us say, to the multiculturalist efforts toward Albanians at the University of Klagenfurt in Austria.

Let us now shift the "postcolonial" into the frame of the "new immigrant" and return to the woman in metropolitan multiculturalism after our global tour. A second take.

In the previous chapters, tracking the native informant, we have scoured Europe. Here we circle with the United States as our moving base. We must therefore recognize that, since its inception, the United States has been a nation of immigrants. The winner among the first set of European immigrants claimed, often with violence, that the land belonged to them, because the Industrial Revolution was in their pocket. And the story of its origin has been re-presented as an escape from old feudalism, in a general de Tocquevillian way. It is well known that in the Founders' Constitution, African slaves and the Original

---

108. Thus Foucault's archaeological notion of a subject-position assigned in the folds of a text (*Archaeology*, pp. 91–92), is read as an invitation to self-dramatize; what Schiller supposedly did to Kant.

109. "[I]t matters little what strange thoughts occur to people in Albania or Burkina Faso, for we are interested in what one could in some sense call the common ideological heritage of mankind" (Francis Fukuyama, "The End of History?" *The National Interest* 18 [1989]: 9). I am not proposing comparing Fukuyama to Kant. The first time as tragedy, the second time as farce.

Nations were inscribed as property in order to get around the problem of the representation of slaves as wealth.[110]

These are extreme cases of marginalization where the term itself gives way: de-humanization, transportation, genocide. When situating New Immigration in the New World Order, we cannot begin in that scene of violence at the origin, but rather with the phenomenon that has gradually kicked us—marginal voices—from opposition to the perceived dominant in the U.S. cultural space. We cannot use "cultural identity" as a permission to difference and an instrument for disavowing that eurocentric economic migration (and eventually even political exile) persists in the hope of justice under capitalism. That unacknowledged and scandalous secret is the basis of our unity. This is what unites the "illegal alien" and the aspiring academic. We can reinvent this basis as a springboard for a reading/writing/teaching that counterpoints these times.

Since the "national origins" of new immigrants, as fantasized by themselves, have not, so far, contributed to the unacknowledged and remoter historical culture of the United States, what we are demanding is that the United States recognize *our* rainbow as part of its history of the present.[111] Since most of our countries were not *territorially* colonized by the United States, this is a transaction that relates to our status as New Americans, not primarily to the countries of our origin. Indeed,

---

110. "The key slogan in the struggle against the British had been 'no taxation without representation.' . . . The acceptance that slaves as wealth should entitle Southern voters to extra representation built an acknowledgement of slavery into the heart of the Constitution." Robin Blackburn, *The Overthrow of Colonial Slavery: 1776–1848* (London: Verso, 1988), pp. 123, 124.

111. Note for example, this detail about the Indian-American case, since I, as Indian resident alien, know it best. Given its focus on its so-called Hindu heritage, and the specific profile of the Hindu in the United States, the Hindu Students Council—a U.S. multiculturalist initiative with ties in India (see Mathews, et al., "Vasudhaiva")—cannot and does not claim, as do other minority groups, that the curriculum erases the Hindu historical experience in the United States. Hence it uses the general "Orientalism-cum-Aryanism" of South Asia area studies as well as the India-mystique in a still-residual bit of U.S. popular culture, to construct a culturally "unmarked" face.

and relatively speaking, our self-representation as marginal in the United States might involve a disavowed dominant status with respect to our countries of national origin; which bears something like a relationship to John Stuart Mill's admission that he was a democrat at home and a despot abroad.[112]

We must no doubt claim some alliance with liberal multiculturalism, for on the other side are Schlesinger and Brzezinski.[113] It is no secret

---

112. This is a grounding theme of John Stuart Mill, "On Liberty," in Richard Wohlheim, ed., *Three Essays* (Oxford: Oxford Univ. Press, 1975), pp. 5–141. Homi Bhabha brings this out in his conversation with Bhikhu Parekh ("Identities on Parade," *Marxism Today* 33.6 [1989]: 27).

113. These are liberal white cultural supremacists (not to be confused with either *racist* white supremacists on the one hand, or *liberal* multiculturalists on the other). This group remains embattled within the nation. "Our task is to combine due appreciation of the splendid diversity of the nation with due emphasis on the great unifying Western ideas of individual freedom, political democracy, and human rights" wrote Arthur M. Schlesinger, Jr. in *The Disuniting of America* (New York: Norton, 1992), p. 138. "Recognition both of the complexity and the contingency of the human condition thus underlines the *political* need for shared moral consensus in the increasingly congested and intimate world of the twenty-first century," wrote Zbigniew Brzezinski in *Out of Control: Global Turmoil on the Eve of the Twenty-First Century* (New York: Scribner's, 1993), p. 231. One is writing with rousing confidence in the American Dream, the other with alarm about the world. Liberal multiculturalism has become visible in the high waters of the academic mainstream, as witness Charles Taylor, *Multiculturalism and "The Politics of Recognition": An Essay* (Princeton: Princeton Univ. Press, 1992); Bruce Ackerman, *The Future of Liberal Revolution* (New Haven: Yale Univ. Press, 1992); and John Rawls, *Political Liberalism* (New York: Columbia Univ. Press, 1993). These important books can obviously not be discussed in a footnote. Here suffice it to say that the three texts have something like a relationship with the civilizing mission of imperialism seriously credited. Ackerman's position is openly based on a "we won, you lost" attitude, and it is not surprising that, at the 1994 Pacific American Philosophical Association convention, he advanced his position as a justification both for foreign aid and for the emancipation of the women of developing nations. His book is specifically addressed to the needs of the New World Order; "The Meaning of 1989" (pp. 113–123) is one of his chapters. John Rawls, by far the most astute of the three, recognizes the limits of liberalism as politics in order to save it morally and doctrinally as "the 'background culture' of civil society" (p. 14). Charles Taylor reduces the value of his thoughtful study by deducing the subject of multicultural-

that liberal multiculturalism is determined by the demands of contemporary transnational capitalisms. It is an important public relations move in the apparent winning of consent from developing countries in the dominant project of the financialization of the globe. (I am arguing that, having shifted our lives from those nations to this, we become part of the problem if we continue to disavow its responsibility.) U.S. transnational corporations (TNCs) regularly send students specializing in business administration abroad to learn language and culture. Already in 1990, the National Governors' Association Report queried: "How are we to sell our product in a global economy when we are yet to learn the language of the customers?" National language departments (including some at my own university) hook up with the business community in the name of cultural studies in order to attract not only native speakers of those languages, but especially new immigrant students from the former colonies of the particular nation-state, so that they too can enter that white-clone enclave. If we are to question this distorting rationale for multiculturalism while utilizing its material support, we have to recognize also that the virulent backlash from the current *racist* dominant in this country is out of step with contemporary geo-politics. *We* are caught in a larger struggle where one side devises newer ways to exploit transnationality through a distorting culturalism and the other knows rather little what transnational script drives, writes, and operates it. It is within this ignorant clash that we have to find and locate our agency, and attempt, again and again, to unhinge the clashing machinery. It is not enough to use "culture" as Foucault uses "power."

The basis of the sympathy and the feeling of same difference among

---

ism (difficult for me to imagine as a unicity) from the "European" historical narrative of the emergence of secularism. I now realize that this is unavoidable when the presence of these diverse elements must be secured in the matricial civil society of a so-called developed state. Duncan Kennedy's thoughtful book, *Sexy Dressing, etc.: Essays on the Power and Politics of Cultural Identity* (Cambridge: Harvard Univ. Press, 1993) shares the same characteristic. For him the time of immigration is solidly in the past (pp. 50–55). The turmoil of new Eurocentric economic immigration cannot be understood by him. With Rorty and Huntington we have sublated the opposition. Of all these writers, Kennedy is the only one who has the intuition that to be human is to be called by the other. He puts it in beguilingly down-home language: "day-to-day experiences in which it seems at the local level that everything has already been determined from somewhere else" (ix).

the various national origins of new immigration is the general social case already mentioned: that we have all come with the hope of finding justice or welfare within a capitalist society. (Even within economic migration, women often remain exilic. The definition is, as usual, gender-sensitive.) We have come to avoid wars, to avoid political oppression, to escape from poverty, to find opportunity for ourselves and, more important, for our children: with the hope of finding justice within a capitalist society. Strictly speaking, we have left the problems of post-coloniality, located in the former colony (now a "developing nation" trying to survive the ravages of neo-colonialism and globalization) *only* to discover that the white supremacist culture wants to claim the entire agency of capitalism—re-coded as the rule of law within a democratic heritage—*only* for itself; to find that the *only* entry is through a forgetfulness, or a museumization of national origin in the interest of class mobility; or yet coding this move as "resistance!" In the liberal multicultural classroom we go for the second choice, thinking of it as resistance to forgetfulness, but necessarily in the long-term interest of our often disavowed common faith in democratic capitalism: "a necessity which the agent *constitutes* as such and for which [s]he provides the scene of action without actually being its subject." This necessity is what unites us and unless we acknowledge it ("and even if we do") we cannot hope to undertake the responsibility of the emerging dominant.[114] High theory, "passing" as "resistance," is part of the problem.

The obstinate among us might want a broader perspective that does not merely *refer* to the international division of labor, but also takes the trouble to acquire transnational literacy in the New World Order that has come and is coming into being in the last decade of the second milennium: command, if you like, of a diversified historical and geographic information system; a little more than cognitive mapping. Why confuse capital's need for uniformity and rationalism with the substantive though abstract equality of democracy? Fredric Jameson exhorts us to eschew moralism and to think of capitalism as both good and bad. That too is not enough for the New Immigrant dissatisfied with ro-

---

114. Pierre Bourdieu, "The Philosophical Institution," in Alan Montefiore, ed., *Philosophy in France Today* (Cambridge: Cambridge Univ, Press, 1983), p. 2. Emphasis mine.

mancing hybridity. For the poison one has chosen to become medicine, one must learn a planning and measuring skill, and presuppose at least the half-healing of persistently arresting the disease of uncontrollable financialization. In high colonialism the native informant could often be foreclosed. What might *we* think about when urged to be native-informant-cum-hybrid-globalist?

When we literary folk in the United States do multiculturalist feminist work today, in the areas of our individual research and national origin, we tend to produce three sorts of thing: identitarian or theoretist (sometimes both at once) analyses of literary/filmic texts available in English and other European languages; accounts of more recognizably political phenomena from a descriptive-culturalist or ideology-critical point of view; and, when we speak of transnationality in a general way, we think of global hybridity from the point of view of popular public culture, military intervention, and the neocolonialism of *multinationals*.

How might we broaden our perspective into greater transnational literacy?

However transnationalized or globalized today's world might be, the boundaries of a civil society still mark out the individual state and are still nationally defined. I have suggested above that a hyperreal class-consolidated so-called international civil society is now being produced to secure the post-statist conjuncture, even as religious nationalisms and ethnic conflict can be seen as "retrogressive" ways of negotiating the transformation of the state in capitalist postmodernization. From my arguments above it would follow that feminists with a transnational consciousness would also be aware that the very civil structure *here* that they seek to shore up for gender justice can continue to participate in providing alibis for the operation of the major and definitive transnational activity, the financialization of the globe, and thus the suppression of the possibility of decolonization—the establishment and consolidation of a civil society *there*, the only means for an efficient and continuing calculus of gender justice *everywhere*.

The painstaking cultivation of such a contradictory, indeed aporetic, practical acknowledgment is the basis of a decolonization of the mind. But the disenfranchised new or old diasporic woman cannot be called upon to inhabit this aporia. Her entire energy must be spent upon successful transplantation or insertion into the new state, often in the name of an old nation in the new. She is the site of global public culture privatized: the proper subject of real migrant activism. She may also be the victim of an exacerbated and violent patriarchy that operates in the name of the old nation as well—a sorry simulacrum of women in nationalism. Melanie Klein has allowed us the possibility of thinking of this male violence as a reactive displacement of the envy of the Anglos and the Anglo-clones, rather than proof that the culture of origin is necessarily more patriarchal.[115]

The disenfranchised woman of the diaspora—new and old—cannot, then, engage in the *critical* agency of civil society—citizenship in the most robust sense—to fight the depradations of "global economic citizenship."[116] Thus we do not silence her, we do not ignore her suffering

---

115. Melanie Klein, *Envy and Gratitude* (London: Tavistock, 1957). Here of course is the basis for developing an active historical critique of the Rorty-Huntington position.

116. As I mention in Chapter 3, economic citizenship based in the world financial market, rather than individual nation-states, as site of authority and legitimacy, is a concept in Saskia Sassen's *Losing Control*. It is operative in the United States too. Look how the press attempts to make it comic. The economic citizen is not caught in the so-called democratic process, it simply commands it. Here is how "James Carville, Bill Clinton's 1992 campaign strategist, [who] made a discovery during that campaign: there was a powerful force that had to be appeased, *even though technically it did not vote*," put it. "'The damned *bond* market,' said the counselor. 'Who the hell knew it was so powerful? . . . If I'm ever reincarnated, I want to come back as the bond market. Then everybody will be afraid of me and have to do what I say'" (Adam Smith, "Investing in a Candidate," *New York Times Magazine*, 15 Sept. 1996, p. 28; first emphasis mine; all subsequent quotations are from this page). "I like the idea of the bond market as a skittish beast," the writer, who is also a Public Broadcasting Service (the national "intellectual" channel) host, continues: "a giant something like the dragon Fafner in Wagner's 'Das Rheingold,' guarding the gold ring of wealth." He domesticates postmodern capital by using an earlier semiotic field. I have commented on this in my earlier work, and also in discussing Derrida's discussion of *Timon of Athens* in *Specters of Marx*. The point here is that, in the post-Soviet New World Order, the finance market (bonds), rather than World Trade (stocks) has taken over globalization. Like most "bourgeois economists," who are descriptively correct but politically in denial, Adam Smith ("his real name is Jerry Goodman") obfuscates this issue by marking the difference, but equating the two in significance: "Now we have another election. Are the bond market's

upon some impossible hierarchy of political correctness, and we desist from guilt-tripping her. For her the struggle is for access to the subjectship of the civil society of her new state: basic civil rights. Escaping from the failure of decolonization at home and abroad, she is not yet so secure in the state of desperate choice or chance as to even conceive of ridding her mind of the burden of transnationality. But perhaps her daughters or granddaughters—whichever generation arrives on the threshold of tertiary education—can. And the interventionist academic

---

nostrils flaring? What about *the other* dragon of wealth and power, the stock market?" (emphasis mine). The same loop holds for his location of the moment of resistance: "the unanticipated." "The twin dragons have an un-dragon-like ability: they know everything in the newspapers. And everything the rest of us know, they have already digested." The antic dragon metaphor successfully screens the more with-it postmodernist figure: they are in the fastest lane (*Gedankenschnelle*, Marx had anticipated) on the information highway; electronic capital. "[S]o it is only the surprises, the unanticipated, that makes them react." But the unanticipated is not confined to the vicissitudes of presidential elections in the United States. It is also the countless "local" resistances in the globe-girdling movements. This footnote can become an infinite progression: on (20 Sept. 1996 *CBS This Morning* offered a jocular byte on Linda the Supercow, bred with the bovine growth hormone, who takes her place with the Cow that Jumped over the Moon, or Mrs. O'Leary's Cow who started the Chicago Fire (same difference here in terms of an earlier moment: scapegoating Irish immigration). Here is *Frontier:* "The crassly utilitarian norms that are guiding innovations have so far produced animals to be used as factories for producing drugs [please relate to Farida Akhter on women, page 387]. . . . Government, agribusiness, pharmaceutical and chemical capital has [*sic*] been moving apace for the last twenty years to create what may be called bio-holocaust. Those who are busy to highlight the nuclear fallout from atomic test and champion the 'No Hiroshima' movement, never really utter a word about bio-hazards which are no less bone-chilling than nuclear hazards. Changes in patent laws, particularly after the GATT agreement, are fueling aggressive efforts to monopolize novel gene combinations and the living things in which they are introduced. The once-unthinkable idea that a microbe, a plant variety or an animal breed could be owned has become accepted practice under the changed patent law imposed by the new imperialist institution WTO. . . . Not only the gene-rich ecosystems of Third World countries but also the cells and genes of indigenous peoples are now envisioned as lucrative targets. . . . The 'animal pharm' syndrome is new in many third world countries. . . . Who needs bovine growth hormone (BGH)? . . . The answer seems to be the four leading U.S. multinationals—American Cyanamide, Eli Lilly, Monsanto and Upjohn—that are promoting BGH worldwide" (24 Aug. 1996, pp. 2–3).

can assist them in this possibility rather than participate in their gradual indoctrination into an unexamined culturalism.

This group of gendered outsiders inside are much in demand by the transnational agencies of globalization for employment and collaboration. It is therefore not altogether idle to ask that they should think of themselves collectively, not as victims below but as agents above, resisting the consequences of globalization as well as redressing the cultural vicissitudes of migrancy. It may be a material challenge to the political imagination to rethink their countries of origin not only as repositories of cultural nostalgia but also as part of the geopolitical present, to rethink globality away from the U.S. melting pot. The possibility of persistently redirecting accumulation into social redistribution can be within their reach if they join the globe-girdling Social Movements in the South through the entry point of their own countries of origin. Liberal multiculturalism without global socialist awareness simply expands the U.S. base, corporate or communitarian.

Arrived here, I must acknowledge that this group is my implied readership. It is to this group that I say: all the narcissistic seductions of liberal multiculturalism notwithstanding, the so-called immediate experience of migrancy is not necessarily consonant with transnational literacy, just as the suffering of individual labor is not consonant with the impetus of socialized resistance.

The figure of the New Immigrant has a radical limit: those who have stayed in place for more than thirty thousand years. We need not value this limit for itself, but we must take it into account. Is there an alternative vision of the human here? The tempo of learning to learn from this immensely slow temporizing will not only take us clear out of diasporas, but will also yield no answers or conclusions readily. Let this stand as the name of the other of the question of diaspora. That question, so taken for granted these days as the historically necessary ground of resistance, marks the forgetting of this name. Friday? Yet here too lies the experience of the impossible that will have moved capital persistently from self to other—economic growth as cancer to redistribution as medicine: *pharmakon.*

Otherwise the binary opposition between liberal-democrat and the leaders of underclass multiculturalist activism waver to no end. For both, "culture" is invaginated in civil society. It remains a difference in vector: conservative or critical (page 333), but the designation remains "my people."[117] Here "one could reconsider . . . the pairs of opposites . . . on which our discourse lives, not in order to see oppositon erase itself but to see what indicates that each of the terms must appear as the . . . other different and deferred in the economy of the same."[118] Aboriginal groups are not outside this tug of war.

When I invoke the possibility of an alternative vision, I am not thinking to romanticize the actual Aboriginal, just as much as, unlike Kant or Fukuyama (the first time as tragedy, the second time as farce), I am not interested in finding in him a negligible example of humanity as such. The small specific group I was speaking about, is, as I made clear, a recently "decriminalized tribe."[119]

How does the Aboriginal subaltern from the intermediate group (to which Bhubaneswari Bhaduri *structurally* belonged), "act[ing] in the interests of the [dominant national group] and not in conformity to their own social being," insert themselves in this conservative/critical tug-of-war?

Reading Petchesky reading Akhter, I suggested that U.S.-based feminism could not recognize theoretical sophistication in the South. This is a lack that transnational literacy may hope to supplement. Let us see how ravaged and compromised subalterns wish to insert themselves into the metropolitan multiculturalist différance between underclass migrant and liberal democrat. This is rather different from diagnostic theories of mimicry or hybridist triumphalism as an end in itself.

To distinguish the heterogeneities of the repositories of these systems, one calculates the moves made by different modes of settler colonizations. And out of the remnants of one such settlement, we were

---

117. Bessie Head's "mad" Elizabeth figures our argument, in a version of the free indirect style: "When someone says 'my people' with a specific stress on the blackness of those people, they are after kingdoms and permanently child-like slaves"(*A Question of Power* [London: Heinemann, 1974], p. 63).

118. Derrida, "Differance," p. 17. This is Derrida's summary of Nietzsche's program.

119. It is again instructive that, mining "indigenous knowledge" or the DNA of "the subaltern body," transnational organizations are aware that the real source is the smaller and remoter groups, historically distanced from the cultures of domination, for whatever reason.

able to glean a bit of theory that gave the lie to ontopology and to identitarian culturalisms.

This lesson in theory is contained in the philosopheme "lost our language," used by Australian Aborigines of the East Kimberly region: teleological reason come full circle.[120] This expression does not mean that the persons involved do not know their Aboriginal mother-tongue. It means, in the words of a social worker, that "they have lost touch with their cultural base." They no longer compute with it. It is not their software. Therefore what these people, who are the inheritors of settler colonial oppression, ask for is, quite appropriately, mainstream education, insertion into civil society, and the inclusion of some information about their culture in the curriculum; under the circumstances the only practical request. The concept-metaphor "language" is here standing in for that word which names the main instrument for the performance of the temporizing that is called life. What the Aboriginals are asking for is hegemonic access to chunks of narrative and descriptions of practice so that a representation of that instrumentality becomes available for performance as what is called theater (or art, or literature, or indeed culture, even theory).[121] Given the rupture between the many languages of Aboriginality and the waves of migration and colonial adventure clustered around the Industrial Revolution narrative, demands for multilingual education would be risible.[122]

---

120. Kaye Thies, *Aboriginal Viewpoints on Education: A Survey in the East Kimberley Region* (Needlands: Univ. of Western Australia, 1987).

121. Recently I found corroboration of both "loss of language" and access to cultural performance in what Lee Cataldi and Peggy Rockman Napaljarri have written about the Warlpiri of central north Australia in *Yimikirli: Warlpiri Dreamings and Histories* (San Francisco: Harper Collins, 1994), pp. xx–xxii. I have no primary knowledge here, but I want to progress slowly into an understanding of "culture as translation." I presented the first fragile tendrils of this reaching out at the annual convention of the European Association for Commonwealth Literatures in Oviedo Spain in February 1996. I have no doubt that I will be involved in this for a long time to come.

122. See Gordon Brotherston, *Book of the Fourth World: Reading the Native Americas through Their Literature* (Cambridge: Cambridge Univ. Press, 1992); and, in the context of contemporary Canadian bilingualist struggle, Merwan Hassan, "Articulation and Coercion: The Language Crisis in Canada," in *Border/Lines* 36 (Apr. 1995): 30–35.

After the Massacre at Wounded Knee, Sitting Bull's cabin was taken to the 1892 Exposition in Chicago. In this case the dominant claims the right to theater, exactly the opposite of what I am commenting on. Or, not quite exactly. For the historically subordinated "had" the language to lose, which the dominant only destroyed. Somewhere in between is Buffalo Bill Cody, who acquired the freedom of Wounded Knee participants so that they could show "Wounded Knee." Today's restricted multicultural diasporists would find in Cody their prototype. It is Capital in the abstract that "frees" the subject of Eurocentric economic migration to stage "culture" in First World multiculturalism.

Buffalo Bill Cody acquired the freedom of Wounded Knee participants so that they could show "Wounded Knee." This is not an altogether ignoble rôle; on the other hand, this is not exactly the subaltern speaking. And it must be distinguished from the demands of those who know they have "lost their language." Today's multicultural diasporists would find in Cody their prototype. I would like to take up the singular case of another woman from a subaltern group, lost in a show where women are freed by the diasporic so that they can show "woman" in the theater.

Derrida had brilliantly reprimanded Lévi-Strauss for thinking that the Nambikwara were "without writing":

> Is not ethnocentrism always betrayed by the haste with which it is satisfied by certain translations or certain domestic equivalents? To say that a people do not know how to write because one can translate the word which they use to designate the act of inscribing as "drawing lines," is that not as if one should refuse them "speech" by translating the equivalent word by "to cry," "to sing," "to sigh?" Indeed "to stammer?" [French *balbutier* ← Greek *barbaros* = speak brokenly, possibly make noise rather than utter meaningful sounds; thus "barbarian"] (*OG* 123)[123]

---

123. In Coetzee's *Waiting for the Barbarians* (New York: Penguin, 1982), the impossible eruption of radical alterity is represented as the separation of subject and voice at the moment of impending death: "the noise comes out of a body that

Let us see how the gendered subaltern as native informant is silenced by a version of this same ethnographic prejudice—that the noble savage is without writing—working within the hyperreal of a universalist feminist solidarity.

In the spring of 1996, the Alexander S. Onassis Center for Hellenic Studies showed "Rifts of Silence." It was a brave piece, a moving performance, where Greek and Turkish women, nine Christians and two Muslims, spoke their female bodies, composed in Greek in a creative writing workshop organized in Komotini, "a borderland hosting Muslim, Christian, Gypsy, Armenian, and Russian-Pontian animosities," by Christiana Lambrinidis, "a playwight and scholar with degrees from Wellesley College and Brown University."[124] I do not know modern Greek. I cannot know how much of the "poetry" part of the utterances was the product of workshop editing. There was a degree of uniformity in the English translation, which may have been due to the single translator. I was troubled by the participants' giving witness to the well-placed diasporic's good politics—her workshop opened them up

---

knows itself damaged perhaps beyond repair and roars its fright. Even if all the children of the town should hear me I cannot stop myself: let us only pray that they do not imitate their elders' games. . . . 'He is calling his barbarian friends,' someone observes. 'That is barbarian language you hear.' There is laughter" (p. 121). This passage is a warning not to read a later passage, introduced by "dreams of how to die" and marked by a dystaxia precisely about elders imitating children, as the author's opinion: "It is the fault of Empire! Empire has created history" (p. 133). Living off the empire in its belly, such essentialized scapegoating is a cheap thrill. Coetzee breaks this controlled daydream—"I am not unaware of what such daydreams signify"—so unlike the loss of control earlier, precisely by the power of parataxis. The long periodic sentence released by "Empire!"—that very word is like a bell—ends with the abrupt break of a short sentence: "There is no moon" (p. 134).

124. "Rifts in Silence: How Daring Is Taught," Program Notes, n.p. Lambrinidis, a powerful and sympathetic woman, is a member of the "international civil society." "Her most recent play, 'Women of Tuzla: Mythography of Courage,' a play consisting of twenty texts from Bosnian women in a refugee camp in Tuzla, w[as to] be performed in Antwerp on March 12, 13, and 14, 1996 with the support of the European Parliament, the Green Party, and women's organizations of Belgium" ("Rifts in Silence"). I have brought up the question of the use of art as unmediated evidence in connection with the work of Petchesky.

to their femininity (and brought them to the United States). I chastised myself for being too critical of a well-intentioned project.

One woman was not with the group: Hanife Ali. By the trick of alphabetization, her name came first in the "Biographical Notes *by* the Writers/Actors" (emphasis mine). All the other entries begin in the first person. Hers begins "She is."[125] The only Gypsy, she had not been allowed by her husband to come to the United States. And, we were told verbally, she always "drew" her letters.

At the discussion following the performance, I waited till the very end and brought up the question of Hanife. I was told that after all the showings in Europe and America, I was the first one to have brought up her name. The others, I thought uncharitably, were busy with the abundantly speaking traveling subalterns.

It turned out that Hanife was no "pure" Gypsy "other." She was the cusp-person of the Gypsy community, the one who translated for the visiting American. And it was not her husband who had denied her permission; it was her partner. In the room at New York University's Tisch Center where the discussion was being held, there were quite a few women and men who lived with partners to whom they were not legally married. There was never a problem with calling such people "partners," or some equivalent word. The man with whom Hanife lived was consistently referred to as, "you would call him her husband, I suppose."

And how had he denied her permission? It transpired that everytime Lambrinidis went to Komotini, she had to approach her through him. This could "mean" many things, of course. As in the case of the Rani of Sirmur, we can only speculate. But given the international feminist tendency to matronize the Southern woman as belonging to gender-oppressive second-class cultures, this can at least be read as a decision not to buy apparent gender-freedom at the expense of race and class; a resistance, however inchoate and remote, to Ackerman, Rorty, Hunt-

---

125. Apparently some of the first-person material in her poems is translated in the third person. It seems, further, that the "stream of consciousness" passages in her Greek material is translated as straight prose poetry, whereas this is not the case with the other contributors. I am grateful to Ioannis Mentzas for helping me with this.

ington. And in the end, it was through this route that Lambrinidis had learnt that Hanife could not come.

Upon further questioning, it emerged that Hanife was not such a subservient character, after all. When she came to the workshop, she would sit neither with the Greek and Turkish women, nor with the workshop leader. She would sit at the other end of the table, in a position equivalent to the leader of the workshop.[126] She would make suggestions for the set, and had specifically suggested a red satin sofa, which was of course reported with an indulgent smile. (I myself thought that it would have added a welcome note of bizarrerie to the resolutely understated living theater decor.)

And she "drew" her letters.

When I asked for an explanation of this, many in the audience pitched in. She was closer to the very source of her experiences and was drawing unmediated ideograms. And so on. But I persisted, for in the last few years I had gained considerable experience in teaching letters to children and adults who did not come from conventionally literate backgrounds. "Conventional" is the operative word here. There is nothing proper to the letter in the convention of its writing. The letter is unmotivated. We who "have writing" perform writing in its convention. Those "newly lettered" from backgrounds "without writing" wrench the performance of writing outside of its felicity:

> Is not ethnocentrism always betrayed by the haste with which it is satisfied by certain translations or certain domestic equivalents? To say that a [person does] not know how to write because one can [describe] the act that they use to [perform] the act of inscribing as "drawing [letters]," is that not as if one should refuse them "speech" by translating the equivalent word by "to cry," "to sing," "to sigh?" (see page 405)

"The subaltern cannot speak" had referred to a single and singular example. As "Can the Subaltern Vote?" points out, "being made to

---

126. And thus is she accidentally placed in the program notes. She is at one end, equivalent to the three Americans, who are at the other end, and are also described in the third person. In between are the official testimonialists, in the first person.

unspeak" is also a species of silencing. That is the mode in which Hanife, the new native informant, is made to support the new global hyperreal: the North is solidary with the South; "woman" is important, not race, class, and empire. "Gender *and* development," not "women *in* development," is the new slogan. The text of textile, the very last movement of this book, will not tell us any different. The woman whom the charismatic diasporic designer "silences" is not there at all, although much visible on the small screen.

Re-enter the web of textile in conclusion.

First, the briefest glimpse of the cultural self-representation of Britain in textile in colonialism; next, a look at contemporary Northern "social dumping," with the female child worker, specifically in the garment industry, being made to support the new global hyperreal. This bit is written without scholarly research, with the fieldwork contacts developed by an embarrassingly part-time activist.[127] It is also New York that brings me an awareness that some of us must continue to place the South in the history of its own present, instead of treating it as a locus of nostalgia and/or human interest.

Doubletake: a coda of how I can temporize my own critical path during the writing of this book. But textility escapes the loom into the dynamics of world trade.

First, then, colonial discourse; a reminder of *Jane Eyre* in the making. If I had wanted simple cases of rampant neo-colonialism in the fashion world, I could have chosen more blatant examples such as the renewed inscription of an unrecognizable "India" and "Africa" into fashion after the films and videos of the Raj and in the legacy of *Out of Africa*. I am, however, predictably more interested in the implicit working of the axiomatics of imperialism in the vocabulary of radical critique. I have, therefore, chosen a subtler example. In order to narrativize the consti-

---

127. "Fieldwork" for me has come to mean something else, working in the field to learn how not to formalize too quickly, for one's own benefit in learning to resonate with responsibility-based mind-sets; rather than a generally hasty preparation for academic and semi-academic transcoding.

tution of the self-consolidating other by way of a discourse of fashion freely assuming a radical aesthetic vocabulary into those axiomatics, I will step back a couple of centuries and refer more elaborately to a text I have cited in an earlier chapter: Rudolf Ackerman's *Repository of Arts, Literature, Commerce, Manufacture, Fashion and Politics*, published from 1809 to 1829 (see page 119).

Each issue of this compendium magazine contained (along with market reports, bankruptcy lists, and detailed lists for a convincing life-style for the aspiring British bourgeoisie) sketches of the season's fashions, of course, but also what was called "Allegorical Presentations containing examples of British Manufactures."

Typically, each design is filled in by drawings of British Palladian architectural themes, whose general connotation, with vague invocations of Rome, is Empire. They "mark deeper, more enduring claims upon a national present as part of a past."[128] Holding up the design are, generally two, sometimes three, massive and decent Graeco-Roman figures, genitalless if male, draped if female. The design itself is two, three, or four pieces of actual textile material, manufactured presumably in nineteenth-century Britain. It is eerie to handle these actual pieces of cloth or silk, more mutely empirical than human bones, nearly two hundred years old, less overtly legitimized than the genuine antique in a museum, so precariously fixed on these brittle pages. It seems curious that no explanation or key is ever given for the "allegories," although they are specifically called that, in issue after issue. Short descriptions of the textile material are all that is provided, with brief hints for their proper use. The stuff is often coarse imitations of Chinese or Indian material, although they are never called that, of course. What significance might we assign to this specific denomination— "allegory"—if the figure so designated is not going to be interpreted? Is an allegory, in the sense accessible to Rudolph Ackerman, not precisely an at least second-level semiotic code that exists to be decoded?

---

128. I have turned Charles W. J. Withers's statement around ("Place, Memory, Monument: Memorializing the Past in Contemporary Highland Scotland," *Ecumene* 3.3 [July 1996]: 327), because, in colonialism, the colonizing impulse appropriates and reterritorializes a "past" to temporize itself more grandly. Marx notes this in "Eighteenth Brumaire" in terms of the bourgeois revolution's reterritorializing of postfeudal Europe.

We can, of course, assume that these "allegories" simply allude to the presence of a vast organization of signification, under the authority of the Empire, which charges the female British class subject's everyday self-representation with a lexical burden far beyond her own grasp; a reminder, as it were, of the responsibility simply of being such a subject in the geopolitical context. (One can imagine Jameson's pedagogic project of "cognitive mapping" for the male U.S. class subject to be a good countermeasure to corresponding ideological formations in operation today.)[129]

There can also be another indexical reading of this ostentatious foregrounding of the "allegorical" status of these representative designs. They dissimulate another narrative—the text of the *production* of these collages (in the strictest sense—these are "stick-on" affairs) in an unwitting allegory of the fixing of the imperial textile trade as a special place of signification, a referentially privileged discursive field.[130] The entire design marks something like "management," covering over the exploitative and violating aspects of colonialism by ostentatiously pointing at some other rusing thing. This "thing" is the representational material, at least five times "historically" inscribed (Greek to Roman to Christian through English to Imperial), which foregrounds itself but is not decoded. The "real" bits of cloth, in the English simply "stuff" or "material," insert themselves into the acknowledged realm of representations, empire of signs, and are coded carefully. There are no named subjects (Van Gogh, Warhol, Portman, Perelman in Jameson's essay) celebrating the coding, and no sign of a euphoric utopia. This "metaphoric" utopia is part of the "concept" of imperialist commerce, the manipulation of the consumer for the cloth trade. In my fancy, the allegorical material signals mutely to the indefinite possibility of the thickening or complicating of the signifying potential of the bits of material as such, themselves literal metonyms—one might mark the

---

129. Anne McClintock, *Imperial Leather* (New York: Routledge, 1996) elaborates this.

130. "To dissimulate is to feign not to have what one has" (Baudrillard, *Simulations*, p. 5). Baudrillard is writing of disease. Shall we speak of colonial greed as a disease, as Marshall McLuhan will speak of "too many people and too little food" as a "cancer [that] enhances cell reproduction . . . and transforms itself into self-consumption"? Cotton, that labor-intensive industry that was the motor of the large slave acquisitions in the American South, is part of the same disease.

oxymoron—of a *text fabricated* out of *raw* material and then staged in a theater of exploitation that provided "the individual (female) subject" a model to imitate. Fashion is not the normative narrative of aesthetic styles in the cultural dominant isomorphically lockstepped to a narrative of modes of production. This is rather the story of the production of the dominant self-representation of the clamorous "individual subject," the *source* of cultural explanations. Jameson's or Baudclaire's stunning intuitions about "our world" as well as the trendy self-assured patter of the New York radical can be serialized with this. Today's "social dumping," by contrast, silences the new subaltern.

Increasingly and metaleptically, transnationality, a new buzzword for cultural studies, is becoming a synonym for the movement of people. To recode a change in the determination of capital as a cultural change is a scary symptom of cultural studies, especially feminist cultural studies. Everything is being made "cultural." I hope the reader will notice the difference and alliance between this statement and Jameson's (page 315).

As the United Nations Library on Transnational Corporations tells us, a transnational corporation is an enterprise that owns value-added activities in two or more countries.[131]

The word "value" stands for me here as a mockery of both Marx and academic marxism, which apparently gave the Marxist notion of "value" a decent burial by showing that it was not theoretically viable (just as, in terms of another kind of theory, Hindess and Hirst laid "mode of production" to rest).[132] Yet because "value" or "worth" (German *Wert*) (for Marx the "simple contentless form" that allows any kind of measure-

---

131. "Transnational corporations are enterprises which own or control value-added activities in two or more countries. The usual mode of ownership and control is by foreign direct investment (FDI), but TNCs may also engage in foreign production by means of corporative alliances with foreign firms" ("Introduction: The Nature of Transnational Corporations and Their Activities," in John H. Dunning, ed., *The Theory of Transnational Corporations* [New York: Routledge, 1993], p. 1). I am grateful to Sonali Perera for bringing this to me when I wanted "the simplest possible definition."

132. I have discussed the question of value at greater length in Spivak, "Scattered Speculations on the Question of Value," in *In Other Worlds*.

ment) is as slippery a word as "supplement," it now measures the difference between the "cheapness" of *their* labor and the expenses of *our*
enterprise: value-added—in a hyperreal electronic simulation of mercantile capitalism.

The relations of production in a TNC is FDI—foreign direct investment—which is finessed as the occasion for the transfer of a package of
resources—technology or management skills—over national boundaries and, thus, once again provides support for the global hyperreal; via,
sometimes, the silenced subaltern's relocated great-granddaughter. I
should like to use a humble anecdotal example to prove this obvious
point.

Before I do so, let me explain why, whenever I speak of transnationality and alternative development, I move to Bangladesh. As long as the
work was focused on colonial/postcolonial discourse, general knowledge of Hindi (the national Indian language), basic knowledge of Sanskrit (the Hindu classical language), bilinguality in Bengali (mother
tongue) and English, and the politico/cultural mulch of a conscientized
diasporic allowed me to plough along, as long as I did not profess South
Asian expertise. As interest developed in the history of the transnational
present, two things came clear: First, that the real front against globalization was in the countless local theaters of the globe-girdling movements. Bangladesh, a small subcolonial country that came into being
when transnational electronic exploitation was beginning to take hold,
offered a much more active terrain of resistance; although India certainly had its share of large, well-publicized movements. I also realized
that if one wanted to intervene—rather than stop at exchanging ideas
with the activist leaders—and learn from those seemingly "local" initiatives, one had to know the language well enough to move with dialectal
shifts, and that for me was Bengali, the national language of Bangladesh.

The difference between India and Bangladesh in terms of transnationality was rather important. Indian independence was the first
large-scale negotiated decolonization. The 1947–1949 constitution was
written at the inception of neocolonialism, when one could imagine
that the nascent Bretton Woods organizations would dispense global
social justice. That constitution provided for an economic structure
somewhat protected from the depredations of international exploitation. And the situation of West Bengal, my native state, where Bengali

is the local language, was doubly different because its government had been Left Front for more than two decades. Thus neither India (with its protected economy), nor, and especially, West Bengal (with its Left Front government) was a fertile field for foreign direct investment. (The situation is of course rapidly changing under post-Soviet economic restructuring.)

To place the export-based garment industry in transnationality, then, allow me to use a bland everyday happening that I put in a frame for a seminar on feminist cultural studies, to explain that transnationality did not primarily mean people moving from place to place, although labor export was certainly an important object of investigation.

The example is Gayatri Spivak on a winter's day at an opening in New York's New Museum. I was wearing a jacket over a sari, and, to layer myself into warmth I was wearing, under the jacket, a full-sleeved cotton top, rather an unattractive duncolored cheap thing, "made in Bangladesh" for The French Connection. By contrast, the sari I was wearing, also made in Bangladesh, was an exquisite woven cloth produced by the Prabartana Weavers' collective under the coordination of Farida Akhter and Farhad Mazhar. Until I saw these weavers at work, I had had no idea how the *jāmdāni*s that I had so admired in my childhood and youth were fabricated. It is complicated teamweaving and simultaneous embroidery at speed, hard to believe if you haven't actually seen it, certainly as delicate and difficult as lacemaking. As a result of the foreign direct investment related to the international garment industry, the long tradition of Bangladeshi handloom is dying. Prabartana not only subsidizes and "develops" the weavers' collective, but it also attempts to undo the epistemic violation suffered by the weavers by recognizing them as artists. This is not merely a reversal, but also a displacement of Ackerman's *Compendium;* there is no allegory-referenced transcoding here. Thus I was standing in the museum wearing the contradiction of transnationalization upon my body, an exhibit, though no one knew it. No persons or groups had moved much to make this possible. There *can* be labor migrancy associated with transnationalization, but in fact it is not necessary—with postfordism and export processing zones. The demographic determining factors for labor migrancy lie elsewhere, and are beyond the scope of these concluding pages.

What I am about to write is not a commentary on the traffic in children in general. It is not even about child labor everywhere, the eradication of which would be an unquestionable good. It is about making human rights a trade-related investment issue. It is about the easy goodwill of boycott politics. It is about the lazy cruelty of moral imperialism. It is about doing deals with local entrepreneurs, themselves bound by their own greed and the greed of global trade resulting in no labor laws. It is about finding in this a justification for a permanent involvement in a country's affairs through foreign aid. Once again, the writer's plea is for the recognition of the agency of the local resistance, as it is connected with the peoples' movements that girdle the globe.

With the comparative opening of the markets after the signing of the General Agreement on Tariffs and Trade in 1994, it seemed as if Northern markets would be swamped with garments manufactured in the South. This was the reason why, after the closure of GATT in 1995, and the establishment of the World Trade Organization as independent and permanent watchdog, what is now called "social dumping" began to be enforced on specifically the export-based *garment* industry: boycott their products because they employ child labor. Nationalism and racism were deployed to unify Northern labor behind management in this regard. The infamous Harkin Bill passed by the U.S. Senate in 1993 ("Child Labor Deterrent Act of 1993") was based on a report compiled by the AFL-CIO, which often works in conjunction with the American Asian African Free Labor Institute (AAAFLI) to undermine labor demands in the South. Betwen the first and final versions of the act, an NBC television report revealed to the public that 52 percent of FDI-related clothing manufactured in Bangladesh (not my sari, in other words, but my French Connection top—the sari is yet another textile text, in history and economics) came to U.S. markets; next *The Wall Street Journal* reported that Wal-Mart, the biggest retail sale outlet in the United States, had lost $0.75 per share as a result of importing clothing manufactured by child labor.[133]

---

133. Cited in Seema Das Seemu, "Garment Shilper Shishu Sromik: 31 Octoberer par kee hobey?" *Chinta* 4.15 (30 Oct. 1995). In the same issue, Shahid Hossain Shamim brings up the important question of the discursive constitution of

At a gender studies meeting at my own university, an explanation of this interested use of "child labor" as a way of blocking export from developing countries was summarily dismissed in an absurd cultural relativist way by a U.S.-nationalist (domestic) welfare sociologist: as if child labor was just a part of Bangladeshi culture and we should not interfere! It is beyond the scope of this book to develop further the social textuality of this one impatient gesture. Suffice it to say that precisely as colonialism made and makes interested use of patriarchy, transnational capital makes use of racism and thus divides a trades union movement already focused on little more than job security in the rank-and-file and management-collaboration at the top (incidentally inhabited by the U.S. academic, willy-nilly, thanks to the Yeshiva decision of the U.S. Supreme Court in 1980). The sorry story of the Second International is played out again with a global focus.

Complicity with patriarchy puts the blame for the exhaustion of the world's resources between the legs of the poorest women of the South, leading to pharmaceutical dumping of dangerous coercive long-term contraception, an unexamined population control rigorously to be distinguished from family planning. The transnationally illiterate benevolent feminist of the North supports this wholeheartedly, with "ignorant goodwill."[134] Any critique is put down to a culturally conservative position *against* family planning.

Similarly, complicity with racism allows the benevolent transnationally illiterate liberal to stop at supporting sanctions against Southern garment factories that use child labor. (It will occur to people of goodwill that the point may be to make the labor less "cheap"—raise the cost of variable capital—by implementing fairer labor laws, but that is, in the "hot peace," a pipe dream; the World Bank is a force against unionization. I am no longer sure of this, given Rorty's easy duping [see note 59]. The real project is, clearly, that "[a]dult workers in the United States and other developed countries should not have their jobs imper-

the "child," much debated in metropolitan feminist theory in connection with the ideology of motherhood. Here one risks censorship for fear of instant dismissal as "a supporter of child labor"!

134. So that I am not accused of abuse, I hasten to add that this phrase is taken from Yeats, "Easter 1916," *Collected Works* (New York: Macmillan, 1963), p. 203.

iled by imports produced by child labor in developing countries" ["Child Labor Deterrent Act of 1993," clause 9]. The U.S. government is not duped.) Human interest videos are already in place, such as the one that lyrically films the backbreaking day of the Pakistani girl who makes bricks, with an "empowering" voiceover relaying her Urdu; and the one about the carpet-weaving boys. Their viewers are neither willing nor able to read or hear the countless dispassionate factual brief testimonies given by the so-called child workers to labor activists in the field.[135] The children certainly do not present their working conditions

---

135. These videos ("Rights and Wrongs: Child Labor," nos. 305 and 414, International Center for Global Communications Foundation) are basically about bonded labor, whereby, in "repayment" of a debt, adults and children are supposed to work under slavery conditions, at such savage rates of interest that the labor sometimes continues over generations. They are excellent videos, and the U.S. public should certainly be educated. Their message to the citizen as consumer is boycott goods produced by child labor, although checking labor conditions in production is next to impossible. Children are shown producing bricks and carpets. Oriental rugs are a luxury item. And, although Pakistan is singled out, India certainly, and China, Turkey, Iran, Tibet, Nepal and the like, probably, use child labor. It is highly unlikely that the conspicuous consumer will suddenly boycott carpets, or that a fall in the carpet trade is going to bring about the infrastructure for children's education. Iqbal Masih, a ten-year-old boy who attempted to break through into resistance, was separated from local resistance groups and transmogrified into a glorified native informant. He was brought to Boston, given a Human Rights award, picked up by U.S. national television ("I want to be like Abraham Lincoln"), and then simply sent home. Thus thrust into unprotected visibility, he was killed by a bullet. Although it has not been proved that this was a trade-related killing, his death can serve as an allegory of how the question of the children themselves is separate from the spectacle of U.S. benevolence. Both videos are frames for documentaries produced by the Swedish videographer Magnus Bergmar. The documentaries do point at local resistance, although the women's speech is inadequately translated, sometimes drowned out by voiceover. (Sweden is an enlightened donor country.) The frame material, spoken by an African-American woman, really focuses only on the garment industry, which is rather different from bonded labor ("traditional" in some South Asian countries), since the work is performed for foreign direct investment under sweatshop conditions. (My text deals with the micrology of "social dumping," specifically in the garment industry, in Bangladesh.) The tone is consistently U.S. nationalistic—even the language is not politically correct—using "underdeveloped" where approved usage dictates "developing." It reaches a high when the talk-show hostess Kathie Lee Gifford

favorably. But, in the absence of any redress or infrastructural support, they find the remote American decision to take their jobs away altogether confusing.[136]

What happens to the innocent restricted enthusiasts who cannot see beyond an easy moralism and hear how the child is made to "unspeak"

---

weeps on camera, beginning her conversion to child-labor-activist-cum-watchdog-for-boycott-support from purveyor-of-child-labor-produced-garments-under-her-label speech with the words, "I was born in a wonderful country." By contrast *The Small Hands of Slavery* (New York: Human Rights Watch, 1996), produced by two anonymous interviewers, remains focused on bonded labor in India and never mentions the garment industry. Many of the sources are concerned academics. (The first footnote reference, Tanika Sarkar, both of whose parents were my teachers, went to the same school and college in India as I did.) The ignored "critical voice of the South"—local non-governmental organizations—is often recorded and correctly assigned the task of helping and policing the state. The bulk of the pamphlet, also quite correctly, faults the Indian government for criminal negligence of laws and constitutional guarantees that are in the books, the oldest for seventy-six years! Nothing can condone this, of course. However, when this excellent book cites the role of the World Bank, once or twice, as part of the local NGOs' analyses, it never integrates it into the general problematic of the bank's economically restructuring imperatives for the State, which severely hamper redistributive activities. And, when this book is cited under "bonded labor" on the Internet (Alta Vista has 1,246,120 matches to the phrase), the only imperative— "What You Can Do in India"—is boycotts and sanctions. Under "Activism," for bonded labor, a representative entry is "Ethical Considerations in Corporate Takeovers," which turns out to be an account of a church-based seminar attended by plenty of CEOs, think tanks, and banks, among them the World Bank and Chase Manhattan. No Human Rights Watch will ever comment on the followup record of these financial institutions. Capitalism *is* better than bond-slavery. But is exploitation the only way out? *Small Hands* records one single instance of "community-based savings and credit program" that "will strike a significant blow against bonded child labor" (p. 147). This, alas, is the door through which credit-baiting without infrastructural reform enters under globalization, for the sake of the complete financialization of the globe; or, it provides justification for the opening of the world's poor to the commercial sector, when the officers of such sponsors of microenterprise are asked to offer examples of social involvement. We have already taken note of Salman Rushdie's dismissal of Indian-language literatures. And Chapter 2 has already pointed at Mahasweta Devi's analysis of the postcolonial polity in "Pterodactyl." Here I will cite a passage from "Douloti the Bountiful": "There are people for passing laws, there are people to ride jeeps, but no one to light the fire" (Devi, "Douloti," in *Imaginary Maps* [New York: Routledge, 1995], p. 88). Rushdie would dismiss this as "parochial." It should still be pointed out that, by contrast to the triumphalist U.S. moral imperialism, the represented agent of judgment, the

herself? For reasons already given, I can only discuss the Bangladeshi case. Any theoretical conclusions must be made mutatis mutandis. The case of Bangladesh will not fit the entire South. It is easier to speak of postnationalism when one participates in a single-state civil society in the metropolis. Economic descriptions of developing countries depend on the history of the nation upon the geopolitical map. A ready cosmopolitanism can be an alibi for geopolitics.

In a chapter going back at least to Rudolph Ackerman, we must consider the text of capital as it manipulates textile. The garment industry did not establish itself upon uninscribed earh to inaugurate "development" for women. It is certainly true that women who would otherwise have been homebound went to work in factories and thus entered the world. But to enter a world without infrastructural support is not an unquestioned good; that is where the caring reader must reintroduce the singularity of ethics. In this respect, the encouragement of women's microenterprise—credit-baiting with no infrastructure—is a comparable phenomenon in the arena of finance capital.

When the boycott began, the factories sometimes employed children with their ages altered. When the children did lose their jobs, they became twenty-four-hour domestic workers for little or no pay, or perhaps prostitutes—perhaps they starved. Sometimes the girl children had come to work with their older female relatives. This is, of course, last-ditch "child care." But with no infrastructural followup, the loss of this was pretty crucial for the child worker, silenced subaltern. And the words of the Harkin Bill: "The employment of children under the age of 15, often at pitifully low wages, undermines the stability of families" (clause 8) seemed an incomprehensible mockery to her.

---

character who speaks the quoted words, is Bono Nagesia, a resistant Aboriginal and, as the last instance of the judgment of the criminal state there is the laboring body of the Aboriginal woman, which passes judgment on independent India: "Filling the entire Indian peninsula from the oceans to the Himalayas, here lies bonded labor spread-eagled, kamiya-whore Douloti Nagesia's tormented corpse, putrefied with venereal disease, having vomited up all the blood in its desiccated lungs. Today, on the fifteenth of August, Douloti has left no room at all in the India of people like Mohan for planting the standard of the Independence flag. . . . Douloti is all over India" (p. 93).

136. Most of these accounts are to be found in handwritten field reports. I have heard some of these first-hand. For a small but representative sampling (in Bengali), see the detailed report published in *Chinta* 5.16–17 (15 May 1996).

Early in 1995, the Bangladesh Garment Manufacturers and Exporters Association entered into an agreement with various indigenous NGOs, with a statement of support from the International Labor Organization and the U.S. Ambassador to Bangladesh, that the parents of the children in question would be financially compensated and the children given primary education. Not big money—about $7.50 a month at the current rate of exchange; and, for education, "[t]he unit cost is approximately U.S. $36 per child per year."[137]

Let us first note that the "education" to be provided is materially useless, because it is in no way continuous with the national education system. Admission into the schools has been made contingent upon showing the keypunch machine IDs that had gone with their jobs. Since two or more years often pass before the former child worker even sees one of these schools, the card is not always available. Fifteen parents in the Pyarabag shantytown in Dhaka said that they were ready to give up their monthly allowance if the children were admitted without those useless attendance cards (not photo IDs), but they were refused. The recalcitrant and reduced payment of compensation requires constant agitation by the fieldworkers. The numbers reported on television from time to time bear little relation to reality. Understandably, there is extreme reluctance to part with information. The righteous anger of a Harkin Bill or the benevolence of a long-distance benefactor lose all plausibility when confronted with the actual indifference and deception that follow the dismissal of these children. My own direct involvement is with the nature, quality, effectiveness, and relevance of the teaching in ground-level schools. I can say with conviction that those questions cannot be raised in the hapless situation that follows the so-called restoration of the sanctity of childhood at the direct foreign investment garment factories.[138]

I promised my informant Seema Das, who did the actual footwork, that I would mainstream this information in the mainest of streams, so that the video campaign of pathos, sensationalism, and human interest would not make the girl unspeak herself. (Both she and I have an un-

---

137. "Proposal for the Provision of Primary Education for Displaced Under-Age Workers," mimeograph, Gonoshajja Sangstha. Apr. 1995, p. 10.

138. Unpublished documentation available upon request.

justified confidence in the power of yet another academic book outside the field.) When I spoke, with some hesitation (and upon request), to a small group of writers, journalists, university students and intellectuals in Dhaka about deconstruction, Seema left the group quietly after the first ten minutes. Intellectual, activist, and entrepreneur are not necessarily united there, as they are not here. And in that three-point division, I place this trivial book.

In this chapter I have tried to examine the interplay between multiculturalism and globality. Is postmodernism the cultural logic of late capitalism? Wading through this debate, I have worked up through the textural stream of textile to let myself be encountered by that other book that I have had to keep pushing away while I have revised this one. I could perhaps re-state Jameson's thoughtful title this way: the casualties of economic postmodernization are not culturalists; they teach us to keep our glance fixed at the crossed-out capital logic of postmodernity. The point may not be to think well and ill of capitalism at the same time. Please decide rather, as the web of text and textile roll out asymptotically, if one can stitch together Kant's *Third Critique* and documents like *Chinta* (see notes 133 and 136) without the everyday or corrupt version of the switch from determinant to reflexive judgment—primary/secondary, data/research, fieldwork/ethnography, native-informant / master discourse—that we perform in our studies and classrooms; and the other way around.[139] Marx could hold *The Science of Logic* and the Blue Books together; but that was still only Europe; and in the doing it came undone.

------

139. It must be acknowledged that Derrida attempted such a stitching in *Glas*, in the interest of a critique of phallogocentrism. But that, too, is only European-focus. His attempts at intervening in globality (*Specters*) or at speaking for (from?) Algeria or as Franco-Maghrebian must remain on another register.

The Setting to Work of Deconstruction

The term "deconstruction" was coined by the French philosopher Jacques Derrida (1930–) between the two appearances of the material that, in its second version, became part of *De la grammatologie* (1967). In its first appearance, in 1965–1966, as a series of reviews in the French journal *Critique*, it contained the term "destruction." The word owed something to Martin Heidegger (1889–1976), especially to the projected second part of his *Kant and the Problem of Metaphysics* (1929), which was to have had the title of *The Fundamental Characteristics of a Phenomenological Destruction of the History of Ontology under the Guidance of the Problematic of Temporality*. The naming of "deconstruction," then, is, among other things, something like a definitive modification of a Heideggerian program. It should be remembered that Heidegger was a strong reader of Friedrich Nietzsche (1844–1900), in whose work also "destruction" played a special part.

This essay interprets deconstruction specifically in Jacques Derrida's work.

Deconstruction, as it emerged in Derrida's early writings, examined how texts of philosophy, when they established definitions as starting points, did not attend to the fact that all such gestures involved setting each defined item off from all that it was not. It was possible, Derrida said, to show that the elaboration of a definition as a theme or an argument was a pushing away of these antonyms. Such demonstrations involved tracking the rhetorical maneuvers performed by words such as "supplément" in Jean-Jacques Rousseau (*Grammatology*), or *pharmakos* and *hama* in Plato and Aristotle ("Plato's Pharmacy," 1968, in *Dissemination:* "Ousia *and* Grammè: *Note on a Note from* Being and Time," 1968, in *Margins*). What these maneuvers seemed to conceal was the track of the first *différance* (a word coined by Derrida)—the setting off described above—as well as its continuation—the pushing away, also described above. This track, of a previous differentiation and a continuous deferment, is called "trace."

The structuralists had emphasized language, or rather sign-systems, as explanatory models of the last instance. In *Of Grammatology*, Derrida submitted that Ferdinand de Saussure (1857–1913) had not been able to admit in his work the implications of his insight that the origin of the possibility of language was the capacity to articulate differences among linguistic and verbal units rather than some internalized knowledge or reservoir of chunks of language. In "Speech and Phenomena" (1967, in *Speech and Phenomena*), Derrida argued that Edmund Husserl's (1859–1938) phenomenological notion of "the living present" entailed the subject's death, since it implied a present extending before and after any given subject's livingness or life. In "Différance" (1968, in *Margins of Philosophy*), an important theoretical intervention presented before the Société française de philosophie, he named this inevitability of the differentiation (setting off) from, and deferment (pushing away) of the trace or track of all that is not what is being defined or posited, as *différance*. It was a "necessary but impossible" move (a formula to become useful for deconstruction); because, in being named, *différance* has already submitted to its own law, as outlined.

This irreducible work of the trace not only produces an unrestricted economy of same and other, rather than a relatively restricted dialectic of negation and sublation, in all philosophical oppositions. It also places our selfhood (ipseity) in a relationship of différance with what can only be "named" radical alterity (and thus necessarily effaced). This rich essay suggests certain rules of thumb for the deconstructive philosopher.

In "Signature Event Context" (1977, in *Margins*), Derrida suggested that J. L. Austin (1911–1960), in founding Speech Act theory, which investigates language as not merely statement but act, acknowledged the rôle of force in signification. He could not, however, admit the consequences of his irreducibly "locutionary" perception of language: that truth-telling is also a performative convention, producing an effect not limited to the transference of a semantic content. Each effective situation alters the truth iterated. "Speech" shares the structure we commonly call "writing," which is given over to the openness of use in unmarked and heterogeneous situations.

Derrida's kinship with other philosophers such as Immanuel Kant (1724–1804), Georg Friedrich Hegel (1770–1831), Søren Kierkegaard (1813–1855), Friedrich Nietzsche, Sigmund Freud (1856–1939), Edmund Husserl, Walter Benjamin (1892–1940), and Emmanuel Levinas (1906–1995), to name only a few, has been established. But it cannot be denied that, all through these philosophical essays and his other early work, the Heideggerian theme of the priority of the question (of Being, to all ontological investigation, as indicated in the projected title of the Kantbook 2, for example) is never absent. It is therefore significant that, in "Violence and Metaphysics: An Essay on the Thought of Emmanuel Levinas" (1964, in *Writing and Difference*), Derrida embraced Levinas's critique of Heidegger, even as he subjected it to a dismantling similar to the ones already mentioned.

Such critical intimacy—rather than the usual critical distance—is a mark of affirmative deconstruction.

In "The Ends of Man" (1968, tr. 1972, in *Margins*), Derrida once again laid out his own project by distinguishing it from Heidegger's. That essay was perhaps Derrida's first articulation of the argument, continued in *Of Spirit* (1987) and beyond, that after the famous turn or *Kehre* of the thirties, Heidegger betrayed his insistence that, at the start of all investigative questioning was a prior question that could not be adequately answered. It is to be noted that Derrida's important essay is open-ended, signaling toward an indefinite future.

At the conference entitled "The Ends of Man" held in 1982 at Cerisy-la-Salle, Derrida described a movement in his own work as well. It was a turn from "guarding the question"—insisting on the priority of an unanswerable question, the question of *différance*—to a "call to the wholly other"—that which must be differed-deferred so that we can posit ourselves, as it were. As we have seen in our discussion of radical alterity in "Différance," a similar double program was figured in his work from the start. The movement now announced by Derrida—

understood as an other-directed swerve away from mere philosophical correctness, alerts us to a greater emphasis on ethics and its relationship to the political.

An early text prefiguring the turn is "Declarations of Independence" (1976, tr. 1982, in *New Political Science* 15). Here Derrida, borrowing terminology from Austinian Speech Act theory, argues that the constitutional subject is produced by the performative of a declaration of independence, which must necessarily state itself as already given, in a constative statement of national identity. (For the important distinction between "performative" and "constative," see J. L. Austin, *How to Do Things with Words* [1962].) This text illuminates Derrida's many incursions into the question of philosophical nationalisms, and indeed his readings of all acts of institution.

"Force of Law: the 'Mystical Foundation of Authority'" (1989) can be identified as the central statement of Derrida's ethical turn: from "guarding the question" to a "call to the wholly other [radical alterity]." If we consider *Given Time* (1991), *The Gift of Death* (1992), and *Aporias* (1993) with it, we will see some major ideas in play.

The earlier work—broadly grasped as the necessary yet impossible argument from *différance*—insisted that all institutions of origin concealed the splitting off from something other than the origin, in order for the origin to be instituted. This was a making indeterminate of any answer to questions of origin, as to what it was from which the supposedly original thing or thought, in description or definition, was being differantiated. It is this question, instituted at the origin, that had to be guarded or kept as a task in the first phase of deconstruction.

If Derrida's own ad hoc periodization is to be credited, the second phase is more "affirmative," a word he used in the mid-seventies. The affirmative call or appeal to the wholly other presumably addressed whatever may be prior to the trace of the other-than-origin instituting the origin; most often through the new concept-metaphor of "the experience of the impossible." If radical alterity was earlier conceived of as a methodologically necessary presupposition that is effaced in being named, now the category of presupposition is deliberately blurred and made more vulnerable as "experience."

Now such imponderables as justice and ethics can be seen as "experiences of the impossible:" experiences of radical alterity. As such, they are undeconstructible, for to open them to deconstruction is to open them to the law of *différance*. Decisions based on such experiences involve aporias, or non-passages. Aporias are distinguished from logical categories such as dilemmas or paradoxes; as experience is from presupposition. Aporias are known in the experience of being passed through, although they are non-passages; they are thus disclosed in effacement, thus experience of the impossible. Formalization is acheived by passing through or "solving" aporias, treating them as practical logical problems. In the second phase of deconstruction, then, formalizations can therefore be seen as a halfway house toward the open end of a "setting to work." (The last theme had been broached in a text of the early eighties: "The Principle of Reason: The University in the Eyes of its Pupils," 1983, invoking not only a Heideggerian text of the same title, but also the older philosopher's famous rectorate address of 1933.)

"Law is not justice, [although] it is just that there be law," says "Force of Law" (notice that the connective has to be supplied; Derrida philosophizes interactively—the reader provides connections in order to make the text work—because he uses the rhetorical dimension of language).

Justice cannot pass in a direct line to law; that line is a non-passage, an aporia. Yet justice is disclosed in law, even as its own effacement. This is the peculiar nature of the deconstructive embrace. Ethics as "the experience of the impossible" and politics as the calculus of action are also in a deconstructive embrace. The space of being is the gift of time (so to speak)—we fall into time, we begin to "be," unanticipatably. To call it a gift is to solve that aporia by thinking of some other (one) that "gives" time. Thus life is lived as the call of the wholly other, which must necessarily be answered (in its forgetting, of course, assuming there had been a gift in the first place in the subject's unanticipatable insertion into temporality), by a responsibility bound by accountable reason. Ethics as experience of the impossible—therefore incalculable—is lived as the possible calculus that covers the range between self-interest and responsibility that includes the politico-legal. Justice and law, ethics and politics, gift and responsibility are structureless structures because the first item of each pair is neither available nor unavailable. It is in view of justice and ethics as undeconstructible, as experiences of the impossible, that legal and political decisions must be made, empirically scrupulous but philosophically errant. (Even this opposition, of course, is not tenable to the last degree.) Here is a summary, made in view of the possibility that to summarize is to efface necessary discontinuities: The calculus of the second item in each pair such as the ones named above is imperative for responsible action, always in view of this peculiarity. These pairs are not interchangeable, but move on an unconcatenated chain of displacements. In each case, the "and" in the pair opens up the task entailed by what Derrida had formalized in "The Supplement of Copula: Philosophy before Linguistics" (1971): that the copula "and" is a "supplement"—that slippery ("undecidable") word that he had first tracked in Rousseau—covering an indefinite variety of relationships, since the supplement both supplies a lack and adds an excess. As "Principle of Reason" and "*Mochlos*; or, The Conflict of the Faculties" (1980, tr. 1984, in *Logomachia*) argue, if responsible action is fully formulated or justified within the system of the calculus, it cannot retain its accountability to the trace of the other. It must open itself to being judged by a setting to work that cannot be defined from within the system. One instantiation of this is to be found in the discussion of messianism in *Specters of Marx* (1993).

Is there a relation of reinscription between this "setting to work" and the rather carefully defined "*ins Werke setzen*"—setting or positing in the work—to be found not only in *Being and Time*, but most particularly elaborated in the later Heidegger's "Origin of the Work of Art" (1935, tr. 1950 and 1960), a piece discussed by Derrida in *The Truth in Painting* (1978)? In this brief compass, suffice it to say that whereas in Heidegger every conflict of worlding upon resistant ground is posited *in* the lineaments of the work of art as work, for Derrida what the word "work" marks is outside and discontinuous with the formulations of philosophy as an end in itself, with a logical systematicity that is mere calculus. This idea of a work outside or beside the disciplinary work of philosophy is laid out by Derrida, thematically as well as rhetorically, in parts of essays entitled exergue or parergon. In "Of Grammatology as Positive Science," Derrida had repeatedly stated that grammatology could not be a positive science because the philosopher could not or would not "venture up to the perilous necessity" of facing unanswerable questions at the origin. It is as if the mature philosopher now acknowledges the peril and steps out of "the shelter" he had invoked in the earlier text. At the origin now is the necessary experience of the impossible, which is lived as a calculus without guarantee.

Literature—more specifically, poetry—remains a figure that provides an experience of the impossible; as suggested in the discussion of

APPENDIX

Paul Celan's work in *Schibboleth* (1986). Derrida's earlier discussions of Stéphane Mallarmé ("The Double Session," 1970, in *Disseminations*), Francis Ponge (*Signsponge*, 1975), and Maurice Blanchot (in *Parages*, 1986), circulate and cluster around this position. His intuitions about the visual arts are not inconsonant, but less assured. *Truth in Painting*, 1978, focusing on "Peasant Boots" by Vincent Van Gogh, the picture that Heidegger considers in the essay mentioned above, asks the simple question: what would be "idiom" (a subsystemic production of meaning) in art, a signifying logic that could lead to a calculable meaning system, which would then provide a springboard for any investigation of "truth" in painting?

It is a curious fact that many so-called ethno-philosophies (such as the Tao, Zen, Sunyavāda, the philosophy of Nāgārjuna, varieties of Sufi, and the like) show affinities with parts of deconstruction. This may relate to their critique of the intending subject. Insofar as they transcendentalize extra-subjective authority, they are not quite "the same thing" as deconstruction. But insofar as they locate agency in the radically other (commonly called "fatalism"), the ex-orbitancy of the sphere of work in the ethical as figured by Derrida has something like a relationship with them. Thus, although Derrida himself is at best cautious about resemblances between his own system and any "theologies" ("Onto-Theology of National-Humanism: Prolegomena to a Hypothesis," 1992, in *Oxford Literary Review* 14.1–2), deconstruction after the turn, in its "setting-to-work" mode, may be of interest for many marginalized cultural systems as a development from within the aftermath of the Kantian Enlightenment, whereby their own calculuses, dominant in reaction, have become as compromised (especially gender compromised) and stagnant as anything perceived by Heidegger in the Kantian line itself. Of course, the possibility of these connections remains dubious as long as the "setting-to-work" mode remains caught within the descriptive and/or formalizing practices of the academic or disciplinary calculus. And as long as the othering of deconstructive philosophy remains confined to discourses at least accessible to related academic disciplines (such as literature, architecture, theology, or feminism), it gives rise to restricted but useful debates.

Currently the most critical and dynamic enclave of marginalized cultural systems is in counterglobalist or alternative-development activism (just as the financialization of the globe is the most robust vanguard of the Enlightenment). In this area, the "setting-to-work" mode of deconstruction breaks hesitantly into an active resistance to the inexorable calculus of globalization, where "democratization" is often a description of the political restructuring entailed by the transformation of state capitalisms and their colonies to tributary economies of rationalized financialization; or it may be engaged in displacing the binary opposition between economic growth and well-being by proposing alternatives to "development." These efforts do not, of course, produce a sustained formalized theory that is recognizably deconstructive. This is the risk of a deconstruction without reserve.

The aporia of exemplarity is most keenly felt here. The subjects and collectivities that produce the examples are in an aporetic bind with those who, far from and often ignorant of their field of work—globalization and development—yet produce the systematic formalizations. The situation may be described by way of the definition of irony (akin to our general sense of allegory) given by the U.S. deconstructionist literary critic Paul de Man (1919–1983): permanent parabasis or sustained interruption from a source relating "otherwise" (*allegorein* = speaking otherwise) to the continuous unfolding of the main system of meaning—both the formalization of deconstruction and, on another level of abstraction, the logic of global development. Further, if the splitting off of socialism from capitalism is perceived as grounded in the prior economy between self-preservation and the call of the other, this setting-to-work of deconstruction without reserve, quite unlike the failures of establishing an alternative system, may be described as a constant pushing away—a differing and a deferral—of the *capital*-ist harnessing of the *social* productivity of capital.

The structureless structure described above, where an item of a pair is both available and unavailable in an experience of the impossible, can be aesthetically figured in various ways. In the novel *Beloved* (1987), Toni Morrison places the "Africa" that is the prehistory of Afro-America or New World African—to be strictly distinguished from the named contemporary continent—in the undeconstructible experience of the impossible. As this call of the other is lived in the calculus of an Afro-America conscious of its rights, *Beloved* figures this disclosure, in effacement, as a maternal sacrifice, "not to be passed on." History requires it on the impossible passage, and does not stay the mother's hand. The central character kills her child to save it from the white world. The ring of the covenant—the brand on her own nameless slave-mother's breast—does not ensure continuity. Historiality is not changed into genealogy.

Two matters should be mentioned in conclusion. First: Derrida's own position, as a Franco-Maghrebian—being of Algerian Jewish extraction he has described himself this way—tends not toward global struggles in a general rather than a deconstructive way: in the call for an economically aware human rights vision, advanced in *Specters*. His more elaborated arguments are drawn from migrancy: the double responsibility of the New Europe (*The Other Heading*, 1991), a critique of "on topology"—something like (multi)cultural identitarianism—"an axiomatics linking indissociably the ontological value of present-being [*on*] to its *situation*, to the stable and presentable determination of a locality, the *topos* of a territory, native soil, city, body in general," *Specters*, p. 82); and figures of the absolute *arrivant* (the undeconstructible figure of alterity which is lived as any calculable diaspora). When he refers to his early years in Algeria ("Circumfessions," 1991, in *Jacques Derrida*), Derrida is not speaking of a country that has undergone a recent national liberation and is therefore not "postcolonial" in any precise sense. And second: the scholarship on Derrida's ethical turn and his relationship to Heidegger as well as on postcolonialism and deconstruction, when in the rare case it risks setting itself to work by breaking its frame, is still not identical with the setting to work of deconstruction outside the formalizing calculus specific to the academic institution.

Aborigines: of Australia, 26, 49, 352, 385, 404; of India, 141–142, 144, 145, 228, 229, 236, 384–385, 419n

Abraham, Nicolas, 5

Absolutist State (Anderson), 92

abyss, of nature, 14–15, 21, 23, 24, 30

Ackerman, Rudolf, 119, 410, 414, 419

Adam, John, 213, 225, 226

aesthetic judgment, 135

Aesthetics (Hegel), 39

Africa, 52n, 92, 94, 172, 196, 357, 430; colonial, 202; cultural identity and, 8; encounter with capitalism, 72; Hegel on, 43; national identity and, 371; origin of name, 188

African-Americans, 376

Agacinski, Sylviane, 27n

agency, 71, 85, 108; in alterity, 293; capitalist, 182; class, 261, 262; disavowal of, 9; in ethno-philosophies, 429; feminist, 183; humanism and, 322n; individual and collective, 77; of local resistance, 415; native and, 194; representation and, 260; suicide and, 299; of women, 193, 270, 295

Ahearn, Edward, 155

Ahmad, Aijaz, vii, 41n, 273n

Akhter, Farida, 386–387, 388, 403, 414

Albright, Madeleine, 376

Algeria, 18n, 358, 431

alienation, 59

allegory, 53, 127, 132, 137, 140, 156n, 180, 324, 346, 410–411, 414

Allegory of Reading (de Man), 34

alterity, 8, 76, 196, 328; absolute, 241; categorical imperative and, 123; native informant and, 352; radical, 290, 425, 426

Althusser, Louis: on class instinct and position, 255n, 257; on culture, 315; on ideology, 252–253, 254, 356; on philosophy, 16–17, 247

Althusserians, 99

Amin, Samir, 37, 59, 86, 89, 93, 101

Anderson, Benedict, 369

Anderson, Perry, 72, 78, 86, 88, 93

Aneignung (appropriation), 59, 60

animal, boundary with human, 121, 125, 187, 285

anthropology, 29n, 67, 153, 170, 196, 242, 245, 388; ethnicity and, 60; ethnography/ethnology and, 73n, 191; native informant in, 49, 142; structuralist, 109–110

anthropomorphism, 16, 18, 32–33

Anti-Oedipus (Deleuze and Guattari), 58, 103, 105–106, 110, 217n, 251–252, 263, 266n

apartheid, 190

aporias, 175, 217n, 326, 327; class instinct and position, 255n; in *Foe* (Coetzee), 183, 184; as non-passages, 427; racism and Development, 378; subject and object, 304

appropriation, 59, 320, 342

architecture, 331, 332, 334, 337, 429

433

archives, 202–203, 204, 239
Ariel (Shakespearean character), 117–
    118, 131, 137, 165, 352
Aristotle, 196n, 197n, 370n, 424
Arjuna, 39, 45, 50–51, 54, 55, 56
Arnold, David, 163
Aronowitz, Stanley, 70
art, 256, 316, 404, 428; Hegel on, 40, 41;
    in India, 48n; Kant on, 19–20; Mini-
    malism, 347–351; postmodern, 324,
    325
Aryans, 63, 64, 229, 232, 236
Asia, 94, 357
Asiatic Mode of Production (AMP), 71–
    73, 79, 80, 110, 290; Deleuze and Guat-
    tari on, 107–108; diagrammed, 343;
    imperialism and, 89–90; in India, 86–
    88; Marx's view of, 85, 102; primitive
    communism and, 82–83; transgressive
    potential of, 92–97; value-form and,
    101. See also modes of production
Attridge, Derek, 174, 183, 186, 187
aufheben/Aufhebung. See sublation
Austin, J. L., 424, 426
author, death of, 98
auto-affection, 52
autobiography, 6, 132, 153, 208
autocritique, 121n, 170, 200
autoreferentiality, 318
Aztec civilization, 117

Balibar, Etienne, 68n, 69n, 330n
Bandung conference (1955), 375
Bangladesh, 380, 386, 389; child labor in,
    416, 419–421; contrast with India, 413–
    414; ecological culture in, 383n; gar-
    ment industry in, 377, 378, 419–420
Bank of England, 101, 102, 179
Bardhan, Kalpana, 361
Barthes, Roland, 98, 336, 342–345, 347,
    349
Baudelaire, Charles, 148–149, 150, 152–
    157, 159, 250–251, 334, 342, 412
Being and Time (Heidegger), 428
Benjamin, Walter, 157, 162, 250, 425
Bhabha, Homi, 190, 200n

Bhaduri, Bhubaneswari, 306–308, 309,
    310–311, 403
Bhagavadgītā. See Srimadbhagavadgītā
Bhaskar, Roy, 365
binary oppositions, 116, 186, 332, 392n;
    growth and well-being, 430; intention
    and form, 349; male and female indi-
    vidualism, 133; multiculturalism and,
    402; philosophy and literature, 112;
    positivism/essentialism and "theory,"
    282–283
Birch, Geoffrey, 211, 212, 213, 217, 226–
    227, 229; Rani of Sirmur and, 231,
    233, 234, 237
Blanchot, Maurice, 429
body-without-organs, 76, 105, 106, 252,
    328
bourgeois society, 31, 174, 221
Brahman caste, 57, 230, 234–235, 286n,
    297, 298
Brecht, Bertolt, 334
Bretton Woods organizations, 95, 276,
    381, 413
Britain (England), 7, 8, 99, 119, 154, 172;
    feminism in, 282; fictive, 127; Raj in In-
    dia, 235–236, 270; Roman Empire and,
    246; scholarship in languages, 162n;
    textiles and colonialism, 409, 410
Brontë, Charlotte, 115, 121, 136–137

Caliban (Shakespearean character), 117–
    118, 130, 137, 165, 352
capital, 80, 100, 212, 245n; capitalist's re-
    lation to, 77, 258, 262; finance, 220;
    homeopathic nature of, 101; industrial,
    100; international division of labor
    and, 269; national economies and, 380;
    normative logic of, 72; value and, 103
Capital (Marx), 74, 75–76, 79, 99–103,
    327, 328, 329, 387
capitalism, 3n, 67, 68, 330, 398; capitali-
    zation of land, 87, 179; colonialism
    and, 87; emergence of, 108; exploita-
    tion and domination under, 263; impe-
    rialism and, 281; industrial, 201, 274,
    317; Marxism and, 83; multinational,

316, 330, 341; patriarchy and, 233n, 237, 296, 304; post-industrial, 84; re-coding of, 354n; Robinson Crusoe and, 177; socialism and, 245; sublation and, 327–330; as supplement to "weak" feu-dalism, 90; technology and legitima-tion of, 365. *See also* political economy; postfordism

Cartwright, Nancy, 365

castes, 57, 58, 141, 165–167, 230, 286n, 298

castration, 134

catachresis, 53, 142, 179, 254, 285; defined, 14; desire as, 251–253; graphe-matic, 322; History as, 331; Indian nationhood and, 141n–142n; psycho-analysis and, 207; as timebound nam-ing, 188; value and, 105, 251

categorical imperative, 123, 136

Celan, Paul, 184, 195n, 429

Chaudhury, Ajit K., 273

child labor, 415–418, 419–420

China, 72, 82, 83, 88, 249n, 344; "China" as referent, 246, 331–335, 375

"Chinese prejudice," 280

chrematistics, 100n

Christianity, 63, 137–138, 305n; ethics of, 123; Hegel on, 43; imperialism and, 216; Kant on, 31; liberation theology, 382, 383

chromatism, 164–166, 291

chronotypography, 66

citizen, figure of, 31

civilization, 61, 91, 93, 117

civil society, 31, 116, 142n, 309, 316; cul-ture in, 402; limits of rational struc-tures of, 353; metropolitan, 356; postnationality and, 399, 400

Cixous, Hélène, 176

class consciousness, 77, 258, 261, 269, 282

classes: alliances and formation of, 60; capitalism and, 80; class composition of colonizing power, 213, 214; colonial elites, 359; formation of, 231; in India, 50, 240; Marx on, 257–262; telematic secessionist, 392–393

classism, 32n, 52n

class struggle, 80

clothing, 337–342, 347, 414

coding, 103, 105–106, 108, 109, 181, 245, 247

Cody, Buffalo Bill, 405

Coetzee, J. M., 174–175, 177, 178, 182, 186, 191, 194, 405n–406n

cognition, 10, 22–23, 25, 26

Cold War, 360, 370

colonialism, 1, 88, 177, 274; biodiversity and, 391; capital and, 246; chromatism and, 167; civilizing mission of, 223n; defined, 172; denegation of, 63; in In-dia, 201, 202, 205, 209–211, 224, 240, 241, 295; Kant's view of, 13n; national-ism and, 60–61, 82; politics and eco-nomics, 225; scapegoating, 371; in South Africa, 190–191; speech and, 187; unequal development and, 85; value coding of, 190

commodity-form, 68n, 75, 78, 177, 317, 387

communism, 76, 80, 82–83

Communist Manifesto, The (Marx), 67, 74, 101

community, 120, 260, 261

companionate love, 116

comparative scholarship, 8

Confessions (Rousseau), 135

consciousness, 261, 273, 274. *See also* class consciousness

consumerism, 275–276

Coomaraswamy, Ananda, 296

cosmograph, 54

creative imagination, 119, 132

credit-baiting, 223n, 237, 243n, 255, 259, 419

Critical Theory, 99

Critique of Judgment, The (Kant), 10–14, 19–36, 57

Critique of Practical Reason, The (Kant), 10

Critique of Pure Reason, The (Kant), 10

cryptonymy, 5, 41, 111

Culler, Jonathan, 282

cultural dominants, 313–315, 338, 347, 348
cultural relativism, 6
cultural studies, 196, 208, 374–375; languages and, 397; national (postcolonial), 99, 359–360; North-South exchange and, 200; transnationality and, 104, 414
culture: initiation into humanity, 30; Kant on, 12–13; material and spiritual, 61; multiculturalism and, 334, 353–358; nature and, 264, 385; postmodernism and, 312–320; primitive man and, 14; reason and, 31
"Cygne, Le" (Baudelaire), 148–154

Darstellung/darstellen (re-presentation), 257, 258–259, 260, 263, 264, 276, 364. See also representation
decoding, 190
decolonization, 40, 358, 359, 360, 362n, 363, 399, 413
deconstruction, 1, 3n, 110–111, 195, 198; appropriations and, 35; axiomatics of imperialism and, 37; battle with Marxism, 314–315; catachresis and, 251–252; challenge of, 98; critics of, 244; (de)centering of subject and, 323–324; de Man's version of, 18–19, 30; in Derrida's work, 423–431; everyday life and, 238; exotic texts and, 52n; Heidegger and, 212–213; "historical moment" and, 331–332; imperialist, 125; Jameson's appropriation of, 320; of the male, 113; of Marx, 81, 92–93, 104; of non-European development models, 96; postcolonial double bind and, 173; reading of philosophy and, 17; of reason, 34; speech of the native and, 190, 191; of subjectivity, 27n; "third world woman" and, 304; of "three worlds" concept, 70; tropological, 24–25, 34, 147, 151, 163, 168; writing and, 38
Defoe, Daniel, 174, 177, 179, 187, 192
Deleuze, Gilles, 58n, 253, 272, 279; on coding, 105, 107–108; critique of psychoanalysis, 207, 217n; on desire, 103,
252; on identity, 261; Marxism and, 263, 273; Other as Subject, 268, 269; representation and, 255–256, 258; "third world" and, 277; on workers' struggle, 248, 249–250
de Man, Paul, 16, 18–19, 27n, 34; on allegory, 156n; on irony, 430; on Schiller, 31; wartime writings of, 106n
democracy, 88, 92, 143, 240, 257n
denegation, 59–60
Derrett, J. D. M., 288
Derrida, Jacques, 1, 17, 69, 184, 204, 247; critique of ethnocentrism, 279–281; deconstruction and, 98, 175, 423–431; différance concept, 3n, 175; on ethics, 5, 15n, 175, 304n; on ethnocentrism, 405; as exemplary postmodernist, 320–325; on friendship and margins, 193–194; "hieroglyphist prejudice," 280, 286; on history, 238; on Kant, 34–35; Marrano and, 17n–18n, 280n; on Nietzsche and Nazism, 97; on Sartre, 171; on travelogue, 350; on writing, 52n
Descombes, Vincent, 27n
desire, 20–21, 103, 105, 249, 264; as catachresis, 251–253; coincident with interest, 258; faith and, 24; Krishna's view of, 51; law and, 216, 217; psychoanalytic transference and, 206; reason and, 35; site of, 207; woman's, 302
desiring-production, 105, 106, 108
determinant judgment, 26, 28
deterritorialization, 279
development, 275, 291, 296, 304, 368, 371, 430; ecosystems and, 380; feminism and, 388; gender and, 377, 386; justifications for, 330, 366; resistance to, 390; "sustainable," 372–373. See also capitalism; colonialism; imperialism
Devi, Mahasweta, 115, 140–141, 143, 310. See also "Pterodactyl"
Dewey, John, 355n
Dharmāsastra, 235, 286, 291, 292–294, 298, 301
dialectic, 39, 83, 316, 326, 330; Asiatic Mode of Production (AMP) and, 97; colonizer-colonized, 192; Jameson on,

315; of law and history, 55; in Marx, 74, 75, 90; master-slave, 272; *Sri-madbhagavadgītā* and, 58

différance, 3n, 112, 175, 241, 424; alterity and, 425, 426–427; of capitalism and socialism, 67, 70, 83, 85, 89, 245; knowledge and, 199

difference: Asiatic Mode of Production (AMP) and, 72, 79, 82; effacement of, 86; identity and, 340, 341, 344; knowledge and, 199; Marx's views of, 73, 79, 82; narrative of history and, 90; original, 198n; race vs. language, 73n; racial, 187; reading of philosophy and, 17; self-identity of normative subject and, 78; sexual, 29, 38n, 105, 274

discursive field, 120–121, 200

discursive formations, 3n, 103

divine law, 189

domination, 263, 278, 293

Duval, Jeanne, 152n, 153

Eagleton, Terry, 122, 124, 322

East India Company, 86, 148, 156, 164, 203, 211, 213, 214; archives of, 287; dissolution of, 224; Marx on, 221n; Rani of Sirmur and, 227; state formation and, 220–221

East India Company (1784–1834), The (Philips), 223–224

ecology, 87, 366, 380–382, 385, 390

Economic and Philosophical Manuscripts (Marx), 73, 74, 329

écriture, 320, 348

education, 215, 383, 420; "aesthetic," 30–31; imperialism and, 229–230, 268, 275; of the monster in *Frankenstein* (Shelley), 137; sanctioned ignorance and, 2

Egypt, 41

Eighteenth Brumaire of Louis Bonaparte, The (Marx), 257–260, 269, 272

Eliot, T. S., 151, 232

Empire of Signs (Barthes), 342, 344, 345

Engels, Friedrich, 72, 76, 107, 109, 110

England. *See* Britain

Enlightenment, 28n, 37, 85, 103, 141,

143, 239, 429; defensibility of, 345; financial globalization and, 429–430; Ideological Subject and, 356; reason and, 353

Entäusserung (alienation), 59

Entfremdung (estrangement), 59, 60

epic narrative, 46–47

"episteme," 288

epistemograph, 41

epistemology, 41

Essays on the Gītā (Ghose), 62–63

essentialism, 172, 259, 264, 271, 282–283, 386

estrangement, 59

ethicotheology, 23

ethics, 30, 78, 382, 419, 427; as alterity, 426; Christian, 123; ethical singularity, 383–384; Foucault and, 238; history and, 110; Kantian, 21, 264n; programs and decisions, 27n; responsibility and, 4–5, 15n

ethnicity, 30, 60, 110

ethnocentrism, 306, 354

ethnography, 6, 49, 58n70, 67, 191, 386

Eurocentric economic migration, 79, 209, 277n, 357, 363n, 395, 405

Eurocentrism, 66n, 69n, 173; Asiatic Mode of Production (AMP) model and, 72; origins of imperialism and, 289n; progress and, 91

Europe, 8, 33, 81; development of capitalism in, 96, 97; ethico-political subject of, 9; literature of the female subject, 114; origins of imperialism and, 37; Other of, 122, 265–266; relations with Latin America, 117–118; rise of, 90n; self-identity of, 72, 209, 211; self-representation of, 163; as Subject, 254

exchange, 105, 141, 177, 263

exploitation, 263, 278

Fabian, Johannes, 109

faith, 36, 37

false consciousness, 254

family, 119–120, 122, 133, 261–262, 264

fashion, 337–342, 352, 412

Female Castaway, The (story within story), 180, 185, 186

feminism, 109–110, 352, 429; bourgeois (nineteenth-century), 13, 112; celebration of the female, 198; class and, 258; complicity with the institution, 146–148; constituency of, 242; end of radical feminism, 256n; ethnography and, 191; Hinduism and, 306; in imperialism, 114, 139; individualist, 116, 118–119, 122, 132, 148; Japanese, 338n–339n; in literature, 128; marginality and, 176–177; multiculturalism and, 399; postcolonial, 114; postmodernism and, 359n; race and racism within, 167–169; theory and, 282, 283; third-worldist, 164–165, 170, 269; universalist, 13n, 102n, 220n, 250, 252, 361; U.S., 116, 164, 176, 282, 384n, 388, 403

fetishism, 134, 177, 204, 317

feudalism, 55n, 81, 83, 88, 89–90, 91; absence of in United States, 394; Asiatic Mode of Production (AMP) and, 108; discourse of, 225, 226; transition to capitalism, 96, 281, 289, 388

Feyerabend, Paul, 365

Fichte, Johann G., 8n

finance capital, 3n, 89, 101, 220, 419

financial capitalism, 69n

First World, 278, 382

Fish, Stanley, 194

Fitzgerald, Edward, 232

Foe (Coetzee), 132, 174, 178–190, 191–194

foreclosure, 4, 6; of the "Aboriginal," 52n; art-historical periodization and, 352; Asiatic Mode of Production (AMP) and, 88; covering over of, 330; culture and imperialism, 60; Marxism and, 68–69, 71, 75; subject and narrative, 9

foreign trade, 100–102

Foucault, Michel, 7, 33, 204, 215, 258; civil society and, 356; critique of Marx and Marxism, 103–104, 273, 278–279; on desiring identity, 261; on the

"episteme," 288; on history, 238; on ideology, 252, 253, 254–255; on Other as Subject, 268, 269, 270; *pouvoir/savoir* concept, 121; on power, 103, 248, 249, 265, 353, 354, 397; "third world" and, 277

"fourth world," 380

Fox-Genovese, Elizabeth, 118–119

France, 7, 258, 334; Althusserians in, 99; bourgeoisie of, 119; colonialism of, 154, 358; style and, 246; "third world" and, 277

Francis, Philip, 86

Frankenstein (Shelley), 114, 132–140, 179, 297

freedom, 21–22, 24, 327–330, 388

French Revolution, 15n

Freud, Sigmund, 4, 5, 17n, 38, 59, 207, 425; metapsychology and ego psychology, 387–388; Oedipal scene, 15; on repression, 254n, 285; science and, 217–219; women and, 283–284

Freudianism, 134, 214

Fukuyama, Francis, 394, 403

fundamentalism, religious, 60, 65, 176, 364, 373

Gandhi, Mahatma, 298

garment industry, 415–416, 419

Geist (spirit), 39, 40, 41

gender/gendering, 85, 88, 104–105, 176–177; colonialism and, 227; development and, 290, 409; nationalism and, 272

General Agreement on Tariffs and Trade (GATT), 102, 382, 383n, 415

Genet, Jean, 17n

German Ideology, The (Marx), 74–75

Germany, 7–8, 99, 163, 358

Ghose, Aurobindo, 62

Gilbert, Sandra, 122, 124

Gitā. See Srimadbhagavadgitā

globality, 356, 358, 363–364, 382

globalization, financial, 3, 18n, 89, 190, 208; as Americanization, 361; Asiatic Mode of Production (AMP) and, 96; capitalism and socialism in, 70; de-

authorization of the state and, 220; desire as catachresis and, 252; as "development," 79; essentialist politics and, 259; gender and development, 200–201; globality and, 164, 363–364; modernization and imperialism, 290; multicultural liberalism and, 397; national liberation and, 309–310, 311; "postnationalism" and, 381; resistance to, 413; subalternity and, 102, 255; technology and, 366; telecommunications and, 275; transnationality and, 357; as tributary system, 95
Global Village (McLuhan), 364, 371
God, 23, 26, 52, 63; death of, 98; as Father, 30; as governor, 36; Judeo-Christian, 280; as Maker of Man, 133, 134; production of, 34
Goethe, Johann Wolfgang von, 42, 241
Gordimer, Nadine, 194, 195
grammar, 56
grammatology, 428
Gramsci, Antonio, 6, 83, 269, 376
graphematic structure, 321–322, 327, 348
Greece, ancient, 43
ground rent, 86, 89
Grundrisse (Marx), 75, 80, 326
Guattari, Félix, 58n, 253, 263, 279; on coding, 105, 107–108; critique of psychoanalysis, 207, 217n; on desire, 103, 252
Gubar, Susan, 122, 124
Guha, Ranajit, 86, 212, 270, 271, 272, 276

Habermas, Jürgen, 8n, 312
Hall, Stuart, 99
Hamacher, Werner, 48n
Hegel, Georg W. F., 3, 17n, 37, 68, 71, 110, 425; on art, 40, 41; on caste, 57n; on difference, 78–79; essentialism and, 282; native informant and, 6, 52, 53; *Srimadbhagavadgītā* and, 39, 43–44, 47–49, 52–54, 58, 63, 64, 209; "universal" narrative of, 8; view of India, 47–48, 54
Hegelianism, 58–59, 63, 65, 88

Heidegger, Martin, 106n, 171, 303, 324, 376, 425; on art as work, 115n, 212, 428–429; deconstruction and, 423; history and, 238
Herder, Johann Gottfried von, 8
hermeneutics, 256
heterogeneity, 314, 315, 316, 320
"hieroglyphist prejudice," 280, 286
Hindess, Barry, 93–96, 316, 345, 412
Hinduism, 42n, 53n; British imperialism and, 229, 230; in literature, 141, 144, 145–146; nationalism and, 62–65, 96, 210n, 228n, 240, 241, 289n, 362–363, 373–374; philosophy and, 54n; *sati* and, 235–236, 295n, 297, 298–302; social behavior and, 58
Hindu Law, 267–268, 288, 297
Hindusthani language, 162
Hindu View of Life, The (Radhakrishnan), 62, 63
Hirst, Paul Q., 93–96, 316, 345, 412
historicism, 331, 334
historiography, 54, 55, 198, 203, 206, 270, 274, 285
history: archives of, 202–203, 204; as figuration, 65; Hegel's view of, 39–40; in India, 44, 48; law and, 43, 51–55, 55, 58, 67; narrative of, 116, 118, 266; norms and aberrations in, 96; nostalgia films and, 202; periodizing of, 316; perspectivism and, 92; philosophy and, 90; in the *Srimadbhagavadgītā*, 50–51; women as subject for, 176, 182; writing of, 205, 238–239, 244
History of Sexuality (Foucault), 103, 304, 353n
Hölderlin, Friedrich, 19
Home and the World, The (film), 240
Homer, 149, 152
homeworking, 67, 68, 391
Horkheimer, Max, 39n
How to Do Things with Words (Austin), 426
human, boundary with animal, 121, 125, 187, 285
humanism, 17, 60, 98, 109, 171, 250, 322n
Husserl, Edmund, 424, 425

hybridity, 17n-18n, 28n, 157, 319n, 399; American context of, 332; ethnicity and, 155; of language, 163, 164; post-colonialism and, 361
hysteria, 134

identity, 6, 27n, 73; desiring, 261; differ-ence and, 340, 341, 344; English cul-tural identity, 133; essentialism and, 282; history and, 238; hybridity of, 155; imperialism and, 125–126, 127; multiculturalism and, 334; narrative of development and, 371; national, 64, 426; nationalism and, 188, 247; post-colonial elites and, 359; women's, 112
identity politics, 69n, 374n
ideology, 64, 66, 75n, 76, 77, 205, 265; al-liance politics and, 279; Althusser on, 252–253; consumerism of, 275–276; critique of, 217, 249, 257; as false con-sciousness, 254; gender and, 68; imperi-alism and, 215; Marx's critique of, 106
Iliad, 368
imaginary, the, 128
Impératif catégorique, L' (Nancy), 123
imperialism, 1, 19; access of colonized to culture of, 60; archives of governance, 132, 146, 205; Asiatic Mode of Produc-tion (AMP) and, 89–90; benevolent, 160; British Raj, 235–236, 270; capital-ism and, 101, 340; civilizing mission of, 6, 14, 36, 113, 116, 121, 179, 214, 290, 296, 303, 371; critique of, 7, 199–200; culture of, 191; defined, 3; discursive production and, 4; as dream-work, 218; ecology and, 380; Eurocentrism and, 37; feminism and, 113, 139; justification of, 201–202; language and, 162–163, 369n; limits of cognition and, 26; literature and, 131, 136–138; Marx's view of, 95n-96n; modes of pro-duction and, 290; narrative(s) of, 267, 279; Other and self in, 130, 131; patri-archy and, 234, 235; philosophy and, 123–124; postcolonial identity and, 30; *pouvoir-savoir* of, 120–122; prejudices of, 58n; scholarship and, 8–9; shifting

formations of, 102; socialization and, 67–68; territorial, 64, 190, 274, 275, 277, 279, 359; time and, 49
Incan civilization, 117
indeterminacy, 22, 36, 121, 125, 153, 276
India, 37, 46, 344, 373, 389; aboriginal population of, 141, 384–385; art in, 41–42; Asiatic Mode of Production (AMP) in, 72, 86–88; in Baudelaire's poetry, 154; British, 201, 202, 205, 209–211, 224, 240, 241, 295; Christianizing of, 216; contrast with Bangladesh, 413–414; decolonization in, 363; diaspora intellectuals and, 67n; East India Com-pany and, 220–221; gendering and ex-ceptionalism, 58; Hindu Law in, 267–268, 288; independent, 240; in lit-erature, 131, 136, 158–162; nation-hood and, 141n, 221, 222, 247; religion and power in, 383; representation of, 303–304; stereotyping of, 232
India (Spear), 226
individualism, 109, 118–119, 282; female, 181, 182; feminism and, 148; in litera-ture, 116; sex and, 134–135
Indonesia, 66n
industrial capitalism, 100, 201, 274, 317, 389
Industrial Revolution, 394, 404
inside-outside dynamic, 5
intellectuals, 250, 259, 265–266, 268, 270, 272
internal colonization, 172
International Monetary Fund (IMF), 101
International Workingmen's Association, 75–76
Internet, 300, 325, 393
interpellations, 112, 116, 164
Interpretation of Dreams (Freud), 218
Invention of Africa, The (Mudimbe), 199
ipseity, 76, 424
irony, 430
Islam, 88, 96
Italy, 269

Jameson, Fredric, 99, 105n, 244, 398, 411, 412; on Asiatic Mode of Production (AMP), 71–72, 79, 97; on "political unconscious," 208n; on postmodernism, 312–320, 322, 324–238, 330, 332, 347–349, 421; "third world literature" and, 109; on U.S. "nostalgia film," 202

Jane Eyre (Brontë), 114–115, 120–122, 146, 178, 409; Christian psychobiography in, 124–125, 139; family in, 119–120; imperialism in, 124–125, 138, 214; Jane's subjectivity, 116

JanMohammed, Abdul, 190

Japan, 338–340, 343–346, 352

Jardine, Lisa, 155

jauhar, 300

Jesus, 63

Johnson, Barbara, 132

Jones, William, 8

Judaism, 63

Judeo-Christian myth, 280

justice, 247, 328; as alterity, 426; in capitalist society, 395, 398; ecological, 380–382; historians and, 301n; homeworking and, 391; impossibility of, 199, 246; Law and, 427; legitimation and, 368

Kali (goddess), 63, 241–242

Kalidasa, 42, 241

Kane, P. V., 294, 301

Kant, Immanuel, 3, 4, 70, 71, 98, 394, 421, 425; on aesthetic judgment, 135; on categorical imperative, 123, 136; *Critique of Judgment*, 10–14, 19–36; *Critique of Practical Reason*, 10; *Critique of Pure Reason*, 10; on desires, 35–36; on faith, 36–37; foreclosure of subject and, 9, 110; on freedom, 21–23; on humanity of primitive peoples, 27n–28n; Marxist-feminists and, 68; native informant and, 6, 110; on rational will, 325–326; on reflexive judgment, 80; Schiller and, 15–16; on the sublime, 10–13, 15–16, 19–20, 325; "universal" narrative of, 8; view of woman, 13

Kantianism, 264

Kawakubo, Rei, 247, 338, 339, 340, 341, 342, 352

Kealiinohomoku, Joann, 353, 354

Keith, Arthur Berriedale, 229

Kierkegaard, Søren, 355n, 425

Kim (Kipling), 62n

Kipling, Rudyard, 62n, 156, 157–160

Klein, Melanie, 198n, 217n, 291, 335n, 400

knowledge, 94, 216, 266; difference and, 199; imperialism and, 267; limits of, 291; notational, 349; object of, 227, 304; power and, 103, 104; production of, 360; in the *Srimadbhagavadgitā*, 52

Kofman, Sarah, 27n, 283

Kosambi, D. D., 45, 46, 50, 56n

Krishna, 43–44, 45, 50–52, 56, 64; 54–55

Kristeva, Julia, 66n, 268n

Ksatriya caste, 57

Kuhn, Thomas, 365

labor, division of: culture and, 316; international, 227, 250, 255–256, 265, 269, 275, 398; sexual, 274

labor unions, 84, 382, 416

Lacan, Jacques, 4, 5, 204, 208n, 335n, 376

LaCapra, Dominick, 202, 204–207, 208n

Lambrinidis, Christiana, 406, 407, 408

language, 215, 322, 379, 425; acquisition of, 187; alterity and, 8; difference and, 73n; discourse and, 265; globalization and, 397; in India and Bangladesh, 413; as metaphor, 404; origin of, 72; structuralism and, 424; translation and, 162

Language of Psycho-Analysis, The (Laplanche and Pontalis), 4

late capitalism, 317, 328, 348

Latin America, 117–118, 130, 148n

Law, 51, 55, 67, 215; deconstruction and, 304; democracy and civil rights, 65; desire and, 216, 217; divine, 189; European subjectivity and, 248; Hindu Law, 267–268; history and, 58; imperialism and, 205, 275; justice and, 427; in literature, 121, 125, 138; natural, 189; patriarchy and, 262; power as, 103;

Law (continued)
  representation and, 257; subject-constitution and, 266
Law, Thomas, 87
Lawrence, D. H., 351
legitimation, 368, 370–371, 377
Lenin, Vladimir, 83
Lentricchia, Frank, 322
Levinas, Emmanuel, 355n, 425
Levine, George, 132
Lévi-Strauss, Claude, 110, 405
liberalism, 388, 396–398, 402
liberation theology, 382, 383
Lineages of the Absolutist State (Anderson), 86
literature, 8, 369, 404, 428–429; archives and, 203; history writing and, 205; imperialism and, 113–115; "nationalist," 205; women and, 112–113
Lyotard, Jean-François, 104, 110, 312, 335–336, 364–365, 368, 369–370

Macaulay, Thomas, 268, 276
Macdonnell, Arthur, 229
macrology, 263–264, 269, 279
Mahābhārata, 44–45, 46, 47, 368
Mallarmé, Stéphane, 429
Man, name of, 5, 6, 34
Maoism, 249
Mao Zedong, 83
Marcuse, Herbert, 315
marginality, 171, 174, 176, 180–181, 239, 333
Marrano, figure of, 17n–18n, 280n
marriage, 181–182, 298, 388
Marx, Karl, 3, 4, 64, 154, 217, 376, 421; agency and, 357; Asiatic Mode of Production (AMP) and, 102; on conspirators, 250–251; difference and, 73, 80; early life and writings, 73–79; economics and, 84; essentialism and, 282; ghost of, 98; globality of, 71; Hegelianism of, 58–59; on India, 221n; on labor power, 387; as Marrano, 18n; mode-of-production concept, 94; native informant and, 6; on nature and humanity, 328–329, 388; on representation, 257–

264; on Robinson Crusoe, 177–178; on social interests, 272; theory of practice in, 321; "universal" narrative of, 8–9; on value, 99–105, 412–413; on women and production, 67
Marxism, 67, 68, 91, 209, 269, 357; apology for imperialism, 227; battle with deconstruction, 314–315; critical nature of, 84; "internationalist," 273, 274; masculine framework of, 262; nationalism and, 82; postmodernism and, 324; theory of power, 263; vanguard and, 71
Marxism and the Bhagvat Geeta (Sardesai and Bose), 62
Marxist-feminists, 68
masculism, 134, 179, 282, 352; celebration of the female, 148; deconstruction of, 151–152, 163, 168; Oedipus complex and, 110
master-slave relation, 140
masturbation, 52n
Matilal, Bimal Krishna, 45, 46, 50, 310
Mayan civilization, 117
Mazhar, Farhad, 414
McLaren, Malcolm, 344
McLuhan, Marshall, 364–366, 369–370, 385
mercantilism, 212, 221n, 225, 290, 394, 413
metalepsis, 14, 23
Metamorphoses (Ovid), 126
micrology, 263–264
Mill, John Stuart, 396
Miller, Jacques-Alain, 265
mimicry, 353, 364
Minimalism, 347–351
Mode of Production and Social Formation (Hindess and Hirst), 93–94
modernism, 313, 315, 317, 333, 361
modernity, 28n, 33, 61, 368
Modern Language Association (MLA), 169
modes of production, 76, 82; critique of concept of, 72, 93–94, 95; culture and, 316; Enlightenment context, 103; narrative of, 219–220, 244–245, 276, 290;

revolution and, 83. *See also* Asiatic Mode of Production (AMP)

money, 99–102, 263

Monier-Williams, Monier, 229

monotheism, 31, 42n

moralism, 315, 324, 326, 330, 332, 377, 398, 418

morals, 9, 12–13, 14, 19, 20, 33, 90, 135

Morgan, Lewis H., 107

Morris, Robert, 110, 347–348

Morrison, Toni, 305n, 430

mothering, 181, 182–183, 193

mother-right, 45n

Mrs. Dalloway (Woolf), 131

Mudimbe, V. Y., 199

multiculturalism, 79, 102, 169, 316, 374; concept of culture, 353–358; liberalism and, 396–398, 402; literature and, 176; metropolitan, 394, 405; national identity and, 334; vanguardism and, 176

multinational capitalism, 316, 330, 341

Mutloatse, Mothobi, 195

Nagarjuna, 429

Nagel, Thomas, 46

name of Man, 5, 6, 34

Name of the Father, 129, 192, 262, 272

Nancy, Jean-Luc, 27n, 123

Nandy, Ashis, 294

Napoleonic Code, 262

Narcissus, 126, 127–128, 344

narrative, 3, 185–186, 193; of capital(ism), 89, 328; coding and recoding, 108; crisis of, 340; cultural history and, 312–313; of dominant European subject, 8–9, 359; foreclosure of subject and, 9; in *Frankenstein* (Shelley), 137, 139; of history, 71, 78, 111; of imperialism, 65; legitimation and, 368; of *Mahābhārata*, 46; modes of production and, 6, 290, 330; narrative closure, 368; psychoanalysis and, 4

nationalism, 49, 60–62, 399, 467; as coding, 247; elitism and, 270; in Europe, 75, 76; gendering in, 88; Hindu, 62–65, 96, 240, 241, 289n, 362–363, 373–

374; identity and, 188; metropolitan intellectuals and, 67n; U.S., 379

nation-state, 223n, 242, 357; East India Company and, 225; European model of, 91; globalization and, 95, 364, 373; territorial imperialism and, 277; workers' struggle and, 250

native informant, 4, 9, 35, 52, 342; agency and, 85; alterity and, 352; anthropology and, 142; Asiatic Mode of Production (AMP) and, 101; being human and, 5–6; diasporic, 169; displaced subject-position of, 170; DNA patenting and, 388n; foreclosure of, 76, 89, 103, 110, 111, 113; in *Frankenstein* (Shelley), 135, 136; indigenous elite as, 270; knowledge production and, 360; Marxism and, 68–70, 98; postcolonial nationhood and, 141; production of, 30; as reader, 33, 49, 53, 66–67; as revolutionary vanguard, 71; woman as, 70

natural law, 189

natural philosophy, 135, 136, 138

nature: art and, 348, 349, 351; cognition of, 10; culture and, 385; ecology and, 382; family and, 261, 264; as female principle, 52; infinity of, 14–15, 21, 23, 24, 30; in Marx, 76–77, 80–81, 289–290, 328–329; as mother, 30; purposiveness of, 22, 25; relation to freedom, 135; sexual difference and, 15n; in the *Srimadbhagavadgītā*, 52; sublime in, 12, 14, 20; teleology and, 20–21

Nazca lines, Minimalism and, 348–350, 351, 352

Nazism, 97

necessity, freedom and, 327–330, 388

negation, 59

Negri, Antonio, 376

neocolonialism, 2n, 85, 177, 190, 359, 361, 398; defined, 3, 172; discourse of, 225; gendering and, 105n; ideology and, 255; inception of, 413; intellectuals and, 118; multinational corporations and, 399

neo-Hegelianism, 326

neoliberalism, 357
Nepal, 210, 211, 231
New Critics, 203–204
New Hollander, 26, 30, 32, 35, 36, 394.
    See also Aborigines; Tierra del Fuego,
    inhabitant of
New Immigrant, 393–394, 398–399, 402
New Philosophy, 249
New Social Movements, 381
New Woman, 157, 158
New World Order, 13n, 274
Nietzsche, Friedrich, 17n, 19, 97, 98,
    217, 423, 425
Non-Governmental Organizations
    (NGOs), 372, 378, 381, 386
North-South divide, 2, 6, 95; alliance
    politics and, 279; cultural studies ex-
    changes, 200; ecological justice and,
    380–382, 386, 390; feminism and, 167–
    169; literature and, 114, 170; wage
    competition and, 377–378
nostalgia, 202, 306
noumenon, man as, 26n-27n, 32, 34, 36,
    124

Ochterlony, David, 213–214, 217, 225,
    229, 233
Odyssey, 368
Oedipus, 110, 127–129, 344
Of Grammatology (Derrida), 322, 424
Olsen, Tillie, 181
ontograph, 54, 55
oriental despotism, 58n
Oriental Despotism (Wittfogel), 71
orientalism, 42n, 48n
Orientalism (Said), 95n, 232n
Origin of the Family, Private Property, and
    the State (Engels), 110
Other, 7, 9, 110; assimilation of, 280,
    281; Europe as, 199–200; of Europe,
    265–266; feminists and, 113; in
    Frankenstein (Shelley), 138; intellectu-
    als and, 249, 250, 268, 270; not-yet-hu-
    manness of, 122; racial, 30, 147, 185,
    197; Self and, 126–127, 130, 138, 171,
    209, 211; self-consolidating, 207; as
    Subject, 268; "third world" as, 278

overdetermination, 183, 184, 193, 218,
    219, 299, 303
Ovid, 126

Paradise Lost (Milton), 137
Paris Commune (1871), 75
Parry, Benita, 190, 191, 217n
patriarchy, 29, 45n, 68, 400; capitalism
    and, 233n, 237, 296, 304; colonialism
    and, 416; family's role in, 262; feminist
    opposition to, 252; historians and,
    301n; inheritance law and, 127; mar-
    riage and motherhood, 181, 183; op-
    posed to capitalism, 74; sati and, 234,
    235, 236, 294; sexual division of labor,
    163; subalternity and, 102n
patronymic. See Name of the Father
Pax Britannica, 201–202
Pax electronica, 370
Persia, 41
Petchesky, Rosalind, 386, 387, 388, 389,
    403
phallocentrism, 350–351
phallus, 80, 134
phenomenality, 53, 56, 58, 103
phenomenal representation, 56
Philips, C. H., 223
philology, 8
philosophy, 8, 123; Christianity and, 31;
    deconstruction and, 423; history and,
    90; in India, 54n; literature and, 112;
    marginality and, 175; politics and, 16–
    17, 33; representation and, 256; of sci-
    ence, 365; Species-Being and, 78;
    sublation of, 74; sublime and, 24; tele-
    ology and, 20
Philosophy of History, The (Hegel), 39, 43,
    57n
Philosophy of Right, The (Hegel), 39
phonocentrism, 149
physicotheology, 23
physiocracy, 212, 225
Pilgrim's Progress (Bunyan), 124
Plato, 349, 424
Pletsch, Carl, 2, 3, 6, 9, 70, 360n
political economy, 60, 87, 90, 109–110,
    177, 257

Political Liberalism (Rawls), 281
Political Unconscious, The (Jameson), 267n
politics, 20, 256, 259, 276–277, 278, 368
polytheism, 31
Ponge, Francis, 429
population control, 68, 385, 390, 416
positivism, 260, 262, 273, 282, 283
postcolonial discourse, 1, 9, 39, 107, 141
postcoloniality, 33n, 172, 191, 239, 358, 373, 398
postfordism, 337, 376, 414; postmodernism and, 317, 365; subaltern woman and, 67, 68, 276, 386, 390; telecommunication and, 275. *See also* capitalism
Postmodern Condition, The (Lyotard), 364–365, 371
postmodernism, 312–320, 323, 334; in architecture, 337; critique of, 336; (de)centered subject and, 347; feminism and, 359n; information and, 392–393
post-Soviet world order, 2, 3, 25, 102, 275, 276; disappearance of nonalignment in, 372; feminism in, 114, 250; immigration patterns in, 393n; multiculturalism and, 169n; nation-states in, 95; privatization and, 357; recoding of capitalism in, 92. *See also* Soviet Union
poststructuralism, 249, 250, 264, 312, 313, 320, 356
pouvoir-savoir (making-sense-ability), 120–122, 164, 356, 370, 390
power, 103–104, 249, 252, 264; class interest and, 263; Foucault on, 254, 265, 278; knowledge and, 215; Marxism as analysis of, 315
practical reason, 32, 36, 37, 136, 326; double bind of, 22, 25; in literature, 135
Pre-Capitalist Modes of Production (Hindess and Hirst), 93
primitive communism, 82–83
primitive man, 13, 14, 26, 32, 123–124
Principles of Hindu Law (Mulla), 302
privatization, 392n

profit, rate of, 99
progress, 93, 348
proletariat, 68n, 69n, 74, 75, 92, 275, 278
"proper signification," 22, 23, 25
property, 80, 86, 294
prostitution, 388
Proust, Marcel, 19, 142
psychoanalysis, 4–5, 109–110, 217, 247; critique of, 106–107; desire and, 105; ethnography and, 58n; normative male subject and, 128; "political unconscious," 208n; transference situation, 206–207, 208
psychobiography, 110, 154; Christian, 124, 139; of female subject, 117; Hindu, 52n, 298; *sati* and, 274, 285n, 286n, 291
"Pterodactyl, Pirtha, and Puran Sahay" (Devi), 140–146
Puranas, 42, 298
Pythagoras, 64

race, 13n, 32n, 112, 227, 231, 282; difference and, 73n; discourse of, 229; *sati* and, 285, 287, 289, 303; as species, 26
Racine, Jean, 149
racism, 52n, 94, 121, 373; chromatism and, 164–165; Marxism and, 274; migrants and, 382; multiculturalism and, 397; nationalism and, 96; reverse, 377
Radhakrishnan, Sarvepalli, 57, 62, 63
Raghunandana, 300–301, 302
Ramayana, 368
Rani of Sirmur, 201, 208, 209, 222, 233, 239, 241–244, 407; in archives, 231, 234, 236–237, 246–247; as instrument of British imperialism, 207, 228, 269, 308; as object of knowledge, 227
rape, 300
rational will, 10, 325–326
Rawls, John, 281, 396n
raw man. *See* primitive man
Ray, Satyajit, 240
Real, the, 5
Reason, 123, 353, 355; as compulsion, 24–25; culture and, 31; duty and, 21; as empiricist individualism, 68; freedom

Reason *(continued)*
    and, 11; limits of, 22–23; negation of,
    189; sublime and, 15, 30
reflective judgment, 28–29, 80
Reich, Robert, 392, 393
Reich, Wilhelm, 254, 284
religion, 20, 215, 230; comparative, 8;
    ecological justice and, 382–383; nation-
    alism and, 64; philosophy and, 31, 54n–
    55n, 123. *See also specific religions*
Remembrance of Things Past (Proust), 142
Renaissance, 7, 162–163
Repository (Ackerman), 119
representation, 172, 196, 211; East India
    Company and, 224; of England to the
    English, 113; of Europe, 199; gender
    and marginality, 180–181; historical ar-
    chives and, 202–203; imperialism and,
    218, 303; intellectuals and, 272; theory
    and action, 256–257; two senses of,
    257–264
reproductive rights, 68
responsibility, ethics of, 355n, 382, 427
Retamar, Roberto Fernandez, 117–118,
    130
revolution, 15n, 39n, 79, 83, 85, 97, 329
Rg-Veda, 235, 286, 291, 301, 302, 383
Rhodes, Cecil, 13n
Rhys, Jean, 115, 125–132, 146, 153, 178,
    262
Richetti, John, 187
Riedel, Manfred, 31
Robinson Crusoe (Defoe), 179, 180, 185,
    186, 193, 196; language and speech in,
    187, 189; marginality and, 174; Marx
    on, 177–178
Rodó, José Enriqué, 117
Rome, ancient, 43
Rorty, Richard, 345, 347, 354, 355
Ross, Robert, 227–230, 229, 230, 231
Rousseau, Jean-Jacques, 18, 19, 34, 72,
    135, 424, 428
Roxana (Defoe), 174, 180
Rubayyat of Omar Khayyam, 232
Rubin, Gayle, 109–110
Rule of Property for Bengal, A (Guha), 86–
    88, 92, 212

Russia, 82, 83

Said, Edward, 95n, 265, 270
Sakuntala (Kalidasa), 42
Sanskrit, 8, 47n, 48n, 136, 413; British
    imperialism and, 229–230; as "high cul-
    ture," 268
Sartre, Jean-Paul, 171, 173, 208, 327
sati (widow self-immolation), 232, 234
    236, 238, 267, 274, 289; bride burning
    in modern India, 307n; British aboli-
    tion of, 285, 287, 290, 296, 298; British
    collaboration with, 295–296, 297;
    Dharmasāstra and, 292–294, 298;
    Hindu Law and, 297, 298–302; in mod-
    ern India, 294; sublation of ideology
    of, 306, 307. *See also* suicide
Saussure, Ferdinand de, 424
Schiller, Friedrich von, 15–16, 30–31, 325
science, 153, 207, 216; imperialism and,
    7; philosophy and, 8; philosophy of,
    365; psychoanalysis and, 4
self-identity, 78
"self-knowledge" (Hegel), 40
self-representation, 7, 9, 73, 163, 165;
    British colonialism and, 409, 411; cul-
    tural, 340–341; of marginals in the
    United States, 396; politics of, 318; re-
    territorialized, 240; United States and
    decolonization, 360
semiotics, 264, 342
Sen, Amartya, 379
Serote, Mongane, 194
sexism, 32n, 52n, 274, 391
sexual difference, 29, 38n, 105, 160n;
    global sisterhood and, 148; in Kipling,
    158–159; subaltern subject and, 274;
    whiteness and, 165
sexuality, as labor power, 181–182
sexual reproduction, 123, 124, 128, 133,
    134, 139
Shakespeare, William, 37, 117
Shastri, Mahamahopadhyaya, 230, 268
Shelley, Mary, 115, 132–140, 153
Shiva, Vandana, 87n, 103
signification, 41, 424
signifiers, 89, 200, 256, 274; absence of,

264; autoreferentiality and, 318; simulacra and, 317
signs, 89, 149, 193
slavery, 389
smriti, 293
social engineering, 96, 135
social formations, 103
socialism, 88, 357, 387; Marx's goal for, 78; relation to capitalism, 67, 76, 80, 83, 245, 430; Second International, 373, 416
social sciences, 3, 9, 84
Social Text group, 99
soul making, 123, 124, 128, 134
South Africa, 190–191, 194, 195, 376
Southern Question, The (Gramsci), 269
Soviet Union, 68, 79, 96, 275. *See also* post-Soviet world order
Spain, 17n
Spear, Percival, 222
Species-Being, 76, 78, 79, 80, 81, 379, 388
Species-Life, 76, 79, 80–81, 106, 379, 388
Specters of Marx (Derrida), 70, 98, 330n, 400n, 428, 431
speech, 26, 186–189, 257, 269, 321, 425
Speech Act theory, 424, 426
Srimadbhagavadgitā, 37, 38, 42, 45–47; cultural representation and, 61–65; Hegel and, 39, 43–44, 47–49, 52–54, 58, 64, 209
sruti, 293, 301
Stalin, Joseph, 79, 83
State, the, 107–108
state capitalism, 223n, 330
state tax, 86, 89
sthitaprajna, 64
structuralism, 424
subaltern, 67, 68, 89, 102, 104, 117, 242; in British India, 215, 216; intellectuals and, 255, 257; in literature of postcolonial India, 140–146; multiculturalism and, 405; psychoanalysis and, 107; silencing of, 353, 373, 386, 412; speech and subjectivity, 269–270, 272–273, 281, 308–309; sublation of *sati* ideology, 306–308; voting and, 309–310
subalternity, 141, 201n, 271n, 309, 310

Subject, 16, 58, 112, 263, 286; as agent of history, 71; colonial, 33n, 127, 140, 187, 215, 266, 268, 359, 360; constitution/formation of, 133, 134, 139, 164, 235, 257, 283, 298, 303; culture and, 14; death of, 347, 348; (de)centered, 320, 322–324, 347; essentialist, 306; ethical, 244; Europe as, 199–200, 265; foreclosure of, 9; gendering of, 324–325; geopolitically differentiated, 31; globalized, 223n, 243n; Hegelian critique of, 258, 264; ideological, 252, 356; "interpellation" of, 116; Kantian, 10, 135, 136; multicultural, 256n; nature as, 76–77; normative male, 128, 133, 176; noumenal, 26n–27n, 32, 34, 36, 78; postcolonial, 33n; power and desire and, 264–265; self-identity and sameness, 113; undivided, 254; Western, 27n, 248
subjectivity, 40, 116, 346
subject-position, 313, 339, 341, 343
sublation, 50, 53, 56, 60; Being and, 59; *différance* and, 70; in Hegel, 78–79; of ideology of *sati*, 306, 307; in Marx, 74, 76, 77–78, 79–80, 90, 327–330; Nazca lines and, 351
Sublime, concept of (Kant), 10–13, 15–16, 20, 23, 135, 325
subreption, 11, 12, 20, 23, 24
Sudra caste, 57
suicide, 45n, 292–293, 297, 306–308. See also *sati*
Suleiman, Susan, 181
supplementation, 22, 23, 37
surplus value, 261, 263, 278, 279, 328, 387
Suttee (Thompson), 231, 303
svabhāva, 57n
svadharma, 57n
Sweden, 373–374, 375
Symbolic (Freudian), 5, 128
Symbolic (Hegelian), 47, 58, 71, 80

Tagore, Rabindranath, 296
Taussig, Michael, 28n
telecommunications, 275, 365, 370

teleology, 19–21, 24, 34, 58, 326; absence of, 370–371; of capitalism, 89; imperialism and, 30; in Marx, 87n, 328–329; Marxism and, 315; moral, 36; reason and, 404; subordination of nature, 33
Tempest, The (Shakespeare), 192
Thapar, Romila, 228
theology, 429
theoretical reason, 135
theory, 256–257, 264, 283
"third world," 2–3, 49, 60, 173; alliance politics and, 276–278; Bandung conference (1955), 375; coding and, 108; dismantling of, 9; feminism and, 164–165, 170, 269; literature and, 114, 170; poststructuralism and, 250; primitivist conception of, 209; religious tyranny in, 66; technology and, 365–366; "Third World Woman" as signifier, 131; U.S. pedagogy of, 65
Thompson, Edward, 230, 231, 296, 303, 304
Thousand Plateaus, A (Deleuze and Guattari), 58, 253, 266n
Tierra del Fuego, inhabitant of, 26, 26n–28n, 30, 32, 35, 36, 394. *See also* Aborigines; New Hollander
Time, 37–38, 45, 48n, 55, 67; *aufheben/Aufhebung* (sublation) and, 60; labor and value and, 178; as law, 43, 51; in Marx, 81
To Every Birth Its Blood (Serote), 194
Torok, Maria, 5
totalitarianism, 97, 176, 323
translation-as-violation, 162–164
transnational capital, 317, 388, 394, 397
tribal societies, 58, 71–72, 141, 142n
tribute, imperialism and, 89, 91, 93
tropology, 16, 18–19, 25, 34; historiography and, 203; masculism and, 148, 151–152, 163, 168; representation as, 259

Unconscious Symbolic, 71, 80
Un-ease of Civilization, The (Freud), 5
Unequal Development (Amin), 86, 89, 92
United Nations (UN), 13n, 69, 384n; feminism and, 252, 361; gender and de-velopment, 245n, 250, 259, 370; global state and, 276; NGOs and, 372
United States, 66, 99, 339; diasporic students in, 376; East India Company and, 225; internal colonization in, 172; literary criticism in, 169; multiculturalism in, 334; as nation of immigrants, 394–396; nostalgia films in, 202; post–Cold War, 223n; third worldism in, 209, 278, 360
universalism, 35, 63, 147–148, 168, 354
Upanisads, 232
use value, 261, 263
utopias, 316, 318, 411

Vaisya caste, 57
value, 71, 79, 83, 99–105, 261; production and coding of, 181; sex/gender and, 109; theoretical viability of, 412–413; use and exchange, 177–178, 263
vanguardism, 176, 196, 357
Vedas, 42
Verneinung (negation), 59
Vertretung/vertreten (representation), 259, 260, 262, 264, 276, 364. *See also* representation
Vietnam, 378
Virgil, 149, 152
viswarūpadarsana (vision of universal form), 54

war, 35
Weber, Max, 57n
welfare state, 374, 377
Western world, 17, 88; defined, 6; feminism in, 112–113; Japan and, 240, 344; material and spiritual culture of, 61; as Subject, 248; technology in, 365
West Germany, 8n
White, Hayden, 202, 203–204, 208n
Wide Sargasso Sea (Rhys), 114, 125–132, 146
will, female, 295–296, 298, 299
Williams, Bernard, 46, 194
Williams, Patricia, 386, 389
Williams, Raymond, 4, 69n, 99, 314, 325
Wittfogel, Karl, 71, 88

Wolf-Man (Freud case), 4–5

women: alliance politics and, 277, 278; capitalist, 386; class-privileged, 201; credit-baiting of, 223n, 237, 243n, 255, 259, 419; development and, 290, 377, 419; dismissed from philosophy, 112; economic resistance of, 104; foreclosure of, 6, 75; history and, 176; imperialist use of, 244; Kant's view of, 13; as maker of children, 133; in Marxism and nationalism, 82; in masculist poetry, 150–154; as monolithic collectivity, 262; names of, 232–233, 287; natural and social, 386–387; in philosophy, 29n, 30; protection of, 288, 291; as reader, 98n; representation of, 111, 259; in *Robinson Crusoe* (Defoe), 179, 196; as subaltern, 270, 281–282, 283, 405; as support of production, 67, 68; world trade and, 220

"women of color," 165, 168

World Bank, 372, 378–379, 416; "bonded labor" and, 418n; gender and, 200n; labor unions and, 382; resistance to, 85, 377

"worlding," 114, 115n, 118, 200, 211, 228, 428

World Trade Organization (WTO), 102, 370, 378, 415

writing, 38, 188, 192, 281, 348, 425

Yeats, William Butler, 19

Zizek, Slavoj, 206n